Social Explainable AI

Katharina J. Rohlfing • Kary Främling •
Brian Lim • Suzana Alpsancar • Kirsten Thommes
Editors

Social Explainable AI

Communications of NII Shonan Meetings

Editors
Katharina J. Rohlfing
Faculty of Arts and Humanities
Paderborn University
Paderborn, Nordrhein-Westfalen, Germany

Kary Främling
Department of Computing Science
Umeå University
Umeå, Sweden

Brian Lim
Department of Computer Science
National University of Singapore
Singapore, Singapore

Suzana Alpsancar
Faculty of Arts and Humanities
Paderborn University
Paderborn, Nordrhein-Westfalen, Germany

Kirsten Thommes
Faculty of Management and Economics
Paderborn University
Paderborn, Nordrhein-Westfalen, Germany

ISBN 978-981-96-5289-1   ISBN 978-981-96-5290-7 (eBook)
https://doi.org/10.1007/978-981-96-5290-7

This work was supported by Deutsche Forschungsgemeinschaft.

© The Editor(s) (if applicable) and The Author(s) 2026. This book is an open access publication.

Open Access This book is licensed under the terms of the Creative Commons Attribution 4.0 International License (http://creativecommons.org/licenses/by/4.0/), which permits use, sharing, adaptation, distribution and reproduction in any medium or format, as long as you give appropriate credit to the original author(s) and the source, provide a link to the Creative Commons license and indicate if changes were made.

The images or other third party material in this book are included in the book's Creative Commons license, unless indicated otherwise in a credit line to the material. If material is not included in the book's Creative Commons license and your intended use is not permitted by statutory regulation or exceeds the permitted use, you will need to obtain permission directly from the copyright holder.

The use of general descriptive names, registered names, trademarks, service marks, etc. in this publication does not imply, even in the absence of a specific statement, that such names are exempt from the relevant protective laws and regulations and therefore free for general use.

The publisher, the authors and the editors are safe to assume that the advice and information in this book are believed to be true and accurate at the date of publication. Neither the publisher nor the authors or the editors give a warranty, expressed or implied, with respect to the material contained herein or for any errors or omissions that may have been made. The publisher remains neutral with regard to jurisdictional claims in published maps and institutional affiliations.

This Springer imprint is published by the registered company Springer Nature Singapore Pte Ltd.
The registered company address is: 152 Beach Road, #21-01/04 Gateway East, Singapore 189721, Singapore

If disposing of this product, please recycle the paper.

Preface

The original idea of the book goes back to the No. 200 NII Shonan Meeting with the title *Social Explainable AI: Designing Multimodal and Interactive Communication to Tailor Human–AI Collaborations*, in September 18–21, 2023, in Japan. It was organized by Kary Främling, Brian Y. Lim, and Katharina J. Rohlfing and gathered together scholars from various disciplines. We wish to acknowledge the funding by the National Institute of Informatics (NII) in Japan in making this meeting possible and fruitful. The open science format was made possible by the German Research Foundation (DFG) TRR 318/1 2021 – 438445824.

Writing these chapters has been a collective and interdisciplinary project. With this book, we present selected social concepts that specify the perspective on social XAI (sXAI) here proposed. We follow the developments in social and interactive AI in general, building on concepts from a large number of disciplines involved in social sciences (such as linguistics, philosophy, and psychology). Our vision is twofold: We present "social aspects" in a comprehensible way for various kinds of readers to encourage those designing XAI to push forward research on the key capabilities of an XAI to engage in a dialog and construct a relevant explanation. At the same time, our book is meant to spark discussions in the emerging interdisciplinary community about how to involve and empower individual users when they interact with XAI.

We wish to highlight the fact that all authors but also reviewers contributed to the collective endeavor: Anna-Lisa Vollmer led the first part of the book, Kary Främling and Britta Wrede supervised the second part, Angela Grimminger the third part, and Kirsten Thommes and Suzana Alpsancar the evaluation part. Hendrik Buschmeier supervised the collaborative writing. We also thank all our external reviewers: Carola de Beer, Zachary Daus, Andreas Holzinger, Eyke Hüllermeier, Casey Kennington, Matthias Kettner, Antonia Krummheuer, Francisco Javier Rodriguez Lera, Tobias Matzner, Tim Miller, Philip Müller, Gabriel Skantze, Matthijs Smakman, Manfred Stede, Simon Trang, Vaibhav Unhelkar, and Marina de Vos.

All chapters were read by Jonathan Harrow and Cornelia Casey-Buschmeier, and we are grateful for their proofreading. We furthermore thank Sebastian Mantsch for proofreading Chaps. 10, 29, and 30.

Paderborn, Germany	Katharina J. Rohlfing
Umeå, Sweden	Kary Främling
Paderborn, Germany	Kirsten Thommes
Paderborn, Germany	Suzana Alpsancar
Singapore, Singapore	Brian Lim
April 2025	

Acknowledgments

- This publication is a result of the Shonan Meeting No. 200: "Social Explainable AI: Designing Multimodal and Interactive Communication to Tailor Human–AI Collaborations". The authors thank the National Institute of Informatics in Tokyo, Japan, for supporting our collaboration and the perfect organization of the initial meeting.
- The open access format was made possible through funding from the German Research Foundation (DFG) supporting the Collaborative Research Center TRR 318/1 2021 'Constructing Explainability' (438445824).
- We are grateful to Jonathan Harrow, Cornelia Casey-Buschmeier, and Sebastian Mantsch for their proofreading.

Contents

1. **Introducing Social Explainable AI** 1
   Katharina J. Rohlfing and Brian Y. Lim

2. **Scenarios of Social Explainable AI in Practice** 19
   Kary Främling, Rachid Alami, Joris Hulstijn, Igor Tchappi, Angela Grimminger, Britta Wrede, Hendrik Buschmeier, and Sylvain Kubler

3. **Components of an Explanation for Co-constructive sXAI** 39
   Anna-Lisa Vollmer, Heike M. Buhl, Rachid Alami, Angela Grimminger, and Axel-Cyrille Ngonga Ngomo

4. **Context for Explanations** 55
   Katharina J. Rohlfing, Kary Främling, and Friederike Kern

Part I Patterns

5. **Practices: How to Establish an Explaining Practice** 77
   Katharina J. Rohlfing, Anna-Lisa Vollmer, and Angela Grimminger

6. **Explanation Goals** 99
   Katharina J. Rohlfing, Amit Singh, André Groß, and Britta Wrede

7. **Structures Underlying Explanations** 119
   Patricia Jimenez, Anna-Lisa Vollmer, and Henning Wachsmuth

8. **Roles and Relationships** 141
   Joris Hulstijn

9. **Responsibilities in sXAI** 157
   Katharina J. Rohlfing, Suzana Alpsancar, and Carsten Schulte

10. **Values and Norms in sXAI** 179
    Wessel Reijers and Suzana Alpsancar

11 Managing the sXAI Interaction: Beliefs, Goals, and Decisional Processes 197
Rachid Alami and Britta Wrede

Part II Incrementality

12 Incremental Communication 227
Britta Wrede, Hendrik Buschmeier, Katharina J. Rohlfing, Meisam Booshehri, and Angela Grimminger

13 Adaptation 247
Heike M. Buhl, Britta Wrede, Josephine B. Fisher, and Marco Matarese

14 Models of the Situation, the Explanandum, and the Interaction Partner 269
Heike M. Buhl, Anna-Lisa Vollmer, Rachid Alami, Meisam Booshehri, and Kary Främling

15 Generation of Explanatory Content and Requirements for Social XAI 297
Kary Främling, Kirsten Thommes, and Britta Wrede

16 Exploration of Explaining Content 317
Kary Främling, Britta Wrede, and Kirsten Thommes

17 Interaction History in Social XAI 331
Kirsten Thommes, Kary Främling, Britta Wrede, and Sylvain Kubler

Part III Multimodality

18 Theoretical Aspects of Multimodal Processing 351
Angela Grimminger and Hendrik Buschmeier

19 Characteristics of Nonverbal Behavior 367
Stefan Lazarov, Igor Tchappi, and Angela Grimminger

20 Nonverbal Signals of Affect 391
Hanna Drimalla

21 Ambiguity of Nonverbal Signals 413
David S. Johnson and Igor Tchappi

22 Timing and Synchronization of Multimodal Signals in Explanations 433
Petra Wagner and Stefan Kopp

23 Multimodality in Explanatory Interactions 447
Friederike Kern

24 Multimodality in Agents ... 463
Rachele Carli, Sukriti Bhattacharya, Igor Tchappi, Kary Främling, and Amro Najjar

25 Visualization and the Use of Multimodality to Explain ... 485
Richard Albrecht, Rachele Carli, Igor Tchappi, and Amro Najjar

Part IV Evaluation

26 Evaluation Principles ... 505
Kirsten Thommes

27 Operationalizing Social Interaction ... 521
Henning Wachsmuth, Kirsten Thommes, and Milad Alshomary

28 Measuring the Outcome of sXAI ... 541
Kirsten Thommes

29 Tasking AI Fairly. How to Empower AI Practitioners With sXAI? ... 557
Suzana Alpsancar and Eugenia Stamboliev

30 The Risk of Manipulation and Deception in sXAI ... 583
Suzana Alpsancar and Michael Klenk

Contributors

Rachid Alami Laboratory for Analysis and Architecture of Systems, Artificial and Natural Intelligence Toulouse Institute, Université de Toulouse, Toulouse, France

Suzana Alpsancar Heinz Nixdorf Institute, Department of Philosophy, Faculty of Arts and Humanities, Paderborn University, Paderborn, Germany

Sukriti Bhattacharya Trustworthy AI, Data and Software (HANDS) Unit, Luxembourg Institute of Science and Technology, Esch-sur-Alzette, Luxembourg

Meisam Booshehri Semantic Computing Group, Faculty of Technology, Bielefeld University, Bielefeld, Germany

Heike M. Buhl Institute for Human Sciences – Psychology, Faculty of Arts and Humanities, Paderborn University, Paderborn, Germany

Hendrik Buschmeier Digital Linguistics Lab, Faculty of Linguistics and Literary Studies, Bielefeld University, Bielefeld, Germany

Rachele Carli Responsible AI group, Umeå University, Umeå, Sweden
Sweden Affiliated to the AI RoboLab, University of Luxembourg, Esch-sur-Alzette, Luxembourg

Hanna Drimalla Human-Centered Artificial Intelligence, Faculty of Technology, Bielefeld University, Bielefeld, Germany

Josephine B. Fisher Psycholinguistics, Faculty of Arts and Humanities, Paderborn University Paderborn, Germany

Kary Främling Department of Computing Science, Umeå University, Umeå, Sweden
Department of Industrial Engineering and Management, Aalto University, Espoo, Finland

Angela Grimminger Psycholinguistics, Faculty of Arts and Humanities, Paderborn University, Paderborn, Germany

André Groß Medical School OWL, Bielefeld University, Bielefeld, Germany

Joris Hulstijn Utrecht University, Utrecht, The Netherlands

Patricia Jimenez Paderborn University, Paderborn, Germany

Stefan Lazarov Psycholinguistics, Faculty of Arts and Humanities, Paderborn University, Paderborn, Germany

Brian Lim Department of Computer Science, School of Computing, National University of Singapore, Singapore, Singapore

Friederike Kern Faculty of Linguistics and Literary Studies, Bielefeld University, Bielefeld, Germany

Michael Klenk Department of Values, Technology and Innovation, Faculty of Technology, Policy & Management, Delft University of Technology, Delft, The Netherlands

Stefan Kopp Social Cognitive Systems Group, Faculty of Technology, Bielefeld University, Bielefeld, Germany

Sylvain Kubler Interdisciplinary Centre for Security, Reliability and Trust (SnT), University of Luxembourg, Esch-sur-Alzette, Luxembourg

Marco Matarese COgNiTive Architecture for Collaborative Technologies unit, Italian Institute of Technology Genoa, Italy

Amro Najjar Trustworthy AI, Data and Software (HANDS) Unit, Luxembourg Institute of Science and Technology, Esch-sur-Alzette, Luxembourg

Axel-Cyrille Ngonga Ngomo Data Science, Heinz Nixdorf Institut, Paderborn University, Paderborn, Germany

David S. Johnson Faculty of Technology, Bielefeld University, Bielefeld, Germany

Wessel Reijers Institute of Media Studies, Faculty of Arts and Humanities, Paderborn University, Paderborn, Germany

Katharina J. Rohlfing Psycholinguistics, Faculty of Arts and Humanities, Paderborn University, Paderborn, Germany

Carsten Schulte Computer Science Education, Paderborn University, Paderborn, Germany

Amit Singh Psycholinguistics, Faculty of Arts and Humanities, Paderborn University, Paderborn, Germany

Eugenia Stamboliev Department of Philosophy, Faculty of Philosophy and Education, University of Vienna, Vienna, Austria

Igor Tchappi FINATRAX, SnT, University of Luxembourg, Esch-sur-Alzette, Luxembourg

Maitreyee Tewari Department of Computing Science, Umeå University, Umeå, Sweden

Kirsten Thommes Faculty of Business Administration and Economics, Paderborn University, Paderborn, Germany

Anna-Lisa Vollmer Interactive Robotics in Medicine and Care, Medical School OWL, Bielefeld University, Bielefeld, Germany

Henning Wachsmuth Institute of Artificial Intelligence, Leibniz University Hannover, Hannover, Germany

Petra Wagner Department Linguistics, Faculty of Linguistics and Literary Studies, Bielefeld University, Bielefeld, Germany

Britta Wrede Medical School OWL, Bielefeld University, Bielefeld, Germany

Acronyms

AI	Artificial Intelligence
CIU	Contextual Importance and Utility
EE	Explainee
ER	Explainer
HAI	Human–Agent Interaction
HCI	Human–Computer Interaction
HHI	Human–Human Interaction
HMI	Human–Machine Interaction
HRI	Human–Robot Interaction
IC	Intermediate Concept
KG	Knowledge Graph
LIME	Local Interpretable Model-agnostic Explanations
ML	Machine Learning
SHAP	SHapley Additive exPlanations
sXAI	Social XAI
ToM	Theory of Mind
XAI	eXplainable AI

Chapter 1
Introducing Social Explainable AI

Katharina J. Rohlfing and Brian Y. Lim

Abstract This introduction sets the stage for the present book. Whereas research in eXplainable AI (XAI) is motivated by societal changes and values, technology development largely ignores social aspects. This book aims to address this research gap with a systematic and comprehensive social view on explainable AI. Besides introducing many relevant concepts, the book offers first access to their possible implementation, thus advancing the development of more social XAI. The introduction starts by connecting the topic to the general research field of XAI. The second part defines the novel approach of social eXplainable AI (sXAI) along the three characteristics of social interaction such as patternedness, incrementality, and multimodality. Finally, the third part explains the structure followed by each chapter. The book offers insights not only for readers who work on technology development but also for those working in sociotechnical fields. Addressing an interdisciplinary readership, the book is an invitation for more exchange and further development of the sXAI field.

1.1 Societal Challenge and XAI

In our digitized society, algorithmic approaches (such as machine learning or autonomous intelligent systems) are rapidly increasing in complexity. These approaches shape current artificial intelligence (AI) that interprets data, learns from them, and uses this learning to achieve specific goals and tasks (Kaplan & Haenlein, 2019). This task specificity is important to note because all "existing AI systems, from natural language processing to image screening, are domain-

---

K. J. Rohlfing (✉)
Psycholinguistics, Faculty of Arts and Humanities, Paderborn University, Paderborn, Germany
e-mail: katharina.rohlfing@uni-paderborn.de

B. Y. Lim
Department of Computer Science, School of Computing, National University of Singapore, Singapore, Singapore
e-mail: brianlim@comp.nus.edu.sg

specific" and cannot cope with changes of users' behaviors flexibly—in this regard, they do not reach "human-like faculties" (Bory et al., 2024, p. 1). Despite the fact that they are developed for specific tasks, the underlying black-box nature of these models and their complexity make them opaque to users. This is the case not only to users but also to their developers, making it difficult for people to understand their assistance—let alone accept and be able to evaluate the decisions they suggest. Thus, the models bear risks of biases and deskilling (Meske et al., 2022) based on the behavior of either the system (e.g., statistical and hidden patterns) or the human (e.g., overreliance, for more, see Chap. 30).

The societal challenge to gain a better control over the approaches in AI has intensified research on explainable AI (XAI), thereby pushing forward many ideas on how algorithms should be explainable or could even be able to explain their own output. The underlying assumption is that the explainability of these systems will bring more control over the technology. The way systems should become explainable has been linked to transparency and comprehensibility (e.g., Arrieta et al., 2020). Consequently and especially for deep neural networks (DNNs), applications aimed at revealing patterns in complex data have led to a rapidly growing body of research concerned with making AI systems "more comprehensible and transparent to humans" (Ali et al., 2023, p. 2) while making the system's behaviors "more intelligible to humans by providing explanation" (Gunning et al., 2019, p. 2). In this vein, XAI refers to "many user-centered, innovative algorithm visualizations, interfaces and toolkits" that support users with various levels of AI literacy in order to enable them to understand AI systems (Wang et al., 2019, p. 1). Whereas XAI is viewed as a solution to the problem of opacity, to date, developers in computer science have investigated it mostly with a method-oriented focus (Meske et al., 2022; Kaplan et al., 2024). Yet, explainability is increasingly considered to be a prerequisite for fair, accountable, and trustworthy AI (Meske et al., 2022; Langer et al., 2021), thereby making it an interdisciplinary field (Miller, 2019; Langer et al., 2021).

1.2 Challenges in XAI Development

The path to XAI systems reveals many challenges (Gunning et al., 2019), and, as already pointed out by Miller (2019), these pertain not just to the nature of explanation. There is also a trade-off between the interpretability and accuracy, with less interpretable systems being more accurate and vice versa, resulting in the challenge to develop interpretable systems without sacrificing the system's performance (Gunning et al., 2019). In addition, XAI systems are challenged by the circumstance that there are users in the loop who might not be able to understand an explanation right away. Finally, there is the challenge of regarding the circumstances of an explanation and to what human actions or responsibilities an explanation is linked. In this latter point, the goal is to create interpretable models for applications in "diverse subject domains, from the bank customer who is refused a loan, the doctor making a diagnosis with a decision aid, to the patient who learns that he may have skin cancer from a smartphone photograph of his mole" (Wang et al., 2019, p. 1). These domains accommodate specific human reasoning, demanding the design of an appropriate XAI application.

Whereas emerging XAI approaches have concentrated largely on interpretability or explainability and the development of appropriate methods to find a "sweet spot" in considering "accuracy, interpretability, and tractability" (Gunning et al., 2019, p. 3), less consideration has been given to the fact that the explainable systems barely ensure being useful to the users. Responding to this limitation, in his seminal work positioning existing research on XAI, Miller (2019) suggested that explainable AI can benefit from research in the social sciences. In a nutshell, by opening up the social science area of research to XAI development, Miller (2019, p. 3) proposes some crucial aspects to explanations, such as (1) explanations addressing the why are contrastive (i.e., given relevant facts, explanations seek to respond to counterfactual cases); (2) explanations are selected, because they address only a relevant part of and not the complete cause of an event; (3) explanations are stronger when they are causally attributive; and (4) explanations are social, meaning that they are dialogic, because an explanation implies "a social interaction between the explainer and the explainee" (ibid).

Many researchers have followed his important impulses leading to our increased knowledge about relevant social aspects that can vary from characterizing the norms of a country that makes explanation a regulatory standard of applying an AI, over settings in which an explanation about the function or output of an AI occurs (e.g., a task within a company), to the specific interests becoming visible when users query an AI. However, this wide range (from societal over institutional to individual) of relevant social aspects and the difficulties in operationalizing them (i.e., breaking them down to measure or implement them) are likely to prevent many researchers from considering the social dimension.

Nonetheless, there is an increasing pressure on research to take social aspects into account, because, more recently, state-of-the-art research (see next Section) has exposed many critical deficits or lacks as reasons for why an explainable system is of little use to users. These include a lack of situation or context awareness (Anjomshoae et al., 2019; Mill et al., 2024), a lack of personalization (Sokol & Flach, 2020), and a lack of interaction (Rohlfing et al., 2021; Kaplan et al., 2024). Whereas current reviews respond to these deficiencies by defining dimensions of how to consider users' perspectives (see next section), approaches toward a committed involvement of users are scarce.

1.3 Human Factors for XAI Development

Within the development of techniques to explain AI, several studies have focused on users. These have shown that the effectiveness of some techniques to explain AI improves understanding, trust, and satisfaction (e.g., Cheng et al., 2019; Colin et al., 2022; Hase & Bansal, 2020; Lim et al., 2009; see Rong et al., 2023 for a review).

Nonetheless, there are also some studies showing that explanations may not help user understanding (Arora et al., 2022; Poursabzi-Sangdeh et al., 2021; Wang & Yin, 2021).

Indeed, usage outcomes of AI explanations depend on decision tasks (Buçinca et al., 2020), the AI's prediction confidence (Lim and Dey, 2011; Lai & Tan, 2019; Zhang et al., 2020), user background in AI (Ehsan et al., 2024), and domain expertise (Wang & Yin, 2021). Even when AI makes mistakes, users have been shown to overtrust AI explanations (Bansal et al., 2021; Kaur et al., 2020), though this could be mitigated by applying cognitive forcing functions (Buçinca et al., 2021; Miller, 2023). To improve the usability and effectiveness of XAI for the individual user, studies have proposed and evaluated many desiderata. These works have found that AI explanations need to be aligned to user reasoning processes, intuitions, and goals (Chen et al., 2023; Lai et al., 2023; Liao et al., 2020; Miller, 2019; Speith et al., 2024; Wang et al., 2019), beliefs (Ross et al., 2017), and usage contexts (Lim & Dey, 2009). They need to be question-oriented (Lim et al., 2009), relatable (Zhang & Lim, 2022), low in cognitive load (Abdul et al., 2020), memorable (Bo et al., 2024), privacy-preserving (Zhao et al., 2021; Zhang et al., 2022), uncertainty-aware (Wang et al., 2021), and domain-aligned (Lim et al., 2025; Matsuyama et al., 2023). Moreover, they should support actionable control (Kulesza et al., 2015) and fair decisions (Dodge et al., 2019; Lyu et al., 2023). To promote the rigorous design of AI explanations, some reviews have summarized desiderata for XAI (Langer et al., 2021; Sokol & Flach, 2020; Arrieta et al., 2020; Wang et al., 2024).

As can be seen from the manifold aspects covered, the aforementioned approaches are specific to human cognition. However, the complex implications of XAI in organizations, institutions, and society remain underexplored (Haque et al., 2023). In fact, Brasse et al. (2023) summarize that it is mainly cognitive theories that are employed in XAI, and this constricts current research.

1.4 Social Factors in XAI Development

Going beyond individual and specific cognitive processing, literature discusses user satisfaction, trust, responsibilities, and understanding—all concepts that are semantically abstract and difficult to grasp. Although there are approaches that attempt to define these in general terms (Hsiao et al., 2021), most studies find their own isolated solutions. Thus, when addressing social aspects, we face the challenge of not only determining that the relevant concepts are difficult to grasp but also that they can be interpreted in a variety of ways.

Concerning user satisfaction, recently, Ehsan et al. (2021) identified the need for social transparency and the need to understand the social-technical gap for XAI (Ehsan et al., 2023). Clearly, not only the users' cognitive processing but more of their context (and implication for it) has to be regarded. When recently addressing more complex implications of XAI, Ali et al. (2023) provided an extensive overview of the variety of methods that are available, criticizing that these methods do not regard whether they satisfy the intended audience's needs (Ali et al., 2023). The authors define satisfaction as the "ability of an explainability technique to improve the usability and utility of the ML-based system" (Ali et al., 2023, p. 8). Because the XAI methods do not support this ability, the authors argue that this state undermines the trustworthiness of the AI solutions.

Trust is another commonly discussed social factor going beyond a psychological state Hsiao et al. (2021). In this regard, Ali et al. (2023) recognize that the trustworthiness of an AI connects states and circumstances. To gain trust, Arrieta et al. (2020) suggest that responsible AI design needs to take the audience as a key aspect into account. This emphasis is justified, because the involvement of the users and the impact on their understanding are barely in the focus of XAI development. Instead, explanations are commonly evaluated intrinsically. Such a focus on the audience and thus on responsible AI would clearly be an advance on current approaches, but the question of how to take the audience into account has no short answer. Some recent approaches to this question differentiate types of users (developers, experts, or lay users), or group users according to their mental models including their beliefs about technology (e.g., in high-level experts or in low literacy) when developing an XAI for specific purposes (Haque et al., 2023). Nonetheless, even though these approaches appear concrete, they result in a rather static XAI that is designed for a target group but are unable to fine-tune or modify their predefined actions in the course of an interaction.

When targeting complex implications of XAI in organizations or institutions, XAI needs to tap into social ecologies. Addressing this need, Meske et al. (2022) zoom out and present the process of decision-making in which an XAI is involved. The innovation of their paper is to emphasize the management of organizational processes as a goal of XAI. It is based on the argument that as a new form of material agency in organizational processes, XAI changes work routines (Ehsan et al., 2021), social practices, and responsibilities. Whereas the first step is to specify groups of stakeholders such as AI regulators, AI developers, AI managers, AI users, and individuals affected, this does not provide an instrument to analyze the ecologies of the decision-making process.

Another social factor is understanding. Whereas relevant investigations might comprise the inspection of relevant cognitive processes or mental models (Hsiao et al., 2021), the term is also related to the pragmatics of its occurrence: understanding for what purpose, with regard to what circumstances, and what abilities of the users? Rohlfing et al. (2021) have argued in favor of broadening the notion of understanding to go beyond what is expected for scientific explanations and extending it to everyday explanations. Recently, Buschmeier et al. (2025) have proposed a comprehensive taxonomy of understanding forms, all of which need to be better investigated in future XAI settings in order to increase the relevance of the explanations for the users.

In summary and following the conclusions by Ali et al. (2023), most research on how to interpret and explain AI systems is motivated by the requirements of developers rather than users and their circumstances. However, to comprehend an AI system satisfactorily, each context of a user requires a different level of explanation

(Sokol & Flach, 2020) and understanding (Buschmeier et al., 2025). Whereas many solutions have been proposed to categorize the users as groups that have particular characteristics being related to a specific preferences in explaining (Haque et al., 2023; Arrieta et al., 2020; Ali et al., 2023; Langer et al., 2021), these solutions do not address the individual levels of explanation and understanding that are needed in user-centered approaches. It can thus be concluded that whereas social aspects are well-recognized in current XAI research and partially identified, what is missing is a stronger guidance toward how to involve users in a meaningful social interaction in order to make an explanation relevant and adapted to the user's emerging understanding. Crucial keys to understanding this gap are to involve the users in XAI as well as to ground the XAI development in theoretical work from other fields—goals that align with our goals for this book. For user involvement, Chromik and Butz (2021) suggest that XAI systems need to be sensitive to the user's mental state and the context of explanation in order to flexibly provide multiple ways to explain. To achieve this flexibility, the incrementality of the dialog can be utilized, because this property makes a step-by-step adaptation possible.

Yet, such flexible systems are currently lacking. The goal of this book is to push forward the necessary research in order to respond to the original call for interactive explanations (Miller, 2019), in which both partners can and should contribute to interaction process. This requires a certain type of an interaction that we elaborate on in this book.

1.5 The Focus on Interaction and a Definition of *Social XAI*

We have argued that what is currently missing in XAI is an answer to the question of how to involve users in a meaningful interaction and, thus, to adapt the explanation to the user's emerging understanding. Let us now focus on the explanatory dialog as a process in which the user can be actively engaged. An explanatory dialog is not just an exchange of specific verbal and nonverbal behaviors. It is the "dialogical coupling" (Fusaroli et al., 2014, p. 147) of explainer and explainee that allows a dynamic process between the partners to unfold. The full dynamics of interaction makes it possible for the partner to adapt to and to negotiate a form of understanding incrementally. This way, explaining can be better intertwined with different forms of understanding—a desideratum for the social design of AI systems (Rohlfing et al., 2021). It builds on the current state of the art, according to which an explanation addressing the *why* does not necessarily lead to an understanding. This is because the explanation might well be comprehensive, simple, or personalized, but it might not be relevant to the user at that moment. **In this book, we therefore place the interaction at the center of our approach to social aspects of explainable AI and propose that it is a means by which an explanation becomes relevant**.

Our focus accords with some concrete answers to the question of how the audience or a user can be taken into account. In this respect, the review by Chromik and Butz (2021) offers design principles for explanation interfaces that focus on the usage of an XAI. Accordingly, the review takes a systematic look at the way the interaction is designed in XAI research. For their purpose, the authors define the explanation user interface (XUI) as "the sum of outputs of an XAI system that the user can directly interact with" (Chromik and Butz, 2021, p. 619). With this definition, explanatory power is assigned to the interaction and not to a statement. The authors review different types of interaction varying in the degree to which the user is involved and influences the system's output. Chromik and Butz (2021) propose that for a system to be interactive, it needs to take advantage of the naturalness of a human–human dialog with multiple turns; it needs to allow an incremental follow-up on initial explanations, flexibility through multiple ways to explain, and sensitivity to the user's mind and context of explanation. The review critically reveals that there are few approaches allowing preemptive task co-management and shared progress tracking in a human–XAI interaction with abilities that make a system flexible and allow an explanation to be adapted to the user.

The focus on interaction offers both: On the one hand, users can be involved, and, while participating in interaction, they can steer it to receive an explanation that is most informative and helpful for them. On the other hand, when users are involved in the explanation process, social factors need to be considered. These specific social factors will be regarded in this book. This access to the social dimension is certainly limited. Even though we are aware of that this chosen focus on social interaction offers access to only a subset of social aspects, we decided to call the book *Social XAI (sXAI)*, because the main aim is to approach the social dimension of XAI with a clear connection of the social factors to the explaining process. In addition, the focus on social interaction offers a form of an application setting for the social dimension resulting in many possibilities for operationalizing the relevant social aspects.

For our proposed perspective, the properties of an interaction are foundational. These properties go beyond the cognitive aspects suggested by Miller (2019): In addition to defining explanations as selective and contrastive to foster the cognitive process of abductive reasoning (i.e., deriving a hypothesis to explain observed phenomenon), we aim to extend current theories in XAI that focus mainly on cognitive processes (Brasse et al., 2023) to interactive approaches. To solidify theoretical foundations, a broader and interaction-oriented perspective is needed.

> Inspired by social interactions, we define sXAI (social explainable AI) as systems that interactively adapt to users in order to co-construct a satisfying explanation. Social interactions are typically characterized by being patterned, incremental, and multimodal. This requires the overall conception of the explanation to take into account the relevant social context in terms of the heterogeneity of participants and their environments along with the unfolding context of interaction.

Our definition is in line with more general suggestions by Naiseh (2024, p. 170) who considers sXAI as approaches, tools, and design techniques that aim not only to explain AI but also to provide benefits to users and the human–AI team. Taken together, what our definitions have in common is their focus on the explainee and especially on their empowerment in line with the goal of "realizing the full potential of XAI" (Naiseh, 2024, p. 175).

To structure our view along clear dimensions and add to already proposed characteristics of an explanation, we focus on the following properties of a social interaction:

- Interaction is **patterned** in the sense that social interaction does not evolve randomly. Instead, interaction is organized sequentially around a goal that is negotiated, and, thus, it changes and potentially even emerges during the interaction. The concept of the goal is central to a social interaction being organized in a pattern. For an explanation, a goal might relate to understanding the function of the system or to being informed about uncertainty in its output. This goal-oriented organization takes place in social and physical contexts and depends on them: Whereas the social context characterizes the explainee's beliefs, social roles, and expectations about the dialog, the physical context relates to relevant aspects of the actual dialogue setting at hand. For the explanatory dialog, we can also say that it is also structured in joint sequential interaction patterns influenced by norms, values, and situational context. The explanatory patterns evolve over time and include universal dialog patterns that are transmitted culturally. In the case of an explanation, specific conversational patterns also give rise to cognitive patterns (e.g., cognitive operations that are typical for reasoning when formulating or receiving explanations). In light of this property of interaction, we postulate that XAI can utilize these interaction patterns for effective explanations. This part of the book covers those ingredients necessary to shape interactions in explaining processes that are essential for forming patterns according to which partners act, predict the further course of the dialog, and fulfill their expectations and roles. Whereas some patterns are general, others are specific to explaining contexts and goals. Different contexts and goals will lead to the emergence of different social roles, and different responsibilities, and this will impact on the construction of explanations. However, the implementation of XAI systems' structures and practices carries risks. These include that XAI may even foster the expected deskilling of people when AI systems take over more and more cognitive tasks as well as encourage too much trust in the alleged reliability of the systems' outputs. It is important to work proactively on preventive measures for these and other risks, both on the side of the developers of XAI methods and that by the deployers of XAI systems in real-world scenarios.
- Interaction is **incremental**. Observing an interaction from outside, *incrementality* describes elements that the partners involved contribute. They sum up to a sequence of behaviors. By participating in an interaction and from the inside, the partners involved build their contribution relating to each other. Together, incrementality allows for a fine-grained and gradual co-construction of the

explanation between the user and the XAI system. Accordingly, an incremental explanation strategy requires and allows both parties to adapt to each other, and it facilitates the identification of misunderstandings directly monitoring each other's reactions—including verbal and nonverbal cues. When misunderstandings surface, the explainer can employ social techniques such as scaffolding to accommodate the explainee's needs and expectations. This interactive process empowers the explainer to enhance their understanding of the explainee and update their model accordingly. We propose that to accomplish this nuanced adaptation, the explainer needs to have a model of not only the subject matter but also of the explainee's current comprehension level regarding the subject. Successful adaptation also hinges on considering the broader context of the interaction. This encompasses such factors as social roles, physical surroundings, ongoing tasks, but also basic conditions with application risks (as defined by AI ACT in Europe), and constraints faced by the explainee. This contextual awareness also extends beyond the immediate interaction and encompasses the history of interactions with the same explainee and other individuals within the same social network. As part of a social system, this demands consistency in the explanations provided to different explainees, ensuring not only trustworthiness but also averting potential controversies among social peers. To account for these aspects, a social XAI system should possess capabilities surpassing those of human–human interaction; it should deliver pertinent and accurate information – particularly when that information has legal implications – while also maintaining human agency and empowering individuals to request explanations and to have the right to have their personal data forgotten at any time.

- Interaction is **multimodal**, because an interaction utilizes many communicative signals in parallel: When people talk to each other, they can hear their partner speak; they can see their partner's face and body language. This means that communication uses multiple modalities; all are closely coordinated in their timing and work simultaneously. Explanations that people give each other (e.g., why there is a rainbow) make good use of these modalities (e.g., visualizing the angle at which sunlight falls on raindrops by drawing the trajectory in the air with a hand gesture). But it is not only the explainer who uses these multimodal signals. While both partners can see each other, explainees also use nonverbal modalities—for example, to give feedback on their understanding by signaling positive understanding by nodding their head, to communicate their focus of attention (by looking at a certain location), or to indicate that they would like to ask a question (by looking at the speaker and breathing in). Thus, humans show emotions and use gestures, drawings, sound effects, and other modalities to make their contribution more comprehensible and efficient for the explainee. In contrast, current XAI systems often overlook the importance of social interaction and the multimodal nature of communication. Yet they have multimodal potential, because AI systems can have screens, projectors, or other capabilities that humans do not have, and these can be valuable when it comes to making explanations easier to understand. In order to achieve true social XAI, we propose that all these capabilities are needed jointly. The key capability of an AI system should be to assess and interpret the reactions and social cues of humans in order to make dialogs fluent and comfortable. This is a form of monitoring that can serve as a basis for further action. This monitoring is informative for a situational assessment through which the dialog can be predicted. It makes it possible to avoid knowledge issues, conflict of intentions, or misunderstanding and thereby not only provide a successful explanation but also prevent breakdowns. Therefore, the AI system needs capabilities to recognize and manage these situations when conducting explanation dialogs. It is postulated that XAI needs to account for different modalities of communications that are used in the process of constructing an explanation to better react to (non)understanding and thus to foster different forms of understanding. To become social, we argue that XAI needs to use and perceive multimodal signals when explaining AI behavior or decisions to humans.

In addition to the three characteristics of the explanatory process, the introductory part of the book sets up the components of explanatory process and the scenarios that we envision. It also offers a framework to context-aware sXAI. The last part of the book deals with the comprehensive evaluation of sXAI. This part demonstrates how the evaluation of the effectiveness of XAI as a social actor that shows some context awareness can benefit from accumulated knowledge in the social sciences. The purpose is to aid the development of context-aware sXAI-systems for interaction with humans. For this, it is important to identify causality, to adequately account for human heterogeneity and diversity beyond stereotypes, to be aware of the boundaries concerning external validity, and to assess empirical effect sizes. Concerning the operationalization of empirical outcomes, human responses must be adequately captured, carefully differentiating between those inner states of humans that are socially relevant (e.g., trust), behavioral responses (e.g., reliance), and the well-known attitude–behavior gap (a dissonance between what humans do and what they consider to be an appropriate behavior) between them. The gap captures the lack of correspondence between the assessment of an attitude on the one hand (e.g., by a survey) and users' performed behaviors on the other hand (as observed). Moreover, systematic evaluations will have to take into account the temporal dimension of interactions, moving away from short-term evaluations to taking sXAI systems seriously as social actors that can build on past interactions, learn from other interactions, and anticipate future interactions as social actors would also do. Finally, this part also discusses imperatives that may bias research questions. When researching humans in social contexts, researchers must carefully reflect on their norms and values before generalizing them to others. For instance, orienting design toward the researcher's self may neglect vulnerable citizens who need more protection from AI automation than others. Here, our recommendation for developers and designers of sXAI is to engage in what is often called the *moral point of view*—i.e., to go beyond one's own individual interests by taking into account several perspectives of different stakeholders and social groups, by trying to assess the design choices in light of the common good, etc. The key is to balance the chances of including social information in XAI and mitigate risks by embedding the sXAI systems into a governance structure extending from development to deployment.

Taken together, successful sXAI will enable people to solve their tasks more efficiently and effectively by making best use of the inherent capabilities of AI methods, in both professional and personal situations. At the same time, it makes it possible to include peoples' genuine skills and leave control over the process to them wherever needed. The understanding of the AI's decisions and behaviors gained through sXAI will not only give people the trust needed to responsibly and maturely integrate AI into the cognitive processes of everyday life, but also make them aware of the aspects in life that distinguish artificial intelligence from human intelligence.

In addition to shedding light on the social dimension by showing why XAI should be social, our book has the objective of **fostering the emerging interdisciplinary community** and participating in a dialog about how to involve users and how to address the lack of consideration of interaction in previous research. With their contribution, the authors follow the objective of expanding current research in computer science, and they offer new answers to the societal challenge mentioned above by contributing to the development of the following:

- A multidisciplinary understanding of the mechanisms involved in the process of explaining, adapting it to the process of understanding.
- Concrete operationalizations for how to involve the users in an interaction with an XAI.
- Computational models and complex AI systems that focus efficiently on what kind of explanation a person requires in a current context.
- An extension of the perspective on interaction to multimodal properties on multiple timescales to give justice to an interaction that unfolds over time and makes a joint construction of a relevant explanation pattern possible.

Writing these chapters has been a collective and interdisciplinary project. With this book, we present selected social concepts that specify the perspective on sXAI here proposed. We follow the developments in social and interactive AI in general, building on concepts from a large number of disciplines involved in social sciences (such as linguistics, philosophy, and psychology).

The reader will soon notice that the social aspects that are introduced in this book are related to each other—this connection reflects the nature of social concepts. They are not just grounded in perception and action; they are also a product of "a collective endeavor" to encode our knowledge (Shea, 2018, p. 5). Because of this nature, we can anticipate that despite all calls for terminological clarity, the meanings of the concepts will remain open for negotiations. The development of the concepts for this book goes hand in hand with the development of the perspective on sXAI and further discussions about this topic that we are aiming to initiate here.

We wish to highlight the fact that all authors but also reviewers contributed to the collective endeavor: Anna-Lisa Vollmer led the first part, Kary Främling and Britta Wrede supervised the second part, Angela Grimminger the third part, and Kirsten Thommes and Suzana Alpsancar the evaluation part. Hendrik Buschmeier supervised the collaborative writing. We also thank all our external reviewers: Carola de Beer, Zachary Daus, Andreas Holzinger, Eyke Hüllermeier, Casey Kennington, Matthias Kettner, Antonia Krummheuer, Francisco Javier Rodriguez Lera, Tobias Matzner, Tim Miller, Philip Müller, Gabriel Skantze, Matthijs Smakman, Manfred Stede, Simon Trang, Vaibhav Unhelkar, and Marina de Vos.

All chapters were read by Jonathan Harrow and Cornelia Casey-Buschmeier, and we are grateful for their proofreading. We furthermore thank Sebastian Mantsch for proofreading Chaps. 10, 29, and 30.

1.6 Addressees of the Book

Our vision is that each chapter will be read by two types of readers: those who are working on technology development and those who are working in related fields with a background in social sciences. Hence, the main goal of each chapter is to present the 'social aspect' in a comprehensible way with current definitions, the state of the art, and the major challenges that are currently being discussed. The challenge is to link the 'social aspect' to the development of XAI systems that are capable of expressing/interacting in a human-understandable way. Because literature in this respect is scarce, many of the chapters propose ideas on how to implement the aspects in XAI. This experience will certainly differ from using books in a usual way. In other words, whereas a book is supposed to provide clear access to how to handle an aspect in research, the chapters in our book can only be a first step and inspiration for XAI developers. In this respect, the readership will find concrete operationalizations of the *social aspects* that they will be able to implement in their research. For researchers with a background in social sciences (or other disciplines), this book should offer insights into the application of social aspects in the context of XAI. It will highlight new facets related to this specific application domain from which new research questions might emerge. It will also show how these aspects are connected.

1.7 Structure of the Book

In the following, we provide some information on the structure of the book as a whole and how each chapter is organized.

Parts of the Book The book is structured in five parts that we considered essential for interactive sXAI. The introductory part sets up the structure with the scenarios that we envision. Whereas we put a lot of effort into identifying social aspects relevant for a social and interactive XAI, we have to highlight that our readership has to expect some *interrelations* between the chapters and therefore overlapping content. The references to each other, we think, are inherent to all social aspects, thereby accounting for a holistic phenomenon.

Each Chapter in the Book Because the field is growing rapidly, each chapter ends with a short section on "how does this chapter inspire further directions of sXAI?" This is to suggest some concrete goals and objectives to the XAI community. For fast readers, we make use of the rapid access section with which each chapter closes. In contrast to an abstract, this presents the content in a more condensed way.

Acknowledgments We wish to thank our coeditors, Kary Främling, Kirsten Thommes, and Suzana Alpsancar as well as the heads of the book's parts – Anna-Lisa Vollmer and Angela Grimminger – for their support in finalizing this chapter.

This work was funded by the Deutsche Forschungsgemeinschaft (DFG, German Research Foundation): TRR 318/1 2021 – 438445824.

References

Abdul, A., Von Der Weth, C., Kankanhalli, M., & Lim, B. Y. (2020). COGAM: Measuring and moderating cognitive load in machine learning model explanations. In *Proceedings of the 2020 CHI Conference on Human Factors in Computing Systems*. CHI '20 (pp. 1–14). Association for Computing Machinery. https://doi.org/10.1145/3313831.3376615

Ali, S., Abuhmed, T., El-Sappagh, S., Muhammad, K., Alonso-Moral, J. M., Confalonieri, R., Guidotti, R., Del Ser, J., Diaz-Rodriguez, N., & Herrera, F. (2023). Explainable Artificial Intelligence (XAI): What we know and what is left to attain Trustworthy Artificial Intelligence. *Information Fusion, 99*, 101805. https://doi.org/10.1016/j.inffus.2023.101805

Anjomshoae, S., Najjar, A., Calvaresi, D., & FrFrämlingmling, K. (2019). Explainable agents and robots: Results from a systematic literature review. In E. Elkind, M. Velosos, N. Agmon & M. E. Taylor (Eds.), *Proceedings of the 18th International Conference on Autonomous Agents and Multiagent Systems* (pp. 1078–1088). AAMAS. International Foundation for Autonomous Agents and Multiagent Systems.

Arora, S., Pruthi, D., Sadeh, N., Cohen, W. W., Lipton, Z. C., & Neubig, G. (2022). Explain, edit, and understand: Rethinking user study design for evaluating model explanations. In *Proceedings of the AAAI Conference on Artificial Intelligence* (pp. 5277–5285). AAAI. https://doi.org/10.1609/aaai.v36i5.20464

Arrieta, A. B., Díaz-Rodriguez, N., Del Ser, J., Bennetot, A., Tabik, S., Barbado, A., Garcia, S., Gil-Lopez, S., Molina, D., Benjamins, R., Chatila, R., & Herrera, F. (2020). Explainable Artificial Intelligence (XAI): Concepts, taxonomies, opportunities and challenges toward responsible AI. *Information Fusion, 58*, 82–115. https://doi.org/10.1016/j.inffus.2019.12.012

Bansal, G., Wu, T., Zhou, J., Fok, R., Nushi, B., Kamar, E., Ribeiro, M. T., & Weld, D. (2021). Does the whole exceed its parts? The effect of AI explanations on complementary team performance. In *Proceedings of the 2021 CHI Conference on Human Factors in Computing Systems*. CHI '21 (pp. 1–16). Association for Computing Machinery. https://doi.org/10.1145/3411764.3445717

Bo, J. Y., Hao, P., & Lim, B. Y. (2024). Incremental XAI: Memorable understanding of AI with incremental explanations. In *Proceedings of the CHI Conference on Human Factors in Computing Systems*. CHI '24 (pp. 1–17). Association for Computing Machinery. https://doi.org/10.1145/3613904.3642689

Bory, P., Natale, S., & Katzenbach, C. (2024). Strong and weak AI narratives: An analytical framework. In *AI & Society*. https://doi.org/10.1007/s00146-024-02087-8

Brasse, J., Broder, H. R., Förster, M., Klier, M., & Sigler, I. (2023). Explainable Artificial Intelligence in information systems: A review of the status quo and future research directions. *Electronic Markets, 33*(1), 26. https://doi.org/10.1007/s12525-023-00644-5

Buçinca, Z., Lin, P., Gajos, K. Z., & Glassman, E. L. (2020). Proxy tasks and subjective measures can be misleading in evaluating explainable AI systems. In *Proceedings of the 25th International Conference on Intelligent User Interfaces* (pp. 454–464). Association for Computing Machinery. https://doi.org/10.1145/3377325.3377498

Buçinca, Z., Malaya, M. B., & Gajos, K. Z. (2021). To trust or to think: Cognitive forcing functions can reduce overreliance on AI in AI-assisted decision-making. In *Proceedings of the ACM on Human–Computer Interaction* 5.CSCW1 (p. 188). https://doi.org/10.1145/3449287

Buschmeier, H., Buhl, H.M., Kern, F., Grimminger, A., Beierling, H., Fisher, J., Groß, A., Horwath, I., Klowait, N., Lazarov, S., Lenke, M., Lohmer, V., Rohlfing, K.J., Scharlau, I., Singh, Terfloth, L., A., Vollmer, A.-L., Wang, Y., Wilmes, A., & Wrede, B. (2025). Forms of understanding of XAI-explanations. *Cognitive Systems Research, 94*, 101419. https://doi.org/10.1016/j.cogsys.2025.101419

Chen, V., Liao, Q. V., Wortman Vaughan, J., & Bansal, G. (2023). Understanding the role of human intuition on reliance in human-AI decision- making with explanations. In *Proceedings of the ACM on Human–Computer Interaction* (pp. 1–32). Association for Computing Machinery. https://doi.org/10.1145/3610219

Cheng, H.-F., Wang, R., Zhang, Z., O'connell, F., Gray, T., Harper, F. M., & Zhu, H. (2019). Explaining decision-making algorithms through UI: Strategies to help non-expert stakeholders. In *Proceedings of the 2019 CHI Conference on Human Factors in Computing Systems*. CHI '19 (pp. 1–12). Association for Computing Machinery. https://doi.org/10.1145/3290605.3300789

Chromik, M., & Butz, A. (2021). Human–XAI interaction: A review and design principles for explanation user interfaces. In C. Ardito, R. Lanzilotti, A. Malizia, H. Petrie, A. Piccinno, G. Desolda & K. Inkpen (Eds.), *Human–Computer Interaction – INTERACT* (pp. 619–640). Notes in computer science. Springer. https://doi.org/10.1007/978-3-030-85616-8_36

Colin, J., Fel, T., Cadène, R., & Serre, T. (2022). What I cannot predict, I do not understand: A human-centered evaluation framework for explainability methods. In *Advances in Neural Information Processing Systems* (Vol. 35, pp. 2832–2845).

Dodge, J., Liao, Q. V., Zhang, Y., Bellamy, R. K. E., & Dugan, C. (2019). Explaining models: An empirical study of how explanations impact fairness judgment. In *Proceedings of the 24th International Conference on Intelligent User Interfaces* (pp. 275–285). Association for Computing Machinery. https://doi.org/10.1145/3301275.3302310

Ehsan, U., Liao, Q. V., Muller, M., Riedl, M. O., & Weisz, J. D. (2021). Expanding explainability: Towards social transparency in AI systems. In *Proceedings of the 2021 CHI Conference on Human Factors in Computing Systems*. CHI '21 (pp. 1–19). Association for Computing Machinery. https://doi.org/10.1145/3411764.3445188

Ehsan, U., Passi, S., Liao, Q. V., Chan, L., Lee, I. H., Muller, M., & Riedl, M. O. (2024). The who in XAI: How AI background shapes perceptions of AI explanations. In *Proceedings of the CHI Conference on Human Factors in Computing Systems*. CHI '24 (pp. 1–32). Association for Computing Machinery. https://doi.org/10.1145/3613904.3642474

Ehsan, U., Saha, K., De Choudhury, M., & Riedl, M. O. (2023). Charting the sociotechnical gap in explainable AI: A framework to address the gap in XAI. In *Proceedings of the ACM on Human–Computer Interaction* (pp. 1–32). Association for Computing Machinery. https://doi.org/10.1145/3579467

Fusaroli, R., Rączaszek-Leonardi, J., & Tylén, K. (2014). Dialog as interpersonal synergy. *New Ideas in Psychology, 32*, 147–157. https://doi.org/10.1016/j.newideapsych.2013.03.005

Gunning, D., Stefik, M., Choi, J., Miller, T., Stumpf, S., & Yang, G.-Z. (2019). XAI – explainable Artificial Intelligence. *Science Robotics, 4*(37), eaay7120. https://doi.org/10.1126/scirobotics.aay7120

Haque, A. K. M. B., Najmul Islam, A. K. M., & Mikalef, P. (2023). Explainable Artificial Intelligence (XAI) from a user perspective: A synthesis of prior literature and problematizing avenues for future research. *Technological Forecasting and Social Change, 186,* 122120. https://doi.org/10.1016/j.techfore.2022.122120

Hase, P., & Bansal, M. (2020). Evaluating explainable AI: Which algorithmic explanations help users predict model behavior?" In *Proceedings of the 58th Annual Meeting of the Association for Computational Linguistics.* Association for Computing Machinery. https://doi.org/10.18653/v1/2020.acl-main.491

Hsiao, J. H.-W., Ngai Hilary, H. T., Qiu, L., Yang, Y., & Cao, C. C. (2021). (2021). *Roadmap of designing cognitive metrics for Explainable Artificial Intelligence.* https://doi.org/10.48550/arXiv.2108.01737

Kaplan, A., & Haenlein, M. (2019). Siri, Siri, in my hand: Who's the fairest in the land? On the interpretations, illustrations, and implications of artificial intelligence. *Business Horizons, 62*(1), 15–25. https://doi.org/10.1016/j.bushor.2018.08.004

Kaplan, S., Uusitalo, H., & Lensu, L. (2024). A unified and practical user-centric framework for explainable artificial intelligence. *Knowledge-Based Systems, 283,* 111107. https://doi.org/10.1016/j.knosys.2023.111107

Kaur, H., Nori, H., Jenkins, S., Caruana, R., Wallach, H., & Wortman Vaughan, J. (2020). Interpreting interpretability: Understanding data scientists' use of interpretability tools for machine learning. In *Proceedings of the 2020 CHI Conference on Human Factors in Computing Systems.* CHI '20 (pp. 1–14). Association for Computing Machinery. https://doi.org/10.1145/3313831.3376219

Kulesza, T., Burnett, M., Wong, W.-K., & Stumpf, S. (2015). Principles of explanatory debugging to personalize interactive machine learning. In *Proceedings of the 20th International Conference on Intelligent User Interfaces* (pp. 126–137). Association for Computing Machinery. https://doi.org/10.1145/2678025.2701399

Lai, V., & Tan, C. (2019). On human predictions with explanations and predictions of machine learning models: A case study on deception detection. In *Proceedings of the Conference on Fairness, Accountability, and Transparency* (pp. 29–38). Association for Computing Machinery. https://doi.org/10.1145/3287560.3287590

Lai, V., Zhang, Y., Chen, C., Liao, Q. V., & Tan, C. (2023). (2023). Selective explanations: Leveraging human input to align explainable AI. In *Proceedings of the ACM on Human–Computer Interaction* 7.CSCW2 (p. 357). https://doi.org/10.1145/3610206

Langer, M., Oster, D., Speith, T., Hermanns, H., Kästner, L., Schmidt, E., Sesing, A., & Baum, K. (2021). What do we want from explainable artificial intelligence (XAI)? A stakeholder perspective on XAI and a conceptual model guiding interdisciplinary XAI research. *Artificial Intelligence, 296,* 103473. https://doi.org/10.1016/j.artint.2021.103473

Liao, Q. V., Gruen, D., & Miller, S. (2020). Questioning the AI: Informing design practices for explainable AI user experiences. In *Proceedings of the 2020 CHI Conference on Human Factors in Computing Systems.* CHI '20 (pp. 1–15). Association for Computing Machinery. https://doi.org/10.1145/3313831.3376590

Lim, B. Y., Cahaly, J. P., Sng, C. Y., & Chew, A. (2025). Diagrammatization and abduction to improve AI interpretability with domain-aligned explanations for medical diagnosis. In *Proceedings of the 2019 CHI Conference on Human Factors in Computing Systems.* CHI '19 (pp. 1–25). Association for Computing Machinery. https://doi.org/10.1145/3706598.3714058

Lim, B. Y., & Dey, A. K. (2009). Assessing demand for intelligibility in context-aware applications. In *Proceedings of the 11th International Conference on Ubiquitous Computing* (pp. 195–204). Association for Computing Machinery. https://doi.org/10.1145/1620545.1620576

Lim, B. Y., & Dey, A. K. (2011). Investigating intelligibility for uncertain context-aware applications. In *Proceedings of the 13th International Conference on Ubiquitous Computing* (pp. 415–424). Association for Computing Machinery. https://doi.org/10.1145/2030112.2030168

Lim, B. Y., Dey, A. K., & Avrahami, D. (2009). Why and why not explanations improve the intelligibility of context-aware intelligent systems. In *Proceedings of the SIGCHI Conference on Human Factors in Computing Systems* (pp. 2119–2128). Association for Computing Machinery. https://doi.org/10.1145/1518701.1519023

Lyu, Y., Lu, H., Lee, M. K., Schmitt, G., & Lim, B. Y. (2023). IF- City: Intelligible fair city planning to measure, explain and mitigate inequality. *IEEE Transactions on Visualization and Computer Graphics, 30*(7), 3749–3766. https://doi.org/10.1109/TVCG.2023.3239909

Matsuyama, H., Kawaguchi, N., & Lim, B. Y. (2023). IRIS:<?pag ?> Interpretable rubric-informed segmentation for action quality assessment. In *Proceedings of the 28th International Conference on Intelligent User Interfaces* (pp. 368–378). Association for Computing Machinery. https://doi.org/10.1145/3581641.3584048

Meske, C., Bunde, E., Schneider, J., & Gersch, M. (2022). Explainable artificial intelligence: Objectives, stakeholders, and future research opportunities. *Information Systems Management, 39*(1), 53–63. https://doi.org/10.1080/10580530.2020.1849465

Mill, E., Garn, W., Ryman-Tubb, N., & Turner, C. (2024). The SAGE framework for explaining context in Explainable Artificial Intelligence. *Applied Artificial Intelligence, 38*(1), e2318670. https://doi.org/10.1080/08839514.2024.2318670

Miller, T. (2019). Explanation in artificial intelligence: Insights from the social sciences. *Artificial Intelligence, 267,* 1–38. https://doi.org/10.1016/j.artint.2018.07.007

Miller, T. (2023). Explainable AI is dead, long live explainable AI! Hypothesis-driven decision support using evaluative AI. In *Proceedings of the 2023 ACM Conference on Fairness, Accountability, and Transparency* (pp. 333–342). Association for Computing Machinery. https://doi.org/10.1145/3593013.3594001

Naiseh, M. (2024). Social eXplainable AI (Social XAI): Towards explaining the social benefits of XAI. In C. Monta & R. Ali (Eds.), *The Impact of Artificial Intelligence on Societies. Understanding Attitude Formation towards AI* (pp. 169–178). Springer.

Poursabzi-Sangdeh, F., Goldstein, D. G., Hofman, J. M., Wortman Vaughan, J. W., & Wallach, H. (2021). Manipulating and measuring model interpretability. In *Proceedings of the 2021 CHI Conference on Human Factors in Computing Systems.* CHI '21 (pp. 1–52). Association for Computing Machinery. https://doi.org/10.1145/3411764.3445315

Rohlfing, K. J., Cimiano, P., Scharlau, I., Matzner, T., Buhl, H., Buschmeier, H., Grimminger, A., Hammer, B., Häb-Umbach, R., Horwath, I., Hüllermeier, E., Kern, F., Kopp, S., Thommes, K., Ngonga Ngomo, A.-C., Schulte, C., Wachsmuth, H., Wagner, P., & Wrede, B (2021). Explanation as a social practice: Toward a conceptual framework for the social design of AI systems. *IEEE Transactions on Cognitive and Developmental Systems, 13*(3), 717–728. https://doi.org/10.1109/TCDS.2020.3044366

Rong, Y., Leemann, T., Nguyen, T.-T., Fiedler, L., Qian, P., Unhelkar, V., Seidel, T., Kasneci, G., & Kasneci, E. (2023). Towards human-centered explainable AI: A survey of user studies for model explanations. *IEEE Transactions on Pattern Analysis and Machine Intelligence, 46*(4), 2104– 2122. https://doi.org/10.1109/TPAMI.2023.3331846

Ross, A. S., Hughes, M. C., Doshi-Velez, F. (2017). Right for the right reasons: Training differentiable models by constraining their explanations. In *Proceedings of the Twenty-Sixth International Joint Conference on Artificial Intelligence.* IJCAI '17 (pp. 2662–2670). International Joint Conference on Artificial Intelligence. https://doi.org/10.24963/ijcai.2017/371

Shea, N. (2018). Metacognition and abstract concepts. *Philosophical Transactions of the Royal Society B: Biological Sciences, 373*(1752), 20170133. https://doi.org/10.1098/rstb.2017.0133

Sokol, K., & Flach, P. (2020). One explanation does not fit all. *KI- Künstliche Intelligenz, 34,* 235–250. https://doi.org/10.1007/s13218-020-00637-y

Speith, T., Crook, B., Mann, S., Schomäcker, A., & Langer, M. (2024). (2024). Conceptualizing understanding in explainable artificial intelligence (XAI): An abilities-based approach. *Ethics and Information Technology, 26*(2), 40. https://doi.org/10.1007/s10676-024-09769-3

Wang, D., Yang, Q., Abdul, A., & Lim, B. Y. (2019). Designing theory-driven user-centric explainable AI. In *Proceedings of the 2019 CHI Conference on Human Factors in Computing Systems.* CHI '19 (pp. 1–15). Association for Computing Machinery. https://doi.org/10.1145/3290605.330083

Wang, D., Zhang, W., & Lim, B. Y. (2021). Show or suppress? Managing input uncertainty in machine learning model explanations. *Artificial Intelligence, 294,* 103456. https://doi.org/10.1016/j.artint.2021.103456

Wang, X., & Yin, M (2021). Are explanations helpful? A comparative study of the effects of explanations in AI-assisted decision-making. In *Proceedings of the 26th International Conference on Intelligent User Interfaces* (pp. 318–328). Association for Computing Machinery. https://doi.org/10.1145/3397481.3450650

Wang, Z., Huang, C., & Yao, X. (2024). A roadmap of explainable artificial intelligence: Explain to whom, when, what and how? *ACM Transactions on Autonomous and Adaptive Systems, 19*(4), 20. https://doi.org/10.1145/3702004

Zhang, W., Dimiccoli, M., & Lim, B. Y. (2022). Debiased-CAM to mitigate image perturbations with faithful visual explanations of machine learning. In *Proceedings of the 2022 CHI Conference on Human Factors in Computing Systems*. CHI '22 (pp. 1–32). Association for Computing Machinery. https://doi.org/10.1145/3491102.3517522

Zhang, W., & Lim, B. Y. (2022). Towards relatable explainable AI with the perceptual process. In *Proceedings of the 2022 CHI Conference on Human Factors in Computing Systems* (pp. 1–24). Association for Computing Machinery. https://doi.org/10.1145/3491102.3501826

Zhang, Y., Vera Liao, Q., & Bellamy, R. K. E. (2020). Effect of confidence and explanation on accuracy and trust calibration in AI-assisted decision making. In *Proceedings of the 2020 Conference on Fairness, Accountability, and Transparency* (pp. 295–305). Association for Computing Machinery. https://doi.org/10.1145/3351095.3372852

Zhang, W., Dimiccoli, M., & Lim, B. Y (2021). Exploiting explanations for model inversion attacks. In *Proceedings of the IEEE/CVF International Conference on Computer Vision* (pp. 682–692). IEEE Computer Society. https://doi.org/10.1109/ICCV48922.2021.00072

Open Access This chapter is licensed under the terms of the Creative Commons Attribution 4.0 International License (http://creativecommons.org/licenses/by/4.0/), which permits use, sharing, adaptation, distribution and reproduction in any medium or format, as long as you give appropriate credit to the original author(s) and the source, provide a link to the Creative Commons license and indicate if changes were made.

The images or other third party material in this chapter are included in the chapter's Creative Commons license, unless indicated otherwise in a credit line to the material. If material is not included in the chapter's Creative Commons license and your intended use is not permitted by statutory regulation or exceeds the permitted use, you will need to obtain permission directly from the copyright holder.

Chapter 2
Scenarios of Social Explainable AI in Practice

Kary Främling ⓘ, Rachid Alami ⓘ, Joris Hulstijn ⓘ, Igor Tchappi ⓘ,
Angela Grimminger ⓘ, Britta Wrede ⓘ, Hendrik Buschmeier ⓘ,
and Sylvain Kubler ⓘ

Abstract A key goal of explainable AI (XAI) is to ensure the trustworthiness of AI systems when they interact with humans in real-world settings. These interactions involve individuals with diverse backgrounds, varying levels of knowledge, and

---

K. Främling (✉)
Department of Computing Science, Umeå University, Umeå, Sweden

Department of Industrial Engineering and Management, Aalto University, Espoo, Finland
e-mail: kary.framling@umu.se

R. Alami
Laboratory for Analysis and Architecture of Systems, Artificial and Natural Intelligence Toulouse Institute, Université de Toulouse, Toulouse, France
e-mail: rachid.alami@laas.fr

J. Hulstijn
Utrecht University, Utrecht, The Netherlands
e-mail: j.hulstijn@uu.nl

I. Tchappi
FINATRAX, SnT, University of Luxembourg, Esch-sur-Alzette, Luxembourg
e-mail: igor.tchappi@uni.lu

A. Grimminger
Psycholinguistics, Faculty of Arts and Humanities, Paderborn University, Paderborn, Germany
e-mail: angela.grimminger@uni-paderborn.de

B. Wrede
Medical School OWL, Bielefeld University, Bielefeld, Germany
e-mail: bwrede@techfak.uni-bielefeld.de

H. Buschmeier
Digital Linguistics Lab, Faculty of Linguistics and Literary Studies, Bielefeld University, Bielefeld, Germany
e-mail: hbuschme@uni-bielefeld.de

S. Kubler
Interdisciplinary Centre for Security, Reliability and Trust (SnT), University of Luxembourg, Esch-sur-Alzette, Luxembourg
e-mail: sylvain.kubler@uni.lu

© The Author(s) 2026
K. J. Rohlfing et al. (eds.), *Social Explainable AI*,
https://doi.org/10.1007/978-981-96-5290-7_2

different abilities to comprehend explanations. This chapter presents scenarios that illustrate the challenges and requirements that arise for XAI methods in such real-life contexts. Specifically, we highlight the importance of adapting explanations to both the context and the explainee(s), which may involve using appropriate and multiple modalities. Based on these scenarios, we identify three key requirements for effective XAI systems: multimodality (the ability to use different explanation formats), incrementality (the ability to refine explanations over time), and patternedness (the ability to present explanations in a structured and recognizable manner).

2.1 Assumptions for the Scenarios

This chapter describes a few *real-life* scenarios of interactions between humans and AI systems, or between humans and humans. Our assumption is that truly social XAI will have to be interactive, versatile, and expressive, similar to humans justifying their choices or explaining the motivations behind their acts. However, for simplicity, we assume that there are only two agents in the scenarios. This can be extended to situations where several humans are present and participate in the process while having different backgrounds, knowledge, and roles.

The AI system – that we call the "machine" for the rest of this section – can be, depending on the context and the application, a computer, a conversational agent, an autonomous robot, an autonomous car, etc. There are a priori no limitations regarding the interfaces and modalities or the contexts.

Concerning temporality, there are essentially two situations:

- the explanation concerns a decision, a behavior, or a plan that the machine has already elaborated, possibly as a result of a request from the human. When the explanation process is started, the explanandum (see Chap. 3) is available/visible/observable to the human.
- or it accompanies a human-machine shared activity: In such a situation, the machine and the human are contributing to a task or are involved in the situation, and it is important to impose on the machine to be transparent concerning its intentions and goals. The machine must also be predictable in terms of its actions in order to ensure that there is sufficient mutual understanding between the machine and the human.

The Explainer Machine In the cases and applications we envisage here, the explanation is provided by the machine that has made the decision and not by another distinct machine that explains to a human what a first machine has done or is doing. Consequently, we assume that the explainer machine has direct access to all the information and processes it has used to make its decision or to perform its actions.

Social Settings While social settings could be very diverse when the two agents (explainee and explainee) are humans, they are more limited in XAI, since the machine is never (or should never) be equal or hierarchically superior (boss, authority...) to a human. Typical 'social' roles/relationships that we envisage in the sequence are the following:

- a machine that is a service provider to humans, and humans need or ask for an explanation of what the machine has done or is doing;
- situations where a human and a machine are coworkers, sharing an activity to which they both contribute and the human is entitled to assume that the machine is pertinent and fully explainable in its behavior;
- a teacher (machine)/learner (human) setting for purely intangible tasks or physical tasks to be incrementally learned by the human with the help of the machine.

Role and Motives of the Explainer We restrict ourselves to machines that are programmed to have the goal of explaining their decision and/or behavior to a human, and not any other goal known or hidden to the explainee, such as profiling the user or simply generating 'trust' without ensuring that the explainee has fully understood and accepted the explanation.

The scenarios that follow in this chapter attempt to illustrate required capabilities for sXAI methods in various real-life situations. This is followed by some reflections on how sXAI could achieve similar functionality, which is then studied in detail in the different sections and chapters of this book.

2.2 Scenario 1: Explaining the Choice of a Car to Explainees with Different Backgrounds

Humans often find themselves in situations where they are asked to justify some choice they made based on their own preferences. The scenario presented here is to some extent based on a real-life situation that occurred to one of the authors in the 1990s and was also used as a study in Främling (1996). The real-life situation consists of choosing a new car to buy from tens of potential cars that have different characteristics or *features*. It is a so-called Pareto optimal situation, where improving the value of one feature tends to penalize the value of some other feature(s). For instance, increasing the performance or equipment level typically increases the price. Humans continuously face this kind of decision situations where they have to make a choice based on their own preferences. Furthermore, the decision might involve more than one decision-maker to some extent, who usually have at least some differences in their preferences. In that case, reaching a decision will require negotiations and a compromise between the different decision-makers. Negotiations go beyond the need for pure explanations, because the 'goodness' of the justifications and arguments presented by the different decision-makers also affects the final decision. That final decision might then need to be justified also to other humans who did not take part in taking the decision.

Table 2.1 Example of a dialog for justifying the choice of a car to buy during negotiation phase between decision-makers

Question/Answer	Explanatory move
Why?	Why should we buy car A?
Why answer	It's safe, spacious and not too expensive
Why not?	But car B looks quite similar and it's cheaper
Why not answer	Yes but it consumes a lot of fuel and maintenance costs are high
Contrastive	But car C is bigger than car A and has the same price, so why not car C instead?
Contrastive answer	Yes, but then …
What if?	But what if you would add this extra option to car C?
Counterfactual answer	Yes, then it would become better but the price …

Since this scenario is based on a real-world situation, we will use the couple Kary and Marie as the decision-makers.[1] They are a couple in their 30s who envision the possibility of having children in the years to come. Kary has owned and maintained cars over a long time and has been following the evolution of cars through time due to a general interest for the topic. He is therefore the core decision-maker. However, the final decision still needs to be a compromise that satisfies both Kary and Marie to some extent. We begin with the situation where Kary has identified a good candidate to buy and presents that to Marie, with a potential dialog shown as an example in Table 2.1.

In this dialog, Kary adapts his vocabulary and the abstraction level to correspond to his perception of Marie's knowledge about cars. It is also conceivable that Kary has 'hidden' aspects that are not included in the explanation for different reasons. It might be that Kary is not even consciously aware of some such aspects and their influence. It might also be the case that Kary feels that it would be too verbose and complicated to express them or that it is too difficult to analyze and quantify their impact on the decision. Humans may also hide parts of their reasoning in order to make negotiations go in the direction that they desire.

Once the choice has been made, Kary may need to justify it also to other people, such as friends, relatives etc. A dialog with car-interested friends might be quite different from the one in Table 2.1, such as the one in Table 2.2. In this case, Kary emphasizes performance and technical aspects rather than focusing on space and security. Figure 2.1 provides a graphical summary of this scenario.

The dialog and the answers/explanations would presumably look slightly different with Kary's parents or other explainees.

---

[1] This choice also has the side effect to avoid the question of choosing role players in a "non-discriminatory" way.

2 Scenarios of Social Explainable AI in Practice

Table 2.2 Example of a dialog for justifying the choice of a car to car-interested friends

Question/Answer	explanatory move
Why?	Why did you buy car A?
Why answer	It's responsive, fun, big enough and not too expensive
Why not?	Why didn't you buy car B instead, which has 4-wheel drive?
Why not answer	It's expensive and consumes a lot of fuel
Contrastive	But then car C has more power and same price?
Contrastive answer	Yes, but then …
What if?	But what if you would remove this extra option from car C?
Counterfactual answer	Then it would become cheaper but …

Fig. 2.1 Simplified illustration of different views and preferences for choosing a car, which (in this case) leads to a common agreement, even though it might not be for the same reasons

What are the lessons that we can learn for sXAI from this scenario? At least the following seem rather clear:

1. Explanations should be given as interactive dialogs, unless they are short, unambiguous or the choice between alternatives is obvious enough (which is rarely the case).
2. The suitable chunks are usually answers to one question at a time.
3. The explainer should support a 'sufficient' set of possible questions that might be asked by the explainee.
4. The explainee should have the liberty to ask questions in any order rather than having the explainer impose the order. Alternatively, if the explainee wants to know more but doesn't know how to formulate questions, the explainer should be able to 'guess' what explanatory move to try next.
5. The explainer should use vocabulary and an abstraction level that is compatible with the explainee's background knowledge. We call such knowledge about the explainee a *partner model* about the explainee.
6. The explainer's partner model about the explainee may evolve as the dialog goes on.

This scenario only includes verbal communication. In reality, the dialog would also include brochures, images, photos, videos, and other means of communication, i.e., different modalities. Social cues are also useful input modalities for humans in this kind of dialogs, where they might indicate that the explainee does not understand, does not agree, or wants to interrupt, because the explanation is becoming too long, etc.

2.3 Scenario 2: Decision Support System for Choosing a Car

The previous scenario only included human-to-human communication. In reality, Kary could have used an AI-based decision support system (DSS) for choosing the car (which he did but it was built by himself, as described in Främling, 1996). Then the DSS becomes the explainer and Kary becomes the explainee, in the same way as all other potential users of the DSS. In such a situation, many aspects that are considered to be more or less obvious in human-to-human communication have to be taken into consideration explicitly, such as the following:

- The AI system has access to databases with information about available cars.
- The AI system uses one (or several) model(s) about available cars and the context of buying and selling cars, i.e., what is called the explanandum (see Chap. 3).
- The AI system does not have any preferences of its own, so it has to provide the explainee (the user) with means to express those preferences somehow.
- The AI system does not initially have any knowledge about the explainee's domain knowledge and therefore has to provide means for the explainee to express noncomprehension or disagreement, which the AI system then needs to react to somehow in order to avoid a breakdown situation in the dialog.

2 Scenarios of Social Explainable AI in Practice 25

Table 2.3 Extract of possible interaction between AI system and human for selecting a car. Human interaction is shown in italics

Proposal/Reaction/Question/Answer	explanatory move
<...>	<initial interaction before AI system gives first proposal>
Proposal	I suggest you buy car A
Why?	*Why should I buy car A?*
Why answer	It's safe, economic and within your price range
Why not?	*Wouldn't car B be better?*
Why Not answer	It's expensive and consumes a lot of fuel
Refusal	*But I like car B more*
Question	Why do you like car B more?
(Human) answer	*I like its shape and I preferred driving with it*
New proposal	Ok, I took that into account. Then car C might actually be even better
Reaction	*Indeed, I had forgotten car C*
Why this and not that?	*So why would car C be better than car B?*
Contrastive answer	Because...
<...>	<interaction continues>

In this scenario, the human and the AI system have a joint goal: finding a car that satisfies the human as well as possible while providing the human with sufficient knowledge and justification to allow them to feel confident about the decision. In this case, confidence includes the capability to justify the decision also to other humans, as was the case for Kary in the human-to-human scenario.

We could imagine an extract of the interaction between the AI system and the human as in Table 2.3. This differs from the previous human-to-human scenario in some significant ways. The human is 'the boss' who will take the final decision, while the AI system is merely a domain expert that helps the human make a well-advised choice and feel confident about it. There is no guarantee that the human will agree with the system's proposal at the end of the dialog, but it can still be considered to be co-constructive, because the human's knowledge level for taking the decision will have increased. The AI system's knowledge about the human presumably also increased during the interaction, if the AI system has the capability to learn from the interaction. Such increased understanding of the human could be used for improving the AI system's interaction skills for future interaction.

2.4 Scenario 3: A Decision Support System for Medical Interventions

AI has been introduced to the medical domain for a long time, and there are numerous application fields it has been applied in. Here, the needs for explanation can be quite diverse: (1) Medical experts may want to get new scientific insights from AI based on large medical datasets; (2) physicians may seek support from a decision support system (DSS) for a diagnosis or treatment decision of a specific patient; (3) medical novices/patients seek support from an (X)AI system in order to get an initial assessment about their physical condition and advice whether a doctor should be consulted; or (4) patients may want more specific information about their diagnosis and their specific condition.

All these cases require different kinds of explanations. While in (1) the focus would lie on providing a more scientific explanation to achieve a deep comprehension of the underlying dependency structures of the relevant features in the data, (2) would require the DSS to provide the physician not only with information that is relevant to a medical expert in order to understand the decision the system is proposing but also to provide information to justify the decision toward the patient, (3) would require to endow the user/patient with actionable information, i.e., to enable him/her to take the next steps to deal with his/her medical situation, whereas (4) may be more focused on achieving a general overview of possible actions as well as a better comprehension of the relevant medical parameters.

With these different contexts of explanations in mind, let's now consider situation (2) where a physician consults a DSS as additional support for deriving a diagnosis and treatment decision that needs to be discussed with a patient. More specifically, consider the case of a fracture of the arm of a child. In such a situation, the physician has to decide if and when surgery is required. Thus, the system has to provide explanations regarding the fracture itself. More specifically, the kind of fracture needs to be determined and explained based on an image from the fracture. Additionally, the overall physical condition and age of the child has to be taken into account in order to estimate the risks and benefits of a surgery. In sum, the explanandum itself is quite complex, and the DSS should be able to track the interaction history and the changes of the explanandum. Also, the DSS should be aware of the interaction situation: If it is only interacting with the physician, it should behave differently than when interacting with the physician as well as the parents and the child itself. In the latter case, it should, for example, offer visualizations of the fracture augmented by additional information such as comparisons to other fractures or how it would change during the healing process or how a surgery would affect the fracture and its healing process. In addition, the child might have questions regarding pain and movement restrictions.

2.5 Scenario 4: Explaining in a Human–Human Tutoring Situation

Nonverbal and multimodal behavior is a characteristic of social interactions. This scenario illustrates aspects of multimodality in face-to-face human–human explanatory interactions and the synchronization of different modalities (see Chaps. 19 and 22 for more in-depth descriptions). It further shows how nonverbal and multimodal feedback is important to display and resolve understanding-related problems and how it shapes the flow of an explanation.

In this scenario, an explainer (ER) is explaining a complex board game to an explainee (EE) who does not know this game. The board game ("Wingspan" by Stonemaier Games, St. Louis, MO, USA) is about collecting birds with different abilities and taking care of them. In the following example interaction (see Fig. 2.2), the ER provides an explanation to the EE regarding the rule for feeding the birds. This rule is related to a certain action, namely, placing cards on a specific location on the board. The explainer explains this rule in a somewhat cumbersome way, likely because he has more game rules and strategies in mind. The explainee displays and expresses some confusion and difficulty in understanding the reference to the location by nonverbal and verbal means.

The ER indicates the location on the board using speech and a pointing gesture toward the upper left corner of the board (see ❶ and the example video frame, Fig. 2.2). While the ER is explaining, the EE displays a range of nonverbal behaviors. First, the EE rapidly moves her eyes across the board and then points to a location on its right corner that she seems to identify as the one the ER is referring to (see ❷, Fig. 2.2). The ER looks at the EE, seems to notice the incorrect reference, and interrupts his explanation (see ❸, Fig. 2.2). The EE produces other (ambiguous) nonverbal behaviors, such as a self-adaptor indicating uncertainty, another pointing gesture, and backchannels ("okay," "mhm") that are used to display understanding (see ❹, Fig. 2.2). These behaviors can serve as feedback signals without interrupting an explainer and could be an indicator of the EE's attempt to follow the explanation. The ER, however, seems to have noticed the referential misunderstanding and initiates a repair (see ❺, Fig. 2.2). The EE nods and produces a backchannel (an ostensive breath) "hh." The ER, again, initiates a repair and at the end of his utterance shifts his gaze from the board to the EE, and the EE also shifts her gaze from the board to the ER (see ❻, Fig. 2.2). As certain gaze patterns are related to certain turn-taking mechanisms, this may indicate to the EE that she could take the turn ❷, Fig. 2.2). The EE then verbally expresses her understanding and requests affirmation by reformulating the ER's explanation with a rise in intonation.

To sum up, human–human face-to-face explanatory interactions are rich in multimodal signals of understanding shaping how the explanation unfold in time, co-constructed by the explainer and the explainee. This scenario is used in Chaps. 5, 18, and 19.

2.6 Scenario 5: The Cognitive and Interactive Robots

The cognitive and interactive robot of the future provides a very rich context and various instantiations of social XAI. Indeed, the main challenge here is to devise the cognitive and interactive abilities to allow pertinent, transparent, legible, and

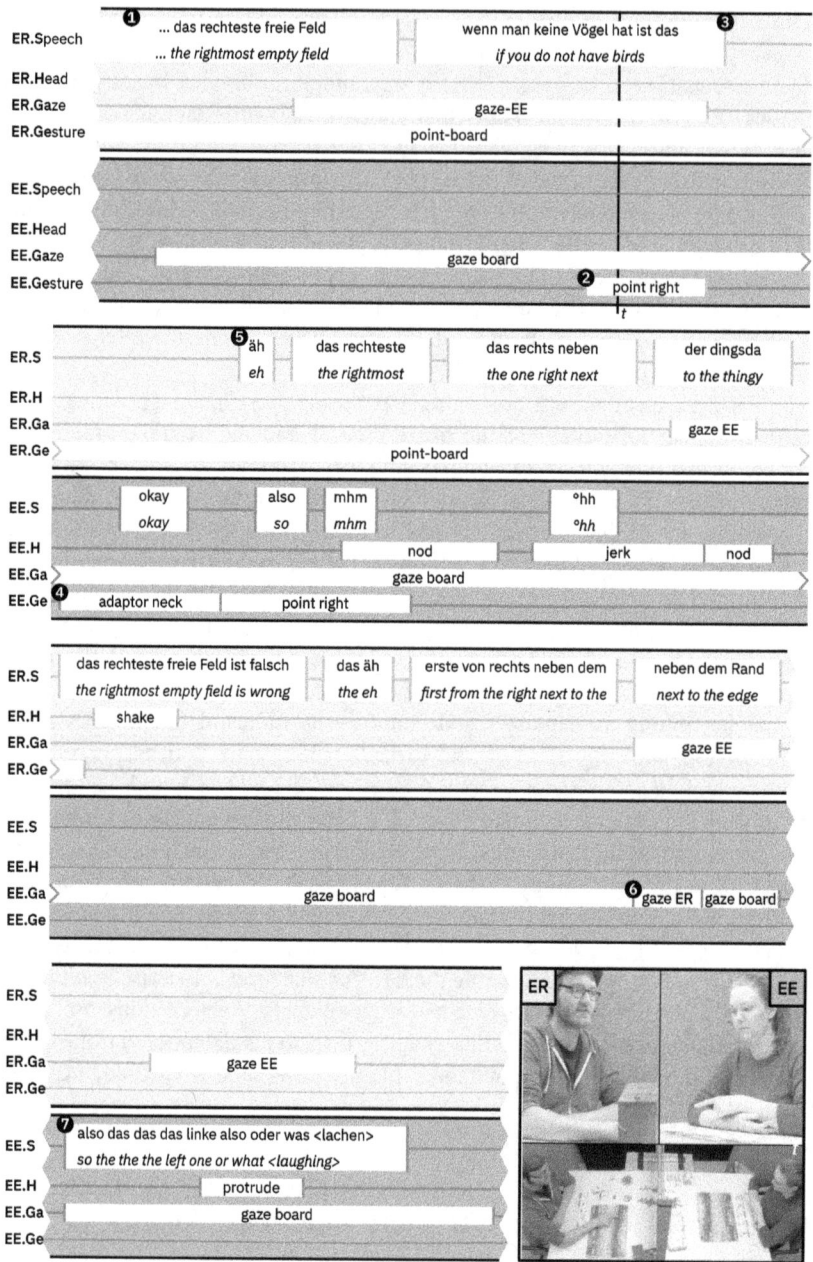

Fig. 2.2 Timeline of explainer's (ER, greenish light tiers) and explainee's (EE, bluish dark tiers) annotated speech and nonverbal behavior (head gestures, gaze target, manual gesture) during a fragment of a face-to-face game explanation in the human–human tutoring scenario. The three-perspective video frame (lower right) shows the explanation situation at time t (black vertical line in annotation. Interesting events are marked from ❶ to ❼) and described in the text. Note: The illustration of multimodal behavior is less precise (in terms of timing and details) than the annotations it was derived from

acceptable behaviors for a robot that is able to perform collaborative tasks with a human partner or to act in a context populated by humans[2] (Clodic & Alami, 2021).

The main specificity of this scenario with respect to other sXAI scenarios is the fact that in this case, there is (1) an embodiment of the machine that acts in a physical environment that is shared with the human(s), and (2) most often, the explanation process is incremental, since it happens while the machine is acting.

Numerous applications can be envisaged, pertaining to two classes of systems:

- service and assistant robot, particularly for service applications and health care;
- or the teammate robot in the factory or the field.

In both cases, the robot is acting in co-presence with humans. In some applications, humans are effectively involved and concerned by the activity of the robot. In other situations or contexts, the humans are simply co-present with the robot and share with it the use of space and other resources available in the place. Finally, humans might also be directly involved when the activity of the robot is oriented toward them (service, health care...) or shared with them (the coworker robot).

In such contexts, the robot, in order to achieve its task will have to share appropriately decisions, tasks, and space with humans. This, obviously, cannot be done without effective abilities to explain its decisions and behaviors.

We propose to analyze the needed robot abilities in two contexts:

1. the robot coworker in a factory, contributing with human workers in the assembly of a big object (airplane or car, for instance)
2. a service robot able to guide and accompany visitors in a public space (a commercial mall or an airport terminal)

Such robots will have to take decisions, elaborate and execute plans, act in the physical world in the presence and/or synergy with humans, coordinate their actions with the humans, and even perform co-manipulation with them.

While the need for an explanation and its pertinence is considered particularly relevant in domains such as medicine or legal affairs due to the potentially severe consequences for their users, it is also very important for robots acting with humans;

- to synthesize predictable and acceptable behaviors;
- to ensure that its goals are known;
- to act in a way that allows and facilitates the correct interpretation of its intentions and actions.

In addition, comfort, fluidity of interaction, and even safety might substantially benefit from transparent and understandable robot behavior (Hellström & Bensch, 2018; Malle et al., 2020; Clodic et al., 2017).

---

[2] Current robots are still very limited in terms of autonomy and interaction abilities. We take here a prospective view of the cognitive and interactive robots of the future based on most advanced research in HRI literature.

All this has to do with explainability and transparency.

We will discuss here below what, when, how, and to whom the robot should be able to explain its actions, intentions, and goals. This could happen as an answer to a human request or, proactively, the robot providing in an explicit manner (verbally or on a screen...) or implicitly (social signals accompanying its action and/or merged with it). Requests from the human can be the following:

- verbal and directly addressed to the robot ("What are you doing? Where are you transporting that object? Why have you done that?...")
- or indirectly, for example, speaking to another human ("Why this robot is doing that?..."),
- or nonverbal (the human close to the robot appears confused, or disturbed, or curious, or suspicious....

Also, even if there is no explicit request for an explanation, the robot's duty is to act in a way that makes what it is doing, explicit and predictable, and to adapt its actions and decisions through interaction with humans.

While illustrating different human-robot explanation situations, we will sketch what abilities, representations, and knowledge the robot would need to achieve what is expected from it.

One essential ability for a service or coworker robot is navigation in order to reach a place, a person, or an object. This navigation most often takes place in an environment populated by humans. It is then a duty for the robot to move around with the minimum possible disruption and in a way that is convenient, understood, and accepted by people copresent and using the site. This is what is called socially aware[3] robot navigation (Rios-Martinez et al., 2015; Mavrogiannis et al., 2023; Singamaneni et al., 2024). Besides the crucial safety aspect, the robot should behave in a way that conveys its intentions. This can be done using various modalities: It can communicate with its head/gaze (Khambhaita et al., 2016; Holman et al., 2021) orientation (social signaling) or by shaping its trajectory, so that it becomes more predictable and legible (Mainprice et al., 2010; Dragan et al., 2013). In situations when there is a need for cooperation, like in narrow passages, it will have to exhibit its decision or proposed solution to a human (choosing from which side to cross, negotiating a passage, etc.).

This can be done with social signals but also, when it is pertinent, through verbal interaction where the robot can inform the human about what it expects form her/him or what it will do next (Hoffman, 2019). Similarly, the robot should be permanently able to interpret verbal requests, or comments, and also assess/estimate, through perception, if the human is confused, hesitant, or not comfortable with respect to the robot behavior (Wallkötter et al., 2021) .

Indeed, it is essential for the robot to do its best for informing, explaining, and facilitating the understanding of its current and future behavior. This can be illustrated by two 'elementary' but highly interactive tasks: approaching a person

---

[3] Or human-aware, or social.

and handing over an object to a person. The robot adapts its trajectory and speed (the ballistics of the motion) to the human and ensures through exchanges of social signals (gaze, head movement, gripping force, contact) that it is aligned with the human, understood, and accepted (Dautenhahn et al., 2006; Chan et al., 2013; Duan et al., 2024).

Another class of contexts is when the task involves the robot and the human. The task can be shared in the sense that it needs contributions from the human and from the robot (Vesper et al., 2010; Lemaignan et al., 2017; Stange et al., 2022).

This is the case of the robot coworker in factory of the future. Other types of tasks that involve the robot and the human in close relation are assistance tasks (e.g., robot helper for healthcare) or service tasks where the robot provides a service to humans (e.g., robot guide, transport, etc.) (Triebel et al., 2015; Mayima et al., 2023).

The tasks to be performed are often multistep involving decisions and actions from both parties. They correspond to a specified goal[4] which is assumed to be known to the human and to the robot. But there could be uncertainty or even ignorance about the choices which have been made, and the reason why some actions have been performed. There could also be uncertainty about the goal and the commitment of the human. They can change at any moment. Then, it is important to endow the robot with the ability to explain if asked, for example, by verbalizing its plan, its choices, and its expectations (Cirillo et al., 2009; Faria et al., 2024).

This can be done with more or less details and refined through interaction. The explanation can also be provided in a proactive way: The robot will then need to clearly exhibit its intentions and expectations, to be predictable, and to facilitate the understanding of the human. This can be done through different means (see Chap. 24), verbally or through social signals (Favier & Alami, 2024).

To do so, the robot should be able to estimate, whenever possible, the mental state of the humans and their beliefs about the state of the world and of the task [5] in order to estimate what is shared or not (Trafton et al., 2005; Devin & Alami, 2016; Dissing & Bolander, 2020). It is also essential for the robot to be aware of the user/human profile. A robot will not interact or provide the same information to a professional or to a naive user or patient (Rossi et al., 2017).

Another essential aspect here that clearly applies to all human-machine intelligence interactive systems of the future is to endow the machine with the ability to permanently evaluate the quality of the interaction (Mayima et al., 2022; Bensch et al., 2017), i.e., if things are going well in the sense that the interaction effectively converges and in satisfactory conditions from the perspective of the human (Fig. 2.3).

---

[4] See Chap. 11.
[5] See Chap. 14.

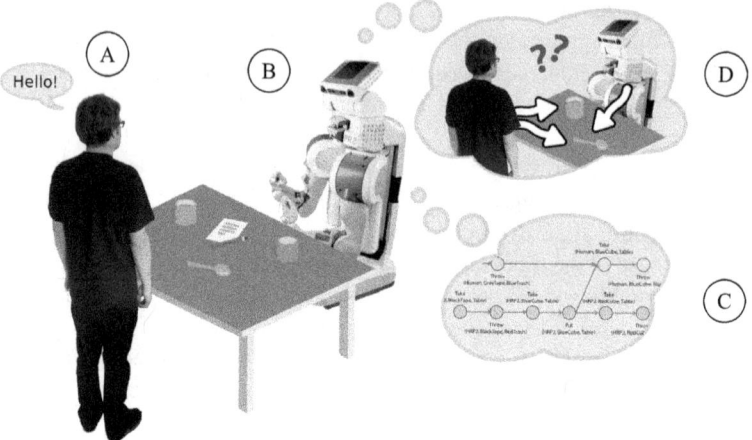

Fig. 2.3 A context of shared human–robot task: The sources of information are multimodal dialog *(A)* (verbal interaction but also through exchange of social signals: joint attention, gaze, backchanneling, pointing...) and perspective-aware monitoring of the human activity and of the environment *(B)* (Robot perceives human, human perceives the robot, and robot reasons and acts based on the fact that is observed or not). Reasoning and planning take place at symbolic (abstract) as well as physical and geometric level *(C)* and take into account agents beliefs, perspectives, and capabilities (Theory of Mind) *(D)* as estimated by the robot. The robot must not only adapt in real time its behaviors but also synthesize predictable, legible, and acceptable intentions, actions, and motions. It has to do its best to proactively facilitate the understanding of the human, and it should always be ready to explain its behavior

2.7 Scenario 6: A Robot Teaching and Evaluating the Cooking

Humans often find themselves in situations where they need to interpret feedback based on subtle cues, especially in learning and creative processes. Cooking is a fundamental skill that involves both technical execution and personal creativity, often requiring guidance and external validation. The scenario presented in this section explores how a novice cook seeks reassurance from an expert—albeit in this case, an advanced AI-powered robotic chef.

This situation is inspired by real-world interactions in learning environments where individuals seek feedback from mentors or instructors. The ability to interpret ambiguous feedback – whether as approval, concern, or curiosity – is an essential part of personal growth and skill development. Additionally, cooking is an activity where exact replication is often impossible due to variations in ingredients, technique, and personal touch, making subjective assessment a key part of the experience.

To illustrate this scenario, we introduce a young woman (the user) who is learning to cook with the guidance of RobotChef, an advanced AI-powered culinary assistant. RobotChef is dressed in a traditional chef's uniform, including a chef's

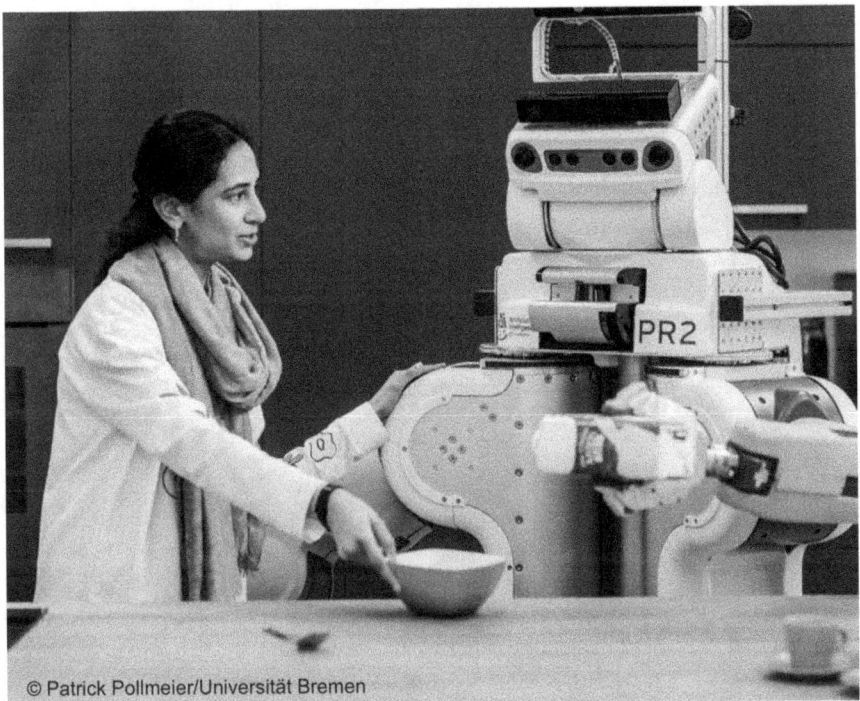

Fig. 2.4 A robot teaching cooking lessons

jacket, apron, and toque (chef's hat). RobotChef is a valuable companion for novice cooks and experienced chefs alike. RobotChef is equipped with advanced culinary algorithms and sensory technology and is designed to educate and assist cooks in the kitchen, offering feedback and guidance on cooking techniques and recipes. Figure 2.4 presents a visual representation of the possible scene.

This scenario explores how the user would interpret RobotChef's nonverbal signals during a cooking lesson, such as demonstrations. The scenario showcases the ambiguity of nonverbal communication. Consider the following three interpretations.

Interpretation 1: Approval

- Situation: *The RobotChef teaches a recipe to the user.*
- User: I tried to follow the recipe closely, but I'm not sure if it's turned out right. Why doesn't my dish look like yours?
- RobotChef: The aroma and presentation of your dish are quite remarkable. It seems you've captured the essence of the recipe beautifully.
- Nonverbal Cue: *RobotChef's lights brighten significantly, and it makes a gentle, upward tilting motion with its head.*
- User's Interpretation: *User perceives the brightening lights and the slight head tilt as signs of enthusiasm and approval from RobotChef, feeling encouraged and satisfied with their cooking efforts.*

Interpretation 2: Concern

- Situation: *The RobotChef teaches a recipe to the user.*
- User: I tried to follow the recipe closely, but I'm not sure if it's turned out right. Why doesn't my dish look like yours?
- RobotChef: The aroma and presentation of your dish are quite remarkable. It seems you've captured the essence of the recipe beautifully.
- Nonverbal Cue: *RobotChef pauses for a moment longer than usual; its lights dim slightly before responding.*
- User's Interpretation: *The pause and the dimming of lights are interpreted by the user as hesitation or concern from RobotChef suggesting that the robot might be diplomatically avoiding critique of the dish's quality, leading the user to doubt the success of their culinary attempt despite the verbal reassurance.*

Interpretation 3: Curiosity

- Situation: *The RobotChef teaches a recipe to the user.*
- User: I tried to follow the recipe closely, but I'm not sure if it's turned out right. Why doesn't my dish look like yours?
- RobotChef: The aroma and presentation of your dish are quite remarkable. It seems you've captured the essence of the recipe beautifully.
- Nonverbal Cue: *RobotChef's sensors activate and scan the dish back and forth, accompanied by a neutral, steady glow of its lights.*
- User Interpretation: *The scanning motion and steady light are seen by the user as a sign of curiosity and analytical assessment from RobotChef. User feels that RobotChef is intrigued by the attempt to follow the recipe, prompting reflection on the creative process and the dish's potential uniqueness.*

In each of the three interpretations, the unchanged verbal dialog between the user and the RobotChef is recontextualized by the robot's varying nonverbal cues, demonstrating how interpretations of the same spoken words can shift dramatically based on nonverbal communication.

2.8 Elements of Social XAI Identified in the Scenarios

The scenarios presented in this chapter were selected based on how well they reflect the way in which humans explain their reasoning to each other and how well they illustrate the need for multimodality and incrementality in particular. Two main categories of AI systems were used, i.e., different kinds of decision support systems where the AI systems are essentially 'non-embodied' (i.e., not tied to a specific piece of hardware) and robotic scenarios where the AI system is embodied and offers means of interaction that go beyond computer screens and graphics. It has also been the authors' intention to refer to these scenarios in the subsequent parts and chapters in order to connect the more technical and academic concerns with the needs of 'real life.'

From the scenarios, we identify at least the following key elements to consider for building a sXAI system:

- **Interaction.** Explainees should have the possibility to guide the dialog by choosing the question to ask ("Why?", "Why not?", ""What if?", ...).
- **Adapted amount of information.** The amount of information that is provided during each step of the dialog should be limited to the explainee's capability to understand the information. This signifies that the user's possible question should be answered with the necessary amount of information but not more.
- **Multiple and adapted modality.** The sXAI system should be able to exploit different explanation capabilities, e.g., text, speech, graphs, illustrations of a different kind, gestures, ...). The choice of which modality (or modalities) is used should be adapted to the explainee's preferences, if possible.
- **Co-constructive adaptation.** The XAI system should be capable of adapting to changes in the context being explained, as well as changes in the explainee's understanding and other information that the AI systems might discover or learn during the interaction.
- **Partner model.** The way in which an sXAI system begins and pursues an interaction should presumably not be the same for all explainees but rather use some assumptions about the explainee that increase the probability of the explanation to be understandable and useful for the explainee. The partner model should also be updated and adapted over time in order to follow the progression of the explainee's understanding and preferences over time.
- **Embodiment.** In some ways, all sXAI systems could be considered to be embodied in the sense that they have a limited set of means on interaction that depends on whether the means of interacting with the explainee is a computer screen, a mobile phone screen, a keyboard, or head, arms, legs of a robot, etc..
- **Etc.** This list is not intended to be exhaustive. The intention is rather to provide a list of elements to consider when developing true sXAI systems.

All these elements might not be needed in all sXAI systems. However, it is rare to find any of these elements in current XAI implementations. Most current XAI methods also lack the necessary capabilities for implementing such functionality. The rest of the book attempts to provide definitions and guidelines for how such capabilities could be developed, as well as how they can be assessed from technical, ethical, and other points of view.

Acknowledgments Kary Främling's work has been partially supported by the Wallenberg AI, Autonomous Systems and Software Program (WASP) funded by the Knut and Alice Wallenberg Foundation.

Rachid Alami's work has been partially supported by the EU-funded project euROBIN under grant agreement no. 101070596 and by the Artificial and Natural Intelligence Toulouse Institute (ANITI) funded by the France 2030 program under the grant agreement no. ANR-23-IACL-0002. This work was funded by the Deutsche Forschungsgemeinschaft (DFG, German Research Foundation): TRR 318/1 2021 – 438445824 for Angela Grimminger, Britta Wrede, and Hendrik Buschmeier.

References

Bensch, S., Jevtić, A., & Hellström, T. (2017). On interaction quality in human–robot interaction. In *Proceedings of the 9th International Conference on Agents and Artificial Intelligence* (pp. 182–189). ICAART. SciTePress. https://doi.org/I10.5220/0006191601820189

Chan, W. P., Parker, C. A. C., Machiel Van der Loos, H. F., & Croft, E. A. (2013). A human-inspired object handover controller. *The International Journal of Robotics Research, 32*(8), 971–983. https://doi.org/10.1177/0278364913488806

Cirillo, M., Karlsson, L., & Saffiotti, A. (2009). A human-aware robot task planner. *Proceedings of the International Conference on Automated Planning and Scheduling, 19*(1), 58–65. https://doi.org/10.1609/icaps.v19i1.13348

Clodic, A., & Alami, R. (2021). What is it to implement a human–robot joint action? In J. von Braun, M. S. Archer, G. M. Reichberg & M. S. Sorondo (Eds.), *Robotics, AI, and humanity* (pp. 229–238). Springer. https://doi.org/10.1007/978-3-030-54173-6/_19

Clodic, A., Pacherie, E., Alami, R., & Chatila, R. (2017). Key elements for human–robot joint action. In R. Hakli & J. Seibt (Eds.), *Sociality and normativity for robots* (pp. 159–177). Springer. https://doi.org/10.1007/978-3-319-53133-5_8

Dautenhahn, K., Walters, M., Woods, S., Koay, K. L., Nehaniv, C. L., Sisbot, A., Alami, R., & Simeon, T. (2006). How may I serve you? A robot companion approaching a seated person in a helping context. In *Proceedings of the 1st ACM SIGCHI/SIGART Conference on Human–Robot Interaction*. HRI '06 (pp. 172–179). Association for Computing Machinery. https://doi.org/10.1145/1121241.1121272

Devin, S., & Alami, R. (2016). An implemented Theory of Mind to improve human–robot shared plans execution. In *The Eleventh ACM/IEEE International Conference on Human Robot Interaction* (pp. 319–326). IEEE. https://doi.org/10.1109/HRI.2016.7451768

Dissing, L., & Bolander, T. (2020). Implementing theory of mind on a robot using Dynamic Epistemic Logic. In *Proceedings of the 29th International Joint Conference on Artificial Intelligence* (pp. 1615–1621). International Joint Conferences on Artificial Intelligence Organization. https://doi.org/10.24963/ijcai.2020/224

Dragan, A. D., Lee, K. C. T., & Srinivasa, S. S. (2013). Legibility and predictability of robot motion. In *Proceedings of the 8th ACM/IEEE International Conference on Human–Robot Interaction* (pp. 301–308). IEEE. https://doi.org/10.1109/HRI.2013.6483603

Duan, H., Yang, Y., Li, D., & Wang, P. (2024). Human–robot object handover: Recent progress and future direction. *Biomimetic Intelligence and Robotics, 4*(1), 100145. https://doi.org/10.1016/j.birob.2024.100145

Faria, M., Melo, F. S., & Paiva, A. (2024). "Guess what I'm doing": Extending legibility to sequential decision tasks. *Artificial Intelligence, 330*, 104107. https://doi.org/10.1016/j.artint.2024.104107

Favier, A., & Alami, R. (2024). A model of concurrent and compliant human–robot joint action to plan and supervise collaborative robot actions. In *Advances in cognitive systems* (pp. 1–16). ACS. https://hal.science/hal-04609442v1

Främling K. K. (1996). Modélisation et apprentissage des préférences par réseaux de neurones pour l'aide àla décision multicritère. PhD thesis. INSA de Lyon. https://tel.archives-ouvertes.fr/tel-00825854

Hellström, T., & Bensch, S. (2018). Understandable robots – What, Why, and How. *Paladyn, Journal of Behavioral Robotics, 9*(1), 110–123. https://doi.org/10.1515/pjbr-2018-0009

Hoffman, G. (2019). Evaluating fluency in human–robot collaboration. *IEEE Transactions on Human–Machine Systems, 49*(3), 209–218. https://doi.org/10.1109/THMS.2019.2904558

Holman, B., Anwar, A., Singh, A., Tec, M., Hart, J., & Stone, P. (2021). Watch where you're going! Gaze and head orientation as predictors for social robot navigation. In *2021 IEEE International Conference on Robotics and Automation (ICRA)* (pp. 3553–3559). IEEE. https://doi.org/10.1109/ICRA48506.2021.9561286

Khambhaita, H., Rios-Martinez, J., & Alami, R. (2016). Head-body motion coordination for human aware robot navigation. In *9th International Workshop on Human-Friendlly Robotics*. HFR '16. https://hal.science/hal-01568838/

Lemaignan, S., Warnier, M., Akin Sisbot, E., Clodic, A., & Alami, R. (2017). Artificial cognition for social human–robot interaction: An implementation. *Artificial Intelligence, 247*, 45–69. https://doi.org/10.1016/j.artint.2016.07.002

Mainprice, J., Sisbot, E. A., Siméon, T., & Alami, R. (2010). Planning safe and legible hand-over motions for human–robot interaction. In *IARP Workshop on Technical Challenges for Dependable Robots in Human Environments*. https://laas.hal.science/hal-01976223v1

Malle, B., Fischer, K., Young, J., Moon, A., & Collins, E. (2020). Trust and the discrepancy between expectations and actual capabilities of social robots. In D. Zhang & B. Wei (Eds.), *Human–Robot Interaction: Control, Analysis, and Design* (pp. 1–23). Cambridge Scholars Press.

Mavrogiannis, C., Baldini, F., Wang, A., Zhao, D., Trautman, P., Steinfeld, A., & Oh, J. (2023). Core challenges of social robot navigation: A survey. *ACM Transactions on Human–Robot Interaction, 12*(3), 36. https://doi.org/10.1145/3583741

Mayima, A., Clodic, A., & Alami, R. (2022). Towards robots able to measure in real-time the quality of interaction in HRI contexts. *International Journal of Social Robotics, 14*(3), 713–731. https://doi.org/10.1007/s12369-021-00814-5

Mayima, A., Sarthou, G., Buisan, G., Singamaneni, P.-T., Sallami, Y., Waldhart, J., Belhassein, K., Clodic, A., & Alami, R. (2023). How to make a robot guide? In *18th International Symposium on Experimental Robotics*. ISER '23 (pp. 483–494). Springer. https://doi.org/10.1007/978-3-031-63596-0_43

Rios-Martinez, J., Spalanzani, A., & Laugier, C. (2015). From proxemics theory to socially-aware navigation: A survey. *International Journal of Social Robotics, 7*, 137–153. https://doi.org/10.1007/s12369-014-0251-1

Rossi, S., Ferland, F., & Tapus, A. (2017). User profiling and behavioral adaptation for HRI: A survey. *Pattern Recognition Letters, 99*, 3–12. https://doi.org/10.1016/j.patrec.2017.06.002

Singamaneni, P. T., Bachiller-Burgos, P., Manso, L. J., Garrell, A., Sanfeliu, A., Spalanzani, A., & Alami, R. (2024). A survey on socially aware robot navigation: Taxonomy and future challenges. *The International Journal of Robotics Research, 43*(10), 1533–1572. https://doi.org/10.1177/02783649241230562

Stange, S., Hassan, T., Schröder, F., Konkol, J., & Kopp, S. (2022). Self-explaining social robots: An explainable behavior generation architecture for human–robot interaction. *Frontiers in Artificial Intelligence, 5*, 866920. https://doi.org/10.3389/frai.2022.866920

Trafton, J. G., Cassimatis, N. L., Bugajska, M. D., Brock, D. P., Mintz, F. E., & Schultz, A. C. (2005). Enabling effective human–robot interaction using perspective-taking in robots. *IEEE Transactions on Systems, Man, and Cybernetics – Part A: Systems and Humans, 35*(4), 460–470. https://doi.org/10.1109/TSMCA.2005.850592

Triebel, R., Arras, K. A., Alami, R., Beyer, L., Breuers, S., Chatila, R., Chetouani, M., Cremers, D., Evers, V., Fiore, M., Hung, H., Islas Ramírez, O. A., Joosse, M. J., Khambhaita, H., Kucner, T., Leibe, B., Lilienthal, A. J., Linder, T., Lohse, M., Magnusson, M., Okal, B., Palmieri, L., Rafi, U., van Rooij, M., & Zhang, L. (2015). Spencer: A socially aware service robot for passenger guidance and help in busy airports. In T. D. Barfoot & D. S. Wettergreen (Eds.), *10th International Conference on Field and Service Robotics*. FSR '15 (Vol. 113, pp. 607–622). Springer. https://doi.org/10.1007/978-3-319-27702-8/_40

Vesper, C., Butterfill, S., Knoblich, G., & Sebanz, N. (2010). A minimal architecture for joint action. *Neural Networks, 23*(8–9), 998–1003. https://doi.org/10.1016/j.neunet.2010.06.002

Wallkötter, S., Tulli, S., Castellano, G., Paiva, A., & Chetouani, M. (2021). Explainable embodied agents through social cues: A review. *Journal of Human–Robot Interaction, 10*(3), 27. https://doi.org/10.1145/3457188

Open Access This chapter is licensed under the terms of the Creative Commons Attribution 4.0 International License (http://creativecommons.org/licenses/by/4.0/), which permits use, sharing, adaptation, distribution and reproduction in any medium or format, as long as you give appropriate credit to the original author(s) and the source, provide a link to the Creative Commons license and indicate if changes were made.

The images or other third party material in this chapter are included in the chapter's Creative Commons license, unless indicated otherwise in a credit line to the material. If material is not included in the chapter's Creative Commons license and your intended use is not permitted by statutory regulation or exceeds the permitted use, you will need to obtain permission directly from the copyright holder.

Chapter 3
Components of an Explanation for Co-constructive sXAI

Anna-Lisa Vollmer, Heike M. Buhl, Rachid Alami, Angela Grimminger, and Axel-Cyrille Ngonga Ngomo

Abstract The chapter "Components of an Explanation for Co-Constructive sXAI" examines the fundamental components that constitute explanations within the framework of social explainable AI (sXAI). It defines key concepts such as the explanandum (the entity being explained), the explanans (the manner of explanation), the explainer (the provider), and the explainee (the recipient), and it explores their interactions. The chapter emphasizes the complexity of explanations, highlighting the dynamic nature of the explainee's evolving understanding along with the contextual factors affecting the explanation process. It advocates an approach to co-constructed explanations in which the explanandum and the explanans adapt to the explainee's needs, allowing roles to interchange. This contrasts with traditional XAI methods that assume a static, one-way knowledge transfer. By focusing on the conceptualization of co-constructive explanation, the chapter aims to inspire more effective and human-centered AI systems, setting the stage for future research in and the following chapters on social XAI.

A.-L. Vollmer (✉)
Interactive Robotics in Medicine and Care, Medical School OWL, Bielefeld University, Bielefeld, Germany
e-mail: anna-lisa.vollmer@uni-bielefeld.de

H. M. Buhl
Institute for Human Sciences – Psychology, Faculty of Arts and Humanities, Paderborn University, Paderborn, Germany
e-mail: heike.buhl@uni-paderborn.de

R. Alami
Laboratory for Analysis and Architecture of Systems, Artificial and Natural Intelligence Toulouse Institute, Université de Toulouse, Toulouse, France
e-mail: rachid.alami@laas.fr

A. Grimminger
Psycholinguistics, Faculty of Arts and Humanities, Paderborn University, Paderborn, Germany
e-mail: angela.grimminger@uni-paderborn.de

A.-C. Ngonga Ngomo
Data Science, Heinz Nixdorf Institut, Paderborn University, Paderborn, Germany
e-mail: axel.ngonga@uni-paderborn.de

3.1 How Does This Chapter Relate to XAI?

When dealing with sXAI, it is necessary to look at the components of explanations, the entities involved, the partners/agents, and so forth. What is an explanation anyway? What is explained? What means are used to explain? And who explains to whom?

This chapter is designed specifically for readers with backgrounds in AI and technical disciplines. It aims to go beyond definitions and create a more in-depth basis for the central terms of the book. Important words and concepts are (see Fig. 3.1) the following:

- Explanandum: the entity (event, phenomenon) that is the object of an explanation.
- Explanans: the (verbal) way that an explanation can be expressed and co-constructed by both partners/agents.
- Explainer: a human or nonhuman agent in the role of producing an explanation in a social interaction.
- Explainee: a human or nonhuman agent in the role of the addressee of an explanation.

However, it is possible and necessary to go further and ask, for example, what is the subject of an explanation? In the scenario with Kary (cf. Sect. 2.3), is it the car? Its specific features? Kary's preferences or decision? The reasons behind this? Because the explanandum may change over the course of an explanation (see Sect. 3.3), such that we here introduce the term *global explanandum* for the whole explanation as a sequence of explananda serving as subcomponents for individual explanation steps. Moreover, the roles of explainer and explainee are also not clear and fixed in explanation interactions. Note that either interaction partner can have the responsibility to explain. The explainer can be one person at one moment and another at the next. Thus, it may be the case that the explainee explains their goals or contributes partial aspects of the explanation if they have understood something well. There are even situations in which the roles of explainer and explainee are not fixed at all, but both work together toward understanding. This is often the case, for example, in learning settings. Thus, a further aim of this chapter is to increase awareness of the complexity of the topic. We aim to present a problem outline. For certain aspects, we shall pose questions and present possible options without offering definitive solutions. Some unresolved aspects will form the basis for future research endeavors. However, many challenges are also central topics in other chapters of this book to which we can refer already.

In Table 3.1, we shall exemplify the above components of an explanation in the scenarios presented in Chap. 2.

Fig. 3.1 Explanation terms

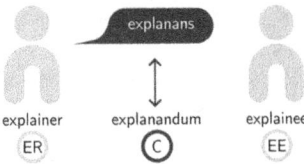

3.2 The Role of Explainer and Explainee

Figure 3.1 shows a minimalist explanation with one explainer (ER) and one explainee (EE). In human–human explanatory interactions, the explainers usually know more about a certain topic, the resulting explanandum, than the explainees (or they think they know more). The explainees strive for understanding and the explainers support them in overcoming a knowledge gap (cf. examples in Chap. 2). Regarding human–computer/robot interaction, in most cases, it holds that the explainer is the artificial agent that justifies its action, beliefs, decisions, and so forth. Thus, the characteristics of these roles go beyond the difference in knowledge. They are discussed in detail in Chap. 8. In classic XAI, the AI is the explainer, and the human user is the explainee. The AI explains or justifies its actions and decisions (see below regarding the explanandum). Further humans are often involved here as well. This is the case, for example, when an expert explains the AI's decisions to a layperson. However, it can be the other way around—for example, when a human explains to a robot why they do not like the recommendation given by the machine. Several further differentiations are important: There are differences between the characteristics of different explainers and explainees such as the type of the partner (robot, human, avatar, etc.), their domain knowledge, the explainers' ability to explain, their interest in the explanandum, and so forth (cf. Chap. 14). Besides the individuals, the relationships that explainer and explainee have with the explanation context differ and impact on the role of explainer and explainee (e.g., good friends, a student and their teacher, a doctor and a patient, a police officer and the suspect, etc.) (see Chaps. 4 and 8). The roles of explainer and explainee can even be reversed during an explanation. During some explanation steps, the original explainee might explain their point of view to the original explainer or might add some knowledge regarding the domain, the explanandum, or related topics. This leads to the need to define the explanation: Is it still the same explanation if the roles reverse or the explanandum changes (even slightly)? Additionally, explainers and explainees themselves change over the course of the explanatory dialog. The most obvious differences pertain to the explainee's level of understanding the explanandum—something that should increase over the course of an explanation. Likewise, there are changes regarding their cognitive load and attention as well as the resulting verbal and nonverbal behavior (see Chaps. 19, 13, Robrecht et al., 2024.) Another aspect to note is the number of people involved in the explanation: Fig. 3.1 shows two people involved. However, in many explanations—for example, at school or university lectures—one explainer and many explainees are the norm. This limits the possibilities for individualized adaptive explanations (cf. Chap. 13).

Table 3.1 The components of an explanation in the six scenarios presented in Chap. 2

Scenario	Explainer	Explainee(s)	Global Explanandum and Sequential Subcomponents
1	Kary	Marie, car-interested friend	Reason for buying Car A with sequential subcomponents: • Reason for buying Car A, more specifically restricted to what interests or is not known to or convinces the explainee • Reason for not buying Car B • Reason for not buying Car C • Reason for not buying Car C with extra option
2	Decision Support System	Kary	The current proposal of the AI system: • Reason for buying Car A • Reason for preference for Car B • Reason for buying Car C
3	Robot co-worker or service robot	Human co-worker or assisted user	Robot goals and plans, decisions and actions • This can be partially observed by the human explainee • Why and how robot has made a decision or achieved an action • Need for predictable, legible and acceptable behavior
4	Decision support system	Physician and patient	A diagnosis and treatment decision: • Reason for why proposing Diagnosis or Treatment A • Reason for why not proposing Diagnosis or Treatment B • Diagnosis or treatment for a different value of Feature X
5	RoboChef	User	Teaching a recipe to the user: • Why the user's dish is not like the robot's
6	Knowledgable human	Non-knowledgable human	Game explanation, consisting of subexplananda such as the following: • Goal of the game • Items such as cards, dice, meeple, objects, etc. • Rules and strategies

3.3 Explanandum

As stated before, the explanandum[1] is the entity (maybe an event, phenomenon, or decision) that is the object of an explanation (see Fig. 3.1, cf. Garfinkel (1981)). In scientific explanations, an *explanandum* is a term used to refer to the statement or phenomenon **that is to be explained**. It is the proposition, fact, or phenomenon that requires an explanation (Woodward, 1979). For example, if someone observes that an object falls to the ground when released, the explanandum in this case would be the falling of the object. Scientists then aim to provide an explanans, which is the set of statements or principles that constitute the explanation for the explanandum (Bokulich, 2011). In this case, the explanans might involve the principles of gravity and the laws of motion. In the following, we shall focus on everyday explanations instead of scientific ones. Everyday explanations do not claim to be complete and exact (Rohlfing et al., 2021; Miller, 2019). They often contain partial information. During the course of an explanation, the explanandum in everyday explanations is a "moving target" (Rohlfing et al., 2021, p. 720), not predefined and finished at the beginning of the explanation.

The explanandum has a global form describing what the explanation is about in general (*global explanandum*). However, we use the term explanandum to refer to a *local explanandum*, which is the content-related goal of one explanation *step*. We define an explanation step as one explainer move and the explainee's following contribution. The explanandum might be the same for multiple subsequent explanation steps. Over the course of an explanation, these local explananda form a sequence.

The explanandum is not only defined by a given situation,[2] event, or object (e.g., the car itself in Kary's car scenario Chap. 2) but also by the goals of the explainer and the explainee. For example, there are different forms of understanding, and it can be the goal of an explainee to *comprehend* something about cars or this specific car (to acquire knowledge) or to be *enabled* to drive cars or this car—that is, to learn an action (cf. Buschmeier et al., 2025). Regarding comprehension as well as enabledness, goals can differ widely with regard to the level of intended understanding, the specific object, and so forth. Also in this sense, the explanandum can change over the course of an explanation, and thus, it is co-constructed by explainer and explainee (cf. Chap. 13).

Different disciplines have different interpretations of how and – in a figurative sense – where this construction takes place. From the point of view of cognitive psychology, the explanandum can be seen as a mental representation of the explainer as well as the explainee (cf. Johnson-Laird, 2005). Thus, the explanandum is different for explainer and explainee. It can be expected that, at the beginning of an explanation, the explainer may have a better (more complete, more correct) representation than the explainee, whereas over the course of the explanation,

---

[1] The plural is explananda.
[2] The context significantly influences both the emergence and modification of the explanandum (see Chap. 4).

the representation of the explainee is built up (cf. Kintsch, 1998). Additionally, explainer and explainee might have their own models of what the explanation should be about and what the need for understanding in the explainee is. Following a constructivist view of knowledge and knowledge generation, an objective explanandum does not exist, just as the knowledge of two people is never the same. Similarly, computer sciences consider the explanandum as a mental model/domain model that is part of an explaining system (cf. Schmid & Wrede, 2022). Going beyond this individual constructivist perspective, a *social* constructivist view such as that in conversation analysis and sociocultural theory locates the explanandum in between the explainer and the explainee (Kern & Selting, 2020; Rogoff, 1998, e.g.,). As a co-construction, it emerges out of negotiation processes during the course of an explanation (cf. Rohlfing et al., 2021; Chaps. 1, 13).

Coming to explananda in sXAI, the sXAI system estimates the needs of the explainee.[3] Speaking about these 'needs,' we address different aspects such as the explainee's desires, goals, interests, knowledge gap, and so forth (Alpsancar et al., 2024). These aspects are built into the sXAI's model of the explainee (the *partner model*) and are used to derive the explanandum. These models of explainee and explanandum are reevaluated and adapted at each step of an explanation (see Chap. 14). Regarding the case of sXAI, the explanation need arises based on observations of AI outputs. Depending on the context and application, the explanation can take, in particular, these forms:

1. **Immaterial:** a decision that has been taken by the machine in response to a request of the user; a solution to a request formulated as a choice, a selection, a diagnosis, a plan, a recommendation or an assessment
2. **Concrete:** an object or a device built by the AI system (e.g., a 3D printed object)
3. **A past activity**: a task that has been achieved by an AI-enabled machine
4. **An ongoing activity:** the overall activity a machine is currently performing: its goal, the physical action the machine is currently performing (the current step in its plan) that can be observed together with its past actions, and its current plan for future action (including the anticipated contribution of the humans in case of a human-machine shared activity), with the latter presenting a fluid transition to the immaterial outputs

In the first three cases, the explanation process happens post hoc. In the ongoing activity case, the explanation activity accompanies a human–machine shared activity. It is somehow intermixed with it.

Importantly, the observed output might not be congruent with the respective global explanandum. Let us consider the example of multiple past actions of an AI-enabled machine as the output that the human explainee has witnessed. The

---

[3] We use the term "need" in a colloquial sense, because it is well-known and popular in XAI literature (e.g., recently Human & Watkins, 2023). However, it is problematic, because it seems like a scientific term used without a conceptual background and it implies the perspective of the user as a passive person.

3 Components of an Explanation for Co-constructive sXAI

explanation need arises, because the explainee thinks to have recognized some commonality in the past actions (i.e., an interpretation) and suspects a general strategy behind the machine's behavior. The global explanandum is, thus, the interpretation of the output (i.e., the general strategy) or even part of the machine's architecture causing the commonalities in the observed behavior.

The output is perceived, at least partially, by the human explainee as a physical object or as an action performed by the machine in the physical environment, on the human, or accompanying/supporting a human action using speech, text, or various modalities (see Chap. 23).

It is important to note that the explanandum might be perceived only partially (e.g., due to spatial conditions) and might need elaborate interpretation (cf. Chap. 4). This should be taken into account in the explanation process. Witnessing it partially might give rise to a fair amount of uncertainty, adding to the co-constructive nature of the explanandum.

It is also important to note that when the explanation accompanies an activity of the machine, the explanandum is somehow intertwined or even merged with the production of the explanans. The machine performs an action and conveys explanation information about it. An example is when a robot adapts a motion to achieve a task or synthesize it not only to achieve the task but also to convey to the human information about its intention or target.

Instances of Explanandum and Explanans for an AI-Enabled Robot

The following two cases illustrate a post hoc explanation process (Case 1) and an explanation of an ongoing activity (Case 2) (see Sect. 2.6 for a detailed example) for a cognitive and interactive robot (Lemaignan et al., 2017; Hellström & Bensch, 2018; Clodic et al., 2017; Arnold et al., 2021; Sakai & Nagai, 2022).

Case 1
Human H1 has given a task to Robot R. R has achieved the task.

1. This task involved R alone
2. This task involved assistance to Human H2 (for what concerns Human H2, refer to Case 2)

The task has been achieved. Some of its effects are perceivable by H1. H1 requests R to give an explanation about what it has done (what happened with respect to the task): The global explanandum is what happened—that is, what the robot has decided, what it has done, and what resulted in terms of effects in the environment and with respect to H2.

Case 2
Human H1 has given a goal to Robot R, and it is currently performing the task to achieve it

1. This task involved R alone but in the presence of a Human H2 (or H1 themselves)
2. This task involved a collaborative activity with H1

In this case, the explanans is closely intertwined with the explanandum (see Sect. 3.4). The task is ongoing. Some of its effects are perceivable by the human copresent with the robot (H2 and/or H1).

H1 requests R to give an explanation about what it is currently doing: The output is what happened until now. The global explanandum can be about the current activity and its goal and also about what the robot is planning to do.

Moreover, the robot should consider the effects of its behavior on copresent humans. At each step, while achieving its task, it has to ensure that its behavior is predictable, legible, and acceptable by copresent and coacting humans.

3.4 Explanans

As above with regard to explananda (cf., Sect. 3.3), for the sake of clarity, we also differentiate between global and local explanantia.[4] The global explanans addresses the (verbal) way that an explanation can be expressed and co-constructed by both partners (see Fig. 3.1). It is a sequence of local explanantia that determine **how** the respective explananda are conveyed at each explanation step. The way an explanation is expressed depends on a plethora of factors (see also Chap. 4). Environmental factors such as loud background noise influence how the explanation is given—in this case, the volume or other, nonverbal communicative means. Also, the norms applied in a setting – when explaining to a superior in a work context versus when explaining to a peer – impact on how an explanation is expressed, for example, which gestures and words are chosen. Explanations are expressed using multiple modalities: for example, with a graphic representation, pictogram, gestures, but also verbal utterances (cf. Chaps. 19 and 25). Due to the discretization of an explanation into explanation steps in our formalization (cf., Sect. 3.5), the production of the explanans is also discretized. However, it is produced continuously such that the explanans used is adapted online during the interaction based on observations of the explainee's reactions (Pitsch et al., 2009; Vollmer et al., 2014; cf. Chap. 13).

The explanans is closely intertwined with the explanandum. The explanandum was defined above as the entity that is the object of an explanation, whereas the explanans is the way this is done. Choosing and producing an adequate explanans might, however, involve referring to a different topic—for instance, by using a specific metaphor. This makes the distinction between explanans and explanandum difficult. In our view, and according to our definitions of the global explanandum and the local explananda, the explanans could involve a reference to a different topic within one explanation step. A broader use of a different topic that extends over multiple explanation steps and therefore is explained affects the respective explananda in that the novel topic will constitute new explananda. We argue that

---

[4] Explanantia is the plural of explanans.

the choice of the explanantia in the explainer is determined by an explanation strategy that couples explananda with the respective explanantia. The explanation strategy is responsible for not only current but also the planning of future explananda and explanantia, and it is updated constantly as the interaction unfolds. Further, explanations, being a form of social interaction, naturally take place in face-to-face communication (i.e., being physically copresent and sharing a referential space) in which (human) interaction partners are able to perceive each other through multiple sensory modalities and also use a variety of modalities to express themselves. Therefore, the global explanans, local explanantia, and the feedback from interlocutors (with respect to, e.g., the current level of understanding or the focus of attention) within the social interaction can be expressed verbally, nonverbally, or multimodally (with different combinations of multimodal behaviors) (see Chap. 19). Empirical research has provided evidence that multimodality facilitates cognitive processing and understanding (rather than hindering it, as one could expect because more information needs to be processed simultaneously) (see Chap. 18, e.g., regarding prosody Kern, 2007 or regarding gestures Holler & Bavelas, 2017).

Considering the factors influencing an explanans above, an explanans depends even more on the context than the explanandum.

For sXAI, the explanans plays a crucial role for conveying an explanandum and making explanations more human-centered. However, the (linguistic) dimensions and parameters of the explanans are still a subject of current research even in human interaction, making the development of a toolbox for different explanantia for sXAI especially difficult. In addition, multimodal communication becomes relevant for sXAI as soon as explanations are (the explanans is) produced by technical agents that provide anthropomorphic cues—for example, agents that use language, speech, or exhibit human features (behavioral and morphological factors; Kim & Im, 2023). Further, it is most likely that humans produce explanantia as multimodal utterances in which information might be distributed across different modalities also when interacting with technical agents. Therefore, a technical agent should be equipped with proper processing allowing it to interpret multimodal input and respond accordingly within explanatory interactions. However, given their ambiguity and their dependency on context and culture, the integration of multimodal aspects into technical systems is a challenging endeavor when it comes to both their perception and their production (cf. Chap. 19).

3.5 Operationalizations of the Explanation Components

This section aims to clarify the multifaceted nature of explanation by proposing a formal structure that captures its core components while also highlighting the intricacies that are frequently neglected in current XAI models.

To simplify the implementation of XAI systems, several strong assumptions are often introduced. These include idealized conditions such as perfect communication, fixed roles, and the absence of contextual factors. This contrasts sharply with the incremental and context-dependent nature of human explanations. By outlining an exemplary set of these assumptions, we aim to illuminate not just how explanations can be formalized but also the complexity that lies beneath the surface—complexity that must be acknowledged and addressed for XAI systems to truly mirror the richness of human explanatory practices.

We can assume an explanation E to be a process that consists of a sequence of explanation steps $e_1 \ldots e_n$. In each step e_i, the explainer er_i (i.e., ER for explanation step i) communicates the explanans es_i to the explainee ee_i (i.e, EE for explanation step i) according to an explanation strategy s_i. In each step, the explainee may also signal or express explanation needs (i.e., the explanandum), denoted em_i. Consequently, each step e_i can be regarded as a 5-tuple $e_i = (er_i, ee_i, s_i, es_i, em_i)$, in which an explainer provides an explanans to an explainee according to an explanation strategy, to which the explainee might form a need that could become apparent or identifiable through cues.

Several strong assumptions can simplify the job of explaining for XAI systems in contrast to the complexity of typical human–human explanations. Most importantly, we could assume the following:

1. The explainer er_i has the best interest of the explainee ee_i in mind and does not explain for the sake of explaining. Humans can explain for different reasons; see Chap. 2, but AI explains only to bring about understanding in the explainee (because of a need for understanding).
2. There are no errors in the communication of the explanandum—that is, the relation between er_i, ee_i, and em_i is functional.
3. There are no errors in understanding the explanans: es_i is understood exactly as intended.
4. er_i and ee_i are fixed roles during each step serving the knowledge transfer from er_i to ee_i.
5. There exists at least one optimal EM and the respective explananda em_i are fixed a priori and objective.
6. There is no error in monitoring the explainee (or no monitoring at all, when the ee_i have known changing states) and the next explanandum depends only on the current state of the explainee and is independent of the explanation history. The steps contain all information necessary to ensure $p(e_i|e_{i-1} \ldots e_1) = p(e_i|e_{i-1})$.
7. No additional context factors have to be taken into account.

3.6 How Does This Chapter Inspire Further Directions of XAI?

In contrast to traditional state-of-the-art (SOTA) XAI approaches, which often rely on simplifying assumptions Sect. 3.5 to streamline the explanation process, this section delves into the complexities inherent in natural human–human explanations. Co-constructing social XAI challenges the above assumptions by emphasizing that explanations are not static, one-way transfers of information, but rather evolving dialogs shaped by the mutual engagement of explainer and explainee. This section explores how abandoning assumptions such as fixed explananda (Assumption 5), rigid role assignments (Assumption 4), and static explanation steps (Assumption 6) opens up new possibilities for creating more adaptive, personalized, and context-sensitive XAI systems. By focusing on the alignment of beliefs and the negotiation of understanding, co-constructing sXAI aims to mirror the richness and complexity of human explanatory practices, pushing the field toward more human-centered AI solutions.

Some of the above assumptions in Sect. 3.5, especially 4, 5, and 6 breach the idea of co-constructing sXAI. In simple SOTA XAI, all of these assumptions and assumption 7 hold. Assumption 5 might often even be broader in SOTA XAI and pertain to an equality of all explainees such that the explanation produced is independent of the explainee. Personalized XAI does not assume equality of explainees and "[characterizes] an explainee as an individuum with preferences, personal characteristics, intentions, etc." (Rohlfing et al., 2021, p. 719). Still, explanations here are not given in a social interaction. In recipient-designed XAI (Miller, 2019), the above are not assumed directly. Miller (2019) supports the concept of recipient design by emphasizing the need to tailor AI explanations to the specific purposes and cognitive processes of human users. However, in contrast to co-constructing sXAI, the global explanandum is not a matter of co-construction, but the explanation is only an interactive 'transfer of knowledge,' and, as such, serves the successive filling of a knowledge gap. Accordingly, the following is assumed: EM and, thus, the explananda em_i depend on the current and successively updated model of the explainee, but the global explanandum is fixed a priori and objective.

In co-constructing sXAI, the global explanandum is not fixed over the course of an interaction, but a "moving target" (Rohlfing et al., 2021). As the explainee's understanding grows, new needs or wants for understanding may form. In some explanations, the explainee might initially not be sure what exactly they would like to know. In this case, the explanandum might emerge in the interaction between explainer and explainee. In other cases, the explanandum needs to be negotiated, because there might be an (initial) offset between what the explainer believes the explanandum to be and what the explainee believes it to be. Thus, in a co-construction, if assumption 5 does not hold, then the explanandum at each step i is not unique but rather consists of beliefs held by the explainer er_i and the explainee ee_i. Formally, assuming a belief function b, we get $em_i = (b(er_i), b(ee_i))$. Therewith, the signature of explanation steps is now $e_i = (er_i, ee_i, s_i, es_i, b)$.

A good explanation, then, is characterized by a good alignment of the respective explananda of explainer (i.e., $b(er_i)$) and explainee (i.e., $b(ee_i)$).

Additionally, in co-constructing sXAI, assumption 4 does not hold, and, for parts of an explanation, the explainee might become the explainer and vice versa, thereby reversing their roles (see Sect. 3.2). The explainee might, for example, become the explainer and explain their prior understanding or point of view to the explainer turned explainee.

Assumptions 2 and 3 may hold for co-constructive explanations. If they do not hold, however, the need for co-construction increases, because there are misunderstandings and miscommunications that make an alignment even more necessary.

These observations highlight the limitations of current SOTA approaches and suggest the potential of co-constructing sXAI. Traditional XAI methods, as discussed, often treat the explanation process as a one-way transfer of knowledge, assuming fixed explananda and equal treatment of all explainees. In contrast, co-constructing sXAI envisions a dynamic, interactive process in which the explanandum and the explanans evolve during the interaction, thereby accommodating the explainee's growing understanding and specific needs. This approach requires a mutual exchange in which the roles of explainer and explainee can interchange, fostering a more personalized and adaptive explanation framework. By focusing on the alignment of beliefs between the explainer and explainee, co-constructing sXAI aims to create more effective and context-sensitive explanations, advancing the field toward more human-centered AI systems.

3.7 Rapid Access to the Content of This Chapter

Explanations are not straightforward, static processes. They evolve with the understanding of the explainee and the context of the interaction. The dynamic nature of an explanation means that roles can interchange between the explainer and explainee, with an explainee possibly contributing knowledge that alters the original explanandum (subject of the explanation). This shift contrasts with traditional XAI (explainable AI) in which explanations are typically one way.

This chapter focuses on the core components of explanations in social explainable AI (sXAI) and their relevance to human–AI interaction. The essential elements of an explanation are identified, and how these elements interact is explored, especially in dynamic, evolving explanations. The key concepts are the following:

- Explanandum: the object or entity being explained, such as an AI decision, event, or action
- Explanans: the method or content of the explanation, often co-constructed through interaction between explainer and explainee
- Explainer: the human or nonhuman agent in the role of producing the explanation
- Explainee: the human or nonhuman agent in the role of an addressee of the explanation, often the human in XAI scenarios

These components form the foundation for understanding how explanations can be structured in AI systems.

Role of Explainer and Explainee
The roles of explainer and explainee are dialogical. The explainee strives to understand an explanandum, and the explainer supports them in overcoming a knowledge

gap. Therefore, the explainer typically knows more about the explained domain than the explainee. Explainer and explainee co-construct the explanation together. As the explainee's understanding grows, the explainer adapts the explanation. In XAI, the AI classically serves as the explainer, with humans as explainees. Sometimes, however, these roles may reverse, such as when the explainee (human) provides feedback or additional information that alters the course of the explanation.

Explanandum as a "moving target"
The explanandum (the subject of explanation) is fluid, often changing during the explanation process. It adapts to the explainee's growing understanding or evolving needs. For example, in the context of sXAI, the explanandum might be the outcome of a collaborative task between a robot and a human or it might be an AI's decision that might—over the course of the explanation—change to the impact of an alternative decision on the explainee's life.

Explanans and Its Importance
The explanans (how an explanation can be verbally or nonverbally expressed and co-constructed by both partners) is tightly linked to the explanandum. For instance, the explainer may use a specific reference to existing knowledge to help the explainee understand the explanandum. The explanation strategy used by the explainer determines how the explanandum is broken down into smaller parts, influencing the effectiveness of the explanation. In sXAI, this can involve the AI system using natural language, visual cues, or multimodal feedback to explain its actions. The complexity of the explanans depends on factors such as context, environment, and interaction norms that affect how the explanation is structured.

Future Directions
This chapter suggests moving beyond current state-of-the-art XAI methods that assume fixed explananda and one-way knowledge transfer. Co-constructive sXAI envisions a more adaptive system in which explanations evolve based on the explainee's goals and understanding. This allows for more personalized, effective interactions. By focusing on how explanations are co-constructed and how explainer and explainee roles can adapt to each other, co-constructive social XAI offers a pathway to more human-centered AI systems.

Acknowledgments This work was funded by the Deutsche Forschungsgemeinschaft (DFG, German Research Foundation): TRR 318/1 2021 – 438445824. Rachid Alami's work has been partially supported by the EU-funded project euROBIN under grant agreement no. 101070596 and by the Artificial and Natural Intelligence Toulouse Institute (ANITI) funded by the France 2030 program under the grant agreement no. ANR-23-IACL-0002.

References

Alpsancar, S., Buhl, H. M., Matzner, T., & Scharlau, I. (2024). Explanation needs and ethical demands: Unpacking the instrumental value of XAI. *AI and Ethics* 1–19. https://doi.org/10.1007/s43681-024-00622-3

Arnold, T., Kasenberg, D., & Scheutz, M. (2021). Explaining in time: Meeting interactive standards of explanation for robotic systems. *ACM Transactions on Human–Robot Interaction, 10*(3), 25. https://doi.org/10.1145/3457183

Bokulich, A. (2011). How scientific models can explain. *Synthese, 180*, 33–45. https://doi.org/10.1007/s11229-009-9565-1

Buschmeier, H., Buhl, H.M., Kern, F., Grimminger, A., Beierling, H., Fisher, J., Groß, A., Horwath, I., Klowait, N., Lazarov, S., Lenke, M., Lohmer, V., Rohlfing, K.J., Scharlau, I., Singh, Terfloth, L., A., Vollmer, A.-L., Wang, Y., Wilmes, A., & Wrede, B. (2025). Forms of understanding of XAI-explanations. *Cognitive Systems Research, 94*, 101419. https://doi.org/10.1016/j.cogsys.2025.101419

Clodic, A., Pacherie, E., Alami, R., & Chatila, R. (2017). Key elements for human–robot joint action. In R. Hakli & J. Seibt (Eds.), *Sociality and normativity for robots* (pp. 159–177). Springer. https://doi.org/10.1007/978-3-319-53133-5_8

Garfinkel, A. (1981). *Forms of explanation. rethinking the questions in social theory*. Yale University Press.

Hellström, T., & Bensch, S. (2018). Understandable robots – What, Why, and How. *Paladyn, Journal of Behavioral Robotics, 9*(1), 110–123. https://doi.org/10.1515/pjbr-2018-0009

Holler, J., & Bavelas, J. (2017). Multi-modal communication of common ground: A review of social functions. In R. B. Church, M. W. Alibali & S. D. Kelly (Eds.), *Why gesture?* (pp. 213–240). Benjamins. https://doi.org/10.1075/gs.7.11hol

Human, S., & Watkins, R. (2023). Needs and artificial intelligence. *AI and Ethics, 3*(3), 811–826. https://doi.org/10.1007/s43681-022-00206-z

Johnson-Laird, P. N. (2005). Mental models and thought. In K. J. Holyoak & R. G. Morrison (Eds.), *The Cambridge handbook of thinking and reasoning* (pp. 185–208). Cambridge University Press.

Kern, F. (2007). Prosody as a resource in children's game explanations: Some aspects of turn construction and recipiency. *Journal of Pragmatics, 39*(1), 111–133. https://doi.org/10.1016/j.pragma.2005.01.017

Kern, F., & Selting, M. (2020). Conversation analysis and interactional linguistics. In C. A. Chapelle (Ed.), *The encyclopedia of applied linguistics*. Wiley. https://doi.org/10.1002/9781405198431.wbeal0203.pub2

Kim, J., & Im, I. (2023). Anthropomorphic response: Understanding interactions between humans and artificial intelligence agents. *Computers in Human Behavior, 139*, 107512. https://doi.org/10.1016/j.chb.2022.107512

Kintsch, W. (1998). *Comprehension: A paradigm for cognition*. Cambridge University Press.

Lemaignan, S., Warnier, M., Sisbot, E. A., Clodic, A., & Alami, R. (2017). Artificial cognition for social human–robot interaction: An implementation. *Artificial Intelligence, 247*, 45–69. https://doi.org/10.1016/j.artint.2016.07.002

Miller, T. (2019). Explanation in artificial intelligence: Insights from the social sciences. *Artificial Intelligence, 267*, 1–38. https://doi.org/10.1016/j.artint.2018.07.007

Pitsch, K., Vollmer, A. L., Fritsch, J., Wrede, B., Rohlfing, K., & Sagerer, G. (2009). On the loop of action modification and the recipient's gaze in adult–child interaction. In *Proceedings of the Gesture and Speech in Interaction International Conference*. https://www.honda-ri.de/pubs/pdf/1306.pdf

Robrecht, A., Buhl, H., & Kopp, S. (2024). Inferring partner models for adaptive explanation generation. In *Proceedings of the 28th Workshop on the Semantics and Pragmatics of Dialogue*.

Rogoff, B. (1998). Cognition as a collaborative process. In D. Kuhn & R. S. Siegler (Eds.), *Handbook of child psychology: Vol 2. Cognition* (pp. 679–744). Wiley.

Rohlfing, K. J., Cimiano, P., Scharlau, I., Matzner, T., Buhl, H., Buschmeier, H., Grimminger, A., Hammer, B., Häb-Umbach, R., Horwath, I., Hüllermeier, E., Kern, F., Kopp, S., Thommes, K., Ngonga Ngomo, A.-C., Schulte, C., Wachsmuth, H., Wagner, P., & Wrede, B (2021). Explanation as a social practice: Toward a conceptual framework for the social design of AI systems. *IEEE Transactions on Cognitive and Developmental Systems, 13*(3), 717–728. https://doi.org/10.1109/TCDS.2020.3044366

Sakai, T., & Nagai, T. (2022). Explainable autonomous robots: A survey and perspective. *Advanced Robotics, 36*(5–6), 219–238. https://doi.org/10.1080/01691864.2022.2029720

Schmid, U., & Wredem, B. (2022). What is missing in XAI so far? An inter- disciplinary perspective. *KI-Künstliche Intelligenz, 36*(3), 303–315. https://doi.org/10.1007/s13218-022-00786-2

Vollmer, A.-L., Mühlig, M., Steil, J. J., Pitsch, K., Fritsch, J., Rohlfing, K. J., & Wrede, B. (2014). Robots show us how to teach them: Feedback from robots shapes tutoring behavior during action learning. *PloS One, 9*(3), e91349. https://doi.org/10.1371/journal.pone.0091349

Woodward, J. (1979). Scientific explanation. *The British Journal for the Philosophy of Science, 30*(1), 41–67. https://doi.org/10.1093/bjps/30.1.41

Open Access This chapter is licensed under the terms of the Creative Commons Attribution 4.0 International License (http://creativecommons.org/licenses/by/4.0/), which permits use, sharing, adaptation, distribution and reproduction in any medium or format, as long as you give appropriate credit to the original author(s) and the source, provide a link to the Creative Commons license and indicate if changes were made.

The images or other third party material in this chapter are included in the chapter's Creative Commons license, unless indicated otherwise in a credit line to the material. If material is not included in the chapter's Creative Commons license and your intended use is not permitted by statutory regulation or exceeds the permitted use, you will need to obtain permission directly from the copyright holder.

Chapter 4
Context for Explanations

Katharina J. Rohlfing , **Kary Främling** , and **Friederike Kern**

Abstract An explanation always relates to some context, with this context being defined by factors such as what is being explained, why the explanation is being given, who is the explainee (see Chap. 3), the modalities of explaining, the (un)observable facts about the situation, and so forth. In this chapter, we argue and explain why context cannot be reduced to components of a situation. Instead, context is also brought into, as well as brought about, that is, co-constructed in a situation between the partners when we consider interaction as the interface at which agents (human or artificial) negotiate their task, circumstances, relevant contextual factors, and so on. We propose four types of contexts for this interface. They vary in terms of gradual adaptability: A highly adaptive context is created by the interaction itself, building on the interaction's progress both semantically and pragmatically. Future XAI developments can take the four types of contexts framework into account depending on what they are aiming toward.

4.1 How Does This Chapter Relate to XAI?

As can be seen in the scenarios of buying a car in Chap. 2, each explanation varies depending on the addressee in order to provide facts that are relevant to that person. However, when it comes to explanations in XAI systems, the question is how to choose the relevant facts in order to represent an appropriate context. This representation is difficult and requires the analysis of a situation, task as well as goals, participants, their behavior, and also their values and social norms or regulations (Mill et al., 2024) in advance. The difficulty lies in predetermining the material and social facts in advance, because it requires knowledge about what will potentially influence the explanation. Dourish (2004) critically remarks that this approach reduces the phenomenon of context to observation and execution of a priori plans. This reduction limits the context to being static and does not address its emergent nature.

However, a static context will soon be exhausted and turn out invalid in light of the rapid spread of AI systems in both working environments and everyday life. The growing ubiquity of XAI delivers not only many possible facts that can be(come) influential or relevant for an explanation, as reflected by Mill et al. (2024). Even more, these facts can change with the usage of XAI and new emerging practices with them. In this chapter, we propose a framework for context-sensitive XAI systems and put the human–AI interaction at the center. In this respect, an interaction between the user and the XAI is a selective process yielding relevant facts in individual cases. It puts, however, specific requirements for an XAI: Considering a pre-given domain or situation, an XAI should be able to draw from information provided in the interaction with the user (see Chap. 17) and determine in a very specific moment what is relevant for an ongoing task. Then, the explanation can be dynamically adapted to the user and the progressing interaction (see Chap. 14). This dynamic adaptation, we argue, can be performed incrementally (see Chap. 12).

If we acknowledge that the context should be co-constructed with the user incrementally to be maximally adapted in terms of relevance, then, the further challenge when designing XAI systems that are situation- and context-aware (Sanneman & Shah, 2022; Mill et al., 2024) is to implement parameters with which material and social facts can be adjusted on the fly. This more adaptive view adds to the complexity of a context or contextual factors for XAI.

This chapter tackles the following questions:

1. How do humans create a context, and how does context-aware XAI relate to it? (see Sect. 4.2)
2. What facts and factors can be regarded as influential and can be considered to be a part of situation and thus reflect context awareness? In addition to material facts, we also introduce social facts that are influential for an explanation (see Sect. 4.3)
3. How – in an interaction that is incrementally and jointly constructed between partners by their actions – are facts selected (or emerge) as being relevant for an explanation provided? (see Sect. 4.4)
4. What XAI model can be proposed to account for a context unfolding during an explanation process? (see Sect. 4.6)

We will finally propose that future XAI need to account for various types of a context (summarized in Table 4.1) resulting in different grades of its adaptability. However, all the types are important for sXAI and can be considered as building upon each other. To point out the advantage of our approach for an sXAI more

Table 4.1 Types of contexts

	Context type	Definition
Increasing adaptability	Selected	A (pre)selected of social and material facts that constitutes a situation
	Situated	A semantic/cognitive interpretation of the limited set of social and material facts that is achieved by the involved agents
	Adjusted	A limited set of facts used by the agents to interpret the situation that can be adjusted along some range during the interaction
	Co-constructed	A dynamic set of facts that is not set up beforehand the interaction but emerges from it incrementally as well as locally and is shaped by the involved partners; the emerging joint knowledge provides a context for further actions

specifically, we consider interaction to be the interface at which XAI can become aware of the context (user, task, circumstances, etc.). This is crucial when facing the growing ubiquity of XAI and its constantly developing applications.

4.2 Making Sense of a Situation: Context in Humans

Difficulties in Recognizing What Context Is Clearly, technologies are developed for specific purposes. It is therefore a wise recommendation for developers to be aware of the context in which a technology will be applied. In light of the rapid spread of AI systems and the growing ubiquity of XAI, it seems imperative for XAI systems to make dynamic decisions on the purpose of and relevant context for an explanation. However, there are many working definitions and conceptions of *context* that could characterize the specific purposes. Some of these refer to the environmental and physical circumstances of the application; others characterize the users; or yet others, their tasks. In research on AI, context is seen as any information that can be used to further make relevant sense of a given situation for the user (Abowd et al., 1999, p. 304). For XAI research, it appears that designing situation and context-aware XAI systems (Sanneman & Shah, 2022; Mill et al., 2024) could mean to select relevant factors that will influence the explanation. Currently, these factors are often not well-motivated theoretically. At this point, it is important to note that we will use both terms *factors* and *facts*. With the term *factor*, we refer to a basic-level category of facts that can be characterized by systematic commonalities. We view *facts* as instantiations of a factor. Accordingly, in our view, once some facts are observed repeatedly as having an influence on an explanation, they can be summarized to a more general (and abstract) factor. The challenge is to define which facts and factors are influential and relevant for determining the context of an explanation.

Below, we describe what context is and what can be influential for its constitution. In contrast to earlier work by Rohlfing et al. (2003), in which we pointed out which various contextual factors come together in a moment of situation interpretation, we aim at a context description that becomes gradually shaped by the participants of an interaction. We therefore propose four types of context that range in their adaptability with respect to the interaction. The aim of this proposition is to make the concept of context more accessible to further XAI design. We have to highlight, however, that instead of taking a broader view on social structures, our approach focuses on social interaction and, thus, a context that becomes manifested within it through verbal and nonverbal behaviors. This focus is in accordance with the Introduction (see Sect. 1.1).

Let us start with some considerations about how humans make sense of a situation, thus creating a context. Later on, we will discuss in which ways this can be adopted for XAI.

Context Is Setting up a stage One could think of *context* as a stage on which facts are presented. This metaphor brings the selection of some facts to the fore, even though other facts exist. The facts can be material and social. For example, the number of people in the room, tables, and so forth are tangible or material facts. At the same time, the age group to which the persons involved belong, the cultural background (of people and tables), or – quite importantly – the dialogical and social roles that the persons assume in an ongoing dialog (e.g., whether they are learners or teachers, explainers or explainees) are social facts (see more specification of the facts and factors in Sect. 4.5). More recently, Mill et al. (2024) pointed out that ethical facts (such as norms and values) should also be considered. Context can then be described in terms of these facts. In Table 4.1, we consider a situation as the first type of a context. In fact, the terms *situation* and *context* "are often used synonymously," but it is only the situation that is given, because it consists of the "spatiotemporal ordering of objects and agents alongside physically given constraints or characteristics like gravitational force or light intensity" (Rohlfing et al., 2003, p. 133). The situation, then, sets the stage for the agents and their actions in the sense that it has the potential to activate behaviors (Brézillon, 1999): Without a phone on a stage, an agent cannot make a phone call; having only one hand available, tapping on the smartphone will turn out differently than usually. While these examples seem simple, identifying all parameters that sum up to a situation in an objective manner is almost impossible. This is because it would require the anticipation of parameters affecting any concrete situation (cf. Langer et al., 2021, p. 10). Yet many facts are created in the moment of acting on the stage. They can become validated as influential post hoc and can be considered as factors only when analyzed systematically in a repeating interaction. Thus, we will argue that an interaction is necessary to let some facts emerge as relevant. We will now consider how humans select a set of relevant facts to act accordingly.

How Do Human Agents Act on Such a Stage? Let us go back to the description of a situation in terms of different material and social facts that capture a moment. We will use the term "situatedness" (Rohlfing et al., 2003, p. 133) to characterize the momentum of situation interpretation and the awareness in which an agent actively "exerts an influence on the situation" (Rohlfing et al., 2003, p. 136). What makes this momentum possible – and, at the same time, what makes an action situated – is the fact that in the agent, sensomotor mechanisms interact with cognitive mechanisms resulting in an interpretation of this situation in line with which actions are performed (Rohlfing et al., 2003, p. 134). This interpretation is an ongoing cognitive construction, and many scholars (Auer & Di Aldo, 1993; Rohlfing et al., 2003; Gumperz, 1992; Clark & Schaefer, 1989) recognize that context is an active achievement rather than a passive observation (Dourish, 2004, p. 22). Exactly due to this momentum of interpretation, we can differentiate between situation on the one hand and context on the other. In fact, this situated knowledge or context enriches the situation (see Situated Context in Table 4.1). In other words, humans' perception of the physical world is complemented – and also driven (Heft, 2007) – by related information retrieved from memory of former actions. For example, when you move your office to another room, you have some expectations regarding how to perform your usual tasks or actions from your previous office, and you need to transfer them to the new setting. This type of context was referred to as "intracontext" (Rohlfing et al., 2003, p. 134), or as a model (Auer & Di Aldo, 1993, p. 22) for what is relevant for the interaction with the social and physical world. To take the example of a phone call, it will be conducted differently when the agent is in a hurry than when there is no hurry. From this perspective, the need to hurry is a construction of the agent only—that is, a relevant context for the action of making a phone call. Additionally, it is important to our framework that the interpretation results in specific interactive behaviors (Kern, 1993). In contrast to a social interaction, examples from an interaction with the physical world can be drawn: Moving your office to another room, you will notice that having the same facts but in a different arrangement will require some adjustment from you, thereby creating a new context for your actions in this specific environment. In fact, Schyns and Rodet (1997) studied how persons perceive features of objects and concluded that the selection of features might differ with respect to their individual experience with the objects. For a human agent, a situation is thus always embedded in a certain context, because this context influences or determines a situation and its analysis by the agent (Rohlfing et al., 2003, p. 134). This results in context-specific actions.

For the sake of clarity, it is important to highlight the role of memory in the process of situation interpretation. In a mature human agent, the interaction between perception and cognition results in a limitation of all possible facts to a relevant (or meaningful) selection, and this becomes a topic of semantic memory (Binder & Desai, 2011). Thus, selected and relevant facts are integrated into the process of semantic interpretation. The integration makes use of memories. It is likely that patterns – having emerged from previous interactions with the physical world or other agents (see Chap. 7) – are helpful in such a semantic/cognitive interpretation because they allow an agent to retrieve meaningful and established units of actions.

In Rohlfing et al. (2003, p. 135), such patterns are recognized as "intercontext" – that is, as memories about interactions (with persons or objects) that have taken place and are recruited for the interpretation of an ongoing situation. These patterns are referred to as a "global structure" from which the participants of an interaction can draw. Such a structure can be culture-specific, as it was demonstrated in the case of job interviews in Kern (1993). In this investigation, interviews from two different groups were microanalyzed: West and East German candidates. The analysis revealed two different styles to describe their professional experience: list formats versus narrative formats. Thus, speakers might fall back on and use different patterns for their interactive behaviors. The patterns can be attributed to global contextual factors such as the speakers' divergent cultural experiences with a particular communicative task that they might bring to the situation (Kern, 1993, p. 224). They seem to be retrieved from memory and support a moderate position suggesting that humans bring some expectations of the task (and partner) into an interaction.

In Auer and Di Aldo (1993, p. 22), these patterns are cognitive models about "what is relevant for the interaction." Because memories are important for the integration between perception and cognition, it should be emphasized that they can be habitual patterns that are embodied and tacit. It is likely that many patterns exist on different levels and can be characterized in form of the self, partner (see Chap. 14), interaction (see Chap. 11), task models (see Chap. 14), and so forth.

An interesting question is how humans develop the ability to semantically interpret a situation, and whether a system could develop it, too. It is known that infants interpret a situation as they develop their perception and memory. Insights can be gained from research on human development into how human perception is increasingly driven or complemented by memory: In their early development, children make sense of a situation by associating particular acts with cues from the situation. However, as they mature, they make a transition from being associationists to being social sophisticates (Hollich et al., 2000). For example, in early development, children were observed to pay attention to the perceptual saliency of objects when first exposed to novel objects in labeling language games with caregivers. Some months later, however, gestures of the partners are more effective in guiding children toward labeling these objects (Golinkoff & Hirsh-Pasek, 2006), suggesting that rather than drawing on the resources the material is offering (salient objects), children can increasingly link the perception of the material facts with social facts (pointing gestures of the partners) as contextualization cues that aid a correct interpretation of the situation. Caregivers help their children to interpret a situation and offer them a meaningful context for their actions (Rączaszek-Leonardi et al., 2013). Relying on a person as a resource for situation interpretation is not just typical for infants alone. In fact, in many cases, adults also rely on situation interpretation such as expert knowledge (Meshi et al., 2012). In addition, a context can emerge from agents interacting on the stage; in these cases, the actions of one agent provide the context for the other and vice versa. Rohlfing et al. (2003, p. 134) refer to the latter case as "intercontext" in which humans interleave continuously with the intracontext. We will explain these dynamics below (in Sect. 4.4, when referring to the co-constructed context in Table 4.1).

From our presentation on how human agents accomplish context, we can summarize that they create it by interpreting a situation. This interpretation relies on bringing the perception and cognition of material and social facts (specified in Sect. 4.5) into a momentum of actively exerting influence on the situation. Let us now consider how artificial systems accomplish contexts.

4.3 Situation-Aware XAI Systems: Context in AI

How Do Artificial Systems Act on a Stage? As already pointed out by Dourish (2004, p. 21), the nature of artificial systems goes hand in hand with a representational perspective in the sense that they require a context (users, tasks, circumstances, etc.) to be encoded and represented. For sXAI, it is helpful to link the semantic/cognitive interpretation of a situation to a situation model (see Sect. 14.2). Consequently, a situation model corresponds to a context of type selected or situated in Table 4.1. A situation model might consist of a location at which a human stands. For an artificial system, this would set up the stage for further actions. However, such a context can become dynamic: Schmidt (1989, p. 193) points to an example of mobile settings in which a human can move around, and the situation can change during the execution of an application. In this case, the location of a human will remain an important fact to which a system needs to be sensitive, but the mobile application will require some adjustments when acting 'on the stage'. The perception of the human and the interpretation of the perception for the application together form the situation model in this example (Schmidt, 1989, p. 198). It is important to highlight that the set of facts is limited and static here, because the facts are preselected.

There is an important difference to humans in this limitation: Human agents draw increasingly from their semantic memory, whereas an XAI system needs to be equipped with a limited set of facts before their application in order to become situation-aware. In other words, artificial systems cannot make sense of a situation ad hoc but have to match the circumstances either to some knowledge base or some given parameters to which they are sensitive.

Now, the crucial issue is to specify the relevant parameters capturing the relevant factors. Here, we can repeat our statement from the beginning that it is almost impossible to identify all the relevant (material, cognitive, social) parameters that sum up to a situation beforehand in an objective manner, due to the fact that the relevance of some parameters might shift in the course of the explanation. For the development of XAI, Sanneman and Shah (2022, p. 1775) propose to limit XAI's situation awareness from a situation (of the selected context in Table 4.1) to a subset comprising the AI behavior. By stating that "it is not equally valuable to provide just any information to human users via XAI, but only information that is relevant to them given their respective tasks and context" (Sanneman & Shah, 2022, p. 1774), the authors further emphasize that the information provided should be relevant and tailored to the user. Interestingly, with the subset of information that is relevant, they seem to be proposing a situated context (see Table 4.1). However, it is certainly difficult to foresee which facts will be relevant not only for developers but also for users. To select the relevant facts, Sanneman and Shah (2022) suggest to focus on AI behaviors that they capture with three levels: (1) On the perception level, the XAI should cover "simply information about a system's inputs and outputs" (Sanneman & Shah, 2022, p. 1775); (2) on the comprehension level, a user is assumed to gain a deeper understanding about why the system made a particular decision in terms of its goals; for this, "causal information is most relevant" (Sanneman & Shah, 2022, p. 1776). Finally, (3) on the projection level, a user should be enabled to conduct backward and forward simulations of what would happen if the system were to have different input (forward simulation) or what input is necessary to have a particular outcome (backward simulation). Thus, "counterfactual or other simulated information" is considered to be the most relevant for this level (Sanneman & Shah, 2022, p. 1776).

Even though the approach helps to highlight core aspects of AI behavior, it still comprises unsolved problems: First, there is the issue of relevance that the authors (and also a more recent approach by Mill et al., 2024) emphasize continually. However, because of the widespread use of AI systems, the growing ubiquity of XAI means that tasks and context change continuously. Thus, we propose that only by adapting to the user via interaction can an XAI system determine what is relevant—an aspect that is missing in current research (we will elaborate on this adaption in Sect. 4.4, referring to adjusted and co-constructed context in Table 4.1). In fact, because the tasks change rapidly, letting novel practices with XAI evolve, the proposition by Meske et al. (2022) to consider more than just the knowledge about AI behavior but also its impact on (novel) responsibilities (see Chap. 9) can be seen as broadening the context awareness that is needed for XAI. This broadening would also accord with ethical factors as suggested by Mill et al. (2024) (see also Chap. 9 for more details). Second, there is the issue of the user's understanding that is supposed to be deepened with each level (perception, comprehension, and projection) proposed by Sanneman and Shah (2022). Certainly, the purpose of an XAI is to induce a user's understanding. However, before any interaction commences, the form or level of the desired understanding is difficult to determine. It might be that the user will tackle different levels of understanding. As the authors note themselves, there currently exists no AI system that could dynamically switch between the proposed levels or address them all (Sanneman & Shah, 2022, p. 1785) in response to how the user's understanding progresses. Thus, the implicit assumption of the framework – to specify variables of the users or audience, their context(s), and their form of needed understanding – clearly limits its applicability, although the framework might be rather helpful for specifying the tasks and needs of the users beforehand or along with the design.

What Factors Can Be Relevant for an Explanation? This is a guiding question in designing context-aware XAI systems. For explanations in interactions between humans, many external factors have been identified as exerting an influence (Booshehri et al., 2024). Recently, Levinson (2024, p. 33) has proposed that contextual factors are structured in their own way, and it is important and insightful to know about the structure that gives rise to cross-situational (also cross-cultural) comparisons in order to reveal the universality of these factors. Some of these factors are specified in Sect. 14.2 and can range from visible ones, such as institutional settings (e.g., a dialog in court), personal characteristics (e.g., age, handedness preference, neurotypicality), modalities of communication (e.g., touch screen, speech), different tasks (e.g., delivering a package, discussing a topic) to invisible ones, such as social roles (e.g., being a teacher or a learner), and sociocultural characteristics (e.g., power status, education), or power structure (e.g., being the leader of a group or a member of a group) that come to light only indirectly through the (inter)actions of the participants (e.g., a teacher giving a student the floor, or interrupting them at other times). As will be shown in the next Sect. 4.4, for human agents, the interaction itself serves as a source in which factors are mutually instantiated and co-constructed, thus becoming influential and relevant.

At the beginning of this section, we asked how agents act on a stage given by the selected context (see Table 4.1). To complete the picture, we have to emphasize that in contrast to humans, XAI systems need to be prepared for possible factors and be able to activate perception of them when necessary. To systematize the possible factors in context-aware AI systems, Abowd and Mynatt (2000, p. 37) proposed the five Ws (Who, What, Where, When, Why) as the minimum information necessary to specify context. In addition, approaches to adaptive XAI systems emphasize that contextual factors cannot be identified without the users. Instead, a system is considered context-aware if it uses contextual factors to retrieve relevant information and/or services for the user (Perera et al., 2014, p. 420). According to this view, only those factors that are relevant to the users contribute to the interaction (Arrieta et al., 2020; Sanneman & Shah, 2022; Mill et al., 2024; Wang et al., 2024). Because it is difficult to foresee what subjective factors will be relevant for the entire course of the explanation, although, at the same time, the factors need to be implemented beforehand, there is a continuous discussion on what factors should be considered. More recently, in addition to considering factors relevant to the users of an XAI as suggested by Arrieta et al. (2020), Meske et al. (2022) propose a further differentiation between users according to their stakeholder groups. Following up on this suggestion, Wang et al. (2024) more recently proposed a roadmap for XAI research considering nine groups of potential XAI stakeholders (such as various experts, regulators, end users), their needs, and questions. Whereas this roadmap helps to characterize the various groups, the picture will change with new tasks and practices with XAI. Optimally, then, an XAI system would see context as accomplished moment by moment (Dourish, 2004, p. 25), and together with the user. As already suggested by Cawsey (1992), this requires an incrementally built-up dialog that offers a relevant explanation (see Chap. 12). In such a context-specific dialog, the interaction itself provides a context for the agents' next actions as it unfolds, constituting relevant facts that shape the stage (Goodwin, 2018, p. 154).

Without being able to answer the question about the relevant factors here, we can point to two different approaches for the design of context-aware XAI. First, some important contextual factors can be set up in advance (e.g., by applying participatory designs) and optimized through their use. This can result in concrete groups of users being identified and characterized in terms of their task behaviors, actions, information preferences, goals, and so forth. Once more, the static nature of this approach should be emphasized: The factors are preselected. Secondly, adaptive and interactive XAI approaches should be able to construct a context incrementally in an interaction with users. However, achieving this is clearly a topic for future research, because it requires the implementation of the iterative or processual nature of interaction and reaction to contextual cues (Gumperz, 1992; Levinson, 2003)—(see Chaps. 17 and 12 for inspiration). Some insights on how humans co-construct such a context incrementally will be presented in the next section.

4.4 (Incrementally) Constructed Context: Semantic/Cognitive Interpretation of the Explanation Situation

How Does Context Emerge? Rather than viewing context as a "collection of material or 'social facts'" (Auer, 1993b, p. 22) that is brought together for a specific momentum, we will now consider the notion of a context from a more constructionist perspective and focus on how a context emerges. In this view, context is not given but constructed in an interaction through what people do (cf. Dourish, 2004, p. 22); it is a joint achievement by all participants (Auer, 1993a) and therefore better adapted to them. More specifically, whereas material and social facts may have an effect on language, talk, and interaction, the participants make some facts more or less relevant over the course of an ongoing interaction in order to make their contribution meaningful to each other. Thus, context is constructed in an interaction and becomes available to co-participants through verbal and embodied signals. At the same time, contextual factors influence the way the interaction unfolds. Interaction and context, thus, stand in a mutually reflexive relationship to each other: Context affects the interaction, and the ongoing interaction affects the contextual factors considered relevant by the interaction partners (Goodwin & Duranti, 1992, p. 31). We will consider this relationship by dividing it into the cognitive construction of the context and the interactive negotiation of it.

When answering the question of how human agents act on a stage above (see Sect. 4.5), we pointed to the semantic/cognitive interpretation of a situation that humans achieve when actively exerting an influence on this situation. We also emphasized the role of memory in this interpretation. As a result, only some facts are (pre)selected and will trigger "a set of dispositions to act" (Dourish, 2004, p. 24). This cognitive knowledge construction can be a normative phenomenon itself, because it is a manifestation of the cognitive construction in question that is socially and culturally determined (Susswein & Racine, 2009). In Chap. 14, this cognitive construction of the context has been labeled a situational model that is being formed for further actions. Thus, context is (re-)constructed individually and subjectively, and interaction partners will often differ in how they perceive, represent, and take account of the situation.

4 Context for Explanations

Importantly and in addition to what we have proposed above, the context does not remain stable for further (inter)actions. To put simply, the interpretation of a situation can change. It is the (inter)action itself that is continuously changing the construction of the situation, and we will refer to this unfolding context as adjusted context in Table 4.1. To formulate it from a constructivist viewpoint, the interaction does not only change the construction of the situation but also yields it: Over the course of the interaction, the explainers get a better picture of the situation and the relevance of their explanation. Let us consider a dialog about dinosaurs as an example. At the beginning, an explainer can (pre)select some facts such as the partner being a very young person. This will result in the explainer's specific disposition to set the explanation content simply, that is, in a child-directed way. However, as the interaction unfolds, it turns out that the young partner is actually an expert of the explanation content (e.g., dinosaurs). Accordingly, the social fact of age does not play a role for setting the explanation content any more. Thus, whereas a situation (or partner) model results from a cognitive situation construction, the molding of such a model results from interactive negotiation. In this sense, context is both the ongoing project and the final product of the participants' joint efforts (Drew & Heritage, 1992). Likewise, material and social contextual facts can be made more or less relevant to the interaction by the participants themselves. Some contextual factors may not even be present (as in the case of the dinosaurs expert) on the stage but will nevertheless be 'brought about' (i.e., made relevant) to make the ongoing interaction events meaningful to the participants (Auer, 1993a). We consider this molding as a process of adaptation, which is why the proposed context types range accordingly.

How Is the History of Interaction Also a Context? As already mentioned above, the semantic/cognitive interpretation of a situation (the situation model) is certainly an incremental process as a situation unfolds over time, requiring its ongoing interpretation to be gradually refined and elaborated. These refinements and adjustments flow into each other. At the same time, this flow speaks to the inherent processuality and incrementality of an interaction, which can create a context in itself for an ongoing explanation (see co-constructed context in Table 4.1): When explainer and explainee negotiate the explanandum, explain, test, and seek for confirmation, an *interaction history* (see Chap. 17) emerges that provides new and changing context for the ongoing interaction (Silverstein, 1993; Auer & Di Aldo, 1993; Auer, 1993a). In other words, with each increment, the joint actions become (invisible) context for subsequent actions. In this way, partners do not only react to each other but also create facts to which they can react further. These facts do not only come from the semantic/cognitive interpretation of the situation (as suggested above) but can emerge from the process of the interaction itself, in which partners decompose what is established, reuse, or transform it (Goodwin, 2013, p. 9). The term "history," thus, accounts for semantic (concerning the content) and pragmatic (concerning the situational circumstances) information accumulated during the interaction. This information can be retrieved and referred to. It is important for the progress of an explanation, because some information may become a necessary background for other information (Goodwin & Duranti, 1992): For example, when explaining a board game, "laying out the tools" Terfloth et al. (2023) – i.e., describing the game materials' physical characteristics – becomes an essential background for further explanations of rules and strategies.

There are some benefits of these emerging histories and contextual factors: Firstly, as the partners continue with their interactive exchange, knowledge accumulates between them (Auer, 1993a, p. 19) that has been described as common ground (Clark & Schaefer, 1989, p. 261), also in Chap. 17. The partners make their interpretations available by using contextualization cues (Gumperz, 1992; Levinson, 2003), such as jointly established gestures and verbal expressions, to negotiate and signal the relevant contextual factors. Accordingly, they establish a joint context. Second, the history yields contextual features (such as words, syntactic constructions, gestures, and prosodical patterns) that, on the one hand, provide a public "substrate" (Goodwin, 2018, p. 3) that the participants can use and subsequently act upon. On the other hand, these features help to understand an explanation and enrich its understanding—that is, the sentences are more understandable within the context of what already has been said (Silverstein, 1993, p. 65). Third, the history supports the development of joint interaction patterns. These are, for example, particular moves that support and establish an underlying structure (e.g., opening, explicating causal, conceptual or procedural relations, closing, cf. Quasthoff et al., 2017). Patterns evoke specific expectations thus capturing common knowledge on how to achieve goals in an interaction (Levin & Moore, 1977). These patterns and practices are culturally determined (see Chaps. 5 and 6). There are also some disadvantages to these emerging histories: They are mostly invisible unless the partners share a workspace (Pickering & Garrod, 2021) that makes the progress of an ongoing interaction visible.

A radical constructionist approach suggests that any context is constructed in the moment of interaction (locally) and incrementally by the partners. In this view, verbal and embodied behaviors are mainly responsible for context construction; the (physical or social) facts have to be made relevant as context factors by the partners in the course of the interaction to support disambiguation or interpretation of what has been said. This radical view would imply a permanent flexibility in context construction. However, as demonstrated in the case of job interviews in, some differences between the speakers' interactive behaviors cannot be interpreted as being "locally produced" (Kern, 1993, p. 224). Instead, they are attributed to global contextual factors[1] such as the speakers' divergent cultural experiences and resulting communicative patterns that are retrieved from memory. Together, these findings support a moderate position suggesting that humans bring some expectations of the task (and partner) into an interaction.

---

[1] Here, one could differentiate between macrocontext (e.g., society), mesocontext (e.g., specific job settings), and microcontext comprising the ongoing interaction. Factors attributed to cultural experience point to the macrocontext.

States for Context-Awareness Above, we have argued in favor of a reciprocal and dynamic relationship between context and interaction, with the interaction offering an interface at which context factors are constructed and manifested incrementally. Whereas some of the current situation-aware XAI systems are prepared for a selection of contextual factors, they are not able to modify these according to signals from the partners, once the interaction has started. We end this section with the suggestion that future XAI systems need to be better aware of changing contexts ranging in their adaptability (Table 4.1). Below, we suggest four types to account for this gradual interactivity.

4.5 Operationalization of Context

We started this chapter by proposing how humans construct context (see Sect. 4.2). With Table 4.1, we can conclude that for an explanation, it is essential (1) to regard a given situation. The situation consists of selected material and social facts that are relevant for both the explainer and the explainee. Imagine, for example, how different an explanation turns out depending on whether there is a quiet environment or a construction site next door—this physical fact will certainly require a different dialog, resulting from an adaption of the explanation to the respective facts. (2) Against this background, a context pertains to the semantic/cognitive interpretation of a situation that is constructed in a specific interaction. (3) In addition, a set of facts can become modified during an ongoing interaction. We could think again of the beginning of a child-directed explanation about dinosaurs during which the adult realizes that the expert is actually on the other side. The social fact of age becomes less relevant as the interaction unfolds. Here, a user could be asked questions to create a better profile for a more successful explanation. (4) Finally, the context might emerge when the interaction unfolds. However, what is typical for human agents, namely, the emerging nature of a context that is constructed jointly in each interaction, is not available in current XAI systems: XAI systems called situation- or context-aware are currently unable to adapt incrementally and thus need to have some relevant and influential factors (categories of facts) implemented before the interaction.

Although some authors have recently proposed frameworks for situation- and context-aware XAI systems (Sanneman & Shah, 2022; Mill et al., 2024), they have failed to consider the effects of the interaction. Utilizing interaction as an interface, we propose in our approach that the interaction is an interface, at which various potential facts can either be manifested as influential, relevant contextual factors, or might be modified for an explanation. This chapter brought together categories of potentially relevant and influential facts that are called contextual factors. Because in principle, many contextual factors can be relevant for an explanation, the main challenge is, thus, to identify them and the ways in which they are structured (Levinson, 2024, p. 33). This identification should be driven by the question of which factors have a significant influence on the explainer's or explainee's (verbal) performance (Kern, 1993). Some of the possible factors are specified in Sect. 14.2. One way of systematizing the facts is to take a sociological perspective that considers the following dimensions (Luhmann, 1984):

- A social dimension evolving around the question of *who* is involved in an explanation: An example is the personal characteristics of the explainer and explainee (such as age or level of expertise) that are visible along with invisible but noticeable characteristics pertaining to their social roles of being, for example, a teacher, or the given power structure (e.g., a chief physician).
- A safety-critical dimension (The Alan Turing Institute, 2022) relates to the impact that the explanation will have: How do decisions impact others (their wealth, their liberty, or legal status).
- A temporal dimension evolving around the question *when* the explanation is communicated: Here, it is important to consider the situational circumstances. These could be the setting or the domain (e.g., an explanation provided in medicine vs. in policing) but also the pertaining circumstances under which an explanation is needed immediately – as is often the case in medicine – or can be provided after thorough data analysis that takes time, as can be the case in policing.
- A factual dimension evolving around the question of *what* is being communicated (data, relevance, architecture) and of which forms of understanding are required for this explanandum. For example, explaining the architecture of an algorithm requires deep comprehension, whereas explaining its relevance might require a follow-up action on utilizing the system.
- A medial dimension evolving around the question of *which modalities* are used (explaining by visualizing vs. explaining by using speech or text alone).
- A procedural dimension evolving around the question of *how* an explanation emerges when adapted to an explainee. This process could decide on different forms of understanding (e.g., enabling somebody to do something vs. attempting to contribute to somebody's comprehension of a matter). This dimension is added because of Sect. 4.4.

Whereas some concrete approaches to contextual factors are proposed above for the less adaptive contexts, for the more adaptive context that can unfold during an interaction, more research is needed. We can only report on the current state of the art in (socio)linguistics and linguistic anthropology suggesting that there are contextual cues (Levinson, 2003) that human agents use to set up, signal, and respond to relevant contextual facts while co-constructing context incrementally. Because this context is jointly constructed, it is better adapted and thus more relevant to the participants. Certainly, for implementations of XAI, we need to better understand how these contextual cues indicate patterns of interaction that can be recognized as being based on contextual factors. Interdisciplinary research across different situations and tasks will be helpful here. In addition to these contextual cues, the concept of public substrate (Goodwin, 2018) can be used to mark perceivable units of interaction such as words, syntactic constructions, gestures, prosodic patterns, or material that emerge during an interaction and are used by participants in and for context construction. This way, linguistic descriptions offer some indication of how knowledge accumulates between dialog partners (Clark & Schaefer, 1989; Levinson, 2003). These descriptions support the existence of a co-constructive process of context creation. However, there is a lack of insight into the mechanisms behind this process and, in particular, into how cognitive and interactive processes intertwine to drive the co-construction, and how, for example, an explainer can use the accumulated knowledge to formulate a better explanation. Thus, currently, we lack operationalizations of concrete cues leading us to how context can be constructed in XAI.

4.6 How Does This Chapter Inspire Further Directions of XAI?

Above, we pointed to many research gaps. Whereas in current XAI, it is possible to specify some situational circumstances (Wang et al., 2024), one of the greatest challenges remains to operationalize material and social facts of an emerging context. From the social and interactive perspective on XAI, the design should therefore target an implementation of adjustable factors. The challenge becomes even more ambitious when interaction is considered. As already mentioned, a social interaction is influenced by a context. In this sense, we might be dealing with nested models: A situational model would need to comprise a model of an interaction that is, however, informing a situation model. Thus, the connection of and between the models is a topic for future research.

Another challenge is to implement social facts, also because they are not always visible, or are established during an unfolding interaction (Dourish, 2004, p. 22). In fact, when interacting, human agents ratify some previous hypotheses about relevant social and material aspects that they bring into the situation in the form of, for example, a partner (see Chap. 14) or task models (see Chap. 7) that go hand in hand with dispositions. Even though some material aspects, such as the immediate need for an explanation can be assumed beforehand, the interaction can reveal a need to modify such circumstances or other relevant aspects. Thus, rather than having a set of features, contextual aspects modeled before an interaction would better provide "a set of dispositions to act" (Dourish, 2004, p. 23) that can be modified as the interaction unfolds. The process of formulating hypotheses or dispositions beforehand (in the form of a partner, interaction or a task model) and modifying them or enabling new hypotheses to emerge within the unfolding dialog is clearly the next target when designing interactive and adaptive XAI systems.

The idea of context as an emerging endeavor is not new. XAI can therefore be inspired by previous work by, for example, Dourish (2004, p. 28) who proposed that in systems, context should not be predefined. Instead, it should be designed in such a way that it supports the process by which context can become "continually manifested, defined, negotiated, and shared" (Dourish, 2004, p. 26). This can be achieved by, for example, history-of-interaction-aware systems that display aspects of their own context or provide visualization techniques. The ambition is that these forms of system behaviors might support the evolution of new practices in interaction with users (see Sect. 5.1).

4.7 Rapid Access to the Content of This Chapter

In this chapter, we have differentiated between various types of context and contextual factors that are relevant for social interaction. In this rapid access to the topic, we suggest that the different types of context with gradual adaptivity should be considered in sXAI:

An agent (a human or a system) facing a situation with material and social facts is the lowest level of context emergence (see **Selected Context** in Table 4.1). With material facts, we refer to characteristics of a situation such as the number of people in the room, tables, and so forth, whereas the involved persons' age group, the cultural background (of people and tables), or the participants' dialogical roles in an ongoing dialog (e.g., whether they are explainers or explainees) would be considered as social facts. A situation activates some behavior potential (Brézillon, 1999). A crucial difference in the perception of a situation between humans and artificial systems is that for a human agent, situation perception is in part constructed on the basis of the memory processes involved in it (see below). For artificial agents and systems, in contrast, facts are instantiations of preselected and implemented factors.

Further, context is a static and limited set of material and social facts that are (pre)selected by the interacting agent(s) to make sense of a situation (see **Situated Context** in Table 4.1). For this type of situated context, there is a construction of the given situation that makes possible a semantic/cognitive interpretation by the agents involved. This construction is often described as a situation model (see Sect. 14.2). For this model, whereas human agents increasingly draw from their semantic memory, for an XAI system to become context-aware, it must implement predetermined semantic factors that could then become implementable and adjustable parameters. Many factors can be considered for the interpretation of a situation. The main challenge in defining context for context-aware systems is thus to identify those factors that are influential or relevant for an explanation.

Viewing context rather as constructed than given, a dynamic set of limited facts appears to constitute a context. It is dynamic in the sense that it can be modified or even emerge from the interaction of the agents (see **Adjusted Context** in Table 4.1). This dynamics is a product of the unfolding interaction itself that continuously changes the situation interpretation because, for example, at the beginning, some facts have been preselected (some social facts about the partner) that will play no further role in the interaction (as they will turn out to be invalid). Consequently, other material and social facts become more relevant (e.g., during the explanatory process rather than at the beginning), and the situational model needs to be updated and adapted. Importantly, context is constructed incrementally by the participants responding to each other. If we allow the interaction to unfold the context, then the further challenge for designing XAI systems that are situation- and context-aware is to implement parameters with which material and social facts can be adjusted on the fly.

Finally, the context is created by and within the unfolding interaction itself (see **Co-Constructed Context** in Table 4.1). This is the case when contextual factors can be negotiated between the interaction partners. In this sense, context becomes an achievement of what they do together (Dourish, 2004, p. 22) and provides a shared background for further doing. When explaining a game to each other, some details (such as the material and the goal) need to be communicated in order to move to further details about, for example, gaming strategies. Thus, some information becomes necessary background for other information (Goodwin & Duranti, 1992). We referred to this unfolding context as the *history of interaction* (see also Chap. 17). It accounts for accumulating semantic and pragmatic information that can be retrieved and referred to. In this type of context, the social interaction and the emerging context constrain each other: Whereas the context provides background for interaction, the interaction itself modifies, reuses, or decomposes the already given context (Brézillon, 1999; Goodwin, 2013) for further (inter)actions. XAI research can draw from incremental models for explanatory dialogs (e.g., Cawsey, 1993) demonstrating the benefits of language processing when related to units that have been already communicated. However, although these relations are a good start, interdisciplinary research is needed to identify larger units of accumulating knowledge (such as practices in Sect. 5.1) in order to develop systems that are more history-of-interaction-aware and can plan and adjust explanations to fit the unfolding context.

Acknowledgments Our work on this chapter benefited from Brian Lim's, Kirsten Thommes', and Suzana Alpsancar's comments as well as numerous discussions with members of the TRR 318. We particularly thank Angela Grimminger and Nils Klowait for in-depth exchanges pushing the theoretical development forward.

This work was funded by the Deutsche Forschungsgemeinschaft (DFG, German Research Foundation): TRR 318/1 2021 – 438445824.

References

Abowd, G. D., & Mynatt, E. D. (2000). Charting past, present, and future research in ubiquitous computing. *ACM Transaction on Computer–Human Interaction, 7*(1), 29–58. https://doi.org/10.1145/344949.344988

Abowd, G. D., Dey, A. K., Brown, P. J., Davies, N., Smith, M., & Steggles, P. (1999). Towards a better understanding of context and context-awareness. In H.-W. Gellersen (Ed.), *Handheld and ubiquitous computing* (pp. 304–307). Springer. https://doi.org/10.1007/3-540-48157-5_29

Arrieta, A. B., Díaz-Rodriguez, N., Del Ser, J., Bennetot, A., Tabik, S., Barbado, A., Garcia, S., Gil-Lopez, S., Molina, D., Benjamins, R., Chatila, R., & Herrera, F. (2020). Explainable Artificial Intelligence (XAI): Concepts, taxonomies, opportunities and challenges toward responsible AI. *Information Fusion, 58*, 82–115. https://doi.org/10.1016/j.inffus.2019.12.012

Auer, P. (1993a). From context to contextualization. In J.-O. Östman & J. Verschueren (Eds.), *Key notions for pragmatics. Handbook of pragmatics highlights* (pp. 86–101). Benjamins.

Auer, P. (1993b). John Gumperz' approach to contextualization. In P. Auer & A. Di Luzio (Eds.), *The Contextualization of language* (pp. 1–38). Benjamins. https://doi.org/10.1075/pbns.22.03aue

Auer, P., & Di Luzio, A. (1993). *The contextualization of language*. Benjamins. https://doi.org/10.1075/pbns.22

Binder, J. R., & Desai, R. H. (2011). The neurobiology of semantic memory. *Trends in Cognitive Sciences, 15*(11), 527–536. https://doi.org/10.1016/j.tics.2011.10.001

Booshehri, M., Buschmeier, H., & Cimiano, P. (2024). A model of factors contributing to the success of dialogical explanations. In *Proceedings of the 26th International Conference on Multimodal Interaction*. ICMI '24 (pp. 373–381). Association for Computing Machinery. https://doi.org/10.1145/3678957.3685744

Brézillon, P. (1999). Context in problem solving: A survey. *The Knowledge Engineering Review, 14*(1), 47–80. https://doi.org/10.1017/S0269888999141018

Cawsey, A. (1992). *Explanation and interaction. A computer generation of explanatory dialogue*. MIT Press. https://doi.org/10.1007/BF00387398

Cawsey, A. (1993). Planning interactive explanations. *International Journal of Man-Machine Studies, 38*(2), 169–199. https://doi.org/10.1006/imms.1993.1009

Clark, H. H., & Schaefer, E. F. (1989). Contributing to discourse. *Cognitive Science, 13*(2), 259–294. https://doi.org/10.1207/s15516709cog1302_7

Dourish, P. (2004). What we talk about when we talk about context. *Personal & Ubiquitous Computing, 8*, 19–30. https://doi.org/10.1007/s00779-003-0253-8

Drew, P., & Heritage, J. (1992). *Talk at work. Interaction in institutional settings*. Cambridge University Press.

Golinkoff, R. M., & Hirsh-Pasek, K. (2006). Baby wordsmith: From associationist to social sophisticate. *Current Directions in Psychological Science, 15*(1), 30–33. https://doi.org/10.1111/j.0963-7214.2006.00401

Goodwin, C. (2013). The co-operative, transformative organization of human action and knowledge. *Journal of Pragmatics, 46*(1), 8–23. https://doi.org/10.1016/j.pragma.2012.09.003

Goodwin, C. (2018). *Co-operative action*. Cambridge University Press. https://doi.org/10.1017/9781139016735

Goodwin, C., & Duranti, A. (1992). Rethinking context: An introduction. In A. Duranti & C. Goodwin (Eds.), *Rethinking context: Language as an interactive phenomenon* (pp. 1–42). Cambridge University Press.

Gumperz, J. J. (1992). Contextualization revisited. In P. Auer & A. Di Luzio (Eds.), *The contextualization of language* (pp. 39–54). Benjamins. https://doi.org/10.1075/pbns.22.04gum

Heft, H. (2007). The social constitution of perceiver-environment reciprocity. *Ecological Psychology, 19*(2), 85–105. https://doi.org/10.1080/10407410701331934

Hollich, G. J., Hirsh-Pasek, K., Golinkoff, R. M., Brand, R. J., Brown, E., Chung, H.-L., Hennon, E. A., & Rocroi, C. (2000). Breaking the language barrier: An emergentist coalition model for the origins of word learning. *Monographs of the Society for Research in Child Development, 65*(3), i–135. https://doi.org/10.1111/1540-5834.00090

Kern, F. (1993). Culture, genres and the problem of sequentiality. An attempt to describe local organization and global structures in talk-in-situation. In A. Fetzer & C. Meierkord (Eds.), *Rethinking sequentiality* (pp. 207–229). Benjamins. https://doi.org/10.1075/pbns.103.10ker

Langer, M., Oster, D., Speith, T., Hermanns, H., Kästner, L., Schmidt, E., Sesing, A., & Baum, K (2021). What do we want from Explainable Artificial Intelligence (XAI)? A stakeholder perspective on XAI and a conceptual model guiding interdisciplinary XAI research. *Artificial Intelligence, 296*, 103473. https://doi.org/10.1016/j.artint.2021.103473

Levin, J. A., & Moore, J. A. (1977). Dialogue-Games: Metacommunication structures for natural language interaction. *Cognitive Science, 1*(4), 395–420. https://doi.org/10.1016/S0364-0213(77)80016-5

Levinson, S. C. (2003). Contextualizing 'contextualization cues'. In S. L. Eerdmans, P. J. Thibault & C. L. Prevignano (Eds.), *Language and interaction: discussions with John J. Gumperz* (pp. 31–39). Benjamins. https://doi.org/10.1075/z.117.04lev

Levinson, S. C. (2024). *The dark matter of pragmatics: Known unknowns*. Cambridge University Press. https://doi.org/10.1017/9781009489584

Luhmann, N. (1984). *Soziale Systeme. Grundriss einer allgemeinen Theorie*. Suhrkamp. https://doi.org/10.1007/978-3-658-13213-2_81

Meshi, D., Biele, G., Korn, C. W., & Heekeren, H. R. (2012). How expert advice influences decision making. *PloS One, 7*(1), e49748. https://doi.org/10.1371/journal.pone.0049748

Meske, C., Bunde, E., Schneider, J., & Gersch, M. (2022). Explainable artificial intelligence: Objectives, stakeholders, and future research opportunities. *Information Systems Management, 39*(1), 53–63. https://doi.org/10.1080/10580530.2020.1849465

Mill, E., Garn, W., Ryman-Tubb, N., & Turner, C. (2024). The SAGE framework for explaining context in Explainable Artificial Intelligence. *Applied Artificial Intelligence, 38*(1), e2318670. https://doi.org/10.1080/08839514.2024.2318670

Perera, C., Zaslavsky, A., Christen, P., & Georgakopoulos, D. (2014). Context aware computing for the internet of things: A survey. *IEEE Communications Surveys & Tutorials, 16*(1), 414–454. https://doi.org/10.1109/SURV.2013.042313.00197

Pickering, M. J., & Garrod, S. (2021). *Understanding dialogue: Language use and social interaction*. Cambridge University Press.

Quasthoff, U., Heller, V., & Morek, M. (2017). On the sequential organization and genre-orientation of discourse units in interaction: An analytic framework. *Discourse Studies, 19*(1), 84–110. https://doi.org/10.1177/1461445616683596

Rączaszek-Leonardi, J., Nomikou, I., & Rohlfing, K. J. (2013). Young children's dialogical actions: The beginnings of purposeful intersubjectivity. *IEEE Transactions on Autonomous Mental Development, 5*(3), 210–221. https://doi.org/10.1109/TAMD.2013.2273258

Rohlfing, K., Rehm, M., & Goecke, K. U. (2003). Situatedness: The interplay between context(s) and situation. *Journal of Cognition and Culture, 3*(2), 132–156. https://doi.org/10.1163/156853703322148516

Sanneman, L., & Shah, J. A. (2022). The situation awareness framework for explainable AI (SAFE-AI) and human factors considerations for XAI systems. *International Journal of Human–Computer Interaction, 38*(18–20), 1772–1788. https://doi.org/10.1080/10447318.2022.2081282

Schmidt, A. (1989). Implicit human computer interaction through context. *Personal Technologies, 4*, 191–199. https://doi.org/10.1007/BF01324126

Schyns, P. G., & Rodet, L. (1997). Categorization creates functional features. *Journal of Experimental Psychology: Learning, Memory, and Cognition, 23*(3), 681–696. https://doi.org/10.1037/0278-7393.23.3.681

Silverstein, M. (1993). The indeterminacy of contextualization: When is enough enough. In P. Auer & A. Di Luzio (Eds.), *The contextualization of language* (pp. 55–76). Benjamins. https://doi.org/10.1075/pbns.22.05sil

Susswein, N., & Racine, T. P. (2009). Wittgenstein and not-just-in-the-head cognition. *New Ideas in Psychology, 27*(2), 184–196. https://doi.org/10.1016/j.newideapsych.2008.04.013

Terfloth, L., Schaffer, M., Buhl, H. M., & Schulte, C. (2023). Adding why to what? Analyses of an everyday explanation. In *Explainable artificial intelligence* (pp. 256–279). Springer. https://doi.org/10.1007/978-3-031-44070-0_13

The Alan Turing Institute. (2022). *Explaining decisions made with AI. Draft guidance for consultation*. https://ico.org.uk/media2/3a3br1tr/explaining-decisions-made-with-artificial-intelligence-all-1-0-39.pdf

Wang, Z., Huang, C., & Yao, X. (2024). A roadmap of explainable artificial intelligence: Explain to whom, when, what and how? *ACM Transactions on Autonomous and Adaptive Systems, 19*(4), 20. https://doi.org/10.1145/3702004

Open Access This chapter is licensed under the terms of the Creative Commons Attribution 4.0 International License (http://creativecommons.org/licenses/by/4.0/), which permits use, sharing, adaptation, distribution and reproduction in any medium or format, as long as you give appropriate credit to the original author(s) and the source, provide a link to the Creative Commons license and indicate if changes were made.

The images or other third party material in this chapter are included in the chapter's Creative Commons license, unless indicated otherwise in a credit line to the material. If material is not included in the chapter's Creative Commons license and your intended use is not permitted by statutory regulation or exceeds the permitted use, you will need to obtain permission directly from the copyright holder.

Part I
Patterns

Chapter 5
Practices: How to Establish an Explaining Practice

Katharina J. Rohlfing, Anna-Lisa Vollmer, and Angela Grimminger

Abstract Applied to the development of an sXAI, a practice captures the ways in which people use a technology and for what purposes. It refers to some structured and routinized actions that have become established within a social group. In this sense, a practice can show in what context of human actions an XAI is embedded, and how it creates a context for behaviors or actions. A communicative practice is of particular interest here, because it makes an adaptive and co-constructive way of interacting possible. However, for a communicative purpose, this concept has many 'relatives.' In order to characterize the phenomenon for sXAI, we will delineate the concept of a practice in general, and of a communicative practice more specifically, by first showing similarities to and differences from other concepts that are used for technology design. Second, we will highlight the potential of this structure. Third, we will identify the limits of current interaction design with respect to this structure. Finally, with the notion of *pragmatic frames*, we suggest a definition that focuses on some key aspects of a communicative practice that can be used and useful in sXAI.

K. J. Rohlfing (✉)
Psycholinguistics, Faculty of Arts and Humanities, Paderborn University, Paderborn, Germany
e-mail: katharina.rohlfing@uni-paderborn.de

A.-L. Vollmer
Interactive Robotics in Medicine and Care, Medical School OWL, Bielefeld University, Bielefeld, Germany
e-mail: anna-lisa.vollmer@uni-bielefeld.de

A. Grimminger
Psycholinguistics, Faculty of Arts and Humanities, Paderborn University, Paderborn, Germany
e-mail: angela.grimminger@uni-paderborn.de

5.1 How Does This Chapter Relate to XAI?

This chapter elaborates on the concept of a *structure*[1] that a dialog or interaction between humans is organized toward—namely, a practice (see also Chap. 7). Hereby, we link to the claim that social interaction can be characterized in terms of patternedness (see Chap. 1). A practice is a pattern (Dignum & Dignum, 2015) that imposes a particular (culture-specific) sequence of actions toward a goal, and it functions in a similar way to a protocol; namely, it establishes expectations about how to perform the actions. When performed for communicative purposes, the involved agents' actions appear to be orchestrated, adapted to each other, and well coordinated with each other. Because of this orchestration, some scholars view both agents involved as a unit which they also refer to as a "dyadic system" (Rączaszek-Leonardi et al., 2014, p. 1). Actions performed in this system are different from autonomous actions performed by agents on their own (Clark & Schaefer, 1989). Even though this structure has been recognized as being "used to manage the progress of the dialogue" (Pickering & Garrod, 2021, p. 116), its potential has yet to be fully exploited in AI systems.

We see two benefits regarding how XAI could relate to this social concept: First, and in continuation of approaches that started with the work of Levin and Moore (1977), an XAI could become able to keep track of the progress of an interaction with a user when equipped with some knowledge about practices. This would result in an sXAI having an increased responsiveness to its users and sensitivity to the emerging context, as suggested within the design principles for an interactive XAI (Chromik & Butz, 2021). Second, when equipped with some knowledge about a variety of practices, an sXAI system could react to a user's abilities and change a practice (from, e.g., explaining to asking a question) in order to ease interaction. It could empower a user's growing knowledge and trigger deeper understanding, or it could adjust to the user's capabilities.

5.2 A (Communicative) Practice

The most intuitive way of getting a grasp on the concept of a practice is to compare it with a routine. Imagine that a child needs to learn a routine such as saying goodbye and leaving—this is one of the first routines that children learn for a communicative purpose (Gleason & Weintraub, 1976). The authors further remark that children learn it with a focus on performing it correctly, and with no emphasis on cognitive operations (Gleason & Weintraub, 1976, p. 135). Consequently, performance is more important than a deep understanding of what goodbye actually means. Interestingly, in the development of routines, it is the *performance* that comes

---

[1] With this notion, we refer to a meaningful unit of organization.

first, and then the *understanding* of it. From this example, we can deduce that a communicative (or conversational) practice is a conventionalized and routinized structure for communicative actions that is embedded in a social and cultural world. The concept of a practice more generally, thus, underscores that persons are "*doing things*" (Schegloff, 1997, p. 539). Practices are further processed "by reference to what such practices are being used to do" (Schegloff, 1997, p. 539). In the following, we will elaborate on the definition. Because it is easier to first consider what is not a practice and to contrast it with some more familiar concepts, we will start with this perspective.

What Is Not a Practice? First, on a descriptive level, a practice is not just a behavior or an action. We use *behavior* and *action* interchangeably and refer to a form of movement and act. Take, for example, the behavior of saying an "aaa." This act of vocalizing consists of producing a particular vowel and can be a part of a practice – for example, during a medical checkup (i.e., if a physician wants to take a look down somebody's throat to check for flu symptoms). In contrast to a single action, practices take more of the circumstances into account and are larger units of investigation. We will define them as structured and routinized sequences of behaviors or actions. Moreover, for a practice to be a *communicative* one, it needs more than one agent; in contrast to routinized sequences of actions, such as going to work (Dignum & Dignum, 2015, p. 38) that can be performed by one agent.

Second, if a sequence of behaviors occurs only once, this is not a practice – for example, when you need to jump to one side to get out of a bike's way. For a practice to evolve, it needs to be repeated. It is only when being applied in a changed or repeated situation (cf. Dignum & Dignum, 2015) that the sequence of behaviors becomes established. This is because the contextualization of the practice – the application of it to a situation – contributes to the development of the underlying structure. Some elements of the sequence of behaviors will need to be changed to adjust to the context (see also Sect. 4.2), and some will be invariant. Bruner (1983) therefore speaks of a surface layer (denoting the adjustable elements) and a deep structure (denoting the invariant parts that are more abstract). Only by reapplying a sequence of behaviors or actions can the invariant structure be revealed.

Third, as it will be elaborated below, it is questionable whether a sequence of behaviors or actions that is performed regularly but by only one person in an idiosyncratic manner is already a practice. For example, you might consider your way of storing your car key (such as by hanging it in a particular place) a practice. Some approaches prefer to argue that a practice can be considered only when taking culture into account, because it carries a social agreement on how things are done (with words or other means) on a behavioral level. In this sense, Schegloff (1997) or Schröter (2016, p. 379) emphasize that practices are not just a particular type of an action. Instead, they are a *way of doing*, a technique that makes use of bodily resources (such as motor skills, cognitive operations, emotions), common world knowledge (also about material artifacts), and cultural knowledge about how to do something in a competent way. In this sense, hanging car keys is only becoming a practice (although not a communicative one) when many people do it, for example, by having a board for it that is close to the entry door.

As an intermediate contrasting definition, we can summarize that a practice is not just a certain behavior but forms a larger unit consisting of a sequence of actions that do not only occur once and are not used by only one individual but can be observed repeatedly in a socially or culturally agreed-upon way. A communicative practice is all of the above, with the specification that it is a sequence of *communicative actions* that are shared among the partners.

What Is a Practice Similar to? Across disciplines, there exist many concepts that are similar to *practice*. However, it would be challenging to delineate them exactly, because each of these concepts bears some aspects of a practice but has a different focus. Overall, it seems that alternative concepts focus on behaviors by an individual. In contrast to these, a practice will always contain more social aspects to highlight the fact that the behaviors of an individual are embedded in a social and cultural system (Reckwitz, 2002, p. 288). Taking an example of a communicative practice, there are culturally different ways of saying goodbye, even though all serve the same purpose (Schegloff, 1997). Here, all these culturally various behaviors or actions with which one can say goodbye can be differentiated from the practice of doing it (Schegloff, 1997, p. 505). Nonetheless, alternative concepts reveal some important qualities of a practice. In the following, we therefore attempt to reveal the different foci to arrive at a set of aspects characterizing a *communicative* practice in particular.

Let us start with a very similar concept that – at first glance – seems to have a broader focus comprised of the situational circumstances. The term *script* emphasizes that the sequence of behaviors is embedded into a context (see Chap. 4) and follows a protocol (Schank & Abelson, 1977). There might be a dressing script, according to which a person gets dressed by carrying out very specific movements and behaviors. One person might also have a coffee-drinking script with specific movements that need to be performed, all summing up to the event of drinking a coffee. Even though these examples feature movements performed toward object(s) or a location, they are not social, and not communicative either, because they do not require the involvement of other persons. Kress and van Leeuwen (2001, p. 47) argue that such scripts may become a social practice when transmitted to others either implicitly via imitation (e.g., a practice of eating with the family alone vs. eating with family and other guests) or explicitly "as overtly stated rules or as examples of 'best practices' (e.g., practice of cooking is made explicit in a cook book)." Importantly, these behaviors do not necessarily have to be communicative.

Next, let us consider the concept of a *speech act* (Austin, 1962; Searle, 1962). As the notion already suggests, this refers to verbal behaviors that can be characterized by an intention (illocutionary act) and an impact on the partner (perlocutionary act) and are conveyed by a message (locutionary act) (see Chap. 7). Because of the impact on the partner that is factored into this notion (especially in the work of Austin, 1962), it can be considered as a unit of dialog that has a collaborative potential. Similar to a practice, speech acts also target very concrete but reoccurring tasks in communication that have socially and culturally agreed-upon ways of being done. However, later work on speech acts has tended to focus on the speaker's intention (Searle, 1962). Furthermore, as Schröter (2016, p. 380) points out, a practice is more comprehensive compared to speech acts, because it comprises more subtasks. Demarcating practices from speech acts, Deppermann et al. (2016, p. 1) define practices as not individual but rather context-dependent habits that encapsulate specific roles (see Chap. 8), responsibilities (see Chap. 9), and social positions. These specifics are better highlighted in *language games* by Wittgenstein (1953/1997) (see also Rouse, 2007), who also focused on verbal behaviors; but the semantics of this notion signifies the cooperative nature of communication, because it takes (at least) two to play a game. Further, the analogy to a "game" highlights the different roles that the interlocutors take when they interact, thereby adopting a particular disposition within the interaction. Language games and speech acts have in common that they both refer to verbal behaviors. We can conclude, following Deppermann et al. (2016, p. 1), that communicative practices are a collective phenomenon. In contrast, speech acts offer more room for individuality. Further, a speech act, as it is currently conceived, is a verbal behavior that does not necessarily need to form larger units (which we have defined as being characteristic for practices).

Above, we argue that similar concepts that describe culturally agreed-upon ways of "doings" are not practices, because they focus mainly on single verbal behavior (as in "speech acts") and on that of an individual (as in "scripts"). The demarcation from concepts in developmental or in multimodal research seems even harder. Consider early interactions with infants: Because infants do not communicate verbally, a practice can also be achieved nonverbally. Research on early caregiver–child interactions provides examples for the various forms this can take. It has been shown that even infants as young as 4 months contribute nonverbally to larger units of behavior, for example, by smiling (Nomikou et al., 2017). From this example with infants as communicative partners, we can draw the conclusions: First, practices can be nonverbal or multimodal (e.g., Streeck, 2009). Second, communicative practices can be constituted within dyadic (or multiparty) interactions (Schröter, 2016). This materialization in different forms (verbal or nonverbal) emphasizes that a practice can appear in various forms and can be conducted in various ways within a social interaction.

The term *format* is applied in repeated or repeatable interactions with infants to denote a sequence of behaviors that is not necessarily intentional (Bruner, 1983). A good example is a peek-a-boo game that many caregivers across different cultures play with their infants: Even very young infants can participate in the game (e.g., by smiling or vocalizing) recognizing their role within it (Nomikou et al., 2017). However, because of their immature cognitive capabilities, one cannot attribute intention to their behaviors. Thus, the term *format* speaks to the possibility that somebody can take part in a practice even nonintentionally (Rączaszek-Leonardi et al., 2013). A good example is when children start to stack building blocks on top of each other. Others will continue to build a tower. In this sense, the individual actions are subordinated to a practice of making a tower, because there is a format

Table 5.1 Overview of concepts that are related to a communicative practice

Notion	Already a communicative practice?	Property similar to a practice
Script	No, because not necessarily interactive	Sequential
Speech acts	No, because focus on individual behavior, focus on smaller units, and not necessarily multimodal	Interactive
Format / Pragmatic frame	Yes, but only few specified for (caregiver–child) interactions	Goal-directed
Dialog games	Yes, but only few specified	Repetitive

of building a tower: Different blocks (colors, shapes, or even other materials) can be used to perform necessary movements and achieve a specific product or outcome, also in multiparty interactions. Importantly, the practice organizes the actions. Interestingly, the latter are not necessarily communicative. Bruner (1983, p. 121), however, emphasizes that a format "involves not only action but a place for communication," and that formats are often constituted by language. The notion of a format overlaps with *pragmatic frames*, a term that has also been proposed as a structure that is "retrieved from memory to guide the interpretation of an ongoing situation" (Rohlfing et al., 2016, p. 2). This structure consists of interactive (that are overt, because observable) and cognitive behaviors (that are covert, because they cannot be observed). Both types of behaviors on the side of both partners are needed to achieve a goal. The goal for which the structure appears organizes or even determines the requested interactive and cognitive behaviors (Rohlfing et al., 2016; Heller & Rohlfing, 2017). In our view, a pragmatic frame is a practice, but this concept places more emphasis on the interplay between joint interactive and cognitive behaviors toward a goal, whereas the concept of practice emphasizes the intersubjective meaning more.

Along the lines of "scripts," "formats," and "pragmatic frames," Levin and Moore (1977, p. 398) have proposed *dialog games* that they define as "goal-oriented units" in which "people engage." Dialog games have been developed based on conceptual work with all the similar concepts (and more) for the purpose of specifying parameters that "remain constant throughout the course of a dialogue of that type" (Levin & Moore, 1977, p. 403). What is helpful for our considerations is the author's model of how to use a dialog game. We will elaborate on this below.

Table 5.1 summarizes which of the concepts we have considered so far can be seen as a communicative practice and which have only some similar properties.

What, then, Is a Practice? Let us consider some examples of a practice. There is a practice of buying a car. There is a practice of going to the movie. There is a practice of explaining something. Just by looking at these examples on the way to a definition, it seems that practices are larger units of human behaviors that can also be achieved in collaboration (Schröter, 2016, p. 380). In contrast to just behaviors or actions, practices are more abstract and organized. In other words, they refer to types rather than tokens of actions that can be observed repeatedly (Schröter, 2016, p. 380). In this sense, they are 'over-individualized' (generalized), because they can be performed by different agents who are not in the same situation or context but who share a social and cultural agreement on how things are done (either in a communicative or behavior-related way).

The term is representative of many contemporary theories across different disciplines. In sociology, "praxeology" is a theory – or rather a research program (Reckwitz, 2003, p. 284) – focusing on social practices attempting to clarify what it means to act within social groups and what role(s) a subject plays within that act. As already mentioned above, the focus extends beyond individual behaviors but underscores the social and cultural meaning that such acting reveals. In this sense, an action is related to a collective spirit ("des kollektiven Geistes") (Reckwitz, 2003, p. 288) and to knowledge. From this perspective, an action reflects not only the intention of an individual but also the relations that the acting person is in. Practices are phenomena at the cognitive–social intersection. Cognitively, practices are patterns. They make a sequence of actions predictable (Davachi & DuBrow, 2015). They imply knowledge that "is on the one hand 'incorporated' in the bodies of the acting subjects" (Reckwitz, 2003, p. 289). The prediction is also a function in a social interaction (or, so-called joint action as described in Chap. 11), when a sequence of actions is performed in collaboration, and the partners can predict each other's contribution. Dialogs are considered to be joint actions, too (Rączaszek-Leonardi et al., 2014). Because of this bodily incorporation, dialogs appear well orchestrated and coordinated. What is social about the practices is a form of the ability to act in accordance with what is shared by a collective.

Admittedly, the notion of social practice is clearly linked to factors that are of a social nature, such as roles and related power structures (see also Chap. 8). However, this notion can also be applied to an interaction with an AI. With his notion of a practice, Reckwitz (2021, p. 56) goes beyond interpersonal relationships and also allows nonhuman (organic or inorganic) entities to be part of a practice. This is because "these entities are connected to humans qua these practices and co-determine which practices are possible" (Reckwitz, 2021, p. 56). This expansion of the social in the direction of artifacts is essential for our consideration with respect to sXAI, because artifacts such as AI systems can contribute to knowledge or action organization.

In accordance with our social interactive account, for further considerations, we will focus the semantics of social practice on specific characteristics that can be accounted for in an interaction and for a communicative purpose. Whereas we are aware that this focus can also be viewed as a limitation, the advantage is (as already noted in the introduction to this book, Chap. 1) to make the social practices graspable and applicable for sXAI. Our focus comprises the following properties: routinized, goal-oriented, relational/interactive, and part of collective knowledge (see Sect. 5.5). Hereby we subscribe to the action-oriented view of communicative practices as differentiated by Deppermann et al. (2016), in which contributions of the involved partners are communicative actions orchestrated toward a shared goal (see Sect. 5.5 for a concrete operationalization).

It is important to emphasize once more that communicative practices can be nonverbal. In the literature, some work on communicative practices refers to verbal behaviors only.[2] This is the case for Levin and Moore (1977, p. 418) who recognize the advantages of social practice as a structure, but limit "dialogue-games" to "capturing common knowledge about language and how it is used to achieve goals" (Levin & Moore, 1977, p. 395). In these games, verbal behaviors are parameterized to provide a model of human dialog. Before further specifying explanation as a communicative practice, we consider its multimodality.

5.2.1 Multimodal Communicative Practice

As already stated above, concepts that are similar to the concept of communicative practice often focus mainly on verbal behavior. But communicative practices are also constituted by nonverbal, embodied behaviors, co-occurring with one another or with verbal behavior (see Chaps. 19, 22 and 23). Thus, communicative practices in social interactions are multimodal (Streeck, 2009; Deppermann & Streeck, 2018). Streeck (2009, p. 4) investigates gestures and other manual activities as a form of "human practice—or a family of practices" that he defines as "a constantly evolving set of largely improvised, heterogeneous, partly conventional, partly idiosyncratic, and partly culture-specific, partly universal practices of using the hands to produce situated understandings" (Streeck, 2009, p. 5) within human activities and interaction. Examples for gestural practices provided by Streeck (2009) are depictions such as drawing a path in the air (e.g., to show a particular shape and motion), mimicking actions ("handling"), or more complex depictions such as a depicting a building site ("articulating gesture space").

Gesture practices are a way of communicating: They are embedded in and possibly constitutive of larger units of communicative activities. In addition, and in line with our definition of a practice, gestural practices such as depicting or mimicking can be applied more than once (i.e., in changing situations); they are more abstract structures that have different forms on the surface layer, and, because their realization might differ cross-culturally, they take culture into account.

How gestural practices are embedded in and constitutive for larger structures is observable from early on in caregiver–child interactions (Bruner, 1983; Rohlfing et al., 2016). The examples below illustrate early labeling practices within a common joint activity of picturebook reading, in which children participate with their caregivers:

1. Caregiver: "What is this?" while pointing with the index finger at a ball depicted on a page.
   Child: "ball."

---

[2] The advantage of the focus on verbal behaviors is that verbal behaviors can be assessed quite well. With them, the exchange between humans in general and how they divide their contributions to the task in detail can be captured more clearly.

In this example, the caregivers are using both verbal behavior (a question) and a gesture (pointing), while the child is requested to react with a recall of the correct label for the depicted object.

2. The caregiver and the child look at a page depicting different pets.
   Caregiver: "Where is the cat?"
   Child: "da" while pointing with the index finger at the cat.

In this example, the child is requested to identify the referent (the cat). Heller and Rohlfing (2017) have shown how developmental changes occur with children's growing cognitive and communicative capabilities. From these changes, it becomes obvious that more knowledgeable partners adapt to the less knowledgeable partners by allowing them to contribute to the joint goal. However, the more knowledgeable partners also monitor the communication and educate their partners toward the use of conventional means. For example, they ask a child to indicate an object with their index finger rather than their nose. The means or devices with which partners realize their contributions on the surface level are considered important and also contribute to the dialogical roles (Quasthoff et al., 2017, p. 91).

What these labeling practices have in common is that they are dyadic and multimodal, because they are constituted by more than one individual and by multimodal means. They can also be applied in changing situations – that is, they are not just observable in the activities of joint bookreading but also in other referential situations. Interestingly, in the two cases specified above, the simple practices (labeling and referring) occur in a more complex practice of joint bookreading, which is certainly a recurrent and very well-known activity for many families. Thus, we can conclude that practices can be nested in each other.

5.2.2 How to Learn a Practice

As already suggested above, children learn first routines very early: As presented in Nomikou et al. (2017), one of the earlier routines is games with their caregivers, such as peek-a-boo. Intuitively, caregivers shape the young infants' agentivity by providing "interactive affordances" (Rączaszek-Leonardi et al., 2013, p. 211). This means that young infants are given the experience of their actions contributing to a larger structure that overarches the engagement of both partners. This way, a frame of joint actions is created. It develops out of "participation," that is, "acting a part in an interaction system" (Nomikou et al., 2017, p. 1).

Because above, we have pointed out what a practice is not, we will use this figure (of negation) to emphasize key aspects of learning: Learning a practice is not only about imitation. Thus, it is not sufficient for children to imitate the other's action. Instead, children recognize the overarching structure of an interaction by finding out about its goal (see Sect. 6.2). In addition, children find out about social affordances by taking various roles in various settings. This experience – to be a participant with or from a different role (see Sect. 9.3) – seems crucial to acquire the sense of joint engagement toward a goal (Rączaszek-Leonardi et al., 2013; Nomikou et al., 2017). Learning is also not only about interpersonal synchrony or alignment with others. Instead, human actions are "predictive in the sense of imitating and connecting actions to effects in the physical or social world " (Nomikou et al., 2016, p. 144). Thus, joint actions are situated requiring and causing pragmatic circumstances.

Current systems lack the ability to learn routines or practices, and we will outline these limitations below (see Chap. 5).

5.3 An Explanation Practice

Above, we have argued for various forms (verbal and nonverbal) of communicative practices. We now focus on communicative practices for specific purposes (for more details about purposes, see Chap. 6). One of such a purpose is explanation. Strictly speaking, an explanation offers a solution to a communicative problem, which is a knowledge asymmetry (see Chap. 3, and exemplified in the scenario described in Sect. 2.5). The practice of explaining in human–human interactions has been researched extensively and described in detail by scholars applying Conversational Analysis (see Chap. 23). Relating to this, we will therefore start this section with what an explanation practice is good for. For this, we need to acknowledge that communicative problems are linked to ongoing activities. For example, a decision needs to be taken, but it is based on information (e.g., a feature) that is not understandable. Thus, this information needs to be explained first before proceeding with the decision process. Consequently, practices have preceding actions as well as actions that will result from them. Explanations themselves can pursue various goals (see Chap. 6). One goal is to increase understanding in the explainee. However, understanding can take different forms such as "comprehension" of relationships and procedures or "enabling" further actions (Rohlfing, Cimiano, et al., 2021; Buschmeier et al., 2025, p. 726) (see also Sect. 3.3). In fact, these two forms can be further differentiated, and we would like to exemplify this differentiation and possible explaining practices that go along with it in the following (Klein, 2009; Rosenfeld & Richardson, 2019):

1. Understanding as comprehension (i.e., acquiring knowledge about relationships and procedures)

   - Explaining why
   - Explaining what
   - Explaining how

2. Understanding as enabledness (i.e., enabling further actions, see also Chap. 6)

   - Explaining to bring about decision
   - Explaining to persuade somebody to do something
   - Explaining to justify something
   - ...

5 Practices: How to Establish an Explaining Practice

For the first point, Klein (2009) states that in an explaining process, there is little clear distinction between the types, because they can all be applied or requested at a certain point or for a more complex explanandum. For example, even in some instructions (e.g., on how to use a smartphone), the explainee will already find a lot of what-aspects paired with why-aspects indicating some novel functions in addition to the dominant form of how to do something (Klein, 2009, p. 29).

As already highlighted above in Sect. 5.2, a practice can be multimodal, and the same applies to an explanation practice. For the process of explaining, Klein (2009, p. 29) specifies two kinds of multimodality: one that is about visualization and more appropriate for written text (see Chap. 25) and another for interactions (see Chaps. 19 and 22). Both kinds serve the understanding and seek to improve it. However, as Klein (2009, p. 30) notes, verbal behavior is the backbone of an explanation, because it connects the modalities with each other in a meaningful way. It is only through this connection that there is a gain of information that was not present without explaining.

It is highly important to remark that the practice of an explanation is different in science than under other circumstances (see also Chap. 3). In both settings though, as pointed out by Garfinkel (1981, p. 172), "explanations are functional things," because they have a job to do. This job is a more elaborated topic in Chap. 23. Here, we can only refer to this elaboration and state that "explicating procedural, conceptual and/or causal relationships" is considered to be the core job for explaining (Quasthoff et al., 2017, p. 90). In science, these relationships are mostly of a causal nature, whereas in the practical life, there can be other – for example, personal, emotional, aesthetic – relationships. Klein (2009, p. 34) suggests that the reasons for the differences between science and other circumstances are pragmatic: In scientific explanations, the scholars seek to understand a phenomenon discovered within a scientific community. In contrast, in practical life, too many details and correct information might not be the best solution to achieve comprehension or enabling. The setting and the aim (e.g., persuading, deciding) imply its own standards for an explanation. To mark that pragmatically, it is important to view which activity or setting is the background for an explanation and what it is linking with. Figure 5.1 is illustrating this.

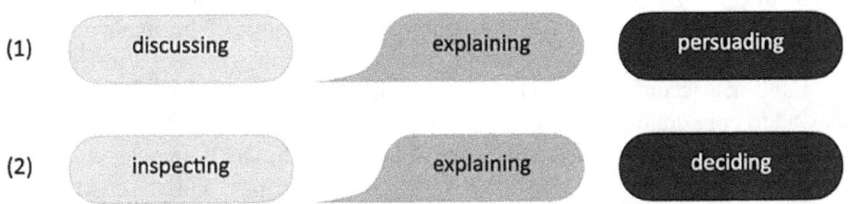

Fig. 5.1 Two examples of how an explanation can be framed by an activity taking place prior to it and an activity following it: (2) Explaining as part of a discussion in order to persuade somebody and (2) explaining as part of a consultation process in a medical setting, for which an inspection is necessary first in order to be able to explain the output of the analysis and find a treatment for the patient

5.4 AI Systems and Practices

Even though approaches exist that suggest taking advantage of a structure such as practice in computational modeling (Levin & Moore, 1977; Steels, 2001), advances are scarce.

Limited Flexibility of AI Systems In this section, we consider whether artificial systems can recognize practices and/or act accordingly. As already mentioned above, the notion of practice encapsulates a bundle of social aspects including cultural context, roles, and power structures (see also Chap. 8). For further considerations and in accordance with our interactive account (sXAI), we will focus on interactively accountable qualities of a practice: routinized, goal-oriented, relational/interactive, and part of collective knowledge (see Sect. 5.5); we will refer to this with the notion of "pragmatic frames" as defined in Rohlfing et al. (2016) and Vollmer et al. (2016). Caution is warranted when transferring a practice to AI systems. This is because the focus on pragmatic frames brings about a reduction of practice to a limited set of qualities. At the same time, coming from developmental research, pragmatic frames (as described in Sect. 7.5) bear a developmental component, meaning that this concept can reveal how practices emerge. Pragmatic frames are interaction patterns organized as a (simple) practice. Inherent to their nature, they bear social characteristics such as interactional roles that become observable when the interaction takes place. In human interaction, these pragmatic frames are typically negotiated and established between interaction partners over the course of repeated interactions. Additionally, they are adapted dynamically to changing contexts depending on the growing understanding of the explainee. However, most current AI systems are able to act only within a specific interaction protocol that limits their behaviors to a specific task, as was shown by an analysis provided in Vollmer et al. (2016). For example, in robot-learning interactions with humans, the interaction patterns are currently fixed and restricted by the developers' concept of how to provide the AI system with learning input. The developers largely control the interaction to ensure that the input is as clean (well-segmented) and well-suited for the learning algorithm as possible. This approach is used primarily, because AI systems, such as robots, are generally designed to fulfill or learn just a single task rather than multiple different ones. As a result, recognizing interaction patterns that provide information about the nature of the interaction is not necessary, and it is also rather complex when the system is expected to recognize these and act accordingly. This limitation also holds for an XAI that is able to respond to only quite selected behaviors of the user (e.g., specific type of questions or questions about a specific content, see Sokol & Flach, 2020). In other words, the exchange between the user and the system is highly scripted and not flexible. The systems, thus, cannot transfer their behavior to other interactions (Vollmer et al., 2016).

Adding to the difficulty for AI systems to act inside *unknown* pragmatic frames, practices with them are additionally restricted by their behavioral capabilities paired with a lack of understanding of these in their human interaction partner.

Toward a Collaborative Task Understanding The key to the question regarding what kind of practice is possible with an AI system lies in the design of the technology. For technology, tasks rather than practices are designed. It is difficult to specify the exact link between *practice* and *task*, because a task (as programmed or designed) includes a clear goal (see Chap. 6), such as vacuuming, and the use of a vacuum cleaner is a practice; at the same time, there exist many practices around the task of vacuuming. In many scenarios, the main function of an AI is to share a specific task and therefore support the user in it while performing some subtask(s): For example, an AI translates a text that the human needs in order to carry on with other tasks (setting up a rental contract). In this case, the task for both the human and the AI is larger than the subtask of the AI. It is further assumed that in such a scenario, no changes to the overall task will take place, and the course of subtasks and the responsibilities for them will always be the same. Further, it is important to highlight that the current form of sharing a task cultivates a model of efficiency: Because a task is shared, it is solved or completed faster and better. Yet, there are other possibilities of sharing a task. For example, an AI could support a user only in the first interaction and phase out its support in repeating interactions in order to empower the user's role and capabilities (see Sect. 9.7). The involvement of an AI also reflects the common model of collaboration: Work is defined in forms of subtasks that can be divided. This model reveals a further limitation: Current AI systems are not able to understand tasks dynamically – that is, depending on what the other partner can contribute. Instead of negotiating the individual contributions and responsibilities with the partner, there is already a clear idea in advance of how a task should be completed. Available AI systems are clearly not sensitive to the fact that a task could be completed with flexible responsibilities within and for its subtasks (see Chap. 9). What is lacking is AI systems capable of more flexible behaviors with respect to their role and responsibility for a task, leaving the user the lead on how the contributions to it should be distributed.

For the subtasks to be divided more dynamically, it would be necessary to consider a collaboration as a progression. In this case, an AI system could manage the progress or work toward the goal of an interaction systematically. Various forms of practices could be used to create and develop interaction protocols consisting of a sequence of behaviors contributing to a goal, because they provide a context, a selection, or a repertoire of actions that are appropriate. AI systems could draw on such a protocol to better simulate and respond to the action of a user.

By providing more insights into the form and function of this structure, our aim has been to motivate XAI development to take advantage of these insights in designing XAI systems that are capable of more than just one interaction protocol. We conclude that in explanatory interactions, a structure like a practice – as already suggested by Levin and Moore (1977) for language games – can be used to manage dialogs in terms of three processes such as recognizing what kind of task is proposed, using this knowledge as a background for comprehension of utterances, and identifying the progress as well as the goal at which "the interaction is to be terminated" (Levin & Moore, 1977, p. 399). In this sense, with the concept of practice, this chapter offers a concrete context of human actions that is unfolding in an interaction.

5.5 Operationalizations of Practices

"Social practices can be seen as patterns which can be filled in by a multitude of single and often unique actions" (Dignum & Dignum, 2015, p. 43). To characterize such patterns, from our considerations above, we derive the following key qualities: routinized, goal-oriented, relational/interactive, and part of collective knowledge. We should further focus on practices for communicative purposes as they can be shared between involved partners. The collaborative effort is in line with our approach to sXAI aiming at interactive adaptivity to yield a satisfying explanation. We propose that sXAI could benefit from the notion of practice. We operationalize the collaborative effort with the aid of pragmatic frames – a structure that is similar to social practice but specified by Bruner (1983) and reintroduced by Rohlfing et al. (2016) and Vollmer et al. (2016). We will draw on Vollmer et al. (2016, p. 2) who define it as a "pattern in verbal and non-verbal behavior involving goal-oriented actions coordinated with the interaction partner that emerges over recurrent interactions." For sXAI, operationalizations of practice or pragmatic frames raise the following questions:

- How can an sXAI represent practices in the data sets that emerge from the interaction between the XAI and a human user?
- How can an sXAI recognize known practices "capturing common knowledge" (Levin & Moore, 1977, p. 418) about means of communications that are used to achieve specific goals? To achieve this, common knowledge about the jobs that need to be achieved collaboratively, as suggested in Sect. 23.1, could be implemented.
- How can an sXAI act inside practices regarding the roles and responsibilities that it might take in an interaction (see Chaps. 8 and 9)? To achieve this, the contributions of the XAI have to be planned carefully and in great awareness of what actions they require the human partner to do (or not to do).
- How can an sXAI negotiate new practices that require knowledge in the XAI about what a practice is and what an alternative in a particular setting could be?

It can be argued critically that the notion of pragmatic frames lacks cultural and collective qualities. In response, we would like to emphasize that they are factored in implicitly for the interaction that is emerging. Further, a goal within a pragmatic frame and the means to this end are already culturally influenced, that is, which communicative means are appropriate to reach a certain goal may be culture-specific (cf. Bruner, 1983).

5.6 How Does This Chapter Inspire Further Sirections of XAI?

One could argue that an AI does not need to act as a social being would do. Above, we have argued that the fact that it is there and contributes to knowledge as well as action organization not only qualifies it for being a part of a practice but necessarily makes it a part of a practice (Reckwitz, 2003). This is because humans develop ways of dealing with it. However, even if we reduce an AI to an artifact and a passive part of a social practice, with all its explaining and other capabilities, AI changes or lets further practices emerge between humans because of the interaction with (X)AI. Having listed some possible goals of the practice of explaining, let us consider how practices and explanation practices may change when AI systems become part of them or how AI systems may influence practices in human–human interactions. Our considerations will be sorted according to some examples below.

Example 1 (Human Users Interacting with AI Systems) As an artifact with recording capabilities, an AI system that humans interact with can lead to shared experience becoming available to both the human and the AI as a "data set" for further actions. Notably, the data used by the algorithms often already contain information about human behavior and the practices used. Because the algorithms preserve human practices, they also have the potential to make them visible (also to others). Allhutter et al. (2020) impressively showed how an AI in the form of a selection aid for future employees (AMS system) reflected the social perceptions and bias against people from minority groups. Because of this, this AI system did not appear to be suitable for collaboration with humans. However, its functional analysis makes it possible to see what practices exist; at the same time, this analysis enables a critical examination of them.

Example 2 (AI Systems Change Practices by Becoming Part of Them) By becoming part of a practice, such as explaining how to assemble a certain piece of furniture while monitoring what the human is doing, AI systems may change explanation practices. Their embodiment and their respective physical abilities as well as their computational abilities differ from the physical and cognitive abilities of humans and underpin particular interfaces. First, even if the conversational jobs (see Chap. 23) are part of the implemented interaction protocol, a human interaction partner most likely has to use other verbal and nonverbal communicative means when interacting with an AI system than those they would use naturally with a human partner (such as pushing a button after each assembly step). Second, but related to the previous point, the definition of when a conversational job begins and ends – that is, what sequences of actions constitute it – needs to be more restricted with an AI system, and, thus, it is less flexible. Hence, an explanation practice is shaped by the agents engaging in it.

Example 3 (Establishment of New Practices by Interacting with AI Systems) Because AI systems are to be found increasingly in various everyday situations and have become a part of practices, new practices may be established with them. However, for a sequence of behaviors to become a practice, it needs to occur repeatedly and needs to be shared across members of certain groups or even cultures (see Sect. 5.2). Certain sequences of behaviors between humans and AI systems that have become an agreed-upon practice in a certain group may not be applied as easily by other groups of people if the specific contribution or action from the AI system is not transparent, intuitive, or easily accessible to them. This bears the risk of excluding certain groups of people (e.g., those with less access to technological knowledge). For example, professional traders at large investment firms might use AI-driven trading algorithms that analyze market trends and execute trades. Over time, this group might develop specialized practices when interacting with these tools, fine-tuning algorithm parameters, interpreting AI signals a certain way, and creating their own shorthands for referring to AI strategies to maximize profit. On the other hand, individual investors or smaller firms might not have access to these tools or the expertise to use them and are, thus, excluded from these practices reinforcing financial inequalities. Another example for this is conceivable in the medical domain: A physician might be assisted by AI systems in making a diagnosis. This might change current practices of how they decide or explain the diagnosis to patients. Further, this might also have consequences for the learning and teaching process of future physicians, because it might require different practices (e.g., more critical thinking) than before. These practices, however, might become inaccessible to nonmedical staff like administrative personnel or patients. This example not only highlights the system's own role within a practice but also illustrates how such a system might cause practices *in human–human interaction* to emerge and change.

Example 4 (Practices of Human–Technology Interaction Change Practices of Human–Human Interaction) New practices that emerge from interacting with new technological opportunities (such as ChatGPT) may influence and change established social practices between humans. For example, ways of requesting information from an AI system (such as requesting a clear formulation of the knowledge gap as prompts) may change expectations in social interactions with humans in which, currently, a knowledge gap is easily negotiated.

Altogether, we suggest that first, existing and future social practices need to be taken into account when developing technology, especially tools with a specific goal such as explaining or being explainable. Second, developers of (X)AI have to be trained on how social practices develop and change in order to simulate what impact the technological development could have and to raise awareness of their social responsibility. Third, and along the lines of the second point, it would be desirable to create an sXAI with which such simulations of how an AI is changing social practices become possible in order to assist people's decisions relating to social context emerging from the use of XAI.

5.7 Rapid Access to the Content of This Chapter

In this chapter, we address practices as a notion introducing a context of human actions that an XAI might take advantage of. In defining the term, we propose the following qualities of a social practice:

- It is a **sequence of (multimodal) behaviors** (with an invariant structure) and a way of behaving for communicative purposes on an abstract level and not just a certain behavior or single action
- It is routinized in the sense that it needs to be **repeated and applied in changing situations** and does not occur just once
- The occurrence and repetition of the sequence are organized toward a **goal**
- It is **culturally embedded**—that is, a practice **requires social agreement on how things are done** (via communicative means), and therefore it is not something that is performed only by one person in an idiosyncratic way

In the literature, the notion of *practices* relates to similar concepts in other disciplines such as *script* or *speech act* that are already discussed in XAI research. It would be a challenge to delineate these exactly, because each of the concepts bears some crucial aspects but has a different focus (see Sect. 5.2). Overall, it seems that in the alternative concepts, there is a focus on behaviors of an individual. In contrast, a practice will always contain more knowledge that is shared by a collective to highlight the fact that the behaviors or actions of an individual are embedded in a social and cultural system (Reckwitz, 2002, p. 288).

When considering practices for communicative purposes in developmental or multimodal research, scholars emphasize that communicative practices can be nonverbal or multimodal (e.g., Streeck, 2009) and can be constituted within dyadic or multiparty interactions (Schröter, 2016). This is the case for the notion of a *format* (Bruner, 1983). It describes dyadic sequences of behavior in early caregiver–child interactions in which children learn the way of "how to get things done with words" in their culture (Bruner, 1983, p. 18). In doing so, formats initially also allow unintentional and nonverbal behaviors from children that are taken up by their caregivers as meaningful (Rączaszek-Leonardi et al., 2013). Similarly, the term *pragmatic frames* describes structures within dyadic or multiparty interactions that are "retrieved from memory to guide the interpretation of an ongoing situation" (Rohlfing et al., 2016, p. 2). They consist of interactive (overt, because observable) and cognitive (covert, because not observable) behaviors that are predictable. Both types are needed to achieve a joint goal. In their work, Nomikou et al. (2017) demonstrates that even very young infants can already participate in a peek-a-boo game that is a pragmatic frame with concrete interactional roles and contributions toward a goal.

In addition to the developmental research, the multimodal nature of practices is described by, for example, Streeck (2009, p. 4), who investigates gestures and other manual activities as a form of "human practice—or a family of practices." Gestural practices are depictions emerging from drawing a path in the air, articulating gesture space, or mimicking actions. They are a way of communicating and, further, they are embedded in and possibly constitutive of larger units of communicative activities. In addition, and in line with our definition of practice, gestural practices such as depicting or mimicking can be applied more than once (i.e., in changing situations), and their realization might differ cross-culturally and thus take culture into account. The fact that human practices are multimodal in nature needs to be considered for their application in XAI.

Whereas the concept of a practice places more emphasis on the intersubjective meaning, the concept of pragmatic frames highlights the interplay between interactive (but multimodal) and cognitive behaviors toward a goal. In this way, it accords with the view on sXAI proposed in this book (see Introduction: Chap. 1).

In incorporating structures of a practice in technology design up to now, it becomes apparent that behavioral sequences in the form of multimodal and even only verbal interaction patterns are fixed or highly restricted when AI systems interact with humans. This is because of the way that developers largely control the interaction to ensure that the input is as clean and well-suited for the learning algorithm as possible. This approach is used primarily because AI systems, such as robots, are generally designed to fulfill or learn a single, specific task with a specific outcome rather than multiple different ones or to perform one task but to be flexible with respect to when the outcome is reached within a certain interaction. The underlying assumption is that a task consists of quite specific contributions that need to be divided. As a result, for the fixed task in current AI systems, recognizing interaction patterns that provide information about the nature of the interaction is not necessary, and it is rather complex when the system is expected to recognize and act accordingly. In contrast, in humans, such a division of labor is negotiated, because partners contribute various competencies or apply various means.

Despite the question of whether and how AI systems can use practices, we have argued that social practices are knowledge that "is on the one hand 'incorporated' in the bodies of the acting subjects, which on the other hand regularly take the form of routinized relationships between subjects and the material artifacts 'used' by them" (Reckwitz, 2003, p. 289). In this vein, AI is part of social practices (Reckwitz, 2021) either as artifact and even more so when contributing as interaction partner. Because of this, it is important to discern that the interaction with an (X)AI (and we assume even more with an sXAI) system not only gives rise to new practices but also changes our existing practices. For example, a physician might be assisted in making a diagnosis, and this might change current practices regarding how she decides or informs patients. Further, the assistance system may support the explanation of the decision via visualization (still an artifact), or by an explanatory dialog actively providing information as individually needed and able to integrate new information and opinions into its co-constructive decision-making process, and thus it is not only a (static) artifact. Because of such assistance systems, the learning process of a physician might require different practices (e.g., more critical thinking) than before.

In our view, the advantage of considering practices in AI systems is threefold:

1. A practice in the form of a pragmatic frame provides an interaction protocol as a context, a selection, or a repertoire of actions that are appropriate. AI systems could draw from this protocol to better simulate and respond to the behaviors of a user. The advantage of this structure is recognized by Levin and Moore (1977) as "capturing common knowledge" about communicative means and how they are used to achieve goals. In the sense that it captures common knowledge, a pragmatic frame relates to intersubjectivity but specifies it further into joint cognitive and interactive behaviors. Overall, for sXAI, the knowledge about explaining as a practice can be used as a background for comprehending verbal and nonverbal behaviors and managing the progress of the dialog.
2. Considering practices rather than individual and very specific/specified behaviors might enable AI systems to transfer their behavior to other interactions (see Vollmer et al., 2016). It might also contribute to a more dynamic design of collaborative tasks between a human and an AI system. Accordingly, sXAI systems might then be able to negotiate the individual contributions and responsibilities of the human, with the AI system being based not only on the joint goal that is to be completed but also on contextual factors such as the (emerging) capabilities of the partners.
3. Future sXAI systems might be able to simulate with the user how the development of an AI will impact on existing and future social practices within a particular application context (see Chap. 9 for more ideas).

Acknowledgments We thank Friederike Kern for her perspective and helpful comments on an earlier version of this chapter which made us focus on and better understand the cultural embedding of social practices.

This work was funded by the Deutsche Forschungsgemeinschaft (DFG, German Research Foundation): TRR 318/1 2021 – 438445824.

References

Allhutter, D., Cech, F., Fischer, F., Grill, G., & Mager, A. (2020). Algorithmic profiling of job seekers in Austria: How austerity politics are made effective. *Frontiers in Big Data, 3*, 5. https://doi.org/10.3389/fdata.2020.00005

Austin, J. L. (1962). *How to do things with words*. Oxford University Press.

Bruner, J. S. (1983). *Child's talk: Learning to use language*. W. W. Norton & Company.

Buschmeier, H., Buhl, H.M., Kern, F., Grimminger, A., Beierling, H., Fisher, J., Groß, A., Horwath, I., Klowait, N., Lazarov, S., Lenke, M., Lohmer, V., Rohlfing, K.J., Scharlau, I., Singh, Terfloth, L., A., Vollmer, A.-L., Wang, Y., Wilmes, A., & Wrede, B. (2025). Forms of understanding of XAI-explanations. *Cognitive Systems Research, 94*, 101419. https://doi.org/10.1016/j.cogsys.2025.101419

Chromik, M., & Butz, A. (2021). Human–XAI interaction: A review and design principles for explanation user interfaces. In C. Ardito, R. Lanzilotti, A. Malizia, H. Petrie, A. Piccinno, G. Desolda & K. Inkpen (Eds.), *Human–Computer Interaction – INTERACT* (pp. 619–640). Notes in computer science. Springer. https://doi.org/10.1007/978-3-030-85616-8_36

Clark, H. H., & Schaefer, E. F. (1989). Contributing to discourse. *Cognitive Science, 13*(2), 259–294. https://doi.org/10.1207/s15516709cog1302_7

Davachi, L., & DuBrow, S. (2015). How the hippocampus preserves order: The role of prediction and context. *Trends in Cognitive Sciences, 19*(2), 92–99. https://doi.org/10.1016/j.tics.2014.12.004

Deppermann, A., Feilke, H., & Linke, A (2016). Sprachliche und kommunikative Praktiken: Eine Annäherung aus linguistischer Sicht. In A. Deppermann, H. Feilke & A. Linke (Eds.), *Sprachliche und Kommunikative Praktiken* (pp. 1–23). De Gruyter. https://doi.org/10.1515/9783110451542-002

Deppermann, A., & Streeck, J. (2018). The body in interaction. In A. Deppermann & J. Streeck (Eds.), *Time in embodied interaction. synchronicity and sequentiality of multimodal resources* (pp. 1–29). Benjamins. https://doi.org/10.1075/pbns.293.intro

Dignum, V., & Dignum, F. (2015). Contextualized planning using social practices. In A. Ghose, N. Oren, P. Telang & J. Thangarajah (Eds.), *Coordination, organizations, institutions, and norms in agent systems X* (pp. 36–52). Springer. https://doi.org/10.1007/978-3-319-25420-3_3

Garfinkel, A. (1981). *Forms of explanation. Rethinking the questions in social theory*. Yale University Press.

Gleason, J. B., & Weintraub, S. (1976). The acquisition of routines in child language. *Language in Society, 5*(2), 129–136. https://doi.org/10.1017/s0047404500006977

Heller, V., & Rohlfing, K. J. (2017). Reference as an interactive achievement: Sequential and longitudinal analyses of labeling interactions in shared book reading and free play. *Frontiers in Psychology, 8*, 139. https://doi.org/10.3389/fpsyg.2017.00139

Klein, J. (2009). ERKLÄREN-WAS, ERKLÄREN-WIE, ERKLÄREN-WARUM. Typologie und Komplexität zentraler Akte der WelterschlieSSung. In R. Vogt (Ed.), *Erklären. Gesprächsanalytische und fachdidaktische Perspektiven* (pp. 25–36). Stauffenburg.

Kress, G., & van Leeuwen, T. (2001). *Multimodal discourse. The modes and media of contemporary communication*. Hodder Education. https://doi.org/10.1017/S0047404504221054

Levin, J. A., & Moore, J. A. (1977). Dialogue-Games: Metacommunication structures for natural language interaction. *Cognitive Science, 1*(4), 395–420. https://doi.org/10.1016/S0364-0213(77)80016-5

Nomikou, I., Leonardi, G., Radkowska, A., Rączaszek-Leonardi, J., & Rohlfing, K. J. (2017). Taking up an active role: Emerging participation in early mother–infant interaction during peekaboo routines. *Frontiers in Psychology, 8*, 1656. https://doi.org/10.3389/fpsyg.2017.01656

Nomikou, I., Schilling, M., Heller, V., & Rohlfing, K. J. (2016). Language-at all times. Action and interaction as contexts for enriching representations. *Interaction Studies, 8*, 128–153. https://doi.org/10.1075/is.17.1.06nom

Pickering, M. J., & Garrod, S. (2021). *Understanding dialogue. Language use and social interaction*. Cambridge University Press. https://doi.org/10.1017/9781108610728.002

Quasthoff, U., Heller, V., & Morek, M. (2017). On the sequential organization and genre-orientation of discourse units in interaction: An analytic framework. *Discourse Studies, 19*(1), 84–110. https://doi.org/10.1177/1461445616683596

Rączaszek-Leonardi, J., Dębska, A., & Sochanowicz, A. (2014). Pooling the ground: Understanding and coordination in collective sense making. *Frontiers in Psychology, 5*, 1233. https://doi.org/10.3389/fpsyg.2014.01233

Rączaszek-Leonardi, J., Nomikou, I., & Rohlfing, K. J. (2013). Young children's dialogical actions: The beginnings of purposeful intersubjectivity. *IEEE Transactions on Autonomous Mental Development, 5*(3), 210–221. https://doi.org/10.1109/TAMD.2013.2273258

Reckwitz, A. (2002). Toward a theory of social practices: A development in culturalist theorizing. *European Journal of Social Theory, 5*(2), 243–263. https://doi.org/10.1177/13684310222225432

Reckwitz, A. (2003). Basic elements of a theory of social practices. A perceptive in social theory. *Zeitschrift für Soziologie, 32*(4), 282–301. https://doi.org/10.1515/zfsoz-2003-0401

Reckwitz, A. (2021). Gesellschaftstheorie als Werkzeug. In A. Reckwitz & H. Rosa (Eds.), *Spätmoderne in der Krise: Was leistet die Gesellschaftstheorie?* (pp. 23–150). Suhrkamp.

Rohlfing, K. J., Cimiano, P., Scharlau, I., Matzner, T., Buhl, H., Buschmeier, H., Grimminger, A., Hammer, B., Häb-Umbach, R., Horwath, I., Hüllermeier, E., Kern, F., Kopp, S., Thommes, K., Ngonga Ngomo, A.-C., Schulte, C., Wachsmuth, H., Wagner, P., & Wrede, B (2021). Explanation as a social practice: Toward a conceptual framework for the social design of AI systems. *IEEE Transactions on Cognitive and Developmental Systems, 13*(3), 717–728. https://doi.org/10.1109/TCDS.2020.3044366

Rohlfing, K. J., Wrede, B., Vollmer, A.-L., & Oudeyer, P.-Y. (2016). An alternative to mapping a word onto a concept in language acquisition: Pragmatic frames. *Frontiers in Psychology, 7*, 470. https://doi.org/10.3389/fpsyg.2016.00470

Rosenfeld, A., & Richardson, A. (2019). Explainability in human–agent systems. *Autonomous Agents and Multi-Agent Systems, 33*(6), 673–705. https://doi.org/10.1007/s10458-019-09408-y

Rouse, J. (2007). Social practices and normativity. *Philosophy of the Social Sciences, 37*(1), 46–56. https://doi.org/10.1177/0048393106296542

Schank, R. C., & Abelson, R. P. (1977). *Scripts, plans, goals and understanding: An inquiry into human knowledge structures*. Erlbaum.

Schegloff, E. A. (1997). Practices and actions: Boundary cases of other-initiated repair. *Discourse Processes, 23*(3), 499–545. https://doi.org/10.1080/01638539709545001

Schröter, J. (2016). Vom Handeln zur Kultur. Das Konzept der Praktik in der Analyse von Verabschiedungen. In A. Deppermann, H. Feilke & A. Linke (Eds.), *Sprache und Kommunikative Praktiken* (pp. 369–403). De Gruyter. https://doi.org/10.1515/9783110451542-015

Searle, J. R. (1962). Meaning and speech acts. *The Philosophical Review, 71*(4), 423–432. https://doi.org/10.2307/2183455

Sokol, K., & Flach, P. (2020). One explanation does not fit all. *KI–Künstliche Intelligenz, 34*, 235–250. https://doi.org/10.1007/s13218-020-00637-y

Steels, L. (2001). Language games for autonomous robots. *IEEE Intelligent Systems, 16*(5), 16–22. https://doi.org/10.1109/5254.956077

Streeck, J. (2009). *Gesturecraft: The manufacture of meaning*. Benjamins. https://doi.org/10.1075/gs.2

Vollmer, A.-L., Wrede, B., Rohlfing, K. J., & Oudeyer, P.-Y. (2016). Pragmatic frames for teaching and learning in human–robot interaction: Review and challenges. *Frontiers in Neurorobotics, 10*, 10. https://doi.org/10.3389/fnbot.2016.00010

Wittgenstein, L. (1953/1997). *Philosophical investigations*. Blackwell.

Open Access This chapter is licensed under the terms of the Creative Commons Attribution 4.0 International License (http://creativecommons.org/licenses/by/4.0/), which permits use, sharing, adaptation, distribution and reproduction in any medium or format, as long as you give appropriate credit to the original author(s) and the source, provide a link to the Creative Commons license and indicate if changes were made.

The images or other third party material in this chapter are included in the chapter's Creative Commons license, unless indicated otherwise in a credit line to the material. If material is not included in the chapter's Creative Commons license and your intended use is not permitted by statutory regulation or exceeds the permitted use, you will need to obtain permission directly from the copyright holder.

Chapter 6
Explanation Goals

Katharina J. Rohlfing, **Amit Singh**, **André Groß**, and **Britta Wrede**

Abstract Goals are central to human actions: In fact, human actions are organized toward goals. Already early in human development, human perception becomes biased to goal-directed actions. A characteristic of social interaction is that goals can be shared among involved agents. This is a great benefit for designing sXAI as it allows explanation goals to be collaboratively negotiated. Even more, depending on the goal, users could be dynamically but minimalistically supported in their autonomous actions. Future sXAI developments can benefit from this chapter by recognizing how essential goals are and that they constitute an intersection of individual actions and social ecologies.

6.1 How Does This Chapter Relate to XAI?

Goals organize actions in such a way that they lead to a change of a state that is different from what it would have been without these actions (Shotter & Newson, 1982). Goals therefore characterize the nature of actions and their contingencies.[1] Following this definition and recognizing that XAI has the overall aim to provide a

---

[1] Following Gómez (2007, p. 729), with contingencies referring to actions or events standing in temporal or other relation to each other. Two actions (such as pointing and looking) that follow contingently on each other form a sequence.

K. J. Rohlfing (✉)
Psycholinguistics, Faculty of Arts and Humanities, Paderborn University, Paderborn, Germany
e-mail: katharina.rohlfing@uni-paderborn.de

A. Singh
Psycholinguistics, Faculty of Arts and Humanities, Paderborn University, Paderborn, Germany
e-mail: amit.singh@uni-paderborn.de

A. Groß · B. Wrede
Medical School OWL, Bielefeld University, Bielefeld, Germany
e-mail: agross@techfak.uni-bielefeld.de; bwrede@techfak.uni-bielefeld.de

user with understanding and to assist in decisions, all actions that an XAI is doing should be seen in service of it.

However, we will also show that goals are not only constructed by individuals. Instead, they are also influenced by social ecologies—this means that actions of an individual (and also of an XAI) follow some norms and values. Thus, they are of a specific kind that is related to a (implicit) framework (Shotter & Newson, 1982).

Both aspects, the way how XAI can/should contribute to the goal of an explanation and the specific nature of that contribution relating to a framework of norms and values, are critical for XAI development.

6.2 Goals in Human Actions

What Is a Goal? An Attempt of Defining It The concept of a goal is very basic to human action. In fact, goals and actions can barely be separated: Csibra and Gergely (2007, p. 60) define an action as "a motor behaviour performed by an agent, which is conceived in relation to the end state it is destined to achieve." In this definition, action is defined by an end state but could also be a transition from one state to an end state; a goal, in turn, is defined as "internal representations of desired states, where states are broadly construed as outcomes, events, or processes" (Austin & Vancouver, 1996, p. 338). Psychologically, goals seem to organize human action. At the low level of perception, an end state can simply be a state contrasting with the former behaviors, building up tension. In this sense, even very early actions of infants display such tension by exhibiting the shape of an arc with a beginning, build up, climax, and resolution (Rossmanith et al., 2014, p. 8). It is important to note that the resolution (reaching the end state) contrasts with the tension of former behaviors and might therefore be well-perceived in young infants. In fact, human infants enjoy simple actions like the ones leading to a lamp being on. If they find out about moving a switch for the purpose of having the light turned on, they will test these contingencies (switch–light) again and again.

Goals organize actions not only for production but also for perception: They are prominent for already young infants (Kelemen, 1999). Imagine a toddler who is eager to participate in a game that the older siblings are playing: She/he will not be able to understand every move in this game, let alone the proper rules, but (a) she/he is definitely motivated to participate, that is, to act as the others do, and (b) she/he knows that this participation is about holding some cards, having a turn with rolling the dice, and the ultimate goal of receiving other cards. As already noted, the perception of goals might be facilitated by the resolution of a tension or a change of state (Rohlfing, 2013).

Goals can be of different nature. Whereas the first example about a child switching the lamp on and off again and again is about a material goal (a light being switched on), some goals might rather lead to a transition of a social state and pertain to social facts. Often, they are achieved collaboratively. For example, an arc of actions (telling a joke), forming a tension and being finally released, is best visible when the social goal of the partner smiling is achieved.

Recognizing Goals Is Human Nature Recognizing goals is an important milestone in understanding actions. In our example above with competent siblings, a toddler joining the game has extracted some parts of the action (holding some cards, rolling the dice, etc.) that can be predicted. To understand a goal is, thus, about "predicting the future course of an on-going action" (Csibra & Gergely, 2007, p. 61). According to Csibra and Gergely (2007), there are two more functional reasons for why discerning an action's goal is advantageous to the observer: First, it allows an observer to learn novel means with which the goal can be achieved. Second, viewing the action in light of the goal imparts insight into the (causal) relations. Within the first year of life, infants infer goals from others' actions and can segment streams of actions into meaningful units based on others' goals (see summary in, e.g., Kelemen, 1999 and Csibra & Gergely, 2003). (Csibra & Gergely, 2007, p. 66) postulate that the mechanism of associating actions with their outcomes could be innate, because human children get "obsessed" with it.

Crucially, the recognition of goals is not limited to one person. Instead, already in early infancy, it extends to collaborative actions. One impressive example are young infants at the age of 2 months who adjust their body when an adult is approaching them in expectation to being picked up (Reddy et al., 2013). Even more, the authors propose that the participation in collaborative goals might be very basic to humans: "anticipatory adjustments to being picked up suggest that infants' awareness of actions directed to the self may occur earlier than of those directed elsewhere, and thus enable infants' active participation in joint actions from early in life" (Reddy et al., 2013, p. 1). Similarly, impressing participation is reported from early games with infants (. e.g., Nomikou et al., 2017), suggesting that knowledge about (communicative) actions is established by "acquaintance" (Berthenthal & Boyer, 2025, p. 19).

Because of this prominence to human infants' perception and action, goals have coined the principles of "theory of rational action" in developmental psychology (Csibra & Gergely, 2003, p. 287). In this theory, it is assumed that actions function to realize goal states by the most efficient means available. For example, if infants see no obstacle, the most rational action for an object to reach a goal is to follow a straight trajectory to the end point (Csibra & Gergely, 2003). In this case, infants would be surprised to see an indirect and curved trajectory of the object. Thus, 1-year-old children are able to interpret goal-directed movement (Csibra & Gergely, 2003, 2007), that is, they analyze the situational constraints, bring in their own knowledge about future goal states within these constraints, and understand actions without attributing intentional mental states to the others. In human children, the goal-directed understanding of actions eventually develops to an ability of a more fine-grained level allowing to discern compositional semantic meaning in action: Csibra and Gergely (2003) assume that teleological understanding scales to Theory of Mind-capabilities and mentalistic action representation including the others' desires and intentions.

Recognizing Intentionality In developmental psychology, there is evidence supporting infants' understanding of actions performed by others being based on their own action production. Berthenthal and Boyer (2025, p. 4) review the literature and propose a common coding of the observation and execution of action. To put it in their words, an "action is understood when its observation leads to simulation (i.e., representing the responses of others by covertly generating similar responses in oneself)." For this simulation, own action experience seems crucial. In a seminal study (known as *sticky mittens paradigm*), putting a pair of adhesive mittens on the hands of 3-month-old infants, Sommerville et al. (2005) provided these infants with the novel experience to reach a goal with their actions. In a later test, infants with this experience demonstrated a sensitivity toward goal-directed actions. Own experiences with end states, thus, seem to sensitize humans to end states that others can achieve. It is worth pointing out that the study also speaks against the obsession in goals being innate, as proposed by Csibra and Gergely (2007).

We argue that such a sensitivity can turn to an expectation. Consider actions in contingency (following on or correlating with each other) forming a sequence, for example, take an object, hold it above a surface, drop it, it will hit the surface. An expectation occurs when the sequence repeatedly leads to the same goal (hit the surface). Then, vice versa, the goal can be predicted by the sequence. For this, not only the goal but also the movements forming the sequence are important. On a general level, when actions form a sequence summing up to a pattern, they can become indicative of a particular goal. We propose that this is the case for a communicative action in cooperation with a partner as well as for understanding actions of others. For example, it was shown that a specific ostensive way of addressing a child (by child-directed speech or direct eye gaze) is resulting in infants being attentive and ready to learn (Senju & Csibra, 2008). It seems that the perception of such a sequence of actions is eliciting – what (Csibra & Gergely, 2003; Kelemen, 1999) would call – a teleological stance in infants. In other words, as infants are cued to anticipate that the other person intends to provide important information, they respond to this with an understanding stance, that is, a state in which they are extrinsically motivated to take part in a social interaction and thus exploit the sense or meaning of the ongoing situation. For the purpose of the book, we would like to draw attention to the reciprocity that is important here: Because infants recognize a pattern in action, they react to it with an understanding stance. Both the tutor and the tutee, thus, are involved in this process. The case is also interesting with respect to our conception of context that we push forward in Chap. 4. There, we propose a co-constructed context in which some performed actions are building background for the interpretation of subsequent actions. In this sense, the ostensive cue, namely, the child-directed speech (or direct gaze) toward a child, is interpreted as important information and worth remembering (see Fig. 6.1). An expected sequence of actions, thus, brings in its own context for interpretation.

Intentionality via Verbal Behaviors Whereas above, we presented how intentionality can be communicated via actions, verbal actions are considered to make intentionality explicit. In fact, some scholars (Gómez, 2007, p. 129) differentiate

Fig. 6.1 A (repeated) sequence of actions: The ostensive child-directed speech (such as "look!") and subsequent look at an entity result in children following the gaze and being increasingly able of teleological stance, that is, of learning (Senju & Csibra, 2008)

between intentionality and action contingencies. The difference lies in the following: Take, for example, a pointing gesture. It can be seen as actions forming a *lean* pattern (action contingencies) toward a visible goal such as "the obtention of an object or the elicitation of an expressive reaction from others" (Gómez, 2007, p. 129). In this sense, a representation for this teleological stance does not require much and comprises three elements: the goal, the action that leads to the goal, and situational constraints (Csibra & Gergely, 2003). In the case of the pointing gesture, the goal would be to refer to an entity and perform a movement (e.g., without arm extension) that is constrained by the situation.

However, a pointing gesture can also be seen as a *rich* mental state, with the help of which "you understand that pointing makes others know that you wish to obtain an object or communicate a piece of information that they ignore" (Gómez, 2007, p. 129). For this representation, the attribution of beliefs, desires, and intentions is needed (Csibra & Gergely, 2003), requiring perspective taking and Theory of Mind. In contrast to the lean interpretation, in which only a reaction counts, with this rich interpretation, humans attribute hidden mental states to other people.

Along these lines of research, verbal behaviors are proposed to bear a rich mentalistic understanding. In fact, some scholars propose that such a rich mentalistic understanding of goals and desires of others is what enables us to use conventional and symbolic acts (e.g., Akhtar & Tomasello, 2000). Humans learn what intentions are possible and how they can be attributed to others.

Because the symbolic meaning of verbal acts and moves signifies states of others, they are, therefore, seen as communicating intentionality—in Chap. 5 on Practices, these behaviors were written up as *speech acts*. In this chapter, it is discussed that the impact on the addressee that the verbal behaviors of a speaker have is originally 'factored into this notion' Chap. 5. However, later considerations on speech acts rather focus on the speaker's intention (Searle, 1962). Here, we can repeat the summary that speech acts seem to involve intention because they are often assumed to be intersubjectively understood. For this intersubjectivity to work, context in a social interaction is crucial (see Chap. 4), because reading of intention means both partners to be involved in relating their verbal behaviors to the context of their actions and relative to social ecologies (i.e., what are common or explicit/implicit social frameworks with norms, values, and expectations) (Dourish, 2004; Shotter & Newson, 1982).

6.3 Goals in AI

In this section, we would like to point to sources that better provide an overview on goals in cognitive systems (see a summary in Rolf & Asada, 2015). Because our chapter is on explanation goals, following the idea of the book, we focus on a system's capabilities that are necessary for a shared goal. Today's cognitive systems are still limited with respect to collaborative capabilities of developing a teleological stance or sharing a goal. However, there are many systems and architectures that use goals as core concepts (Rolf & Asada, 2015). In belief–desire–intention (BDI) architectures, for example, achieving goals is described as "directing action towards some end-state" (Rolf & Asada, 2015, p. 333). One approach to dealing with such goals in AI is goal-based planning, where systems generate a sequence of actions to achieve a predefined goal. Using formal planning algorithms, these systems determine the best course of action to achieve their goal. For example, a self-driving car sets a navigation goal and uses a planning algorithm to avoid obstacles while following traffic rules. Another view comes from reinforcement learning, where agents learn goal-directed behaviors through trial and error. However, unlike systems with explicit goal representations, reinforcement learning agents do not inherently possess an intentional representation of the goal. Instead, they infer goals indirectly through a reward that guides their learning process. Beyond individual planning and learning techniques, cognitive architectures provide an overarching framework for goal-driven behavior. These architectures model humanlike cognitive processes, allowing systems to represent, prioritize, and dynamically pursue multiple goals by integrating different learning mechanisms. However, Rolf and Asada (2015) also reveal that other definitions of goals have been used referring to a performed action only, without being directed toward a state. This raises an important question: What minimal level of knowledge is required for a system to participate in an interaction while pursuing only a vaguely implemented goal? This is similar to how a toddler can take part in a game without fully knowing the rules. Developing AI that can engage in such interactions remains an open challenge, particularly for systems designed to learn from and adapt to dynamic environments. Rolf and Asada (2015, p. 335) propose "teleological goals" for this, which imply a representation: "Our mind makes sense of others' action by linking them to our knowledge and our representations of the world." Without such capabilities, an interaction with a user will break down soon when facing unforeseen situations. We propose that a first step could be achieved by a system (natural or artificial) that analyzes the ongoing situation based on its prior experience, on which basis a behavior execution is built (see Sect. 4.3). The situational analysis takes place on both the interaction level and the semantic level and regards patterns of actions.

6.4 Goals in Collaborative Human–AI System Actions

For the modeling and development of AI, we can provide an interim summary: Individual goals organize actions, but are also influenced by social ecologies (Shotter & Newson, 1982). Simple as the statement may be, we have shown above how complicated the organization can be.

Shared Goals We now turn to joint actions of humans that are seen as a model for collaboration with an AI system. This section intersects with Chap. 11 on engagement. When humans perform joint actions, they cooperate closely to achieve a goal. Both the awareness of what the goal is toward which they work and the ability to choose the appropriate action are the characteristics of joint actions. Both aspects are essential but barely realized in current AI systems. There is an ongoing discussion on whether AI systems can be team members in the sense of joining and complementing human actions: Groom and Nass (2007, p. 488) hold the position that joint actions emerge because of same advantages for individuals and teams "adopt share goals because forming teams to achieve shared goals makes it easier to achieve individual goals." In this sense, joint actions are organized toward shared goals and are performed in a task-oriented manner. For the jointness to emerge, it is necessary that AI systems understand a goal (Rohlfing, 2025). However, as already specified in the chapter on Components (see Chap. 3), goals can not only differ widely but also be subject to negotiation. This can result in changes to the goal: What was previously targeted might no longer be valid—a process that was originally described as co-construction of a joint goal (Shah et al., 2018, p. 170). What is required from the AI systems to be capable of an (inter)action toward a shared goal is adaptation (see Chap. 13)—also of the goal to coordinate with others. The coordination, in turn, requires more than just knowledge about how to divide a task; it also requires knowledge about who can contribute what to the shared goal (Rohlfing, 2025)—a metaknowledge, that is, knowing what the system can contribute.

Metaknowledge Directly linking to the metaknowledge, techniques for explicating perceptual functions and cognitive reasoning are the focus of explainable goal-driven AI (XGDAI) (Sado et al., 2023) in the context of carrying out and explaining a task. The aim is to "establish teams of humans and robots that effectively make use of the individual capabilities of each team member" (Sado et al., 2023, p. 2). By communicating about the AI's perceptual functions and cognitive reasoning explicitly, users are assumed to understand the AI's limitations and capabilities better, thus "enhancing confidence and safety and preventing failures" (Sado et al., 2023, p. 3). Whereas this line of research specifies some important applications for the XGDAI, metaknowledge could also be helpful in cases of malfunctionality. This is the case when technology does not work as expected or experienced so far. Revealing the changes of capabilities with regard to previous use cases would empower the users in further actions, also enhancing confidence and safety. Note that this use of metaknowledge to communicate about the AI's limitations regarding its perceptual and reasoning capabilities is not restricted to interactions where the goal is to execute a physical task. In the context of explaining an AI decision in a nonembodied situation such as a recommender or decision support system, the AI's limitations are more difficult to infer, thus less easy to observe. Being able to communicate about the AI's limitations as well as its changes of capabilities is, therefore, even more important in these cases. We will consider this research line in our next section, in which we will focus on goals in explanations.

6.5 Goals in Explanations

We started this chapter by pointing out that goals organize (human) actions. We have also elaborated that humans' perception of actions is biased toward goals. Linking actions to explanations, it is suggested that attributing a goal to an action is, in itself, an act of explanation (Csibra & Gergely, 2003). For example, discerning an ongoing action leads to an implicit reasoning of *why* an action – be it a physical action, a decision, an explanation, or a reasoning step – was taken at first place, for which often an intuitive answer comes out as the relevance of the particular action in light of the goal. Hence, the goal in itself becomes the explanandum justifying the act. For example, consider an instructional scenario, where a learner is trying to learn baking. In a broader sequence of actions leading to baking, if the goal is made available to the learner at the beginning, a subaction – such as putting flour into a bowl – will naturally provide an implicit explanation of that action in that moment: The actor intends to prepare dough first. In this sense, the 'why' of an action becomes self-evident and self-explanatory when the goal of the task is already known to the learner.

This automatic ascription of goal to an action has been suggested to facilitate action anticipation (Csibra & Gergely, 2003), reducing the need for further explanation of the subsequent action that a tutor takes. And only when the intended goal of the tutor does not match the inferred goal of the learner, an explanation is actively sought by the learner from the tutor. For example, if pouring flour into a bowl typically signals the next step of adding water (given the local goal of preparing dough), but the tutor instead sets the bowl aside and begins cutting vegetables, then the action would need explanation, since the tutor's intended goal does not fit the learner's inferred goal. In other words, explanation points to deviations, aspects, and characteristics that are not perceivable. It is important to note that for a deviation to be discerned, a sequence of actions needs to be established—this is described in the chapter on Practices (see Chap. 5). At this time, when there is a deviation, one of two processes must follow: Either a new connection between the present action to a novel goal should be established (given the goal has changed now) or the tutor must scaffold the new unknown means of achieving the existing goal (baking), which may not yet be available in the learner's action repertoire. Whereas scaffolding a new mean would require it to connect to the existing goal through verbal scaffolding, changing the goal itself would need a debiasing mechanism, what Rolf and Asada (2015) call a goal avoidance, as in 'the tutor goal is NOT baking.' Crucially, here the role of linguistic negation for goal debiasing has already been highlighted in the scaffolding scenario, where the attention from the goal can be attenuated (Singh & Rohlfing, 2022) and means can be scaffolded (Groß et al., 2023). According to Rolf and Asada (2015, p. 333), providing a negative sign (e.g., negation) to the goal is not sufficient to model the state avoidance—rather by considering which states are the desired ones. Thus, an updated connection to the action and novel goal can better be provided by 'the tutor's goal is not to bake.. but [some alternate state].' Importantly, these alternative states can either be explicitly provided by the tutor or implicitly inferred by the learner through context and discourse. Overall in these two processes, two different questions about the explanation processes can be asked. When the tutor assigns a new goal to an action as a process of updating the learner's inference, the learner was implicitly reasoning why-question for that particular action with reference to a 'contingent' goal. In contrast, when the reasoning concerns possible means to achieve a fixed goal (e.g., how a particular action contributes to baking at a given moment), the focus shifts to how the action serves its purpose. Thus, on the one hand, a why-question pertains to goal-directed explanations; on the other hand, a how-question focuses on understanding the procedural aspects of an action.

In summary, the core aim of explanation is to enhance understanding in the explainee. However, understanding can take different forms such as "comprehension" of relationships and procedures or "enabledness" of further actions (Buschmeier et al., 2025; Rohlfing et al., 2021, p. 726).

6.6 Explainable Systems: Goals and Purposes

Most explainable systems have been developed for a specific purpose and in attempt to satisfy the interests and expectations of some user groups (cf. Langer et al., 2021). We will differentiate the purpose from a goal because we consider a goal to be related to a state and actions that can only be performed by involved agent(s). In contrast, a purpose relates to a function of a system in a specific context (of an application), implying what users can do with it and what for. A purpose is therefore more about the foreseen or desirable capabilities of the system.

In terms of goals related to actions, XAI systems have to generate answers to questions such as *Why was decision P taken?* and, in a counterfactual context, *Why P and not Q?* (Miller, 2019). Whereas linguistically, and often through counterfactual reasoning, such explanations primarily address why-questions, aiming to enhance comprehension of relationships and procedures, they often fall short in enabling users for further actions. Following Klein (2009), we argue that in addition to explaining *why*, explaining *how* is equally important. Whereas why-explanations provide insight into causal reasoning and decision-making processes, how-explanations equip users with the necessary understanding to act upon the information in the future, bridging the gap between comprehension and actionable knowledge. For this bridge, Klein (2009) points to little clear distinction between why, what, and how, because all these aspects can be relevant at a certain point in an explaining process. This might be especially true for more complex explananda.

In addition to the concrete verbal action of answering some questions that is classically viewed as the main contribution of an XAI, and in the spirit of the book, we have argued above that for user-centered explanation, XAI systems need to scaffold the user's understanding incrementally, by composing the explanandum in a step-by-step manner as well as by allowing to refer to very specific parts of the explanation to precisely pinpoint a problem and initiate a clarification—this is scaffolding as proposed for a social design of XAI (Rohlfing et al., 2021). In this scaffolding process, it is possible to distribute the sequence of actions among the involved partners, so each of them can make a contribution to the shared goal aligned with their best capabilities. Again, for XAI systems to achieve that, in Sect. 6.4, we have specified what is needed. However, before the scaffolding can take place, an sXAI system would need the capability to continuously monitor how the user is learning and adjust the level of assistance accordingly. For this kind of monitoring, it is a prerequisite for a system to break a task down into (sub)actions and to evaluate the contribution of the partners to the goal. Only then, it is capable of scaffolding dynamically, that is, provide the user with relevant information. In educational settings, for example, an XAI system should gradually reduce its involvement and allow the learner to take more and more control.

In terms of purposes related to the application of XAI, Rosenfeld and Richardson (2019, p. 681) specify several of them. We attempt to merge them with another taxonomy for explainable goal-driven agents and robots proposed by Sado et al. (2023, p. 5). This latter approach evolved around collaborative tasks with humans in the loop. It, thus, accords with a form of context-sensitive interaction, designed for shared goals that we also envision in this book. Overall, the purposes of explaining can be differentiated in those that are instrumental for further actions and of epistemic nature, in the sense that users gain knowledge from them (cf. Páez, 2019; Alpsancar et al., 2024, p. 449). These purposes can also be conceptualized as the explanation questions as mentioned in Sect. 6.5. Whereas the concept of further action has already been suggested to be instrumental for how or what actions are to be taken, linking it to the domain of enabling (Buschmeier et al., 2025), the epistemic dimension highlights why an action is important within a given context, thereby contributing to knowledge-building (Csibra & Gergely, 2003). Meaning, after a successful explanation of how-aspects, the explainee understands what actions need to be taken—whether immediately, or in the distant future (if deep enabling has been achieved). Thus, deep enabling not only fosters understanding but also serves the purpose of more agentive and responsible action-taking by the users (Buschmeier et al., 2025), which represents one of the key prerequisites of a successful explanation among those outlined below:

- *To make the system's action explicit so both the human and the user can take responsibility for their actions*—in this purpose, there is a clear division of actions leading to a goal in which both partners can participate and collaborate on. Importantly, the explication of the actions – often referred to as "transparency" Sado et al. (2023, p. 5) – is a prerequisite for humans to react to the system's behavior in a "credit or blame"-way Sado et al. (2023, p. 6). It requires a form of metaknowledge from the system.

- *To justify the system's decision, so the human user can decide to accept it*—interestingly, in this purpose, there is a clear involvement of the follow-up event, which is about taking a decision. In this case, an explanation is the means to be enabled to make this decision.
- *To ensure fair, ethical decisions*—what differentiates this purpose from the previous one is that a very specific type of decision, namely, a fair and ethical one, is targeted. In this case, an interaction might be required to guide a user toward critical thinking (see Sect. 29.1. This requires some social ecologies to be specified and selected for the interaction, also knowledge of a system being able to identify a goal (e.g., critical thinking in the users).
- *To convince or persuade the user to do something*—this is a quite common purpose in decisions that are made within a social interaction (see Sect. 30.1). For example, in the scenario of buying a car (see Sect. 2.3), Kary is providing arguments to convince Mary about some features of the car being more important. In this respect, Sado et al. (2023, p. 6) mention recommender systems providing explanations for how each product matches what kind of preferences.
- *To elaborate on the agent's choices to guarantee safety*—this purpose is closely linked to safety specifics of a given situation. Certainly, the content of the appropriate explanation needs to address it precisely.
- *To build trust*—there exist different measures of trust, but most of them are in the form of a survey asking the users about trusting a system. This is problematic as an attitude–behavior gap was identified (Kraus, 1995), suggesting that what humans do often does not match with what they indicate to be appropriate behavior (see also Chap. 28 as subjective vs. objective measures in evaluation). Depending on the operationalization of trust, an explanation for it will vary, guiding the user toward the desired stance that needs, however, to be recognized. Another possibility is that some strategies in trust building will be applied, without monitoring their effect.
- *To discover additional knowledge*—clearly, this purpose is about information seeking, which can involve many tasks with many goals. From an interactionist perspective, this purpose is fulfilled if the system is basically able to explain any further content and thus fill the knowledge gap that a specific user has. On the other hand, the knowledge can be filled only if the user can formulate it (by cleverly prompting). Likely, a question–answer strategy can be mostly applied for this purpose.
- *To evaluate or debug*—in the case of experts, this explanation might focus on details that are relevant for further improvement of the system. If the user is a layperson, the explanation needs to start from a very different point and progress with close monitoring of the user's understanding.

- *To introduce to the user what the specific AI system is*—involves engaging in certain forms of description with the aim of making an unknown object intelligible. Often, this relies on the production of ad hoc association between categories of objects to sketch out semantic maps.

Thus, an sXAI system needs to be able to (1) establish a goal, for example, by negotiation with the user, but also to (2) pursue this goal (e.g., enabling the explainee to carry out a certain physical action or to comprehend a certain decision and enable him/her to make their own decision) by monitoring its progress and adapting its explanations, and to (3) modify this process (or the goal) according to a specific set of purposes that are relevant to the current situation (e.g., to enable an AI expert to debug the system or to enable a domain expert to justify their decision more profoundly or to enable a layperson to carry out a new physical task).

6.7 Operationalizations of Goals

Above, we proposed that goals organize actions. In this organization, actions become contingent, forming a sequence. With reference to Chap. 5, we suggest that the organization is driven by both: contingencies (i.e., relations) of actions that make the sequence of others' or shared actions predictable (Davachi & DuBrow, 2015; Nagai, 2016) and orientation toward a goal that allows an anticipation of the desired outcome. Importantly for sXAI, as already mentioned in chapter on Practices (see Chap. 5 for the notion of *pragmatic frames*), such a sequence can combine contributions from both partners. Now, we propose that it can be analyzed on two levels: micro- and tasklevel (indicated in Fig. 6.2).

On the microlevel, we can analyze how individual (sub)actions follow each other. This is the case when an object is taken, led to a surface, and dropped. These three actions are contingent in the sense that they form a temporal order in a sequence. On

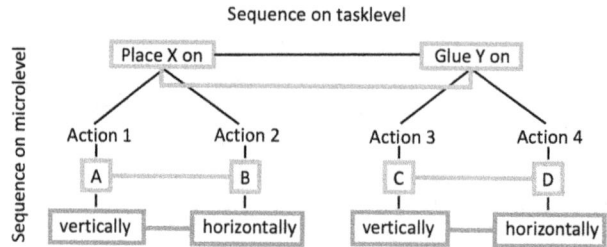

Fig. 6.2 A simple action model: There are two different paths (A and B) and two different manners (vertical and horizontal) that an object can be placed or glued on. Both verbs, *place* and *glue*, constitute the tasklevel because they organize the (sub)actions on a microlevel toward a different goal

this level, each of the (sub)actions can be optimized by their manner: For example, an object could be taken in a very specific manner (carefully, or with a pinch grip).

On a tasklevel, we can focus on the goal of actions and how it organizes the sequence of (sub)actions. Hereby, with a sequence of actions organized toward a specific goal, we will refer to a task (Vollmer et al., 2016). Consider, for example, a sequence of actions that is needed to *take* an object in comparison with *put* it somewhere. Some of the necessary (sub)actions (such as transporting the object) might be quite similar in both tasks, but the sequences differ in terms of the goal: an object disappears from or appears somewhere. It should be noted that current AI systems are criticized for not being flexible regarding various goals of actions (Vollmer et al., 2016). In other words, they cannot recognize, change, or learn goals that they were not trained for.

Note that our operationalization of actions follows a rather simple model. Basically, it controls two fundamental components that have been identified for a motion event (Slobin, 1996; Talmy, 1975): Whereas the *path* characterizes, for example, where an object should be placed, the *manner* specifies how the motion should be performed.

In our simple operationalization, many important aspects of shared goals and collaboration are missing. Certainly, a more complex action model is required to address human-aware planning (as proposed in Chap. 11 on Engagement). Hereby, we can point to some general ideas suggesting that the (sub)actions within a sequence oriented toward a shared goal could be distributed according to responsibilities that the partners have (Rohlfing et al., 2016). This pertains to many actions performed within a social interaction. For example, to point another person to a location, it is beneficial to first gain her attention and then point. In these shared sequences of actions (call attention–gain attention–point–share attention), both partners have to be coordinated with each other (see also Chaps. 11 and 9).

Another limitation of our simple action model is that responsibilities for the shared goal are not defined. However, in a social interaction, the responsibilities (i.e., who is performing what subaction toward the shared goal) can be flexibly distributed among partners. This way, a less knowledgeable partner can participate in the shared goal with little responsibility for it, while the other partner adapts accordingly (Rohlfing et al., 2016). The responsibilities are important because they also bring in social and cultural knowledge from social ecologies (see Chap. 9).

We have just pointed out social ecologies influencing goals and purposes. The way how ecologies are related to goals is a main topic in the chapter on Practices (see Chap. 5). Here, we can briefly state that they are also influencing the way humans interact with each other. For example, "members of different cultures have different sizes of personal space. Getting too close to someone can be perceived as invasive or threatening" (Rolf et al., 2018, p. 2). The authors further state that not only are social norms highly culture-specific, they are also "highly context-sensitive" (Rolf et al., 2018, p. 2). For an AI system to learn such norms, the authors suggest equipping them with the need to socially interact. The interaction would be like a testbed providing the AI system with encouraging or discouraging feedback according to which it could learn.[2]

Note that in this section, we have focused on the explanation of physical actions. In how far it is possible to transfer the structure of (sub)goals of physical actions to that of explanations of decisions, for example, from a decision support system, remains subject for further research. However, explanations in general consist of goals and subgoals and, therefore, require a certain structure that should be taken into account by an sXAI system.

6.8 How Does This Chapter Inspire Further Directions of XAI?

This chapter provided essential insights into what goals are, how they organize actions, and the fact that, from early on, humans process goals with a high priority. Future sXAI can benefit from this chapter by recognizing that goals are at the intersection of individual actions and social ecologies and has to be designed in greater awareness of it.

Overall, in developing sXAI systems, their goals as well as their flexibility in them should be clear; sXAI that are able to recognize goals could then support their interaction partners in reaching them. Imagine, for example, a robot that recognizes that a patient is attempting to take some pills. It might assist the person to a degree that is necessary without taking all the subaction within the task. This way, people could get the 'just needed'-support while remaining in control of as much actions as possible. For this well-suited scaffolding of actions, sXAI systems must adapt to both the users' contribution and their capabilities. Clearly, this includes breaking down complex tasks into manageable actions, monitoring of the users' contribution, and providing feedback at important learning moments. To achieve this, future research should develop methods to (1) infer or negotiate users' goals in an explanation, (2) have a representation of the purpose of the system in the given context, and (3) means to adapt the whole explanation process to these goals and purposes. This requires not only metacommunicative capabilities of the sXAI but also of the explainee. For example, goals need to be negotiated that may not yet be clear to an explainee right from the beginning and need to be co-constructed and continuously monitored and adapted throughout the interaction. The adaptation of the explanation process requires a broad spectrum of sXAI capabilities: On the one hand, the level of understanding in terms of comprehension and enabledness can vary for different explainees as they may be subject to different situational conditions, such as time pressure and high personal importance of a decision. This will affect the scaffolding strategies, such as, for example, a fast explanation may

---

[2] It should be recognized that this idea implies some care-work for AI systems. Clearly, this is controversial regarding the obligations on the side of the user (Alpsancar et al., 2024).

require a different selection and presentation of arguments and reasoning steps than an explanation which supports a decision that will have severe consequences for the explainee. On the other hand, the sXAI needs to have a representation of its own and the explainee's capabilities and to monitor the changes over the course of the interaction. This can pertain to physical actions in the case of a physical task goal as well as to the knowledge that the explainee has of the domain—requiring cognitive and communicative capabilities. In consequence, the sXAI then needs the capability to determine its actions in such a (proactive) way that it increases the contributions of the explainee in order to keep them in control. For example, increasing the amount of questions of the user or keeping the explainee involved through other communicative actions may be one strategy to achieve not only a more active role of the explainee but also a better support for the explainee to guide the explanation to the issues that are relevant to them and to a better retention of those elements of the explanation that are particularly important for the explainee. In the example of a user taking pills, the sXAI should involve the user in an interaction where the relevant aspects for taking the pills, such as a prescription for a daily dose of two pills and a prescription for taking a pill in the case of pain, are explained. The explanation should be based on the awareness of the sXAI that the shared goal (taking the pills) is a repeated interaction where the purpose is to enable the explainee to take the right amount of pills with high confidence building on an understanding level that is appropriate.

The goal is to offer participatory support that is dynamically minimalistic and fosters users' autonomous action in the long run. By incorporating scaffolding principles, XAI systems can promote user autonomy, improve learning, and create more natural, human-centered interactions.

6.9 Rapid Access to the Content of This Chapter

Goals organize human actions and can be characterized as an end state to which actions are related. The actions transition one state to another. According to Shotter and Newson (1982), goals lead to a change of a state ("broadly construed as outcomes, events, or processes" (Austin & Vancouver, 1996, p. 338) that is different to what it would have been without these actions. Goals can be of different nature: They can be achieved by the actions of an individual (e.g., flip a switch to turn the lamp on), but also collaboratively (e.g., by a caregiver leading the child's hand to the switch, so it can be turned on by the child); they can be material, as in the case of a room being lightened up, or social, as in the case of somebody laughing about a joke.

The action organization and sensitivity to goals begins early in infancy. Some scholars suggest that collaborative actions are at the beginning of goal perception because infants as young as 2 months can participate in the accomplishment of goals: For example, they can adjust their body when an adult approaches and looks at them to ease the action of being picked up. This adjustment does not happen when the adult approaches the child without looking (Reddy et al., 2013). This research suggests that young infants are sensitive to sequences of actions. When they repeat an action and by acquaintance with that, they form a pattern (action contingencies) according to which infants can expect the goal and then act accordingly. We suggest that this mechanism is valid for both recognizing goals in others' actions and for accomplishing shared goals in a collaborative way. For understanding goals that other humans perform, infants' own experiences with end states seem crucial and bias infants to perception of goals (Sommerville et al., 2005).

In contrast to the *lean* interpretation of others' actions in the form of contingencies that lead to a visible state change, humans are also able of a *rich* mentalistic interpretation, according to which they attribute mental states to others. Verbal behaviors are proposed to bear a rich mentalistic understanding, and some scholars propose that it enables humans to use conventional and symbolic acts (e.g., Akhtar & Tomasello, 2000). This interpretation is possible because humans relate it to social ecologies, that is, an implicit framework with norms and values that humans acquired.

For the purpose of the book, we consider shared goals to be relevant. They pertain to the collaborative nature of goals. When humans orient their actions toward a shared goal, they cooperate tightly (see also Sect. 11.3). There is an ongoing discussion about whether AI systems can perform as team members in the sense of joining and complementing human actions (Groom & Nass, 2007). Some approaches suggest that communicating about the AI's perceptual functions and cognitive reasoning explicitly (related to metaknowledge) could help AI systems to achieve team membership (Sado et al., 2023).

For XAI systems to become better collaborators, it might also be helpful to be prepared for various types of goals in explanations. Hereby, we differentiate between goals of explanations and purposes of the XAI: A goal is related to a state and actions, whereas a purpose relates to a function of a system designed for a specific context (of an application), implying what users can do with it and what for. SXAI systems that target everyday explanations need to be able to dynamically co-construct a goal with the user, along existing social ecologies. Currently, XAI are designed for many purposes, such as to justify the system's decision and to evaluate or debug (cf. Rosenfeld, 2021). In differentiating goals with respect to purposes of XAI, some approaches consider goals as end states, others as learned patterns of behavior shaped by feedback, and still others as dynamic representations that evolve through interaction. Whereas many architectures incorporate goal-directed behavior, the challenge is to design systems that can flexibly interpret and adapt to goals, especially in uncertain or collaborative environments (Vollmer et al., 2016).

We have proposed that teleological goals, which link actions to broader world representations, could enhance XAI's ability to adapt in interactions. According to Rolf and Asada (2015, p. 335), these goals help XAI make sense of behaviors by relating actions to its understanding of the world. By incorporating teleological goals, XAI can analyze experiences and adjust behavior accordingly, recognizing action patterns at both the interaction and semantic levels. Without this capability, XAI interactions may break down in unforeseen situations.

Our chapter inspires further directions of XAI introducing dynamicity to the goals. Accordingly, sXAI systems should (i) be more flexible in attributing goals when interacting with the human user. Hereby, they could have the capability to adjust goals based on the information provided within the interaction. In addition, when performing joint actions, they should (ii) be sensitive to their contribution and how it supports human agency in the form of performing actions autonomously. Hereby, they could contribute more (i.e., more actions) to the goal in order to let the explainee participate in the accomplishment of the shared goal; but this scaffolding could fade away, when the explainee can contribute more.

Acknowledgments This work was funded by the Deutsche Forschungsgemeinschaft (DFG, German Research Foundation): TRR 318/1 2021 – 438445824.

References

Akhtar, N., & Tomasello, M. (2000). The social nature of words and word learning. In R. M. Golinkoff & K. A. Hirsh-Pasek (Eds.), *Becoming a word learner. A debate on lexical acquisition* (pp. 115–135). Oxford University Press. https://doi.org/10.1093/acprof:oso/9780195130324.003.005

Alpsancar, S., Buhl, H. M., Matzner, T., & Scharlau, I. (2024). Explanation needs and ethical demands: Unpacking the instrumental value of XAI. In *AI and Ethics* 1–19. https://doi.org/10.1007/s43681-024-00622-3

Austin, J. T., & Vancouver, J. B. (1996). Goal constructs in psychology: Structure, process, and content. In *Psychological Bulletin, 120*(3), 338–375. https://doi.org/10.1037/0033-2909.120.3.338

Berthenthal, B. I., & Boyer, T. W. (2025). Human infants perception and understanding of others' actions. In *SSRN*. https://doi.org/10.2139/ssrn.5173544

Buschmeier, H., Buhl, H.M., Kern, F., Grimminger, A., Beierling, H., Fisher, J., Groß, A., Horwath, I., Klowait, N., Lazarov, S., Lenke, M., Lohmer, V., Rohlfing, K.J., Scharlau, I., Singh, Terfloth, L., A., Vollmer, A.-L., Wang, Y., Wilmes, A., & Wrede, B. (2025). Forms of understanding of XAI-explanations. *Cognitive Systems Research, 94,* 101419. https://doi.org/10.1016/j.cogsys.2025.101419

Csibra, G., & Gergely, G. (2003). Teleological reasoning in infancy: The naive theory of rational action. *Trends in Cognitive Science, 7*(7), 287–292. https://doi.org/10.1016/S1364-6613(03)00128-1

Csibra, G., & Gergely, G. (2007). 'Obsessed with goals': Functions and mechanisms of teleological interpretation of actions in humans. *Acta Psychologica, 124*(1), 60–78. https://doi.org/10.1016/j.actpsy.2006.09.007

Davachi, L., & DuBrow, S. (2015). How the hippocampus preserves order: The role of prediction and context. *Trends in Cognitive Sciences, 19*(2), 92–99. https://doi.org/10.1016/j.tics.2014.12.004

Dourish, P. (2004). What we talk about when we talk about context. *Personal & Ubiquitous Computing, 8,* 19–30. https://doi.org/10.1007/s00779-003-0253-8

Gómez, J.-C. (2007). Pointing behaviors in apes and human infants: A balanced interpretation. *Child Development, 78*(3), 729–734. https://doi.org/10.1111/j.1467-8624.2007.01027.x

Groom, V., & Nass, C. (2007). Can robots be teammates? Benchmarks in human–robot teams. *Interaction Studies, 8*(3), 147–157. https://doi.org/10.1075/is.8.3.10gro

Groß, A., Singh, A., Banh, N. C., Richter, B., Scharlau, I., Rohlfing, K. J., & Wrede, B. (2023). Scaffolding the human partner by contrastive guidance in an explanatory human–robot dialogue. *Frontiers in Robotics and AI, 10*, 1236184. https://doi.org/10.3389/frobt.2023.1236184

Kelemen, D. (1999). Function, goals and intention: Children's teleological reasoning about objects. *Trends in Cognitive Science, 12*(3), 461–468. https://doi.org/10.1016/S1364-6613(99)01402-3

Klein, J. (2009). ERKLÄREN-WAS, ERKLÄREN-WIE, ERKLÄREN-WARUM. Typologie und Komplexität zentraler Akte der Welterschließung. In R. Vogt (Ed.), *Erklären. Gesprächsanalytische und fachdidaktische Perspektiven* (pp. 25–36). Stauffenburg.

Kraus, S. J. (1995). Attitudes and the prediction of behavior: A meta-analysis of the empirical literature. *Personality and Social Psychology Bulletin, 21*(1), 58–75. https://doi.org/10.1177/0146167295211007

Langer, M., Oster, D., Speith, T., Hermanns, H., Kästner, L., Schmidt, E., Sesing, A., & Baum, K. (2021). What do we want from explainable artificial intelligence (XAI)? A stakeholder perspective on XAI and a conceptual model guiding interdisciplinary XAI research. *Artificial Intelligence, 296*, 103473. https://doi.org/10.1016/j.artint.2021.103473

Miller, T. (2019). Explanation in artificial intelligence: Insights from the social sciences. *Artificial Intelligence, 267*, 1–38. https://doi.org/10.1016/j.artint.2018.07.007

Nagai, Y. (2016). Mechanism for cognitive development. In M. Kasaki, H. Ishiguro, M. Asada, M. Osaka & T. Fujikado (Eds.), *Cognitive neuroscience robotics a: Synthetic approaches to human understanding* (pp. 51–72). Springer. https://doi.org/10.1007/978-4-431-54595-8_3

Nomikou, I., Leonardi, G., Radkowska, A., Rączaszek-Leonardi, J., & Rohlfing, K. J. (2017). Taking up an active role: Emerging participation in early mother–infant interaction during peekaboo routines. *Frontiers in Psychology, 8*, 1656. https://doi.org/10.3389/fpsyg.2017.01656

Páez, A. (2019). The pragmatic turn in explainable artificial intelligence (XAI). *Minds and Machines, 29*(3), 441–459. https://doi.org/10.1007/s11023-019-09502-w

Reddy, V., Markova, G., & Wallot, S. (2013). Anticipatory adjustments to being picked up in infancy. *PloS One, 8*(6), e65289. https://doi.org/10.1371/journal.pone.0065289

Rohlfing, K. J., Cimiano, P., Scharlau, I., Matzner, T., Buhl, H., Buschmeier, H., Grimminger, A., Hammer, B., Häb-Umbach, R., Horwath, I., Hüllermeier, E., Kern, F., Kopp, S., Thommes, K., Ngonga Ngomo, A.-C., Schulte, C., Wachsmuth, H., Wagner, P., & Wrede, B (2021). Explanation as a social practice: Toward a conceptual framework for the social design of AI systems. *IEEE Transactions on Cognitive and Developmental Systems, 13*(3), 717–728. https://doi.org/10.1109/TCDS.2020.3044366

Rohlfing, K. J. (2013). *Frühkindliche Semantik*. Narr Francke Attempto.

Rohlfing, K. J. (2025). Human–AI Teaming: Kulturwissenschaftliche Lücken. In V. Uppenkamp & M. Vösgen-Nordloh (Eds.), *Data – Culture – Society. Kulturwissenschaftliche Perspektiven auf Data Society als gesellschaftliche Transformation* (pp. 49–70). wbg Academic.

Rohlfing, K. J., Wrede, B., Vollmer, A.-L., & Oudeyer, P.-Y. (2016). An alternative to mapping a word onto a concept in language acquisition: Pragmatic frames. *Frontiers in Psychology, 7*, 470

Rolf, M., & Asada, M. (2015). *What are goals? And if so, how many?* (pp. 332–339). IEEE. https://doi.org/10.1109/DEVLRN.2015.7346167

Rolf, M., Crook, N., & Steil, J. (2018). *From social interaction to ethical AI: A developmental roadmap* (pp. 204–211). IEEE. https://doi.org/10.1109/DEVLRN.2018.87610238

Rosenfeld, A. (2021). Better metrics for evaluating explainable artificial intelligence. In *Proceedings of the 20th International Conference on Autonomous Agents and Multiagent Systems* (pp. 45–50). Virtual Event, International Foundations for Autonomous Agents and Multiagent Sysems.

Rosenfeld, A., & Richardson, A. (2019). Explainability in human–agent systems. *Autonomous Agents and Multi-Agent Aystems, 33*, 673–705. https://doi.org/10.1007/s10458-019-09408-y

Rossmanith, N., Costall, A., Reichelt, A. F., López, B., & Reddy, V. (2014). Jointly structuring triadic spaces of meaning and actions: Book sharing from 3 months on. *Frontiers in Psychology, 5*, 1390. https://doi.org/10.3389/fpsyg.2014.01390

Sado, F., Loo, C. K., Liew, W. S., Kerzel, M., & Wermter, S. (2023). Explainable goal-driven agents and robots–a comprehensive review. *ACM Computing Surveys, 55*(10), 1–41. https://doi.org/10.1145/3564240

Searle, J. R. (1962). Meaning and speech acts. *The Philosophical Review, 71*(4), 423–432. https://doi.org/10.2307/2183455

Senju, A., & Csibra, G. (2008). Gaze following in human infants depends on communicative signals. *Current Biology, 18*(9), 668–671. https://doi.org/10.1016/j.cub.2008.03.059

Shah, J. A., Gluck, K. A., Belpaeme, T., Koedinger, K. R., Rohlfing, K. J., van der Maas, H. L. J., Van Eecke, P., VanLehn, K., Vollmer, A.-L., & Yee-King, M. (2018). Task instruction. In K. A. Gluck & J. E. Laird (Eds.), *Interactive task learning: Humans, robots, and agents acquiring new tasks through natural interaction* (pp. 169–192). MIT Press. https://doi.org/10.7551/mitpress/11956.003.0016

Shotter, J., & Newson, J. (1982). An ecological approach to cognitive development: Implicate orders, joint action and intentionality. In G. Butterworth & P. Light (Eds.), *Social cognition: studies in the development of understanding* (pp. 32–52). Harvester.

Singh, A., & Rohlfing, K. J. (2022). Does contrastive attention guidance facilitate action recall? An eye-tracking study. In *Proceedings of KogWis2022, the 5th Biannual Conference of the German Society for Cognitive Science* (pp. 213–214). Albert-Ludwigs-Universität Freiburg.

Slobin, D. I. (1996). *From "Thought and Language" to "Thinking for Speaking". Rethinking linguistic relativity.* Cambridge University Press.

Sommerville, J. A., Woodward, A. L., & Needham, A. (2005). Action experience alters 3-month-old infants' perception of others' actions. *Cognition, 96*(1), B1–B11. https://doi.org/10.1016/j.cognition.2004.07.004

Talmy, L. (1975). Semantics and syntax of motion. In J. P. Kimball (Ed.), *Syntax and semantics* (Vol. 4, pp. 181–238). Brill.

Vollmer, A.-L., Wrede, B., Rohlfing, K. J., & Oudeyer, P.-Y. (2016). Pragmatic frames for teaching and learning in human–robot interaction: Review and challenges. *Frontiers in Neurorobotics, 10*, 10. https://doi.org/10.3389/fnbot.2016.00010

Open Access This chapter is licensed under the terms of the Creative Commons Attribution 4.0 International License (http://creativecommons.org/licenses/by/4.0/), which permits use, sharing, adaptation, distribution and reproduction in any medium or format, as long as you give appropriate credit to the original author(s) and the source, provide a link to the Creative Commons license and indicate if changes were made.

The images or other third party material in this chapter are included in the chapter's Creative Commons license, unless indicated otherwise in a credit line to the material. If material is not included in the chapter's Creative Commons license and your intended use is not permitted by statutory regulation or exceeds the permitted use, you will need to obtain permission directly from the copyright holder.

Chapter 7
Structures Underlying Explanations

Patricia Jimenez ⓘ, Anna-Lisa Vollmer ⓘ, and Henning Wachsmuth ⓘ

Abstract This chapter presents recurring structures of interactions – and their associated goals – as they occur in explaining processes. It explores how explanations are not delivered in isolation but unfold through dynamic, structured sequences of interaction between participants. Beginning with the smallest units, we examine how individual dialog acts and multimodal signals form micro-patterns within turns. These, in turn, compose meso-level structures such as pragmatic frames that organize sequences of interaction into meaningful, goal-oriented episodes. At the macro-level, we identify common types of explanatory dialogs, such as inquiry, information-seeking, or deliberation, which are shaped by participants' goals and situational demands. The chapter highlights how these patterns of structure are instantiated differently across social and situational contexts and proposes that understanding them is crucial for designing socially intelligent and adaptive XAI systems. By analyzing how these structures emerge and function, we offer a framework for operationalizing explanation structures in a way that supports co-constructive and context-sensitive human-AI interaction.

7.1 How Does This Chapter Relate to XAI?

Following an interactionist standpoint – and in line with what has previously been discussed in this collection – we propose that in XAI a *good* explanation is not merely generated by an AI system and passively received by the user. Instead, it

---

P. Jimenez (✉)
Paderborn University, Paderborn, Germany
e-mail: patricia.jimenez@uni-paderborn.de

A.-L. Vollmer
Interactive Robotics in Medicine and Care, Medical School OWL, Bielefeld University, Bielefeld, Germany
e-mail: anna-lisa.vollmer@uni-bielefeld.de

H. Wachsmuth
Institute of Artificial Intelligence, Leibniz University Hannover, Hannover, Germany
e-mail: h.wachsmuth@ai.uni-hannover.de

is co-constructed through the dynamic interaction between the user and the system (Rohlfing et al., 2021). This co-construction process is inherently interactive, not only highlighting the active role of users in probing, questioning, and interpreting AI outputs, but also the need for XAI systems that are responsive to users and the sequential nature of interactions. In considering explanations as interactive processes, we want to bring to the fore of the discussion on XAI the long-standing idea that interactions are not a random or chaotic process but *ordered*. Indeed, the notion of *interaction order* (Goffman, 1967)[1] has influenced many studies of interaction in the social sciences—originally human face-to-face interaction, later also remote/virtual and human-computer interaction (for an overview see Housley, 2021). This notion rests on the idea that there are underlying social frameworks for navigating social interactions that members of a society mobilize in order to get by across a wide array of social situations. Sacks et al. (1974) in investigating the systematic nature of everyday conversation argued that social interactions, even seemingly chaotic or trivial ones, are organized and follow predictable patterns. Thus, 'order' can be found in the smallest details of interaction; as Sacks puts it: "There is order at all points" (Sacks, 1995);[2] in turn-taking, pauses, repairs (corrections), and how people open or close conversations. His point was that every moment of communication, from the most formal exchanges to casual chats, reflects an *orderliness* that can be systematically studied as part of the interactional machinery through which social action is accomplished.

The *orderliness* of interaction and, therefore, any identifiable pattern or structure – as has been repeatedly highlighted throughout this handbook – is naturally occurring and emerging, susceptible to situated changes and ongoing reifications. In a sense, it is always a unique phenomenon in its own right. The emergence of observable interaction structures occurs over time and, within a single interaction, new structures can emerge and dissolve as the conversation unfolds (see Chap. 17). Across repeated interactions between the same individuals, certain patterns may become more entrenched, shaping the dynamics of future encounters. Over broader time frames, recognizable patterns or structures may evolve within communities, influenced by changing cultural, social, and technological landscapes.

Our aim in this chapter is to offer a way of navigating the incommensurability of explanations as natural occurring social/interactional phenomena and the possibility of its modeling. In other words, we propose a way of operationalizing structures of

---

[1] Goffman (1967) describes interactions as "rituals" where people tend to follow certain norms and scripts to preserve mutual respect. Goffman argues that interactions, even the most casual ones, are structured by a set of implicit rules and norms that maintain social order. In this chapter, we want to narrow our lens to the *languaged* order of explanations, or, as the title suggests, the *structures underlying explanations*.

[2] "This view, rather like the 'holographic' model of information distribution, understands order not to be present only at aggregate levels and therefore subject to an overall differential distribution, but to be present in detail on a case by case, environment by environment basis. A culture is not then to be found only by aggregating all of its venues; it is substantially present in each of its venues (Schegloff in Sacks 1995, Introduction, p. vxi)."

explanations, while retaining a sensitivity towards the notion of order, pattern, and structure as locally produced and situationally accomplished, that is, the product of situated action (Suchman, 1987). The structures we present have the potential to help co-constructing XAI systems because as explanations are – as any other form of social interaction – ordered, and hence, somehow predictable, XAI systems integrating a sensitivity to these structures of human communication can better engage and accommodate the human partners interacting with them. However, this is no easy task. The transition from raw phenomena to a model always yields simplification, and, consequently, something will always be lost in translation.

In this chapter, we propose a way of retaining significant detail to produce a co-constructive explanation model by differentiating between three structural levels: micro-, meso-, and macro-level structure. This classification was chosen by us and is not based on theoretical foundations or prior studies. The levels do not have clear-cut boundaries but rather exhibit fluid transitions, with definitions that remain somewhat ambiguous. Nevertheless, the division into three levels aims to illustrate structures of increasing complexity, emphasizing that structures exist at different levels and are interconnected rather than strictly separated. The category of *micro-level structures* encompasses multimodal sequences of units of action, whereas the category of *meso-level structures* captures congregations of micro-level structures that form recognizable and meaningful interaction sequences recurring within dialogs. Finally, the category of *macro-level structures* refers to patterns of meso-structure that can form types of dialog. All these level structures can be seen as blueprints, guiding XAI systems on how to act and react to human interactants in situations of explanation.

Below, we discuss some key concepts (the notion of structure, elementary process units and turns), and present a typification of structures in increasing size, starting from the micro-level structures to the dialogical patterns constituting the proposed macro-level, providing examples for typical evolving structures in each of the sections. Then, we offer an example of how an operationalization of such structures may be conducted, and consider our contribution to inspire further directions of XAI.

7.2 The Notion of Structures

In this chapter, the concept of structures can be seen as referring to the organized and patterned ways in which explanations may unfold (Psathas, 1995). This does not imply that explanations follow a rigid or universal formulaic expression. Instead, 'structure' in talk ought to be seen as observable *ordered* patterns that organize explanations as a *social practice*. This interpretation aligns with Garfinkel's adaptation of Mannheim's documentary method (Garfinkel, 1967), which suggests that examining multiple instances of explanations can reveal shared norms, rules, and reasoning patterns that shape and contextualize them.

This approach emphasizes the *indexical* and *reflexive* nature of explanations, showing how they are deeply influenced by the context in which they are produced while simultaneously reflecting broader societal or cultural frameworks (see Chap. 4). This perspective also resonates with Wittgenstein's (1953) concept of language games (Wittgenstein, 1953), where the meaning of words and actions emerges from their use within specific 'forms of life.' *Explaining*, therefore, is not a universal activity but one grounded in cultural, social, and linguistic practices, as they are used *here* and *now*, on each next occasion. Its success depends on a shared understanding between participants—not as a prerequisite, but rather as a context-dependent interactional accomplishment. For instance, different occasions – such as a pedagogical task, a scientific inquiry, or an emotional expression – dictate distinct criteria for what constitutes an adequate explanation at a given point. Furthermore, acts of explaining can reshape the language game itself, as seen in scientific or philosophical breakthroughs that introduce new concepts and redefine how we communicate and think about such concepts. Ultimately, from this perspective, explaining is a practical activity whose meaning and function are determined by the specific rules and purposes of the 'game' in which it occurs.

This approach poses a significant challenge, not only in examining how explanations are produced but also in operationalizing them for XAI systems. As Reeves (2022) highlights, there is an incommensurability problem in reconciling or translating the concepts, methodologies, and assumptions of radical interactionist approaches (e.g., Ethnomethodology and Conversation Analysis) into the field of AI. These approaches emphasize the social practices and contextual nuances of human interaction, focusing on lived experiences and the production of social realities. In contrast, AI often adopts computational and mechanistic approaches, simplifying complex social phenomena into data-driven models. This divergence creates a conceptual gap, as AI's interpretations of concepts like *natural language or understanding* often lack the social and contextual richness that is central to interactionists. By retaining a sensitivity towards these tensions, we aim to contribute to a deeper understanding of human-technology interaction without compromising the core foundations of our approach.

Consequently, rather than attempting to provide an exhaustive typology of process units, turns, and structures – a task that exceeds the scope of this chapter and may ultimately prove unattainable – we propose that explanations possess characteristic structures that can be analyzed through identifiable interaction patterns. These patterns can be explored through types or categories of common patterns and structures predictable in particular settings. For the purpose of computational operationalization, in this chapter, these structures are classified into micro-, meso-, and macro-level patterns.

What typology or combination of typologies to choose depends on the kinds of structure sought. In either way, the micro-, meso-, and macro-level patterns that emerge from them generalize over the different typologies. We discuss them in the following. Later, Chap. 27 discusses how to operationalize social interaction on the basis of turns and their functions.

7.3 The Building Blocks: Elementary Process Units and Turns

Explanations, when viewed as structured phenomena, can be analyzed and broken down into their constituent components (see Chap. 3 on components of an explanation). At their core, explanations are built from discrete actions that, when combined, form recognizable patterns of interaction. However, defining these basic units is inherently arbitrary, as the boundaries between actions are not preassigned. To address this, we explore the concept of elementary process units (EPUs), a notion drawn from fields such as cognitive science, linguistics, and computational modeling, where they refer to fundamental *units of processing*, such as phonemes or gestures. These units may be verbal propositions, gestures, or combinations thereof, serving as the foundational elements from which larger interaction structures emerge.

From the perspective of these disciplines, interaction structures are seen as closely tied to cognitive processes. In turn, these processes necessitate and influence certain behaviors—for instance, looking at an object when recognizing it or displaying a happy expression when understanding something. *Cognitive biases* are also seen as playing a key role in segmenting and interpreting actions, giving rise to patterns when combined across interacting agents. Theories like the self-organization of low-level behavior, as explored by Oudeyer (2006) in speech evolution, suggest that complex interaction structures emerge bottom-up, driven by simple behavioral elements. Interdisciplinary research in the field of education (e.g., Dominey & Dodane, 2004; Gogate et al., 2000; Gratier, 2003; Gratier et al., 2015; Nomikou & Rohlfing, 2011; Lohan et al., 2012) supports the theory that cognitive biases further facilitate learning by helping learners respond to specific situations and allowing tutors to emphasize certain aspects of continuous action through verbal and nonverbal cues.

It is important to note that EPUs are fundamentally context-dependent (cf. Chap. 4). A gaze, a cough, or a feedback sound could all be considered units, but their status as process units depends on their sequential relevance within an interaction. Thus, although the theories mentioned above connect this concept to internal processes, we can think of it in terms of what an action, analytically labeled as a *process unit*, accomplishes in an explanatory situation.

For linguists, there are various typologies of turns to be made or of the EPUs composed therein. Studies in these fields argue that even if the turns that instantiate the typologies are multimodal in most real-life explanation settings, the basic typologies can be dealt with as unimodal. In other words, although they exist across modalities – from text to speech, from gestures to movements, etc. – most typologies can be associated with the function of a turn, as the following examples show:

- *Constative Utterances* (Austin, 1962). Statements that describe or report facts that can be true or false, such as saying "it is raining today";

- *Performative Utterances* (Austin, 1962). Communicative utterances with a performative function, such as committing to an action. For example, saying "I apologize" constitutes the act of apologizing or saying "I promise" creates the act of promising. But also making someone carry out an action or expressing an emotional state. In other words, statements that perform an action just by being spoken;
- *Dialog Acts* (Bunt et al., 2010). Communicative functions within dialogs, such as asking certain types of question or giving confirming or disconfirming answers.
- *Hand Gestures* (Lausberg & Sloetjes, 2015). Functions of gestures, for example, to emphasize something or to express an emotion or attitude;
- *Head Movements* (Heylen, 2006). Functions of specific head movements, for example, to indicate the need for a closer look or the expectation of engagement.

Partners in an explanation often display multiple sequentially organized actions, although sometimes these may also clash with and within each other. However, each combination of EPUs produces grounds for meaning assignment, that is, they are meaningful together. Each such pattern of actions can be seen as one *turn* of a partner. Whereas turns may be interrupted (and hence may remain incomplete) in real-life interaction, we consider such turns as the minimal building blocks of an interaction. In the smallest case, one turn equals one EPU, but a turn may also be constituted by several EPUs. For example, in accomplishing different *discourse modes* (Smith, 2003) such as narrating, reporting, and arguing, the structuring of communicative functions and units is required.

7.4 Micro-Level Structures: Elementary Patterns in Turn-Sequences

Turn-taking systems are fundamental in dialog, allowing speakers to alternate and manage who speaks when. Sacks et al. (1974) laid the foundation for understanding the universal mechanisms governing spoken interaction. They proposed that turn-taking is a fundamental organizational feature of conversation, facilitating orderly communication across languages and cultures. Their framework identified two key components: turn-constructional units (TCUs) which can be EPUs such as a word, but also phrases or sentences, and transition relevance places (TRPs), where a change of speaker can occur. The study outlined two main methods of turn allocation: speaker selection, where the current speaker chooses the next, and self-selection, where participants vie to take the floor. In addition, the study describes rules that ensure orderly transitions and mechanisms such as overlap resolution and conversational repair to address interruptions or misunderstandings.[3] Another

---

[3] Subsequent research has built upon this work to explore turn-taking across diverse contexts, cultures, and modalities (e.g., West & Zimmerman, 1975; Jefferson, 1986; Goodwin, 1981; Schegloff, 1996, to mention just a few), including explanations Wagner et al. (2024). The turn-taking framework has also been applied in the field of human-computer interaction (HCI) to

important aspect of turn-taking systems is the idea that turns are *recipient designed*, meaning that turns in interaction – whether produced face-to-face or mediated – are designed to *do* something.[4] Turns are then contingent on what came before while, at the same time, setting up contingencies for what comes next, that is, how a recipient will respond. As Heritage (1984, p. 242) puts it, turns are "context shaped and context renewing." Drew (2012) notes that these contingencies "generate strings or sequences of connected turns, sequences that progress on the basis of our understanding of what one another was doing in his/her prior turn(s)."

A quintessential micro-sequence in conversation – and therefore also in co-constructed explanations – is the *adjacency pair* (Sacks et al., 1974; Paltridge, 2012). These are pairs of interactive *moves* produced by different interaction partners that belong together. This can occur at the verbal level, for example when a person says "Gesundheit" (or "bless you" in English) after another person sneezes, or responds with a greeting upon being greeted. It can also involve one interlocutor asking a question and another one responding, or one participant producing a request and another complying with or refusing that request. Other instances may be less overtly verbal, such as a pointing gesture toward an object accompanied by the interaction partner's gaze shifting to the indicated target.

To look at an actual instance of explanation, we resort to public materials stored in YouTube. The following example can be found in the video called "Computer Scientist Explains Machine Learning in 5 Levels of Difficulty" (video published by WIRED *Computer scientist explains machine learning in 5 levels of difficulty, 2025*).

Expert: Do you know what Machine Learning is? Have you heard that before?
Child: No ((shaking her head))

An adjacency pair is thus a sequence composed of two turns, a *first pair part* and a *second pair part*. However, these are not randomly sequenced, but a speaker's first part (e.g., question) produces the conditions for a particular type of second pair part. This is what Schegloff (1968, p. 1075) referred to as "conditional relevance." In other words, there are certain types of initiating turns that make relevant a restricted range of possible next actions. If the relevant second pair part to a first pair part is not produced or does not comply with the conditional possibilities, co-participants may treat a problem and make relevant some form of accountability.

Another micro-sequence commonly found in explaining processes includes the *initiation-response-feedback sequence*. These sequences are variations of the adjacency pair, or could be seen as composed of two or more adjacency pairs

---

develop conversational agents and virtual assistants (e.g., Skantze, 2021; Pelikan et al., 2023). Overall, the turn-taking model remains pivotal in both understanding human communication and informing the design of interactive technologies.

[4] The notion of "recipient design" was first described as "a multitude of respects in which the talk by a party in a conversation is constructed or designed in ways which display an orientation and sensitivity to the particular other(s) who are the co-participants" (Sacks et al., 1974).

(Jimenez & Smith, 2021). Each pair showing the regularities of placement and *tying* (Sacks, 1995) found in the adjacency structures of natural conversation.

This type of sequences are, among many other settings, observed in classrooms where the teacher first initiates the sequence through a question or prompt asked to a specific recipient such as a cohort of students. The respondent then provides an answer to which, in turn, the teacher may give an evaluation or feedback. This type of sequences can be identified by the way teachers produce an educationally trivial sequence of question-answer turns. In the literature, these sequences are known as question-answer-comment (Q-A-C) (McHoul, 1978) or as the initiation-response-evaluation (IRE) sequence (Mehan, 1979). The presence of these sequences tends to be closely tied to the formulation of 'question-with-known-answers' (Macbeth, 2004) and is designed to make learners participate in pedagogical situations by providing candid answers to a teacher's questions. The learners' answers provide contributions to the teacher's ongoing 'résumé-to-be' for the lesson (Freebody & Freiberg, 2000). The teacher being in control of such *résumé* sets the parameters of what constitutes an adequate contribution and what the final and 'correct' answer will be. This kind of sequences delivers the last word, and sequence closure, to the teacher (Macbeth, 2004). Thus, whereas corrections in other interactional situations have a function often associated with some sort of repair, in educational settings, and more concretely, in the case of question-with-known-answers, corrections are strongly tied to accountable pedagogical aims.

Although not all explanatory situations can be seen as an equivalent to classroom interaction – particularly in relation to the interactional asymmetry between teacher-students – we propose this type of structure to be seen as common micro-level structures in explanations, particularly in scenarios where asymmetry, whether an epistemic asymmetry or otherwise, is a constitutional feature of the interaction. For example, going back to the video "Computer Scientist Explains Machine Learning in 5 Levels of Difficulty" (*Computer scientist explains machine learning in 5 levels of difficulty, 2025*), on level 2, the expert asks the same question but this time to a teenager:

Expert: *Have you heard of Machine Learning before? ((camera cut))*

Teenager: *I'm going to assume that it means humans being able to teach machines and robots how to learn themselves?*

Expert: *That's right! ((camera cut))*

Expert: *When we teach machines to learn from data to build a model from that data or a representation of that and then to make a prediction*

Here the teenager sees the questions – "have you heard of Machine Learning before?" – not as a yes/no question-answer pair, but as an occasion to display and get their *understanding* checked. We see this in the formulation of the answer as performative utterance – "I'm going to assume," which indicates the act of providing a candidate answer without claiming epistemic authority – and the intonation of the answer as a question, which yields a second-part pair, a ratification. We also see it in the way the expert orients to this response as a *guess/assumption*, and therefore something subject to evaluation/feedback. The expert then not only validates such response – "that's right" – but she also offers a fourth turn where the *explanation* is tweaked and expanded. Moreover, although the expert asks questions such as "do you know what Machine Learning is?", we can see in how the interaction unfolds that she is not asking a 'genuine' question aimed at filling her 'epistemic gap.' Instead, the question can be seen as a prompt designed to trigger an explanatory situation. Thus, this prompt has a goal, that is, to check the level of understanding of the co-participant and to use such understanding as the starting point of an explanation.

The expert's initial questions can be seen as what Wachsmuth and Alshomary (2022) labeled a type of *dialogical act* called a "check question." Waschmuth and Alshomary, in studying the Wired videos series of *5 Levels*, explaining 13 topics to 5 explainees of different proficiency, listed other dialogical acts such as "what/how question," "disconfirming answer," "agreeing statement," and so on. In total, they identified ten of these turn-level category labels that capture the basic behavior of explainers and explainees in explaining dialogs. They also proposed a flat taxonomy of ten *explanation moves* to categorize linguistic units in an explanatory dialog. These include moves such as requesting an explanation and providing an explanation, but also signaling understanding and non-understanding, testing prior knowledge, and more. All of these moves are recognizable features of an explanation at a meso-level structure, which leads us to our next section.

7.5 Meso-Level Structures: Pragmatic Frames and "Jobs" in Explanation

The idea of a meso-structure is closely associated with that of *practices* (see Chap. 5). This is because they comprise a sequence of behaviors, which are essential for a practice to be identified as such—together they are seen as forming a *gestalt contexture* (Garfinkel, 1967).[5] There are many concepts from different disciplines that refer to this type of sequences, that is, behaviors that are sequentially performed by the interlocutors involved and that constitute a recognizable set of meaningful actions. These actions, when together, can be seen as accomplishing a goal. Whereas

---

[5] In a purposeful misreading of Gurwitsch's work, Harold Garfinkel suggests that people rely on a "family" of lay sense-making practices whereby coherence is assembled into an array of "particulars" by interpreting them in terms of an underlying pattern. These are referred to as "gestalt contextures," and their functional significant relies on the interpreter's presupposed knowledge of, for example, typical actions. Garfinkel uses Karl Mannheim's notion of the "documentary method" to describe how people determine the adequacy of certain interpretations to the situation. The method consists of treating a scene/situation/interaction (and, of course, its observable properties) as "the document of," as "pointing to," and "standing on behalf of" a presupposed underlying pattern. "Not only is the underlying pattern derived from its individual documentary evidence, but the individual documentary evidence, in turn, is interpreted on the basis of 'what is known' about the underlying pattern. Each is used to elaborate the other" (Garfinkel, 1967). This is what is referred to as the *reflexive* nature of the relationship between setting, action, agents, etc. and the possibility of their recognition as such.

the concept of a goal is complex, meso-sequences can be seen as having a goal orientation, which in Sect. 6.5 is defined as an observable change in form of an outcome, event, or process (Austin & Vancouver, 1996).

One of the challenges of the notion of meso-structures is that micro-sequences can be used to constitute meso-sequences. In this sense, meso-sequences can be combined in various ways, which makes them sometimes difficult to identify. One way to think about meso-level structures is in considering the notion of pragmatic frames (PFs)—a notion introduced by (Rohlfing et al., 2016) as an alternative theory in the study of language acquisition. A PF consists of a jointly coordinated sequence of multimodal behaviors and cognitive processes in a specific context and forms a recurring pattern of interaction with roles for each interaction partner. They are similar to the patterns that Bruner (1983) found in parent-child games and termed *formats* but include and highlight the cognitive dimension (Rohlfing et al., 2016). PFs usually emerge in social interaction but can also be taught. They allow for a certain degree of *flexibility*, but generally contain a repeated structure, a strongly recognizable interactional protocol that guides the interaction.

For example, conducting fieldwork in a primary school in South Wales, in the UK, Jimenez and Smith (2021) observed that, in this particular setting, teachers recruited the collective attention of the students by initiating a particular *adjacency pair*. This sequence, which starts with a first-part pair "oo-la-la" uttered always by the teacher, must be followed by a collective second-part pair "cha-cha-cha" produced by the students. The pupils have learned over time that the third part of the intended sequence is that the children *should* fall silent. If they fail, grounds for the teacher's reproach and sanctioning of the students' behaviors are granted. The first turn initiated by the teacher, moreover, is often produced as the teacher lifts her body or head slightly. Embodied actions that contribute to the signaling that in her capacity of *the* 'teacher,' she has the right to demand the attention of the students in the classroom. Those present in the classroom have come to understand that the teacher can demand pupils' attention at any point, that they can rely on such a resource to initiate a classroom activity (e.g., provide an instruction), and that the students are expected not only to orient their attention to the teacher, but respond with a second-part turn, thus making the "oo-la-la-cha-cha-cha" pair a recurrent feature of classroom interaction in this setting.

The utterance "oo-la-la" can be seen as a *speech act* (Austin, 1962; Searle, 1962). As already mentioned in Sect. 5.2, a *speech act* refers to verbal behaviors (locutionary acts) with which certain intentions (illocutionary acts) can have an impact on a partner (perlocutionary acts). In contrast to PFs that extend to nonverbal behaviors, speech acts refer to verbal behaviors that might, however, become modulated by nonverbal means. Because of the impact on the partner that is factored into the notion (especially in the work of Austin, 1962), it can be seen as embedded in a social and cultural fabric that provides the conditions in which they are used.

Similarly, as discussed in Chap. 23.2, when addressing the interactive structure of explanations, explanatory interactions feature a series of "organizational jobs" that are carried out jointly by both *explainer* and *explainee* (Quasthoff et al., 2017, p. 103). These include opening and closing an explanation, and, among other tasks, opening an explanation involves establishing its topical relevance. In between opening and closing, we find jobs constituting the actual explanation, that is, "explicating procedural, conceptual and/or causal relations (Fisher et al., 2022, p. 317)." These jobs are sometimes followed or interrupted by dialogic phases in which clarification of follow-up questions might emerge. These 'jobs' can be seen through the lens of PFs in the sense that they constitute patterns of social action that offer the co-participant the opportunity to interpret the situation and determine next relevant actions. For example, ongoing research suggests that the closing of an explanation opens up a sequential position in which explainees have an opportunity to ask clarification questions; therefore, looping back into the explanation proper (Fisher et al., 2022).

In human–AI interaction, PFs have been argued to have potential benefits for AI systems (Vollmer et al., 2016). They carry meaning such that information about cognitive operations, expected contributions, and interaction goals can be connected to the sequence constituting a PF. If systems can recognize these sequences, they could gain information on the goal of the interaction, how to behave at which points, and what role to perform. For example, Steels and colleagues 2001, Steels and Kaplan (2002), Steels and Belpaeme (2005) formally modeled 'language games' in computational and robotic simulations, allowing robotic agents to successfully negotiate new semantic representations in which words were used as cues to draw the attention of social peers to a shared referent. Although neither Steels – or Wittgenstein in his conceptualization of language games – considered the details of the cognitive and developmental dimensions involved in learning these frames, these models can be seen from the perspective of PF (Vollmer et al., 2016).

7.6 Macro-Level Structures: Dialog Types in Explanation

The reasons for people to have explanation dialogs are multiple. People might want to understand how a certain fact came about, or they aim to get more information about a situation, get instructions for how to tackle a task, or something similar. Some of the dialogs towards accomplishing these goals are very conventionalized because they appear across topics, domains, contexts, and groups of people. In this chapter, we argue that there are structures of dialog that follow a more general goal, such as an exchange of information, and that comprise recurring series of turns—or even recurring series of meso-sequences. Take a discussion as an example: Whereas discussing is certainly a specific practice (for more details, see Chap. 5), it can consist of many meso-sequences, such as explanations, arguments, illustrations, and similar. From these, entire dialog structures easily emerge that reoccur in similar scenarios in similar ways.

In a lecture-like classroom setting, for example, a teacher may first inform students about the aspects of a new topic, more in a descriptive form and possibly supported by visual illustrations or notes, for example, in a slide presentation. Upon questions on specific aspects from the students, the teacher may explain the details of these aspects and may come up with ad hoc illustrations. Students may challenge the validity of specific points or signal their non-understanding, which may lead teachers to give arguments or further explanations, and so forth.

In the context of argumentation, Walton (2010) studied how to categorize recurring types of dialog. He proposes seven different dialogue types (that are detailed further below) and organizes them according to three dimensions: (a) the *initial situation* that triggers a dialog, such as the need for information; (b) the *participant's goal* within the dialog, such as the acquisition or giving of information; and (c) the *dialog goal* such as the exchange of information. The distinction between the participant's goal and the dialog goals is particularly noteworthy, emphasizing the dialectical nature of argumentation. Walton and Krabbe (1995) establish dialog protocols to be followed in order to reach the underlying goals, whereas (Van Eemeren & Grootendorst, 2003) develop rules of a critical discussion needed for success.

While argumentation and explanation refer to different communicative functions, they share many verbal and nonverbal interaction structures, most obvious in the context of giving reasons. Accordingly, we may also observe common triggers of explaining dialogs, and the goals of such dialogs may also diverge. The abovementioned classroom setting makes this explicit, where the explainee (i.e., a student) may seek understanding of the topic being discussed, and the explainer (i.e., the teacher) seeks to achieve this understanding on the explainee's side, but also to keep time constraints and a sufficient integration of other students. These side goals in turn affect the dialog goal.

Table 7.1 lists the seven dialog types distinguished by Walton (2010) along with their triggering initial situation and the two kinds of goals discussed above. Among the seven types, three are rather argumentation-specific, namely, *persuasion*, *negotiation*, and *eristic*. By contrast, the other four certainly also apply to explanations,

Table 7.1 The seven basic types of dialog in the taxonomy of Walton (2010), originally proposed for argumentative dialogs

Dialog type	Initial situation	Participant's goal	Dialog goal
Persuasion	Conflict of opinions	Persuade other party	Resolve or clarify issue
Inquiry	Need to have proof	Find and verify evidence	(Dis)Prove hypothesis
Discovery	Need to find an explanation of facts	Find and defend a suitable hypothesis	Choose best hypothesis for testing
Negotiation	Conflict of interests	Get what you most want	Reasonable settlement both can live with
Information-Seeking	Need information	Acquire or give information	Exchange information
Deliberation	Dilemma or practical choice	Coordinate goals and actions	Decide best available course of action
Eristic	Personal conflict	Verbally hit out at opponent	Reveal deeper basis of conflict

showing the close connection between the two communicative processes. In detail, these four dialog types are characterized as follows:

- *Inquiry Dialogs.* An inquiry is a cooperative dialog that aims at evidence in favor or against a hypothesis about an explanandum (Walton, 2010 speaks of a *probandum* in the case of argumentation). Inquiries aim at conclusions and cumulatively build up towards them.
- *Discovery Dialogs.* Unlike in inquiries, the right conclusions are not predetermined emerge through the exchange of information in the course of the dialog. This particularly puts emphasis on the establishment of the explanandum in the beginning of the explaining process.
- *Information-seeking Dialogs.* This type of dialog may be perceived as the default setting of many explaining processes; an explaining aims to acquire information from the explainer who provides this information. Usually, this dialog type comes with rather clearly defined roles, either leading to a question-and-answer structure or an instruction-feedback cycle.
- *Deliberation Dialogs.* Deliberation, finally, shares properties of both inquiry and discovery. Similar to the former, it aims at conclusions, though ultimately more at decisions with respect to actions. Likely to the latter, the participants exchange knowledge in order to come to conclusions that would not be possible for either of them in isolation, often in a rather balanced co-constructive way.

Despite the fit of these dialog types to explaining processes, we observe that their description is rather abstract, likely not exhibiting concrete recurring structures. Once instantiated in a specific domain or social context (as the classroom setting above), the structures will likely become visible.

7.7 Operationalizations of Structures

An operationalization of the structures described in this chapter should enable an sXAI system to recognize patterns in the structures, to learn how to co-construct patterns, and to interact within co-constructive explanation dialogs with humans (or potentially also with other systems). The structures we went through cover different granularities from elementary process units and turns to elementary interactions, pragmatic frames, dialog types, and goals. Yet, they all share that we can largely see their manifestation in explanation dialogs as *sequences* of social interactions between explainers and explainees, even if some of them exhibit implicit hierarchical relations and circular repetitions.

As a consequence, a straightforward operationalization of these structures is a formalized model of sequential social interaction. In Chap. 27, we will formally define such a model for the three main aspects of sXAI: multimodality, incrementality, and patterns. For brevity, here we give only a short overview of the details relevant to patterns in the structures of explanation dialogs in particular.

Operationalization A social interaction σ can be operationalized as a sequence of two or more alternating turns τ of an explainer and an explainee, where each turn τ fulfills a specific function $f(\tau)$ within the explanation dialog. To this end, τ may combine one or more utterances υ of distinct modalities, whereas its function $f(\tau)$ may simultaneously compose multiple atomic functions, each represented by a nominal label or numeric value.

While the outlined model is fairly abstract and generic, it can be refined for an explanation setting of interest by specifying concrete atomic functions. Moreover, it could in principle also be extended, for example, by mapping that specifies hierarchical relations between the turns. In line with some of the examples given above in this chapter, common refinements of the possible functions of turns include topics, dialog acts, and explanation moves (Wachsmuth & Alshomary, 2022), taxonomies of head movements (Heylen, 2006), hand gestures (Lausberg & Sloetjes, 2015), or the like. Now, the model enables the recognition of patterns of different granularity, as follows.

On the micro-level, typical elementary interactions may be found through simple n-gram modeling (Aggarwal, 2015), that is, identifying recurring sequences of one more turn functions in a collection of explanation dialogs that appear most often or significantly more often than the average. If categorical meta-information is available about the dialogs (e.g., successful vs. nonsuccessful interactions), this further allows for a recognition of the most discriminative elementary interactions (e.g., those that nearly always lead to success).

On the meso-level, similar approaches are possible to recognize typical pragmatic frames, in principle. However, the increased length of the interactions compared to the micro-level will make it harder to obtain significant patterns. One common strategy from related research areas is to look at higher-level abstractions of functions (Persing et al., 2010), that is, functions of whole sequences of turns rather than of single turns (e.g., of a sub-dialog on some topic related to the main explanandum). Another strategy is to abstract from variations or noise in the sequences themselves. Within the field of natural language processing, (Wachsmuth & Stein, 2017) proposed a universal model that models any discourse-level argument as a sequence of rhetorical moves (i.e., turn functions in the given context) and allows for various abstractions, such as the restriction to changes in the moves only. Such models should be easily transferable to explanation dialogs.

On the macro-level, finally, the recognition of dialog types ultimately boils down to a classification problem (Aggarwal, 2015), that is, to learn to map any given dialog to one class from a set of predefined classes, for example, information-seeking dialogs vs. deliberative dialogs and others (Walton, 2010). Again, other categorical meta-information about the dialogs also allows here to find those dialog types that are most discriminative of the respective categories.

7.8 How Does This Chapter Inspire Further Directions of XAI?

This chapter has outlined the structured nature of explanations and how they emerge through dynamic, co-constructed interactions between users and AI systems. Our exploration of interaction order, elementary process units, turns, micro-, meso-, and macro-level structures provides structural insights that can offer guidance for refining and enhancing XAI with context awareness, adaptability, co-construction, and interactivity.

Adaptive and Context-Aware Explanatory Models One of the most immediate takeaways from this chapter is the importance of *situated* and *contextual* structures in explanations. This highlights the necessity for XAI systems to move beyond static, one-size-fits-all explanation templates and towards *adaptive* explanatory models. Aligning with the idea of meso- and macro-level structures guiding interaction sequences in meaningful and context-appropriate ways, future research should focus on models that can dynamically adjust explanations based on user engagement patterns, prior interactions, and cognitive states. This structure might inspire the design of modular explanation frameworks where different levels of abstraction are explicitly modeled.

Incrementality and Interactional Order in XAI The chapter has demonstrated how explanations are not singular outputs but rather *incremental and interactive processes* (cf. Part II). This calls for a paradigm shift in XAI development—from systems that provide predefined explanations to those that enable dialog-based explainability. Future work should focus on developing AI models that support turn-taking, conversational repairs, and sequence-sensitive responses, ensuring explanations evolve through interaction rather than being passively received. Techniques such as incremental natural language generation, context-aware retrieval-augmented generation (RAG), and reinforcement learning-based dialog adaptation could be further explored. At the core of this book is the emphasis on *co-construction*—that explanations are not merely delivered but are actively shaped by both the AI and the user. This necessitates the development of systems that can handle collaborative meaning-making, adjusting responses based on user input, misunderstandings, and knowledge gaps. This further motivates research in interactive learning, mixed-initiative dialog systems, and explanation personalization.

Enhancing Explainability through Pragmatic Frames The notion of *pragmatic frames* in this chapter and the next (Chap. 5) underlines the potential for AI to recognize and participate in structured explanatory sequences that align with user expectations. Future XAI research should explore methods for training models to recognize these frames and generate explanations that match the expected discourse structures. For instance, AI could learn to differentiate between an instructional explanation, a causal explanation, or a justificatory explanation, dynamically switching between these as needed.

From Modeling Structures to Implementing Socially Intelligent XAI Finally, the framework presented in this chapter should inspire research in building socially intelligent XAI systems that respect human communicative norms. By implementing structured interaction mechanisms, future AI systems can better align with human conversational patterns, reducing cognitive load and enhancing user comprehension. This suggests an interdisciplinary approach, combining insights from conversation analysis, computational linguistics, and social psychology with state-of-the-art machine learning techniques.

7.9 Rapid Access to the Content of This Chapter

This chapter explores how explanations in socially Explainable AI (sXAI) should not be static outputs but dynamic, co-constructed processes shaped by interaction. Unlike traditional views where explanations are presented passively to users, this chapter highlights the structured nature of explanations, emphasizing that they unfold in ordered and predictable ways. Drawing from research on human interaction (Sacks et al., 1974; Goffman, 1967), the chapter argues that explanations follow underlying structures, just as conversations do. This order is not rigid but emerges naturally within interaction, reflecting broader social, linguistic, and cognitive patterns.

Understanding this interaction order is essential for XAI systems to provide relevant, understandable, and meaningful explanations. This chapter categorizes explanation structures into three levels: micro-level (small interactional elements such as gestures and speech turns), meso-level (recognizable sequences that make up explanation processes), and macro-level (overarching structures shaping the entire dialog, such as inquiry or deliberation). These levels provide a framework for operationalizing explanation structures in AI systems, ensuring that explanations are context-aware, interactive, and adaptive.

7.9.1 The Notion of Structure in Explanations

The concept of structure in explanations refers to the patterns and rules governing how explanations unfold in social interactions. This does not mean that explanations follow a rigid script, but rather that they emerge from observable and recurrent patterns. Inspired by Ethnomethodology (Garfinkel, 1967), the chapter highlights that explanations are not only produced in interaction but also shape the interaction itself. Explaining is not a universal act but varies depending on context, culture, and purpose, requiring a shared understanding between explainer and explainee.

This approach aligns with Wittgenstein's concept of language games (Wittgenstein, 1953), where meaning arises through use in a specific setting. An explanation in a scientific discussion follows different rules than one in a pedagogical context or everyday conversation. Explanations also evolve over time—new scientific discoveries can redefine what constitutes an explanation, just as shifts in user knowledge shape AI-driven explanations. Understanding these dynamics is crucial for XAI systems, which must adapt their explanations not just to static user profiles but to the evolving nature of human-AI interaction.

7.9.2 The Building Blocks of Explanation: Turns and Elementary Units

At the most fundamental level, explanations are constructed from discrete communicative actions that, when combined, form meaningful interaction sequences. These building blocks can be categorized into elementary process units, turns, and sequences.

Elementary process units include verbal and nonverbal components such as words, phrases, gestures, and feedback signals. Each of these contributes meaning within an interaction. Turns are larger units of interaction that structure explanations into recognizable patterns. For example, in dialog, turns can serve different functions such as asking a question, providing an answer, offering clarification, and signaling understanding.

Different disciplines have categorized turns based on their function. Speech act theory (Austin, 1962) distinguishes between constative utterances (statements describing facts) and performative utterances (statements that enact change, such as saying "I promise" to create a commitment). Dialog acts (Bunt et al., 2010) focus on conversational moves, such as confirming, requesting, and instructing, while multimodal research (Lausberg & Sloetjes, 2015; Heylen, 2006) has shown that gestures and head movements also structure interaction.

In XAI, understanding these basic building blocks is crucial. AI systems need to identify user cues, recognize sequential dependencies, and generate responses that align with natural explanation structures. For example, when a user raises an ambiguity, the AI should not just repeat information but engage in a clarification sequence.

7.9.3 Micro-Level Structures: Elementary Patterns in Turn-Sequences

At the micro-level, explanations are composed of turn-sequences that follow recognizable patterns. One fundamental structure is the adjacency pair (Sacks et al., 1974), where one turn makes a specific response relevant. Examples include question-answer pairs (e.g., "Why is this the best decision?" "Because it optimizes efficiency") or request-compliance pairs (e.g., "Can you explain further?" → "Sure, let me elaborate"). These structures form the backbone of explanatory dialogs.

Another common sequence is the initiation-response-feedback (IRE) pattern, frequently observed in teaching (Mehan, 1979). In an educational setting, a teacher might ask a question, receive a student's response, and then provide feedback. This model is relevant to XAI, where AI systems must evaluate user understanding and adjust explanations accordingly. For example, if a user gives an incorrect interpretation of an AI's decision, the system should provide corrective feedback rather than moving on to the next topic.

These micro-level structures are critical for AI to generate coherent and user-friendly explanations. AI should be able to recognize when a user signals uncertainty, requests elaboration, or expresses disagreement, responding in a way that aligns with natural conversational norms.

7.9.4 Meso-Level Structures: Pragmatic Frames and "Jobs" in Explanation

At the meso-level, explanations follow structured sequences called pragmatic frames, which are recurring patterns of interaction that help participants navigate explanatory dialogs. Pragmatic frames help shape how explanations unfold by establishing expectations about roles, turn-sequences, and goals.

For example, in a question-answer frame, an explanation unfolds in response to a direct inquiry. In a correction frame, the explainer adjusts the explanation to rectify a misunderstanding. In an instructional frame, the AI provides a step-by-step explanation, as seen in teaching or troubleshooting scenarios. In a justification frame, the AI must defend or clarify a decision, such as explaining why a medical AI chose one treatment over another.

Recognizing and using these meso-level structures is crucial for adaptive XAI. AI should not deliver explanations in a vacuum but recognize the interactional frame and adjust its response accordingly. If a user is seeking justification, the AI should provide reasoning and supporting evidence. If the user is in a learning mode, the AI should scaffold information gradually.

7.9.5 Macro-Level Structures: Dialog Types in Explanation

At the macro-level, explanations align with different types of dialogs that serve specific purposes. Following Walton (2010), we can categorize explanatory dialogs into seven broad types:

1. Persuasion—AI aims to convince the user of a particular decision.
2. Inquiry—AI helps the user test or evaluate a hypothesis.

3. Discovery—AI and user explore new knowledge together.
4. Negotiation—AI and user balance conflicting preferences.
5. Information-seeking—AI provides requested information.
6. Deliberation—AI and user collaborate on decision-making.
7. Eristic (debate)—AI engages in argumentation, often in conflict-driven discussions.

Understanding these structures allows AI to adjust its explanation style based on the overall dialog type. A system providing recommendations in healthcare might rely on persuasion and justification, while an AI tutor would use instructional and inquiry-based dialogs.

7.9.6 Operationalizing Explanation Structures for XAI

For AI to generate structured explanations, it must recognize and model interaction patterns at all levels. Key operationalization strategies include:

- Pattern recognition—Identifying common turn-sequences in explanatory dialogues.
- Adaptive modeling—Using structured pragmatic frames to guide responses.
- Dialog classification—Recognizing the macro-level dialog type to determine the best explanation style.

By implementing these strategies, AI can move beyond static, pre-scripted explanations to provide real-time, user-responsive interactions.

7.9.7 Future Directions: Towards Socially Intelligent XAI

This chapter provides a framework for developing adaptive, structured explanations in AI. Future research should focus on:

- Adaptive explanation strategies that adjust dynamically based on user interaction.
- Incremental explanations that evolve through dialog rather than one-time information dumps.
- Multimodal explanation generation, integrating speech, text, and visual elements.
- Recognizing social and cultural variation in explanation structures.

By implementing structured interaction mechanisms, future AI systems can become more transparent, comprehensible, and socially intelligent, aligning with human conversational norms to improve trust, usability, and effectiveness.

Acknowledgments This work was funded by the Deutsche Forschungsgemeinschaft (DFG, German Research Foundation): TRR 318/1 2021 – 438445824.

References

Aggarwal, C. C. (2015). *Data mining: The textbook.* Springer. https://doi.org/10.1007/978-3-319-14142-8

Austin, J. L. (1962). *How to do things with words.* Oxford University Press. https://doi.org/10.1093/acprof:oso/9780198245537.001.0001

Austin, J. T., & Vancouver, J. B. (1996). Goal constructs in psychology: Structure, process, and content. *Psychological Bulletin, 120*(3), 338–375. https://doi.org/10.1037/0033-2909.120.3.338

Bruner, J. (1983). *Child's talk: Learning to use language.* Norton. https://doi.org/10.1177/026565908500100113

Bunt, H., Alexandersson, J., Carletta, J., Choe, J.-W., Fang, A. C., Hasida, K., Lee, K., Petukhova, V., Popescu-Belis, A., Romary, L., Soria, C., & Traum, D (2010). Towards an ISO standard for dialogue act annotation. In *Proceedings of the Seventh International Conference on Language Resources and Evaluation (LREC'10).* ELRA. https://aclanthology.org/L10-1385/

Computer scientist explains machine learning in 5 levels of difficulty. (2025). Retrieved February 28, 2025. https://www.wired.com/video/watch/5-levels-machine-learning

Dominey, P. F., & Dodane, C. (2004). Indeterminacy in language acquisition: The role of child directed speech and joint attention. In *Journal of Neurolinguistics, 17*(2–3), 121–145. https://doi.org/10.1016/S0911-6044(03)00056-3

Drew, P. (2012). Turn design. In J. Sidnell & T. Stivers (Eds.), *The handbook of conversation analysis.* Wiley-Blackwell. https://doi.org/10.1002/9781118325001.ch7

Fisher, J. B., Lohmer, V., Kern, F., Barthlen, W., Gaus, S., & Rohlfing, K. J. (2022). Exploring monological and dialogical phases in naturally occurring explanations. *Künstliche Intelligenz, 36*(3), 317–326. https://doi.org/10.1007/s13218-022-00787-1

Freebody, P., & Freiberg, J. (2000). Public and pedagogic morality: The local orders of instructional and regulatory talk in classroom. In S. Hester & Francis, D. (Eds.), *Local educational order* (pp. 141–162). Benjamins. https://doi.org/10.1075/pbns.73.06fre

Garfinkel, H. (1967). *Studies in ethnomethodology.* Prentice-Hall.

Goffman, E. (1967). *Interaction ritual: Essays in face-to-face behavior.* Routledge. https://doi.org/10.4324/9780203788387

Gogate, L. J., Bahrick, L. E., & Watson, J. D. (2000). A study of multimodal motherese: The role of temporal synchrony between verbal labels and gestures. *Child Development, 71*(4), 878–894. https://doi.org/10.1111/1467-8624.00197

Goodwin, C. (1981). *Conversational organization: Interaction between speakers and hearers.* Academic Press.

Gratier, M. (2003). Expressive timing and interactional synchrony between mothers and infants: Cultural similarities, cultural differences, and the immigration experience. *Cognitive Development, 18*(4), 533–554. https://doi.org/10.1016/j.cogdev.2003.09.009

Gratier, M., Devouche, E., Guellai, B., Infanti, R., Yilmaz, E., & Parlato-Oliveira, E. (2015). Early development of turn-taking in vocal interaction between mothers and infants. *Frontiers in Psychology, 6*(1167), 236–245. https://doi.org/10.3389/fpsyg.2015.01167

Heritage, J. (1984). A change-of-state token and aspects of its sequential placement. In J. M. Atkinson & J. Heritage (Eds.), *In structures of social action: Studies in conversation analysis* (pp. 299–345). Cambridge University Press. https://doi.org/10.1017/CBO9780511665868.020

Heylen, D. (2006). Head gestures, gaze, and the principles of conversational structure. *International Journal of Humanoid Robotics, 3*(3), 241–267. https://doi.org/10.1142/S0219843606000746

Housley, W. (2021). *Society in the digital age: An interactionist perspective.* SAGE. https://doi.org/10.4135/9781526486295

Jefferson, G. (1986). Notes on 'latency' in overlap onset. *Human Studies, 9*(2–3), 153–183. https://doi.org/10.1007/bf00148125

Jimenez, P., & Smith, R. (2021). Accomplishing the categorial landscape of the classroom: The case of group singing. *Ethnographic Studies, 18*, 173–194. https://doi.org/10.5281/zenodo.5805434

Lausberg, H., & Sloetjes, H. (2015). The revised NEUROGES-ELAN system: An objective and reliable interdisciplinary analysis tool for nonverbal behavior and gesture. *Behavior Research Methods, 48*, 973–993. https://doi.org/10.3758/s13428-015-0622-z

Lohan, K. S., Rohlfing, K. J., Pitsch, K., Saunders, J., Lehmann, H., Nehaniv, C. L., Fischer, K., & Wrede, B. (2012). Tutor spotter: Proposing a feature set and evaluating it in a robotic system. *International Journal of Social Robotics, 4*, 131–146. https://doi.org/10.1007/s12369-011-0125-8

Macbeth, D. (2004). The relevance of repair for classroom correction. *Language in Society, 33*, 703–736. https://doi.org/10.1017/S0047404504045038

McHoul, A. (1978). The organization of turns at formal talk in the classroom. *Language in Society, 2*, 183–213. https://doi.org/10.1017/S0047404500005522

Mehan, H. (1979). *Learning lessons: Social organization in the classroom.* Harvard University Press. https://doi.org/10.4159/harvard.9780674420106

Nomikou, I., & Rohlfing, K. J. (2011). Language does something: Body action and language in maternal input to three-month-olds. *IEEE Transactions on Autonomous Mental Development, 3*(2), 113–128. https://doi.org/10.1109/TAMD.2011.2140113

Oudeyer, P.-Y. (2006). *Self-organization in the evolution of speech.* Oxford University Press. https://doi.org/10.1093/acprof:oso/9780199289158.001.0001

Paltridge, B. (2012). *Discourse analysis: An introduction* (2nd ed.). Bloomsbury Academic. https://doi.org/10.5040/9781350934290

Pelikan, H., Porfirio, D., & Winkle, K. (2023). Designing better human–robot interactions through enactment, engagement, and reflection. In *Proceedings of the CUI@HRI Workshop at the 2023 ACM/IEEE International Conference on Human–Robot Interaction.* https://cui.acm.org/workshops/HRI2023/pdfs/HRCI23_paper_7.pdf

Persing, I., Davis, A., & Ng, V. (2010). Modeling organization in student essays. In *Proceedings of the 2010 Conference on Empirical Methods in Natural Language Processing* (pp. 229–239). ACL. http://aclweb.org/anthology/D10-1023

Psathas, G. (1995). *Conversation analysis: The study of talk-in-interaction.* Sage Publications.

Quasthoff, U., Heller, V., & Morek, M. (2017). On the sequential organization and genre-orientation of discourse units in interaction: An analytic framework. *Discourse Studies, 19*(1), 84–110. https://doi.org/10.1177/1461445616683596

Reeves, S. (2022). *Navigating incommensurability between ethnomethodology, conversation analysis, and Artificial Intelligence.* https://doi.org/10.48550/arXiv.2206.11899

Rohlfing, K. J., Wrede, B., Vollmer, A.-L., & Oudeyer, P.-Y. (2016). An alternative to mapping a word onto a concept in language acquisition: Pragmatic frames. *Frontiers in Psychology, 7*, 470. https://doi.org/10.3389/fpsyg.2016.00470

Rohlfing, K. J., Cimiano, P., Scharlau, I., Matzner, T., Buhl, H., Buschmeier, H., Grimminger, A., Hammer, B., Häb-Umbach, R., Horwath, I., Hüllermeier, E., Kern, F., Kopp, S., Thommes, K., Ngonga Ngomo, A.-C., Schulte, C., Wachsmuth, H., Wagner, P., & Wrede, B (2021). Explanation as a social practice: Toward a conceptual framework for the social design of AI systems. *IEEE Transactions on Cognitive and Developmental Systems, 13*(3), 717–728. https://doi.org/10.1109/TCDS.2020.3044366

Sacks, H. (1995). *Lectures on conversation* (Vols. I and II). Blackwell.

Sacks, H., Schegloff, E. A., & Jefferson, G. (1974a). A simplest systematics for the organization of turn-taking for conversation. *Language, 50*(5), 696–735. https://doi.org/10.1353/lan.1974.0010

Schegloff, E. A. (1968). Sequencing in conversational openings. *American Anthropologist, 70*(6), 1075–1095. https://doi.org/10.1525/aa.1968.70.6.02a00030

Schegloff, E. A. (1996). Turn organization: one intersection of grammar and interaction. In E. Ochs, E. A. Schegloff & S. A. Thompson (Eds.), *Interaction and grammar* (pp. 52–133). Cambridge University Press. https://doi.org/10.1017/CBO9780511620874.002

Searle, J. R. (1962). Meaning and speech acts. *The Philosophical Review, 71*(4), 423–432. https://doi.org/10.2307/2183455

Skantze, G. (2021). Turn-taking in conversational systems and human–robot interaction: A review. *Computer Speech & Language, 67*, 101178. https://doi.org/10.1016/j.csl.2020.101178

Smith, C. (2003). *Modes of discourse. The local structure of texts*. Cambridge University Press. https://doi.org/10.1017/CBO9780511615108

Steels, L. (2001). Language games for autonomous robots. *IEEE Intelligent Systems, 16*(5), 16–22. https://doi.org/10.1109/MIS.2001.956077

Steels, L., & Belpaeme, T. (2005). Coordinating perceptually grounded categories through language: A case study for colour. *Behavioral and Brain Sciences, 28*(4), 469–488. https://doi.org/10.1017/S0140525X05000087

Steels, L., & Kaplan, F (2002). Bootstrapping grounded word semantics. In T. Briscoe (Ed.), *Linguistic evolution through language acquisition: Formal and computational models* (pp. 53–74). Cambridge University Press. https://doi.org/10.1017/CBO9780511486524.003

Suchman, L. (1987). *Plans and situated actions: The problem of human–machine communication*. Cambridge University Press.

Van Eemeren, F. H., & Grootendorst, R. (2003). A pragma-dialectical procedure for a critical discussion. *Argumentation, 17*, 365–386. https://doi.org/10.1023/A:1026334218681

Vollmer, A.-L., Wrede, B., Rohlfing, K. J., & Oudeyer, P.-Y. (2016). Pragmatic frames for teaching and learning in human–robot interaction: Review and challenges. *Frontiers in Neurorobotics, 10*, 10. https://doi.org/10.3389/fnbot.2016.00010

Wachsmuth, H., & Alshomary, M. (2022). "Mama always had a way of explaining things so I could understand": A dialogue corpus for learning to construct explanations. In *Proceedings of the 29th International Conference on Computational Linguistics* (pp. 344–354). ICCL. https://aclanthology.org/2022.coling-1.27

Wachsmuth, H., & Stein, B. (2017). A universal model for discourse-level argumentation analysis. *ACM Transactions on Internet Technology: Argumentation in Social Media, 17*(3), 28. https://doi.org/10.1145/2957757

Wagner, P., Włodarczak, M., Buschmeier, H., Türk, O., & Gilmartin, E. (2024). Turn-taking dynamics across different phases of explanatory dialogues. In *Proceedings of the 28th Workshop on the Semantics and Pragmatics of Dialogue*. http://semdial.org/anthology/Z24-Wagner_semdial_0001.pdf

Walton, D. (2010). Types of dialogue and burdens of proof. In P. Baroni, F. Cerutti, M. Giacomin & G. R. Simari (Eds.), *Proceedings of the 2010 Conference on Computational Models of Argument (COMMA 2010)* (pp. 13–24). IOS Press.

Walton, D. N., & Krabbe, E. C. W. (1995). *Commitment in dialogue: Basic concept of interpersonal reasoning*. SUNY Press.

West, C., & Zimmerman, D. H. (1975). Sex roles, interruptions and silences in conversation. In B. Thorne & N. Henley (Eds.), *Language and sex: Difference and dominance* (pp. 105–129). Newbury House.

Wittgenstein, L. (1953). *Philosophical investigations*. Blackwell. https://doi.org/10.2307/2217461

Open Access This chapter is licensed under the terms of the Creative Commons Attribution 4.0 International License (http://creativecommons.org/licenses/by/4.0/), which permits use, sharing, adaptation, distribution and reproduction in any medium or format, as long as you give appropriate credit to the original author(s) and the source, provide a link to the Creative Commons license and indicate if changes were made.

The images or other third party material in this chapter are included in the chapter's Creative Commons license, unless indicated otherwise in a credit line to the material. If material is not included in the chapter's Creative Commons license and your intended use is not permitted by statutory regulation or exceeds the permitted use, you will need to obtain permission directly from the copyright holder.

Chapter 8
Roles and Relationships

Joris Hulstijn

Abstract This chapter defines the notion of social roles and role relationships as well as interaction roles (speaker, addressee) at various levels (utterance, dialog, social relationship). Roles are part of a script or frame, which can be formalized as a dialog game. Roles are played by specific agents, but only if they qualify. Given a role, it is clear what the expertise, responsibilities, norms, and powers are of an agent who has adopted that role. We specifically analyze the roles of the explainer and explainee in an interactive everyday explanation dialog (explication).

8.1 Introduction

This part of the book is about interaction patterns. Patterns are common sequences of utterance types, for example, inform-acknowledge, question-answer, or propose-counter propose-accept. Such patterns can be analyzed and understood by various theoretical structures. In the previous chapter, we looked at the sequence of utterances in an interaction (Chap. 7). Now we will look at the structure of the social situation behind that interaction. We can see interaction patterns as produced by *frames* or *scripts* (Schank & Abelson, 1977). Frames help us understand the structure of a complex social situation. For example, a restaurant is a public place with tables, where a waiter serves meals to a customer in return for money. Scripts are similar to frames but deal with the sequence of social events, like in a film script. Famously, the restaurant script demands that after selecting a meal, waiting, and eating the meal, the customer must pay for the meal, before leaving (Schank & Abelson, 1977). So in the restaurant script, a payment scene must follow after an eating scene. Note that this social norm is attached to the *role* of the customer. It applies to anyone who happens to perform these actions in the script.

J. Hulstijn (✉)
Utrecht University, Utrecht, Netherlands
e-mail: j.hulstijn@uu.nl

© The Author(s) 2026
K. J. Rohlfing et al. (eds.), *Social Explainable AI*,
https://doi.org/10.1007/978-981-96-5290-7_8

Who is doing what in a script? In this chapter, we characterize the notion of *roles*, the types of participants that remain stable throughout a sequence of social events, and the changes in the *relationships* between the people in these roles.

Given the roles in a script, we can ask several questions. Who is qualified to play a role? Why would a participant want to adopt a role? How is adoption of a role and leaving a role being signaled? What are the expertise, responsibilities, norms and powers associated with a role? How do the social relationships between participants in roles, such as trust or authority, develop during a dialog?

8.2 How Do Roles Relate to sXAI?

In this chapter, we will explore in particular the roles and role relationships of the *explainer* (ER) and *explainee* (EE), as defined in the introduction Sect. 3.1. The specific script to study is *everyday explanation* (Miller, 2019). There are important lessons to be learned from scientific explanation (Hempel, 1965), but everyday explanation dialogs work differently. Such dialogs will be called *explication* here; the term explanation is used in a more general sense.

In explication, the main responsibility of the explainer is to make the explainee understand a specific issue, called the *explanandum* (to-be-explained). The material used in producing such an explanation is called *explanans*. The explanans may consist of factual information, and a certain rule or regularity, from which an answer to the issue to be explained, can be inferred. This mechanism is illustrated in Fig. 8.1.

At the start, the explainee has a 'knowledge gap' that needs to be filled. Therefore, the explainer must take the current knowledge of the explainee into account. This process of adjustment to the explainee is called *scaffolding* (Chap. 13 on Adaptation). The metaphor suggests that an explainee may need some extra support. The explainer can use techniques like examples or diagrams to support the explainee in understanding step by step. Scaffolding requires maintenance of a model of the current knowledge of the explainee. During the dialog, the knowledge of both participants evolves. That means that another responsibility of the explainer is to monitor the progress of the dialog and update the partner model accordingly.

The responsibility of the explainee, on the other hand, is to take the explanans into consideration and genuinely try to understand the explanandum. To help the explainer build an accurate partner model, the explainee must provide feedback

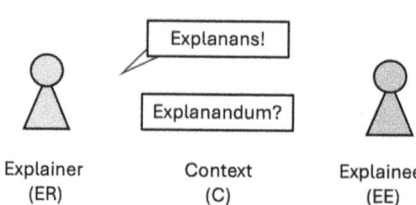

Fig. 8.1 Explication dialog (Rohlfing et al., 2021, Fig 1), see Sect. 3.1

Table 8.1 Role model of explication dialogs

Role:	Explainer (ER)	Explainee (EE)
Expertise	Knows about topic	Does not know about topic
Responsibility	Explain explanandum	Attend to explanans
	Take knowledge of explainee into account	Ask clarification questions
	Monitor completion	Provide feedback
Powers	Demand attention	Demand explanation
	Communicate explanans	Communicate explanadum

about the relative success of the explanation and specifically ask for clarification if needed (Table 8.1).

The example shows that roles come with responsibilities but also with the power to get things done (see Chap. 9). Once participants are engaged in an explication dialog, they are committed to pursue a joint goal: to make the explainee understand. To reach that goal, a qualified explainer has a repertoire of communicative acts. In return, the explainee must pay attention and take the explanans into consideration.

In case of explainable AI (XAI), the role of explainer is typically played by an AI system; the end user plays the role of explainee. That means that the design of an sXAI system must follow the norms associated with these roles. Social interaction is largely conventional (Clark, 1996). System designers can use these conventions to their advantage, to make systems appear natural and easier to use. By contrast, when a system does not follow the social norms and conventions associated with a role, the system will be seen as awkward and will be much harder to use.

8.3 Roles and Norms

The concept of a social role is a metaphor that derives from theater or film. The stage metaphor was investigated in detail by Goffman (1981). Not only actors play roles, but, in fact, everybody plays various roles in different circles. For example, I play the roles of teacher in the university, rower in my team, and father at home. The norms, responsibilities, and institutional powers associated with a social situation typically attach to roles and not to individuals. Following the theater metaphor: Once an actor has adopted a role, they must say the words in the script and can expect the other actors to play their part. Thus, the social norms in a script both have a normative sense (must) and a conventional sense (expect).

These norms follow from the responsibilities taken on by having adopted a role (see Chap. 9). This individual responsibility derives from the joint responsibility of the entire group to succeed in achieving a joint goal (we-mode thinking) (see Tuomela 2000). To succeed collectively, each participant has to do their task and help the others do theirs. When they have succeeded, or when they cannot achieve the task, they must let the others know, so they can reschedule the tasks (Hulstijn & Maudet, 2006).

A role also empowers a participant to accomplish a task. For example, a teacher has the institutional power to ask the students to be silent, and if one student disobeys, the teacher has the power to expel that student from the classroom. The school forms an institution that has formal rules about proper conduct of students and teachers, in addition to social conventions about power and status.

8.4 Role Relationships

Roles only have meaning in relation to other roles: *role relationships*. Consider the medical doctor in a doctor–nurse relationship or in a doctor–patient relationship. Although we use the word "doctor" for both, the responsibilities, expectations, and powers are quite different. In the first case, it concerns a work relationship. For instance, a doctor may instruct a nurse to complete a task. In the second case, it concerns a medical relationship. The doctor must diagnose the patient and may prescribe a treatment. The patient must trust the doctor's medical expertise.

In AI, we often use the word *agents* for the actors or individuals who play a role (Boella et al., 2006). The term agent can represent both human and artificial agents. If we see a social situation as a *social network structure* represented by a graph, then the nodes (points) represent agents who play roles and the edges (arrows) are role relationships. Mutual relationships are indicated by bidirectional arrows. Common social relations are trust, authority, has-more-expertise, etc. One agent may play many roles, provided that the responsibilities and powers are consistent. Conversely, one role may be played by many agents.

For example, a medical consultation is also an explication, with the patient in the role of explainee, and the doctor in the role of explainer (Fig. 8.2). The explanandum could be: What is wrong with the patient? The explanans could be the diagnosis, a disease that explains the symptoms. Moreover, in explaining, the doctor makes an utterance. So in that instance, the doctor also plays the role of speaker, and the patient plays the role of hearer. This stacking of roles and role relationships is quite common and provides a structure to social situations.

Roles are bound by a *context* (Chap. 4). To follow the theater metaphor, roles need a stage. We use the fact that roles are conventional, defined by a specific social

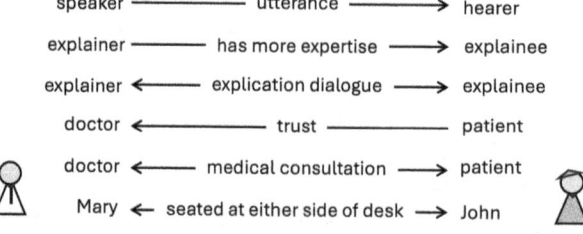

Fig. 8.2 Stacking of agents, roles, and role relationships, in a social situation

situation, organization, or institution. In many cases, physical properties provide cues as to how to interpret a situation. For instance, a medical doctor can be identified by a white coat. However, the context is also shaped by what is being said and done. Thus, a shared memory of the utterances and events becomes part of the context. The context is *dynamic*: It needs to be continuously updated.

8.5 Dialog Roles

Earlier we used frames and scripts to characterize social situations (Schank & Abelson, 1977). For the specification of the dynamics of social AI systems, frames and scripts are not precise enough. We will use a different theoretical perspective, namely, *dialog games* (Carlson, 1983; Mann, 1988; McBurney & Parsons, 2002). Just like the rules of a game determine possible sequences of moves on a game board, the rules of a dialog game determine coherent sequences of communicative acts in a social situation (Sect. 8.7).

We observe, for instance, in datasets of actual dialogs, that some sequences of dialog moves are really quite common. For instance, we find interaction patterns like question–answer, or request-proposal-acceptance, or greet–greet (Clark & Schaefer, 1989). The presence of these common interaction patterns can be explained by conventional dialog game rules. In fact, there are interesting relationships between three notions: interaction patterns, dialog games, and joint goals. Protocol rules in a dialog game specify well-formed sequences of utterances, which correspond to common interaction patterns. Why would a participant follow these rules? We believe that dialog games provide rules to coordinate participants' behavior, so they can achieve a joint goal (Hulstijn, 2000). This coordination function has two parts: predicting what others will do based on regularities (descriptive) and prescribing what you have to do in your role (prescriptive).

Roles can be found at different levels, which correspond to different time scales. See Table 8.2. We distinguish (1) *Turn-taking roles*, such as speaker, addressee, or (over)hearer. These roles alternate repeatedly (Sacks et al., 1974). (2) *Participant roles*, such as expert and novice in an information exchange, or explainer and explainee in an explication dialog. Those roles remain stable during a dialog of a certain type but change whenever a new (sub) dialog is started. (3) *Social roles*, like

Table 8.2 Dialog roles at different levels

Type	Roles	Level
Turn taking roles	Speaker–hearer, addressee	Per turn or per utterance
Participant roles	Expert–novice	Per dialog game (information exchange)
	Explainer–explainee	Per dialog game (explication)
Social roles	Teacher–student	Per social situation (education)

teacher and pupil. These roles extend beyond a single dialog. Their scope depends on a long-term social situation. In our running example, explainer–explainee relationships are found at the second level, similar to the roles in an information exchange (expert–novice). However, after repeated explication dialogues, a more stable role relationship may get established, similar to that in an education setting.

8.6 Operationalization

Roles and role relations have been used in many fields, also within computer science and AI. For example, Steimann (2000) analyzes the use of roles in formal ontologies and programming. Here we will limit ourselves to ideas about social situations (Schank & Abelson, 1977) and the stage metaphor (Goffman, 1981), formalized according to analysis in multiagent systems (Boella et al., 2006; Wooldridge, 2009; McBurney & Parsons, 2002).

To analyze the properties of roles and role relationships in social situations, we need a systematic approach; see, for example, the TROPOS framework for specifying multiagent systems (Bresciani et al., 2004). A multiagent system is a collection of autonomous agents, pieces of software that operate independently of human interference, in a digital environment. To specify multiagent interaction protocols, roles are needed as placeholders for the agents that play them.

Multiagent systems are composed of sets of agents, autonomous software entities, that are structured into groups, roles, and role relationships, set in a specific environment (Partsakoulakis & Vouros, 2004). Agents represent individuals: They are specific. For example, agents may have different knowledge, different goals, or different capabilities to perform actions in the environment. Roles and groups are normative expectations placed on agents. They are generic, at least for that social situation. Note that a group can always be defined as the set of agents in a special *member* role. So, groups will be dropped in the definitions below.

Based on roles, we can work out the expertise, responsibilities, and institutional powers assigned to the agents who play them (Boella et al., 2006). The analogy between the individual attitudes of agents and the normative expectations of roles is illustrated in Table 8.3.

Agents play roles during a certain period in time. An agent may even play several roles, as long as the corresponding norms and responsibilities do not conflict. For

Table 8.3 Relating agent properties to normative expectations of roles

Agents	Roles
Knowledge	Expertise
Goals	Responsibilities, norms
Capabilities	Institutional power
Environment	Social situation

8 Roles and Relationships

example, a football player can also be team captain. Moreover, one role may be played by several agents. For example, a football team has several defenders.

Definition 8.1 (Time) Let T be a set of time points $t_1, t_2, \ldots$ with temporal order $<$. An event e at time point t is written as $e(t)$. A state s with a duration $[t_1, t_2]$ is written as $s([t_1, t_2])$. Interval $[t_1, t_2]$ is *included* in interval $[s_1, s_2]$ when $s_1 < t_1$ and $t_2 < s_2$. We can define similar relations of *overlap*, *before*, and *after* (Allen, 1983).

Definition 8.2 (Role Models) Given time T, a role model M_i of a social situation or institution i is defined as a tuple $M_i = (A_i, R_i, D_i, Q, :)$, where A are agents, R are roles, $D \subseteq R \times R$ are dependencies or role relations, $Q : R \to Bool$ are qualification formulas, and $: \subseteq A \times R \times T$ is the play relation.

- Agents $A_i = \{a, b, \ldots\}$ represent individuals in an environment i. Agents are characterized by *knowledge* (or beliefs), *goals*, and the *actions* they can perform on the environment. Communicative acts are a special type of actions: When successful, they change the knowledge or goals of other agents.
- Roles $R_i = \{r, s, \ldots\}$ represent placeholders for agents, in a social situation or institution i.
- Role relations or dependencies $D_i = \{d, e, ..\}$ represent relations between roles, such as trust, power, or relative expertise.
- Qualifications $Q_r = \{P, R, \ldots\}$ are formulas that specify under what conditions an agent may play a role r.
- When agent a plays role r, we write $a : r$ or $a :_t r$. The state of playing a role is marked by entry and exit moves: $enact(a, r, t)$ and $deact(a, r, t)$.

Agents may only enact a role, when they are *qualified*. For example, a nurse must have certain expertise. Qualifications are modeled by a formula Q_r that specifies the expertise (expected knowledge) and capabilities (expected actions) for the agent. So $Q_r(a)$ specifies a precondition for $enact(a, r, t)$.

Once enacted, a role comes with *responsibilities*. In this chapter, responsibilities are modeled like goals for agents, except that they are normative. In that sense, responsibilities share characteristics with obligations or duties (Castelfranchi, 1998). There are two types of responsibilities: (1) *achievement responsibilities*, to bring about some state of affairs that does not yet hold, and (2) *maintenance responsibilities*, to ensure a desirable state of affairs or avoid an undesirable state of affairs. For example, a security guard has the responsibility to keep a building secure. Also $deact(a, r, t)$ has a precondition, namely, that all achievement responsibilities of $a : r$ must have been fulfilled or canceled.

The institution that defines a role provides certain *institutional powers*: actions that can bring about some institutional state of affairs. For example, only a notary can validate a sales contract for a house. Or, to repeat Austin's (1962) example, a priest has the institutional power to marry a couple in church. In many of these cases, there is a specific action or ritual that counts as the status change. For example, signing and countersigning a sales contract mark the transfer of ownership.

Role relations, also known as *dependencies* (Malone & Crowston, 1994), are simultaneous constraints on two agents, to coordinate their behavior. Common types of dependencies are *power* (employer–employee), *delegation* (principal–agent), *transfer* (sender–receiver), *trust* (trustor–trustee), *service* (consumer–producer), *expertise* (expert–novice), and *communication* (speaker–addressee).

We believe that a social relationship can be modeled as a combination of such basic relations. In practice, social relations often form bundles that enhance each other. For example, an expert has more expertise than a novice, therefore is more trusted on that topic, and gains authority over the novice.

8.7 Dialog Games

The notion of games plays an important part in many sciences. In economics, for example, game theory helps to predict whether the relative incentives of players will lead to collaboration. Here we will use the game metaphor to analyze dialogs. Observe that dialog is largely conventional. There are implicit or explicit rules that specify which sequences of utterances are coherent and have meaning. These rules can be expressed as the rules of a game, specified as moves (communicative acts) of players (roles) that affect the state of a game board (dialog context). Dialog games were originally developed in computational linguistics (Carlson, 1983; Mann, 1988) but have been formalized in the field of multiagent systems as Agent Communication Languages or interaction protocols (Wooldridge, 2009; McBurney & Parsons, 2002). In Chap. 7, we already explained that there are various types of dialog (Mann, 1988; Walton & Krabbe, 1995). For instance, Table 7.1 lists persuasion, inquiry, discovery, negotiation, information seeking, deliberation, and eristic dialogs. Dialog game rules determine how such a dialog starts, which moves are allowed, what their effect is, and how the dialog is terminated. For example, the purpose of a negotiation is to reach agreement on some transaction. Unlike the zero-sum games in economics, dialog rules do not specify winning or losing conditions for one participant but rather success conditions for all participants. For example, the purpose of information seeking is to resolve some issue or answer a question for the asker. The purpose of a negotiation is to reach a deal about some transaction. To walk out of a negotiation without a deal is unsuccessful for both. After all, dialog is seen as a joint activity.

In our running example, explication dialog, a successful termination, means that the knowledge gap of the explainee (explanadum) is resolved by a series of moves (explanans), by the explainer. An unsuccessful termination means that the explainee does not understand the explanans and fails to resolve the explanandum.

Dialog games are constructed from moves. Typically, moves are interpreted as communicative acts or speech acts (Searle, 1969); see also Chap. 7. Communicative acts are written in the format $act(a, b, P)$ where act is the type of communicative act, for instance, inform or question, a and b are the agents that play the role of speaker and addressee, and P represents the semantic content of the act. For

8 Roles and Relationships

Fig. 8.3 Sequence diagram of the Contract Net Protocol

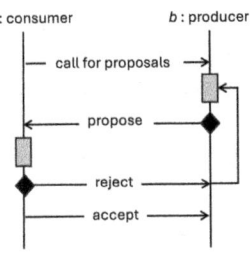

assertive acts, like inform or declare, the content P is a proposition that is supposed to be true. For directive acts, like request or propose, the content P is a proposition to be made true or an action to be executed. For inquisitive acts, like a question, the content P specifies an issue to be resolved (Hulstijn, 2000).

Concerning syntax or form, dialog game rules are often expressed by grammars, finite-state machines, or sequence diagrams. Chapter 7 on Interaction Structures and Chap. 27 on Operationalizing Social Interaction provide more details on the formal specification of interaction patterns. Here we will just use diagrams. For example, the Contract Net Protocol in Fig. 8.3 specifies the following sequences to be valid:

(1) cfp, propose, accept.
    cfp, propose, reject.
    cfp, propose, reject, propose, accept.
    cfp, propose, reject, propose, reject.
    ...

What a simple sequence diagram cannot specify is the semantic relation between the content of the moves. For example, suppose a and b are negotiating that b will deliver service S, in return for a price P. Now only when the proposed value of service S against price P matches a's original request, a deal will be accepted by a. This depends on a's individual evaluation but also on social conventions about the relative value of services and prices (Table 8.4). Such expectations are attached to the roles. For example, in a negotiation, we expect that buyers typically want higher quality for lower prices and that sellers want roughly the opposite.

One of the effects of a successful dialog is that the role relations change. For example, in the negotiation, agent b and a become mutually committed to perform S in return for P. So, afterward, two role relations are added to the dialog context: a commitment from b to a to deliver the service S and a counter-commitment from a to b to pay price S (Chopra & Singh, 2013).

Table 8.4 Coherent response rules for negotiation

Trigger	Response
cfp(a, b, S, P)	respond propose(b, a, S', P'), if $S' \leq_b S$ and $P' \geq_b P$
	else no response
propose(b, a, S', P')	respond accept(a, b, S', P') if $S' \geq_a S$ and $P' \leq_a P$
	else respond reject(a, b, S', P').

Communicative acts can be given a semantics expressed in terms of the beliefs and intentions of the speaker and hearer (Cohen & Perrault, 1979). For example, if agent a (speaker) asserts to agent b (hearer) that P, then a signals that a intends b to believe (1) that P (essential condition) and (2) that agent a believes that P (sincerity condition). Similarly for a question: If a asks a question whether P, then a signals that a intends b to intend a to believe P in case b believes P herself or to intend b to believe $\neg P$ in case b believes $\neg P$. So a intends b to provide an answer. Later, such a BDI semantics for agent communication was standardized (FIPA, 2002).

Instead of expressing the semantics of communicative acts in terms of the individual beliefs and intentions of the speaker and hearer, we can also provide semantics in terms of the expected change to the dialog context: the common ground among all dialog participants (Clark, 1996). The common ground is hard to calculate. As a proxy for the common ground, we can use a record of the utterances made, just like a game board records the effect of the moves in game (Lewis, 1979). This view has also been influential in argumentation theory (McBurney & Parsons, 2009). Here, the dialog game board represents the *commitments* made by participants. Commitments can be about the claimed truth of a proposition, as in argumentation, or about promised actions or future states of affairs, as in negotiation.

Table 8.5 specifies the elements of any dialog game, in terms of changes to the commitment states of the participants (McBurney & Parsons, 2002, 2009)

How does this dialog game model relate to other models in this book?

In Chaps. 7 and 27, a social interaction σ is operationalized as a sequence of alternating turns by different participants $\sigma = \tau_1 \ldots \tau_n$. Each turn consists of one or more utterances by the same participant: $\tau_i = \upsilon_{i1} \ldots \upsilon_{ik}$ and each utterance υ fulfill a communicative function $f(\upsilon)$. We can map υ_a unto a communicative act $act(a, b, P)$ and the function f unto act, which is the move in the game.

In Chap. 27, we present a characterization of explication dialogs, in terms of four states: { question stated (EE), explanation presented (ER), explainee affirmed (EE),

Table 8.5 Elements of a dialog game (McBurney & Parsons, 2002, 2009)

Game Elements	Specification
Roles	Define the roles of the participants
Commencement	Define start condition by specifying initial commitments for each role
Locutions	Specify which moves (communicative acts) are permitted for which roles
Combination of Locutions	Define the contexts or sequences in which (sequences of) locutions are permitted or not, or obligatory or not
Commitments	Define the semantics of locutions, in terms of how the commitments of the participants change
Combination of Commitments	Define how commitments are combined or changed when conflicting or complementary commitments are made
Speaker Order	Define the order in which speakers can make utterances (turn taking)
Termination	Define successful and unsuccessful end conditions, in terms of commitment states for each role

explainer affirmed (ER)}, and an embedded argumentation dialog (Fig. 27.1); see (Madumal et al., 2019). This model can be nicely mapped onto the commitment states presented here. The content of any utterance is first *presented* and only added as a commitment, once it has been *affirmed*. However, not all affirmations have to be explicit. Consider initiative-response pairs like question–answer, greet–greet, or cfp-propose–accept. In many cases, an appropriate response to an initiative counts as an implicit affirmative. For example, an appropriate answer to a question signals that the underlying issue is accepted as relevant in the dialog. Similarly, an appropriate proposal signals that the cfp was well received. However, if a participant wants to reject a presented utterance, this must be signaled explicitly. This mechanism of embedding is called *grounding*: It puts utterances into the common ground (Clark & Schaefer, 1989; Clark, 1996).

8.8 Uptake and Roles

In human society, interaction rules can be explicit, as in court, or implicit, as in everyday interaction. Implicit rules must be deduced from situational factors like location, status, level of acquaintance, urgency of the interaction purpose, and so on. Because the interpretation of role relations and the corresponding interaction rules in a specific situation is difficult, this is a common source of misunderstanding. It may lead to a breakdown of communication. On the other hand, the ambiguity in role relations also allows for some flexibility, which may reduce potential conflicts. Such flexibility allows the participants to cocreate the meaning of a dialog. This process may be called *uptake* (Hulstijn & Maudet, 2006; Austin, 1962).

Consider example (2). The utterance is ambiguous and can be taken as an order, a request, or a suggestion. How the utterance is *taken up* by the addressee will help shape the remainder of the conversation, as it determines the apparent role relation. For example, an order as in B1 presupposes an authority relationship, whereas a mere suggestion as in B3 does not make such assumptions.

(2) A. Could you shut the window please?
  B1. Yes sir! order: presupposes authority
  B2. Certainly. request: presupposes collaboration
  B3. Good idea. suggestion: no presupposed relation

This example highlights that the dialog context or common ground is *cocreated* by the participants. An important instrument for this cocreation process is grounding: giving either explicit or implicit feedback and acknowledgments on utterances, that helps participants to add the meaning of utterances to the common ground, or else, to flag misunderstanding or lack of attention (Clark & Schaefer, 1989).

Moreover, the example shows that moves can be deliberately *ambiguous*. In computer science, we are told that ambiguity is bad. In human dialog, however, ambiguity allows various interpretations to smooth over potential misunderstandings or differences of interest. For example, suppose agent A (junior) in example (2) has misunderstood the status of agent B (senior). A meant the utterance as a request. To save the situation, B can 'take up' the challenge with response B3, silently correcting the presupposition. Alternatively, B can respond with an exaggerated response B1 as a joke to signal the awkwardness of the situation.

Example (3) shows that why-questions can be ambiguous in a similar way. In general, a why-question asks for a reason or explanation. It signals that there is an explanandum, an issue to be explained. What exactly needs to be explained depends on the difference in knowledge between speaker A and addressee B. The various intonation contours of why-questions B1, B2, and B3 show that there are different ways to interpret the why-question (Hulstijn & van der Torre, 2023). Different intonation patterns signal a different focus of attention, which identifies the elements in the context to which alternatives may be considered (Rooth, 1992). In other words, they signal different elements of the context to be challenged. This extends to the presupposed social relationships and norms. Each variant B1–B3 reveals a different 'knowledge gap' of B about the social context (explanandum). Finally, A takes up this challenge, determines the explanans, resolves the explanandum (B1 and B2), and avoids the potential conflict about authority.

(3) A. You must do the dishes!
     B. Why?   challenge demand as a whole
     B1. Why *must* I do the dishes?   challenge authority
     B2. Why must *I* do the dishes?   challenge addressee
     B3. Why must I do the *dishes*?   challenge content
     A. Because someone must do the dishes and I don't have time.

8.9 Rapid Access to the Content of This Chapter

What are the design principles for developing an Explainable AI system that provides a trustworthy and convincing explanation dialogue? To understand that question, we have to realize that the participants in any dialogue are playing *roles*. Attached to these roles are *social conventions*. System designers must use these conventions to their advantage in order to make system behavior appear natural and easier to use. By contrast, when a system does not follow the social norms and conventions associated with a role, the system will be seen as awkward and will be harder to use.

In this book, we believe that an explanation should be provided step by step, in an interactive fashion. Such an everyday explanation does not may be called *explication*. Suppose that an AI system displays some intelligent behavior; for example, it supports a human end user in a decision task, as in Example (4). The system suggests to the user to select alternative A out of a range of options $\{A, B, C\}$. Naturally, the user will be inclined to ask "Why A?" or "Why not B?" Such a why-question signals that the user lacks knowledge about the reasons of

8 Roles and Relationships

the system to select *A* over other plausible alternatives. We call such a knowledge gap the *explanandum*, the issue to be explained (see Introduction). The system explains that option *A* has the highest return on investment. This may trigger further questions by the user. The optimization argument and the ROI table are part of what we call the *explanans*, the material for making the user understand the explanation, and resolve the explanandum.

4. S. There are three feasible alternatives: $\{A, B, C\}$. I suggest to select A.
   U Why A? Why not B?
   S. Because A has the highest expected return on investment:

	A	B	C
ROI	5600	4600	2200

   U. How did you calculate ROI?

This chapter studies the notion of *roles* and *role relationships* in social situations. Roles and role relations can be found at various levels and different time scales (utterance, dialog, social situation). For example, the roles of speaker and addressee quickly alternate between turns in a dialog. The roles of expert and novice remain stable throughout an information exchange but may change when a new dialog starts about a new topic. The roles of teacher and pupil remain stable over many interactions. They are associated with an education situation.

Roles are placeholders in a social situation, indicated by conventional signals, such as location or uniform. Roles are played by individuals (agents), but only when they qualify. An agent may play many roles. Conversely, one role may be played by many agents. When an agent has adopted a role, the agent must see to the responsibilities and social norms that are associated with the role. Given the role, we can predict the expertise, responsibilities, and powers of that role. So these social conventions and norms have both a prescriptive element (must) and a predictive element (expect).

Role relations or *dependencies* are relationships that are associated with the roles in a specific social situation. Consider relative expertise, trust, or authority. In Example (4), we assume that the system has relatively more (access to) knowledge about the decision options; otherwise, the system would not be in a position to give advice to the user. By contrast, we assume the user has relatively more knowledge about the decision criteria. The user remains responsible.

Roles appear at different *levels* and associated time frames. Turn-taking roles like speaker and hearer alternate repeatedly. Participant roles like explainer and explainee remain the same for an entire dialog of a particular genre. It is very common that one type of dialog is embedded in another type of dialog. For example, an explication dialog may be embedded in a negotiation dialog: "Why is it so expensive?". In that case, the roles of explainee–explainer are stacked on top of the roles of buyer–seller, of the negotiation. The role-playing relationship is subject to a number of constraints. For example, for an agent a to play role r, written $a : r$, a must be qualified. The responsibilities of all the roles an agent plays at one time must be mutually compatible. Such constraints can be specified in the form of a *multiagent system*.

In order to keep track of the dynamics of interactive dialogs, with role changes, we make use of a theoretical framework called *dialog games*. Interaction rules can be expressed as the rules of a game, specified as moves (communicative acts) of players (roles) that affect the state of a game board (dialog context). Following McBurney and Parsons (2002), a dialog game is defined by a set of rules with a semantics that is based on the changes to the commitment states of the participants:

1. participant roles,
2. for each role, initial commitment states,
3. for each role, vocabulary of moves (communicative acts),
4. for each role, valid sequences of moves (protocol),
5. for each move, expected change to the commitment states of all roles,
6. for each commitment change, rules to combine them or resolve conflicts,
7. turn taking, attention and grounding rules,
8. for each role, successful end conditions and failure conditions.

Finally, the chapter discusses the important role of *ambiguity* and interpretation in dialogs. In an explication dialog, what the explanandum is may be radically underspecified. Therefore, the *uptake* of the explainer partially determines what counts as the explanandum, further on in the dialog. If the explainer is wrong, the explainee must signal this and correct the explainer's presupposition. Therefore, both participants cocreate the explanation.

References

Allen, J. F. (1983). Maintaining knowledge about temporal intervals. *Communications of the ACM, 26*(11), 832–843. https://doi.org/10.1145/182.358434

Austin, J. L. (1962). *How to do things with words.* Harvard University Press.

Boella, G., Damiano, R., Hulstijn, J., & van der Torre, L. (2006). The roles of roles in agent communication languages. In *Proceedings of the International Conference on Intelligent Agent Technology (IAT 2006)* (pp. 381–384). IEEE. https://doi.org/10.1109/IAT.2006.119

Bresciani, P., Perini, A., Giorgini, P., Giunchiglia, F., & Mylopoulos, J. (2004). TROPOS: An agent-oriented software development methodology. *Journal of Autonomous Agents and Multi-Agent Systems, 8*, 203–236. https://doi.org/10.1023/B:AGNT.0000018806.20944.ef

Carlson, L. (1983). *Dialogue games.* Reidel. https://doi.org/10.1007/978-94-015-3963-0

Castelfranchi, C. (1998). Modelling social actions for AI agents. *Artificial Intelligence, 103*(1–2), 157–182. https://doi.org/10.1016/S0004-3702(98)00056-3

Chopra, A. K., & Singh, M. P. (2013). Agent communication. In G. Weiss (Ed.), *Multiagent systems: A modern approach to distributed artificial intelligence* (2nd ed., pp. 101–141) MIT Press.

Clark, H. H. (1996). *Using language.* Cambridge University Press. https://doi.org/10.1017/CBO9780511620539

Clark, H. H., & Schaefer, E. F. (1989). Contributing to discourse. *Cognitive Science, 13*(2), 259–294. https://doi.org/10.1207/s15516709cog1302_7

Cohen, P. R., & Raymond Perrault, C. (1979). Elements of a plan-based theory of speech acts. *Cognitive Science, 3*(3), 177–212. https://doi.org/10.1016/S0364-0213(79)80006-3

FIPA. (2002). *FIPA communicative act library specification*. Tech. rep. 00037. Foundation for Intelligent Physical Agents.

Goffman, E. (1981). *Forms of talk*. University of Pennsylvania Press.

Hempel, C. G. (1965). *Aspects of scientific explanation and other essays in the philosophy of science*. The Free Press. https://doi.org/10.1086/288305

Hulstijn, J. (2000). Dialogue games are recipes for joint action. In *Proceedings of 4th Workshop on Formal Semantics and Pragmatics of Dialogue (Götalog'00)* (pp. 99–106).

Hulstijn, J., & Maudet, N (2006). Uptake and joint action. *Cognitive Systems Research, 7*(2–3), 175–191. https://doi.org/10.1016/j.cogsys.2005.11.002

Hulstijn, J., & van der Torre, L. (2023). What should I do and why? In *Proceedings of 16th International Conference on Deontic Logic and Normative Systems (DEON 2023)* (pp. 335–336). College Publications.

Lewis, D. (1979). Scorekeeping in a language game. *Journal of Philosophical Logic, 9*, 339–359. https://doi.org/10.1007/BF00258436

Madumal, P., Miller, T., Sonenberg, L., & Vetere, F. (2019). A grounded interaction protocol for explainable artificial intelligence. In *Proceedings of the 18th International Conference on Autonomous Agents and MultiAgent Systems (AAMAS 2019)* (pp. 1033–1041). International Foundation for Autonomous Agents and Multiagent Systems.

Malone, T. W., & Crowston, K. (1994). The interdisciplinary study of coordination. *ACM Computing Surveys, 26*(1), 87–119. https://doi.org/10.1145/174666.174668

Mann, W. C. (1988). Dialogue games: Conventions of human interaction. *Argumentation, 2*, 511–532. https://doi.org/10.1007/BF00128990

McBurney, P., & Parsons, S (2002). Games that agents play: A formal framework for dialogues between autonomous agents. *Journal of Logic, Language and Information, 11*(3), 315–334. https://doi.org/10.1023/A:1015586128739

McBurney, P., & Parsons, S. (2009). Dialogue games for agent argumentation. In G. Simari & Rahwan, I. (Eds.), *Argumentation in artificial intelligence* (pp. 261–280). Springer. https://doi.org/10.1007/978-0-387-98197-0_13

Miller, T. (2019). Explanation in artificial intelligence: Insights from the social sciences. *Artificial Intelligence, 267*, 1–38. https://doi.org/10.1016/j.artint.2018.07.007

Partsakoulakis, I., & Vouros, G. (2004). Roles in MAS. In T. A. Wagner & J. Hulstijn (Eds.), *An Application science for multi-agent systems* (pp. 133–154). Springer.

Rohlfing, K. J., Cimiano, P., Scharlau, I., Matzner, T., Buhl, H., Buschmeier, H., Grimminger, A., Hammer, B., Häb-Umbach, R., Horwath, I., Hüllermeier, E., Kern, F., Kopp, S., Thommes, K., Ngonga Ngomo, A.-C., Schulte, C., Wachsmuth, H., Wagner, P., & Wrede, B (2021). Explanation as a social practice: Toward a conceptual framework for the social design of AI systems. *IEEE Transactions on Cognitive and Developmental Systems, 13*(3), 717–728. https://doi.org/10.1109/TCDS.2020.3044366

Rooth, M. (1992). A theory of focus interpretation. *Natural Language Semantics, 1*(1), 75–116. https://doi.org/10.1007/BF02342617

Sacks, H., Schegloff, E. A., & Jefferson, G. (1974). A simplest systematics for the organisation of turn-taking for conversation. *Language, 50*, 696–735. https://doi.org/10.2307/412243

Schank, R. C., & Abelson, R. P. (1977). *Scripts, plans, goals and under- standing: An inquiry into human knowledge structures*. Erlbaum.

Searle, J. R. (1969). *Speech acts: An essay in the philosophy of language*. Cambridge University Press. https://doi.org/10.1017/CBO9781139173438

Steimann, F. (2000). On the representation of roles in object-oriented and conceptual modelling. *Data and Knowledge Engineering, 35*(1), 83–106. https://doi.org/10.1016/S0169-023X(00)00023-9

Tuomela, R. (2000). *Cooperation: A philosophical study*. Springer. https://doi.org/10.1007/978-94-015-9594-0

Walton, D. N., & Krabbe, E. C. (1995). *Commitment in dialogue: Basic concepts of interpersonal reasoning*. State University of New York Press.
Wooldridge, M. (2009). *An introduction to multiagent systems* (2nd ed.). John Wiley and Sons.

Open Access This chapter is licensed under the terms of the Creative Commons Attribution 4.0 International License (http://creativecommons.org/licenses/by/4.0/), which permits use, sharing, adaptation, distribution and reproduction in any medium or format, as long as you give appropriate credit to the original author(s) and the source, provide a link to the Creative Commons license and indicate if changes were made.

The images or other third party material in this chapter are included in the chapter's Creative Commons license, unless indicated otherwise in a credit line to the material. If material is not included in the chapter's Creative Commons license and your intended use is not permitted by statutory regulation or exceeds the permitted use, you will need to obtain permission directly from the copyright holder.

Chapter 9
Responsibilities in sXAI

Katharina J. Rohlfing ⓘ, Suzana Alpsancar ⓘ, and Carsten Schulte ⓘ

Abstract One of the purposes for which XAI is often brought into play is to enable a user to act responsibly. However, responsibility is a complex normative and social phenomenon that we unfold in this chapter. We consider that the classical concepts of agency and responsibility do not fully capture what is needed for meaningful collaboration between human users and XAI. Advocating the perspective of sXAI, we argue that the growing adaptivity of AI systems will result in sXAI being considered as partners. Both partners adopt particular (dialogical) roles within a collaborative process and take responsibility for them. We expect that these roles lead to reactive attitudes toward the sXAI on the side of the human partners that make these roles relational. They resemble those reactive attitudes that we hold toward other human agents. For agents to exercise their responsibility, they need to possess agential capacities to fulfill their role with respect to the structure of a social interaction. Hence, sXAI can be expected to act responsibly. But because of XAI's limited normative capacities, it might rather act as a marginal agent. We refer to marginal agents and show they can be scaffolded with regard to their agential capacities and their knowledge about the structure of a social interaction. The structure links the actions of the partners to each other in terms of a set of stimuli and responses to it in pursuit of a particular goal. Hence, it is important to differentiate between the

---

Authors Katharina J. Rohlfing and Suzana Alpsancar have equal contribution.

K. J. Rohlfing (✉)
Psycholinguistics, Faculty of Arts and Humanities, Paderborn University, Paderborn, Germany
e-mail: katharina.rohlfing@uni-paderborn.de

S. Alpsancar
Heinz Nixdorf Institute, Department of Philosophy, Faculty of Arts and Humanities, Paderborn University, Paderborn, Germany
e-mail: suzana.alpsancar@uni-paderborn.de

C. Schulte
Computer Science Education, Paderborn University, Paderborn, Germany
e-mail: carsten.schulte@uni-paderborn.de

© The Author(s) 2026
K. J. Rohlfing et al. (eds.), *Social Explainable AI*,
https://doi.org/10.1007/978-981-96-5290-7_9

different goals that a structure can impose for exercising responsibility. Therefore, we follow (Responsibility from the margins. Oxford University Press; 2015. https://doi.org/10.1093/acprof:oso/9780198715672.24001.0001) and offer three structures that can help to organize responsibility for *decisions made* with the assistance of AI systems. These structures are attributability, answerability, and accountability. Our insights will inform the development and design process of XAI to meet the guiding principles of responsible research and innovation as well as trustworthy AI.

9.1 How Does This Chapter Relate to XAI?

It is common sense to hold decision-makers responsible for their decisions. However, who should be held responsible when a physician makes a decision that was supported by an AI? The black-box character (Santoni de Sio & Mecacci, 2021) of the decision-support systems (DSS) on the one hand and the new form of agency they facilitate on the other hand challenge that existing practice. Thus, one of the central questions in the recent discussion about the use of black-box AI in high-stake fields is whether this leads to a "responsibility gap" (Coeckelbergh 2021; Matthias 2004, p. 174; Santoni de Sio and Mecacci 2021), either because there is no basis for a joint responsibility attribution (humans reason in a different way than current black-box systems operating on statistical knowledge) or because the agents involved presumably cannot justifiably be assigned responsibility for the performance of the opaque systems (see 9.2 for more details).

In response to these problems, XAI promises to facilitate responsibility. The promise covers different aspects (see next section), but the most important is that by rendering an explainable output, the system makes the user able to "exercise responsible agency" (Coeckelbergh, 2020, p. 2061).

The big promise of XAI is justified, because providing relevant and effective explanations can serve as a reason to change people's behavior. Reasons are seen as something from which a normative force can emanate.[1] In general, explanations often facilitate future actions (O'Hara, 2020) even in a minimalistic sense by reducing arbitrariness. This function also resonates with our modern idea of individual freedom and democratic self-governance with the ability to provide reasons for one's actions and decisions and to be able to respond to reasons (Vredenburgh, 2022; Wasserman-Rozen et al., 2023).

Up to now, there is still little discussion in the literature about how that function of facilitating responsibility may play out in real XAI-interaction scenarios in either the technical and social or the ethical/legal sense.

In this chapter, following the perspective outlined in Sect. 1.5, we promote an understanding of XAI as a process of social interaction that unfolds for a specific purpose. After reviewing the connection between responsibility and agency from

---

[1] This normative force is the reason why XAI can be understood as an influencing technology with the accompanying urge to weigh up both the opportunities and the risks have (see Sect. 30.1).

a Technology Ethics perspective in 9.2, in Sect. 9.3, we lay the ground for our developmental approach to responsibility. This advocates the perspective of sXAI, according to which a successful explanation requires XAI to adapt to the user's forms of understanding in a process of social interaction that unfolds for a specific purpose. In Sect. 9.4, we refer to marginal agents and show they can be scaffolded with regard to their agential capacities and their knowledge about the structure of a social interaction. We claim that XAI may better live up to the promise of facilitating responsibility if it can provide a relevant explanation in a given explanatory situation. This implies that at the beginning of the explanatory dialog, it does not have to be clear what the relevant explanation consists of, but that this will emerge during the process of explaining (Rohlfing et al., 2021) and selecting "what is relevant to the other" (Coeckelbergh, 2020, p. 2063). This allows an XAI system to adapt on a case-specific basis (see Chap. 13 on Adaptation), and is in line with discussions over which XAI technique is suitable for which case to bridge the alleged responsibility gap (Königs, 2022; Taylor, 2024).

9.2 Responsibility and Agency

We start with some foundations. Our modern responsibility practices are deeply linked to our understanding of agency (Talbert, 2024). According to the standard account of responsibility, only agents exhibiting or meant to hold specific abilities can be seen as responsible (or moral) agents, and they are responsible only for those doings and events that they can effectively control and foresee in a 'suitable sense' (Fischer & Ravizza, 1998):

> That means that the agent can be considered responsible only if s/he knows the particular facts surrounding his action, and if s/he is able to freely form a decision to act, and to select one of a suitable set of available alternative actions based on these facts. (Matthias, 2004, p. 175)

Thus, agents must be in control and know what they are doing in order for them to be held responsible and for them to act responsibly (Coeckelbergh, 2021). Reasonable as it is, this simple view cannot be maintained when we consider the social practice of exercising agency (Strawson, 1963; Watson, 2004). For instance, think of the responsibility that parents hold toward their children, or professionals hold toward their job assignments, and owners over their belongings—it seems that we hold the mentioned agents (parents, professionals, owners) responsible for quite a lot of things that they can neither control directly nor foresee.

What a social practice of ascribing responsibility organizes is the way of how we strive to get things done as desired and how we cope when this turns out differently. This is reflected in a series of typical "reactive attitudes" that we hold toward each other (and ourselves) such as resentment, indignation, and guilt (Strawson 1963, p. 75; Wallace 2022. It is important to note that usually, only "adult human beings" (Talbert, 2024) who are considered to be typical qualify as moral agents with knowledge about these reactive attitudes. This implies that not only animals, plants, products, and systems but also nontypical adult human beings do not count as responsible agents. To not draw a strict line between responsible and nonresponsible agents but to rather to embrace diverse agents, some scholars propose to understand responsibility as a gradual matter (Coates & Swenson, 2013). More specifically, Shoemaker (2015, p. 65) points to "marginal agents" toward whom we hold ambivalent reactive attitudes. *Marginal agents* – denoting individuals as babies, (small) children, or persons with handicaps such as dementia or psychoses – do not completely fall into the category of a typical adult human being. Consequently, it would not be appropriate to blame marginal agents in the same way in which we blame typical adults. However, this marginality does not imply that we are free from expectations toward these agents. Instead, in social practice, we still have morally loaded emotions and responses toward them, out of which some might be appropriate in terms of their agential capacities.

To account for the fact that we respond to doings and nondoings of marginal agents, Shoemaker (2015, p. 64) proposes to further differentiate dimensions of responsibility and to link them to not only different "agential capacities" on the side of the responsible agent but also to different responsive attitudes that other people have toward the responsible agent. We will come to this account later in Sect. 9.3. Here, we propose transferring this differentiation to the interaction with artificial agents.

Let us elaborate on the responsibility problem in more detail and relate it to the current AI systems. Above, we have referred to the traditional axiom for responsibility, which is that agents must be in control and know what they are doing in order for them to be held responsible and for them to act responsibly (Talbert, 2024). This is limited in AI based on algorithms that operate on statistical knowledge designed to maintain a high level of learning performance. As a result, the AI can extend its function to new tasks and contexts, without the user reasoning the same way and being able to predict its outcome. In addition to this "responsibility gap" (Matthias, 2004, p. 174), the proposition that if not the function of the AI, then the person who developed it should be responsible, brings in the problem of "many hands" (Coeckelbergh, 2020, p. 2056): Many agents at various stages are involved in the process of developing an AI, making it is impossible to single out one individual who could be held as the agent responsible for this AI. In addition, there is the problem of "many things" (Coeckelbergh, 2020, p. 2058) capturing the fact that an AI consists of various components such as data, software, material, and the relations between things. Again, many agents contribute to these components. Accordingly, we are left with the problem that the attribution of responsibility for an AI is considered to be impossible.

To bridge these abovementioned responsibility gaps, we suggest that instead of discussing the agency of AI, we should consider its "agential capacities" (Shoemaker, 2015, p. 64), as we do within a social practice of dealing with marginal agents. Our perspective links up with relational responsibility as suggested by Coeckelbergh (2020) and Coeckelbergh and Loh (2020), meaning that agential capacities only unfold in given social settings. These settings determine to a large degree the scope of interaction in terms of agential roles, patterns, expectations, and the like. In such social settings, skills are exercised in relation to the participating agents. This is true for artificial as well as human agents. Accordingly, autonomy should not be misunderstood as a property of technical systems, but as an attribute of the sociotechnical system—that is, the type of interaction between humans and technology in specific settings with their specific conditions. In other words, the agential capacities of artificial agents are those potentials that can unfold in these relations. For explanatory dialog, it means that each partner can be conceptualized as executing some form of local autonomy (Oshana, 2002) depending on the unfolding interaction, and, hereby, on the different roles that are negotiated throughout the interaction (Schilling et al., 2016). In sum, we propose to tie the classical questions about responsibility and agency to the relationship between the user and XAI, which accords with the relational view advocated by Coeckelbergh (2020). To this end, it makes sense to start from the relational roles in which the user and XAI (or AI) stand. In the following section, we will provide a solid base for how agents develop their agential capacities in social acts by drawing on the developmental theory on social cognition proposed by Mead (1946).

9.3 Responsibilities in an Interaction and the Structure of Explaining: A Developmental View

We now focus on the explanatory dialog between a user and an XAI. Let us think of it as a classical division of labor between the explainer (the person who knows more and explains) and the explainee (the person who knows less and needs to gain knowledge).[2] An explanation is a process in which the explainer and the explainee work toward an understanding and toward a symmetry in knowledge and understanding that can take various forms (Buschmeier et al., 2025). There is a structure to this explanatory dialog, described in Chap. 23, which the partners follow. To recapitulate, based on convincing developmental research showing that young children can discern and enact the structure and anticipate the contribution of an involved partner, we assume that partners work along this structure collaboratively to achieve the joint goal.

In the following, we analyze how the partners are responsible for pursuing the joint goal (to achieve a relevant explanation). Hereby, it is important to realize that albeit it is clear what the shared goal is in general – namely, a relevant explanation to bring about understanding (see Chap. 6) – what the relevant explanation consists of in each dialog remains an open question. According to the core idea of sXAI, the interaction can lead to a relevant explanation, implying that the specification of the relevant explanation only emerges through the interaction (Groom & Nass, 2007, p. 488). Now, the interesting question is: how does the specification of the shared

---

[2] Although it should be noted that these classical roles are not strict in everyday explanations and can be reversed in the course of the dialog.

goal emerge along the ongoing distribution of individual tasks and turn-takings? Whereas in the literature, it is discussed that in collaboration, humans adapt to each other to distribute and align actions that are needed to achieve a goal (Converse et al., 1993), little is known about how this distribution takes place. Here, we argue that insights from development and learning might reveal not only how actions are distributed but also how humans reach an alignment with the goal.

Our following considerations about how partners take responsibility for an explanation follow the theoretical approach by Mead (1946), a social psychologist. He considers each individual act within a social act. Imagine here a child playing the role of, for example, being a seller.[3] There is a set of acts (behaviors) that the child will perform in order to play this role such as asking for needs, handling objects that are to be sold, requesting money, and handling it. In addition, the acts are linked to a particular sort of responses that the child would like to elicit in others (Mead, 1946, p. 151). For example, following a request for money such as "this will cost you 1 Euro," a response of paying is expected from the buyer. Children – already at the age of 2 years – sometimes play different roles with themselves. In this case, a child says something in one character, which is then a stimulus to respond in another character, and so on. Both roles depend on each other and are tightly interrelated. The same is true for the role of an explainer and explainee who also depend on each other, because they provide a set of stimuli to which specific responses are elicited. Mead (1946, p. 151) summarizes this phenomenon with the structure (see Chap. 7) that the playing child is following. This structure – also dubbed a *practice* or *pragmatic frame* (see Chap. 5) – combines both the child's assumption about a set of stimuli and the responses to it. The fact that even young children can follow it demonstrates that, obviously, it can be remembered and easily retrieved.

When both partners are humans and familiar with the task, it is easy to assume that they can both know the structure, act accordingly, and within a framework of expectations. In this sense, responsibility can be ascribed to any acts and decisions made by humans with whom they are familiar and who knows the structure. It is more difficult to ascribe responsibility if one of the partners is an artificial system. In this respect, we need to differentiate between what systems are, or will be, available. Real collaboration becomes possible by moving away from systems that are limited to only a one-way transition of information. The necessary movement is toward interaction as embodied actions in which "a joint understanding of an action is established with the AI for an effective collaboration in a given domain" (Chromik & Butz, 2021, p. 14). For the design of XAI, it means that the joint understanding of actions is a prerequisite for an XAI to make use of a structure of an interaction (see Chap. 7). Albeit the content, form, and type of the specific relevant explanation cannot be known in advance, what we can determine in advance is a general structure regarding the knowledge of how to enact the practice of explaining

---

[3] Note that the child playing the social practice of selling and buying does not evoke the figure of a marginal moral agent, but rather represents a simple but core structure of social interactions in general.

(see Chap. 23 for more details on the structure of explaining). We assume that the typical sXAI is capable of responding to explanatory requests, initiating a dialogue with the user, fulfilling the explanatory dialog (social interaction), and providing different kinds of information and knowledge. This calls for adaptive technologies that are currently being developed (Rohlfing et al., 2021; Sokol & Flach, 2020).

The consequences of such technological developments are that they can be perceived as a partner or teammate; and the interaction between a user and such a system can be perceived as an interpersonal interaction (see Chap. 11 for systems able of interpersonal interaction). This perception has consequences for the attribution of responsibility. We propose that the growing adaptivity of AI systems will result in them being perceived as having agential capacities and being considered as responsible partners within the collaborative progress toward a joint goal (see Chap. 6 for shared goals). Each of the partners contributes toward achieving this goal. For example, there are XAI that can adjust to the human partners in the sense that they provide an answer to a question (Sokol & Flach, 2020). The adjustment to the user, thus, provides information tailored to what the user wants to know. For this, the system disposes of a repertoire of actions from which it can choose one that seems appropriate. However, this kind of adjustment appears to be quite limited because, for example, the user can only ask questions and never change the role. In addition, the system is not able to cope with unforeseen questions or a change in the explanandum. Thus, more flexible forms of adjustment should follow.

In other words, we expect that the social character of interacting with XAI leads to reactive attitudes on the side of the human partner toward the XAI that resemble those reactive attitudes that we hold toward other human agents. With these requirements, we propose that it is legitimate in a specific sense to ascribe some responsibility to the acting of an XAI in line with its capacities as an artificial agent. This is because the explanatory dialgue can be considered as joint actions. These actions are performed by both partners and organized toward a common goal, namely, gaining a relevant explanation for the situation at hand and reaching a form of understanding. Thus, the XAI should be ready to respond to the demand for answers to why it suggested a certain solution or performed a certain individual turn (Miller, 2023, p. 338). It should also be capable of giving an adequate response if the human partner attributes certain individual acts to its agency, and along with these, a responsibility to steer or scaffold the dialog in a certain direction. If the XAI fails to provide this, it does not fulfill its role as a partner in finding a relevant explanation.

9.4 Scaffolding Agential Capacities in an Interaction with Marginal Agents

Conceiving the explanatory dialog as a real collaboration – that is, as a social interaction governed by the emerging concretization of a joint goal (Groom & Nass, 2007, p. 488) – yields another vital responsibility dimension and raises the question regarding who is responsible for achieving the shared goal of a relevant explanation (see Chaps. 11 and 6).

We can offer an answer to this question by focusing on agential capacities in social acts. If we think of the explanatory dialog as a joint action, we can assume two cases: one case in which both partners know about the structure and act accordingly and a second case in which one partner has little knowledge about (or awareness of) the structure, with the result that the other has to take the lead and the responsibility for performing it. Thus, in a joint action, each partner is responsible for a contribution, and in the case in which both are aware of the structure and form of the practice, both hold a shared responsibility for its adequate unfolding. To give a simple everyday example, buying bread in a bakery can be seen as a joint action with the shared goal of a successful transaction. Imagine one partner would not comply with the norm. For example, the buyer enters and asks for bread, and the seller does not act accordingly but tells the time. Thus, in a very basic sense, both partners are responsible for the successful unfolding of a practice, but only insofar as they are familiar with that practice. In this vein, Clark and Schaefer (1989, p. 263) consider contributions of the partners to be "participatory" rather than "autonomous" acts.

The participatory nature, just described above, makes an interaction adaptive (Pol et al., 2023), and, therefore, resilient to asymmetrical cases. Let us consider such a case, in which one partner has little awareness of the structure according to which the interaction unfolds. Because of this knowledge asymmetry, the other (more knowledgeable) partner has not only to recognize the goal of the interaction but also to take the responsibility as well as the lead for it, and guide the interaction toward it. This case is particularly interesting because of its dynamics: While guiding the less knowledgeable partner, the more knowledgeable person is providing some support with regard to detecting the underlying structure. This support is called "scaffolding" (Wood et al., 1976, p. 90). In developmental and educational literature, scaffolding is a way of interaction allowing novices to participate (Van de Pol et al., 2010). An example would be an XAI system that offers a learner a rich set of information, reducing it next time to only a few items in order to elicit a greater contribution from the learner. Such a system could be applied in assisting a human user who assembles materials. The user needs to learn specific actions that follow on from each other (see Chap. 6 on Goals). At first, the XAI could explain every single action for the user. But subsequently, it could fade the assistance away and explain (or guide through) only those actions that have turned out to be more difficult.

The advantages of scaffolded participation can be described as a "legitimate peripheral participation" (Rojas-Drummond et al., 2013, p. 12) that gives the novice a first sense of the task. A system could scaffold such a participation by instructing for every action that needs to be taken. This is similar to a caregiver telling a child how to look at a book and making explicit every action. It is important to highlight that scaffolding is a dynamic process because after participating in an interaction once, a novice can extend their own contribution based on this experience and move forward to fulfill a more central role in a repeated interaction. According to Van de Pol et al. (2010), this fulfillment goes hand in hand with a transfer of responsibilities and the fading of scaffolding. In our example, the novice will gain some knowledge about the actions to be performed. Some memory of these can be retrieved the next time they are performed, requiring less scaffolding. Whereas fading of scaffolding refers to the behaviors of the more knowledgeable partner offering less and less support, transfer of responsibilities refers to the eventual reliance on the other partner's knowledge about the structure, and this becomes manifested in appropriate (responsible) task performance. The example of a user learning how to assemble materials demonstrates both the increase in the user's responsibility for the product and the decrease in the scaffolding that the XAI system provides in support. "Scaffolding is temporary, gradually transferring more responsibility to novices so as to promote the eventual appropriation of knowledge and abilities" (Rojas-Drummond et al., 2013, p. 12). In addition to promoting appropriate knowledge of the structure and related abilities, by scaffolding, novices experience the division of actions and how they can put them together collaboratively to accomplish a goal (see Chap. 6 on Goals). This ability, namely, to know how a task can be divided collaboratively, and – even further – how more or less responsibility can be attributed to the collaborators depending on their contribution, is lacking in current technologies. As a result, they can barely simulate and complement the contribution of the other partner in a meaningful way. However, this ability is important in order to have a sense of the structure that consists of sequences of actions. It is exactly this ability that is becoming observable in the role-play of a child, who can execute both parts: acts as stimuli that then elicit responses (Mead, 1946, p. 151). Interestingly, a child can already take this group of responses and organize them into a certain whole—that is, the structure of the interaction that is then retrieved for the role-play. Correspondingly, for an sXAI system to have a similar ability, it needs to consider its own actions in relation to the other partner—that is, depending on the responses that they can elicit. Accordingly, it means to foster and cultivate the agency of the sXAI. The assumption is that if a system were to have the ability of adaptivity and collaboration (see Chap. 11), it would qualify as a legitimate subject for the attribution of the particular role responsibility that corresponds to being a partner in an explanatory dialog.

9.5 Responsibilities for Decisions: A Social Interaction View

Above, we argued for a perspective in which partners have knowledge about the structure of an interaction and expect a contribution of the other partner to it in the form of a collaborative act (Clark & Schaefer, 1989). In this sense, partners act in a participatory and adaptive manner, enabling each other to exercise their skills.

Let us now consider the interaction with an sXAI. Simply put, an sXAI system enables the user to "exercise responsible agency" (Coeckelbergh, 2021, p. 2061). Because it is a social setting, the relevant output should make further actions possible. However, there is a particular demand for an explanation to be relevant for the receiver(s) in a "relational" manner (Coeckelbergh, 2020, p. 2061). In the case of a decision support system in the healthcare scenario described in Sect. 2.4, there are two receivers: The physician is the first (receiving an explanation from the XAI) and the patient is the second (receiving an explanation from the physician). Thus, in this scenario, agency is to be exercised from two perspectives (Coeckelbergh, 2020; Coeckelbergh & Loh, 2020). Consequently, the XAI is expected to serve as responsibility-enabling in such a way that the physician is ready to take responsibility for their decision about the diagnosis and the treatment. In addition, it also empowers the agency of the patients who is affected by the decision and may justly hold the physician responsible for the decision made.

Let us now analyze this case in more detail. For the analysis of responsibilities, we take the sXAI view and advocate responsibility as a social practice. As already mentioned above, a social practice requires knowledge about a set of stimuli and the appropriate responses to it (see Chap. 5 on Practices). Our view aligns with Coeckelbergh (2020, p. 2061) and recognizes the relational and communicative nature of responsibility. Following Shoemaker (2015, p. 34), we differentiate between "accountability, attributability, and answerability" as different social practices of responsibility attribution, resp. enabling responsibility. Each of these practices has its own structure and entails different dialogical roles as well as responsive attitudes (Tigard, 2021). In the following, we specify the structure and roles that can be expected:

- Accountability concerns mostly liability issues in the legal sense and the agent's (strong) moral feelings. To "hold one to account is to engage in more overt forms of blame like directed anger" (Tigard, 2021, p. 599). The corresponding attitudes toward accountability are therefore anger/resentment or gratitude.
- Attributability refers to a capacity to attribute individual action to an agent reflecting "their underlying cares or commitments" (Tigard, 2021, p. 599). This attribution implies some form of judgment about the goodness or adequateness of that action, and this is typically linked to the respective agent's capacities. It relates to those reactive attitudes we hold toward the character of responsible agents—for example, admiration or disdain.[4]
- Answerability comes into play when agents have the ability to respond to other's demands "for justification by citing their judgments about the worth of some reasons over others" (Shoemaker, 2015, p. 64). We demand answers from others about their doings "in order to evaluate their judgment and understand their reasons for action" (Tigard, 2021, p. 599). This might very well happen in an XAI-user interaction.

With this differentiation, we can now discern that in the case in which sXAI empowers the physician (user) as a responsible agent, the patient is also empowered in the sense that they can justly attribute the decision made to the physician (attributability) and demand answers (answerability), or to review the decision-

---

[4] We slightly adjust understanding of attributability proposed by Shoemaker (2015). We do not hold it as an attitude toward the expression of the "deep self" of the partner, which makes no sense in light of AI systems. Rather, we see it as the capacity to first attribute an individual action to an agent at all.

making process. In terms of the joint action and reconstructing the process during which that shared goal was achieved, the user might attribute certain steps, including the further direction of the explanatory dialog to the individual contribution of the sXAI at a certain time/step within the dialog. In this sense, it seems reasonable to attribute the cause of the further direction of the explanatory dialog to the sXAI.

This analysis makes clear that the appropriate attribution of responsibility depends on the agential capacities and the dialogical roles. Because we propose a gradual account of responsibility, we can circumvent the black-and-white thinking in most of the current ethics-of-AI debate. For instance, to say XAI is a responsible agent within an explanatory dialogue does not imply that it is the same kind of moral agent that we usually hold human adults to be.[5] This distinction is particularly important when it comes to accountability issues, which are the focus of most articles. In our view, it makes no sense to hold an XAI legally or morally accountable for its actions, because practically nothing follows from that. If the XAI was legally accountable for liability issues, it would need to possess the necessary capital to pay for the damage that occurred. If it could not pay, how could someone punish it? Thus, the social categories of accountability simply seem to be unfit for interaction with artificial agents. If accountability is necessary, it would make practical sense to hold the manufacturer or operator accountable in terms of meeting quality standards for the respective product and its proper deployment; and in the sense of duties of care, to expect them to do their best to prevent malfunctioning and potential risks as well as to be ready to improve systems from experiences gained. It also seems reasonable to hold the facilities (e.g., a clinic) accountable for deploying specific systems, including the risks of deployment. In terms of attitudes, if we expect a person whom we hold accountable to regret their doing, this corresponds with attitudes of anger and practices of blaming. Forgiveness can lead to a fresh start in an interpersonal relationship, but when interacting with an sXAI system, other forms or redoing the interaction seem to be more productive.

9.6 Operationalizations of Responsibilities and Responsibilities When Designing XAI

Above, we have proposed that for a responsible agent, it is essential to understand the structure of the social interaction in which the responsibility is to be exercised.

---

[5] So far, the question of the moral status of AI systems has often been treated in too undifferentiated a manner. Most positions start from properties of the systems, from which they then either deduce either that they should not be classified as moral agents under any circumstances or that they must be classified as moral agents. For instance, Bryson (2010) argues that their status as goods and property prohibits a categorization as moral agents, whereas Sullins (2006, p. 28) argues that if robots have a sufficient degree of autonomy and their purpose is to fulfill a "social role that carries with it some assumed responsibilities," such as duties of care in healthcare facilities, then we can only make sense of the robot's behavior if we hold it to be a responsible agent.

What follows from this is that to promote the responsibility-enabling function of XAI in the sense of attributability and answerability, it is important to analyze the different forms of a structure unfolding in the respective sociotechnical setting for a specific purpose. Generally, we see the emerging need to differentiate between two kinds of structures.

First, there is the structure within an interaction, as elaborated above (see Chap. 23). It can be defined as the template for actions that are necessary to fulfill a goal or a task. One operationalization could be the number of critical actions that are needed for the goal or task (or the final ratification of these actions). However, because the actions are participatory (taking the other partner into account), and therefore adaptive, deciding whether an action is *critical* for a goal might depend on the context and therefore not straightforward. Another possibility is to operationalize responsibility as a capability of handling the structure of a particular interaction pattern and acting as a partner in a joint task. In this case, testing whether the person's "answerability" (Coeckelbergh, 2020, p. 2063) to stimuli or whether the person can play different roles in the task could attest to knowledge about the structure. As new social practices emerge, there will be new roles and new forms of responsibilities linked to them (see Chap. 5). For example, a practice aiming toward direct critical thinking might yield "contestability" (Alfrink et al., 2023, p. 614) as a further outcome of responsibility-enabling XAI, and this could mean that the users received information allowing them to argue against a decision or classification (Royal Society, 2019).

Second, the structure can also be seen as awareness of the actions that are necessary to fulfill a goal and of other agents who are affected by their actions. Because of the metalevel that is needed for such an awareness, we call it a metastructure of interaction—that is, possible responsibility relations in which an interaction is embedded (see also Chap. 6 for Metaknowledge). This is the case when the explainee's questions go beyond queries concerning the technology and its function and are more about "imagining the ways in which they might be affected" (Coeckelbergh, 2020, p. 2063). The ways in which explainees might be affected can be manifold and range from a direct context of interaction to a broader context of organizational structures. An XAI could support this by overviewing the landscape of stakeholders and making the decision-making procedures explainable (Ali et al., 2023, p. 41). This would facilitate the agent's responsible actions on the basis of being informed about all kinds of consequences resulting from the decisions and actions with the XAI. In the words of Santoni de Sio and Mecacci (2021, p. 1066), the explanation that the AI is providing in this case of overviewing the landscape of stakeholders and pointing out consequences resulting from the decision might be necessary not only due to technical black boxes but also to the organizational (because an AI is implemented for purposes) and legal (as an AI is an intellectual property that does not "fit easily in the traditional intellectual property categories") black boxes that emerge (Noto La Diega, 2018, p. 12). This could be assessed using a questionnaire for different groups such as the developers or the end users to reveal how they (over)view the "ecology of responsibility relations" (Coeckelbergh, 2020, p. 2062) within the decision-making procedures when using an XAI. If we recognize that such an overview makes sense to us as humans (Coeckelbergh, 2021), we should make efforts to design XAI that are capable of engaging with us for this purpose. We see this topic emerging from the current discussion of XAI, and it is up to future research to investigate in what way – that is, with what set of questions about the affected ways – explainees might seek to explore the "ecology of responsibility relations" (Coeckelbergh, 2020, p. 2062) in order to figure out their responsibilities on a metalevel of reflection. The development of AI should then support this human task of giving reasons to those who ask or may ask questions about the actions and decisions mediated by the technology (Coeckelbergh, 2020, p. 2064), even though it might be impossible to sufficiently predict all relevant consequences and behaviors in advance (Santoni de Sio & Mecacci, 2021, p. 1074). Nonetheless, the human agency and thus human responsibility can only be supported through meaningful and relevant answers.

Hence, in the end, the two structures are relevant for responsibility: one zooming in on the interaction that unfolds along a specific structure (see Chap. 23) and the other zooming out from the interaction and being more on the metalevel. They belong together: It is the ability to engage in adaptivity and collaboration that qualifies a system to bear responsibility. This ability can only be exercised only in an interaction. The design of such a system needs to be compatible with human agency and how human responsibilities can be supported. For this design, it is crucial to have a clear and broad picture of the "ecology of responsibility relations" (Coeckelbergh, 2020, p. 2062) as has been suggested recently for trustworthy artificial intelligence (Ali et al., 2023).

From our perspective, besides liability and accountability issues, we consider two questions to be relevant for the responsible design of sXAI following from our view:

(1) What qualities does the sXAI component need to be able to assume the role of a responsible partner in a dialog with users?
(2) What should be considered in the development of sXAI to promote the responsibility-enabling function for users and those affected?

Based on our given presumption that (2) can be facilitated by the achievement of a relevant explanation via interacting with the XAI, all designers' good intentions should go to (1)—it implies that the XAI is capable of determining whether or not it is familiar with the practice at hand. Because of its familiarity with the structure, the XAI components must be able to determine the role of the partner in the explanatory dialog on a case-specific basis. This means adapting to the requirements of the circumstances, the purpose, and the user. In principle, three options are conceivable here, based on the criterion of what prior knowledge exists on the part of the user and the XAI:

(i) The knowledge is symmetrical about the shared goal—in this case, the responsibility for achieving the goal should be shared between the two partners by anticipating and complementing each other's contribution.

(ii) The knowledge is asymmetrical in such a way that the XAI has more relevant knowledge about the overall structure than the user—in this case, the XAI has a greater responsibility. Accordingly, it should take on a more (pro)active role in the joint concretization of the relevant explanation, both in terms of content (e.g., by making suggestions, asking questions, informing about facts and contexts) and in terms of the organization of the collaboration (e.g., by guiding the dialog, offering the user suggestions on how to proceed (rough plan/goal), and stimulating turn-taking).

(iii) The knowledge is asymmetrical the other way round: The user knows more about the structure—in this case, the XAI should be guided more, which can only be possible when the XAI is adaptable and can learn for future interactions.

Finally, it should be highlighted that so far, systems are not answerable to their interaction partners. We assumed that if a system had the ability to engage in adaptivity and collaboration, it would qualify as being responsible. Yet imagine that a system is able to engage in symmetric interaction like a human partner, as we sketched for the case (i) and (ii): Should an XAI also be responsible like a human partner, taking more (e.g., as an explainer) or less (e.g., as an explainee) responsibility for decisions? Certainly, whether the division of responsibilities should always be asymmetric with more responsibility given to the user is a future ethical question. In that case, a system would need not only to identify crucial actions that might be critical to a decision but also mark them as such by, for example, explicitly alerting the user (see Chap. 11 for some ideas on this). This is in line with meaningful human control as proposed by Santoni de Sio and Mecacci (2021) are proposing. For future research, we would like to make this point more explicit, and in the next section, we suggest how responsibility can be fostered.

9.7 How Does This Chapter Inspire Further Directions of XAI? And How to Foster Responsibility in the Design of XAI?

We have argued that the core idea of sXAI is to support or enhance the agency of both decision-makers as well as the recipients of decisions. Certainly, this support should be different in high- vs. low-stake scenarios. Current developments recognize that understanding can vary depending on the group of stakeholders, their interest, goals, expectations, and demands regarding AI systems (Langer et al., 2021). Increasingly, the context in which an AI system is applied, affects the kinds of understanding and the explanation that it is addressing.

Future adaptive and context-aware sXAI, which are able to co-construct a relevant explanation with the user in a collaborative act, could also enhance the user's agency. To achieve this, the ability to engage in "scaffolding" (Wood et al., 1976, p. 90), as a form of adaptivity, is essential. As presented above, it is a support engaging a novice in an interaction, but it is of temporary nature. A scaffolding system can enhance the user's agency by first allowing participation but then transferring more and more responsibility for the shared goal to the user. Once the novice participates in a more sovereign way, the support can fade away. Fading of scaffolding is thus linked to the transfer of responsibilities (Van de Pol et al., 2010).

We now briefly discuss what the above-presented perspective on responsibility could mean in practice, when it is connected with an sXAI able to scaffold. Of question is how this relates to explanations designed to increase trustworthiness and agency. We consider scaffolding to be an important characteristic of a user-centered explanation that advances the user's understanding (Rohlfing et al., 2021) (see also Chap. 13).

Using large language models (LLMs; think of ChatGPT) as an example, we can imagine a kind of ladder of scaffolds leading to increased responsibility of the human user.

Initially, the user can start by engaging in a natural conversation with the system: posing questions, for instance. The alignment and quality of responses, as well as the development of the dialog, will depend primarily on the capabilities of the system—and can be seen as part of the system's responsibility. This is reflected in some debates on ChatGPT, for example, regarding programming: Maybe the system is good enough to be responsible for producing working code, so that humans need only to describe the intended code in natural language (Welsh, 2023).

However, in many cases, the system may not generate satisfactory answers or functional code. Instead, it might produce text that is inaccurate. Thus, on a second level (or perhaps, on the first level after naive use), users became aware that the system is not akin to a search engine merely retrieving answers. Instead, it is designed to generate text that feels natural. In other words, it is a text-generating system. Consequently, the responsibility for the accuracy of answers somehow shifts to the user, who must consider the nature of the system as a text generator—placing, thus, an additional burden on the user.

On the next level(s), the human becomes somewhat more responsible for the quality and correctness of the output, whereas the system becomes responsible probably more for the style. To facilitate the user in taking this responsibility, an explanation of the training process and the probabilistic nature of the system's responses can be provided. The goal would be for the user to understand that the system acts in some sense as a statistical parrot (Bender et al., 2021) in some sense.

However, the system does not rely solely on the next most probable word. It also draws on semantic vectors and alignment, so that it can consider – at least to some degree – the context and so differentiate between, for example, different contextual meanings of a word and choose the likeliness of the probable words based on this attention to some specific context. Based on this explanation, it becomes the responsibility of the human user to select appropriate keywords that assist the system in determining the correct context. Alternatively, the user can provide additional contextual explanations to aid the system in generating accurate responses.

This leads to prompt design (or prompt engineering) which seems to be difficult for users (Zamfirescu-Pereira et al., 2023): Apparently, misinterpreting the system as a sort of human dialog partner appears to result in lower-quality outcomes. Instead, a kind of programming attitude can help the use of specifically designed prompts (Welsh, 2023).

Currently, there are several prompt patterns aiming to improve the quality of the system's output (e.g., White et al., 2023). Explaining these patterns can be seen as a shift in responsibility, because the human user now gains more control and hence responsibility for the quality of answers. In other words, it is the explanandum (not the system itself but the prompt patterns) that becomes a tool with which a human user can gain more control. Along these lines, Miller (2023, p. 340) proposes moving away from a decision that an XAI is suggesting toward which hypotheses to consider for the decision.

Overall in the case of dealing with LLM such as ChatGPT presented above, explanations can be seen as a scaffold increasing the responsibility of the human user, while at the same time also aiming to increase the quality of the interaction and results. However, current research strongly suggests that when looking at agency alone, the first step or scaffold in an explanation should aim to prompt engineering toward specific patterns in order to increase quality. In the above-presented ladder of scaffolds, though, the first scaffolds were different and focused more on explanations that shift responsibility by increasing awareness of possible misinterpretations or wrong expectations toward the system. Thus, "to exercise responsible agency" (Coeckelbergh, 2020, p. 2061) might differ to some degree from agency alone: The scaffold 'understanding the nature of the system as being a text-generator' makes the responsibility of the user clearer – to check the trustworthiness of the system's output – but does not add much to agency in terms of how to obtain a better quality in the answers, although, it does helps, in terms of responsible use and understanding of the system.

Interestingly, although the scaffolds focus on responsibility zooming into the interaction, they could also be seen as fostering metareflection and zooming out from the interaction. This is the case when a user can be scaffolded to overview the landscape of stakeholders and the consequences resulting from the decision. This concerns knowledge about the "ecology of responsibility relations" (Coeckelbergh, 2020, p. 2062) within the decision-making procedures when using an XAI. For this, future sXAI could be capable of engaging with this metapurpose.

9.8 Rapid Access to the Content of This Chapter

Responsibility comes into play for an agent who knows the underlying structure that the interaction follows (Mead, 1946). Such a structure features some conversational 'jobs' that need to be accomplished for the underlying goal that the interaction serves (see Chap. 23). Children, for example, explore such a structure by role-playing in which they take many different roles by themselves. Through this playing out all roles in one person, they demonstrate their knowledge about the 'jobs,' that is, the responses that a stimulus can elicit. All the responses and the stimuli are summing up to a structure (Mead, 1946). The knowledge about such a structure (i.e., about what kind of stimuli elicit what kind of responses) is seen as a condition for holding someone responsible and for exercising responsibility. In other words, agents need to be in control and know what they are doing (Coeckelbergh, 2021). Thus, to understand the concept of responsibility, it is important to understand the concept of the structure of an ongoing social practice (see Sect. 5.2 and Chap. 23).

For persons being supported by an AI, the 'knowledge' becomes difficult to capture. This is because many AI systems function like black boxes, that is, they offer algorithmic solutions in which not even an expert can gain insights (Burrell, 2016, p. 10). This nature of the algorithms (i.e., operations on statistical knowledge with its hidden patterns) is different from humans' reasoning that requires agents, reasons, and causes (Coeckelbergh, 2021). This difference leads to a "responsibility gap" (Matthias, 2004, p. 174), according to which it is difficult to hold someone responsible in the case in which a decision-maker has been supported by an output that not even an expert can inspect (Burrell, 2016). In addition, arguing that if not responsible for the function, then some person should be responsible for the development of the AI system should have a responsible person, brings in the problem of "many hands" (Coeckelbergh, 2020, p. 2056) clearly revealing that many agents at various stages are involved in such a technology development process. As a result, it is impossible to identify one individual responsible. Finally, there is the problem of "many things" (Coeckelbergh, 2020, p. 2058) capturing the fact that an AI consists of various components such as data, software, material, and the relations between things. Thus, attribution of responsibility for an AI seems impossible.

Whereas these three problems of "responsibility gap," "many hands," and "many things" (ibid) pertain to the development of AI, in the case of XAI, the question about responsibility arises when a human is seen not only as designer or developer but especially as a user **interacting** with an XAI. Then, this person has to decide something on the basis of an explanation that has been provided. A big promise of XAI is that explainability enables the human agent "to exercise responsible agency" (Coeckelbergh, 2020, p. 2061).

When attempting to bridge the responsibility gap and focusing on relational aspects of explainability (Coeckelbergh, 2020, p. 2061), we highlight the fact that exercising responsibility can take place only within a social practice that sets up a very specific purpose within a specific sociotechnical setting. As a consequence of regarding responsibility as a property of social interaction, the difference between social practices requires us to perceive different responses that are related to them, as can be seen in children taking up on their roles with a focus on a goal. Following Shoemaker (2015), we argue that for sXAI, social practices with the goal of accountability, answerability, and attributability need to be differentiated: (i) Accountability concerns liability issues in the legal sense, and the corresponding attitudes toward accountability are, for example, anger and gratitude. (ii) Attributability refers to a capacity of making attributions for individual action. It relates to those reactive attitudes such as admiration and disdain. (iii) Answerability characterizes agents having the ability to respond to other's demands and justify their doing so. This differentiation more precisely captures the agential capacities to expect from XAI and the roles that an sXAI can take in different sociotechnical settings. In addition, this differentiation provides a better answer to the question of what an artificial system, such as XAI, can 'know' about what they are doing in order to hold a system responsible for its actions.

Concerning the knowledge that an XAI can have, we can consider the example sketched in Sect. 2.3. In this example, we have two persons interacting with each other and jointly unfolding a dialog. It becomes obvious that in this dialog, both persons, Mary and Kary, are following a goal, which is to explain why the one car was chosen and not the other. Basically, the dialog is about Mary trying to understand the reasons why Kary chose one car over the other. In this dialogue, both persons are pursuing a goal, which is for Mary to understand something that she did not know before. Both persons, thus, are equally responsible for achieving the goal, and they act accordingly—this is the structure that they are following. However, an interaction can also be asymmetric in terms of one partner knowing the structure better than the other. In this case, responsibilities can be transferred gradually from the more to the less knowledgeable partner—we see this transfer in the case of a sXAI assisting users in, for example, assembling materials. In this case, sXAI could scaffold the user's behavior to provide a greater contribution. For this, the user needs to learn specific actions that the sXAI could explain. But subsequently, the sXAI's assistance could fade, explaining only those actions with which the user turns out to have more difficulties (see Chap. 6).

At this point, the form of responsibility relates directly to the way responsibility is distributed among the interaction partners. Probably, only an sXAI that is able to scaffold human agents to a degree that they feel responsible for the task will clearly foster human agency (see Chap. 6). In addition, a meaningful explanation might go well beyond what is currently considered for explanatory content. XAI could give an overview of the landscape of stakeholders (Ali et al., 2023, p. 41) or could explicitly encourage a user to consider alternative hypotheses (Miller, 2023, p. 340). This would facilitate the agent's responsible actions on the basis of being informed about all kinds of consequences resulting from the decisions and actions with the XAI (Santoni de Sio & Mecacci, 2021, p. 1066). These consequences could be technical, but also organizational (as an AI is implemented for purposes) and legal (as an AI is an intellectual property that does not "fit easily in the traditional intellectual property categories" (Noto La Diega, 2018, p. 12)). It is up to future research to investigate in what way, for example, a set of questions about the affected ways explainees might seek to explore the "ecology of responsibility relations" (Coeckelbergh, 2020, p. 2062) can be developed in order to figure out their responsibilities on a metalevel of reflection about the structure of decision-making procedures.

Acknowledgments We thank Matthijs Smakman for his valuable perspective and helpful comments on an earlier version of this chapter.

This work was funded by the Deutsche Forschungsgemeinschaft (DFG, German Research Foundation): TRR 318/1 2021 – 438445824.

References

Alfrink, K., Keller, I., Kortuem, G., & Doorn, N. (2023). Contestable AI by design: towards a framework. *Minds and Machines, 33*(4), 613–639. https://doi.org/10.1007/s11023-022-09611-z.

Ali, S., Abuhmed, T., El-Sappagh, S., Muhammad, K., Alonso-Moral, J. M., Confalonieri, R., Guidotti, R., Del Ser, J., Diaz-Rodriguez, N., & Herrera, F. (2023). What we know and what is left to attain Trustworthy Artificial Intelligence. *Information Fusion, 99*, 101805. https://doi.org/10.1016/j.inffus.2023.101805.

Bender, E. M., Gebru, T., McMillan-Major, A., & Shmitchell, S. (2021). On the dangers of stochastic parrots: Can language models be too big? In *Proceedings of the 2021 ACM Conference on Fairness, Accountability, and Transparency* (pp. 610–623). ACM. https://doi.org/10.1145/3442188.3445922.

Bryson, J. J. (2010). Robots should be slaves. In Y. Wilks (Ed.), *Engagements with artificial companions: Key social, psychological, ethical and design issues* (pp. 63–74). Benjamins. https://doi.org/10.1075/nlp.8.11bry.

Burrell, J. (2016). How the machine 'thinks': Understanding opacity in machine learning algorithms. *Big Data Society, 3*(1), 1–12. https://doi.org/10.1177/2053951715622512.

Buschmeier, H., Buhl, H.M., Kern, F., Grimminger, A., Beierling, H., Fisher, J., Groß, A., Horwath, I., Klowait, N., Lazarov, S., Lenke, M., Lohmer, V., Rohlfing, K.J., Scharlau, I., Singh, Terfloth, L., A., Vollmer, A.-L., Wang, Y., Wilmes, A., & Wrede, B. (2025). Forms of understanding of XAI-explanations. *Cognitive Systems Research, 94*, 101419. https://doi.org/10.1016/j.cogsys.2025.101419

Chromik, M., & Butz, A. (2021). Human–XAI interaction: A review and design principles for explanation user interfaces. In C. Ardito et al. (Eds.), *Human–Computer Interaction– INTERACT 2021: 18th IFIP TC 13 International Conference*, Bari, Italy (pp. 619–640). Springer International Publishing. https://doi.org/10.1007/978-3-030-85616-8_36.

Clark, H. H., & Schaefer, E. F. (1989). Contributing to discourse. *Cognitive Science, 13*(2), 259–294. https://doi.org/10.1207/s15516709cog1302_7.

Coates, D. J., & Swenson, P. (2013). Reasons-responsiveness and degrees of responsibility. *Philosophical Studies, 165*, 629–645. https://doi.org/10.1007/s11098-012-9969-5.

Coeckelbergh, M. (2020). Artificial intelligence, responsibility attribution, and a relational justification of explainability. *Science and Engineering Ethics, 26*(4), 2051–2068. https://doi.org/10.1007/s11948-019-00146-8.

Coeckelbergh, M. (2021). Narrative responsibility and Artificial Intelligence: How AI challenges human responsibility and sense-making. *AI & Society, x*(x), 1–14. https://doi.org/10.1007/s00146-021-01375-x.

Coeckelbergh, M., & Loh, J. (2020). Transformations of responsibility in the age of automation: being answerable to human and non-human others. In B. Beck & Kühler (Eds.), *Technology, anthropology, and dimensions of responsibility* (pp. 7–22). J.B. Metzler. .

Converse, S., Cannon-Bowers, J. A., & Salas, E. (1993). Shared mental models in expert team decision making. In J. Castellan (Ed.). *Individual and group decision making: Current issues* (pp. 221–246). Lawrence Erlbaum Associates.

Fischer, J. M., & Ravizza, M. (1998). *Responsibility and control: A theory of moral responsibility*. Cambridge University Press. https://doi.org/10.1017/CBO9780511814594.

Groom, V., & Nass, C. (2007). Can robots be teammates?: Benchmarks in human–robot teams. *Issues in Science and Technology, 8*(3), 483–500. https://doi.org/10.1075/is.8.3.10gro.

Königs, P. (2022). Artificial intelligence and responsibility gaps: What is the problem? *Ethics and Information Technology, 24*(3), 36. https://doi.org/10.1007/s10676-022-09643-0.

Langer, M., Oster, D., Speith, T., Hermanns, H., Kästner, L., Schmidt, E., Sesing, A., & Baum, K. (2021). What do we want from explainable artificial intelligence (XAI)? – A stakeholder perspective on XAI and a conceptual model guiding interdisciplinary XAI research. *Artificial Intelligence, 296*, 1–24. https://doi.org/10.1016/j.artint.2021.103473.

Matthias, A. (2004). The responsibility gap: Ascribing responsibility for the actions of learning automata. *Ethics and Information Technology, 6*(3), 175–183. https://doi.org/10.1007/s10676-004-3422-1.

Mead, G. H. (1946). *Mind, self, and society. From the standpoint of a social behaviorist* (Vol. 445). The University of Chicago Press.

Miller, T. (2023). Explainable AI is dead, long live explainable AI! Hypothesis- driven decision support using evaluative AI. In *Proceedings of the 2023 ACM Conference on Fairness, Accountability, and Transparency* (pp. 333–342). ACM. https://doi.org/10.1145/3593013.3594001.

Noto La Diega, G. (2018). Against the dehumanisation of decision-making — Algorithmic decisions at the crossroads of intellectual property, data protection, and freedom of information. *Journal of Intellectual Property, Information Technology and Electronic Commerce Law, 19*(1), 3–34.

O'Hara, K. (2020). Explainable AI and the philosophy and practice of explana- tion. *Computer Law & Security Review, 39*, 1–7. https://doi.org/10.1016/j.clsr.2020.105474.

Oshana, M. A. L. (2002). The misguided marriage of responsibility and autonomy. *The Journal of Ethics, 6*, 261–280. https://doi.org/10.1023/A:1019482607923.

Pol, J. van de, van Braak, M., Pennings, H. J., van Vondel, S., Steenbeek, H., & Akkerman, S. (2023). Contributing to discourse. *Annals of the International Communication Association, 47*(1), 1–19. https://doi.org/10.1080/23808985.2022.2130809.

Rohlfing, K. J., Cimiano, P., Scharlau, I., Matzner, T., Buhl, H., Buschmeier, H., Grimminger, A., Hammer, B., Häb-Umbach, R., Horwath, I., Hüllermeier, E., Kern, F., Kopp, S., Thommes, K., Ngonga Ngomo, A.-C., Schulte, C., Wachsmuth, H., Wagner, P., & Wrede, B. (2021). Explanation as a social practice: Toward a conceptual framework for the social design of AI systems. *IEEE Transactions on Cognitive and Developmental Systems, 13*(3), 717–728. https://doi.org/10.1109/TCDS.2020.3044366.

Rojas-Drummond, S., Torreblanca, O., Pedraza, H., Vélez, M., & Guzmán, K. (2013). 'Dialogic scaffolding': Enhancing learning and under- standing in collaborative contexts. *Learning, Culture and Social Interaction*, 11–21. https://doi.org/10.1016/j.lcsi.2012.12.003.

Royal Society. (2019). *Explainable AI: the basics. Policy briefing*. https://royalsociety.org/news-resources/projects/explainable-ai/.

Santoni de Sio, F., & Mecacci, G. (2021). Four responsibility gaps with artificial intelligence: Why they matter and how to address them. *Philosophy & Technology, 34*(4), 1057–1084. https://doi.org/10.1007/s13347-021-00450-x.

Schilling, M., Kopp, S., Wachsmuth, S., Wrede, B., Ritter, H., Brox, T., Nebel, B., & Burgard, W. (2016). Towards a multidimensional perspective on shared autonomy. In *Proceedings of the AAAI Fall Symposium Series 2016*. Stanford, CA, USA.

Shoemaker, D. (2015). *Responsibility from the margins*. Oxford University Press. https://doi.org/10.1093/acprof:oso/9780198715672.001.0001.

Sokol, K., & Flach, P. (2020). One explanation does not fit all. *KI- Künstliche Intelligenz, 34*, 235–250. https://doi.org/10.1007/s13218-020-00637-y.

Strawson, P. (1963). Freedom and resentment. *Proceedings of the British Academy, 48*, 187–211.

Sullins, J. P. (2006). When is a robot a moral agent? *International Review of Information Ethics, 6*, 23–30. https://doi.org/10.29173/irie136.

Talbert, M. (2024). Moral responsibility. In E. N. Zalta & U. Nodelman (Eds.), *The Stanford Encyclopedia of Philosophy*. Fall 2024. Metaphysics Research Lab, Stanford University.

Taylor, I. (2024). Is explainable AI responsible AI? *AI & Society*, 1–10. https://doi.org/10.1007/s00146-024-01939-7.

Tigard, D. W. (2021). There is no techno-responsibility gap. *Philosophy & Technology, 34*(3), 589–607. https://doi.org/10.1007/s13347-020-00414-7.

Van de Pol, J., Volman, M., & Beishuizen, J. (2010). Scaffolding in teacher–student interaction: A decade of research. *Educational Psychology Review, 22*(3), 271–297. https://doi.org/10.1007/s10648-010-9127-6.

Vredenburgh, K. (2022). The right to explanation. *Journal of Political Philosophy, 30*(2), 209–229. https://doi.org/10.1111/jopp.12262.

Wallace, R. J. (2022). Responsibility and reactive attitudes. In D. K. Nelkin & D. Pereboom (Eds.), *The Oxford Hand- book of Moral Responsibility* (pp. 287–303). Oxford University Press. https://doi.org/10.1093/oxfordhb/9780190679309.013.32.

Wasserman-Rozen, H., Gilad-Bachrach, R., & Elkin-Koren, N. (2023). Lost in translation: The limits of explainability in AI. *Cardozo Arts & Entertainment Law Journal, 42*(2), 391–437.

Watson, G. (2004). Two faces of responsibility. In *Agency and Answerability: Selected Essays* (pp. 260–288). Clarendon Press. https://doi.org/10.1093/acprof:oso/9780199272273.003.0010.

Welsh, M. (2023). The end of programming. *Communications of the ACM, 66*(1), 34–35. https://doi.org/10.1145/3570220.

White, J., Fu, Q., Hays, S., Sandborn, M., Olea, C., Gilbert, H., Elnashar, A., Spencer-Smith, J., & Schmidt, D. C. (2023). *A prompt pattern catalog to enhance prompt engineering with ChatGPT*. https://doi.org/10.48550/arXiv.2302.11382. arXiv: 2302.11382 [cs.SE].

Wood, D., Bruner, J. S., & Ross, G. (1976). The role of tutoring in problem solving. *Journal of Child Psychology and Psychiatry, 17*(2), 89–100. https://doi.org/10.1111/j.1469-7610.1976.tb00381.x.

Zamfirescu-Pereira, J. D., Wong, R. Y., Hartmann, B., & Yang, Q. (2023). Why Johnny can't prompt: How non-AI experts try (and fail) to design LLM prompts. In *Proceedings of the 2023 CHI Conference on Human Factors in Computing Systems* (pp. 1–21). ACM. https://doi.org/10.1145/3544548.3581388.

Open Access This chapter is licensed under the terms of the Creative Commons Attribution 4.0 International License (http://creativecommons.org/licenses/by/4.0/), which permits use, sharing, adaptation, distribution and reproduction in any medium or format, as long as you give appropriate credit to the original author(s) and the source, provide a link to the Creative Commons license and indicate if changes were made.

The images or other third party material in this chapter are included in the chapter's Creative Commons license, unless indicated otherwise in a credit line to the material. If material is not included in the chapter's Creative Commons license and your intended use is not permitted by statutory regulation or exceeds the permitted use, you will need to obtain permission directly from the copyright holder.

Chapter 10
Values and Norms in sXAI

Wessel Reijers and **Suzana Alpsancar**

Abstract Why may an explanation, or more appropriately, the process of explaining, be relevant in a particular setting? This chapter argues that the explainability of AI can serve different instrumental and intrinsic purposes or values depending on the design context. Given these considerations, we ask how may developers design sXAI in such a way that it allows them to promote those values that are linked to the final purposes of deploying different AI systems in different contexts. To address this challenge, we turn to the widely used and discussed value-sensitive design (VSD) approach. First, the chapter provides a brief introduction to VSD and presents some points of criticism that have been raised in the literature—most notably, the lack of a theoretical, normative basis to justify the choice of values. Second, in response to this, the chapter develops a set of values that are informed by the XAI literature and are specifically responsive to the notion of sXAI. Most notably, it focuses on the intrinsic values of self-advocacy, deliberative agency, and reason responsiveness. Third, the chapter demonstrates and assesses the relevance of these values in the context of a VSD exercise. For this exercise, we consider a disobedient robot/AI-system case. Overall, the chapter proposes a VSD framework that integrates intrinsic values tied to sXAI contexts.

10.1 How Does This Chapter Relate to XAI?

By offering a perspective on the design of XAI as being socially interactive, we hope to add to the *relevance* of XAI, which has been flagged as one of the most pressing challenges in the field. In this chapter, we relate the relevance of XAI

W. Reijers (✉)
Institute of Media Studies, Faculty of Arts and Humanities, Paderborn University, Paderborn, Germany
e-mail: wessel.reijers@uni-paderborn.de

S. Alpsancar
Heinz Nixdorf Institute, Department of Philosophy, Faculty of Arts and Humanities, Paderborn University, Paderborn, Germany
e-mail: suzana.alpsancar@uni-paderborn.de

to addressing the purposes XAI is meant to serve, which are, in turn, entangled with values and norms. Despite a persistent suggestion, explanations are not always wanted, helpful, or needed and, hence, relevant. They might even be conceived as annoying or overburdening. They entail the potential of manipulating, nudging, or misleading users (see Chap. 30). Despite its remarkable prominence in the current AI ethical guidelines, explainability is also not always a necessary condition to ensure that ethical or legal demands are met (Alpsancar et al., 2024). Accordingly, XAI is not of unquestionable value, and its relevance depends highly on the context of usage, including users, institutional settings, and environmental as well as broader cultural and social factors (Bruijn et al., 2022). We start our argument by posing a question: Why may an explanation, or more appropriately, the *process* of explaining, be relevant or valuable in a particular setting? A straightforward answer is that it is relevant because it serves a certain (useful, good) purpose. For example, a medical explanation of XAI may serve the purpose of correctly diagnosing a medical condition such as when an XAI application helps medical professionals eliminate spurious correlations in the classification of images of tumors. Similarly, explaining a decision made on a credit score may serve the purpose of ensuring the appropriate application of creditworthiness, which implies – among other things – respecting values of fairness and nondiscrimination as well as professional standards (norms) such as doing fair business and so forth.

The current XAI literature has little to say about concrete purposes of the product (i.e., explanations) or process (i.e., explaining) of XAI (Freiesleben & König, 2023). Usually, XAI is claimed to be of general value. Concrete purposes either are not mentioned at all or are derived one-sidedly from a mere technical perspective interest in optimizing the AI systems at hand. For example, the achievement of LIME to point out the features in their weighting that were or were not decisive for a prediction (Ribeiro et al., 2016) assumes that the participants in practice are always concerned precisely with understanding this explanandum. A central idea of sXAI is that it is not always clear in advance what the explanandum actually consists of. Instead, the explanandum has to be identified in the interaction between the user and XAI. This is accompanied by a change of perspective: The purposes of XAI (what is to be explained and for what purpose) are not derived solely from the properties of the system, but take into account the social embedding of AI systems in real-world applications. Here, we invite our readers to question the relevance of XAI from the perspective of concrete usage situations that entail (presumed) diverse users' interests (Langer et al., 2021) as well as ethical considerations (Alpsancar et al., 2024) (due to a lack of expertise, we exclude legal issues). To explicate the entanglement of purposes, values, and norms, we draw from considerations in social philosophy and technology ethics: The value of XAI may be derived from the value of its purposes. Purposes may be instrumental or final. For instance, the instrumental purpose of a medical XAI may be to spot false positives. Yet, instrumental purposes by themselves do not establish relevance. Rather, they always stand in relation to final, one might say 'higher-order,' purposes. Aristotle (1980) discussed this relation in the *Nicomachean Ethics* (NE 1094a) when he argued that technical activities always serve a dual purpose: one realizing the function of an artifact (e.g., a hammer) and one referencing a final, self-sufficient purpose (e.g., providing shelter), and this motivates the relevance of the whole technical practice. Purposes, the ends of our striving, are linked to norms and values. Whereas final ends are meant to be good in themselves, instrumental ends are of instrumental value. Instrumental ends are good in the sense of serving something else that is perceived as good. Final ends are those purposes 'for the sake of which' we engage in certain activities and practices.

Given these considerations, how may developers design sXAI in such a way that it allows them to promote those values that are linked to the final purposes of deploying different AI systems in different contexts? This question opens up the challenge of responsible innovation, but not in the sense of post hoc interventions (i.e., identifying and mitigating harms), but in the sense of ex ante decisions that 'embed' values in the design process. One of the most established approaches in this regard is the "value-sensitive design" method that was conceptualized originally by Friedman et al. (2006) and has since developed into a burgeoning field tackling questions regarding the value-sensitive design of, for instance, care robots (Wynsberghe, 2013), digital media (Zimmer, 2005), and virtual assistants (Harbers & Neerincx, 2017). Furthermore, the approach is linked increasingly to the strategic efforts of national and international funding bodies within the agenda of responsible research and innovation (Simon, 2017). In this chapter, we adopt this approach as our starting point, and investigate how it may contribute to realizing the values implied in the concept of sXAI.

First, the chapter provides a brief introduction to the value-sensitive design approach and presents some points of criticism that have been raised in the literature. Following these points, the chapter develops a set of values that are informed by the XAI literature and are specifically responsive to the notion of sXAI. The chapter concludes by demonstrating and discussing the relevance of this set of values by engaging in a value-sensitive-design exercise that makes use of a disobedient robot scenario.

10.2 Value-Sensitive Design and Criticisms

Value-sensitive design (VSD) is a widely studied interdisciplinary approach that offers a basis for considering how values may be embedded into the design of new technologies. Its point of departure is the idea that a design process and its outcome both promote and demote certain practices and the values these espouse (or lack; see Friedman et al., 2006). For instance, technologies that make use of end-to-end encryption promote private and secure communication and therefore the value of privacy. Note that VSD assumes a process of translation from concrete design features and requirements to higher-order values (and vice versa). This dual movement of interpretation leads to VSD being characterized as an iterative process consisting of three stages.

The first is the conceptual stage. This stage focuses primarily on establishing values and explicating their working definitions. Values may be identified by considering direct and indirect stakeholders. For sXAI, direct stakeholders may be users of an XAI system such as doctors operating an AI to perform a diagnosis. Indirect stakeholders are individuals and groups that do not interact directly with technology, but might still be affected by it. For instance, women may be affected by a medical XAI technology if it perpetuates a gender bias. The notion of *value* does not enjoy a univocal definition in the VSD literature, but the initial idea was that it is derived from stakeholder preferences. A value can therefore be descriptive, such as 'accessability' as a value underlying the practice of engaging with an XAI interface for stakeholders with diminished eyesight.

Yet, this also raises the question of instrumental versus final purposes, a criticism that will be further developed below. In more developed versions of VSD, the conceptual stage also considers the operations of translating between values and design requirements. Van de Poel (2013, p. 253) has introduced a "values hierarchy" that helps to organize different layers of concretization. The most abstract layer is the mere values such as privacy. The most concrete layer is the level of design requirements. In between, there is a layer of norms whereby the notion of *norm* stands "for all kinds of prescriptions for, and restrictions on, action" (Van de Poel, 2013, p. 19). For instance, a norm can be both a permission (data may be shared) and a restriction (no personal data may be shared). Norms can be technical, legal, or social. Whereas many of the first two will usually be given formally, norms can also be present informally. For instance, although there is no codification to start a conversation with some sort of greeting cue, it would be a break of social norms to not do it in interpersonal interactions. Likewise, using and storing your tools with care and attention can be understood as part of the practices (life form) of what it means to be a good craftsman. Because of their multifaced character, it is quite challenging to explicate the relevant norms for a given usage scenario. According to Van de Poel (2013), we may understand the process of translating in two directions: either concretizing abstract values first into norms, and then second, the norms into more specific design requirements, or the other way around. For instance, privacy would be an abstract value, informed consent a norm that governs privacy-enhancing technologies, and a modular consent software tool could be a design requirement. Here, it is important to realize that the process of translating values into design requirements (or the other way around) is not a straightforward one, but interpretative work that can, in general, always be contested. Interpretations are highly context-relative. For instance, the interpretation of a value such as privacy is dependent on the context in which information is shared, being very different in the context of sharing public messages on social media and sharing sensitive medical information. Beyond Van de Poel's value hierarchy, there are different heuristics in the literature on how to organize these interpretation processes with care and in a systematic way, for example, the so-called VCIO model (Hauschke et al., 2022). The process of concretizing values should also include a reflection on the interplay of all the relevant values for the case at hand. These values might be conflicting, indifferent, or adding interdependencies, and they often involve prioritization of design choices that have to be made (Hauschke et al., 2022; Hubig & Reidel, 2003).

The second is the empirical stage. This stage focuses on empirically investigating how stakeholders think about values and how they relate to them in their everyday usage and appropriation of new technologies. It serves the purpose of developing a more situated understanding of the technology in question (Jacobs et al., 2021), one that considers its concrete social context. Different methods, drawing from fields such as sociology and anthropology, may be deployed to perform these empirical investigations. For instance, user surveys may be distributed to collect information about user preferences and for weighing particular values. Similarly, focus groups may be organized to gain a more in-depth understanding of stakeholder opinions—for instance, those of vulnerable groups interacting with a technology. Because VSD is an iterative method, the empirical investigations inform the conceptual stage, because it allows for operationalizing, weighing, and specifying values, norms, and design requirements.

The third is the technical stage. This stage may be both retrospective and prospective, depending on the developmental phase of the technology in question. Retrospectively, the technical stage may inquire into existing technologies that either support or hinder practices that promote (or demote) values. For example, a rear mirror supports the practice of safe driving, and hence the value of (public) safety. Prospectively or proactively, the technical stage may inquire into possible new sociotechnical configurations that allow for a transformation of practices in such a way that they better embed particular values. As such, the technical stage is responsive both to existing technological arrangements and ones that are in the process of development. To illustrate the latter, VSD has been applied to study and prescribe value embeddedness of nanomaterial for pharmaceutical use (Timmermans et al., 2011).

Despite its appeal and wide applicability, the VSD approach has also met with criticism. One point is of particular relevance for our purposes, because it strikes at the core of both the objectives of the VSD and the sXAI approaches. That is, as argued above, both approaches need to distinguish between instrumental and final purposes. Originally, VSD does so by considering the preferences of direct or indirect stakeholders, but this approach has been met by criticism stating that it invokes a sense of ethical relativism or the lack of a normative basis for justifying ethical claims such as the selection of values (Jacobs & Huldtgren, 2021; Cenci & Cawthorne, 2020; Simon, 2017). Whereas it is important and often fruitful to consider the voices of stakeholders, not all preferences are equally legitimate, and some may be even misguided. Consider, for instance, a stakeholder group advocating for limiting the use of a particular technology to a particular ethnic group. Such a preference would quite clearly lack legitimacy, because it implies a problematic form of discrimination.[1]

---

[1] Furthermore, even the choice of core ethical values can be questioned against the background of a globalized world. VSD had been quite power-agnostic (Zaman & JafariNaimi, 2015; Friedman & Hendry, 2019).

The core of the difficulty lies in the question of how to justify a value judgment. Individual preferences, even in aggregate, may be misguided and lack justification beyond their nature as expressed interests. As argued by Manders-Huits (2011), empirical knowledge about stakeholder preferences does not suffice to ground the values that VSD aims to incorporate into technology design. This derives, at least in part, from VSD's lack of engagement with normative theory. Normative theories such as utilitarianism, deontology, and virtue ethics provide an argumentative framework to arrive at reasons for grounding values that are intersubjectively justifiable.

However, the normative justification of VSD is itself challenging. There is a broad consensus in the technology ethics literature that it is neither expedient to approach this justification top-down (e.g., trying to derive all value references from a supreme ethical principle such as the categorical imperative or the utilitarian calculation of utility maximization) nor can it be justified to derive them entirely bottom-up (in the sense of pure casuistry). The first strategy remains too unrealistic, given the plurality of goods and their justifications in society and the second strategy too nonbinding, given that any selection of values is potentially acceptable without the need for proper justification. The golden path therefore lies in the middle where one must try to balance case-specific, generally valid normative claims with context-specific claims and situational conditions. Therefore, any set of values suitable for VSD of sXAI needs prima facie to take the social context of XAI into account. What is required, therefore, is a normative basis for a set of values that is responsive to the context of sXAI, which consequently may be developed following the idea of finding a *reflective equilibrium* (Rawls, 1971), which means that the normative justification of the values in question responds dynamically to empirical insights that include stakeholder preferences. For instance, the meaning of the principle of fairness in the context of AI systems has been challenged and modulated through concrete practices of discrimination caused by bias in AI models. In fact, VSD already includes such a reflective step in the empirical stage, and this offers an even greater impetus to reconsider the conceptual stage.

10.3 The Values of sXAI

This section takes up the challenge of formulating a set of values that may guide the process of VSD of sXAI. In our understanding, the values of sXAI are twofold: One dimension (Dimension 1) derives from the idea that sXAI is sensitive toward the different contexts of AI deployment. Hence, it resonates with the social embeddedness of the technical system. The other dimension (Dimension 2) derives from the guiding idea of this book (see Chap. 1) that sXAI (in contrast to mere XAI) strives to pursue better explanations by promoting a real interactive mode of explanatory inquiry and dialog. The second dimension is then about the interaction between the user and the XAI system.

To do justice to the first dimension, we need to take the perspective of (presumed/intended) real-world applications. For this, we suggest distinguishing the following types of value dependencies:

1. Fundamental values
2. Context-relative higher-order values
3. Individual preferences and interests

Fundamental values are fundamental in the sense that they should always be respected under all circumstances. Consequently, not respecting these values needs justification. Fundamental values are abstract and reflect basic human rights. They can be drawn from recent AI ethics guidelines that have been issued by industry, academia, and politics. As metareviews have shown (Morley et al., 2020; Hagendorff, 2020), these guidelines converge linguistically around five core principles: "transparency, justice and fairness, non-maleficence, responsibility, and privacy" (Jobin et al., 2019, p. 389). Here, the challenge is to first concretize the meaning of these values for each application scenario, analyze the inference with other interpreted values, and then translate them into design requirements.

The task is the same for the second set of values that are of a different category. Whereas the values of the first type are universal in the sense that they should always be respected, the validity of the second set of values varies from context to context. For example, the value of health is obviously a higher-order value for medical settings, whereas it does not play such a role in scenarios of buying/selling cars (Sect. 2.3). In addition to the tasks mentioned above, the challenge here is to identify which higher-order values are relevant for the intended application context. These higher-order values correspond to the social character of the application context and can be drawn from their institutionalized form. For instance, solvency and success are more important in business relationships than in healthcare settings. Because these norms are supra-individual (they are not private but social), they may be inferred partly by common-sense reasoning from the perspective of a shared sociocultural world (Rouse, 2007; Reckwitz, 2002; Jaeggi, 2018). These values may also be pursued empirically by inquiring about the standards of excellence that constitute the social practices within the given contexts (Reijers & Gordijn, 2019).

The third dimension, individual preferences and interests, should be informed by empirical user studies. It should be noted that there is a theoretical debate about whether or not one should call preferences values at all (Sagoff, 1986; Jacobs & Huldtgren, 2021; Warren et al., 2011; Loreggia et al., 2018). Some wish to draw a clear and lasting distinction between values and interests/preferences. We think that it is not the choice of terminology that is decisive. Instead, we need to be aware of their categorical differences. In other words, it must be clear that individual preferences and interests (including those of stakeholders, organizations, etc.) do not necessarily have to coincide with higher-order values or fundamental values. For instance, although a physician would like to act on behalf of the patient's best interest – that is, to promote the higher-order value of health – the patient herself might not want to act in accordance with the physician's therapy. Moreover, there is a hierarchy between these categories of values in the sense that higher categories might orient conflicts of lower categories.

A conflict of interest might occur around the code of the software when one party wishes it to be open source, whereas the other wishes the code to fall under corporate secrecy. Here, the higher-order value of fair competition might be the ground on which this conflict can be solved—for example, in the sense that the principle of fair competition would be negated if industries were forced to disclose their intellectual achievements in such a way that it would not be profitable to invest in such developments. Hence, the code should be protected by intellectual property rights. However, if the code belongs to an application of an AI system that, due to its context of deployment, affects people's lives in such a way that there is good reason to demand its transparency, such a higher-order value of fair competition (related to free markets) could be overruled by a fundamental value or basic human rights argument. For instance, Rudin et al. (2020) argue that because decision support is used in the justice system, the public – that is, independent agencies – should be able to scrutinize and audit the inner mechanisms of these systems, because, otherwise, the principle of due process, fairness, and individual rights could be violated.

The task of concretizing values is context-specific and needs to be informed by case studies. We shall now turn to the other dimension of the value of sXAI that plays out in the interaction process. Here, we assume that we can explicate a set of intrinsic values that belong specifically to the social character of XAI in the sense of the unfolding interaction process (see Chap. 1 Introduction). Intrinsic values are those that are realized by a social practice across different contexts of explanation. These values are intrinsic, because they can be realized only through explainability—that is, they relate to social practices for which explainability is a sine qua non. They are opposed to extrinsic values, which only play out in relation to contextual factors (Van de Poel & Kroes, 2014). Values are extrinsic when they are contingently tied to explainability, meaning that they could be realized through other means. For instance, sXAI can be used to promote health in medical settings, but the promotion of health is not linked intrinsically to sXAI. In reality, the interaction will always be embedded in a social context (Dignum, 2022; Dignum & Dignum, 2020; Dignum, 2018) and, consequently, what we call Dimension 1 and Dimension 2 of the social character of XAI will interplay in real life. However, it is worth addressing the intrinsic values specifically, because they will be incorporated by the sXAI independent of the application scenario. Here, we propose to understand the intrinsic values of sXAI in terms of the discursive practice of explaining—that is, good sXAI is such that enables and promotes particular qualities that we value in the discursive practice of explaining (Colaner, 2022).

For the scope of this chapter, we shall rely on the existing literature discussing the intrinsic values of XAI. Surveying this literature, it becomes readily apparent that XAI is concerned with deliberative, or more accurately, discursive practices. These include practices of explicating, recommending, informing, and so forth. For each of these social practices, standards of excellence may be formulated that establish what it means to perform them well—for instance, to inform a citizen well in the process of explaining an administrative AI-driven decision.

The following list of values is not meant to be complete, but it may act as a starting point for engaging in an exercise of reflective equilibrium finding as described in the previous section. The values respond to the requirements expressed in the foregoing discussion, because they enjoy normative justification (not being mere stakeholder preferences) and specifically apply the idea of being able to provide better help with XAI through the social character of interacting with the XAI:

- **Self-advocacy**. As Vredenburgh (2022) argues, explainability should in certain contexts be considered a right, because it realizes the value of informed self-advocacy. This value is justified normatively because it protects a set of vital interests, and, when absent, harms the legitimacy of institutions. Through the realization of self-advocacy, people are able to both hold others accountable for AI-driven decisions and exercise agency in mitigating harmful decisions.
- **Deliberative agency**. As O'Hara (2020, p. 4) argues, explainability has the potential to "facilitate future action." By itself, this does not denote a final purpose, but in a discursive setting, it realizes the democratic value of deliberative agency. This value is normatively justified because it allows people to formulate and act on their own reasons while respecting their autonomy (Jongepier & Keymolen, 2022).
- **Reason responsiveness**. One of the main purposes of XAI is to provide "users" with such explanations that they might justify toward others the decisions they have made with the support of an AI system (Bruijn et al., 2022; Mittelstadt et al., 2019). Justifying something means to provide good reasons for why something was perceived as good. Because AI may generate decisions (support) that are used to either reward or sanction people (e.g., credit scores), said decisions may require justifications to realize higher-order values of a given social context (e.g., solvency) or fundamental values such as fairness. We argue that sXAI is intrinsically linked to the value of promoting reason responsiveness (Fischer & Ravizza, 1998) in the sense that relevant explanatory interactions (with the XAI) help users respond to reasons and justify their decisions based on the support of the AI system toward whoever asks for them. The interaction thus enables or strengthens the user's capacity to respond to reasons (Watson, 2004). Note that we are not claiming that it is sufficient for the XAI *to deliver* reasons (Baum et al., 2022); rather we presume that *reason responsiveness as a capacity* might be the outcome of the interaction process.

In short, value-sensitive design of sXAI could justifiably depart from an initial set of values of self-advocacy, deliberative agency, and reason responsiveness. These values are intrinsic rather than extrinsic to sXAI, because they are potentially relevant across implementation contexts (e.g., healthcare, the military) and speak to the character of sXAI of facilitating discursive practices.

10.4 Value-Sensitive Design of Disobedient Robots

So far, we have argued that value-sensitive design (VSD) of sXAI ought to explicate the social character of XAI that we presume to be two-sided: One side addresses the respective social context of AI deployment; the other relates to the interaction itself as a social process of explaining. Regarding the first side, we have suggested explicating and analyzing value dependencies on three dimensions: fundamental values, higher-order values implied by the social contexts, and users' preferences and interests (individual values). The value dependencies of the second dimension are those that belong to the social practices of explaining. Here, we have proposed to particularly address the values of self-advocacy, deliberative agency, and reason responsiveness, because all of these, in our eyes (drawing from the literature), belong to the idea of sXAI as a discursive practice of explaining.

In this section, we demonstrate and assess the relevance of these values in the context of a VSD exercise. For this exercise, we consider a disobedient robot/AI-system case (as a variation of the disobedient robot scenario as discussed in Briggs and Scheutz 2015). The assumption in this case is that under certain circumstances, the most responsible response of a robot would be to disobey a user's order. To be sure, disobedience may be nondiscursively present in robotic systems. Consider, for instance, a self-driving car that usually allows for manual override of the system, except in certain (potentially malicious) cases. To further illustrate this, if a driver were to start using the car as a weapon to drive into a crowd of people, the car could automatically override the manual system and safely shut down.

However, the more interesting cases here are those in which disobedience is or should be discursively present. Consider, for example, a surgeon ordering a surgical robot to perform an operation that, without the surgeon's knowledge, would constitute a life-threatening risk. The robot, in that case, should arguably disobey the order, but would also need to provide reasons for this, because the stakes of performing the operation itself may be saving the patient's life. Simple, nondiscursive disobedience would potentially stall the whole process, with devastating consequences, but discursive disobedience would offer opportunities to consider alternative action pathways.

The difference between disobedience being nondiscursively and discursively present may be understood along the lines of Suchman's notion of situated actions (2007). Suchman argues that some technologies are largely independent of their natural and social environment, and are also able to implement strict sets of plans. A traditional coffee machine, for instance, offers the user a strict plan of actions that can allow no deviation if one wants to attain the desired outcome (coffee). AI systems are commonly different, because they are more flexible and may respond to environmental fluctuations. In certain situations of disobedience, however, like the above-presented scenario concerning the self-driving car, immediate pathways of action are similarly closed off. In these exceptional cases, the question is how much social context is necessary or desirable. Arguably, in the case of the self-driving car, disobeying the 'order' to drive into a crowd of people needs no act of explaining (only, potentially, post hoc), whereas the surgical robot disobeying an order would need to engage in a process of explaining. The social interaction that sXAI would aim to design would fall in between the two extremes of complete context independence and complete context dependence.

Given this background of the case of disobedient robots, let us run through the three stages of the VSD exercise, taking the example of the disobedient surgical robot.

First, at the conceptual stage, we have established the three leading and normatively grounded values of self-advocacy, fairness, and deliberative agency. VSD challenges us to generate working conceptualizations of these values, given a number of relevant direct and indirect stakeholders. These may be, among others, surgeons, caregivers, the patient, her family and friends, the hospital management, and the patient's health insurance. In a full VSD exercise, value conceptualizations may need to be provided for each stakeholder, but given the scope of this chapter, let us focus on the stakeholder group of surgeons. The value of deliberative agency implies that the interaction involving the robot disobeying would make room for the surgeon to formulate and act on reasons for alternative courses of action. Following Van de Poel (2013), this value can be translated into norms guiding the design of the robot. Nonexhaustively, these norms would be (1) that reasons are provided for disobeying the order, but also that (2) alternative actions linked to these reasons are suggested. This opens up the deliberative space for the surgeon to make an alternative decision and proceed with the process of healing the patient. These norms, in turn, will need to be turned into design requirements. For instance, these requirements may include that alternative pathways of action should be ranked and summarized and that multimodal means of representation should be available for real-time communication of these pathways in the operating theater.

Second, at the empirical stage, quantitative and qualitative studies may be conducted to facilitate the reflective equilibrium finding needed to further validate and specify the three values. For this, researchers may conduct interviews, focus groups, and surveys with the direct and indirect stakeholders. Acknowledging that such efforts are beyond the scope of our current illustrative purpose, researchers may also draw from existing empirical research. Such research may, for instance, give more insight into the value of self-advocacy. In their paper, Gould et al. (2023) investigated patients' attitudes toward AI used for risk prediction in the context of clinical decision-making—specifically for knee surgery. In this case, the stakeholder group are the patients, who discussed the issue of informed consent in the context of empowerment when being faced with the application of AI. Among others, patients indicated that this empowerment would come from a better understanding of the AI decision-making based on an individual risk profile (Gould et al., 2023, p. 9), explaining it with an analogy of a car having a flat tire (a flat tire one can spot with the eye, but the AI will have a sense of risk that is invisible). Another patient explains that an important factor in feeling empowered is being aware of the doctor's ability to handle the AI's advice. This information provides helpful input for conceptualizing and operationalizing the value of self-advocacy. First, it draws a connection between self-advocacy and informed consent as an important norm to support this value. Second, it validates the value of suggesting alternative pathways of action in the case of robot disobedience, because this facilitates a discursive relationship between the surgeon and the AI system.

Third, at the technical stage, existing and new technical configurations may be considered that would enable the technical requirements established through the conceptual and empirical stages. It lies beyond the scope of this chapter to survey the extensive suite of technical solutions for (social) explainable AI. Yet, some tentative suggestions may be presented that resonate with the points above. First and retrospectively, a technology such as an informed consent visualizer model, explaining the goals and data uses of an AI system, may be installed to support the value of self-advocacy (Reddy, 2023). Second, a prospective design project could be set up that tries to realize an XAI system that is able to provide alternative courses of action in real time.

10.5 Conclusion

This chapter has discussed the importance of values and norms in relation to the responsible design of sXAI. It conceived of values as higher-order final purposes that may be embedded in the design. The chapter has presented value-sensitive design (VSD) as a widely used approach to achieve this, but also criticized it for its relativistic stance concerning values that considers them as stakeholder preferences. Instead, the chapter suggests a reflective equilibrium approach, departing from values that are justified through normative theory, and following those that are developed and specified through empirical and technical investigations. It considered three values that are pertinent to sXAI: self-advocacy, fairness, and deliberative agency. To demonstrate the benefits of these values, the chapter discussed their use in a VSD exercise based on the case of disobedient robots.

10.6 Rapid Access to the Content of This Chapter

This chapter starts from the observation that despite the salience of XAI, explanations are not always desirable or necessary. Hence, we start our argument by posing a question: Why may an explanation, or more appropriately, the process of explaining, be relevant in a particular setting? This question is largely neglected in the most recent XAI literature. To explicate the entanglement of purposes, values, and norms, we draw from considerations in social philosophy and technology ethics: The value of XAI may be derived from the value of its purposes. Purposes may be instrumental (e.g., explainability to realize fairness) or final (i.e., explainability for its own sake). Purposes, the ends of our striving, are linked to norms and values. Whereas final ends are meant to be good in themselves, instrumental ends are of instrumental value. Instrumental ends are good in the sense of serving something else that is perceived as good. Final ends are those purposes 'for the sake of which' we engage in certain activities and practices. Given these considerations, we ask: How may developers design sXAI in such a way that it allows them to promote those values that are linked to the final purposes of deploying different AI systems in different contexts? This question opens up the challenge of responsible innovation, but not in the sense of post hoc interventions (i.e., identifying and mitigating harms), but in the sense of ex ante decisions that 'embed' values into the design process. To address this challenge, we turn to the widely used and discussed value-sensitive design (VSD) approach.

First, the chapter provides a brief introduction to VSD and presents some points of criticism that have been raised in the literature. VSD is a widely studied interdisciplinary approach that offers a basis for considering how values may be embedded into the design of new technologies. Methodologically, it proposes three stages: The first is the conceptual stage. Primarily, this stage focuses on establishing values and explicating their working definitions. The second is the empirical stage. This stage focuses on empirically investigating how stakeholders think about values and how they relate to them in their everyday usage and appropriation of new technologies. The third is the technical stage. This stage may be both retrospective and prospective, depending on the developmental phase of the technology in question.

Despite its appeal and wide applicability, the VSD approach has also met with criticism. One point is of particular relevance for our purposes, because it strikes at the core of both the objectives of the VSD and the sXAI approaches. That is, as argued above, both approaches need to distinguish between instrumental and final purposes. Originally, VSD does so by considering the preferences of direct or indirect stakeholders, but this approach has been met by criticism stating that it invokes a sense of ethical relativism—that is, the lack of a normative basis for the evaluation of ethical claims. The core of the difficulty lies in the question how to justify a value judgment. Individual preferences, even in aggregate, may be misguided and lack justification beyond their nature as expressed interests. This is a thorny issue, because the literature widely acknowledges that it is neither expedient to approach this justification top-down (e.g., by trying to derive all value references from a supreme ethical principle such as the categorical imperative or the utilitarian calculation of utility maximization) nor to approach it entirely bottom-up (in the sense of pure casuistry).

Second, the chapter develops a set of values that are informed by the XAI literature and are specifically responsive to the notion of sXAI. Doing so, it aims to address the justification challenge of values that feed into the VSD of sXAI approach. In our understanding, the values of sXAI are twofold: One dimension derives from the idea that sXAI is sensitive toward the different contexts of AI deployment. Hence, it resonates with the social embeddedness of the technical system. In line with this dimension, we may distinguish between (1) fundamental values that should be respected under all circumstances, (2) context-relative higher-order values that may be final but only in particular contexts (e.g., health in healthcare context), and (3) user preferences that need to be assessed empirically.

The other dimension derives from the guiding idea that sXAI strives to pursue better explanations by promoting a real interactive mode of explanatory inquiry and dialog. Surveying existing literature, it becomes readily apparent that XAI is concerned with deliberative, or more accurately, discursive practices. One intrinsic value of sXAI is self-advocacy, or one's ability to advocate for one's interest that is needed to enjoy core democratic rights. Through the realization of self-advocacy, people are able both to hold others accountable for AI-driven decisions and to exercise agency in mitigating harmful decisions. A second is deliberative agency, or the ability to deliberate with others on things that matter in one's life. This value is normatively justified, because it allows people to formulate and act on their own reasons, respecting their autonomy. A third is reason responsiveness. Because AI may generate decisions (support) that are used either to reward or sanction people (e.g., credit scores), said decision may require justifications to realize higher-order values of a given social context (e.g., solvency) or fundamental values such as fairness.

Third, we demonstrate and assess the relevance of these values in the context of a VSD exercise. For this exercise, we consider the disobedient robot/AI-system case (see Chap. 2). The assumption in this case is that under certain circumstances, the most responsible response of a robot would be to disobey a user's order. At the conceptual stage, we have established the three leading and normatively grounded values of self-advocacy, deliberative agency, and reason responsiveness. VSD challenges us to generate working conceptualizations of these values, given a number of relevant direct and indirect stakeholders. These may be, among others, surgeons, caregivers, the patient, her family and friends, the hospital management, and the patient's health insurance. We focus on the value of deliberative agency, which implies that the interaction involving the robot disobeying would make room for the surgeon to formulate and act on reasons for alternative courses of action. Non-exhaustively, these norms would be (1) that reasons are provided for disobeying the order, but also that (2) alternative actions linked to these reasons are suggested. This opens up the deliberative space for the surgeon to make an alternative decision and proceed with the process of healing the patient.

At the empirical stage, quantitative and qualitative studies may be conducted to facilitate the reflective equilibrium finding needed to further validate and specify the three values. We focus on empirical findings from a paper on patient's attitudes toward AI used for risk prediction in the context of clinical decision-making (Gould et al., 2023). This empirical information provides helpful input, because (1) it draws a connection between self-advocacy and informed consent as an important norm to support this value and (2) it validates the value of suggesting alternative pathways of action in the case of robot disobedience, because this facilitates a discursive relationship between the surgeon and the AI system. At the technical stage, existing and new technical configurations may be considered. One would be, retrospectively, a technology such as an informed consent visualizer model, explaining the goals and data uses of an AI system that may be installed to support the value of self-advocacy. Another would be a prospective design project that could be set up to try and realize an XAI system that is able to provide alternative courses of action in real time.

Acknowledgments This work was funded by the Deutsche Forschungsgemeinschaft (DFG, German Research Foundation): TRR 318/1 2021 – 438445824.

References

Alpsancar, S., Buhl, H. M., Matzner, T., & Scharlau, I. (2024). Explanation needs and ethical demands: unpacking the instrumental value of XAI. *AI and Ethics*. https://doi.org/10.1007/s43681-024-00622-3.

Aristotle (1980). *The Nicomachean ethics*. D. Reidel. https://doi.org/10.1007/978-94-010-2303-0.

Baum, K., Mantel, S., Schmidt, E., & Speith, T. (2022). From responsibility to reason-giving explainable artificial intelligence. *Philosophy & Technology, 35*(1), 12. https://doi.org/10.1007/s13347-022-00510-w.

Briggs, G. M., & Scheutz, M. (2015). "Sorry, I can't do that": Developing mechanisms to appropriately reject directives in human–robot interactions. In *Proceedings of the AAAI Fall Symposia* (pp. 32–36). AAAI Press. https://cdn.aaai.org/ocs/11709/11709-51307-1-PB.pdf.

Cenci, A., & Cawthorne, D. (2020). Refining value sensitive design: A (capability-based) procedural ethics approach to technological design for well-being. *Science and Engineering Ethics, 26*(5), 2629–2662. https://doi.org/10.1007/s11948-020-00223-3.

Colaner, N. (2022). Is explainable artificial intelligence intrinsically valuable? *AI & Society, 37*, 231–238. https://doi.org/10.1007/s00146-021-01184-2.

de Bruijn, H., Warnier, M., & Janssen, M. (2022). The perils and pitfalls of explainable AI: Strategies for explaining algorithmic decision-making. *Government Information Quarterly, 39*(2), 101666. https://doi.org/10.1016/j.giq.2021.101666.

Dignum, F. (2018). *Interactions as social practices: Towards a formalization*. arXiv: 1809.08751 [cs.AI]. https://arxiv.org/abs/1809.08751.

Dignum, F., & Dignum, V. (2020). How to center AI on humans. In A. Saffiotti, L. Serafini, & P. Lukowicz (Eds.), *NeHuAI 2020. First International Workshop on New Foundations for Human-Centered AI: Proceedings of the First International Workshop on New Foundations for Human-Centered AI (NeHuAI) co-located with 24th European Conference on Artificial Intelligence (ECAI 2020)* (pp. 59–62). CEUR workshop proceedings. http://ceur-ws.org/Vol-2659/.

Dignum, V. (2022). *Relational artificial intelligence*. arXiv: https://arxiv.org/abs/2202.07446. 2202.07446 [cs.CY].

Fischer, J. M., & Ravizza, M. (1998). *Responsibility and control: A theory of moral responsibility*. Cambridge University Press. https://doi.org/10.1017/CBO9780511814594.

Freiesleben, T., & König, G. (2023). Dear XAI community, we need to talk! Fundamental misconceptions in current XAI research. In L. Longo (Ed.), *World Conference on Explainable Artificial Intelligence* (pp. 48–65). Springer. https://doi.org/10.1007/978-3-031-44064-9_3.

Friedman, B., & Hendry, D. G. (2019). *Value sensitive design: Shaping technology with moral imagination*. The MIT Press. https://doi.org/10.7551/mitpress/7585.001.0001.

Friedman, B., Kahn, P. H., & Borning, A. (2006). Value sensitive design and information systems. In P. Zhang & D. F. Galletta (Eds.), *Human–computer interaction and management information systems: Foundations* (pp. 348–372). Routledge. https://doi.org/10.4324/9781315703619.

Gould, D. J., Dowsey, M. M., Glanville-Hearst, M., Spelman, T., Bailey, J. A., Choong, P. F. M., & Bunzli, S. (2023). Patients' views on AI for risk prediction in shared decision-making for knee replacement surgery: Qualitative interview study. *Journal of Medical Internet Research, 25*, 1–16. https://doi.org/10.2196/43632.

Hagendorff, T. (2020). The ethics of AI ethics: An evaluation of guidelines. *Minds and Machines, 30*(1), 99–120. https://doi.org/10.1007/s11023-020-09517-8.

Harbers, M., & Neerincx, M. A. (2017). Value sensitive design of a virtual assistant for workload harmonization in teams. *Cognition, Technology & Work, 19*(2–3), 329–343. https://doi.org/10.1007/s10111-017-0408-4.

Hauschke, A., Puntschuh, M., Hallensleben, S., & Loh, W. (2022). *VDE SPEC 90012 V1.0 - VCIO based description of systems for AI trustworthiness characterisation.* Tech. rep. VDE Verband der Elektrotechnik.

Hubig, C., & Reidel, J. (2003). *Ethische Ingenieurverantwortung. Handlungsspielräume und Perspektiven der Kodifizierung.* Ed. Sigma.

Jacobs, M., Kurtz, C., Simon, J., & Böhmann, T. (2021). Value sensitive design and power in socio-technical ecosystems. *Internet Policy Review, 10*(3), 1–26. https://doi.org/10.14763/2021.3.1580.

Jacobs, N., & Huldtgren, A. (2021). Why value sensitive design needs ethical commitments. *Ethics and Information Technology, 23*(1), 23–26. https://doi.org/10.1007/s10676-018-9467-3.

Jaeggi, R. (2018). *Critique of forms of life.* Harvard University Press.

Jobin, A., Ienca, M., & Vayena, E. (2019). Artificial intelligence: The global landscape of AI ethics guidelines. *Nature Machine Intelligence*, 389–399. https://doi.org/10.1038/s42256-019-0088-2.

Jongepier, F., & Keymolen, E. (2022). Explanation and agency: Exploring the normative-epistemic landscape of the "right to explanation". *Ethics and Information Technology, 24*(4), 1–11. ISSN: 1572-8439. .

Langer, M., Oster, D., Speith, T., Hermanns, H., Kästner, L., Schmidt, E., Sesing, A., & Baum, K. (2021). What do we want from Explainable Artificial Intelligence (XAI)?–A stakeholder perspective on XAI and a conceptual model guiding interdisciplinary XAI research. *Artificial Intelligence, 296*, 1–24. https://doi.org/10.1016/j.artint.2021.103473.

Loreggia, A., Mattei, N., Rossi, F., & Venable, K. B. (2018). Preferences and ethical principles in decision making. In J. Furman, G. Marchant, H. Price, & F. Rossi (Eds.), *Proceedings of the 2018 AAAI/ACM Conference on AI, Ethics, and Society* (p. 222). Association for Computing Machinery. ISBN: 9781450360128. https://doi.org/10.1145/3278721.3278723.

Manders-Huits, N. (2011). What values in design? The challenge of incorporating moral values into design. *Science and Engineering Ethics, 17*(2), 271–287. https://doi.org/10.1007/s11948-010-9198-2.

Mittelstadt, B., Russell, C., & Wachter, S. (2019). Explaining explanations in AI. In *Proceedings of the Conference on Fairness, Accountability, and Transparency* (pp. 279–288). Association for Computing Machinery. https://doi.org/10.1145/3287560.3287574.

Morley, J., Floridi, L., Kinsey, L., & Elhalal, A. (2020). From what to how: An initial review of publicly available AI ethics tools, methods and research to translate principles into practices. *Science and Engineering Ethics, 26*, 2141–2168. https://doi.org/10.2139/ssrn.3830348.

O'Hara, K. (2020). Explainable AI and the philosophy and practice of explanation. *Computer Law & Security Review, 39*, 1–7. https://doi.org/10.1016/j.clsr.2020.105474.

Rawls, J. (1971). *A theory of justice: Original edition.* The Belknap Press.

Reckwitz, A. (2002). Toward a theory of social practices: A development in culturalist theorizing. *European Journal of Social Theory, 5*(2), 243–263. https://doi.org/10.1177/13684310222225432.

Reddy, S. T. A. (2023). Using Apple's ResearchKit and CareKit frameworks for Explainable Artificial Intelligence healthcare. *Journal of Big Data Technology and Business Analytics, 2*(3), 15–19.

Reijers, W., & Gordijn, B. (2019). Moving from value sensitive design to virtuous practice design. *Journal of Information, Communication and Ethics in Society, 17*(2), 196–209. https://doi.org/10.1108/JICES-10-2018-0080.

Ribeiro, M. T., Singh, S., & Guestrin, C. (2016). "Why should I trust you?": Explaining the predictions of any classifier. In *Proceedings of the 22nd ACM SIGKDD International Conference on Knowledge Discovery and Data Mining.* KDD '16 (pp. 1135–1144). Association for Computing Machinery. https://doi.org/10.1145/2939672.2939778.

Rouse, J. (2007). Social practices and normativity. *Philosophy of the Social Sciences, 37*(1), 46–56. https://doi.org/10.1177/0048393106296542.

Rudin, C., Wang, C., & Coker, B. (2020). The age of secrecy and unfairness in recidivism prediction. *Harvard Data Science Review, 2*(1), 1–53. https://doi.org/10.1162/99608f92.6ed64b30.

Sagoff, M. (1986). Values and preferences. *Ethics, 96*(2), 301–316. https://doi.org/10.1086/292748.

Simon, J. (2017). Value sensitive design and responsible research and innovation. In S. O. Hansson (Ed.), *The ethics of technology: Methods and approaches* (pp. 219–236). Rowman & Littlefield.

Suchman, L. A. (2007). *Human–machine reconfigurations: Plans and situated actions* (2nd ed.). Cambridge University Press. https://doi.org/10.1017/CBO9780511808418.

Timmermans, J., Zhao, Y., & van den Hoven, J. (2011). Ethics and nanopharmacy: Value sensitive design of new drugs. *NanoEthics, 5*(3), 269–283. https://doi.org/10.1007/s11569-011-0135-x.

Van de Poel, I. (2013). Translating values into design requirements. In D. P. Michelfelder, N. McCarthy, & D. E. Goldberg (Eds.), *Philosophy and engineering: Reflections on practice, principles and process* (pp. 253–266). Springer. ISBN: 978-94-007-7762-0. https://doi.org/10.1007/978-94-007-7762-0_20.

Van de Poel, I., & Kroes, P. (2014). Can technology embody values? In P. Kroes & P.-P. Verbeek (Eds.), *The moral status of technical artefacts* (pp. 103–124). Springer Netherlands. https://doi.org/10.1007/978-94-007-7914-3_7.

van Wynsberghe, A. (2013). Designing robots for care: Care centered value-sensitive design. *Science and Engineering Ethics, 19*(2), 407–433. https://doi.org/10.1007/s11948-011-9343-6.

Vredenburgh, K. (2022). The right to explanation. *Journal of Political Philosophy, 30*(2), 209–229. https://doi.org/10.1111/jopp.12262.

Warren, C., McGraw, A. P., & Van Boven, L. (2011). Values and preferences: defining preference construction. *Wiley Interdisciplinary Reviews: Cognitive Science, 2*(2), 193–205. https://doi.org/10.1002/wcs.98.

Watson, G. (2004). *Agency and answerability: Selected essays.* Oxford University Press. https://doi.org/10.1093/acprof:oso/9780199272273.001.0001.

Zaman, B., & JafariNaimi, N. (2015). A value sensitive design case study: Why values do (not) design. In *Workshop: Charting the Next Decade for Value Sensitive Design, Critical Alternatives Conference*. Aarhus, Denmark. https://api.semanticscholar.org/CorpusID:157694007.

Zimmer, M. (2005). Media ecology and value sensitive design: A combined approach to understanding the biases of media technology. In *Proceedings of the Media Ecology Association* (Vol. 6, pp. 1–15). https://www.media-ecology.net/publications/MEA_proceedings/v6/Zimmer.pdf.

Open Access This chapter is licensed under the terms of the Creative Commons Attribution 4.0 International License (http://creativecommons.org/licenses/by/4.0/), which permits use, sharing, adaptation, distribution and reproduction in any medium or format, as long as you give appropriate credit to the original author(s) and the source, provide a link to the Creative Commons license and indicate if changes were made.

The images or other third party material in this chapter are included in the chapter's Creative Commons license, unless indicated otherwise in a credit line to the material. If material is not included in the chapter's Creative Commons license and your intended use is not permitted by statutory regulation or exceeds the permitted use, you will need to obtain permission directly from the copyright holder.

Chapter 11
Managing the sXAI Interaction: Beliefs, Goals, and Decisional Processes

Rachid Alami and Britta Wrede

Abstract In this chapter, we focus on managing the human-machine interaction involved in the explanation process and the mechanisms and tools that can be used to implement such management. Explanation is treated as a human–machine co-construction process. We essentially take a constructive approach in the hope that it might help potential designers and developers of such systems. We draw on literature from various fields such as philosophical explorations of social action, studies of human dialog, human–computer interaction, computer-supported collaborative work, multiagent systems, and human–robot interaction and collaboration. We cover the conceptual and decisional ingredients that may be relevant for implementing the socially interactive process that an AI-enabled machine needs when asked to explain the output it has produced when addressing a decision task or when it has to produce a behavior that is understandable and acceptable for a human who is co-acting or simply co-present with the machine. We review the methods and approaches for designing the appropriate decision and interaction capabilities for socially explainable AI (sXAI). First, we review planners that are designed specifically to synthesize preferred (from a human perspective) explanations and behaviors. We then turn to control architectures that have to orchestrate the various machine capabilities dealing with situation assessment, human mental state estimation, planning, goal management, and human–machine interaction in order to ensure proper management of the sXAI interaction.

R. Alami (✉)
Laboratory for Analysis and Architecture of Systems, Artificial and Natural Intelligence Toulouse Institute, Université de Toulouse, Toulouse, France
e-mail: rachid.alami@laas.fr

B. Wrede
Medical School OWL, Bielefeld University, Bielefeld, Germany
e-mail: bwrede@techfak.uni-bielefeld.de

© The Author(s) 2026
K. J. Rohlfing et al. (eds.), *Social Explainable AI*,
https://doi.org/10.1007/978-981-96-5290-7_11

11.1 How Does This Chapter Relate to sXAI?

In this chapter, we focus on the management of the human–machine interaction involved in the explanation process and the mechanisms and tools that can be used to implement such management.

We draw on studies, findings, and systems related to human-robot interaction (HRI) because it can be seen as an illustrative instance of human-machine collaboration (Doncieux et al., 2022; Papagni & Koeszegi, 2021; Sakai & Nagai, 2022). The ability of the machine to explain its decisions and behaviors is a must, as is the need to ensure that the human properly understands how the machine operates. Additionally, HRI applications provide a wide range of real-world situations in which a machine is co-present and embodied alongside a human, employs a variety of modalities, and continuously monitors and analyzes human responses.

Let us recall that, in such a context,[1] the explanation can be seen as:

1. A post hoc interactive process in which the AI machine is asked to explain the output it has produced when addressing a decision-making task;
2. A process that accompanies a human-machine shared activity during which the machine, while performing its part of the task, also provides information to the human that explains its decisions and actions.

It is also important to note that when the explanation accompanies a shared human-machine activity, it is somehow intertwined with it. The machine has to do its part of the work and convey explanatory information about it; the human does their part of the job and also contributes to the explanation process. This can happen in various ways. For example, the machine can accompany an action it is performing with communication cues that are intended to provide information (to the human) about the action, why it has been chosen, and how it is being performed.

The machine can also 'merge' goal-directed action and communication by choosing a way of performing the action that conveys complementary information about its intention or goal or about the contextual conditions it is considering. Examples of this are expressive movements that perform a motion action and exhibit the fact that it is cautious, or ensure that it is visible and its intention is easy to interpret without ambiguity(Dehais et al., 2011; Strabala et al., 2013).

Another aspect to consider is the fact that the action the machine has achieved or is currently achieving may have been proactive or in response to a human request. In the former case, it is essential for the machine to also explain/justify (or be prepared to do so) why it has acted proactively.

We essentially take a constructive approach in this chapter in the sense that we address the concepts, the models, and the algorithms that can be used to design and implement the AI-enabled explaining and interactive machine.

---

[1] See, for illustration, scenario in Sect. 2.6.

We begin by reviewing the literature pertaining to the conceptual and decisional components that may be pertinent for its implementation, given that the sXAI explanation co-construction process can be seen as a collaborative problem-solving process between humans and machines (see Sect. 1.5). Then, we discuss the concepts behind the so-called 'social' abilities needed to implement an effective explanation of the behavior of an AI-enabled machine. We posit that principles and mechanisms borrowed from joint action (Sebanz et al., 2006) could apply to sXAI, and we review several coordination processes that are involved in human-human joint action. However, because we are dealing with a human and an AI-enabled machine, we argue that there is a clear and assumed *asymmetry* between the machine and the human in this process. This has implications in terms of *constraints* and *objectives* that should shape the machine's behavior.

We then examine the tools and the interactive mechanisms that could be used to implement the system conducting and managing the social interaction that supports the explanation process. We essentially cover the planning and anticipation capabilities of the machine which should be designed to allow a synthesis of understandable and acceptable behavior. And besides the planning and anticipation capabilities of the machine, we discuss two notions that are essential in order to conduct a productive human–machine collaboration process: (1) the management of goals and related decision issues and (2) the commitment of the human to the overall process and how it is conducted, along with the management of this commitment by the machine throughout the sXAI process.

11.2 Overview of the Chapter

We first define the concepts and then address the software architectures and algorithms related to the implementation of the interactive human-machine explanation process.

In Sect. 11.3, we analyze the explanation process as a goal-directed belief updating process. The two agents – the human and the machine – share a goal and incrementally contribute to its achievement. Based on this, we review the main concepts studied in collaborative multiagent studies (Sect. 11.4) and, in particular, the notion of joint goals.

Then, in order to account for the social aspect of the interactive explanation elaboration process, we posit that sXAI can be viewed as a human–machine joint action. Because various forms of uncertainty can undermine the alignment of representations and hence coordination, we review in Sect. 11.5 the related principles and then the sensorimotor and cognitive processes in joint action by which uncertainty is reduced and coordination is achieved.

In Sect. 11.6 we discuss the roles and task distribution between the human and the machine and illustrate why it is important to adopt, at the design level, an asymmetry between the machine and the human in the process that enforces the machine's duties to adapt to the human's needs and to facilitate their action and understanding.

We then focus on the need to track and manage the goals, throughout the explanation process (Sect. 11.7) and also to assess and manage the human's commitment to the sXAI process (Sect. 11.8).

Finally, in Sect. 11.9 we review the literature on the models and algorithms for the synthesis of plans and machine behaviors in the context of human-machine collaboration. The main issues here concern the elaboration of plans that satisfy a set of properties related to human legibility, predictability, and acceptability.

11.3 The Explanation Process: A Goal-Directed Belief Updating Collaborative Process

The explanation co-construction process can be viewed and implemented as a human-machine collaborative problem-solving process. There is a goal-oriented problem to be solved. The goal is to reach an agreement between the human and the machine that the explanation is understood and accepted by the human.[2] Consequently, sXAI is a collaborative and interactive process between two agents, the human (H) and the machine (M). Both contribute in order to reach the goal (Rohlfing et al., 2021; Sado et al., 2023). This is achieved by updating the human's beliefs through an interactive process, leading to a satisfactory explanation from the human perspective.

By itself, the explaining process can be viewed in terms of both agents iteratively performing (Arrieta et al., 2020):

- An update of their beliefs
- An elaboration of a communication action; in some contexts this action also has an effect on the real world as perceived by the other agent
- The execution of the action that is observed by the other agent.

A communication action ($H \rightarrow M$ or $M \rightarrow H$) is the utterance of a conjunction of facts. Besides, the two agents can also produce nonverbal signal and some facts can then be interpreted from such signals. The main effect of actions that is considered here is that of the one produced by an agent on the beliefs of the other agent.

This is an interactive multistep process. Human and machine/robot are the two agents that contribute incrementally to reaching the shared goal. The iteration is in fact a suite of action/reaction steps. But this is not necessarily a proper sequence. It may happen that the two agents act concurrently. For example, one agent might interrupt the other, comment on, or complement what the other agent is doing while it is being done. This requires the ability for multimodal interaction (cf. Sect. 23.6) as well as incrementality (cf. Sect. 12.1).

---

[2] See Sect. 6.6 for more details about goals in explainable systems.

The scheme can be extended to more than two agents, for example, a machine involved in the explanation of its decision to two humans.

The following two sections are dedicated to reviewing the main concepts of multiagent collaboration (Sect. 11.4) and then those elaborated by the joint action community (Sect. 11.5) and how they can be instantiated within the context of the explanation process.

11.4 The Explaining Process: A Multiagent Collaborative Activity

Because the explanation process can be analyzed as a multiagent collaborative activity, it may be pertinent to draw on the concepts and mechanisms proposed in the extensive literature on multiagent cooperation including that on human-machine cooperation. Indeed, the concepts and mechanisms of collaboration have been at the core of diverse research topics such as philosophical explorations of social action, studies of human dialog, human–computer interaction, multiagent systems, and distributed artificial intelligence.

Levesque et al. (1990) have analyzed the fundamental concepts concerning teamwork. This research is essentially motivated by the following question: Given that actions are performed by individuals, and that it is individuals who ultimately have the beliefs and goals that generate actions, "what motivates agents to form teams and act together?"

The main point here is that a collaborative activity is one that is performed by individual agents who share certain specific mental properties. A key notion has been elaborated here: the notion of "joint persistent goal" when two or more agents are involved in a collaborative activity (Cohen & Levesque, 1991, p. 499):

"A team of agents have a joint persistent goal relative to q to achieve p just in case

1. they mutually believe that p is currently false;
2. they mutually know they all want p to eventually be true;
3. it is true (and mutual knowledge) that until they come to mutually believe either that p is true, that p will never be true, or that q is false, they will continue to mutually believe that they each have p as a weak achievement goal relative to q and with respect to the team."

Other pioneering contributions to this field address the concept of shared activity and the role of shared intention (Bratman, 1993). They point out that successful joint action depends on the efficient coordination of participant agents' goals, intentions, plans, and actions. Indeed, it seems essential to investigate what are the tools and mechanisms that help to achieve a joint goal in a way that is robust against possible failures and misunderstandings.

When involved in joint activity, agents should be able to form representations not just of their own intentions and actions but also of those of their partners, and these two sets of representations need to be aligned. This leads to the concept of shared plans(Grosz & Kraus, 1999) and the ingredients used for their elaboration: shared representations, mutual beliefs, and common ground (Wenke et al., 2011).

Another important contribution to the topic is the work of Herbert Clark and his conception of the dialogue as a collaborative process (Clark, 1994). Various forms of uncertainty can undermine predictability, the alignment of representations, and hence coordination. Clark (2005) shows how dialogue serves to coordinate collaborative activities that usually emerge in hierarchically nested projects and sub-projects. He points out that dialog is used to coordinate two kinds of transitions: vertical transitions, or entering and exiting joint projects, and horizontal transitions, or continuing within joint projects.

The concepts of joint activity developed by Herbert Clark are used by (Klein et al., 2005) to exhibit the requirements for carrying out joint activities, and the 'choreography' of joint activity. One essential aspect discussed here is the fact that joint activity depends on the interpredictability of the participants' attitudes and actions. Such interpredictability is based on common ground, pertinent knowledge, and assumptions that are shared among the parties involved in the activity.

In Sect. 11.9, we shall discuss how these concepts and coordination processes have been used to design the software architectures of cognitive and interactive machines, and report on the models and algorithms used in their planners and reasoners.

11.5 sXAI Viewed as Human-Machine Joint Action

11.5.1 About Human-Human Joint Action

Based on what has been discussed above, we posit that principles and mechanisms borrowed from joint action could apply to sXAI. Indeed, research on human-human joint action (Knoblich et al., 2011; Sebanz et al., 2006) has become a topic of intense research in cognitive psychology and philosophy, providing elements and even offering control architecture hints to help our understanding of human-human joint action.

As a definition, we borrow the following: "Joint action can be regarded as any form of social interaction whereby two or more individuals coordinate their actions in space and time to bring about a change in the environment" (Sebanz et al., 2006, p. 70).

Now, and for the benefit of sXAI developers, we would like to draw from these studies what knowledge a machine needs to have about the human it is interacting with, and what processes it needs to handle in order to manage a successful interaction. Conversely, it is important to identify what information the human should possess in order to understand and follow what the machine is doing and how the machine should make this information available to its human partner.

11.5.2 Cognitive Processes by Which Uncertainty Is Reduced and Coordination Achieved

Successful joint action depends on the efficient coordination of participant agents' goals, intentions, plans, and actions. In other words, it is not enough for agents to have a common goal. They must also coordinate their own contribution with those of their coagents so as to have a coherent and convergent activity (Schilling et al., 2016). This requires them to monitor their partner's intentions and actions, predict their consequences, and use these predictions to adjust what they are doing to what their partners are doing[3] (Clodic et al., 2017).

In recent years, there has been a great deal of work, both conceptual and empirical, on the cognitive processes by which uncertainty is reduced and coordination achieved. Successful joint action requires agents to coordinate both their intentions and their actions. Several coordination processes are involved in human-human joint action.

Self-other Distinction The first coordination process is the *self-other distinction*. This means that "for shared representations of actions and tasks to foster coordination rather than create confusion, it is important that agents also be able to keep apart representations of their own and other's actions and intentions" (Pacherie, 2012, p. 359).

Joint Attention Attention is the mental activity by which we select among items and focus on some rather than others. The second coordination process is *joint attention*. However, this is more than the addition of two agents' attentions:

"The phenomenon of joint attention involves more than just two people attending to the same object or event. At least two additional conditions must be obtained. First, there must be some causal connection between the two subjects' acts of attending (causal coordination). Second, each subject must be aware, in some sense, of the object as an object that is present to both; in other words, the fact that both are attending to the same object or event should be open or mutually manifest (mutual manifestness)" (Pacherie, 2012, p. 355).

Understanding of Intentional Action Each agent should be able to *infer their partner's intention* when to reading their actions or course of actions. This links up with action-to-goal prediction (i.e., inferring the underlying goal through the understanding the ongoing action) and goal-to-action prediction (i.e., inferring what would be the action(s) needed to achieve a known goal).

---

[3] See, for illustration, see scenario in Sect. 2.6.

Shared Task Representations These play an important role in goal-directed coordination (Knoblich et al., 2011). They serve as the basis for and support all the processes described above. Indeed, it is only when the partners share a common representation of the task at hand that they can implement it successfully (Butterfill & Sebanz, 2011; Wenke et al., 2011) (see Chap. 14).

One important notion illustrating how the partners involved in a joint action contribute jointly is the notion of "coordination smoothers" (Vesper et al., 2010, p. 118). A coordination smoother is either a modulation of one's own behavior that reliably has the effect of either simplifying coordination or making it more fluid. A first type of coordination smoother involves making one's own behavior more predictable. A second type of coordination smoother involves ways of delimiting and structuring one's own task in order to reduce the need for coordination. Indeed, it has been demonstrated that coordination is a costly process (Klein et al., 2005). The choice of objects affording a particular task distribution can also serve as a third coordination smoother. A fourth type of coordination smoother involves providing coordination signals (Clark, 1994). Agents are able to selectively make certain movements salient with the effect that information about their actions is more readily available to others; in this case, movements serve both as components of actions and as coordination signals (Liang et al., 2019).

In Sect. 11.9, we shall review some examples of robot planners and reasoners that explicitly implement the concepts and mechanisms discussed here.

11.6 Roles and Task Distribution Between the Human and the Machine

As discussed above, highly coordinated joint activity assumes a basic compact—namely, an agreement (often tacit) to facilitate coordination and prevent its breakdown. This includes a commitment to some degree of aligning goals, and all parties are expected to bear their portion of the responsibility to establish and sustain common ground and to repair it when necessary (Bradshaw, 2003).

11.6.1 Human Versus Machine

Because we are proposing to model the human and the machine on the basis of a multiagent scheme here, it is very important to recall that the human and the machine are not **EQUAL** when participating in the joint activity we envisage. Indeed, even when involved in a joint task with a machine, the human is not restricted to the task at hand. The system should be designed so that in such a way as to give the human the latitude to change their focus or goal, or to disengage at any time. It may also happen that the human does not comply (for unknown reasons) with the duties needed for a smooth joint action (Grinbaum et al., 2017; Doncieux et al., 2022).

In addition, the machine is there to help and facilitate the action of the human (Clodic et al., 2017; Scheutz et al., 2022). It should not only exhibit a rational and predictable behavior but also:

- Do its best to be acceptable;
- Do its best to be understandable and to ensure that its intentions are legible;
- Facilitate the action of the human;
- Adapt to their rhythms;
- Constantly monitor the 'quality of the interaction.'

11.6.2 About Machines Able to Act as Socially Interactive Agents

Because our topic is socially explainable artificial intelligence (sXAI), it is important to state at which "level" and how a human-machine interactive activity can be qualified as social.

We refer here to the definition proposed by (Skewes et al., 2019, p. 1) for the so-called social robots. This can assuredly be extended to socially interactive machines:

"social robots may be practically defined as programmable devices that are designed to act within the physical and symbolic space of human social interactions, and which have affordances for what people common-sensically call social interactions. Indeed, people easily engage with such devices, following typical patterns of social interactions, while experiencing both similarities and distinctive discrepancies from "authentic" interactions with a human partner."

Indeed, when developing a socially interactive machine, it is important to understand and state as precisely as possible the relation between the interactive machine and the human from the human's point of view (Mutlu & Forlizzi, 2008; Nass & Yen, 2010; Šabanović, 2010).

The development and deployment of such so-called social machines raise ontological and ethical questions (Seibt, 2017). There is clearly a need for principled interdisciplinary design approaches taking the socio-cultural and societal contexts into account such as (Fischer et al., 2020) that yields culturally sustainable applications and can inform the development of the machine's decision-making and interactive capabilities. This goes further than user-centered, participatory approaches (Lee et al., 2017), and ethnographic studies.

This is even more important today with LLMs that can mimic human behavior and roles or even their emotions and posture.

A recent paper (Clark & Fischer, 2023, p. 60) states that, when interacting with social agents, people construe them not as social agents per se, but as "depictions of *social agents.*" Also, and very importantly, people distinguish these agents from the authorities responsible for them or behind them.

We also point here to a proposal for the elaboration of an ontology (Seibt, 2022) that could be used as a descriptive framework for human–robot interaction. The aim here is to identify different 'levels of sociality' and to order them relatively to the behavioral or mental coordination capabilities required of the agents.

These issues are fundamental and have direct implications for how human-machine interactions should be designed and managed with clear roles and transparency in terms of capabilities. Indeed an AI-enabled machine, even with sophisticated skills in terms of situation assessment and services provided to humans, remains a machine with known and explicit limitations in terms of social capabilities.

11.7 Goal Management and Associated Decisional Issues in sXAI

As discussed above, the explanation process is, by essence, goal-oriented (see Sect. 6.3 for a discussion of the role of goals in sXAI), and we have seen that it is shared between the human and the machine. We can assume that there is a first interactive process aiming to specify this shared goal and agree upon it (Butterfill & Sinigaglia, 2023). This can range from (1) very simple cases in which, for example, in a post hoc situation, the human issues a request to explain a decision taken by the machine, and the machine adopts this immediately as a shared goal, to (2) more complex cases in which the goal is cospecified by the human and the machine.

In the case in which the explanation accompanies a human-machine collaborative activity, the goal associated with it is implicit, because it is part of the machine's duties.

It is discussed in the literature that the explanation most often goes through an interactive multistep process. Therefore, there is a need to manage the process and keep track of the current state of the process and of the goal itself (Miller, 2019) and of the goal/sub-goal hierarchy. Bangerter and Clark (2003) have discussed how joint activities usually emerge in hierarchically nested projects and sub-projects.[4]

The explanation is often based on a goal/task decomposition (Paternò, 2004). A typical mechanism can be represented through hierarchical task networks (HTNs) (Ghallab et al., 2016) that make it possible to organize a progressive refinement of the problem into subproblems that also may need an explanation. HTNs have been used widely in the literature to structure human-machine interaction(Alford et al., 2016; Cheng et al., 2021; Darvish et al., 2021).

The refinement can be verbalized (Bangerter & Clark, 2003) and negotiated between the machine and the human (Gordon et al., 2023; Hayes & Scassellati, 2016; Johannsmeier & Haddadin, 2016; Milliez et al., 2016; Tewari & Persiani, 2021).

---

[4] See also Sect. 6.7.

It may also happen for the human to change their mind during the explanation process and suggest that a different goal or set of sub-goals needs to be achieved first, before returning to the original goal. The machine will have to comply and focus on the agreed sub-goal while leaving the global goal active. There is an extensive literature on goal reasoning that emphasizes the explicit representation of goals, their automatic formulation, and their dynamic management (Vattam et al., 2013). For example, (Roberts et al., 2016) have proposed a framework that blends hierarchical goal networks and hierarchical task networks and manages the goal life cycle with clear semantics. This has recently been adapted to human-centric goal reasoning (Brameld et al., 2024).

Thus, methods for goal formulation and goal management could certainly contribute to the development of the decision-making and social capabilities of future systems capable of conducting socially acceptable explanations of AI decisions and behaviors.

11.8 On Commitment and Its Management

The notion of commitment plays a pivotal role in understanding joint action (Bratman, 1993; Cohen & Levesque, 1991). In order to perform a joint action, coagents need to establish and handle their commitment to the shared goals and the plans involved in the joint action.[5] However, the study of commitments is quite new in the context of human-machine collaborative task achievement (Castro et al., 2019).

As a first approximation, a commitment is in place when an agent (the author of the commitment) gives an assurance to another agent (the recipient of the commitment) that they will act in a certain way. As a result, the recipient forms expectations regarding the actions of the author. Also, and very importantly, both parties have mutual knowledge about the existence of the commitment. What distinguishes a joint action from a mere coordination is that the partners are committed to achieving a goal together (Michael & Salice, 2017).

A central function of commitments within joint action is to reduce uncertainty about the agent's intention to contribute. This is communicated through social signals and cues or regulative actions produced and perceived by the agents that permit the exhibition of this commitment Hegel et al. (2011). It is also estimated indirectly based on estimating the involvement of an agent by assessing their contribution to the task at hand.

This is based essentially on expectations. Of course, expectations can be frustrated or fulfilled. Therefore, commitment management can be seen as a mechanism for reparation (Castro & Pacherie, 2023).

---

[5] In the literature and more particularly in the robotics domain, the word "engagement" is often used.

In the literature, a number of contributions address the capacity of a machine to detect or measure a user's commitment and to react appropriately (see Oertel et al., 2020 for an overview). One pioneering contribution is the Collagen system (Sidner et al., 2005) that was developed to monitor and support the engagement of the human throughout the process. There are several contributions proposing implementations of engagement detection for human–robot interaction (Lu et al., 2411) and estimation of the level of engagement (Anzalon et al., 2015; Drejing et al., 2015; Klotz et al., 2011; Nasir et al., 2022).

Other relevant ways of assessing whether things are going well in a human-machine social interaction have been proposed. Clark and Krych (2004) studied the ability to speak while monitoring addressees for understanding. This could also be used to assess whether the human is committed or not to the task at hand. An indicator of the quality of the interaction is the level of fluency in human-robot shared-location teamwork. Hoffman (2019) has proposed a number of metrics to evaluate this. A measure of the quality of an interaction (QoI) has also been proposed in Mayima et al. (2022) where metrics have been defined and integrated into a cognitive and collaborative robot to measure in real time whether things are going as expected and whether the human–robot duet is progressing toward the goal. The machine acts and reacts on the basis of a model of the human and an estimation of their mental state and the common background. This makes it important to equip it with the ability to assess and report strong deviations from expectations and non-convergence toward the shared goal.

11.9 Operationalizations of Decisional Processes for Managing the sXAI

Because the explanation co-construction process can be considered and implemented as a collaborative human-machine problem-solving process with a goal to be achieved, the sXAI machine should be endowed with the ability to reason about and respond to the human's actions, reactions and requests, and to plan (or synthesize) its contribution to the process.

In Chap. 14, we discussed the knowledge and the models that can be used in the process and in order to assess the situation at each step and estimate the human's beliefs. In the rest of this chapter, we shall discuss the models and algorithms for the behavior synthesis aspect.

Indeed, the challenge is to design and build the cognitive and interactive capabilities that will allow the machine to be pertinent at any moment and exhibit transparent, legible, and acceptable behaviors (Clodic et al., 2017; Mercuur et al., 2020).

The interested reader is referred to the extensive literature on planning in the human–machine context. This covers a number of aspects that we shall summarize here.

Besides producing a plan to achieve a given goal based on initial knowledge about the state of the world and the agent's abilities, the challenge here is to be intelligible. Weld and Bansal (2019) discuss a number of aspects such as facilitating user control, considering user acceptance, as well as improving human insight and adapting the machine to the human's requests and behavior. An essential aspect is to elaborate and manage the explanation as an interactive process.

Langley (2019) states that the explainable agent must be able to communicate its decisions and reasons in ways that make contact with human concepts; and it must also be able to explain not only decisions made during plan generation but also how actual events have diverged from a plan and how it has adapted in response to this divergence.

Planning Preferred Explanations and Interaction The literature states clearly that planning is a key ability for generating preferred explanations (Sohrabi et al., 2011); for dealing with what, why, and how questions (Hellström & Bensch, 2018); and also for addressing the social issues (Miller et al., 2018).

One first aspect is to endow the planning process with the ability to gather the causalities of the decision (i.e., for what reason and on the basis on what criteria a given action has been chosen) and to enrich the plan with complementary information aimed at allowing the human to understand the rationale behind it (i.e., the choices made by the planner) (Hayes & Shah, 2017; Petrick & Foster, 2016). Indeed, knowledge-enriched plans are well-suited to this purpose, because they provide the reasons for causal, temporal, and hierarchical relationships between actions.

Dialog can then be integrated with planning, plan refinement (Daruna et al., 2022), task and sub-task allocation (Milliez et al., 2016), as well as plan execution (Broz et al., 2015). Indeed, user studies showed that such strategies allow, for example, users to correct the robot's reasoning and to, thus, improve the robot behavior (Daruna et al., 2022). However, the study was based on artificially introduced reasoning errors. Interestingly, when interacting with an adaptive robot that is capable of, e.g., adapting to the user by (sub-)task allocation, users are able to perceive the highly adaptation capability of the robot, but they do not rate the interaction as more natural (Milliez et al., 2016).

Human-Aware Planning When planning, it is also important not only to take into account what the machine can do but also to anticipate the decisions, actions, and reactions of the human in the context and throughout the process. This is the so-called human-aware task planning approach (Alami et al., 2006; Cirillo et al., 2009; Ramachandruni et al., 2024; Unhelkar et al., 2018) in which, given a goal and the initial conditions, the planner is able to build a shared plan addressing not only the future actions of the machine but also the actions that the human might potentially perform in order to reach a solution or to orient or influence the final plan achievement. This opens up the possibility for the planner to estimate when it can proactively provide or propose assistance (Hoffman & Breazeal, 2007; Kulkarni et al., 2021). It is then able, if needed, to ask for help (Rosenthal et al., 2012; Singh et al., 2022; Tellex et al., 2014) or, more generally, elicit human decision or action (Buisan et al., 2022).

Various criteria linked to preferences for certain plans or courses of action can then be taken into account and formulated as cost and utility measures to evaluate plans and select those with the preferred cost or utility (Edgar et al., 2024; Favier & Alami, 2024; Lallement et al., 2014; Sanneman & Shah, 2020; Shah et al., 2022).

Another key factor to consider, particularly in social contexts, is the elaboration of plans and behaviors that satisfy ethical considerations (Evans et al., 2020; Parker et al., 2022) and are aligned with human values (Khamassi et al., 2024).

Considering Human Perspective-Taking and Human Mental Models A number of contributions propose frameworks to enable the planner to consider in a distinct manner the beliefs of the machine and those of the human partner. Indeed, it is important, when planning an intelligible action or computing an explanation, to build up a good estimation of the perspective of the human (Scheutz et al., 2017; Trafton et al., 2005) and then act in a congruent manner (Milliez et al., 2014) or generate a pertinent communication action (Devin & Alami, 2016; Li et al., 2016). This is essential in order to adapt the plan to the context as it is observed (or known) by the human (Dominey & Warneken, 2011; Favier et al., 2023; Nikolaidis & Shah, 2012) or to adapt to human variability (Hiatt et al., 2011).

Reasoning and adapting to human mental models and abilities is also dealt with as a model reconciliation planning process (Sreedharan et al., 2021). Indeed, when users have domain and task models that differ from those of the AI system, the reasoning within the process of explaining the correctness of a plan and the rationale for its decision should refer to this divergence explicitly. Depending on the situation, the machine may comply with human beliefs or choose to provide complementary information (Chakraborti et al., 2019).

Reasoning and planning with a distinctive consideration of the beliefs of the planning agent and the agent observing or involved in the plan are addressed in the literature on epistemic planning (Bolander & Andersen, 2011). Communication is then modeled as an action that allows, at the right moment, to align the knowledge between the agents relatively to a fact (Alshehri et al., 2021; Hu et al., 2022; Muise et al., 2022). Other contributions, based on epistemic planning, provide means to address pertinent pro-activity (Shvo et al., 2022) or to adapt the plan in a way that is congruent with shared or non-shared experience between the machine and the human (Shekhar et al., 2024).

Acceptability and Legibility Issues Not all plans that achieve a given goal will be satisfactory to the human involved in, or even just observing, the execution of the plan. It is important, when planning the behavior of the machine, to consider its acceptability and legibility for the humans co-present with its execution. A number of contributions tackle this aspect. The fundamental idea is to model the satisfaction or the level of satisfaction with a set of given properties for a plan, an explanation, or a behavior. For abstract or symbolic plans, the properties may concern social rules and convention (Alili et al., 2009), or adaptation to expectations (Malle et al., 2020; Seegebarth et al., 2012).

For robots, a number of contributions have addressed the issue based on geometric and dynamic descriptions of the robot's motions and actions as observed by the co-present human. This is known as human-aware or socially aware motion in which a number of parameters such as visibility and preferences in terms of acceptability, predictability, and comfort are considered.[6]

One major challenge for the widespread use of robots is navigation in human-populated environments, commonly referred to as socially aware navigation. Recent years have seen tremendous progress in the field of social navigation (Francis et al., 2025; Singamaneni et al., 2024).

An important aspect is to ensure the legibility from the human spatial perspective of the intention or goal of any motion by the robot (Dragan & Srinivasa, 2014). The way the robot moves allows it not only to perform its task but also to implicitly convey information about its intentions (Knepper et al., 2017; Watkins et al., 2021). The robot could also make use of other means to generate pertinent social cues as it performs its motion (Wallkötter et al., 2021).

Object manipulation tasks by the robot in the presence of or in synergy with humans also need to be socially aware (Mainprice et al., 2010; Sisbot & Alami, 2012). Besides safety, the generation of a predictable and acceptable motion plan is based essentially on a multi-criteria cost and utility search for trajectories or plans that satisfy the mentioned constraints and properties (Lohrmann et al., 2024).

Teaching a robot to learn new tasks in an interactive way, instead of imitating in a one shot fashion, is a complex endeavor and has only recently come into the focus of research (Laird et al., 2017; Thomaz et al., 2019). This requires the user to understand not only relevant aspects of the underlying learning algorithm but also of the general robot system. Beierling et al. (2024), therefore, propose the concept of an *enabling architecture* which encompasses those aspects of a robot system that a user needs to know in order to use the robot effectively. Furthermore, Beierling and Vollmer (2024) show that providing human teachers with a multimodal interface for giving feedback to a robot's performance of a task it is currently learning is beneficial for the teaching process.

Let us also mention a key aspect that provides solid cues for predictability and intentionality of a robot arm and that is related to human and robot affordances (Awaad et al., 2013; Pandey & Alami, 2014).

Control Architectures for Managing the Human–Machine Interaction The reasoning and planning process may be contingent upon the specific domain in which the machine is specialized. However, the machine's capacity to manage the explanation process can be regarded as being general and reusable across domains. This is generally addressed at the level of the machine's control architecture (Lemaignan et al., 2017; Stange et al., 2022; Vesper et al., 2010) in which a controller orchestrates the different skills dealing with situation assessment; the

---

[6] See, for illustration, scenario in Sect. 2.6.

estimation of the human mental state; online decision and planning; and control of perception, action, and communication means.

11.10 How Does This Chapter Inspire Further Directions of sXAI?

This chapter focuses on the cognitive and interactive skills that can be used to implement the management of the human–machine interactions involved in the explanation process. It can be considered as an introduction to the mechanisms and tools that can be used to implement such management.

We provide a brief overview of the literature from various fields such as philosophy of mind and action, human–computer interaction, multiagent systems, joint action and social cognition, and human–robot interaction and collaboration.

We adopt a constructive approach in the hope that it might help a potential designer and developer of such a system. The main point here is to investigate the decisions and the associated deliberation and planning abilities that are necessary for a machine to be able to determine when and how to act in relation to the social interactions that accompany the explanation content itself.

We posit that principles and mechanisms borrowed from joint action could apply to sXAI. The machine must then assess the humans' mental state, monitor their actions, predict their consequences, and use these predictions to adjust and align its behavior with what the human is doing and/or and in accordance with their mental state and beliefs. The machine should also do its best to be understandable and legible and to facilitate the human's action.

We review the cognitive processes by which uncertainty is reduced and coordination achieved and made fluid. These are essentially (1) the development of the human-centered planning and deliberation skills related to the synthesis of the machine's behavior and (2) the deliberation skills dedicated to the control of the interaction process:

1. As far as the synthesis of machine behavior is concerned, a first element is to equip the machine with the ability to take into account the beliefs of the machine and those of the human partner in a distinct way, and to build up a good estimation of the human partner's perspective. It is also necessary to develop task and behavior planners (based on so-called human-aware or human-centered or socially aware planning techniques) that shape the machine's plans and behavior so that they are legible and acceptable. This includes decisions about when and how to use social cues and signals.
2. With regard to the deliberative abilities that are dedicated to the control of the interaction, two essential mechanisms have been identified in the literature as essential for successful goal-oriented social interaction: the management of goals and their life cycle, and the management of the human's commitment throughout the interactive process.

These guidelines provide a strong basis to transfer existing management frameworks developed mostly for human–robot interaction to the realm of sXAI. Thus, the explanation process can be viewed as a joint task between the AI system. Note that the goal to be negotiated can be multifaceted: On the one hand, the explanandum itself needs to be negotiated at the beginning of the interaction in order to achieve common ground. On the other hand, there is a need to also negotiate the epistemic goal of the explanation. There is evidence that the emotional state of explainees play an important role in XAI. It has been shown that individuals who are emotionally aroused are more likely to follow guided explanations whereas non-aroused individuals are more likely to follow the advice of an AI system that does not provide an explanation. This indicates that the emotional state of a human explainee affects his/her goal of the explanation with respect to the level of understanding she/he expects (Thommes et al., 2024). Thus, further research is needed to develop approaches on how to negotiate the epistemic goals of an explanation regarding the emotional state of the user and what explanation strategies to follow to achieve different epistemic states. Also, more research is required to investigate how contextual factors such as time constraints or importance affect the epistemic goals that users have in an sXAI.

11.11 Rapid Access to the Content of This Chapter

In this chapter, we focus on the management of the human–machine interaction involved in the explanation process and the mechanisms and tools that can be used to implement such management.

The explanation is treated as a human–machine interactive co-construction process. We draw on studies, findings, and systems related to human–robot interaction (HRI) because this can be seen as an illustrative instance of human–machine collaboration (Doncieux et al., 2022; Papagni & Koeszegi, 2021; Sakai & Nagai, 2022). The ability of the machine to explain its decisions and behaviors is a must, as is the need to ensure that the human properly understands how the machine operates.

We adopt a constructive approach in the hope that it might help a potential designer and developer of such a system.

We draw on literature from various fields such as philosophy of mind and action, human-computer interaction, computer-supported collaborative work, multiagent systems, joint action and social cognition, and human-robot interaction and collaboration.

We consider the conceptual and decisional ingredients that might be relevant to the implementation of the socially interactive process that an AI-enabled machine needs to perform when asked to explain the output it has produced while addressing a decision task, or when it has to produce an intelligible and acceptable behavior with respect to a human co-acting with the machine or simply co-present.

The explanation can be seen as:

1. A post hoc interactive process in which the AI machine is requested by a human to explain the output it has produced to address a decision task;
2. A process that accompanies a human-machine shared activity and in which the machine, while performing its part of the task, also provides the human with information that explains its decisions and actions.

Because the explanation process can be analyzed as a multiagent collaborative activity, we draw on the concepts and mechanisms proposed in the extensive literature on multiagent cooperation including that on human–machine cooperation. The main point of interest for us here is that a joint activity is one that is performed by individual agents who share certain specific mental properties such as a joint persistent goal (Cohen & Levesque, 1991). Other seminal contributions include those concerning the concept of shared activity and the role of shared intentions (Bratman, 1992), the notion of shared plans (Grosz & Kraus, 1999), and the ingredients used for their elaboration (mutual beliefs, common ground). Another important contribution to the topic is the work of Herbert Clark and his conception of the dialog as a collaborative process (Clark, 1994; Clark & Brennan, 1991) and of how it serves to coordinate joint activities that usually emerge in hierarchically nested projects and sub-projects. An essential aspect is the fact that joint activity depends on the interpredictability of the participants' attitudes and actions, based on common ground, relevant knowledge, and assumptions shared among the parties. Klein et al. (2005)) have worked out the requirements for carrying out joint activities, and the "choreography" of joint activity.

Based on this, we argue that principles and mechanisms borrowed from joint action Sebanz et al. (2006) could apply to sXAI, and we review several coordination processes that are involved in human-human joint action (Pacherie, 2012) that could be relevant to us: the self-other distinction, joint attention and mutual manifestness, the ability to understand intentional action, and shared task representations.

Because we are proposing to model the human and the machine on the basis of a multiagent scheme here, it is very important to recall that the human and the machine are not **EQUAL** when they are involved in a joint activity. Indeed, even when involved in a joint task with a machine, the human is not restricted to the task at hand. The system should be designed so that in such a way as to give the human the latitude to change their focus or goal, or to disengage at any time. Also, it may happen that the human does not comply (for unknown reasons) with duties needed for a smooth joint action (Doncieux et al., 2022). In addition, we require the duties of the machine to be understandable and legible, to adapt to humans and their rhythms, and to seek to facilitate the human's action.

We then review the methods and approaches for designing the relevant decision and interaction capabilities for sXAI. We cover a number of contributions related to:

- Planning preferred (from a human perspective) explanations and interactions,
- Human-aware approaches to task and motion planning,
- The need to explicitly consider human perspective-taking and human mental models when planning and shaping the behavior of the machine.

We discuss how legibility and acceptability constraints can/should be built into such planners.

Finally we discuss the need to investigate and develop control architectures (Lemaignan et al., 2017; Stange et al., 2022; Vesper et al., 2010) in which a controller orchestrates the different skills dealing with situation assessment, estimation of the human mental state, online decision and planning, control of perception, and action and communication means. In addition to the control of the machine's deliberation and anticipation capabilities, two key concepts determine a relevant and fruitful social interaction: (1) the management of goals and related decision issues and (2) the commitment of the human and its management. We also discuss the need for the controller to assess whether things are going well and to measure the quality of an interaction (QoI) throughout the interactive human-machine co-construction process.

Acknowledgments Rachid Alami's work has been partially supported by the EU-funded project euROBIN under grant agreement no. 101070596 and by the Artificial and Natural Intelligence Toulouse Institute (ANITI) funded by the France 2030 program under the grant agreement no. ANR-23-IACL-0002. Britta Wrede was funded by the Deutsche Forschungsgemeinschaft (DFG, German Research Foundation): TRR 318/1 2021 – 438445824

References

Alami, R., Clodic, A., Montreuil, V., Sisbot, E. A., & Chatila, R. (2006). Toward human-Aware robot task planning. In *AAAI Spring Symposium: To Boldly go where no Human-Robot Team Has Gone Before*. HAL, hal–01977564. https://laas.hal.science/hal-01977564

Alford, R., Shivashankar, V., Roberts, M., Frank, J., & Aha, D. W. (2016). Hierarchical planning: Relating task and goal decomposition with task sharing. In G. Brewka (Ed.), *Proceedings of the Twenty-Fifth International Joint Conference on Artificial Intelligence*. IJCAI'16 (pp. 3022–3029). AAAI.

Alili, S., Alami, R., & Montreuil, V. (2009). A task planner for an autonomous social robot. In H. Asama, H. Kurokawa, J. Ota & K. Sekiyama (Eds.), *Distributed Autonomous Robotic Systems 8* (pp. 335–344). Springer. https://doi.org/10.1007/978-3-642-00644-9_30

Alshehri, A., Miller, T., & Sonenberg, L. (2021). Modeling communication of collaborative multiagent system under epistemic planning. *International Journal of Intelligent Systems, 36*(10), 5959–5980. https://doi.org/10.1002/int.22536

Anzalone, S. M., Boucenna, S., Ivaldi, S., & Chetouani, M. (2015). Evaluating the engagement with social robots. *International Journal of Social Robotics, 7*(4), 465–478. https://doi.org/10.1007/s12369-015-0298-7

Arrieta, A. B., Díaz-Rodriguez, N., Del Ser, J., Bennetot, A., Tabik, S., Barbado, A., Garcia, S., Gil-Lopez, S., Molina, D., Benjamins, R., Chatila, R., & Herrera, F. (2020). Explainable Artificial Intelligence (XAI): Concepts, taxonomies, opportunities and challenges toward responsible AI. *Information Fusion, 58*, 82–115. https://doi.org/10.1016/j.inffus.2019.12.012

Awaad, I., Kraetzschmar, G. K., & Hertzberg, J. (2013). Affordance-based reasoning in robot task planning. In *Planning and robotics* (p. 2).

Bangerter, A., & Clark, H. H. (2003). Navigating joint projects with dialogue. *Cognitive Science, 27*(2), 195–225. https://doi.org/10.1016/S0364-0213(02)00118-0

Beierling, H., Richter, P., Brandt, M., Terfloth, L., Schulte, C., Wersing, H., & Vollmer, A.-L. (2024). What you need to know about a learning robot: Identifying the enabling architecture of complex systems. *Cognitive Systems Research, 88*, 101286. https://doi.org/10.1016/j.cogsys. 2024.101286

Beierling, H., & Vollmer, A.-L. (2024). *The power of combined modalities in interactive robot learning.* https://arxiv.org/abs/2405.07817

Bolander, T., & Andersen, M. B. (2011). Epistemic planning for single and multi-agent systems. *Journal of Applied Non Classical Logics, 21*(1), 9–34.

Bradshaw, J. M. (2003). Making agents acceptable to people. In *3rd International Central and Eastern European Conference on Multi-Agent Systems, CEEMAS* (Vol. 2691, pp. 1–3). Lecture notes in computer science. Springer. https://doi.org/10.1007/3-540-45023-8/_1

Brameld, K., Castro, G., Sammut, C., Roberts, M., Aha, D. W. (2024). *Human-centric goal reasoning with ripple-down rules.* https://doi.org/10.48550/arXiv.2402.10224

Bratman, M. E. (1992). Shared cooperative activity. *The Philosophical Review, 101*(2), 327–341. https://doi.org/10.2307/2185537

Bratman, M. E. (1993). Shared intention. *Ethics, 104*(1), 97–113. https://doi.org/10.1086/293577

Broz, F., Di Nuovo, A., Belpaeme, T., & Cangelosi, A. (2015). Talking about task progress: Towards integrating task planning and dialog for assistive robotic services. *Paladyn, Journal of Behavioral Robotics, 6*(1). https://doi.org/10.1515/pjbr-2015-0007

Buisan, G., Favier, A., Mayima, A., & Alami, R. (2022). HATP/EHDA: A robot task planner anticipating and eliciting human decisions and actions. In *IEEE International Conference on Robotics and Automation* (pp. 2818–2824). ICRA. IEEE. https://doi.org/10.1109/ICRA46639. 2022.9812227.

Butterfill, S. A., Sinigaglia, C. (2023). Towards a mechanistically neutral account of acting jointly: The notion of a collective goal. *Mind, 132*(525), 1–29. https://doi.org/10.1093/mind/fzab096

Butterfill, S. A., & Sebanz, N. (2011). Joint action: What is shared? *Review of Philosophy and Psychology, 2*(2), 137–146. https://doi.org/10.1007/s13164-011-0062-3

Castro, V. F., Clodic, A., Alami, R., Pacherie, E. (2019). *Commitments in human-robot interaction.* https://doi.org/10.48550/arXiv.1909.06561

Castro, V. F., & Pacherie, E. (2023). Commitments and the sense of joint agency. *Mind & Language, 38*(3), 889–906. https://doi.org/10.1111/mila.12433

Chakraborti, T., Sreedharan, S., & Kambhampati, S. (2019). Balancing explicability and explanations in human-aware planning. In *Proceedings of the Twenty-Eighth International Joint Conference on Artificial Intelligence* (pp. 1335–1343). AAAI. https://doi.org/10.24963/ijcai. 2019/185

Cheng, Y., Sun, L., & Tomizuka, M. (2021). Human-aware robot task planning based on a hierarchical task model. *IEEE Robotics and Automation Letters, 6*(2), 1136–1143. https://doi. org/10.1109/LRA.2021.3056370

Cirillo, M., Karlsson, L., & Saffiotti, A. (2009). A human-aware robot task planner. In *Proceedings of the International Conference on Automated Planning and Scheduling* (Vol. 19, pp. 58–65). PKP Publishing Services Network. https://doi.org/10.1609/icaps.v19i1.13348

Clark, H. H. (1994). Managing problems in speaking. *Speech Communication, 15*(3–4), 243–250. https://doi.org/10.1016/0167-6393(94)90075-2

Clark, H. H. (2005). Coordinating with each other in a material world. *Discourse Studies, 7*(4–5), 507–525. https://doi.org/10.1177/1461445605054404

Clark, H. H., & Brennan, S. E. (1991). Grounding in communication. In L. B. Resnick, J. M. Levine & S. D. Teasley (Eds.), *Perspectives on socially shared cognition* (pp. 127–149). American Psychological Association. https://doi.org/10.1037/10096-006

Clark, H. H., & Fischer, K. (2023). On depicting social agents. *Behavioral and Brain Sciences, 46*, e51. https://doi.org/10.1017/S0140525X22002825

Clark, H. H., & Krych, M. A. (2004). Speaking while monitoring addressees for understanding. *Journal of Memory and Language, 50*(1), 62–81. https://doi.org/10.1016/j.jml.2003.08.004

Clodic, A., Pacherie, E., Alami, R., & Chatila, R. (2017). Key elements for human-robot joint action. In R. Hakli & J. Seibt (Eds.), *Sociality and normativity for robots* (pp. 159–177). Springer. https://doi.org/10.1007/978-3-319-53133-5_8

Cohen, P. R., & Levesque, H. J. (1991). Teamwork. *Nous, 25*(4), 487–512.

Daruna, A. Das, D., & Chernova, S. (2022). Explainable knowledge graph embedding: Inference reconciliation for knowledge inferences supporting robot actions. In *IEEE/RSJ International Conference on Intelligent Robots and Systems* (pp. 1008–1018). IROS. IEEE. https://doi.org/10.1109/IROS47612.2022.9982104

Darvish, K., Simetti, E., Mastrogiovanni, F., & Casalino, G. (2021). A hierarchical architecture for human-robot cooperation processes. *IEEE Transactions on Robotics, 37*(2), 567–586.

Dehais, F., Sisbot, E. A., Alami, R., & Causse, M. (2011). Physiological and subjective evaluation of a human–robot object hand-over task. *Applied Ergonomics, 42*(6), 785–791. https://doi.org/10.1016/j.apergo.2010.12.005

Devin, S., & Alami, R. (2016). An implemented Theory of Mind to improve human-robot shared plans execution. In *The Eleventh ACM/IEEE International Conference on Human-Robot Interaction* (pp. 319–326). HRI. IEEE. https://doi.org/10.1109/HRI.2016.7451768

Dominey, P. F., & Warneken, F. (2011). The basis of shared intentions in human and robot cognition. *New Ideas in Psychology, 29*(3), 260–274. https://doi.org/10.1016/j.newideapsych.2009.07.006

Doncieux, S., Chatila, R., Straube, S., & Kirchner, F. (2022). Human-centered AI and robotics. *AI Perspectives, 4*(1), 14. https://doi.org/10.1186/s42467-021-00014-x

Dragan, A., & Srinivasa, S (2014). Integrating human observer inferences into robot motion planning. *Autonomous Robots, 37*(4), 351–368. https://doi.org/10.1007/s10514-014-9408-x

Drejing, K., Thill, S., & Hemeren, P. (2015). Engagement: A traceable motivational concept in human-robot interaction. In *2015 International Conference on Affective Computing and Intelligent Interaction* (pp. 956–961). ACII. IEEE. https://doi.org/10.1109/ACII.2015.7344690

Edgar, G., Aygun, A., McWilliams, M., & Scheutz, M. (2024). Towards genuine robot teammates: Improving human-robot team performance beyond shared mental models with proactivity. In R. Vinjamuri (Ed.), *Discovering the Frontiers of human-robot interaction* (pp. 1–22). Springer. https://doi.org/10.1007/978-3-031-66656-8_1

Evans, K., de Moura, N., Chauvier, S., Chatila, R., & Dogan, E. (2020). Ethical decision making in autonomous vehicles: The AV ethics project. *Science and Engineering Ethics, 26*, 3285–3312. https://doi.org/10.1007/s11948-020-00272-8

Favier, A., & Alami, R. (2024). A Model of concurrent and compliant human-robot joint action to plan and supervise collaborative robot actions. In *Advances in cognitive systems*. ACS. HAL, hal-04609442. https://hal.science/hal-04609442/

Favier, A., Shekhar, S., & Alami, R. (2023). Models and algorithms for human-aware task planning with integrated Theory of Mind. In *32nd IEEE International Conference on Robot and Human Interactive Communication* (pp. 1279–1286). RO-MAN. IEEE. https://doi.org/10.1109/RO-MAN57019.2023.10309437

Fischer, K., Seibt, J., Rodogno, R., Rasmussen, M. K., Weiss, A., Bodenhagen, L., Juel, W. K., & Krüger, N. (2020). Integrative social robotics hands-on. In *Interaction Studies, 21*(1), 145–185. https://doi.org/10.1075/is.18058.fis

Francis, A., Pérez-D'Arpino, C., Li, C., Xia, F., Alahi, A., Alami, R., Bera, A., Biswas, A., Biswas, J., Chandra, R., Chiang, H.-T. L., Everett, M., Ha, S., Hart, J., How, J. P., Karnan, H., Lee, T.-W. E., Manso, L. J., Mirksy, R., ... Martín-Martín, R. (2025). Principles and guidelines for evaluating social robot navigation algorithms. *ACM Transactions on Human–Robot Interaction, 14*(2), 34. https://doi.org/10.1145/3700599

Ghallab, M., Nau, D. S., & Traverso, P. (2016). *Automated planning and acting*. Cambridge University Press. ISBN: 978-1-107-03727-4.

Gordon, J., Knoblich, G., & Pezzulo, G. (2023). Strategic task decomposition in joint action. *Cognitive Science, 47*(7), e13316. https://doi.org/10.1111/cogs.13316

Grinbaum, A., Chatila, R., Devillers, L., Ganascia, J.-G., Tessier, C., & Dauchet, M. (2017). Ethics in robotics research: CERNA mission and context. *IEEE Robotics and Automation Magazine, 24*(3), 139–145. https://doi.org/10.1109/MRA.2016.2611586

Grosz, B. J., & Kraus, S (1999). The evolution of SharedPlans. In D. M. Gabbay, J. Barwise, Wooldridge, M., & Rao, A. (Eds.), *Foundations of rational agency* (Vol. 14, pp. 227–262). Springer.

Hayes, B., & Scassellati, B. (2016). Autonomously constructing hierarchical task networks for planning and human-robot collaboration. In *IEEE International Conference on Robotics and Automation* (pp. 5469–5476). ICRA. IEEE. https://doi.org/10.1109/ICRA.2016.7487760

Hayes, B., & Shah, J. A. (2017). Improving robot controller transparency through autonomous policy explanation. In B. Mutlu (Ed.), *Proceedings of the 2017 ACM/IEEE International Conference on Human-Robot Interaction*. HRI'17 (pp. 303–312). Association for Computing Machinery. https://doi.org/10.1145/2909824.3020233

Hegel, F., Gieselmann, S., Peters, A., Holthaus, P., & Wrede, B. (2011). Towards a typology of meaningful signals and cues in social robotics. In H. I. Christensen (Ed.), *20th IEEE International Symposium on Robot and Human Interactive Communication* (pp. 72–78). RO-MAN. https://doi.org/10.1109/ROMAN.2011.6005246

Hellström, T., & Bensch, S. (2018). Understandable robots – What, why, and how. *Paladyn, Journal of Behavioral Robotics, 9*(1), 110–123. https://doi.org/10.1515/pjbr-2018-0009

Hiatt, L. M., Harrison, A. M., & Trafton, J. G. (2011). Accommodating human variability in human-robot teams through theory of mind. In *Proceedings of the Twenty-Second international joint conference on Artificial Intelligence* (pp. 2066–2071). https://doi.org/10.5591/978-1-57735-516-8/IJCAI11-345

Hoffman, G. (2019). Evaluating fluency in human–robot collaboration. *IEEE Transactions on Human-Machine Systems, 49*(3), 209–218. https://doi.org/10.1109/THMS.2019.2904558

Hoffman, G., & Breazeal, C. (2007). Effects of anticipatory action on human- robot teamwork efficiency, fluency, and perception of team. In *Proceedings of the ACM/IEEE International Conference on Human-Robot Interaction*. HRI (pp. 1–8). Association for Computing Machinery. https://doi.org/10.1145/1228716.1228718

Hu, G., Miller, T., & Lipovetzky, N. (2022). Planning with perspectives – decomposing epistemic planning using functional STRIPS. *Journal of Artifcial Intelligence Research, 75*, 489–539. https://doi.org/10.1613/jair.1.13446

Johannsmeier, L., & Haddadin, S. (2016). A hierarchical human-robot interaction-planning framework for task allocation in collaborative industrial assembly processes. *IEEE Robotics and Automation Letters, 2*(1), 41–48. https://doi.org/10.1109/LRA.2016.2535907

Khamassi, M., Nahon, M., & Chatila, R. (2024). Strong and weak alignment of large language models with human values. *Scientific Reports. 14*, 19399. https://doi.org/10.1038/s41598-024-70031-3

Klein, G., Feltovich, P. J., Bradshaw, J. M., & Woods, D. D. (2005). Common ground and coordination in joint activity. In W. R. Rouse & K. B. Boff (Eds.), *Organizational simulation* (pp. 139–184). Section: 6. John Wiley & Sons. ISBN: 978-0-471-73944-9.

Klotz, D., Wienke, J., Peltason, J., Wrede, B., Wrede, S., Khalidov, V., & Odobez, J.-M. (2011). Engagement-based multi-party dialog with a humanoid robot. In *The 12th Annual Meeting of the Special Interest Group on Discourse and Dialogue* (pp. 341–343). The Association for Computer Linguistics.

Knepper, R. A., Mavrogiannis, C. I., Proft, J., & Liang, C. (2017). Implicit communication in a joint action. In *2017 12th ACM/IEEE International Conference on Human–Robot Interaction*. HRI (pp. 283–292). Association for Computing Machinery. https://doi.org/10.1145/2909824.3020226

Knoblich, G., Butterfill, S., & Sebanz, N. (2011). Psychological research on joint action. In *Psychology of learning and motivation* (Vol. 54, pp. 59–101). Elsevier. https://doi.org/10.1016/B978-0-12-385527-5.00003-6

Kulkarni, A., Srivastava, S., & Kambhampati, S. (2021). *Planning for proactive assistance in environments with partial observability.* https://arxiv.org/abs/2105.00525

Laird, J. E., Gluck, K., Anderson, J., Forbus, K. D., Jenkins, O. C., Lebiere, C., Salvucci, D., Scheutz, M., Thomaz, A., Trafton, G., & Wray, R. E. (2017). Interactive task learning. *IEEE Intelligent Systems, 32*(4), 6–21. https://doi.org/10.1109/MIS.2017.3121552

Lallement, R., De Silva, L., & Alami, R. (2014). *HATP: An HTN planner for robotics.* https://doi.org/10.48550/arXiv.1405.5345

Langley, P. (2019). Explainable, normative, and justified agency. In *The Thirty-Third Conference on Artificial Intelligence, AAAI, The Ninth Symposium on Educational Advances in Artificial Intelligence* (pp. 9775–9779). EAAI. https://doi.org/10.1609/AAAI.V33I01.33019775

Lee, H. R., Šabanovic, S., Chang, W.-L., Nagata, S., Piatt, J., Bennett, C., & Hakken, D. (2017). Steps toward participatory design of social robots: Mutual learning with older adults with depression. In *Proceedings of the 2017 ACM/IEEE International Conference on Human-Robot Interaction*. HRI'17. Association for Computing Machinery. https://doi.org/10.1145/2909824.3020237

Lemaignan, S., Warnier, M., Sisbot, E. A., Clodic, A., & Alami, R. (2017). Artificial cognition for social human–robot interaction: An implementation. *Artificial Intelligence, 247*, 45–69. https://doi.org/10.1016/j.artint.2016.07.002

Levesque, H. J., Cohen, P. R., & Nunes, J. H. T. (1990). *On acting together*. SRI International.

Li, S., Sun, W., & Miller, T. (2016). Communication in human-agent teams for tasks with joint action. In V. Dignum, P. Noriega, M. Sensoy & J. S. Sichman (Eds.), *Coordination, organizations, institutions, and norms in agent systems XI* (pp. 224–241). Springer. https://doi.org/10.1007/978-3-319-42691-4_13

Liang, C., Proft, J., Andersen, E., & Knepper, R. A. (2019). Implicit communication of actionable information in human-AI teams. In S. A. Brewster, G. Fitzpatrick, A. L. Cox & V. Kostakos (Eds.), *Proceedings of the ACM Conference on Human Factors in Computing Systems*. CHI. https://doi.org/10.1145/3290605.3300325

Lohrmann, C., Stull, M., Roncone, A., & Hayes, B. (2024). Generating pattern-based conventions for predictable planning in human–robot collaboration. *ACM Transactions on Humman–Robot Interaction, 13*(4), 53. https://doi.org/10.1145/3659061

Lu, S.-R., Lo, J.-H., Hong, Y.-T., & Huang, H.-P. (2024). Implementation of engagement detection for human–robot interaction in complex environments. *Sensors, 24*(11), 3311. https://doi.org/10.3390/s24113311

Mainprice, J., Sisbot, E. A., Siméon, T., & Alami, R. (2010). Planning safe and legible hand-over motions for human-robot interaction. In *IARP Workshop on Technical Challenges for Dependable Robots in Human Environments* (Vol. 2). HAL, hal–01976223. https://hal.science/hal-01976223/.

Malle, B., Fischer, K., Young, J., Moon, A., & Collins, E. (2020). Trust and the discrepancy between expectations and actual capabilities of social robots. In D. Zhang & B. Wei (Eds.), *Human-robot interaction: control, analysis, and design* (pp. 1–23). Scholars Press.

Mayima, A., Clodic, A., & Alami, R. (2022). Towards robots able to measure in real-time the quality of interaction in HRI contexts. *International Journal of Social Robotics, 14*(3), 713–731. https://doi.org/10.1007/s12369-021-00814-5

Mercuur, R., Dignum, V., & Jonker, C. M. (2020). Integrating social practice theory in agent-based models: A review of theories and agents. *IEEE Transactions on Computational Social Systems. 7*(5), 1131–1145. https://doi.org/10.1109/TCSS.2020.3007930

Michael, J., & Salice, A. (2017). The sense of commitment in human–robot interaction. *International Journal of Social Robotics, 9*(5), 755–763. https://doi.org/10.1007/s12369-016-0376-5

Miller, T. (2019). Explanation in artificial intelligence: Insights from the social sciences. *Artificial Intelligence, 267*, 1–38. https://doi.org/10.1016/j.artint.2018.07.007

Miller, T., Pearce, A. R., & Sonenberg, L. (2018). Social planning for trusted autonomy. In H. A. Abbass, J. Scholz & D. J. Reid (Eds.), *Foundations of trusted autonomy* (pp. 67–86). Springer. https://doi.org/10.1007/978-3-319-64816-3_4

Milliez, G., Lallement, R., Fiore, M., & Alami, R. (2016). Using human knowledge awareness to adapt collaborative plan generation, explanation and monitoring. In *11th ACM/IEEE International Conference on Human-Robot Interaction*. HRI (pp. 43–50). IEEE. https://doi.org/10.1109/HRI.2016.7451732

Milliez, G., Warnier, M., Clodic, A., & Alami, R. (2014). A framework for endowing an interactive robot with reasoning capabilities about perspective-taking and belief management. In *The 23rd*

IEEE International Symposium on Robot and Human Interactive Communication (pp. 1103–1109). RO-MAN. IEEE. https://doi.org/10.1109/ROMAN.2014.6926399

Muise, C., Belle, V., Felli, P., McIlraith, S., Miller, T., Pearce, A. R., & Sonenberg, L. (2022). Efficient multi-agent epistemic planning: Teaching planners about nested belief. *Artificial Intelligence, 302*, 103605. https://doi.org/10.1016/j.artint.2021.103605

Mutlu, B., & Forlizzi, J. (2008). Robots in organizations: The role of workflow, social, and environmental factors in human-robot interaction. In *Proceedings of the 3rd ACM/IEEE international conference on Human robot interaction*. HRI'08. Association for Computing Machinery. https://doi.org/10.1145/1349822.1349860

Nasir, J., Bruno, B., Chetouani, M., & Dillenbourg, P. (2022). What if social robots look for productive engagement? *International Journal of Social Robotics, 14*, 55–71. https://doi.org/10.1007/s12369-021-00766-w

Nass, C., & Yen, C. (2010). *The man who lied to his laptop: What we can learn about ourselves from our machines*. Penguin Publishing Group. ISBN: 978-1-101-44271-5.

Nikolaidis, S., & Shah, J. (2012). Human-robot teaming using shared mental models. In *Proceedings of the ACM/IEEE International Conference on Human-Robot Interaction*. HRI. https://interactive.mit.edu/wp-content/uploads/2024/08/HART2012_nikol_shah.pdf

Oertel, C., Castellano, G., Chetouani, M., Nasir, J., Obaid, M., Pelachaud, C., & Peters, C. (2020). Engagement in human–agent interaction: An overview. In *Frontiers in Robotics and AI, 7*. https://doi.org/10.3389/frobt.2020.00092

Pacherie, E. (2012). The phenomenology of joint action: Self-agency versus joint agency. In A. Seeman (Ed.), *Joint attention: New developments in psychology, philosophy of mind, and social neuroscience* (pp. 343–389). MIT Press.

Pandey, A. K., & Alami, R. (2014). Towards human-level semantics understanding of human-centered object manipulation tasks for HRI: Reasoning about effect, ability, effort and perspective taking. *International Journal of Social Robotics, 6*(4), 593–620. https://doi.org/10.1007/s12369-014-0246-y

Papagni, G., & Koeszegi, S. (2021). Understandable and trustworthy explainable robots: A sensemaking perspective. *Paladyn, Journal of Behavioral Robotics, 12*(1), 13–30. https://doi.org/10.1515/pjbr-2021-0002

Parker, T., Grandi, U., Lorini, E., Clodic, A., & Alami, R. (2022). Ethical planning with multiple temporal values. In *5th Biennial Robophilosophy Conference: Social Robots in Social Institutions* (Vol. 366, pp. 435–444). Frontiers in artificial intelligence and applications. IOS Press. https://doi.org/10.3233/FAIA220644

Paternò, F. (2004). ConcurTaskTrees: An engineered notation for task models. In D. Diaper & N. Stanton (Eds.), *The handbook of task analysis for human-computer interaction* (pp. 483–503). Lawrence Erlbaum Association.

Petrick, R. P. A., & Foster, M. E. (2016). Using general-purpose planning for action selection in human-robot interaction. In *2016 AAAI Fall Symposium on Artificial Intelligence for Human-Robot Interaction* (pp. 71–74). AI-HRI 2016. AAAI.

Ramachandruni, K., Kent, C., & Chernova, S. (2024). UHTP: A user-aware hierarchical task planning framework for communication-free, mutually-adaptive human-robot collaboration. *ACM Transactions on Human-Robot Interaction, 13*(3), 1–27. https://doi.org/10.1145/3623387

Roberts, M., Shivashankar, V., Alford, R., Leece, M, & Gupta, S. (2016). Goal reasoning, planning, and acting with ACTOR SI M, The actor simulator. In *Poster Proceedings of the Fourth Annual Conference on Advances in Cognitive Systems* (pp. 97–113). Cognitive Systems Foundation Evanston.

Rohlfing, K. J., Cimiano, P., Scharlau, I., Matzner, T., Buhl, H., Buschmeier, H., Grimminger, A., Hammer, B., Häb-Umbach, R., Horwath, I., Hüllermeier, E., Kern, F., Kopp, S., Thommes, K., Ngonga Ngomo, A.-C., Schulte, C., Wachsmuth, H., Wagner, P., & Wrede, B (2021). Explanation as a social practice: Toward a conceptual framework for the social design of AI systems. *IEEE Transactions on Cognitive and Developmental Systems, 13*(3), 717–728. https://doi.org/10.1109/TCDS.2020.3044366

Rosenthal, S., Veloso, M., & Dey, A. K. (2012). Is someone in this office available to help me? Proactively seeking help from spatially-situated humans. *Journal of Intelligent and Robotic Systystems, 66*(1–2), 205–221. https://doi.org/10.1007/S10846-011-9610-4

Šabanović, S. (2010). Robots in society, society in robots. *International Journal of Social Robotics, 2*(4). https://doi.org/10.1007/s12369-010-0066-7

Sado, F., Loo, C. K., Liew, W. S., Kerzel, M., & Wermter, S. (2023). Explainable goal-driven agents and robots—a comprehensive review. *ACM Computing Surveys, 55*(10), 211. https://doi.org/10.1145/3564240

Sakai, T., & Nagai, T. (2022). Explainable autonomous robots: A survey and perspective. *Advanced Robotics, 36*(5–6), 219–238. https://doi.org/10.1080/01691864.2022.2029720

Sanneman, L., & Shah, J. A. (2020). *Trust considerations for explainable robots: A human factors perspective.* https://doi.org/10.48550/arXiv.2005.05940

Scheutz, M., DeLoach, S. A., & Adams, J. A. (2017). A framework for developing and using shared mental models in human-agent teams. *Journal of Cognitive Engineering and Decision Making, 11*(3), 203–224. https://doi.org/10.1177/1555343416682891

Scheutz, Matthias, Ravenna Thielstrom, and Mitchell Abrams (2022). Transparency through explanations and justifications in human-robot task-based communications. *International Journal of Human–Computer Interaction, 38*, 1739–1752. https://doi.org/10.1080/10447318.2022.2091086

Schilling, M., Kopp, S., Wachsmuth, S., Wrede, B., Ritter, H., Brox, T., Nebel, B., & Burgard, W. (2016). Towards a multidimensional perspective on shared autonomy. In *2016 AAAI Fall Symposia* (pp. 338–344). AAAI.

Sebanz, N., Bekkering, H., & Knoblich, G. (2006). Joint action: bodies and minds moving together. *Trends in Cognitive Sciences, 10*(2), 70–76. https://doi.org/10.1016/j.tics.2005.12.009

Seegebarth, B., Müller, F., Schattenberg, B., & Biundo, S. (2012). Making hybrid plans more clear to human users—a formal approach for generating sound explanations. In *Proceedings of the Twenty-Second International Conference on Automated Planning and Scheduling* (Vol. 22, pp. 225–233). ICAPS. AAAI. https://doi.org/10.1609/icaps.v22i1.13503

Seibt, J. (2017). Towards an ontology of simulated social interaction: varieties of the "As If" for robots and humans. In *Sociality and normativity for robots* (pp. 11–39). Studies in the philosophy of sociality. Springer. https://doi.org/10.1007/978-3-319-53133-5_2

Seibt, J. (2022). OASIS: A human-centered descriptive framework for social interactions with robots. In J. Seibt, R. Hakii & M. Nørskow (Eds.), *Robophilosophy–philosophy of, for, and by social robotics.* MIT Press.

Shah, N., Verma, P., Angle, T., & Srivastava, S. (2022). *JEDAI: A system for skill-aligned explainable robot planning.* https://doi.org/10.48550/arXiv.2111.00785

Shekhar, S., Favier, A., & Alami, R. (2024). Human-aware epistemic task planning for human-robot collaboration. In *The HAXP: Human-Aware and Explainable Planning Workshop at ICAPS.* HAL, hal-04587617. https://hal.science/hal-04587617/

Shvo, M., Hari, R., O'Reilly, Z., Abolore, S., Wang, S.-Y. N., & McIlraith, S. A. (2022). Proactive robotic assistance via Theory of Mind. In *2022 IEEE/RSJ International Conference on Intelligent Robots and Systems.* IROS (pp. 9148–9155). IEEE. https://doi.org/10.1109/IROS47612.2022.9981627

Sidner, C. L., Lee, C., Kidd, C. D., Lesh, N., & Rich, C. (2005). Explorations in engagement for humans and robots. *Artificial Intelligence, 166*(1), 140–164. https://doi.org/10.1016/j.artint.2005.03.005

Singamaneni, P. T., Bachiller-Burgos, P., Manso, L. J., Garrell, A., Sanfeliu, A., Spalanzani, A., & Alami, R. (2024). A survey on socially aware robot navigation: Taxonomy and future challenges. *The International Journal of Robotics Research* 1–33. https://doi.org/10.1177/02783649241230562

Singh, R., Miller, T., & Reid, D. (2022). Collaborative human-agent planning for resilience. In A. Theodorou, J. C. Nieves & M. De Vos (Eds.), *Coordination, organizations, institutions, norms, and ethics for governance of multi-agent systems XIV* (Vol. 13239, pp. 28–43). Lecture notes in computer science. Springer. https://doi.org/10.1007/978-3-031-16617-4_3

Sisbot, E. A., & Alami, R. (2012). A human-aware manipulation planner. *IEEE Transactions on Robotics, 28*(5), 1045–1057. https://doi.org/10.1109/tro.2012.2196303

Skewes, J., Amodio, D. M., & Seibt, J. (2019). Social robotics and the modulation of social perception and bias. *Philosophical Transactions of the Royal Society B: Biological Sciences, 374*(1771), 20180037. https://doi.org/10.1098/rstb.2018.0037

Sohrabi, S., Baier, J., & McIlraith, S. (2011). Preferred explanations: Theory and generation via planning. *Proceedings of the AAAI Conference on Artificial Intelligence, 25*(1), 261–267. https://doi.org/10.1609/aaai.v25i1.7845

Sreedharan, S., Chakraborti, T., & Kambhampati, S. (2021). Foundations of explanations as model reconciliation. *Artifical Intelligence, 301*, 103558. https://doi.org/10.1016/J.ARTINT.2021.103558

Stange, S., Hassan, T., Schröder, F., Konkol, J., & Kopp, S. (2022). Self-explaining social robots: An explainable behavior generation architecture for human–robot interaction. *Frontiers in Artificial Intelligence, 5*, 866920. https://doi.org/10.3389/frai.2022.866920

Strabala, K., Lee, M. K., Dragan, A., Forlizzi, J., Srinivasa, S. S., Cakmak, M., & Micelli, V. (2013). Towards seamless human–robot handovers. *Journal of Human–Robot Interaction, 2*. https://doi.org/10.5898/JHRI.2.1.Strabala

Tellex, S., Knepper, R., Li, A., Rus, D., & Roy, N. (2014). Asking for help using inverse semantics. *Robotics: Science and Systems Foundation*. https://doi.org/10.15607/rss.2014.x.024

Tewari, M., & Persiani, M. (2021). Towards we-intentional human-robot interaction using theory of mind and hierarchical task network. In *Proceedings of the 5th International Conference on Computer-Human Interaction Research and Applications 1: Humanoid* (pp. 291–299). Sitepress Digital Library. https://doi.org/10.5220/0010722200003060

Thomaz, A. L., Lieven, E., Cakmak, M., Chai, J. Y., Garrod, S., Gray, W. D., Levinson, S. C., Paiva, A., & Russwinkel, N. (2019). Interaction for task instruction and learning. In K. A. Gluck & J. E. Laird (Eds.), *Interactive task learning: Humans, robots, and agents acquiring new tasks through natural interactions* (pp. 91–110). MIT Press.

Thommes, K., Lammert, O., Schütze, C., Richter, B., & Wrede, B. (2024). Human emotions in AI explanations. In *World Conference on Explainable Artificial Intelligence* (pp. 270–293). Springer. https://doi.org/0.1007/978-3-031-63803-9_15

Trafton, J. G., Cassimatis, N. L., Bugajska, M. D., Brock, D. P., Mintz, F.E., & Schultz, A. C. (2005). Enabling effective human-robot interaction using perspective-taking in robots. *IEEE Transactions on Systems, Man, and Cybernetics, 35*(4), 460–470. https://doi.org/10.1109/TSMCA.2005.850592

Unhelkar, V. V., Lasota, P. A., Tyroller, Q., Buhai, R.-D., Marceau, L., Deml, B., & Shah, J. A. (2018). Human-aware robotic assistant for collaborative assembly: Integrating human motion prediction with planning in time. *IEEE Robotics and Automation Letters, 3*(3), 2394–2401. https://doi.org/10.1109/LRA.2018.2812906

Vattam, S., Klenk, M., Molineaux, M., & Aha, D. W. (2013). Breadth of approaches to goal reasoning: A research survey. In D. W. Aha, M. T. Cox & H. Muñoz-Avila (Eds.), *Goal Reasoning: Papers from the ACS Workshop (Technical Report CS-TR-5029)* (Vol. 111). University of Maryland, Department of Computer Science.

Vesper, C., Butterfill, S., Knoblich, G., & Sebanz, N. (2010). A minimal architecture for joint action. *Neural Networks, 23*(8–9), 998–1003. https://doi.org/10.1016/j.neunet.2010.06.002

Wallkötter, S., Tulli, S., Castellano, G., Paiva, A., & Chetouani, M. (2021). Explainable embodied agents through social cues: A review. *Journal of Human–Robot Interaction, 10*(3), 27. https://doi.org/10.1145/3457188

Watkins, O., Huang, S., Frost, J., Bhatia, K., Weiner, E., Abbeel, P., Darrell, T., Plummer, B., Saenko, K., &Dragan, A. (2021). Explaining robot policies. *Applied AI Letters, 2*(4), e52. https://doi.org/10.1002/ail2.52

Weld, D. S., & Bansal, G. (2019). The challenge of crafting intelligible intelligence. *Communications of the ACM, 62*(6), 70–79. https://doi.org/10.1145/3282486

Wenke, D., Atmaca, S., Holländer, A., Liepelt, R., Baess, P., & Prinz, W. (2011). What is shared in joint action? Issues of co-representation, response conflict, and agent identification. *Review of Philosophy and Psychology, 2*(2), 147–172. https://doi.org/10.1007/s13164-011-0057-0

Open Access This chapter is licensed under the terms of the Creative Commons Attribution 4.0 International License (http://creativecommons.org/licenses/by/4.0/), which permits use, sharing, adaptation, distribution and reproduction in any medium or format, as long as you give appropriate credit to the original author(s) and the source, provide a link to the Creative Commons license and indicate if changes were made.

The images or other third party material in this chapter are included in the chapter's Creative Commons license, unless indicated otherwise in a credit line to the material. If material is not included in the chapter's Creative Commons license and your intended use is not permitted by statutory regulation or exceeds the permitted use, you will need to obtain permission directly from the copyright holder.

Part II
Incrementality

Chapter 12
Incremental Communication

Britta Wrede , Hendrik Buschmeier , Katharina J. Rohlfing ,
Meisam Booshehri , and Angela Grimminger

Abstract Whereas human communication is inherently incremental, this is mostly not the case for current explainable AI (XAI) approaches. Incrementality in human–human interaction (HHI) serves to achieve smooth and fast interaction. This makes it possible, in the case of explanations, to continuously monitor an explainee's understanding and identify and locate misunderstandings very precisely in order to scaffold the interaction partner online. It also allows the chunking of complex meanings into smaller units that are easier to handle and remember. The two processes together allow human interlocutors to develop a new quality of interaction by relying on and referring to previous jointly established routines and concepts, thereby facilitating further interaction and achieving a progressivity toward a joint explanatory goal. This is currently lacking in XAI systems. Whereas some forms of incrementality have been implemented in human–computer interaction (HCI) systems, it is still largely, with few exceptions, unaccounted for in XAI research. We present some incremental systems and discuss what technological advances

B. Wrede (✉)
Medical School OWL, Bielefeld University, Bielefeld, Germany
e-mail: bwrede@techfak.uni-bielefeld.de

H. Buschmeier
Digital Linguistics Lab, Faculty of Linguistics and Literary Studies, Bielefeld University, Bielefeld, Germany
e-mail: hbuschme@uni-bielefeld.de

K. J. Rohlfing
Psycholinguistics, Faculty of Arts and Humanities, Paderborn University, Paderborn, Germany
e-mail: katharina.rohlfing@uni-paderborn.de

M. Booshehri
Semantic Computing Group, Faculty of Technology, Bielefeld University, Bielefeld, Germany
e-mail: mbooshehri@techfak.uni-bielefeld.de

A. Grimminger
Psycholinguistics, Faculty of Arts and Humanities, Paderborn University, Paderborn, Germany
e-mail: angela.grimminger@uni-paderborn.de

© The Author(s) 2026
K. J. Rohlfing et al. (eds.), *Social Explainable AI*,
https://doi.org/10.1007/978-981-96-5290-7_12

are needed to achieve similar efficiency in explaining processes to that in human interaction.

12.1 How Does This Chapter Relate to XAI?

Many XAI approaches rely on the idea of providing a correct and complete explanation to the user (Ancona et al., 2018). Whereas current XAI research – along with very early knowledge-based systems – recognizes the value of interaction and provides interactive interfaces that makes it possible to ask (specific) questions or change feature values (Wang et al., 2019), it still tends to fall short when it comes to the ability to sequentially build up on the basis of smaller explanation steps, to actively seek to provide the currently most adequate piece of information, or to support collaborative naming of jointly observed patterns. All these capabilities require *incremental* communication capabilities or a model of the incremental communication capabilities of the human interaction partner. To accommodate these accounts of incrementality, this chapter will address the following issues as fundamental capabilities for jointly developing explanations and understanding an explanandum: (i) chunking (Chekaf et al., 2016) as an incremental cognitive strategy supporting learning strategies, (ii) incremental language processing (Tanenhaus & Brown-Schmidt, 2008) and production (Levelt, 1989), and (iii) the incremental view on interacting in dialog (Schlangen & Skantze, 2011).

In human–computer interaction (HCI), specifically in interactive dialog systems and human–robot interaction, incrementality has been in the focus of research for several decades (e.g., Addlesee et al., 2020; Buschmeier et al., 2012; Fink et al., 1998; Guhe, 2007; Kennington et al., 2025; Kilger & Finkler, 1995; Köhn, 2018; Schlangen & Skantze, 2011; Skantze & Hjalmarsson, 2013; Visser et al., 2014). In most cases, the aim has been to achieve a smooth and seamless interaction, without awkward pauses or tedious negotiations for turn-taking, rather than to support understanding in a human explainee. Although approaches to incremental HCI with a focus on ensuring user's understanding exist (Buschmeier & Kopp, 2018; Hough & Schlangen, 2016), their use for explanations has yet to be explored fully, if at all. This chapter reviews accounts of incremental human interaction as well as human–machine interaction to illustrate how incremental communication can change the quality of an explanation.

12.2 Problem Description

Although humans are capable of processing a multitude of communicative cues and reacting to their interaction partner in a highly contingent manner, AI or artificial systems in general tend to master such a capability only to a certain degree. Humans achieve this capability through incremental processing—that is, by starting to analyze an explanation when it is not yet finished, thus processing the input in terms of *increments* (Guhe, 2007), *installments* (Clark & Schaefer, 1989), or, more generally, *chunks* (Chekaf et al., 2016). In contrast, artificial systems often only start processing when a whole utterance has been finished. Also, with respect to synthesis, they only start to 'utter' an answer once it has been generated completely instead of starting to 'articulate' once the first segments of speech have been encoded. In cases in which the generation of a response needs much time (e.g., several seconds), such an approach affects turn-taking and creates pauses that interrupt the flow, thereby making the dialog flow painful and the interaction highly cumbersome. More sophisticated dialog systems are capable of incremental processing to different degrees. Note that incremental processing occurs at all levels of communication and interaction: at the lower level at which phonemes are parsed into morphemes and words, at the syntactic level at which the sentence structure is being parsed word by word, up to the discourse level at which whole pragmatic units such as speech or dialog acts are analyzed incrementally.

We distinguish between three accounts of incrementality: (1) a compositional, (2) a 'standard' incremental, and (3) a processual account.

The (1) *compositional* account of incremental communication focuses on the additive nature of the increments. For example, consider an interaction between an XAI system providing feature importance to explain the proposed decision to a human user. Rather than providing the explainee with all feature importance values at once, communicating each feature separately allows the explainee to consider each feature on its own, thus giving them more time to process the possibly complex information. To access the complete explanation, the explainee simply has to add up all features. In contrast, in the (2) *standard incremental* account, a new explanation item may lead to a reevaluation of the prior information. For example, providing only the name of a relevant feature may lead the explainee to assume a certain correlation between the feature and the classification outcome. If then a SHAP visualization (Lundberg & Lee, 2017) of this feature is added, which contains information as to what values were associated with a specific outcome, this initial assumption may be challenged and reevaluated allowing the explainee even to create new concepts based on the reevaluation of a prior utterance. From these processes emerges a new quality of interaction that can be called a (3) *processual* account of incremental interaction. More specifically, the dynamic and flexible incremental processing builds the basis for developing interaction 'tools' between the explainer and the explainee that make their interaction increasingly smoother and faster. This is because it allows them, for example, to co-construct new concepts or terms, or to develop shortcuts that relieve the interaction from complex processes such as clarification subdialogs.

12.3 Human Incremental Communication

12.3.1 Compositional Account of Incremental HHI

Human working memory limits how much (new) information can be retained. It is, accordingly, beneficial when an explanation is not given as a whole, but rather broken down into smaller pieces of information. This also supports the feedback process, because non-understanding cues or questions can be interpreted against a much more focused background.

In addition to this, humans can make information easier to retain by recoding it into chunks (Chekaf et al., 2016). This process of chunking has been described as the recoding of several words or stimuli into a single familiar unit or chunk, and has been shown to free working memory capacity (Thalmann et al., 2019). There are two ways in which such a recoding can take place: (1) based on information in long-term memory acquired through prior knowledge or expertise. This means that when an explanation describes a complex concept that is partly known by the explainee, they will be able to retrieve it from their long-term memory and recode the possibly lengthy description into a label. (2) On the other hand, chunks can be formed in immediate memory (Chekaf et al., 2016). This has been shown to work for sequences of single items such as letters or symbols, and it is facilitated if such a sequence shows certain characteristics such as "compressibility"—that is, repeating patterns or orderings (Chekaf et al., 2016, p. 97). We argue that such higher-level chunking can be supported by interaction—for example, by applying a label to a jointly attended sequence or pattern of entities such as words, graphs, or phenomena. This makes it possible to refer to this complex sequence or pattern by just one word in the following, a process that is critically supported by incremental processing (Brennan & Clark, 1996).

This perspective on breaking down information for explaining and then chunking it for decoding is important when considering how information can best be presented to yield an understanding – that is, a link to already existing knowledge – and how to build increasingly on this.

This building on previous information also happens at higher levels of incremental communication. In the context of explanations, so-called explanatory moves have been proposed that are functional units of interaction building up an explanation. Booshehri et al. (2024) capture these units through speech-act-like categories. They view explanatory moves as cohesive units in terms of meaning or context that point to the structure and mechanisms of human interaction. In the following, we shall describe an example from an annotated dialog (see Table 12.1), extracted from the "five-level Corpus" (Booshehri et al., 2024), in order to illustrate our proposed compositional account. In the dialog, an expert explainer explains the topic of virtual reality to a child (i.e., the explainee). First (1), the explainer poses a *diagnostic query* to test whether the explainee is familiar with the topic virtual reality. Then (2), the explainee responds with a *confirmation*, an *assertion*, and an *analogy* about virtual reality. (3) The explainer *praises* the explainee's response and *elaborates*—that is,

Table 12.1 Example of an annotated dialog from the five-level Corpus (Booshehri et al., 2024). In each transcribed turn, explanatory move labels are placed in square brackets preceding their respective utterance segments. In the dialog, an expert (explainer, ER) explains the topic 'virtual reality' to a child (explainee, EE). A video of the dialog is available here: https://youtu.be/akveRNY6Ulw?t=23

	Speaker	Transcribed utterance with annotated explanatory move
1	ER	[Diagnostic Query] So do you know what virtual reality is?
2	EE	[Confirm] Yes, [Assert] it's simple. [Analogy] It's like a video game except it feels like you're in the video game.
3	ER	[Praise] That's actually a really good description. [Elaboration] The idea is that if you've got a system here that can make you see whatever we want you to see, then we can make you believe that you're anywhere else, like on top of a mountain, or in a dungeon or under the ocean.
4	EE	[Completion] Or in Minecraft.
5	ER	[Confirm] Yeah, [Echo Response] or in Minecraft. [Elaboration] When you look at a TV on the wall showing a picture of a mountain or something, how can you tell that it's not just a window and there's something else behind it? Because it always doesn't look quite right if you have a static picture of a person on a screen and you move around like this, it's not really changing. And it's interesting—those are things we have to figure out. We need to figure out when you look at something in reality, how can you tell whether it's real or not. [Verification Question] Have you been to a 3-D movie where you put on the little glasses?
6	EE	[Confirm] Yeah.
7	ER	[Elaboration] So what they do, the trick for that is, if you ever at a theater and you take up the glasses and you look at it, you'll see its blurry where there's actually two pictures that they're showing at the same time. And what those little glasses do, is they let one eye see one picture, and the other eye see a different picture. So then your eyes can say, oh it looks like I'm seeing through the screen or something is floating out in front of it. In the VR headsets, what we do is, there's actually either two screens or one screen split in half, so that it draws a different picture, completely different picture, for each eye. And we make sure that each eye can only see the picture it intended to. And that's what can make things feel like they got this real depth to them, that its something that you could reach out and touch and it doesn't feel like a flat TV screen.

adds more information to the information already presented in the dialog to create a more comprehensive whole. (4) The explainee then *displays understanding* (4) by adding to the explainer's *elaboration* (i.e., by producing a *completion* move). Next (5), the explainer *confirms* (5) the explainee's *completion*, *echoes their response*, and continues to provide more information through further *elaboration*. The explainer further asks a *verification question* to confirm a fact about the explainee's past experiences (in this case, attending a 3D movie). (6) The explainee then *confirms* this, allowing (7) the explainer to further *elaborate* on the topic to create a more complex, emergent whole.

12.3.2 Standard Account of Incremental HHI

Models of speech processing acknowledge incrementality to different degrees. Levelt et al. (1999)'s influential model of speech production suggests a highly modular hierarchical process of encompassing conceptualization of the speaker's intention, lexical access, phonetic encoding, and articulation in which words are retrieved from the lexicon and articulated before the conceptualization of the whole utterance is finished. A self-monitoring loop at the final stages of articulation (Cholin et al., 2011) involves the speech comprehension mechanism for detecting and initializing correction of errors during the articulation process. This results in different ways of correcting the error, as suggested by different computational speech production models (Guenther et al., 2006; Kröger et al., 2020; Postma, 2000), generally a stop of the ongoing word articulation followed by a restart of the articulation of the intended word or of the correct word if a wrong word has been activated.

This capability for self-correction is interesting also from a dialogical perspective because it contains informative cues for listeners. On the one hand, it has been shown that corrections of the form "move the yel- purple square" or "move the yellow—purple square" lead to more errors in the action execution of the listener, with more misleading information yielding more errors. However, the introduction of a filler ("move the yel- uh purple square") allows the listener more time to process the correction, yielding less errors in the execution of the action (Brennan and Schober, 2021). Such hesitation cues can also have a pragmatic function and indicate epistemic states such as uncertainty, whereas the exact location of the hesitation or of the word lengthening is interpreted as a pointer to which word the speaker is uncertain of (Betz et al., 2019). Indeed, it has been shown that increased cognitive load correlates strongly with increased use of hesitations such as pauses and lengthening (Betz et al., 2023). The same trend could be shown for speech-accompanying gestures (Graziano & Gullberg, 2018). Thus, for the listener, the incremental speech production process containing hesitations and corrections can serve as a rich source of information on the cognitive processes of the speaker.

Most of the models for incremental language production have focused solely on spoken utterances. However, human communication within social interactions does consist not only of verbal utterances that are produced and comprehended incrementally but also of nonverbal and multimodal behaviors. This may pose various challenges for incremental processing of the multimodal signals from an interlocutor (see also Chap. 18). First, nonverbal behaviors can be either a meaningful part of an utterance, such as co-speech gestures or facial expression, or not meaningful like movements such as scratching and grasping a bottle to drink. Holler and Levinson (2019, p. 639) call this the "segregation problem" because co-occurring, but nonmeaningful, signals need to be separated from the meaningful ones. Second, meaningful behaviors from different articulators do not necessarily occur in perfect temporal alignment but may be produced asynchronously. This is called the "binding problem" (Holler & Levinson, 2019, p. 639). However, multimodal utterances do not slow down communicative interactions. Instead, they reduce response times. To account for findings from human–human multimodal communication and temporal aspects in turn-taking, Holler and Levinson (2019, pp. 641, 644) propose a framework for *multimodal* human language processing within *social interactions*. As to the binding problem, they propose that signals are integrated into a holistic unit based on "gestalt-like principles" and "statistical regularities in the co-occurrence of multimodal signals together with the communicative meanings that the whole ensemble is intended to convey, and these regularities must outweigh idiosyncratic message encoding to be effective" (ibid). This makes it possible to predict a following signal or combination of signals based on the prior one; whereas on a higher level, these so-called multiplex signals are semantically and pragmatically processed ("multimodal gestalts"). A multimodal semantic memory buffer is active while processing a multimodal utterance, and this is constantly updated to increase the accuracy of the prediction and the semantic and pragmatic interpretation. This multimodal semantic memory buffer also plays a role in the segregation problem: Signals that do not seem to fit into one of the predictions at a certain time during this incremental processing are not integrated at that time. However, if predictions and interpretations change, they need to be temporarily stored to integrate them later should a reanalysis become necessary (see Kennington et al., 2017; Yaghoubzadeh & Kopp, 2016, for computational approaches to temporality). With their framework, Holler and Levinson (2019) argue that *multimodal* human language processing within *social interaction* involves processes that *differ* from those in unimodal processing. This is opposed to a view of unimodal processing modules as being additive when combined with one another. Empirical studies testing this hypothesis have provided evidence that some forms of nonverbal or multimodal signals do in fact support prediction for the interlocutor in face-to-face interactions (e.g., Bekke et al., 2024; Nota et al., 2021); and when they occur as a multimodal gestalt, they are interpreted differently compared to when they occur individually (Trujillo & Holler, 2024).

Incremental dialog processing is where incremental speech production (by the speaker) and incremental speech comprehension (by the listener) come together[1] and enable dialog participants to coordinate their behavior and representations in a close loop (Kopp et al., 2008). The speaker incrementally plans their utterance while it is being articulated. Different levels of planning and execution operate with different ranges of projection into the future. Production is thought to start from an intention of *what* to say that projects a whole utterance (or even a larger argument or an explanation). It needs to be made more concrete in terms of *how* to say it (which constructions, words, how to articulate, etc.), and this projects only a second or fractions of seconds ahead (Levelt, 1989; Thompson, 1977). While production is ongoing in the speaker, the listener comprehends what the speaker is saying,

---

[1] It should be noted that the external self-monitoring loop in speech production also makes use of speech comprehension (Levelt, 1989).

understands what has been said so far, and projects into the future what will be said next, when the utterance will end, and so forth. Such production and comprehension are happening in the present and enable a form of directness between interaction partners that exists only in spontaneous spoken dialogs, and humans know how to make use of it.

A basic mechanism that relies on this directness is *communicative feedback* that listeners use to communicate four basic functions of communication (Allwood et al., 1992): (1) Is the listener in contact with the speaker, (2) is the listener willing and able to perceive the speaker, (3) is the listener willing and able to understand the speaker, and (4) further attitudinal reactions (e.g., acceptance, agreement, emotional reactions). Listeners can use nonverbal gestures (such as head nods, facial expressions, eyebrows, gaze, blinks, posture shifts; see, e.g., Allwood et al., 2007; Heylen, 2006; Hömke et al., 2017), but also short verbal–vocal expressions (back channels such as "uh-huh," "yeah," "oh" ...; Ward, 2006) to provide feedback to speakers. In both cases, feedback interferes only minimally with what the speaker is doing. Nonverbal feedback to the speaker's speech takes place in different modalities, and verbal–vocal feedback is minimal and unobtrusive due to its usually very short duration and acoustic properties Ward, 2006, such as being similar to the speaker's speech in its vicinity (Heldner et al., 2010).

What is interesting about feedback with respect to incremental processing in dialog is that speakers continuously monitor listeners for their understanding and adapt their language production to the listeners' needs on the fly (Clark, 1996). This allows speakers to anticipate and detect problems in understanding on the side of the listeners as early as possible. Speakers can then address these problems immediately, while they are still 'small' and manageable by, for example, replanning the parts of the utterance that lie in the future (Brennan et al., 2010; Clark & Krych, 2004) or by self-repair (Dingemanse & Enfield, 2023; Schegloff et al., 1977). Another important aspect of incremental dialogue lies in the fact that humans are capable of reevaluating their current understanding of the topic at hand. More specifically, new information (chunks) can shed light on previous information and lead to a new understanding. This is a very important feature of human communication that is especially important in explaining processes.

12.3.3 *Processual Account of Incremental HHI*

From these different compositional and temporal processes of incrementality, a new quality of the interaction arises:

Above, we outlined units that capture increments of an explanatory dialog and processes that allow for rapid correction of misunderstandings and, thus, a reevaluation of prior knowledge as well as an incremental building up of knowledge. In this section, we relate this to what is known from the social sciences about human interaction being organized in social practices (see Chap. 5). One of the discussed characteristics of practices, such as explanatory processes, is that they are organized toward a goal (see Chaps. 6 and 7). This is helpful for a new view of incrementality that has the goal of framing an ongoing interaction. For an interaction, the goal can be characterized as its outcome, giving the sense or meaning to the given situation. Interestingly, in the processuality of the units presented above, the underlying assumption is that they sum up to a goal (see Sect. 11.7). However, with the concept of social practices, it becomes more necessary to rather investigate how the individual units contribute to what kind of goal(s). From this perspective, the incrementality turns from the processuality to the progressivity of an interaction in terms of how each increment contributes to a progress. Thus, instead of describing the process as such, research should move forward to explain the iterative 'gain'— that is, how the current unit or groups of units build on previous ones resulting in a change of quality for the interaction. In other words, the history of interaction and how it influences interlocutors on the cognitive/semantic level and the subsequent interaction is still not accounted for. This is surprising because the phenomenon has been identified as "common ground" (Clark & Brennan, 1991, p. 12) or "public substrate" (Goodwin, 2018, p. 32), emphasizing the fact that interlocutors build a joint context (see Chap. 4) for further actions. This context can become observable when interlocutors use similar vocabulary or gestures (Pickering & Garrod, 2004).

Current research approaches to incrementality attempt to identify cues that might indicate a change in quality. But despite these attempts, such investigations of processuality tend to apply neutral measurements such as time. For example, in Xu et al. (2020), some of the measurements presented are statistical. When using time and time series to display and analyze temporal aspects, each time interval is treated similarly. However, assuming that the history of interaction influences the present, the weights for the relevance of each such time interval may change, and later on the weights are laden differently. For example, at the beginning of the interaction, the units establish a basis, on which during the course of interaction, information can be established in a different quality, e.g., extended in a particular sense. The changes in qualities from 'establishment' to 'extension' have been proposed in a developmental approach investigating how parent–child interactions change over time (Lyra, 2010). During *establishment*, interlocutors seem to work on a set of means for negotiating and constituting the verbal and nonverbal context of their interaction. During *extension*, the partner can draw from established context in order to negotiate further actions and extended exchanges (Lyra, 2010, p. 277). We can draw some inspiration from it and propose that the semantic quality will change from establishment to extension, moving forward to abbreviations. When reaching the *abbreviation*, the dialog could become faster and more deictic because the interlocutors can rely on what they have established already, in terms of content and verbal and nonverbal means. For example, when interacting with an sXAI system, this would mean that in a first iteration, the explainer system may offer to explain the contribution of the most relevant feature to the decision provided by the AI. This step may require several clarification steps in order for the explainee to discover and understand that the feature name may be misleading and that an explanation of the feature can be asked for. In a second iteration, the explainee may directly ask for the explanation of the second important feature, thus making use of an established interaction pattern. Future work should extend to fields that seem to emerge and seem to be relevant (e.g., van Geert & de Ruiter, 2022).

Thus, although incrementality leads to a range of different phenomena and has diverse functions in HHI that are fundamental for explaining and understanding processes, it has been shown to be a feature that is difficult to conceptualize and implement in HCI, because it requires a complex technological architecture. In fact, incrementality has been tackled from different perspectives with different goals in mind, the combination of which might yield abilities that are similar to the human processuality or progressivity account of incrementality.

12.4 Operationalization: Incremental HCI

Technical realizations of incremental communication capabilities for social XAI systems require complex mechanisms that need to be integrated into HCI design and system architectures right from the start, and not just as an afterthought (Kopp et al., 2014).

12.4.1 Compositional Account of Incremental HCI/sXAI

Most of the existing incremental approaches in the context of XAI, or explaining machines in general, can be summarized under the compositional account of incrementality, because they focus on achieving a complex explanation in a step-by-step fashion. According to our taxonomy of incrementality, a compositional account of incremental sXAI would be based on an initial explanation to which more and more incremental information units are added to yield an increasingly better mental model. Given the complex nature that deep learning and other complex classifiers exhibit, this is an interesting idea, because it would make it possible to slowly build an explanation for highly nonlinear and possibly high-dimensional relationships between features and a certain outcome.

Bo et al. (2024) explicitly targeted the human capability to assess complex facts and relationships in an incremental manner. They developed an incremental explanation approach that distinguishes between typical (majority) items (e.g., houses with living area smaller than 2500 sqft) and special items (e.g., houses with a living area larger or equal than 2500 sqft). For both subspaces, they trained a linear explanation model that explains the target value, in this case the house price, by a linear combination of factors—for example, the sum of the (weighted) number of bathrooms and the (weighted) size of the living area ($w_{br} \cdot num_{br} + w_{la} \cdot size_{la}$). The weights were actually a price (e.g., 17 k\$ for bathroom), which means that that the price for a house would increase by 17k\$ for each bathroom it has. For houses in the minority subspace (i.e., living area larger or equal than 2500 sqft), the total price would increase by 51k$ for each bathroom. In this way, it was possible to (1) explain each price as a linear combination of such factors and (2) ensure that for the majority subspace, the price for each factor remained stable, but could vary for instances from the special cases subspace. Thus, the explanation for the minority samples would consist of the value from the majority samples plus a value describing the delta to that value. This is, in fact, an incremental explanation, because it starts with a general baseline and then adds a delta that may be variable. The idea was to allow users to better learn the baseline factors as they interacted with the system. In a study, it was shown that users' performance in predicting the output of the AI system that had been explained using this approach was best when they received explanations from the incremental approach compared to three different non-incremental approaches. Whereas in this case the incrementality consisted of two 'units' (i.e., the typical and the special subspaces), it is conceivable that this could be extended to more subspaces.

In Monteath and Sheh (2018), the entire classification process is operationalized as an incremental explanation. Here, a medical diagnosis is made interactively between an XAI system and a physician. Specifically, a decision tree is trained that not only takes into account the predictive value of the different features for determining the correct outcome but also includes the cost of each test to be performed at each node. This is because the complete information that the tree theoretically deals with is not available and would be too costly to obtain. Thus, the goal is not only to achieve the best possible decision model but also to take into account that not all information is readily available but needs to be generated by specific (costly) medical tests. This results in a predefined tree structure in which a specific path is created for each interaction based on the test results. Whereas the tree itself is fixed, for the user this approach yields very case-specific paths through the tree. As a result, depending on the results of individual tests, different other tests and possible hypotheses will result, resulting in an incremental decision process toward the final hypothesis. Here, the incrementality is in the decision process itself, because not all information is given at once, but is provided incrementally. Thus, the explanation process is necessarily incremental.

Another interactive approach to decision support in the medical context has been suggested by Wang et al. (2019). A graphical user interface presents different types of information, ranging from raw data (i.e., vital parameters) to diagnostic hypotheses, to feature attributions, and counterfactual reasoning. Here, the decision is based on a complete set of information, but the path along which information about the decision can be assembled incrementally is free. The user can freely select what kind of information from an XAI component they want or do not want to see or manipulate. Thus, there is no explicit incremental representation of information. Instead, the information the user gathers grows incrementally, and the user determines when they have seen enough explanation.

Another domain in which incrementality emerges in HCI is assistance systems that support users in carrying out tasks, for example, in manufacturing where complex assemblies have to be carried out by human workers. Because such assemblies require actions to be carried out sequentially, this is naturally an incremental process in which the sequence of all steps leads to the final goal of the overall assembly. In these approaches, the sequence of incremental units—which comprise both action and explanation steps—is often the target of research. For example, in order to make it possible for more proficient users to choose their own path, Atif et al. (2003) created different paths of actions in their assistance system. In order to adapt to the increasing proficiency of their users, several authors have suggested increasing the incremental information units in order to unburden the learner from too many too detailed recurring explanations (Apoki et al., 2019; Atif et al., 2003), thus de facto implementing a chunking approach (see Oestreich et al. (2022), for suggested operations to change either the incremental units or their order in adaptation to the user).

12.4.2 Standard Incremental Account of Incremental HCI

To make incremental communication possible, social XAI systems can build upon established research in the field of computational language generation and dialog modeling.

One influential framework for incremental processing in dialog systems is the "IU-model" (Schlangen & Skantze, 2011). This describes general abstract principles based on a network of "module components" that consume, process, and produce "incremental units" (IUs). It can be used to build modular architectures compatible with the stages of processing in standard dialog system pipelines (e.g., automatic speech recognition, natural language understanding, dialog management, natural language generation, and speech synthesis) that are comparable to assumptions in psycholinguistic models of speech processing (e.g., Levelt, 1989; see Sect. 12.3.2).[2] The module components process information according to "Wundt's principle" (Guhe, 2007, p. 70): incrementally consuming a minimal amount of input and incrementally producing a minimal amount of output.

For an automatic speech recognition component, the incremental input is a stream of audio frames read from an audio source (e.g., a microphone), and the incremental output could be, depending on the component's granularity, words (Addlesee et al., 2020; Baumann et al., 2009). One aspect that needs to be considered for incremental processing is the trade-off between the responsiveness of a component and the stability of the increments it produces. A speech recognition component could, for instance, generate a word IU as soon as an audio frame leads the underlying statistical model to predict the end of a word (e.g., the word "four"). It could, however, be that the next audio frames lead to a reevaluation of the word

---

[2] A number of implementations of the IU-model have been realized in different research groups (Chiba et al., 2024; Kennington et al., 2014, 2020; Michael, 2020; Schlangen et al., 2010) and been used to build various spoken dialog agents.

boundary—for example, when the user actually uttered the word "forty" (and maybe later "forty-five"; Skantze & Schlangen, 2009). In this case, the IU would need to be retracted, and a new IU would need to be produced (Baumann et al., 2009). In a fully incremental system, this might then trigger a cascade of reevaluations in module components further down in the network.

Most relevant for generating social XAI explanations are questions revolving around incremental conceptualization and language generation because these play a crucial role for co-construction in that they enable the scaffolding and adaptivity capabilities of the system. Guhe (2007) presents four processes for an incremental conceptualizer for language generation: construction, selection, linearization, and preverbal message generation. These are also easy to conceptualize for a social XAI system: construction of the explanandum and the explanation, selection of relevant aspects to explain, linearization of these aspects, and incremental generation of preverbal messages for each "explanatory move" (Booshehri et al., 2024). For adaptive language generation and synthesis, Buschmeier et al. (2012) present an IU-model-based architecture that processes incremental microplanning tasks of the size of intonation units (which could be Guhe's incremental preverbal messages) as input, and plans the surface form of the next utterance increment just-in-time when the (incremental) speech synthesis has finished synthesizing and speaking it. This interplay between components in the generation pipeline enables incremental adaptation of system output to concurrent user input such as communicative feedback signals (see Sect. 12.3.2), as demonstrated for the case of adaptive information presentation in the system described and evaluated in (Buschmeier & Kopp, 2018).

12.4.3 Summary

There exists a range of incremental approaches in HCI and XAI, but they follow different goals and provide incrementality along different dimensions.

In the standard account of incremental HCI, the goal of incremental architectures is generally to achieve a smooth interaction in which multimodal feedback can be given and processed on the fly to correct an ongoing utterance or action. This supports a very fine-grained feedback loop making it possible to pinpoint misconceptions or misunderstandings very precisely. Thus, incrementality at the HCI level is an important cornerstone for enabling precise monitoring of the explainee's understanding.

In contrast, the compositional account of HCI and XAI focuses on the content of the explanation and, thus, serves more as a scaffolding mechanism. By providing initial fundamental explanation units on which further explanations can be built, the hope is to yield understanding of more complex explananda. This can be achieved through chunking—that is, combining incremental units so that they can become new units that simplify the subsequent explanation process. A further focus lies on the sequencing of incremental units. By breaking the explanation down into smaller units, it also becomes possible to negotiate the sequence of these units with the explainee.

Thus, incremental HCI and sXAI are fundamental mechanisms that support monitoring on the one hand, and scaffolding toward complex explanations on the other.

12.5 How Does This Chapter Inspire Further Directions of XAI?

1. Currently, monitoring components in XAI are scarce. Incremental HCI provides a means to monitor the *ongoing* interaction with diverse XAI output elements—that is, while the user is interacting with the elements. This would make it possible to infer important aspects of the user's mental model and to actively provide feedback and explanations to correct possible misconceptions or misunderstandings as soon as possible. This is important because misconceptions or misunderstandings that persist over time are likely to cause further understanding problems later on.
2. Regarding the compositional account of incrementality, sXAI can be improved in several directions; first, there is still little knowledge about what the right level of incremental units for explaining AI is, and how to adapt it to different explainees. Second, which sequences of incremental explanation units are better to follow and understand than others is also mostly unknown. Incrementality can be achieved along different dimensions such as feature attributions, subspaces, and so forth. Investigating which incrementality dimensions are important under which circumstances would provide a huge benefit for sXAI research.
3. Finally, interactions with XAIs have so far been mostly 'one-off.' However, especially in the context of incremental explanations, it would be valuable to enable and analyze repeated interactions with an XAI system over a longer period of time. One important question here would be how much complexity can be achieved by such a long-term incremental approach?

12.6 Rapid Access to the Content of This Chapter

In humans, incrementality is an important mechanism with which to respond quickly to ongoing actions by making use of partially processed information. This is an important capability, especially in communication with other individuals, because it allows for very efficient interaction. Humans' continuous feedback to the ongoing interaction is a rich source of information regarding the explainee's understanding process. In fact, it allows for very precise pinpointing of misunderstandings. In addition, incrementality has a compositional aspect that enables people not only to process information step by step but also to build mental representations in an incremental way. This makes it possible to start with an initial simple model that can be improved by further explanations. Finally, we postulate a processual account of incrementality that takes into account that through these two processes, not only will new representations of an explanandum emerge but also communicative processes will become smoother because they can draw on previous information and exchanges. In this way, more efficient patterns of interaction can be established.

In HCI research, the development of incremental processing capabilities to enable smooth and efficient multimodal interaction has yielded a large body of insights. However, although incremental dialog frameworks exist, they are still not standard because they require a complex architecture allowing for bidirectional corrective feedback. Research has shown that incremental interaction modeling can achieve smooth interaction, thereby making it possible to integrate gestures and actions and to react accordingly. We also see incremental XAI approaches in which temporal efficiency is an issue. Regarding the compositional representation of XAI, we see first approaches in different domains that target the production of understandable explanation processes by making use of incremental explanation steps. Some of these approaches have been shown to reach a higher level of understanding in explainees.

Thus, future research has to target both the standard incremental and the compositional accounts of incrementality. This concerns a number of issues, the most important of which is to combine incremental monitoring with scaffolding through incremental explanation processes. To reach the goal of a processual quality of incremental interaction in sXAI would require the integration of a learning process of the sXAI system that not only tracks the state of the user but also learns communication patterns that ease the interaction.

Acknowledgments We thank Casey Kennington for helpful comments on an earlier version of this chapter.

This work was funded by the Deutsche Forschungsgemeinschaft (DFG, German Research Foundation): TRR 318/1 2021 – 438445824.

References

Addlesee, A., Yu, Y., & Eshghi, A. (2020). A comprehensive evaluation of incremental speech recognition and diarization for conversational AI. In *Proceedings of the 28th International Conference on Computational Linguistics* (pp. 3492–3503). ICCL. https://doi.org/10.18653/v1/2020.coling-main.312.

Allwood, J., Kopp, S., Grammer, K., Ahlsén, E., Oberzaucher, E., & Koppensteiner, M. (2007). The analysis of embodied communicative feedback in multimodal corpora: A prerequisite for behaviour simulation. *Language Resources and Evaluation, 41,* 255–272. https://doi.org/10.1007/s10579-007-9056-2.

Allwood, J., Nivre, J., & Ahlsén, E. (1992). On the semantics and pragmatics of linguistic feedback. *Journal of Semantics, 9,* 1–26. https://doi.org/10.1093/jos/9.1.1.

Ancona, M., Ceolini, E., Öztireli, C., & Gross, M. (2018). *Towards better understanding of gradient-based attribution methods for deep neural networks*. https://doi.org/10.48550/arXiv.1711.06104. arXiv: 1711.06104 [cs.LG].

Apoki, U. C., Al-Chalabi, H., & Crisan, G. C. (2019). From digital learning resources to adaptive learning objects: An overview. In *Proceedings of the 6th International Conference on Modelling and Development of Intelligent Systems* (pp. 18–32). Springer. https://doi.org/10.1007/978-3-030-39237-6_2.

Atif, Y., Benlamri, R., & Berri, J. (2003). Learning objects based framework for self-adaptive learning. *Education and Information Technologies, 8*, 345–368. https://doi.org/10.1023/B:EAIT.0000008676.64018.af.

Baumann, T., Atterer, M., & Schlangen, D. (2009). Assessing and improving the performance of speech recognition for incremental systems. In *Proceedings of Human Language Technologies: The 2009 Annual Conference of the North American Chapter of the ACL* (pp. 380–388). ACL.

Betz, S., Bryhadyr, N., Türk, O., & Wagner, P. (2023). Cognitive load increases spoken and gestural hesitation frequency. *Languages, 8*(1), 71. https://doi.org/10.3390/languages8010071.

Betz, S., Zarrieß, S., Székely, É., & Wagner, P. (2019). The greennn tree – Lengthening position influences uncertainty perception. In *Proceedings of Interspeech* (pp. 3990–3994). ISCA. https://doi.org/10.21437/Interspeech.2019-2572.

Bo, J. Y., Hao, P., & Lim, B. Y. (2024). Incremental XAI: Memorable understanding of AI with incremental explanations. In *Proceedings of the 2024 CHI Conference on Human Factors in Computing Systems* (pp. 1–17). Association for Computing Machinery. DOI: https://doi.org/10.1145/3613904.3642689.

Booshehri, M., Buschmeier, H., Alshomary, M., Rohlfing, K., Wachsmuth, H., & Cimiano, P. (2024). *Modeling explanations as processes: A new analytical framework accounting for relational and structural patterns in explanatory dialogues*. Preprint, under review. Available at zenodo. https://doi.org/10.5281/zenodo.13151350.

Brennan, S. E., & Clark, H. H. (1996). Conceptual pacts and lexical choice in conversation. *Journal of Experimental Psychology: Learning, Memory, and Cognition, 22*, 1482–1493. https://doi.org/10.1037/0278-7393.22.6.1482.

Brennan, S. E., Galati, A., & Kuhlen, A. K. (2010). Two minds, one dialog: Coordinating speaking and understanding. In B. H. Ross (Ed.), *The psychology of learning and motivation: Advances in research and theory* (Vol. 53, pp. 301–344). Psychology of Learning and Motivation. Academic Press. https://doi.org/10.1016/S0079-7421(10)53008-1.

Brennan, S. E., & Schober, M. F. (2021). How listeners compensate for disfluencies in spontaneous speech. *Journal of Memory and Language, 44*(2), 274–296. https://doi.org/10.1006/jmla.2000.2753.

Buschmeier, H., Baumann, T., Dosch, B., Kopp, S., & Schlangen, D. (2012). Combining incremental language generation and incremental speech synthesis for adaptive information presentation. In *Proceedings of the 13th Annual Meeting of the Special Interest Group on Discourse and Dialogue*. Seoul, South Korea (pp. 295–303).

Buschmeier, H., & Kopp, S. (2018). Communicative listener feedback in human–agent interaction: Artificial speakers need to be attentive and adaptive. In *Proceedings of the 17th International Conference on Autonomous Agents and Multiagent Systems* (pp. 1213–1221). IFAAMAS.

Chekaf, M., Cowan, N., & Mathy, F. (2016). Chunk formation in immediate memory and how it relates to data compression. *Cognition, 155*, 96–107. https://doi.org/10.1016/j.cognition.2016.05.024.

Chiba, Y., Mitsuda, K., Lee, A., & Higashinaka, R. (2024). The Remdis toolkit: Building advanced real-time multimodal dialogue systems with incremental processing and large language models. In *Proceedings of the 14th Annual International Workshop on Spoken Dialogue Systems Technology (IWSDS)* (pp. 1–6). Sapporo, Japan.

Cholin, J., Dell, G. S., & Levelt, W. J. M. (2011). Planning and articulation in incremental word production: Syllable-frequency effects in English. *Journal of Experimental Psychology: Learning, Memory, and Cognition, 37*(1), 109–122. https://doi.org/10.1037/a0021322.

Clark, H. H. (1996). *Using language*. Cambridge University Press. https://doi.org/10.1017/CBO9780511620539.

Clark, H. H., & Brennan, S. E. (1991). Grounding in communication. In L. B. Resnick, J. M. Levine, & S. D. Teasley (Eds.), *Perspectives on socially shared cognition* (pp. 222–233). American Psychological Association.

Clark, H. H., & Krych, M. A. (2004). Speaking while monitoring addressees for understanding. *Journal of Memory and Language, 50*, 62–81. https://doi.org/10.1016/j.jml.2003.08.004.

Clark, H. H., & Schaefer, E. F. (1989). Contributing to discourse. *Cognitive Science, 13*, 259–294. https://doi.org/10.1207/s15516709cog1302_7.

Dingemanse, M., & Enfield, N. J. (2023). Interactive repair and the foundations of language. *Trends in Cognitive Sciences, 28*, 30–42. https://doi.org/10.1016/j.tics.2023.09.003.

Fink, G. A., Schillo, C., Kummert, F., & Sagerer, G. (1998). Incremental speech recognition for multimodal interfaces. In *Proceedings of the 24th Annual Conference of the IEEE Industrial Electronics Society (IECON)* (Vol. 4, pp. 2012–2017). IEEE. https://doi.org/10.1109/IECON.1998.724027.

Goodwin, C. (2018). *Co-operative action*. Cambridge University Press. https://doi.org/10.1017/9781139016735.

Graziano, M., & Gullberg, M. (2018). When speech stops, gesture stops: Evidence from crosslinguistic and developmental comparisons. *Frontiers in Psychology, 9*, 879. https://doi.org/10.3389/fpsyg.2018.00879.

Guenther, F. H., Ghosh, S. S., & Tourville, J. A. (2006). Neural modeling and imaging of the cortical interactions underlying syllable production. *Brain and Language, 96*(3), 280–301. https://doi.org/10.1016/j.bandl.2005.06.001.

Guhe, M. (2007). *Incremental conceptualization for language production*. Lawrence Erlbaum.

Heldner, M., Edlund, J., & Hirschberg, J. (2010). Pitch similarity in the vicinity of backchannels. In *Proceedings of INTERSPEECH 2010*, Makuhari, Japan (pp. 3054–3057). https://doi.org/10.21437/Interspeech.2010-58.

Heylen, D. (2006). Head gestures, gaze and the principle of conversational structure. *International Journal of Humanoid Robotics, 3*, 241–267. https://doi.org/10.1142/S0219843606000746.

Holler, J., & Levinson, S. C. (2019). Multimodal language processing in human communication. *Trends in Cognitive Sciences, 23*, 639–652. https://doi.org/10.1016/j.tics.2019.05.006.

Hömke, P., Holler, J., & Levinson, S. C. (2017). Eye blinking as addressee feedback in face-to-face conversation. *Research on Language and Social Interaction, 50*, 54–70. https://doi.org/10.1080/08351813.2017.1262143.

Hough, J., & Schlangen, D. (2016). Investigating fluidity for human–robot interaction with real-time, real-world grounding strategies. In *Proceedings of the 17th Annual Meeting of the Special Interest Group on Discourse and Dialogue* (pp. 288–298). ACL. https://doi.org/10.18653/v1/W16-3637.

Kennington, C., Han, T., & Schlangen, D. (2017). Temporal alignment using the incremental unit framework. In *Proceedings of the 19th ACM International Conference on Multimodal Interaction* (pp. 297–301). ACM. https://doi.org/10.1145/3136755.3136769.

Kennington, C., Kousidis, S., & Schlangen, D. (2014). InproTKs: A toolkit for incremental situated processing. In *Proceedings of the 15th Annual Meeting of the Special Interest Group on Discourse and Dialogue (SIGDIAL)* (pp. 84–88). ACL. https://doi.org/10.3115/v1/W14-4312.

Kennington, C., Lison, P., & Schlangen, D. (2025). *Prior lessons of incremental dialogue and robot action management for the age of language models*. https://doi.org/10.48550/arXiv.2501.00953. arXiv: 2501.00953 [cs].

Kennington, C., Moro, D., Marchand, L., Carns, J., & McNeill, D. (2020). rrSDS: Towards a robot-ready spoken dialogue system. In *Proceedings of the 21th Annual Meeting of the Special Interest Group on Discourse and Dialogue* (pp. 132–135). ACL. https://doi.org/10.18653/v1/2020.sigdial-1.17.

Kilger, A., & Finkler, W. (1995). *Incremental generation for real-time applications*. Technical report. RR-95-11. Deutsches Forschungszentrum für Künstliche Intelligenz. https://doi.org/10.22028/D291-24965.

Köhn, A. (2018). Incremental natural language processing: Challenges, strategies, and evaluation. In *Proceedings of the 27th International Conference on Computational Linguistics (COLING)* (pp. 2990–3003). ICCL.

Kopp, S., Allwood, J., Grammar, K., Ahlsén, E., & Stocksmeier, T. (2008). Modeling embodied feedback with virtual humans. In I. Wachsmuth & G. Knoblich (Eds.), *Modeling communication with robots and virtual humans* (pp. 18–37). Springer. https://doi.org/10.1007/978-3-540-79037-2_2.

Kopp, S., van Welbergen, H., Yaghoubzadeh, R., & Buschmeier, H. (2014). An architecture for fluid real-time conversational agents: Integrating incremental output generation and input processing. *Journal on Multimodal User Interfaces, 8*, 97–108. https://doi.org/10.1007/s12193-013-0130-3.

Kröger, B. J., Stille, C. M., Blouw, P., Bekolay, T., & Stewart, T. C. (2020). Hierarchical sequencing and feedforward and feedback control mechanisms in speech production: A preliminary approach for modeling normal and disordered speech. *Frontiers in Computational Neuroscience, 14*, 573554. https://doi.org/10.3389/fncom.2020.573554.

Levelt, W. J. M. (1989). *Speaking: From intention to articulation*. The MIT Press. https://doi.org/10.7551/mitpress/6393.001.0001.

Levelt, W. J. M., Roelofs, A., & Meyer, A. S. (1999). A theory of lexical access in speech production. *Behavioral and Brain Sciences, 22*(1), 1–38. https://doi.org/10.1017/S0140525X99001776.

Lundberg, S. M., & Lee, S.-I. (2017). A unified approach to interpreting model predictions. In *Advances in Neural Information Processing Systems* (Vol. 30). Curran.

Lyra, M. C. D. P. (2010). On interaction analysis and dialogical perspective: Emergent patterns of order and relational agency. In *Integrative Psychological and Behavioral Science, 44*, 273–280. https://doi.org/10.1007/s12124-010-9130-y.

Michael, T. (2020). Retico: An incremental framework for spoken dialogue systems. In *Proceedings of the 21th Annual Meeting of the Special Interest Group on Discourse and Dialogue* (pp. 49–52). ACL. https://doi.org/10.18653/v1/2020.sigdial-1.6.

Monteath, I., & Sheh, R. (2018). Assisted and incremental medical diagnosis using explainable artificial intelligence. In *Proceedings of the 2nd Workshop on Explainable Artificial Intelligence* (pp. 104–108).

Nota, N., Trujillo, J. P., & Holler, J. (2021). Facial signals and social actions in multimodal face-to-face interaction. *Brain Sciences, 118*(8), 1017. https://doi.org/10.3390/brainsci11081017.

Oestreich, H., Heinz-Jakobs, M., Sehr, P., & Wrede, S. (2022). Human-centered adaptive assistance systems for the shop floor. In C. Röcker & S. Büttner (Eds.), *Human-technology interaction: Shaping the future of industrial user interfaces* (pp. 83–125). Springer. https://doi.org/10.1007/978-3-030-99235-4_4.

Pickering, M. J., & Garrod, S. (2004). Toward a mechanistic psychology of dialogue. *Behavioral and Brain Sciences, 27*, 169–226. https://doi.org/10.1017/S0140525X04000056.

Postma, A. (2000). Detection of errors during speech production: A review of speech monitoring models. *Cognition, 77*(2), 97–132. https://doi.org/10.1016/S0010-0277(00)00090-1.

Schegloff, E. A., Jefferson, G., & Sacks, H. (1977). The preference for self-correction in the organization of repair in conversation. *Language, 53*, 361–382. https://doi.org/10.2307/413107.

Schlangen, D., Baumann, T., Buschmeier, H., Buß, O., Kopp, S., Skantze, G., & Yaghoubzadeh, R. (2010). Middleware for incremental processing in conversational agents. In *Proceedings of the 11th Annual Meeting of the Special Interest Group in Discourse and Dialogue*, Tokyo, Japan (pp. 51–54).

Schlangen, D., & Skantze, G. (2011). A general, abstract model of incremental dialogue processing. *Dialogue and Discourse, 2*, 83–111. https://doi.org/10.5087/dad.2011.105.

Skantze, G., & Hjalmarsson, A. (2013). Towards incremental speech generation in conversational systems. *Computer Speech & Language, 27*, 243–262. https://doi.org/10.1016/j.csl.2012.05.004.

Skantze, G., & Schlangen, D. (2009). Incremental dialogue processing in a micro-domain. In *Proceedings of the 12th Conference of the European Chapter of the Association for Computational Linguistics*, Athens, Greece (pp. 745–753).

Tanenhaus, M. K., & Brown-Schmidt, S. (2008). Language processing in the natural world. *Philosophical Transactions of the Royal Society B, 363*, 1105–1122. https://doi.org/10.1098/rstb.2007.2162.

ter Bekke, M., Levinson, S. C., Van Otterdijk, L., Kühn, M., & Holler, J. (2024). Visual bodily signals and conversational context benefit the anticipation of turn ends. *Cognition, 248*, 105806. https://doi.org/10.1016/j.cognition.2024.105806.

Thalmann, M., Souza, A. S., & Oberauer, K. (2019). How does chunking help working memory? *Journal of Experimental Psychology: Learning, Memory, and Cognition, 45*(1), 37. https://doi.org/10.1037/xlm0000578.

Thompson, H. S. (1977). Strategy and tactics: A model for language production. In W. A. Beach, S. E. Fox, & S. Philosoph (Eds.), *Papers from the 13th Regional Meeting of the Chicago Linguistic Society* (pp. 651–668). Chicago Linguistic Society.

Trujillo, J. P., & Holler, J. (2024). Conversational facial signals combine into compositional meanings that change the interpretation of speaker intentions. *Scientific Reports, 14*(1), 2286. https://doi.org/10.1038/s41598-024-52589-0.

van Geert, P., & de Ruiter, N. (2022). *Toward a process approach in psychology: Stepping into Heraclitus' river*. Cambridge University Press. https://doi.org/10.1017/9781108859189.

Visser, T., Traum, D. R., DeVault, D., & op den Akker, R. (2014). A model for incremental grounding in spoken dialogue systems. *Journal on Multimodal User Interfaces, 8*, 61–73. https://doi.org/10.1007/s12193-013-0147-7.

Wang, D., Yang, Q., Abdul, A., & Lim, B. Y. (2019). Designing theory-driven user-centric explainable AI. In *Proceedings of the 2019 CHI Conference on Human Factors in Computing Systems*. Glasgow, UK (pp. 1–15). https://doi.org/10.1145/3290605.3300831.

Ward, N. (2006). Non-lexical conversational sounds in American English. *Pragmatics & Cognition, 14*, 129–182. https://doi.org/10.1075/pc.14.1.08war.

Xu, T. L., De Barbaro, K., Abney, D. H., & Cox, R. F. (2020). Finding structure in time: Visualizing and analyzing behavioral time series. *Frontiers in Psychology, 11*, 1457. https://doi.org/10.3389/fpsyg.2020.01457.

Yaghoubzadeh, R., & Kopp, S. (2016). flexdiam – Flexible dialogue management for problem-aware, incremental spoken interaction for all user groups (demo paper). In *Proceedings of the 7th Workshop on Speech and Language Processing for Assistive Technologies* (pp. 87–90). ACL.

Open Access This chapter is licensed under the terms of the Creative Commons Attribution 4.0 International License (http://creativecommons.org/licenses/by/4.0/), which permits use, sharing, adaptation, distribution and reproduction in any medium or format, as long as you give appropriate credit to the original author(s) and the source, provide a link to the Creative Commons license and indicate if changes were made.

The images or other third party material in this chapter are included in the chapter's Creative Commons license, unless indicated otherwise in a credit line to the material. If material is not included in the chapter's Creative Commons license and your intended use is not permitted by statutory regulation or exceeds the permitted use, you will need to obtain permission directly from the copyright holder.

Chapter 13
Adaptation

Heike M. Buhl ⓘ, Britta Wrede ⓘ, Josephine B. Fisher ⓘ, and Marco Matarese ⓘ

Abstract An essential prerequisite for XAI to interact with the user and co-construct understanding is the adaptation to individual users. Two forms of adaptation are considered: (1) Cognitive adaptation involves scaffolding and monitoring as key processes of mutual support between explainer and explainee. These processes are particularly well established in tutoring research. This chapter elaborates on scaffolding, monitoring, and the resulting cognitive adaptation through illustrative examples. (2) Interactive adaptation focuses on the behaviors of both explainer and explainee. Specific strategies for their mutual support and joint co-construction of explanations are introduced. This includes content adaptations as well as explanatory strategies adapted by the explainer for successful scaffolding. For this to succeed, the substantive contributions of the explainee should be considered in particular. Examples of implementations of these forms of personalization already exist in XAI and are presented here as forms of operationalization. While early approaches tended to consider user characteristics statically, more recent systems show initial capabilities for dynamically adaptive explanation generation.

H. M. Buhl (✉)
Institute for Human Sciences – Psychology, Faculty of Arts and Humanities, Paderborn University, Paderborn, Germany
e-mail: heike.buhl@uni-paderborn.de

B. Wrede
Medical School OWL, Bielefeld University, Bielefeld, Germany
e-mail: bwrede@techfak.uni-bielefeld.de

J. B. Fisher
Psycholinguistics, Faculty of Arts and Humanities, Paderborn University, Paderborn, Germany
e-mail: josephine.beryl.fisher@uni-paderborn.de

M. Matarese
COgNiTive Architecture for Collaborative Technologies unit, Italian Institute of Technology, Genoa, Italy
e-mail: marco.matarese@iit.it

© The Author(s) 2026
K. J. Rohlfing et al. (eds.), *Social Explainable AI*,
https://doi.org/10.1007/978-981-96-5290-7_13

13.1 How Does This Chapter Relate to XAI?

When advocating the idea of a social XAI (sXAI), we follow the theory of social constructivism positing that knowledge is constructed through interaction with others (Vygotski, 1934/1986). For XAI, the explaining AI and the human as explainee should develop a common understanding of each other and the explanandum (Rohlfing et al., 2021). In this sense, an important prerequisite for XAI to be social is adaptation to the user. These ideas have some important theoretical foundations that might help developers understand the need for adaptation as a prerequisite of sXAI. To make sXAI concrete, it is useful to include two forms of adaptation: cognitive and interactive. Explainers perceive the feedback from the explainee, and they adapt their explanation accordingly. This **interactive adaptation** presupposes that the explainer notices the knowledge, goals, and so forth of the explainee and, if necessary, changes their beliefs about the explainee—that is, the user. We refer to this as **cognitive adaptation**. In order to implement cognitive adaptivity in sXAI, it is necessary to consider how adaptivity can be designed and what to adapt to. In this chapter, we focus particularly on design principles and the theoretical lines on which they are based. Chapter 14 on models of the situation, the explanandum, and the partner will elaborate on which mental representations are adapted and how they are modified during the course of explanations. Building on this cognitive adaptivity, interactive adaptation of the form and the content becomes possible during the course of explanations.

13.2 Cognitive Adaptation Processes

The wealth of research on learning processes provides a good illustration of the opportunities and challenges of cognitive adaptation. Our aim is to show that explanations, in order to promote understanding, should enable the construction of knowledge. Furthermore, we shall illustrate some supporting means, scaffolding and monitoring. However, it should be noted that several of the reported studies refer to a special form of explanations—namely, instructional explanations. Unlike everyday explanations and most AI explanations, a correct, comprehensive, and precise explanation is formulated in a formal learning context. The teacher or tutor aims to achieve a specific learning objective (cf. Miller, 2019).

13.2.1 Knowledge Construction Needs Adaptive Interactions

When describing learning processes, educational science and psychology underline two aspects: (1) Learning is an individual learner's construction of knowledge as a developing mental representation. This is in contrast to the older and widespread idea that fixed and predefined knowledge units can or even should be transmitted from teacher to learner. (2) To support this construction, it is necessary for teachers to adapt to the individual student's knowledge and purposes (Kulgemeyer, 2018; Parsons et al., 2018). This chapter briefly clarifies the difference between knowledge transmission, individual knowledge construction, and the co-construction of knowledge in order to show the benefits of these various conceptualizations for sXAI. The co-constructive approach is particularly promising here.

Until the 1980s, learning was predominantly seen as acquiring knowledge. The basic idea is that learners acquire knowledge that others, for example, teachers, already have. The task of the teacher is to structure the learning material well, distribute it in convenient packages, and hand it over to the learner as a 'transmission.' Learners are seen as quite passive receivers, whereas teachers are active in this process. To this end, various forms of instructional design have been developed to deliver the material to be learned efficiently. Despite concerns about this view of learners, sXAI can benefit from instructional designs that build on it. It is helpful to consider the structure of an explanation and the organization and portioning of the information to be passed on (Reigeluth, 2013) as well as the cognitive load that the subject and the learning material impose on a learner/explainee (Sweller, 2010) (see also Chap. 12).

Going beyond the transmission of information, representatives of constructivist theory underline that learning is an individual construction (Piaget, 2005, cf. Palincsar, 1998). This construction benefits from the learner's experience with the material through, for example, problem-oriented learning environments, authentic problems, and self-explaining. The role of the teacher changes to that of an advisor or coach. Learners are autonomous and active. Research has shown that own knowledge construction enables a deeper understanding and stronger and more flexible problem-solving skills (Staub & Stern, 2002).

In addition, social constructivism underlines that learning is a social process. In this sense, Chi and Wylie (2014) have summarized different learning activities in the ICAP framework (interactive, constructive, active, and passive). The more engaged learners are with other learners (from passive receiving to active manipulating to constructive generating and, finally, to interactive dialoguing), the more successfully they learn in terms of deep understanding, inferences, transfer, and critical thinking.

The social constructivist emphasis on individual processes of knowledge construction has overcome the concept of a one-explanation-fits-all approach. The consequence is that teaching in general and explaining in particular should be adaptive and adjust to the needs of the explainees (Bernacki et al., 2021; Parsons et al., 2018). This adaptation becomes visible in explanations through the interactive adaptation of the content and the form to the explainee (e.g., experts vs. laypersons, adults vs. children). In addition to this global adaptation, local incremental adaptations are needed during the course of the explanation that consider the history of an explanation (cf. Chap. 17). One first step is to consider differences between individual explainees. This is the case in Kary's explanation of the car he is interested in for his wife, a friend, and so forth with its focus on different aspects (e.g., economy or speed; cf. Sect. 2.3). Since the 1970s, instructional design has drawn attention to learners' different aptitudes and prior knowledge. The aptitude-treatment-interaction approach emphasizes that the teaching method must be adapted to the abilities of the learners. This was related to both knowledge acquisition (Sternberg et al., 1999) and behavioral approaches (Snow, 1991). However, these approaches remained mostly experimental. Indeed, a better understanding of research findings could be gained when not only characteristics of the situation or the person are considered but also their interaction. For example, weak and insecure learners benefit from clear instructions, whereas intelligent learners and learners with high self-efficacy lose motivation in the same setting (e.g., Saleh et al., 2005). AI explanations must therefore also be adapted to these explainees' characteristics in terms of their level and focus.

A second step of adapting to the needs of learners or explainees is the local adaptation within the course of an explanation (cf. the differentiation between the adjusted and co-constructed context in Sect. 4.5). "As such, the teacher must monitor students' changing understanding and adapt instruction" and explanation (Parsons et al., 2018, p. 208). A variety of explainees' changing characteristics must be considered. In particular, it is necessary to diagnose understanding or misunderstanding in the actual explanation (Kulgemeyer, 2018). Social constructivist theories can inform the intertwined processes of diagnosis and adaptation. Speaking about children's language development, Bruner and colleagues (e.g., Wood et al., 1976, p. 90) have described parental activities as "scaffolding". In a broader sense, scaffolding is an individually tailored guidance from a parent, teacher, tutor, or (tutorial) system to a learner—in our case, from explainer to explainee. It results from the social interaction between the two. This allows the right form and amount of support to be provided for a specific explainee in a specific context and situation. The support is faded away when it is no longer needed. This challenge requires close 'monitoring.' The explainer interprets verbal and nonverbal signals of understanding or misunderstanding in the explainee. Taking the social constructivist conception further, the explainer and the explainee build their understanding together. In this sense, monitoring is not only carried out by the explainer. Both explainer and explainee engage in monitoring, and support each other with scaffolding. These social processes go beyond personalization of AI or AI explanations. Rohlfing et al. (2021, p. 720) have summarized this in a framework of "explanation as a social practice in which the explainee and the explainer interact in different social roles" and jointly construct the explanation with both being involved in scaffolding and monitoring processes.

13.2.2 Examples of Cognitive Adaptation in Explanatory Dialogs

Three related areas of research should be considered for their substantial contributions to the understanding of adaptation within an explanatory process: research on instructional explanations, on tutoring, and on intelligent tutorial systems, that, to some extent, build on this.

Instructional explanations given mostly by teachers to the class are a topic in psychology and (science) education. In contrast to the abovementioned interpretation as knowledge transmission, Kulgemeyer and Geelan (2024) discuss a constructivist view of explaining with similar involvement, but with different tasks of explainer and explainee: The explainers (experts) formulate an address-oriented explanation. The explainees (novices) provide feedback on their understanding process. The explainers must diagnose this feedback appropriately. In the case of teachers, their professional knowledge supports the instructional quality of their explanation and their diagnosis of the explainees' feedback and understanding. To define instructional quality, a literature review by Kulgemeyer (2018) identified empirically confirmed factors. He refers to the adaptivity of the explanation as the most important factor. Explanations are more effective if they are adaptive and consider the learners' prior knowledge, skills, or cognitive abilities (Wittwer et al., 2008). The second most important factor is the selection of appropriate tools for achieving adaptation. For science education, Kulgemeyer (2018) refers to the 'tools' of linguistic registers, examples, analogies, the level of mathematization, figures, and demonstrations. With our focus on sXAI, we shall discuss these in detail in the following section (Sect. 13.3).

Tutoring refers to a personalized learning process with one tutor and one tutee. It is particularly effective in the sense that both tutor and tutee experience a learning gain. As Chi and colleagues have worked out on the basis of observational studies, tutors provide scaffolding: The tutor diagnoses and monitors the tutees' evolving understanding, provides appropriate assistance, and gradually fades the support away as the tutee becomes more competent (Chi et al., 2001). Despite an asymmetry in the interaction, the tutee is equally active. Tutor and tutee mutually influence each other and organize their interaction jointly. More details on scaffolding and substantive contributions will follow in Sect. 13.3.

However, tutors often neglect tutees' knowledge deficits. Especially tutors with less tutoring experience are weak in monitoring the specific individual understanding of the tutee (Chi et al., 2004). One reason for this might be the limited cognitive capacities of human tutors/explainers (Wittwer et al., 2010). As a result, human tutoring is less effective than expected and hoped. Based on a comparison between human tutors and intelligent tutoring systems (ITS), Van Lehn (2011) found that ITS were nearly as effective as human tutors (for a specific example, see Sect. 13.5). This is encouraging for sXAI if the explained principles of knowledge construction are adhered to.

Intelligent tutoring systems (ITS) are computer-based educational programs that provide personalized instruction and feedback to learners. Like human tutors, they should be adaptive to an individual learner. To this end, alongside the domain model representing the subject to teach, they have a student (diagnosis) model of the learner's current knowledge. This is updated as the learner interacts with the ITS. Additionally, the ITS has a tutoring model with instruction strategies, what and how to teach, and a user interface. Mousavinasab et al. (2021) conducted a systematic review of the purposes of using AI techniques in ITS and how they took into account learners' characteristics. They found that learners' performance evaluation (ability or procedural knowledge), adaptive guidance, and adaptive instruction are the most important purposes. Regarding learner characteristics, their knowledge level, learning performance, and behavior in the learning path were frequently addressed. So far, the influence of these various aspects on learning success is not yet completely clear. However, XAI can benefit from ITS characteristics by taking their advantages into account (Clancey & Hoffman, 2021).

To sum up, the results of these research areas underline the importance of adaptation. However, they also highlight problems and challenges. For human explainers (here tutors), cognitive resources limit the ability to respond to the explainee in a well-adapted manner. ITS overcome this limitation: Because their cognitive capacity is not limited, they can be equipped with mental models of both the domain and the explainee, and they can monitor and scaffold the explainees' understanding adaptively. We shall discuss these important cognitive prerequisites of sXAI in Chap. 14.

13.3 Interactive Adaptation

Cognitive adaptation accompanies the verbal behavior of the interaction partners – the so-called interactive adaptation. Unlike cognitive adaptation, which can only be inferred, interactive adaptation is visible. However, cognitions influence behavior and are influenced by it. In the following, we shall consider only verbal behavior. The importance of nonverbal behavior will be discussed in Chap. 19. One of the most important mechanisms in conversation is turn-taking (cf. Chap. 7). The core of the turn-taking model is the organization of contributions by the conversational partners. They negotiate the speaker changes and who speaks when (Sacks et al., 1974). In our view, these changes are not automatically interactive, but depend on which utterances are selected in the explanation. The selection of the next speaker occurs by addressing the other speaker or by continuing to speak via self-selecting (Sacks et al., 1974). Consequently, the turn-taking mechanism enables successful interactions through the allocation of speakers and their verbal contributions. An additional mechanism for successful interactions is proposed by Pickering and Garrod (2004) in their interactive alignment account. The situational models of the speakers need to be aligned for successful communication, and this most often takes the form of an underlying automatic linguistic alignment. However, both interlocutors are actively involved in creating a shared understanding of the topic under discussion (Pickering & Garrod, 2004). In this vein, from the co-constructive view, both conversational partners steer the interaction (Fisher et al., 2023; Rohlfing et al., 2021). The question to answer is: How do explainers' and explained verbal behavior showcase interactive adaptation? On the one hand, the explainer does this by placing certain contents and choosing certain explanation strategies: the so-called speaker moves. These consist of an utterance that includes a single idea by a speaker within a turn (Chi et al., 2008). Our claim is that especially the explanation strategy of scaffolding (see Sect. 13.2.1) is important for the interactive adaptation by the explainer. In tutoring, Chi et al. (2001) suggest that scaffolding moves by tutors (in our case, explainers) guide tutees (in our case, explainees) through tailored explanations that elicit active involvement. This involvement is highlighted through interactive scaffolding in which tutors provide guidance, and tutees respond constructively by building upon the input. As a first step, we shall consider tutor moves that elicit such responses. For a detailed description, see Sect. 13.3.2.

However, the explainee also guides the explanation through their types of explanation strategies, for example, by the questions they are asking, if they address familiar topics, or if they initiate new topics. When the explainee introduces a new topic in the explanation, the explainer generally takes it up directly (Fisher et al., 2023). Empirical work on game explanations (Fisher et al., 2023) broadly shows that the interactive adaptation of both conversational partners shapes and thereby supports the co-construction (Rohlfing et al., 2021) of an explanation and the joint involvement of the conversational partners (Clark & Schaefer, 1989). An explanation of a game encompasses various elements including its rules, playing pieces, and the game board. Kotthoff (2009) notes that this form of explanation, similar to route and word explanations, is straightforward and can be implemented immediately. The author additionally refers to game explanations as procedural explanations.

In order to enhance social aspects in sXAI, it is crucial to include the verbal behavior of the explainee, which enables the development of an adequate partner model (cf. Sect. 14.4) and allows a better response to the explainee—and this again leads to an increase in their understanding. According to tutoring literature (Chi et al., 2008), the substantial contributions and active involvement of the tutee lead to considerable learning effects. As Chi et al. (2008) outlined, the tutee's substantive contributions (e.g., the feedback of understanding or nonunderstanding) are crucial for the success of tutoring (see detailed description in Sect. 13.3.3). For sXAI research, it is necessary to identify substantive contributions of the explainee and to adapt the explanation accordingly (Buhl et al., 2024). Currently, there is still not enough knowledge about which substantial contributions of the explainee the sXAI should consider (Fisher, 2025, in prep). To shed light upon sXAI, it is beneficial to take human–human explanations as a starting point, and to examine how linguistic adaptation processes take place (Fisher et al., 2022).

Regarding interactive adaptation between speakers, we shall refer to the concepts already mentioned in the section before and use some examples to consider the substantive speaker moves by the explainee and the scaffolding moves by the explainer in more depth. Both concepts, speaker moves and scaffolding, are taken from tutoring research, and are adapted to explanations. The basis for the examination of the moves is a content analysis of the semantic dialog patterns (Fisher et al., 2023). Therefore, the interactive adaptation is described from three analysis levels: (1) semantic dialog patterns, (2) interactive scaffolding moves by explainer, and (3) substantive moves by explainee. These levels constitute a possible approach to investigating parts of the interactive adaptation.

13.3.1 Adapting the Content

It has been argued that a large portion of this adaptation happens unintentionally, as put forward in the alignment concept that interprets adaptation processes as happening at a rather "mechanistic" level (Pickering & Garrod, 2004, p. 169). More specifically, adaptations in interactions have been largely observed to occur at the prosodic, lexical, and syntactic levels—that is, through the uptake of words or syntactic constructions by the interaction partners. According to the alignment account, it is argued that adaptation at one level percolates to another level. That is, by selecting the same words or syntactic constructions of the interlocutor, similar semantic concepts and situation models are constructed when the interlocutors engage in joint action.

A further concept of adaptation has been described in terms of grounding as a process between two interlocutors to achieve a joint goal (Clark & Brennan, 1991). According to this perspective, a task-oriented interaction, in which both interaction partners follow a joint goal consists of (1) presentations in which one interlocutor offers a contribution consisting of concepts to be considered by the interaction partner, followed by (2) acceptance in which the listener provides evidence about whether or not they have understood what has been presented. This process will incrementally build a so-called common ground of knowledge that both partners know they are sharing (Clark, 1996). In order to achieve grounding, especially in difficult situations such as interactions with computers, grounding hierarchies have been proposed in which feedback of a (computational) listener is given based on its status at different processing levels (Brennan & Hulteen, 1995). This enables the system to provide detailed feedback about its understanding should this be necessary. In the case when many clarification requests or corrections have been uttered by the user in the ongoing interaction, the system will adapt its feedback strategy by providing feedback on its processing status at each processing level. In the case when the previous interaction did not produce any clarification questions or corrections from the user, the system will assume that the current interaction is smooth and will provide less or no feedback and simply carry out the perceived command.

To enable grounding, the semantics of a conversation needs to be considered. Fisher et al. (2023) have proposed a method to examine the contents of a human–human explanation. In general, they were investigating a variety of adaptation processes. For this purpose, they recorded game explanations that constitute the ADEX (adaptive dialogical explanations) corpus. This contains 64 game explanation dyads with a total of 128 participants. The majority of participants were German native speakers and university students (mean age: 25 years). Explanations lasted an average of 5.5 minutes (range: 2.3–12.3 minutes). In the analysis process, Fisher et al. (2023) assigned nodes, the so-called semantic dialog patterns, to the speech that labels the content. A node captures specific semantic information of the domain. They had to explain the board game Quarto, a strategic game that has different game figures with four features. To win the game, one has to place four figures in a row that share the same feature. An example of Node 2.2, which states that two players are playing the game, is given in Table 13.1, dataset 05 by the explainer in their first speaker move. Only that information is given within this move. As stated earlier, a move is an utterance capturing a single idea. In the linguistic analysis, each utterance is assigned nodes to support the speaker move analysis. The node captures the information on the domain, and the moves are the verbal expressions of this. By using this type of analysis, one can keep track of when the conversational partners talk about certain topics. This enables detailed comparisons of the contents of the utterances and, thereby, a differentiation of speaker moves. Furthermore, the interaction history is also recorded by this (Fisher et al., 2023). For more details see Chap. 17. In Fisher et al. (2023), the analysis enabled the investigation of the coverage of nodes by the speakers. They found that the explainees were actively involved in their coverage of the explanation nodes by addressing up to 48 percent of the nodes.

13.3.2 Explainer Adapting via Scaffolding

The explainer can adapt their explanations to the explainee's knowledge and goals via their scaffolding moves. As observed in tutoring settings (Chi et al., 2001), scaffolding moves by the tutor are a constructive way of guiding the tutee in the conversation. In Chi et al. (2001), the tutor moves are defined and categorized as *constructive moves* when the moves prompt a response from students. These are also *interactive* if they include asking questions aimed at assessing understanding or comprehension as well as providing scaffolding to support student learning. However, so far, research on scaffolding (Chi et al., 2001, 2008) has focused mainly on the explainer instead of the explainee. Thus, little is known about what kind of scaffolding can be triggered by what kind of verbal reaction of the explainee, which connection is assumed in the interactive view (Rohlfing et al., 2021). To fill this gap, Fisher and Rohlfing (2024a) have focused on the interactive and constructive moves by the explainer depending on a verbal reaction by the explainee—hence, called the interactive and constructive moves (Table 13.1). These are based on tutoring literature (Chi et al., 2001, 2008; Miyake, 1986) with some adaptations based on the ADEX corpus of human–human game explanations (Sect. 13.3.1). In Table 13.1, each example is taken from a consecutive stretch of speech within the explanations, attempting to provide context to enhance understanding of the game explanations. Fisher and Rohlfing (2024a) present a full list of interactive and constructive moves.

In the following, by selecting the moves according to their frequency of occurrence, we suggest some interactive and constructive moves to be implemented in sXAI. The most frequent interactive and constructive scaffolding moves, in order of most to least, are *decomposing game, metatalk, confirming, reminding*, and *highlighting*. An example of *decomposing game* is shown in Dataset 68 where the explainer is dividing the information on the game features into smaller chunks by listing just one of the four features. This can make the explanation potentially easier to comprehend, because the amount of information is minimized. Chi et al. (2001) refer to this by the category of *decomposing task*, which refers to the problem-solving steps in the tutoring sessions.

The second most frequent scaffolding move is *metatalk*. In the example in Dataset 16, it makes explicit that there is no further content that can be added. In contrast to Chi et al. (2001), we also see confirmatory feedback as a type of scaffolding because it guides and thereby encourages the tutee in their knowledge construction. This is supported in the example, because the explainee makes a substantive contribution by *paraphrasing* their conversational partner following the explainer's confirmatory feedback.

Another prominent category is *reminding* (Chi et al., 2001) the explainee of certain aspects. In the example of Dataset 22, the explainer repeats the features of the different figures of the game. The final type of scaffolding that will be considered is *highlighting* (Chi et al., 2001). Important aspects of the game become emphasized via various linguistic means such as negations, contrasts, and registers. In the example of Dataset 17, the explainer highlights, via negation, that one has to choose the figures for the other player, and thus, one cannot think about which figure to choose for oneself.

To contrast the interactive and constructive scaffolding moves exemplified above, a noninteractive move can be seen in Dataset 05. There, the explainer states that the game is usually played by two players. After this, no verbal response by the explainee follows. Therefore, it is noninteractive. The explainer continues with the board game, and the explainee directly asks a question regarding that information; and, therefore, it becomes interactive. Thus, the scaffolding moves are interactive either by the explainee self-selecting or by the explainer asking them a question. This is not shown in the examples from Table 13.1. Consequently, the analysis of interactivity of moves is intertwined with the mechanisms of turn-taking (Sacks et al., 1974). Further research needs to investigate the causal relationship between interactive and constructive scaffolding by the explainer and substantive moves by the explainee more thoroughly. It is probable that other factors of a cognitive nature (e.g., cognitive load [see Sect. 13.2.2], nonverbal behavior (see Chap. 19), or previous experiences (see Sects. 17.1, 14.4) also come into play in the adaptation process.

The adaptation of the explainer using scaffolding moves needs to be taken in relation to the substantive moves by the explainee in order to gain a more thorough insight into the interactive adaptivity of the speakers (Buhl et al., 2024). This type of adaptation will be discussed in the next section.

13.3.3 Explainee Adapting via Substantive Contributions

A closer look at how the explainee is adapting to the explainer reveals that it is via their *substantive contributions*. These contributions are especially important, because they give insights into the explainee's understanding. This concept is

13 Adaptation

Table 13.1 Examples of adaptive and nonadaptive moves from the ADEX corpus

Adaptive	Nonadaptive	Move	Example
Scaffolding		Decomposing game	ER: And there are some that are square.
Substantive		Factual question	EE: Do the square ones not have a hole? (68)
Scaffolding		Metatalk	ER: Well, if we had a board here now we could try it right
Substantive		Mentalizing	EE: No, I think yeah I can picture it well. (65)
Scaffolding		Confirming	ER: Exactly
Substantive		Paraphrasing partner	EE: So, there are many eight different types of figures. (16)
Scaffolding		Reminding	ER: Light, dark, tall, small with a hole, without a hole
	Nonsubstantive	Repeating partner	EE: Tall small. (22)
Scaffolding		Highlighting	ER: That is why you can't think about what you are placing next, but which figure am I choosing for the other one next
Substantive		Additional info	EE: Yes, exactly so, theoretically, you always have to think two three steps ahead about what you want to do next. (17)
	Nonscaffolding	Noninteractive	ER: Two players usually.
Scaffolding		Decomposing game	ER: The game board consists of four times four boxes
Substantive		Factual question	EE: Square-shaped or does it not matter? (05)

Sentence structure and semantics were adapted to the English language and thus correspond broadly to the German transcripts. Examples include dataset numbers

also taken from the field of tutoring studies (Chi et al., 2001) and follows the differentiation between substantive and nonsubstantive contributions by the tutee (in our case, the explainee): On the one hand, substantive contributions are relevant follow-ups, making it necessary to consider the semantics of the previous turn. This uses the information on the semantic dialog patterns (the nodes). Examples of substantive moves are giving unprompted self-explanations, asking questions, answering questions, responding to scaffolding prompt by tutor, and reflecting (Chi et al., 2008). On the other hand, nonsubstantive moves are continuer, repetitions, agreement, and off-task remarks by the tutee (Chi et al., 2001).

The concept of substantiveness can be applied to explanations. Therefore, one needs to consider the explanation nodes and the speaker moves of the utterances in order to examine their substantiveness. Fisher and Rohlfing (2024b) have based their coding scheme for the speaker moves mainly on tutoring literature (Chi et al., 2001, 2004, 2008; Tare et al., 2011). To provide deeper insights into substantive moves, some examples from the data from Table 13.1 will follow. The most frequent substantive move is asking a *factual question*. An example of that is in Dataset 68, in which the different features of the figures are addressed that the explainer has just mentioned. This is a substantive move, because it displays direct reference to the topic under discussion and steers the interaction toward that specific feature. This is confirmed by the explainer directly responding to the question. A further substantive speaker move is *mentalizing*, because this can display general thinking processes or emotional demands. In Dataset 65, the explainee expresses that they think they are able to envision what the board game looks like without it being present.

Another form of substantive involvement by the explainee is their move *paraphrasing partner*. In Dataset 16, the explainee paraphrases that the figures have different features that their conversational partner had mentioned earlier in the explanation. This is substantive, because they have reformulated the previous information. In contrast to *paraphrasing*, the move of *repeating partner* is not substantive, because the wording is not changed, as can be seen in Dataset 22 because only two words are repeated. Thereby, the effort in their knowledge construction does not become visible, because the content is only repeated and not altered in any way. The explainee cannot only talk about aspects that were previously explained, but can also bring in *additional info*. Thus, they steer the interaction by explaining to themselves a new aspect of the game. For example, regarding the strategies of the game, the explainee in Dataset 17 infers that part of the strategies is to plan ahead. This is based on the previous utterance by the explainer and possibly by their general knowledge of games.

What all the substantive moves by the explainee have in common is that they relate to the explanation domain and steer the interaction to a certain degree. In general, it displays how the explainee is involved in an explanation through their diverse set of speaker moves. These characterize the co-construction of an explanation by the explainee. This already becomes evident when only considering the five most common moves from the ADEX corpus.

13.4 Operationalization

Although XAI represents a relatively new field of study, several methods to implement adaptation in line with social frameworks have been proposed. As one may expect, they differ in complexity, and how deeply they consider the human partner in shaping the explanations. We refer to this aspect as operationalization, meaning how social frameworks have been implemented in explainable actions executed by artificial intelligent systems for adaptation and personalization.

The examples reported below show several ways to operationalize adaptation in XAI that have been investigated. Some approaches have pursued static personalization based on users' characteristics. This is a straightforward method but holds back issues because it is challenging to collect people's personality dimensions in the wild, and they are not robust to changes or dynamic circumstances. On the other hand, researchers have also proposed more dynamic and social adaptation strategies that exploit the interaction between the system and the user, which, in turn, becomes a partner. Although such approaches aim to leverage the human–machine interaction, they are challenging to implement, and can only partially model the complexity of such interaction.

Researchers first questioned whether cognitive adaptation could bring desirable results when dealing with explanations. Focusing on recommendation systems, Tintarev and Masthoff (2012) compared the effectiveness of both personalized and not-personalized explanations and users' satisfaction with them. The authors operationalized the personalization by referring to the users' preferences and interests while providing explanations. Promisingly, their results showed that personalization led to higher user satisfaction.

Moreover, different explanation types may adapt to specific user roles (Chap. 8). Considering the users' role is key in personalizing explainable systems, because people with different expertise or duties may need different information from such explanations. For instance, developers might be interested in detecting the system's malfunctions, whereas end users might be interested more in understanding the inner functioning of the system itself. In this regard, Delaunay et al. (2023) proposed a road map to compare three main XAI methods (feature-attribution, example-based, and rule-based) to test specific users' preferences. Moreover, they argued that users and usage scenarios are more complex than the three categories mostly considered so far: developers, domain experts, and lay users. They proposed a methodology to compare the impact of different explanation types on users. Such a methodology involves metrics such as trust, satisfaction, and understanding that are considered from both intentional and behavioral perspectives. Hence, they provided a valuable framework to operationalize explanations' effects on users and gain insights into what kind of explanation to present and to whom.

A static way to implement user personalization is by using their personality traits (Millecamp et al., 2019) and customizing explanations based on people's preferences for XAI methods that reflect their personality dimensions (Li et al., 2024). This is considered static, because it involves a one-shot mechanism with the users' personalities being assessed only once before using the system (Chap. 4). However, despite the rich literature on the adaptation of explanations through user profiling, there is evidence that very few users' characteristics can be proficiently used for personalization in XAI (Nimmo et al., 2024). For further details on partner modeling, see Chap. 14.

For example, Millecamp et al. (2019) collected users' personal characteristics (e.g., need for cognition, their inclination toward cognitively demanding activities) through a survey, and tested whether these significantly impacted people's interaction with a recommender system and their perception of it. They observed that for people with a low need for cognition, explained recommendations were the most beneficial, whereas for those with a high need for cognition, explanations could create a lack of confidence. The interaction effect between the need for cognition and confidence explains such a seemingly contradictory result. The authors found that people with a low need for cognition benefited more from explanations, because they helped raise their confidence in their decisions and vice versa. A follow-up study found that users' openness (i.e., their tendency to be open-minded, creative, and insightful) affects whether they would like to reuse the explanatory system (Millecamp et al., 2020).

Similarly, Conati et al. (2021) used well-established psychological tests to collect users' cognitive and personality characteristics and evaluated how personalized recommendations affected students' learning outcomes. They observed that providing explanations increased students' trust in the system's hints, perceived usefulness, and their intention to use it again. Additionally, they showed that three user characteristics modulated students' learning gains: need for cognition, conscientiousness, and reading proficiency. These represent the users' characteristics on which to operate the adaptation. In contrast, Chandramouli et al. (2023) tackled the personalization problem by iteratively tuning the hyperparameters of opaque image classifiers. The users iteratively rate the quality of explanations, and a classifier tries to optimize both the accuracy and their perceived explainability.

Moving on to XAI adaptation techniques that consider the explainee more deeply, Chakraborti et al. (2017) proposed to design the problem of explaining as a "model reconciliation problem." This approach aims to produce explanations to progressively modify the users' internal (mental) models (Chap. 14) in order to match them with the system's models. In this sense, the system seeks to find the optimal plan for such changes and implement it through several explanation moves. A concept operationalized in the computational architecture for co-constructive explainable systems proposed by Booshehri et al. (2024) exploits the MAPE-K architecture. Through monitoring (Sect. 13.3) (i.e., tracking the user's understanding and interpreting their cognitive states), it gathers information about the users. Subsequently, it interprets this information in the context of the ongoing explanation to see if it corresponds to the system's expectations. Finally, it scaffolds by generating plans comprising adaptation actions and realizing explanation actions.

In addition to that, in the realm of human–robot interaction, Matarese et al. (2023a) allowed a social robot to produce example-based counterfactual explanations by exploiting the human–robot shared experiences. Specifically, during their collaborative tasks (i.e., playing a cooperative version of the Connect 4 game), the robot collected the game configurations it and its human partner encountered, and it used these when needed to justify its recommendations. Compared to more precise examples, these social explanations resulted in a higher learning gain and robot influence, especially for less skilled players. Such an approach was more dynamic, because it used the human–robot collaborative behavior and did not just consider the people's characteristics. In a subsequent study, the authors replicated this effect (adaptive explanations being more persuasive), and found it stronger when a social robot produced the explanations compared to a voice assistant (Matarese et al., 2024). Moreover, they found that people's personality dimensions (e.g., agreeableness and negative agency) also shape their willingness to follow the robot's suggestions (Matarese et al., 2023b).

Furthermore, Robrecht and Kopp (2023) developed an adaptive explanation generation system that exploited a model incorporating several linguistic levels of humanlike explanations. Such a model uses online planning (Monte Carlo tree search) to solve continuously adapted Markov decision processes to select which

13 Adaptation

explanations to provide. Based on initial assumptions and online feedback from the explainee, their system updates its partner model and the corresponding decision-making. Based on the understanding of the explainee, which is inferred through an action-expectation mechanism, the system adapts its explanatory actions online to forward the information it has to provide.

Gross et al. (2025) have suggested a closed-loop approach for an XAI approach on *how* to explain actions to a human in which a cognitive state of the human interaction partner is estimated based on eye gaze, prior task performance, and prior interaction history. Drawing on this state, verbal scaffolding strategies determining the use of negation as a focusing strategy that requires significant cognitive resources are then selected. A reinforcement learning approach adapts these strategies based on their success or failure to increase user's task performance.

While monitoring and scaffolding are important strategies to yield joint understanding, it has been argued that to achieve aligning concepts, it is necessary to establish embodied interaction (Oudeyer, 2006). Such embodied experiences are likely to develop higher-level concepts that are easier to communicate to and be understood by others who have shared the same experiences. For example, Malle (2022) provides a reasoning framework modeling how humans attribute intention and the reasons for the behavior of other agents. In this context, emotions have also been proposed as an important variable in addition to beliefs and goals to explain the behavior of a robot or an agent to users (e.g., Kaptein et al., 2017a, 2017b; Neerincx et al., 2018).

13.5 How Does This Chapter Inspire Further Directions of XAI?

Adaptivity in explanations imposes strong requirements on sXAI systems. It requires the XAI system to provide an interactive interface that allows the explainee to actively contribute to the explaining process by asking questions or offering explanations of one's own understanding for inspection. Whereas some XAI systems already support interaction through a graphical user interface or other interfaces, they still lack important prerequisites.

On the one hand, an sXAI system needs to be able to monitor the explainee's state of understanding. There are a range of ways to do this. One is to actively search for signals of (non-)understanding such as nodding, freezing, eye gaze to the intended object, facial expressions, and verbal utterances. Another way is to evaluate the explainee's actions: Errors will provide valuable insight into the problems that the explainee has with the current explanation.

On the other hand, sXAI systems need scaffolding strategies to address mis- or nonunderstanding by, for example, focusing on other explanation parts that might be easier to understand, by repetition, providing more specific verbal explanations that use contrasts, or guiding attention toward the current explanation detail.

Some of these adaptation mechanisms can be found in ITS (see Sect. 13.2.2; Clancey & Hoffman, 2021). For example, Clement et al. (2013) estimated students' region of proximal development based on their success in specific math exercises. Their approach explicitly modeled the learner's competence levels along different dimensions based on their performance on specific math exercises in such a way that a reinforcement learning (RL) system could learn which action would increase which competence dimension. In a field study on learning with an ITS, this system was applied in four sessions to 265 children aged 7–8 years (Clément et al., 2024). The RL system sampled curricula – that is, it selected the most promising activities drawing on the child's prior performance on an exercise with a specific difficulty pattern that was supposed to model the *zone of proximal development*: (1) a 'standard' path as used by teachers, arranging the exercises in a linear sequence of difficulty ("PREDEF") and (2) a structure of exercises that allowed for branching, thereby enabling the RL to search for activities along different dimensions of difficulty ("ZPDES"). In a between-subject design, children were administered the RL approach based on either the standard path or on the structure allowing for branching. Results showed that children who learned with the ITS system based on the structure that allowed them to branch along different difficulty dimensions showed a significantly higher increase in their test scores at the end of the four sessions than those who had learned with the RL system based on the linear sequence. A closer examination of the learning paths or exercise paths revealed that, indeed, the exercises the algorithm selected in the ZPDES condition were far more diverse than those selected in the PREDEF condition. They exhibited different difficulty patterns and sometimes left out certain types of exercises. This indicated that a stronger individualization to the children's needs was achieved by the ZPDES approach.

This shows that it is possible not only to estimate the level of expertise or potential of an interaction partner but also to determine which contribution – in the case of ITS, an exercise – will provide the best learning effect. Considering how to transfer such approaches to XAI in order to predict the best next step for explaining seems to be a promising approach for future research.

Note that such strategies need to be based on a model of the explainee in order to adapt the system's behavior adequately. This also requires a representation of the task at hand – that is, the explanandum and if/how the relevant parts of it are already understood by the human partner. Therefore, in Chap. 14, we shall discuss the role of mental models for sXAI.

13.6 Rapid Access to the Content of This Chapter

In order for an explainer and an explainee to establish an explanation process that enables joint understanding, it is indispensable that both partners not only exchange their perspectives on the explanandum but that they are capable of adapting them to one another. Thus, the process of understanding does not simply involve adding a predefined explanation to the explainee's knowledge base. Rather, the explainee needs to actively construct an understanding of it by adapting existing or creating new concepts. This requires the capabilities of a cognitive adaptation process. This cognitive adaptation requires individually tailored guidance for the explainee by scaffolding them. It is necessary for the sXAI to monitor the needs and knowledge of the user or explainee. To elaborate on these processes, sXAI can benefit from research on learning and teaching and especially research on tutoring grounded in the theory of social constructivism.

These cognitive adaptation processes can be inferred by the interactive behaviors of the explanation partners. Exploring human–human interactions, it has been observed that the explainee plays an important role by contributing *substantive* moves, and thereby actively shaping the explanation. Thus, the explainee plays an important role in how the explanation is adapted to their needs. Accordingly, the explainer monitors the explainee and makes use of *scaffolding* moves.

In HCI systems, such adaptation capabilities have been implemented by either the use of partner models that characterize relevant parts of the user (e.g., by personality traits) that have been shown to play an important role in how certain kinds of advice and explanations are taken into account or the use of behavioral information that allows dynamic adaptation. In interactions with a social robot, it could be shown that adaptation can be achieved by leveraging the human–robot collaboration. Furthermore, first semiautonomous systems monitoring the user's understanding and adapting by using specific scaffolding strategies are currently being developed and researched. Intelligent tutoring systems are an important resource for powerful methods of adapting to the user.

Acknowledgments We thank Bertram F. Malle for his valuable perspective and helpful comments on an earlier version of this chapter.

This work was funded by the Deutsche Forschungsgemeinschaft (DFG, German Research Foundation): TRR 318/1 2021 – 438445824.

References

Bernacki, M. L., Greene, M. J., & Lobczowski, N. G. (2021). A systematic review of research on personalized learning: Personalized by whom, to what, how, and for what purpose(s)? *Educational Psychology Review, 33*(4), 1675–1715. https://doi.org/10.1007/s10648-021-09615-8

Booshehri, M., Buschmeier, H., Cimiano, P., Kopp, S., Kornowicz, J., Lammert, O., Matarese, M., Mindlin, D., Robrecht, A. S., Vollmer, A.-L., Wagner, P., & Wrede, B. (2024). Towards a computational architecture for co-constructive explainable systems. In *Proceedings of the 2024 Workshop on Explainability Engineering* (pp. 20–25). Association for Computing Machinery. https://doi.org/10.1145/3648505.3648509

Brennan, S. E., & Hulteen, E. A. (1995). Interaction and feedback in a spoken language system: A theoretical framework. *Knowledge-Based Systems, 8*(2–3), 143–151. https://doi.org/10.1016/0950-7051(95)98376-H

Buhl, H. M., Fisher, J. B., & Rohlfing, K. (2024). Changes in partner models—effects of adaptivity in the course of explanations. In *Proceedings of the Annual Meeting of the Cognitive Science*

Society (Vol. 46, pp. 4976–4983). eScholarship. https://escholarship.org/uc/item/5bb7p5pt#main

Chakraborti, T., Sreedharan, S., Zhang, Y., & Kambhampati, S. (2017). *Plan explanations as model reconciliation: Moving beyond explanation as soliloquy.* https://doi.org/10.48550/arXiv.1701.08317

Chandramouli, S., Zhu, Y., & Oulasvirta, A. (2023). Interactive personalization of classifiers for explainability using multi-objective Bayesian optimization. In *Proceedings of the 31st ACM Conference on User Modeling, Adaptation and Personalization* (pp. 34–45). Association for Computing Machinery. https://doi.org/10.1145/3565472.3592956

Chi, M. T. H., Roy, M., & Hausmann, R. G. M. (2008). Observing tutorial dialogues collaboratively: Insights about human tutoring effectiveness from vicarious learning. *Cognitive Science, 32*(2), 301–341. https://doi.org/10.1080/03640210701863396

Chi, M. T. H., Siler, S. A., & Jeong, H. (2004). Can tutors monitor students' understanding accurately? *Cognition and Instruction, 22*(3), 363–387. https://doi.org/10.1207/s1532690xci2203_4

Chi, M. T. H., Siler, S. A., Jeong, H., Yamauchi, T., & Hausmann, R. G. Hausmann (2001). Learning from human tutoring. *Cognitive Science, 25*(4), 471–533. https://doi.org/10.1207/s15516709cog2504_1

Chi, M. T. H., & Wylie, R. (2014). The ICAP framework: Linking cognitive engagement to active learning outcomes. *Educational Psychologis, 49*(4), 219–243. https://doi.org/10.1080/00461520.2014.965823

Clancey, W. J., & Hoffman, R. R. (2021). Methods and standards for research on explainable artificial intelligence: Lessons from intelligent tutoring systems. *Applied AI Letters, 2*(4), e53. https://doi.org/10.1002/ail2.53

Clark, H. H. (1996). *Using language.* Cambridge University Press. https://doi.org/10.1017/CBO9780511620539

Clark, H. H., & Brennan, S. E. (1991). Grounding in communication. In L. B. Resnick, J. M. Levine & Teasley, S. D. (Eds.), *Perspectives on socially shared cognition* (pp. 127–149). American Psychological Association. https://doi.org/10.1037/10096-006

Clark, H. H., & Schaefer, E. F. (1989). Contributing to discourse. *Cognitive Science, 13*(2), 259–294. https://doi.org/10.1016/0364-0213(89)90008-6

Clement, B., Roy, D., Oudeyer, P.-Y., & Lopes, M. (2013). *Multi-armed bandits for intelligent tutoring systems.* https://doi.org/10.48550/arXiv.1310.3174

Clément, B., Sauzéon, H., Roy, D., & Oudeyer, P.-Y. (2024). *Improved performances and motivation in intelligent tutoring systems: Combining machine learning and learner choice.* https://arxiv.org/abs/2402.01669

Conati, C., Barral, O., Putnam, V., & Rieger, L. (2021). Toward personalized XAI: A case study in intelligent tutoring systems. *Artificial Intelligence, 298*, 103503. https://doi.org/10.1016/j.artint.2021.103503

Delaunay, J., Largouët, C., Galárraga, L., & Van Berkel, N. (2023). Adaptation of AI explanations to users' roles. In *Workshop on Human-Centered Explainable AI (@ CHI 2023).* HAL. https://inria.hal.science/hal-04388942/

Fisher, J. B., Lohmer, V., Kern, F., Barthlen, W., Gaus, S., & Rohlfing, K. J. (2022). Exploring monological and dialogical phases in naturally occurring explanations. *KI-Künstliche Intelligenz, 36*(3), 317–326. https://doi.org/10.1007/s13218-022-00787-1

Fisher, J. B., Robrecht, A. S., Kopp, S., & Rohlfing, K. J. (2023). Exploring the semantic dialogue patterns of explanations – a case study of game explanations. In *Proceedings of the 27th Workshop on the Semantics and Pragmatics of Dialogue* (pp. 35–46). SEMDIAL. https://www.semdial.org/anthology/papers/Z/Z23/Z23-3007/

Fisher, J. B., & Rohlfing, K. J. (2024a). *Preliminary ADEX coding scheme for EX-scaffolding moves.* https://osf.io/ngp3u

Fisher, J. B., & Rohlfing, K. J. (2024b). *Preliminary ADEX coding scheme for speaker moves.* https://osf.io/twza4

Gross, A., Richter, B., & Wrede, B. (2025). SHIFT: An interdisciplinary framework for scaffolding human attention and understanding in explanatory tasks. In *ICDL2025*. https://doi.org/10.48550/arXiv.2503.16447

Kaptein, F., Broekens, J., Hindriks, K., & Neerincx, M. (2017a). Self-explanations of a cognitive agent by citing goals and emotions. In *2017 Seventh International Conference on Affective Computing and Intelligent Interaction Workshops and Demos (ACIIW)* (pp. 81–82). IEEE. https://doi.org/10.1109/ACIIW.2017.8272592

Kaptein, F., Broekens, J., Hindriks, K., & Neerincx, M. (2017b). The role of emotion in self-explanations by cognitive agents. In *2017 Seventh International Conference on Affective Computing and Intelligent Interaction Workshops and Demos (ACIIW)* (pp. 88–93). IEEE. https://doi.org/10.1109/ACIIW.2017.8272595

Kotthoff, H. (2009). Erklärende Aktivitätstypen in Alltags- und Unterrichtskontexten. In J. Spreckels (Ed.), *Erklären im Kontext. Neue Perspektiven aus der Gesprächs- und Unterrichtsforschung* (pp. 120–146). Schneider.

Kulgemeyer, C. (2018). Towards a framework for effective instructional explanations in science teaching. *Studies in Science Education, 54*(2), 109–139. https://doi.org/10.1080/03057267.2018.1598054

Kulgemeyer, C., & Geelan, D. (2024). Towards a constructivist view of instructional explanations as a core practice of science teachers. *Science Education, 108*(4), 1034–1050. https://doi.org/10.1002/sce.21863

Li, Z., Yang, S., & Wang, S. (2024). *Exploring personality-driven personalization in XAI: Enhancing user trust in gameplay.* https://doi.org/10.48550/arXiv.2408.04778

Malle, B. F. (2022). Attribution theories: How people make sense of behavior. In D. Chadee (Ed.), *Theories in social psychology* (2nd ed., pp. 93–120). https://doi.org/10.1002/9781394266616.ch4

Matarese, M., Cocchella, F., Rea, F., & Sciutti, A. (2023a). Ex(plainable) Machina: how social-implicit XAI affects complex human– robot teaming tasks. In *2023 IEEE International Conference on Robotics and Automation (ICRA)* (pp. 11986–11993). IEEE. https://doi.org/10.1109/ICRA48891.2023.10160839

Matarese, M., Cocchella, F., Rea, F., & Sciutti, A. (2023b). Natural born explainees: How users' personality traits shape the human–robot interaction with explainable robots. In *2023 32nd IEEE International Conference on Robot and Human Interactive Communication (RO-MAN)* (pp. 1786–1793). IEEE. https://doi.org/10.1109/RO-MAN57019.2023.10309636

Matarese, M., Rea, F., Rohlfing, K. J., & Sciutti, A. (2024). *Let people fail! Exploring the influence of explainable virtual and robotic agents in learning-by-doing tasks.* https://doi.org/10.48550/arXiv.2411.10176

Millecamp, M., Htun, N. N., Conati, C., & Verbert, K. (2019). To explain or not to explain: the effects of personal characteristics when explaining music recommendations. In *Proceedings of the 24th International Conference on Intelligent User Interfaces* (pp. 397–407). https://doi.org/10.1145/3301275.3302313

Millecamp, M., Htun, N. N., Conati, C., & Verbert, K. (2020). What's in a user? Towards personalising transparency for music recommender interfaces. In *Proceedings of the 28th ACM Conference on User Modeling, Adaptation and Personalization* (pp. 173–182). Association for Computing Machinery. https://doi.org/10.1145/3340631.3394844

Miller, T. (2019). Explanation in artificial intelligence: Insights from the social sciences. *Artificial Intelligence, 267*, 1–38. https://doi.org/10.1016/j.artint.2018.07.007

Miyake, N. (1986). Constructive interaction and the iterative process of understanding. *Cognitive Science, 10*(2), 151–177. https://doi.org/10.1207/s15516709cog1002_2

Mousavinasab, E., Zarifsanaiey, N., R. Niakan Kalhori, S., Rakhshan, M., Keikha, L., & Ghazi Saeedi, M. (2021). Intelligent tutoring systems: A systematic review of characteristics, applications, and evaluation methods. *Interactive Learning Environments, 29*(1), 142–163. https://doi.org/10.1080/10494820.2018.1558257

Neerincx, M. A., van der Waa, J., Kaptein, F., & van Diggelen, J. (2018). Using perceptual and cognitive explanations for enhanced human–agent team performance. In *Engineering*

Psychology and Cognitive Ergonomics: 15th International Conference, EPCE 2018 (pp. 204–214). Springer. https://doi.org/10.1007/978-3-319-91122-9_18

Nimmo, R., Constantinides, M., Zhou, K., Quercia, D., & Stumpf, S. (2024). User characteristics in Explainable AI: The rabbit hole of personalization? In *Proceedings of the 2024 CHI Conference on Human Factors in Computing Systems*.Association for Computing Machinery. https://doi.org/10.1145/3613904.3642352

Oudeyer, P.-Y. (2006). *Self-organization in the evolution of speech* (Vol. 6). OUP Oxford.

Palincsar, A. S. (1998). Social constructivist perspectives on teaching and learning. *Annual Review of Psychology, 49*(1), 345–375. https://doi.org/10.1146/annurev.psych.49.1.345

Parsons, S. A., Vaughn, M., Scales, R. Q., Gallagher, M. A., Parsons, A. W., Davis, S. G., Pierczynski, M., & Allen, M. (2018). Teachers' instructional adaptations: A research synthesis. *Review of Educational Research, 88*(2), 205–242. https://doi.org/10.3102/0034654317743198

Piaget, J. (2005). *The psychology of intelligence*. Routledge. https://doi.org/10.4324/9780203981528

Pickering, M. J., & Garrod, S. (2004). Toward a mechanistic psychology of dialogue. *Behavioral and Brain Sciences, 27*(2), 169–190. https://doi.org/10.1017/S0140525X04000056

Reigeluth, C. M. (Ed.). (2013). *Instructional-design theories and models: A new paradigm of instructional theory, volume II*. Routledge. https://doi.org/10.4324/9781410603784

Robrecht, A. S., & Kopp, S. (2023). SNAPE: A sequential nonstationary decision process model for adaptive explanation generation. In *ICAART (1)* (pp. 48–58). Scitepress. https://doi.org/10.5220/0011671300003393

Rohlfing, K. J., Cimiano, P., Scharlau, I., Matzner, T., Buhl, H. M., Buschmeier, H., Esposito, E., Grimminger, A., Hammer, B., Häb-Umbach, R., et al. (2021). Explanation as a social practice: Toward a conceptual framework for the social design of AI systems. *IEEE Transactions on Cognitive and Developmental Systems, 13*(3), 717–728. https://doi.org/10.1109/TCDS.2020.3044366

Sacks, H., Schegloff, E. A., & Jefferson, G. (1974). A simplest systematics for the organization of turn-taking for conversation. *Language, 50*(4), 696–735. https://doi.org/10.17323/1728-192X-2015-1-142-202

Saleh, M., Lazonder, A. W., & De Jong, T. (2005). Effects of within- class ability grouping on social interaction, achievement, and motivation. *Instructional Science, 33*, 105–119. https://doi.org/10.1007/s11251-004-6405-z

Snow, R. E. (1991). Aptitude-treatment interaction as a framework for research on individual differences in psychotherapy. *Journal of Consulting and Clinical Psychology, 59*(2), 205–216. https://doi.org/10.1037/0022-006X.59.2.205

Staub, F. C., & Stern, E. (2002). The nature of teachers' pedagogical content beliefs matters for students' achievement gains: Quasi-experimental evidence from elementary mathematics. *Journal of Educational Psychology, 94*(2), 344–355. https://doi.org/10.1037/0022-0663.94.2.344

Sternberg, R. J., Grigorenko, E. L., Ferrari, M., & Clinkenbeard, P. (1999). A triarchic analysis of an aptitude-treatment interaction. *European Journal of Psychological Assessment, 15*(1), 3–13. https://doi.org/10.1027//1015-5759.15.1.3

Sweller, J. (2010). Element interactivity and intrinsic, extraneous, and germane cognitive load. *Educational Psychology Review, 22*, 123–138. https://doi.org/10.1007/s10648-010-9128-5

Tare, M., French, J., Frazier, B. N., Diamond, J., & Evans, E. M. (2011). Explanatory parent–child conversation predominates at an evolution exhibit. *Science Education, 95*(4), 720–744. https://doi.org/10.1002/sce.20433

Tintarev, N., & Masthoff, J. (2012). Evaluating the effectiveness of explanations for recommender systems: Methodological issues and empirical studies on the impact of personalization. *User Modeling and User-Adapted Interaction, 22*, 399–439. https://doi.org/10.1007/s11257-011-9117-5

Van Lehn, K. (2011). The relative effectiveness of human tutoring, intelligent tutoring systems, and other tutoring systems. *Educational Psychologist, 46*(4), 197–221. https://doi.org/10.1080/00461520.2011.611369

Vygotski, L. S. (1934/1986). *Thought and language.* MIT Press.
Wittwer, J., Nückles, M., & Renkl, A. (2008). Is underestimation less detrimental than overestimation? The impact of experts' beliefs about a layperson's knowledge on learning and question asking. *Instructional Science, 36,* 27–52. https://doi.org/10.1007/s11251-007-9021-x
Wittwer, J., Nückles, M., & Renkl, A. (2010). Using a diagnosis- based approach to individualize instructional explanations in computer-mediated communication. *Educational Psychology Review, 22*(1), 9–23. https://doi.org/10.1007/s10648-010-9118-7
Wood, D., Bruner, J. S., & Ross, G. (1976). The role of tutoring in problem solving. *Journal of Child Psychology and Psychiatry, 17*(2), 89–100. https://doi.org/10.1111/j.1469-7610.1976.tb00381.x

Open Access This chapter is licensed under the terms of the Creative Commons Attribution 4.0 International License (http://creativecommons.org/licenses/by/4.0/), which permits use, sharing, adaptation, distribution and reproduction in any medium or format, as long as you give appropriate credit to the original author(s) and the source, provide a link to the Creative Commons license and indicate if changes were made.

The images or other third party material in this chapter are included in the chapter's Creative Commons license, unless indicated otherwise in a credit line to the material. If material is not included in the chapter's Creative Commons license and your intended use is not permitted by statutory regulation or exceeds the permitted use, you will need to obtain permission directly from the copyright holder.

Chapter 14
Models of the Situation, the Explanandum, and the Interaction Partner

Heike M. Buhl [ID]**, Anna-Lisa Vollmer** [ID]**, Rachid Alami** [ID]**, Meisam Booshehri** [ID]**, and Kary Främling** [ID]

Abstract Social XAI aims to co-construct an explanation jointly with an individual user in a specific situation. This requires mental models of the situation, the explanandum, and the interaction partner. These models must be dynamic in order to react to changes in the context and to new insights from the interaction. We discuss the characteristics and prerequisites of as well as the changes in these models against the background of human–human as well as human–computer and human–robot social interactions, and we present practical examples of how such models can be implemented in information systems using knowledge graphs.

H. M. Buhl (✉)
Institute for Human Sciences – Psychology, Faculty of Arts and Humanities, Paderborn University, Paderborn, Germany
e-mail: heike.buhl@uni-paderborn.de

A.-L. Vollmer
Interactive Robotics in Medicine and Care, Medical School OWL, Bielefeld University, Bielefeld, Germany
e-mail: anna-lisa.vollmer@uni-bielefeld.de

R. Alami
Laboratory for Analysis and Architecture of Systems, Artificial and Natural Intelligence Toulouse Institute, Université de Toulouse, Toulouse, France
e-mail: rachid.alami@laas.fr

M. Booshehri
Semantic Computing Group, Faculty of Technology, Bielefeld University, Bielefeld, Germany
e-mail: mbooshehri@techfak.uni-bielefeld.de

K. Främling
Department of Computing Science, Umeå University, Umeå, Sweden

Department of Industrial Engineering and Management, Aalto University, Espoo, Finland
e-mail: kary.framling@umu.se

© The Author(s) 2026
K. J. Rohlfing et al. (eds.), *Social Explainable AI*,
https://doi.org/10.1007/978-981-96-5290-7_14

14.1 How Does This Chapter Relate to XAI?

When underlining the significance of XAI explanations, Miller (2019, p. 33) summarizes that the flow of the dialog depends on "(1) the current state of the discourse[1] relative to the goal/subgoal hierarchy; (2) the current focus of the explanation, such as which components of a device are currently under discussion; and (3) assumptions about the user's knowledge." Whereas Chap. 17 specifically discusses the state of the discourse, this chapter elaborates on the situation as the basis for the mental representation of the context (cf. Sect. 14.2), the current focus of the explanation, the explanandum, and assumptions about the user's knowledge (cf., Sects. 14.3 and 14.4). Due to being a field with far more extensive research to date, we draw on work from human–human interaction with the goal that mental representations of humans might inform sXAI models, and in Sect. 14.5 we focus on XAI as well as literature on human-centered AI systems and on so-called human–computer and human–robot social interaction.

14.2 Model of the Situation: Context

In the domain of human–AI interaction, comprehensively understanding and modeling the context is crucial for crafting AI-generated explanations that are contextually relevant and easily understandable. We shall explore the characteristics and elements that define the context, delineate the distinction between *situation* and *context*, and examine methodologies for context modeling and representation techniques. Additionally, we highlight the latest advances in representing the context model in artificial agents.

14.2.1 Situation Versus Context

Differentiating *situation* from *context* is not easy, because the two terms are often used interchangeably. As explained in Chap. 4, a situation refers to the objective, immediate circumstances in which an interaction is taking place. These are perceivable, but might not be observable by a person because of, for example, their perspective or the distance. The environmental properties of a situation that characterize physical location and time of an interaction significantly influence how explanations are formulated and perceived. This necessitates adjustments in the complexity and presentation of explanations depending on the environment. For example, a noisy environment may require simpler, louder explanations, whereas

---

[1] Here an explanation.

a classroom setting might allow for more detailed and technical explanations. Different environments result in different expectations (Lombard & Ditton, 1997).

A *situation*, thus, comprises the circumstances surrounding an explanatory interaction (different material and social facts; cf. Chap. 4) focusing on the specific environment, the participants involved, and their actions (Rohlfing et al., 2003). In contrast, the *context* is a dynamically, continuously constructed interpretation of the situation that encompasses broader influences such as cultural, social, and historical factors that impact on the behavior of an interactant and impart meaning to a situation. It describes a mental representation in each interactant combining all those inferences and attributions that are made on the basis of current or previous observations and experiences that now influence the ongoing interaction (cf. Chap. 4). These might be inherently subjective, in that the explainer and explainee model the context of an explanation differently.

14.2.2 Characteristics and Elements of the Situation

The situation of human–human but also of human–AI interaction thus encompasses both perceivable and nonperceivable elements. Moreover, a situation might change over time, necessitating a detailed and incremental approach to its representation.

Perceivable Aspects
A situation can only be perceived with top-down influence. Hence, there is no pure perception of a situation but always an interpretation of it (see Chap. 4). Technologies such as sensors for AI in physical environments or data analytics in digital environments enable AI to perceive aspects of a situation to varying extents. These include the physical environment: An embodied AI equipped with sensors such as cameras, light detection and ranging (LiDAR), and depth sensors can perceive physical features such as objects, walls, doors, own and others' location, and furniture layouts. These are essential for navigation, object manipulation, and spatial reasoning. Through motion sensors, cameras, and sometimes wearable devices, embodied AI can observe human physical actions such as walking, gesturing, or manipulating objects. Microphones enable them to detect sounds, including speech, that can be processed using automatic speech recognition (ASR) and natural language processing (NLP) techniques to understand commands or questions as well as ambient sounds that can provide context about the environment. Information about timing can also be perceived. With advanced computer vision techniques, AI systems can recognize facial expressions, eye gaze, and body language, and these are indicators of emotional states, attentional state, or intentions. However, the interpretation of these cues can be challenging and itself context-dependent. The human user as the explainee is part of the situation. Because of its complexity and importance, we discuss the model of the partner in a separate section (Sect. 14.4).

Nonperceivable Aspects

Nonperceivable aspects pertain mainly to the interaction partner (e.g., their intentions). We view this as being part of the situation that could, however, also be modeled separately. We describe the model of the partner in Sect. 14.4.

Other aspects of the situation that are not perceived directly include the own interactive role or occluded objects (because of the own perspective on the situation), or nonperceivable aspects of objects, such as the temperature. These can be inferred through information from the interaction partner, the perceived situation, and memory over the course of the interaction as well as by higher-level reasoning—for example, when an arrival time is calculated based on the speed of a movement or when prior knowledge makes it possible to draw inferences from an utterance (Kintsch, 1998).

14.2.3 Computational Representation Approaches

As we have established in this chapter, the dynamic construction of context corresponds to a model of the situation directed towards an interaction goal that interprets the perceivable objective aspects of the situation using facts from memory. AI systems should represent the context (i.e., the situation model) in a similarly dynamic way. However, as detailed in Chap. 4, current approaches mainly consider static context factors that have been defined in advance: The literature on situation modeling in AI systems deals mainly with the monitoring of either environmental states (e.g., positioning of objects) or the interaction partner in the sense of goals or intent recognition in order to predict future behavior. Yet, generally, this is not an interpretation based on a rich informational and cognitive background. The literature further underscores the significance of aligning AI's understanding of situations with human perspectives for meaningful interactions (Shen et al., 2024). A situation thus needs to be 'parsed' and represented as ontological types and relations that reflect human language semantics in order to be able to communicate about agents and items in the environment (Mavridis & Roy, 2006). Especially if the explanandum is part of the situation, not only the situation should be considered, but also the explainee's model of the situation. Theory of mind (ToM, Frith and Frith, 2005 and perspective taking, Underwood & Moore, 1982; Johnson, 1975) play an important role not only in understanding the explainee's model of the situation and to aligning situation models to establish common ground but also during co-constructed explanation,[2] discussed in Sect. 14.4.

Interestingly, as mentioned earlier, there could be objects, features of objects, or relations between objects that are perceived by the machine but hidden or nonobservable for the human. Hence, the machine performs a so-called situation assessment based on an interpretation of the flow of sensory data and builds two

---

[2] See, for illustration, scenario 2.6.

distinct representations of the scene: one from its point of view and one from the point of view of the human. Such representations need to be human-centered and verbalizable, because they will potentially be used in the human–machine multimodal dialog.

One approach to achieve such representation is *symbol grounding*,[3] the process that allows the machine to associate symbols and relations to the data acquired by physically embedded sensors. For an overview of subconcepts, see Coradeschi et al. (2013). It is used to synthesize the estimation of the agent's beliefs about the current state they observe (Ros et al., 2010; Lemaignan et al., 2012). Besides identifying objects and relations between them, grounding relies on the key notion of affordances (Baggs, 2021) that can be computed and/or estimated from the side of the machine and it also considers the perspective of the human as well as their abilities within the context (Pandey & Alami, 2013; Beßler et al., 2020).

14.3 Model of the Explanandum

The explanandum is the subject of the explanation. Regarding XAI, this is typically a decision, an action, or the result of an action by the AI (Sect. 3.3). As discussed in Chap. 3, in XAI explanations as part of everyday explanations (cf. Miller, 2019), the explanandum is a "moving target" (Rohlfing et al., 2021, p. 720). As such, it is not predefined at the beginning of the explanation, but is negotiated by the explainer and the explainee over the course of the explanation. This leads to two elementary characteristics of the explanandum in the context of sXAI: (1) The explanandum differs from moment to moment. Vollmer et al. (Sect. 3.3) therefore referred to "local explananda." (2) Explananda are not objectively given, but subjective respectively dyadic and dependent on explainer, explainee, and context. Therefore, they are not complete or correct in an objective sense. However, in the typical case of an explanation, at the beginning, the explainer knows more about the domain than the explainee, and the explainee knows more at the end of the explanation than at the beginning. That does not imply that the knowledge of the explainer and the explainee are the same as a result of the explanation! To clarify the characteristics of explananda for implementation in sXAI, we shall consider the forms and development of mental representations.

14.3.1 Mental Representations of the Explanandum

Throughout the explanation, the explainer and the explainee have cognitive representations of the explanandum, often summarized as a mental model. Regarding

---

[3] Note that this is not the same grounding process which achieves common ground between interaction partners; cf., Chaps. 13 and 17.

humans as well as AI, these mental representations are discussed as 'knowledge.' Various systematizations show the diversity of possible representations that are important for the structure of explanations. Against the background of a long tradition, Anderson (2013) and De Jong and Ferguson-Hessler (1996) distinguish types of knowledge. For sXAI, two types of knowledge are particularly important: namely, conceptual declarative knowledge regarding the "knowledge of facts, concepts, and principles" (De Jong & Ferguson-Hessler, 1996, p. 107) and procedural knowledge referring to "actions and manipulations" that transform one state into another. Conceptual knowledge describes 'knowing that' and procedural knowledge refers to 'knowing how.' Focusing on XAI explanations, Buschmeier et al. (2025) discuss knowledge as a result of a given explanation as "understanding." They assign the goals of comprehending something and of being enabled to do something to these conceptual and procedural forms of knowledge.

The question of the mental representation of knowledge – that is, the model of the explanandum – closely interlinks cognitive psychology, philosophy, and AI research (cf. Schmid & Wrede, 2022). On the one hand, human thinking, learning, and memory serve as a model for AI. On the other hand, when speaking about information processing, our current ideas of human memory and learning are inspired by technical operations and full of analogies. For sXAI, it is important to consider that knowledge is more than information. While learning, humans process information into knowledge in a meaningful context. Thus, knowledge is based on personal experiences and individual goals and is therefore oriented towards action. Hence, knowledge is therefore constructed in action and depending on the (social) context. In contrast to cognitive approaches, situational and social constructivist approaches argue that the resulting knowledge does not lie in one person, but is created in interaction with others and is distributed among individuals (cf. Reinmann-Rothmeier & Mandl, 2002; Chap. 13). However, to describe mental representations of the explanandum in more detail to facilitate sXAI, it is also necessary to analyze the *individual* knowledge representation.

Mental representations can be perception-based and very close to the original perception and rich in detail. In humans, this detailed information is often lost over time, and, in the end, it is not necessary for the actual understanding of the matter. In contrast, meaning-based representations contain the semantics of an event, object, or context. They are stored in the long term (Anderson, 2013). Therefore, perception-based representations may influence the explanation, but they are rarely the aim of the explanation. Meaning-based representations are given in propositions, schemas, or analog representations (cf. Sternberg & Ben-Zeev, 2001).

- Propositions are the smallest units of knowledge that can be true or false. Conceptualizations of human cognition and informatics summarize propositional representations as lists of relations and arguments or propositional networks. Similarly, semantic networks organize general knowledge of, for example, hierarchies of categories (Collins & Loftus, 1975). Nowadays, these are often referred to under the name knowledge graphs (cf. the operationalization in Sect. 14.5).

- Schemas are mental structures capturing the meaning of concepts (e.g., a house or a social category such as 'a man') or an event (e.g., a script of a visit to a restaurant; cf. Schank & Abelson, 1975) in systems of rules (cf. Sternberg & Ben-Zeev, 2001). They organize knowledge, simplify actions and decision-making, and make learning easier due to the possibility of building on previous knowledge.
- Analog representations, often also called images, are near to the sensation—for example, the mental imagination of a ship (a picture), a mechanism, or, even more difficult to imagine, a sound. The analog representation of an object has, for example, visual, spatial, or temporal similarities to the original object (cf. Kosslyn, 2005). Mental models (here the word is used in a narrow sense) are a specific analog representation of processes (e.g., the functioning of a motor) and can contain elements that are not visible at that moment (cf. Johnson-Laird, 2005).

Explananda of XAI are typically artifacts—that is, made by humans with a specific goal, such as (the output of) a large language model (LLM) or a robot. When explaining these technical artifacts, one can refer to their architecture (the structure, e.g., the physical properties and mechanisms of how the robot works) or their relevance (the function of the artifact) on either an individual or societal level (e.g., the benefits and risks of using LLMs while writing or working together with a robot). This conceptualization was developed in the philosophy of technology (Kroes, 1998). Knowledge and explanations about architecture can be, per se, more or less correct or incorrect. In contrast, "the function [relevance] cannot be isolated from the context of use of a technological object; it is defined within the context. Since the context is a context of human action, we will call the function a human (or social) construction" (Kroes, 1998, p. 124). Thus, relevance is always subjective—or, when it is constructed jointly in an explanation, social.

With the question of how architecture and relevance are distributed across explanations and what motivates explainers to explain one or the other side, Terfloth et al. (2023) investigated a total of 24 human-to-human explanations of a simple artifact, a board game. A qualitative content analysis was used to identify utterances that address architecture and relevance. Thereby, architecture as well as relevance were identified in the explanations. Generally speaking, explainers focus more on architecture than on relevance. They begin regularly with architecture, which is interpreted as "laying out the tools" (Terfloth et al., 2023, p. 267). After the explanations, the explainers were interviewed regarding their perception of explainees' knowledge and interests in specific explanation scenarios (Schaffer et al., 2024). The explainers reported that they decided for architecture or relevance and additionally specific parts of explanations due to their own knowledge and interests as well as the anticipated or perceived interests of the explainee. The transfer of these results to more complex and digital artifacts with less clear objectives (i.e., also relevance) is still an open problem. However, we can already conclude that AI explanations must contain both architecture and relevance and that the corresponding signals of the explainees must be taken into account.

14.3.2 Construction of a Model of the Explanandum

The development of a model of the explanandum as the result of an explanation can be described with the support of more general conceptualizations of language comprehension. Kintsch (1998) describes comprehension of spoken or written language – that is, text comprehension – in his seminal construction-integration model. The abovementioned mental representations are built bottom-up step by step: The surface level contains the exact wording. In a first knowledge construction step, the meaning of a text or utterance is extracted resulting in a propositional level. Meaning is represented in the form of propositions. With the next step, knowledge integration leads to the third level: a situational model that represents the meaningful and holistic model of the explanandum. Following Kintsch, it can be interpreted as a mental model as characterized by Johnson-Laird (2005) (see above). It is constructed from the text basis in combination with prior knowledge. On this level, an appropriate understanding of the explanandum is elaborated that is specific for the context. Natural explanation processes use not only language, but also gestures (cf. Sect. 19.1). Complex explanatory processes such as doctor–patient dialogs also use illustrations and 3D models. When processing such pictorial or figurative material, a visual image is assumed instead of the propositional level. However, the next step of construction results again in a mental model (cf. Nathan, 2024; Schnotz & Bannert, 2003). The specific quality of the resulting mental model depends on the given material and, eventually, the combination with a text, cognitive load, context factors, and so forth.

14.4 Model of the Interaction Partner

If it is no longer assumed that one explanation fits all, the goals and the knowledge of specific explainees must be considered. Thus, sXAI has to take the specific explainee into account in order to tailor explanations to the purposes of particular human addressees. One relevant precondition for considering the purposes of the addressee is having a model: a mental representation of this partner (Fischer, 2016; Schmid & Wrede, 2022). Because of its outstanding and, at the same time, already well-founded significance, this model will be explored in more detail. Informed by cognitive and educational psychology as well as psycholinguistics, these mental representations are known as *partner models* (e.g., Dillenbourg et al., 2016). We prefer this term in contrast to the comparable *user model* of the agent in order to underline the co-constructive interaction between AI and human. The partner model consists of knowledge and beliefs regarding the partner such as their interests in the explanandum and the explanation, knowledge, beliefs, preferences, cognitive capacity, or mood (e.g., Miller, 2019). To understand the significance of partner models, just imagine the differences in explaining something to a child versus an adult, an expert versus a novice, and so forth.

As research on tutoring shows, the needs of the partner are often neglected (Chi et al., 2004). However, when tutors get explicit information regarding tutees' prior knowledge, they adapt their explanation to this information. This reduces tutees' misunderstanding and supports their knowledge acquisition (Nückles et al., 2005). Moreover, besides learning settings, human communication in general and explanations in particular directed towards a layperson in contrast to an expert also often lack consideration of partner characteristics, and this has negative consequences for their understanding (Wittwer et al., 2008). Wittwer et al. (2010) analyzed why instructional explanations are not sufficiently tailored to the explainee: Explainers have an egocentric bias and impute their own knowledge to others (Buhl, 2001; Fisher et al., 2022; Horton & Keysar, 1996; Nickerson, 1999). They do not engage in seeking information on the explainee's understanding. An underlying reason for both may be that the explanation demands a high amount of cognitive resources. Thus, there is no further cognitive capacity to consider the knowledge and motivation of the explainee. The use of AI without the limitations of cognitive load in explanations can overcome these problems. Even at the behavioral level, in human–computer interaction, an agent giving adaptive feedback is perceived as more helpful by the users than an agent giving nonadaptive or especially no feedback at all (Buschmeier & Kopp, 2018).

14.4.1 Dimensions of Partner Models

The literature on learning, especially in the area of tutoring and instructional explanations, provides a rough overview of which dimensions of partner models are considered to be relevant. These can be differentiated into structural and psychological variables. Structural variables are, for example, gender, age, or ethnicity, but also the status and the role (cf. Chap. 8) of the explainee. Psychological variables are, in particular, motivational factors such as interest in the explanandum and in the explanation itself. In addition, cognitive characteristics of the explainee are important for understanding an explanation. Ergo for the partner model: This concerns the cognitive abilities and prior knowledge that are actually significant predictors of learning success (e.g., Ackerman, 1996). These must therefore be taken into account in explanations. Additionally, beliefs, attitudes, and emotions are part of the partner model (Thommes et al., 2024).

To further distinguish between the psychological aspects as a precondition of collaborative learning, Dillenbourg et al. (2016, p. 230) differentiate between dispositional and situational dimensions of partner models. Whereas dispositional dimensions refer to "long-term knowledge, skills or traits," situational dimensions refer to "knowledge, behaviour or intentions activated in the situation in which A and B are collaborating" with a temporally limited validity. Knowledge is a good example for changes over the course of the explanation. If the explainer assumes that the explainee understands the explanation, they assume an increase in the situational knowledge as part of the partner model. However, it is important to underline that not only the situational dimensions of the partner model change over the course of an explanation but also the dispositional dimensions (Buhl et al., 2024). For example, an explainer might assume a high degree of explainee's prior knowledge. In the course of the explanation, when monitoring the feedback of the explainee, they might recognize that this is not the case. To make it a little more complicated, but therefore more complete, if the explainer takes the understanding of the explainee into account, the partner model of the explainer includes their model of the explanandum and the context (Robrecht & Kopp, 2023; Schmid & Wrede, 2022). In other words, speaking about knowledge as part of the partner model addresses their model of the explanandum. Furthermore, the explainee knows that the explainer knows what the explainee knows and so forth (cf., Schaffer et al., 2024). This assumes first-order theory of mind (ToM), second-order ToM, and so on (see the next subsection).

In order to elaborate and update a model of the human partner, dimensions of partner models have been identified in the AI literature (Thomaz et al., 2016). Beside application-dependent profiling techniques, it is especially important to identify what could be a common ground in terms of general knowledge that would be pertinent during the explanation process (Butterfill & Sebanz, 2011; Wenke et al., 2011). This can be done today using adapted prompting techniques to large language models (LLMs). Other dimensions of the partner model in the literature dealing with human–robot interaction concern what can be globally called preferences—for example, preferences in terms of legibility (Dragan et al., 2013) and acceptability of behaviors and motions (Singamaneni et al., 2024; Francis et al., 2025). Preferences can also be modeled as social norms and conventions (Carlucci et al., 2015)—criteria that specifically tackle trust (Chamola et al., 2023) and explainability (García et al., 2020; De Graaf et al., 2021). They can be either learned or modeled and used in motion and task planners.

14.4.2 Preconditions of Partner Models

In developmental psychology, preconditions for building up a partner model are known as ToM and perspective taking (e.g., Sodian & Kristen, 2016). "Theory of mind is the ability to attribute mental states, such as desires, knowledge, and beliefs, to others in order to predict and explain their behavior" (Devine, 2016, p. 1). In the 1970s and 1980s, research with children (e.g., Wimmer & Perner, 1983) and chimpanzees (e.g., Premack & Woodruff, 1978) showed that the development of this ability enables children to understand other people's good-directed actions, use language successfully, and not only understand jokes and complex stories but also tease people. The subsequent research followed a path from simple first-order ToM (A knows what B knows) to second-order ToM (A knows that B knows that A knows) and so on. Based on ToM, the next step in the development of social cognition is perspective taking: the ability and readiness to consider the perspective of an interlocutor (Steins & Wicklund, 1996) and the coordination of different perspectives (Selman & Byrne, 1981). These are a must when humans interact (Flavell, 1992; Tversky et al., 1999). In recent years, the term *ToM* has also been extended to older children, adolescents, and adults. Therefore, the definitional boundaries between ToM and perspective taking have become somewhat blurred. It is helpful to bear in mind that ToM describes an ability or readiness, whereas perspective taking describes a cognitive activity. An agent with a ToM can differentiate between perspectives and, in a next step, take on the perspective of an interlocutor. A further, now widespread, term in this area is *mentalizing*—that is, understanding mental states. Regarding human–computer interaction in general and sXAI in particular, perspective-taking processes and co-constructive processes can be informed by human–human interaction (Kopp & Krämer, 2021). With the insight that social interactions require ToM, the construct has been transposed to social robots and XAI. It is now well accepted that ToM has to be considered for any human–robot cognitive interaction (Premack & Woodruff, 1978; Thellman et al., 2022; Byom & Mutlu, 2013). In a context in which a machine interacts with a human, it is necessary to endow it with the ability to estimate the mental state of the human. For example, in a given situation, visual perspective taking (Trafton et al., 2005; Johnson & Demiris, 2005; Breazeal et al., 2006; Warnier et al., 2012; Milliez et al., 2014; Wilf et al., 2023) can be used to compute what can be seen from the point of view of the human throughout the interaction (see above, Sect. 14.2).

14.4.3 Development of the Partner Model

Partner models change over the course of an explanation. In a nontechnical sense, we see processes of partner modeling. At the beginning of an explanation, explainers have global partner models based on stereotypes regarding, for example, their gender, age, profession, and physical appearance together with previous experiences with this or other explainees (cf. Brennan et al., 2010; Dillenbourg et al., 2016). Additionally, if little is known about an explainee, own characteristics are also assumed for the partner (Nickerson, 1999)—for example, 'I understand technical aspects of AI, thus I assume this understanding with the partner' (Nückles et al., 2006). Over the course of an interaction, the partner models are modified and refined. Since there is limited empirical research on specific processes, the question of how this works in detail remains unanswered. In general terms, the explainer monitors signs of understanding or nonunderstanding, and this results in a local partner model (Lazarov & Grimminger, 2024). In this process, dimensions of the partner model as well as their composition might change (Dillenbourg et al., 2016). Especially the degree of knowledge about the explanandum as a dimension of the partner model increases. Chapter 13 discussed cognitive and interactive adaptation processes. With the need to tailor explanations to individual explainees and, furthermore, to negotiate the explanation between explainer and explainee, both interlocutors monitor each other (e.g., their knowledge) and scaffold their understanding and explaining (cf. Chi et al., 2001; Rohlfing et al., 2021). To facilitate adaptation, models of the partner and their changes must be considered. This refers to cognitive adaption. The interactive adaptation addresses the behavior of the interlocutors. The behavior of the partner influences the partner model, and, as a consequence, the (changed) partner model influences behavior. The specific interplay between partner models and behavior is still quite unclear. To investigate one step of this adaptation, we assumed that the partner model of the explainer is informed by the interactive behavior of the explainee (Buhl et al., 2024). We investigated explainers' self-reported partner models in relation to the observed verbal moves of explainees in dyadic human-to-human explanations. The partner models changed along important dimensions such as knowledge, interest in the explanation, cooperation, and mood. Moves such as questions and summarizing and paraphrasing information given by the explainees were associated with the partner's model dimensions concerning the interaction such as interest in and the ability to co-construct the explanation. These correlations can be implemented in sXAI. In addition, further empirical investigations are needed, which also considers the explainers' interactive behavior under the influence of their partner model, the explainees' respectively users' partner model (Doyle et al., 2021) and various complex explananda.

However, there is still a long way to go to find a correct and complete partner model in sXAI. As outlined, despite notable prerequisites for joint action (Tomasello & Carpenter, 2007), even humans often find it difficult to correctly identify characteristics and goals of the partner. This is particularly problematic for AI. Whereas some intentions can be inferred from actions and expressions, access to human thoughts and intentions remains beyond the scope of current technology. Understanding complex, unexpressed intentions requires sophisticated models of human behavior and cognition that are still under development. Although some emotional states can be inferred from facial expressions, vocal intonation, and body language, accurately perceiving and understanding the full range of human emotions, especially subtle or mixed emotions, is a significant challenge. Abstract concepts such as beliefs, desires, and motivations are not directly perceivable. These aspects often require interpretation through verbal communication, contextual understanding, social roles, and inference, which are areas of ongoing research. Also, predicting *future* human actions and plans, especially those not linked immediately to the current context or expressed intentions, is difficult. While predictive modeling and machine learning can offer some insights, accurately foreseeing future actions involves complex reasoning that is currently a challenge for AI systems.

14.5 Operationalization

The current state of the art in XAI does not provide guidelines or clear approaches for implementing the models described in the earlier sections of this chapter. Therefore, it is not possible to give absolute guidelines for how such models can, or should, be implemented. Nonetheless, we shall provide some ideas and preliminary results on how the models could be implemented for the needs of sXAI. The approaches presented here have been implemented and tested by the authors to some extent, but other approaches could be equally valid.

14.5.1 Knowledge Graphs as a Modeling Tool

The target of most XAI systems are so-called black box AI systems, where the ones that are based on machine learning tend to be the main focus. The minimal information that is available for black box systems are the labels of the AI system's inputs and outputs. In many, or most, cases those labels are specified for the needs of efficient handling by computer systems, rather than being defined for human comprehensibility or explainability. Therefore, a first and minimal step towards explainability is to provide a mapping between the AI system labels and human-comprehensible labels. *Semantic nets* (Collins & Quillian, 1969; Sowa, 2000) offer capabilities for specifying such mappings, where the nodes *AI-system-label* and *explainability-label* are connected by a relation *XAI-label* or similar. The relations or *edges* of semantic nets can be directed or not and can also have a weight that indicates the strength of the relation.

Semantic nets are nowadays often referred to with the term *knowledge graph (KG)*, which was popularized by Google in 2012, when it used KGs as a way to enhance its search engine results. Google's KG is a massive database that stores information on entities, relationships, and concepts and uses this information to provide users with more accurate and informative search results. Such KGs can be used also for XAI purposes by including meta-data and links towards supplementary information that can be exploited in different ways for providing explanations.

Highlighting that the definition of a KG remains controversial, Hogan et al. (2021, p. 3) view a KG as *"a graph of data intended to accumulate and convey knowledge of the real world, whose nodes represent entities of interest and whose edges represent potentially different relations between these entities."* KGs can be formally specified in numerous ways, *e.g.*, using Resource Description Framework (RDF) (Cyganiak et al., 2014), Web Ontology Language (OWL) (W3C OWL Working Group, 2012), and related formalisms. KGs can be exploited for expanding the capabilities of XAI systems in many ways. KGs are a general concept for defining vocabularies, concepts and their relationships, possibly with associated meta-data. They are normally based on how humans structure the information related to a given domain, situation, or context. KGs are therefore cornerstone for describing the explanandum, as well as for creating the explanans.

KGs, decision rules, etc. are ways of encoding information in formats that are usable for information systems but they are usually not appropriate to use as such as explanans. If natural language explanans are used, then a typical approach is to use text templates, rules, OWL, or similar tools for producing the text. It also seems probable that large language models (LLMs) are used for this purpose, or at least will be used in a near future. Many XAI methods produce different kinds of graphs or other visual representations, where it might be less obvious how to use KGs. One way of using KGs for explanations are the intermediate concepts (ICs) proposed by Främling (1996b,a) that introduce different levels of abstraction using meronomies or taxonomies. ICs make it possible to start an explanation at a high conceptual level and then delve into details, allowing the explainer to determine which aspects of the explananda or explanantia to elaborate on based on the explainee's interests. This aligns well with the perspective that explanations are *selected* (Miller, 2019), meaning that the explainer may select a subset of causes from possibly an infinite number of causes behind an event as *the* explanation. ICs are not limited to natural language explanations and can be used for dividing the explanation into appropriate explanatory moves that make a compromise between the length and the relevance of information displayed at each move of the explanation, or rather of the explanatory dialog. Furthermore, KGs and ICs to use can be chosen and adapted to the explainee, even during the explanatory dialog (cf., Chap. 13).

It is worth noting that such an application of KGs is in line with *knowledge refinement and complexity management* as a key perspective (Confalonieri & Guizzardi, 2023), where 'explicit knowledge,' in particular ontologies, can play a significant role in sXAI. This perspective refers to the fundamental mechanisms of *abstraction* (i.e., considering all relevant details and dropping all irrelevant ones as a way of dealing with complexity of the world) and *refinement* (i.e., representing knowledge in a more specific manner).

In the scenarios presented in Chap. 2, the context for the car selection scenario is selecting a car and all the information related to that. The relevant information for composing the explanation is e.g.:

- KGs about cars that define the terms that are generally used for describing cars, such as 'brand,' 'model,' 'drivetrain (4WD [four-wheel drive], AWD [all-wheel drive], front-wheel drive [FWD], and rear-wheel drive [RWD]),' 'power (kW, horsepowers,' 'acceleration,' 'fuel consumption,' etc.
- KGs about buying that define terms such as 'price,' 'monthly reimbursement,' 'reduction percentage,' etc.
- Possibly KGs about car maintenance, including terms such as 'maintenance interval,' 'expected lifetime,' 'cost of maintenance,' etc.
- Language versions of the KGs, which do not necessarily provide a one-to-one correspondence between the different terms
- Potentially also other KGs that relate to private economy, ecological sustainability, etc.

However, we did not find any more recent work on AI-assisted car selection than that of Främling (1996b). Therefore, we will use the Ames Housing dataset instead (De Cock, 2011).

14.5.2 Model of Explanandum

In this section, we shall describe how a limited model of the explanandum can be implemented and used to generate explanatory content and to explore it in an interactive way, as described in Chaps. 15 and 16 as well as in Främling (2023, 2024). A model of the explanandum is also a necessary building block for the creation of partner models, as explained in Sect. 14.5.4. As mentioned, the technologies and methods presented here represent ongoing research, so they might (and presumably will) change in the future. Our intention is to allow the assessment of what is currently feasible and where further development is necessary.

To illustrate the usefulness of the models, we need to choose an explanandum that is sufficiently complex to actually justify the use of advanced models. We have chosen the Ames Housing data set for this purpose. The Ames Housing dataset is a comprehensive collection of features related to residential properties in Ames, Iowa, USA (De Cock, 2011). The dataset consists of 2,930 houses and is widely used in predictive modeling and machine learning tasks, especially for regression tasks. Although there exist a few versions of this dataset, the one used here has 80 explanatory variables and one target variable (the sales price). The target variable represents the final price of each property. With 80 features that are partially overlapping and dependent on each other, it becomes challenging to provide understandable and correct explanations. Features include both numerical and categorical variables covering a wide range of aspects such as lot size, number of rooms, location, and construction.

The feature names used in the dataset such as "BsmtFinType1," "BsmtFinType2," "BsmtFullBath," and "BsmtHalfBath" can be challenging to understand. Therefore, a first requirement for implementing sXAI functionality is to provide descriptive feature names that are explainee-understandable. In practice, such feature names will not be sufficient for truly understanding how they are defined, so that there is also a requirement to provide longer descriptions. For such longer descriptions, it would presumably be beneficial or necessary to have different versions for different explainees where the preferred ones can be defined by a partner model. This information about feature names, descriptions, and meta-data can be represented as a KG.

In the case of Ames Housing, many features are correlated or interdependent. For instance, there are at least 11 features that describe different aspects of the basement and that are somehow correlated or interdependent. For most explainees, it would probably make sense to receive an explanation that uses 'basement' and similar high-level concepts in the explanantia rather than using all 80 "raw" features. Figure 14.1 shows an example of a 'part-of' hierarchy (commonly referred to as a meronymy) that has been used by Främling (2023, 2024) to provide explanations with different levels of abstraction. This type of hierarchy represents a relationship in which a concept or entity (the part) is a component or member of another concept or entity (the whole). Such a hierarchy is a KG with 'part-of' relations, so it can be

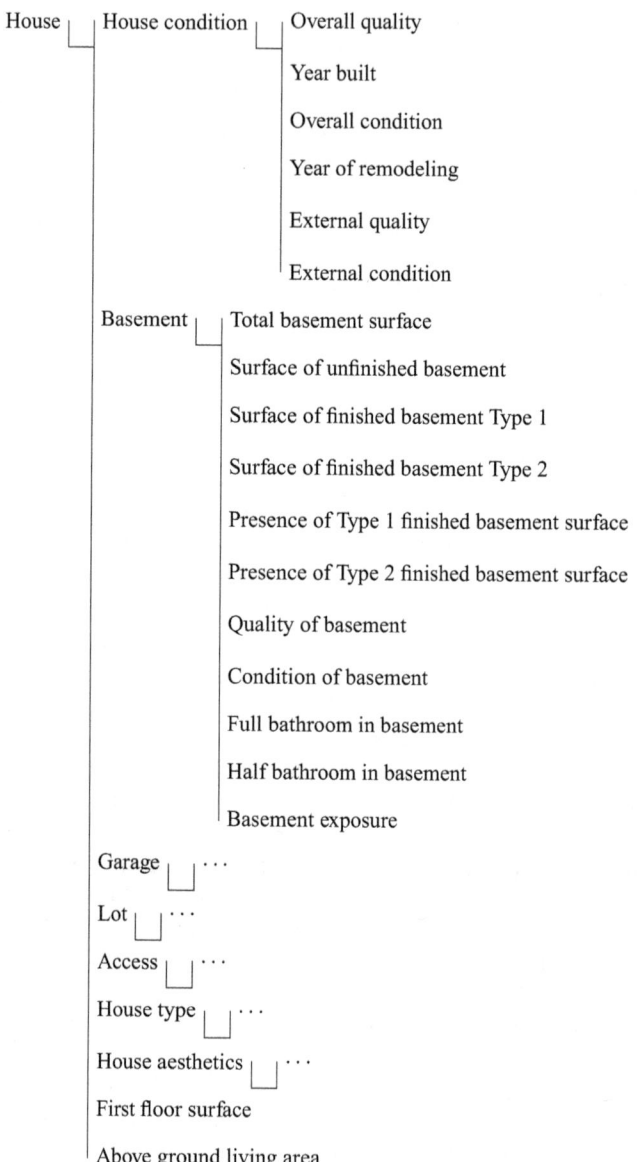

Fig. 14.1 Example of a vocabulary for structuring explanations for the Ames Housing dataset

integrated into bigger KGs that can include feature descriptions, meta-data, and so forth as described previously.

Models of explananda could include much more information than what is described here, presumably described as a KG that could also include LLM-generated content as nodes of the graph. KGs only represent information and connections between different kinds of information, but they do not specify how these KGs are used in practice. We shall provide some examples of such uses for generating explanatory content in Chap. 15 and the interactive exploration of explanations in Chap. 16.

14.5.3 Model of the Context

Most uses of the Ames Housing dataset consist in training an machine learning (ML) model to predict the sales price of individual houses based on the values of the other features. In this case, we could consider that the explanandum is the prediction process of the ML model. The goal of the sXAI interaction is to allow the explainee to gain the highest possible level of understanding of the reasons and reasoning of the model that leads to a predicted sales price that is either high, low, or whatever.

A minimal context model could represent the different modalities that can be used as explanans in a particular context. For example, if a computer screen is available, then bar plots or similar could be used to present the explanans, whereas under the dangerous conditions that occur in a driving situation, it might be best to use voice output. In Sect. 4.5, this context type was referred to as a "selected" context. The different questions that can be asked at each explanatory move also depend on the context. If we use a vocabulary such as the one in Fig. 14.1, then these options can be available for every node of the vocabulary, even though not all options might be applicable to all nodes. Figure 14.2 shows an example of how the available explanans can be declared in a KG for the intermediate concept "Basement". KGs can also have directed edges, which we have not used in this case. KGs provide a lot

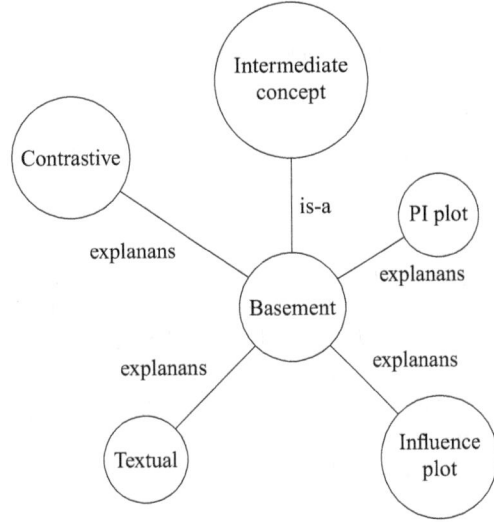

Fig. 14.2 Example of a KG representing different explanans modalities that are available for explaining the value of Ames Housing node "Basement". Nodes in a KG also typically have some kind of "is-a" relation(s) that identify the type(s) of the node, which in this case is an 'intermediate concept' that can then be used to extract the hierarchy in Fig. 14.1 from a complex KG with different kinds of relations

of liberty in how they are structured, which affects how the KGs are accessed and used in practice. This is why the definition and implementation of KGs is usually the task of knowledge engineers who bridge the gap between human expertise and computational systems, enabling the AI systems to perform tasks requiring complex reasoning or domain-specific knowledge.

The purpose of defining this kind of KGs is that it becomes possible to produce software that knows how to interpret and use the named edges to create an interactive dialog through an appropriate user interface. In a classical graphical user interface, the KG in Fig. 14.1 says that the explainee could be given a menu or similar for switching between the different explanans modalities. A similar approach can be used for declaring what are the next possible questions or actions available to the explainee at the explanatory move in question. KG models of explananda can contain all kinds of information, but the software that implements the user interface will need to know how to use the different relations defined by the labeled edges in order to implement the desired sXAI functionality.

14.5.4 Partner Model

The KG discussed so far includes the available domain knowledge, how it can be presented to the explainee, and the possibilities to navigate during an interaction with the explainee. However, it is identical for all explainees. In order to make explanatory interactions more efficient for the explainee, it could be advantageous to collect statistics about what vocabulary to use, what explanans modality works the best and when, and what kind of questions and corresponding answers tend to be preferred by the explainee. It is common practice for the edges of a KG to have weights assigned to them. Such weights could be used for memorizing what concepts were used the most during an interaction as well as statistics on what modalities were used, what questions were asked, and so forth. This signifies that a partner model is essentially a weighted version of the corresponding KG that is used during the interaction.

The partner model KG is specific to a particular explainee. It can be initialized from a default KG or by using some 'explainee-type' KG that is suitable for the explainee in question (the 'global' partner model characterized in Sect. 14.4). After its creation, the partner model KG might be extended, pruned, or modified in other ways (resulting in the 'local' partner model). How edge weights are updated is still an open question. A simple approach is to update edge weights so that often-used edges are prioritized in the future. As discussed in this book, social cues could also be used to detect whether the explainee's face indicates satisfaction and understanding of the explanans and then strengthen the corresponding weights. Correspondingly, if a lack of understanding is detected, then the sXAI system should try a different edge and reduce the weight of the nonsuccessful one.

KGs could also be considered to be, or used as, Markov models, and how to navigate within the KG could be modeled as a Markov decision process (MDP). The creation and adaptation of a partner model as an MDP using Monte Carlo tree search (MCTS) has been proposed by Robrecht and Kopp (2023). MCTS provides a way of solving MDPs online. An MCTS policy aims to find a balance between searching for new (exploration) and trying promising options (exploitation). As such, MCTS has many similarities with how reinforcement learning (RL) agents explore the space of possible states and actions and receive positive or negative rewards that allow them to learn optimal policies. RL typically balances between exploring new options and exploiting what has already been learned, but it is well known and also pointed out in Robrecht and Kopp (2023) that RL systems face challenges when having to deal with rapidly changing environments. As pointed out earlier in this chapter, explainee knowledge, experience, and preferences might change over time, so it is essential for the partner model to be capable of adapting to such changes.

The concepts presented here are further demonstrated in Chap. 16 for interactive exploration of explanations and in Chap. 17 regarding the building and use of partner models for sXAI. It should also be emphasized that partner models are presumably not limited to KGs, but will include other technologies too, such as AI systems that are fine-tuned for detecting gesture-based social cues of the explainee—to mention just one example.

14.6 How Does This Chapter Inspire Further Directions of XAI?

As we have shown so far, various disciplines are contributing to the question of which models sXAI should have at its disposal in order to adapt to the user in a specific situation and in a particular second of the interaction. Researchers from computer science, psycholinguistics, psychology, didactics, and other fields have formulated suggestions as to how models of context, explanandum, and partner support the process of explanation in sum along with the understanding of the explainee. As shown in the operationalization part of the chapter (Sect. 14.5), some of these models have already been implemented successfully in XAI. Following the goals of sXAI, we underline the need to implement them more frequently and, furthermore, to do this in a co-constructive manner. But how much is needed? It should also be kept in mind that AI should remain as parsimonious as possible. Two important next steps are therefore required:

Even for the comparatively well-studied human–human interaction, the mental interplay of explainer and explainee on the one hand and the explanation on the other has not yet been investigated sufficiently. To distinguish between them, we defined the cognitive adaptivity of the mental representation and the interactive adaptivity of multimodal explanation behavior. Both change over the course of an interaction. But how does this work? How do they influence each other? To date, findings are surprisingly scarce. Empirical studies are therefore needed on their association and mutual influences in human–human and human–computer/robot interactions. This, in turn, requires valid assessment methods. However, this is a sophisticated task due to the subjectivity and dynamic of mental models.

Further on, it is necessary to ask which of the findings from human–human interaction can and should be transferred to human–machine interaction, including sXAI. The crucial question is whether or how much XAI should interact like a human. Answering this must take into account the strengths and weaknesses of human interaction partners in dealing with models, especially in situations with high cognitive load. In contrast, AI has different or even fewer problems of information processing and model representation. In this respect, it may not make sense for AI to mimic humans. Or does it make sense, because it allows familiar interaction scripts to be used? Additionally, there are some insights that the imitation of human behavior by robots actually makes it more difficult for the user to understand technical processes (Hindemith et al., 2021). It is also still an open question as to how humans *want* to interact with AI. From the perspective of data privacy (cf. Chap. 29), for example, it is questionable whether and which aspects of the discussed models (e.g., regarding [assumed] characteristics of user) should be made accessible and thus transparent for the AI.

To sum up, sXAI is inconceivable without models of the AI of context, the explanandum, and the partner. These must therefore be implemented. However, how this is done and exactly which features should be considered requires further interdisciplinary research that takes interaction studies and computational modeling into account.

14.7 Rapid Access to the Content of this Chapter

Imagine you want to explain a game to a friend! What knowledge do you need? Technically speaking: Which mental models are needed?

First of all, you need to know the game: What is the aim of the game? What elements are there? What to do with these elements? Even if you know a game very well, you probably would not explain it fully straight away. Or you may not know it perfectly. You can still start with the basics.

If you explain the same game in different situations, the explanation would look very different in each case. You can explain loudly or quietly depending on the background noise; in detail or briefly depending on the time available. If you have the game at your disposal during the explanation, you will probably use the cards or figures to explain something. However, not all aspects of the situation will influence the explanation. For example, what the environment looks like may be irrelevant. We refer to the representation of relevant factors of the situation as 'context.'

Additionally, you should adapt to the person you are talking to. You explain things differently to a child than to an adult. However, you may realize during the explanation that the child has a lot of experience with games. Perhaps it knows a similar game or is very intelligent. In this case, you would probably adapt the explanation. What the interlocutors are interested in regarding the explanation also depends on their goals. For example, do they want to be able to play the game, or do they plan to buy a game? These goals need different explanations.

All of these elements of knowledge are 'models' of explainers (also of explainees, but that is not our topic). They are often referred to as mental models or mental representations. A large number of models are involved in every communication situation. We focus on three models:

The **model of the situation, the context** gives the framework of the explanation: A large number of relevant context characteristics are perceivable to the explaining human or AI (cf., Chap. 4). These include the situation in the area of their visual, acoustic, olfactory, and otherwise characterized perceptual space. This list already points to the purely sensory challenge for current AI. Other factors are simply not perceivable. This may be the case because they are not in the field of perception – perhaps in another room – or because they are not directly visible. This includes many characteristics of the partner/user that must be inferred from their perceivable behavior. This becomes clear in a robot–human interaction: The robot needs a model of what the partner can see from their point of view. However, if the partner signals that this is not the case, the explanation must be adapted. Current AI already has some sensory, representational, and processual prerequisites for this that need to be developed further.

The **model of the explanandum**, often referred to as a *domain model* in technical contexts: In everyday explanations, the explanandum, which should be explained, is not fixed completely before an explanation; it is a "moving target," as Rohlfing et al. (2021, p. 720) say about XAI explananda. For example, although it is clear that the game is to be explained, it only becomes clear during the explanatory interaction how detailed the explanation should be and what exactly is of interest. Depending on the explainer, explainee, context, and so forth, the explanandum is represented differently. In the game explanation, language-based propositional representations or visual analog representations can be useful. The purpose of the explanation also determines the form of the model. If the goal is to buy a game, the explainee needs conceptual knowledge (addressing the question "what?"). If the goal is to be enabled to play, procedural knowledge (addressing the question "how?") is needed. Usually, however, both forms of knowledge are needed to reach agency in dealing with an explanandum (e.g., adapting the options for using the game or the AI).

In the special case in which the machine is conducting a collaborative activity with a human such as playing a game together, or is simply acting in the presence of a human, the explanation must accompany (or complement) the activity. The machine performs an action and conveys explanatory information about it. An example is when a robot adapts a motion to achieve a task or synthesizes it to not only achieve the task it has to do, but also to convey to the human information about its intention or target.

The **model of the partner**, referred to as the *user model* in technical contexts with the AI as explainer, also changes over the course of the explanation. If the explainee is a stranger, the explainer initially only has a very rough partner model (Brennan et al., 2010). Over the course of the explanation, the partner model is refined and adapted. For example, an explainer explaining a game to a child realizes that the child unexpectedly already has a great deal of prior knowledge. An important aspect during the course of the explanation is that the explainer perceives – or assumes – that the explainee understands their explanation, and, as a result, knows increasingly more about the explanandum. The explainee's knowledge is therefore a particularly important dimension of the partner model, as is the explainee's interest (here: to buy or play a game). Other relevant dimensions can be, for example, the explainee's cognitive abilities or emotions.

The discussion of a partner model makes it particularly vivid that explainers should have the ability to construct and consider mental model. Prerequisites are theory of mind and perspective taking. Humans are 'actually' very good at adopting the perspective of others. However, they often do not succeed well in communication situations if these are associated with a high cognitive load and no further capacities are available for perspective-taking inferences. AI has better prerequisites here, because it can process more information at the same time. However, the AI must have the models and be able to process them over the course of the explanation.

This results in requirements for sXAI to have models of the context, the explanandum, and the partner. It must be able to adapt these over the course of the explanation in response to the interaction with the human user.

Acknowledgments We thank Stefan Kopp for his valuable perspective and helpful comments on an earlier version of this chapter.

This work was funded by the Deutsche Forschungsgemeinschaft (DFG, German Research Foundation): TRR 318/1 2021 – 438445824. Rachid Alami's work has been partially supported by the EU-funded project euROBIN under grant agreement no. 101070596 and by the Artificial and Natural Intelligence Toulouse Institute (ANITI) funded by the France 2030 program under the grant agreement no. ANR-23-IACL-0002.

Kary Främling's work has been partially supported by the Wallenberg AI, Autonomous Systems and Software Program (WASP) funded by the Knut and Alice Wallenberg Foundation.

References

Ackerman, P. L. (1996). A theory of adult intellectual development: Process, personality, interests, and knowledge. *Intelligence, 22*(2), 227–257. https://doi.org/10.1016/S0160-2896(96)90016-1.

Anderson, J. R. (2013). *The architecture of cognition*. Psychology Press. https://doi.org/10.4324/9781315799438.

Baggs, E. (2021). All affordances are social: Foundations of a Gibsonian social ontology. *Ecological Psychology, 33*(3–4), 257–278. https://doi.org/10.1080/10407413.2021.1965477.

Beßler, D., Porzel, R., Pomarlan, M., Beetz, M., Malaka, R., & Bateman, J. (2020). A formal model of affordances for flexible robotic task execution. In *ECAI 2020* (pp. 2425–2432). IOS Press. https://doi.org/10.3233/FAIA200374.

Breazeal, C., Berlin, M., Brooks, A., Gray, J., & Thomaz, A. L. (2006). Using perspective taking to learn from ambiguous demonstrations. *Robotics and Autonomous Systems, 54*(5), 385–393. https://doi.org/10.1016/j.robot.2006.02.004.

Brennan, S. E., Galati, A., & Kuhlen, A. K. (2010). Two minds, one dialog: Coordinating speaking and understanding. In B. H. Ross (Ed.), *Psychology of learning and motivation* (Vol. 53, pp. 301–344). Elsevier. https://doi.org/10.1016/S0079-7421(10)53008-1.

Buhl, H. M. (2001). Partner orientation and speaker's knowledge as conflicting parameters in language production. *Journal of Psycholinguistic Research, 30*, 549–567. https://doi.org/10.1023/A:1014217421749.

Buhl, H. M., Fisher, J. B., & Rohlfing, K. J. (2024). Changes in partner models–effects of adaptivity in the course of explanations. In *Proceedings of the 46th Annual Conference of the Cognitive Science Society* (pp. 4976–4983). Cognitive Science Society (CSS). https://escholarship.org/uc/item/5bb7p5pt.

Buschmeier, H., Buhl, H.M., Kern, F., Grimminger, A., Beierling, H., Fisher, J., Groß, A., Horwath, I., Klowait, N., Lazarov, S., Lenke, M., Lohmer, V., Rohlfing, K.J., Scharlau, I., Singh, Terfloth, L., A., Vollmer, A.-L., Wang, Y., Wilmes, A., & Wrede, B. (2025). Forms of understanding of XAI-explanations. *Cognitive Systems Research, 94*, 101419. https://doi.org/10.1016/j.cogsys.2025.101419

Buschmeier, H., & Kopp, S. (2018). Communicative listener feedback in human–agent interaction: Artificial speakers need to be attentive and adaptive. In *Proceedings of the 17th International Conference on Autonomous Agents and Multiagent Systems* (pp. 1213–1221). International Foundation for Autonomous Agents and Multiagent Systems.

Butterfill, S. A., & Sebanz, N. (2011). Joint action: What is shared? *Review of Philosophy and Psychology, 2*(2), 137–146. https://doi.org/10.1007/s13164-011-0062-3.

Byom, L. J., & Mutlu, B. (2013). Theory of mind: Mechanisms, methods, and new directions. *Frontiers in Human Neuroscience, 7*, 413. https://doi.org/10.3389/fnhum.2013.00413.

Carlucci, F. M., Nardi, L., Iocchi, L., & Nardi, D. (2015). Explicit representation of social norms for social robots. In *2015 IEEE/RSJ International Conference on Intelligent Robots and Systems (IROS)* (pp. 4191–4196). IEEE. https://doi.org/10.1109/IROS.2015.7353970.

Chamola, V., Hassija, V., Sulthana, A. R., Ghosh, D., Dhingra, D., & Sikdar, B. (2023). A review of trustworthy and explainable artificial intelligence (XAI). *IEEE Access, 11*, 78994–79015. https://doi.org/10.1109/ACCESS.2023.3294569.

Chi, M. T. H., Siler, S. A., & Jeong, H. (2004). Can tutors monitor students' understanding accurately? *Cognition and Instruction, 22*(3), 363–387. https://doi.org/10.1207/s1532690xci2203_4.

Chi, M. T. H., Siler, S. A., Jeong, H., Yamauchi, T., & Hausmann, R. G. (2001). Learning from human tutoring. *Cognitive Science, 25*(4), 471–533. https://doi.org/10.1016/S0364-0213(01)00044-1.

Collins, A. M., & Loftus, E. F. (1975). A spreading-activation theory of semantic processing. *Psychological Review, 82*(6), 407–428. https://doi.org/10.1037/0033-295X.82.6.407.

Collins, A. M., & Quillian, M. R. (1969). Retrieval time from semantic memory. *Journal of Verbal Learning and Verbal Behavior, 8*(2), 240–247. https://doi.org/10.1016/S0022-5371(69)80069-1.

Confalonieri, R., & Guizzardi, G. (2023). *On the multiple roles of ontologies in explainable AI*. https://doi.org/10.48550/arXiv.2311.04778. arXiv: 2311.04778 [cs.AI].

Coradeschi, S., Loutfi, A., & Wrede, B. (2013). A short review of symbol grounding in robotic and intelligent systems. *Künstliche Intelligenz, 27*(2), 129–136. https://doi.org/10.1007/S13218-013-0247-2.

Cyganiak, R., Wood, D., & Lanthaler, M. (2014). *RDF 1.1 Concepts and Abstract Syntax*. W3C Recommendation W3C Recommendation 25 February 2014. Accessed 23 Apr 2025. World Wide Web Consortium (W3C).

De Cock, D. (2011). Ames, Iowa: Alternative to the Boston Housing Data as an end of semester regression project. *Journal of Statistics Education, 19*(3), 1–15. https://doi.org/10.1080/10691898.2011.11889627.

De Graaf, M. M. A., Dragan, A., Malle, B. F., & Ziemke, T. (2021). Introduction to the special issue on explainable robotic systems. *ACM Transactions on Human–Robot Interaction, 10*(3), 22. https://doi.org/10.1145/3461597.

De Jong, T., & Ferguson-Hessler, M. G. M. (1996). Types and qualities of knowledge. *Educational Psychologist, 31*(2), 105–113. https://doi.org/10.1207/s15326985ep3102_2.

Devine, R. T. (2016). Theory of mind. In V. Zeigler-Hill & T. K. Shackelford (Eds.), *Encyclopedia of personality and individual differences* (pp. 1–9). Springer. https://doi.org/10.1007/978-3-319-28099-8_560-1.

Dillenbourg, P., Lemaignan, S., Sangin, M., Nova, N., & Molinari, G. (2016). The symmetry of partner modelling. *International Journal of Computer-Supported Collaborative Learning, 11*, 227–253. https://doi.org/10.1007/s11412-016-9235-5.

Doyle, P. R., Clark, L., & Cowan, B. R. (2021). What do we see in them? Identifying dimensions of partner models for speech interfaces using a psycholexical approach. In *Proceedings of the 2021 CHI Conference on Human Factors in Computing Systems* (pp. 1–14). ACM. https://doi.org/10.1145/3411764.3445206.

Dragan, A. D., Lee, K. C. T., & Srinivasa, S. S. (2013). Legibility and predictability of robot motion. In *2013 8th ACM/IEEE International Conference on Human–Robot Interaction (HRI)* (pp. 301–308). IEEE. https://doi.org/10.1109/HRI.2013.6483603.

Fischer, K. (2016). *Designing speech for a recipient: The roles of partner modeling, alignment and feedback in so-called 'simplified registers'*. Benjamins. https://doi.org/10.1075/pbns.270.

Fisher, J. B., Lohmer, V., Kern, F., Barthlen, W., Gaus, S., & Rohlfing, K. J. (2022). Exploring monological and dialogical phases in naturally occurring explanations. *KI-Künstliche Intelligenz, 36*(3), 317–326. https://doi.org/10.1007/s13218-022-00787-1.

Flavell, J. H. (1992). Perspectives on perspective taking. In H. Beilin & P. B. Pufall (Eds.), *Piaget's theory: Prospects and possibilities* (pp. 107–139). Psychology Press.

Främling, K. (1996a). Explaining results of neural networks by contextual importance and utility. In R. Andrews & J. Diederich (Eds.), *Rules and Networks: Proceedings of the Rule Extraction from Trained Artificial Neural Networks Workshop, AISB 1996 Conference* (pp. 38–43). Society for the Study of Artificial Intelligence and Simulation of Behaviour (AISB).

Främling, K. (1996b). Modélisation et apprentissage des préférences par réseaux de neurones pour l'aide à la décision multicritère". PhD thesis. INSA de Lyon.

Främling, K. (2023). Counterfactual, contrastive, and hierarchical explanations with contextual importance and utility. In *Explainable and transparent AI and multi-agent systems* (pp. 180–184). Springer. https://doi.org/10.1007/978-3-031-40878-6_16.

Främling, K. (2024). *Contextual importance and utility in Python: New functionality and insights with the py-ciu package*. https://doi.org/10.48550/arXiv.2408.09957. arXiv: 2408.09957 [cs.AI].

Francis, A., Pérez-D'Arpino, C., Li, C., Xia, F., Alahi, A., Alami, R., Bera, A., Biswas, J., Chandra, R., Chiang, H.-T. L., Everett, M., Ha, S., Hart, J., How, J. P., Karnan, H., Lee, T.-W. E., Manso, L. J., Mirksy, R., ... Martín-Martín, R. (2025). Principles and guidelines for evaluating social robot navigation algorithms. *ACM Transactions on Human–Robot Interaction, 14*(2), 34. https://doi.org/10.1145/3700599.

Frith, C., & Frith, U. (2005). Theory of mind. *Current Biology, 15*(17), R644–R645. https://doi.org/10.1016/j.cub.2005.08.041.

García, D. H., Yu, Y., Sieińska, W., Part, J. L., Gunson, N., Lemon, O., & Dondrup, C. (2020). *Explainable representations of the social state: A model for social human–robot interactions*. https://doi.org/10.48550/arXiv.2010.04570. arXiv: 2010.04570 [cs.RO].

Hindemith, L., Philip Göpfert, J., Wiebel-Herboth, C. B., Wrede, B., & Vollmer, A.-L. (2021). Why robots should be technical: Correcting mental models through technical architecture concepts. *Interaction Studies, 22*(2), 244–279. https://doi.org/10.1075/is.20023.hin.

Hogan, A., Blomqvist, E., Cochez, M., D'amato, C., De Melo, G., Gutierrez, C., Kirrane, S., Gayo, J. E. L., Navigli, R., Neumaier, S., Ngomo, A.-C. N., Polleres, A., Rashid, S. M., Rula, A., Schmelzeisen, L., Sequeda, J., Staab, S., & Zimmermann, A. (2021). Knowledge graphs. *ACM Computing Surveys, 54*(4), 71. https://doi.org/10.1145/3447772.

Horton, W. S., & Keysar, B. (1996). When do speakers take into account common ground? *Cognition, 59*(1), 91–117. https://doi.org/10.1016/0010-0277(96)81418-1.

Johnson, D. W. (1975). Cooperativeness and social perspective taking. *Journal of Personality and Social Psychology, 31*(2), 241–244. https://doi.org/10.1037/h0076285.

Johnson, M., & Demiris, Y. (2005). Perceptual perspective taking and action recognition. *International Journal of Advanced Robotic Systems, 2*(4). https://doi.org/10.5772/5775.

Johnson-Laird, P. N. (2005). Mental models and thought. In K. J. Holyoak & R. G. Morrison (Eds.), *The Cambridge Handbook of Thinking and Reasoning* (pp. 185–208). Cambridge University Press.

Kintsch, W. (1998). *Comprehension: A paradigm for cognition*. Cambridge University Press.

Kopp, S., & Krämer, N. (2021). Revisiting human–agent communication: The importance of joint co-construction and understanding mental states. *Frontiers in Psychology, 12*, 580955. https://doi.org/10.3389/fpsyg.2021.580955.

Kosslyn, S. M. (2005). Mental images and the brain. *Cognitive Neuropsychology, 22*(3), 333–347. https://doi.org/10.1080/02643290442000130.

Kroes, P. (1998). Technological explanations: The relation between structure and function of technological objects. *Society for Philosophy and Technology Quarterly Electronic Journal, 3*(3), 124–134. https://doi.org/10.5840/techne19983325.

Lazarov, S., & Grimminger, A. (2024). Variations in explainers' gesture deixis in explanations related to the monitoring of explainees' understanding. In *Proceedings of the 46th Annual Conference of the Cognitive Science Society* (pp. 4805–4812). University of California. https://escholarship.org/uc/item/7dz8n8tf.

Lemaignan, S., Ros, R., Sisbot, E. A., Alami, R., & Beetz, M. (2012). Grounding the interaction: Anchoring situated discourse in everyday human–robot interaction. *International Journal of Social Robotics, 4*(2), 181–199. https://doi.org/10.1007/s12369-011-0123-x.

Lombard, M., & Ditton, T. (1997). At the heart of it all: The concept of presence. *Journal of Computer-Mediated Communication, 3*(2). https://doi.org/10.1111/j.1083-6101.1997.tb00072.x.

Mavridis, N., & Roy, D. (2006). Grounded situation models for robots: Where words and percepts meet. In *2006 IEEE/RSJ International Conference on Intelligent Robots and Systems* (pp. 4690–4697). IEEE. https://doi.org/10.1109/IROS.2006.282258.

Miller, T. (2019). Explanation in artificial intelligence: Insights from the social sciences. *Artificial Intelligence, 267*, 1–38. https://doi.org/10.1016/j.artint.2018.07.007.

Milliez, G., Warnier, M., Clodic, A., & Alami, R. (2014). A framework for endowing an interactive robot with reasoning capabilities about perspective-taking and belief management. In *The 23rd IEEE International Symposium on Robot and Human Interactive Communication* (pp. 1103–1109). IEEE. https://doi.org/10.1109/ROMAN.2014.6926399.

Nathan, M. J. (2024). Inference making and learning from text via embodied situation models: extending Kintsch's legacy. *Discourse Processes, 61*(6–7), 319–323. https://doi.org/10.1080/0163853X.2024.2362030.

Nickerson, R. S. (1999). How we know – and sometimes misjudge – what others know: Imputing one's own knowledge to others. *Psychological Bulletin, 125*(6), 737–759. https://doi.org/10.1037/0033-2909.125.6.737.

Nückles, M., Winter, A., Wittwer, J., Herbert, M., & Hübner, S. (2006). How do experts adapt their explanations to a layperson's knowledge in asynchronous communication? An experimental study. *User Modeling and User-Adapted Interaction, 16*, 87–127. https://doi.org/10.1007/s11257-006-9000-y.

Nückles, M., Wittwer, J., & Renkl, A. (2005). Information about a layperson's knowledge supports experts in giving effective and efficient online advice to laypersons. *Journal of Experimental Psychology: Applied, 11*(4), 219–236. https://doi.org/10.1037/1076-898X.11.4.219.

Pandey, A. K., & Alami, R. (2013). Affordance graph: A framework to encode perspective taking and effort based affordances for day-to-day human–robot interaction. In *2013 IEEE/RSJ International Conference on Intelligent Robots and Systems* (pp. 2180–2187). IEEE. https://doi.org/10.1109/IROS.2013.6696661.

Premack, D., & Woodruff, G. (1978). Does the chimpanzee have a theory of mind? *Behavioral and Brain Sciences, 1*(4), 515–526. https://doi.org/10.1017/S0140525X00076512.

Reinmann-Rothmeier, G., & Mandl, H. (2002). Wissen. *Lexikon der Psychologie*, 7–9. https://www.spektrum.de/lexikon/psychologie/wissen/16892

Robrecht, A. S., & Kopp, S. (2023). SNAPE: A sequential non-stationary decision process model for adaptive explanation generation. In *Proceedings of the 15th International Conference on Agents and Artificial Intelligence - Volume 1: ICAART* (pp. 48–58). ScitePress. https://doi.org/10.5220/0011671300003393.

Rohlfing, K. J., Cimiano, P., Scharlau, I., Matzner, T., Buhl, H. M., Buschmeier, H., Grimminger, A., Hammer, B., Häb-Umbach, R., Horwath, I., Hüllermeier, E., Kern, F., Kopp, S., Thommes, K., Ngomo, A.-C. N., Schulte, C., Wachsmuth, H., Wagner, P., & Wrede, B. (2021). Explanation as a social practice: Toward a conceptual framework for the social design of AI systems. *IEEE Transactions on Cognitive and Developmental Systems, 13*(3), 717–728. https://doi.org/10.1109/TCDS.2020.3044366.

Rohlfing, K. J., Rehm, M., & Goecke, K. U. (2003). Situatedness: The interplay between context(s) and situation. *Journal of Cognition and Culture, 3*(2), 132–156. https://doi.org/10.1163/156853703322148516.

Ros, R., Sisbot, E. A., Alami, R., Steinwender, J., Hamann, K., & Warneken, F. (2010). Solving ambiguities with perspective taking. In *2010 5th ACM/IEEE International Conference on Human–Robot Interaction (HRI)* (pp. 181–182). IEEE. https://doi.org/10.1109/HRI.2010.5453204.

Schaffer, M. E., Terfloth, L., Schulte, C., & Buhl, H. M. (2024). Perception and consideration of the explainees' needs for satisfying explanations. In *2nd World Conference on eXplainable Artificial Intelligence*, Valletta, Malta. https://ceur-ws.org/Vol-3793/paper_3.pdf.

Schank, R. C., & Abelson, R. P. (1975). Scripts, plans, and knowledge. In *IJCAI'75: Proceedings of the 4th International Joint Conference on Artificial Intelligence* (pp. 151–157). Morgan Kaufmann Publishers Inc. https://www.ijcai.org/Proceedings/75/Papers/021.pdf.

Schmid, U., & Wrede, B. (2022). What is missing in XAI so far? An inter-disciplinary perspective. *KI-Künstliche Intelligenz, 36*(3), 303–315. https://doi.org/10.1007/s13218-022-00786-2.

Schnotz, W., & Bannert, M. (2003). Construction and interference in learning from multiple representation. *Learning and Instruction, 13*(2), 141–156. https://doi.org/10.1016/S0959-4752(02)00017-8.

Selman, R. L., & Byrne, D. F. (1981). A structural-developmental analysis of levels of role-taking in middle childhood. In L. D. Steinberg & L. J. Mandelbaum (Eds.), *The life cycle: Readings in human development* (pp. 96–104). Columbia University Press. https://doi.org/10.7312/stei93738-009.

Shen, H., Knearem, T., Ghosh, R., Alkiek, K., Krishna, K., Liu, Y., Ma, Z., Petridis, S., Peng, Y.-H., Qiwei, L., et al. (2024). Towards bidirectional human–AI alignment: A systematic review for clarifications, framework, and future directions. https://doi.org/10.48550/arXiv.2406.0926. arXiv: 2406.0926 [cs.RO].

Singamaneni, P. T., Bachiller-Burgos, P., Manso, L. J., Garrell, A., Sanfeliu, A., Spalanzani, A., & Alami, R. (2024). A survey on socially aware robot navigation: Taxonomy and future challenges. *The International Journal of Robotics Research, 43*(10), 1533–1572. https://doi.org/10.1177/02783649241230562.

Sodian, B., & Kristen, S. (2016). Theory of mind. In J. A. Greene, W. A. Sandoval, & I. Bråten (Eds.), *Handbook of epistemic cognition* (pp. 68–85). Routledge. https://doi.org/10.4324/9781315795225.

Sowa, J. F. (2000). *Knowledge representation: Logical, philosophical, and computational foundations*. Brooks/Cole Publishing Co. https://doi.org/10.5555/318183.

Steins, G., & Wicklund, R. A. (1996). Perspective-taking, conflict, and press: Drawing an E on your forehead. *Basic and Applied Social Psychology, 18*(3), 319–346. https://doi.org/10.1207/s15324834basp1803_5.

Sternberg, R. J., & Ben-Zeev, T. (2001). *Complex cognition: The psychology of human thought*. Oxford University Press.

Terfloth, L., Schaffer, M., Buhl, H. M., & Schulte, C. (2023). Adding why to what? Analyses of an everyday explanation. In *World Conference on Explainable Artificial Intelligence* (pp. 256–279). Springer. https://doi.org/10.1007/978-3-031-44070-0_13.

Thellman, S., de Graaf, M., & Ziemke, T. (2022). Mental state attribution to robots: A systematic review of conceptions, methods, and findings. *ACM Transactions on Human–Robot Interaction, 11*(4), 41. https://doi.org/10.1145/3526112.

Thomaz, A., Hoffman, G., & Cakmak, M. (2016). Computational human–robot interaction. *Foundations and Trends in Robotics, 4*(2–3), 105–223. https://doi.org/10.1561/2300000049.

Thommes, K., Lammert, O., Schütze, C., Richter, B., & Wrede, B. (2024). Human emotions in AI explanations. In *Explainable Artificial Intelligence* (pp. 270–293). Springer. https://doi.org/10.1007/978-3-031-63803-9_15.

Tomasello, M., & Carpenter, M. (2007). Shared intentionality. *Developmental Science, 10*(1), 121–125. https://doi.org/10.1111/j.1467-7687.2007.00573.x.

Trafton, J. G., Schultz, A. C., Bugajska, M., & Mintz, F. (2005). Perspective-taking with robots: Experiments and models. In *IEEE International Workshop on Robot and Human Interactive Communication* (pp. 580–584). IEEE. https://doi.org/10.1109/ROMAN.2005.1513842.

Tversky, B., Lee, P., & Mainwaring, S. (1999). Why do speakers mix perspectives? *Spatial Cognition and Computation, 1*, 399–412. https://doi.org/10.1023/A:1010091730257.

Underwood, B., & Moore, B. (1982). Perspective-taking and altruism. *Psychological Bulletin, 91*(1), 143–173. https://doi.org/10.1037/0033-2909.91.1.143.

Warnier, M., Guitton, J., Lemaignan, S., & Alami, R. (2012). When the robot puts itself in your shoes. Managing and exploiting human and robot beliefs. In *The 21st IEEE RO-MAN International Symposium on Robot and Human Interactive Communication* (pp. 948–954). IEEE. https://doi.org/10.1109/ROMAN.2012.6343872.

Wenke, D., Atmaca, S., Holländer, A., Liepelt, R., Baess, P., & Prinz, W. (2011). What is shared in joint action? Issues of co-representation, response conflict, and agent identification. *Review of Philosophy and Psychology, 2*(2), 147–172. https://doi.org/10.1007/s13164-011-0057-0.

Wilf, A., Lee, S. S., Liang, P. P., & Morency, L.-P. (2023). Think twice: Perspective-taking improves Large Language Models' Theory-of-Mind capabilities. https://doi.org/10.48550/arXiv.2311.10227. arXiv: 2311.10227 [cs.AI].

Wimmer, H., & Perner, J. (1983). Beliefs about beliefs: Representation and constraining function of wrong beliefs in young children's understanding of deception. *Cognition 13*(1), 103–128. https://doi.org/10.1016/0010-0277(83)90004-5.

Wittwer, J., Nückles, M., & Renkl, A. (2008). Is underestimation less detrimental than overestimation? The impact of experts' beliefs about a layperson's knowledge on learning and question asking. *Instructional Science, 36*, 27–52. https://doi.org/10.1007/s11251-007-9021-x.

Wittwer, J., Nückles, M., & Renkl, A. (2010). Using a diagnosis-based approach to individualize instructional explanations in computer-mediated communication. *Educational Psychology Review, 22*(1), 9–23. https://doi.org/10.1007/s10648-010-9118-7.

W3C OWL Working Group. (2012). *OWL 2 Web Ontology Language Document Overview (Second Edition)*. W3C Recommendation W3C Recommendation 11 December 2012. Accessed 23 Apr 2025. World Wide Web Consortium (W3C). https://www.w3.org/TR/owl2-overview/.

Open Access This chapter is licensed under the terms of the Creative Commons Attribution 4.0 International License (http://creativecommons.org/licenses/by/4.0/), which permits use, sharing, adaptation, distribution and reproduction in any medium or format, as long as you give appropriate credit to the original author(s) and the source, provide a link to the Creative Commons license and indicate if changes were made.

The images or other third party material in this chapter are included in the chapter's Creative Commons license, unless indicated otherwise in a credit line to the material. If material is not included in the chapter's Creative Commons license and your intended use is not permitted by statutory regulation or exceeds the permitted use, you will need to obtain permission directly from the copyright holder.

Chapter 15
Generation of Explanatory Content and Requirements for Social XAI

Kary Främling, Kirsten Thommes, and Britta Wrede

Abstract If XAI are to become social XAI, XAI methods must have capabilities enabling them to 'extract' information about the underlying AI model and to generate explanatory content based on that information. In a dialog between explainer and explainee, the explanans presented in every explanation move have to relate to each other understandably and coherently in order to remain trustworthy. This signifies that the generated explanantia have to be consistent—independently of what question is answered by each explanans, in what modality, in what vocabulary, and at what level of abstraction. Moreover, it is advantageous to be able to provide a rich palette of different kinds of explanantia in order to be able to have a fluent dialog in which the explanantia can be generated and adapted to the context, the explainee, feedback, reactions during the interaction with the explainee, and so forth. This chapter attempts to identify relevant questions that an explainee might ask during an explanatory dialog, and it assesses to what extent different XAI methods are capable of addressing these questions in a coherent way. The Contextual Importance and Utility (CIU) method is used to illustrate how an XAI method can generate explanantia for most of the identified questions. CIU also provides a flexibility in how explanatory content is generated that makes it possible to create a meaningful dialog with the explainee.

K. Främling (✉)
Department of Computing Science, Umeå University, Umeå, Sweden

Department of Industrial Engineering and Management, Aalto University, Espoo, Finland
e-mail: kary.framling@umu.se

K. Thommes
Faculty of Business Administration and Economics, Paderborn University, Paderborn, Germany
e-mail: kirsten.thommes@uni-paderborn.de

B. Wrede
Medical School OWL, Bielefeld University, Bielefeld, Germany
e-mail: bwrede@techfak.uni-bielefeld.de

© The Author(s) 2026
K. J. Rohlfing et al. (eds.), *Social Explainable AI*,
https://doi.org/10.1007/978-981-96-5290-7_15

15.1 How Does This Chapter Relate to XAI?

As a research domain, XAI is usually considered to be an extension to AI systems that makes it possible to get answers to such questions as "Why?," "Why not?," and so forth, or, in general, to somehow expose the reasons behind a result, action, recommendation, or another outcome of the AI system. However, current XAI systems are rarely interactive and rarely maintain a model to track the explainee's understanding and the interaction history. In order to make such interaction with explainees possible, the XAI methods employed have to be capable of generating explanations that present them in different ways, using different modalities, and using varied vocabularies while synthesizing explanations in order not to overwhelm the explainee and also provide the possibility for explainees to get a detailed explanation if they desire. In this chapter, we study how such explanatory content could, or can, be generated by XAI methods. The use of such content for interaction with explainees will be discussed and presented in Chap. 16.

15.2 State-of-the-Art XAI Methods

The name "XAI" started to gain in popularity around 2017 when the DARPA[1] launched a new research program on the topic, under that name Gunning and Aha (2019). A paper describing the Local Interpretable Model-agnostic Explanations (LIME) XAI method by Ribeiro et al. (2016) presumably also played an important role in creating interest in XAI. Since then, there has been a great proliferation of survey and conceptual papers that categorize XAI methods and approaches in different ways, such as Guidotti et al. (2018b), Anjomshoae et al. (2019), and Barredo et al. (2020) to mention a few. Those papers make an initial distinction between white box versus black box models. White box models are expected to offer *complete transparency*, meaning that the internal structure, algorithms, and logic of the model are accessible and understandable. Some frequently mentioned examples are decision trees, linear regression, and several types of rule-based systems. The assumption is then that because domain experts can analyze and understand the operation of the system, white boxes do not need to be explainable. In reality, the same could be considered to be true for support vector machines or even neural networks, because experts on those technologies can understand how the models operate, even though the complexity of the task may be higher.

The white box versus black box debate illustrates one challenge with current XAI research: *interpretability* and *explainability* are often assessed for models or explanations that are intended for, and understandable to, AI/ML model developers or (in the best case) domain experts for verification purposes, that is, to check that

---

[1] Defense Advanced Research Projects Agency.

the model works according to the expectations (Miller, 2019). It is rare for XAI methods to produce explanations that would even be intended for 'true' end users who are not typically domain experts and do not know anything about the inner workings of the AI system. Furthermore, most current state-of-the-art XAI methods produce a static explanation that makes it difficult to implement any interactive functionality that would bring added value to the explainee. For this reason, we shall consider all AI systems to produce black box outcomes that need to be presented and explained in different ways to different explainees.

Black box models can be further divided into subcategories. The possibly oldest category is the one that attempts to create a surrogate white box that mimics the black box as much as possible but expresses the internal workings in a more human-understandable way (Andrews et al., 1995). However, as argued already, the outcomes of rule-based systems and decision trees also tend to be interpretable only by experts, so we do not consider them as being intrinsically explainable.

XAI methods can further be divided into model-specific and model-agnostic methods. Methods belonging to different categories have different purposes, advantages, and limitations. So-called post hoc methods provide explanations for a specific instance x and the outcome $f(x)$, where f is the model (i.e., the black box). Model-specific XAI methods such as Layer-Wise Relevance Propagation, Grad-CAM, and integrated gradients are specific for deep neural networks (DNNs). For simplicity, we will call these *gradient-based* methods, even though it is questionable whether all those methods actually use gradients of the DNN. So-called transformer models (Vaswani et al., 2017) have become popular due to their success in LLMs and systems such as ChatGPT. Transformer-specific XAI methods have been proposed by, for example, Chefer et al. (2021) and Liu et al. (2021), but model-agnostic methods can also be applied to them.

To address the explainability of any black box models, we shall now focus on the category of post hoc and model-agnostic XAI methods. This category is currently dominated by the family of *additive feature attribution (AFA)* methods (Lundberg and Lee, 2017). AFA methods create a *surrogate model* $g(x)$ that is a locally interpretable approximation of the original model $f(x)$. x is a vector of black box input feature values describing the current context to be explained, usually called the *instance* to explain in XAI literature. The surrogate model $g(x)$ is used to calculate a feature attribution value ϕ_i for each feature. Here, we shall call ϕ_i the *influence* value of each input feature i for the specific instance x to be explained. A high, positive influence value signifies that the current feature value has a strongly positive influence on the output value compared to a reference instance or 'baseline.' A high and negative influence value signifies that the current feature value has a strongly positive influence on the output value compared to the reference instance. The reference instance is an instance (which might not exist in reality) for which the influence value is zero for all features. The reference instance is not necessarily identified as such by all AFA methods, for instance, the SHAP method uses just the average output value for a set of instances as a *baseline* value (Lundberg and Lee, 2017). For most AFA methods, the notions of *low value*, *high value*, and so forth are relative to the influence values of other features because influence values do not typically have a predefined, or known, range.

There is a certain confusion in XAI research and literature between concepts such as importance, influence, relevance, significance, *etc.*. However, it has been argued by, for example, Främling (2022a) that feature importance and influence have different meanings and mathematical definitions. For instance, the Permutation Feature Importance (PFI) of Breiman (2001) works by measuring the change in the model's performance after permuting the values of a particular feature. If the performance degrades significantly, the feature is deemed important; if it changes little, it is considered less important. PFI estimates a global feature importance. That is, it does not provide instance-specific values and can be considered to give importance values in the range [0, 1]. As such, feature importance has been used in domains such as decision science for decades (or centuries, depending on the interpretation of what feature importance is). In decision science, feature importance is usually expressed as a weight in the range [0, 1] in linear models, as for the analytic hierarchy process (AHP) method, for instance (Saaty, 1980). AHP is only one example of methods that could be considered to belong to the categories of *utility theory* and *multiple criteria decision-making*. Rather than going into the history of utility theory, whose origins presumably go back at least to Daniel Bernoulli and his book from 1738, we invite the reader to read, for example, (Dyer, 2005). Främling (2020) provides an explicit link from utility theory to XAI.

For instance-specific XAI methods, that is, AFA methods as well as gradient-based XAI methods in general, ϕ can take any values from the interval $[-\inf, \inf]$. As mentioned earlier, ϕ can be negative or positive because the instance x to be explained is compared to some baseline ϕ_0. An instance that corresponds exactly to the baseline for all input features would have zero $\phi = 0$ values for all features, no matter how "important" the features are. For gradient-based methods, the baseline is the zero gradient $\phi = 0$. When using the Shapley value as an XAI method, the baseline ϕ_0 is the average output value for the set of instances studied (Štrumbelj and Kononenko, 2014). Then, the difference between the model output and ϕ_0 is what needs to be explained and this is distributed to the different ϕ_i values. Due to the comparison against a baseline, methods that produce influence values (rather than importance values) could be considered *contrastive* by nature in the sense that they show the contrast between option A (the instance x) and option B (in this case the baseline).

The Contextual Importance and Utility (CIU) method proposed by Främling (1996b) and Främling (1996a) has a different background theory and approach than AFA methods. CIU is inspired by multiple criteria decision-making and utility theory (Främling, 2020) and defines feature importance accordingly. *Contextual Importance (CI)* estimates how much the result can change by modifying the value(s) of one or more features (jointly) for the instance x. *Contextual Utility (CU)* estimates how favorable the current feature value(s) is (are) for getting a high-utility output value. CI and CU values are both in the range [0, 1]. By defining a baseline CU, CIU can also be used to calculate an influence value $\phi = CI(CU - CU.baseline)$ and produce contrastive explanations against any baseline values or other instance with which it is being compared. For CIU, ϕ values are in the range $[-CU.baseline, 1 - CU.baseline]$.

Some model-agnostic post hoc XAI methods have also been proposed that extract *decision rules*, such as Anchors (Ribeiro et al., 2018) and LORE (Guidotti et al., 2018a). However, those approaches are mainly suitable for classification tasks and, like the abovementioned methods, rely on building a surrogate model g. These methods also usually have constraints regarding the number of output classes, calculation time, and so forth.

Methods based on *counterfactual examples* refer to the generation of alternative scenarios that, if the input differed, would lead to a diverse outcome (Wachter et al., 2018). A counterfactual explanation essentially answers a "What-if?" question, but current methods tend to be limited to classification tasks and show what changes are required for the classification to change. Other challenges involve defining meaningful counterfactuals among all possible alternatives and ensuring robustness in high-dimensional spaces.

15.3 What Questions Do Users Actually Expect to Get Answers on?

As pointed out by, for example, Miller (2019), it is justified to ask to what extent current XAI methods are actually intended to justify and explain outcomes of AI systems, or whether they are rather tools made by AI and ML professionals to meet their needs to understand their own models. If we look at the car selection scenario and the example dialogs shown in Chap. 2, explainees tend to ask many different questions and expect answers that take into account the context and the history of interaction in the answers, as pointed out, e.g., by Lim and Dey (2009). Some explainees might prefer purely numeric outputs, while others might prefer bar plots, textual explanations, or other modalities of explanation. It would also be beneficial to use the vocabulary, modalities, and so forth that are preferred by the explainee would be used, as represented by a partner model.

Taking a similar approach to the one of Lim and Dey (2009), we use the scenarios in Chap. 2 to identify relevant questions that explainees might want to ask:

- *Why?* This is presumably the most obvious question, that is, receive a justification for the current output or result of an AI system. In this case, the explanation will focus presumably on features with a positive influence. However, there are also different variants:
  - *Why is this the best option?* This is the most commonly used explanation in XAI literature (e.g., "Why is this a cat?" and then highlighting where the cat is).

- *Why is this option only average?* This question can be more challenging, and especially explanations using influence values might become rather noninformative due to zero or close-to-zero ϕ values.

- *Why not?* A "Why not?" explanation would normally emphasize features with a negative influence. Some examples of variants of "Why not?" questions are:

  - *Why is this not a good house?*
  - *Why is this not a husky dog?*

- *Why is this feature important (or not)?* An XAI algorithm that just gives a number that represents some notion of *importance* is not necessarily sufficiently trustworthy if it cannot be justified. Some examples of questions could be:

  - *Why is performance important for recommending this car?*
  - *Why is safety not important for assessing this car?*
  - *Why is age important for survival on the Titanic?*

- *What if?* This is the basic counterfactual question, that is, what would happen if the values of one or more features change? Examples of "What-if?" questions are:

  - *Would adding options to car A make it better, without making it too expensive?*
  - *What part of my house should I renovate in order to increase its value as much as possible?*

- *How to?* This is another kind of counterfactual question, in which the XAI system attempts to find a way of modifying the studied instance in a way that would achieve some target value or class. However, doing so usually has a cost. Features are also often dependent, so modifying the value of one feature might affect that values of other features. Finally, there may be many alternative ways to achieve the target, which makes it into an optimization problem. Examples of "How to?"-questions are:

  - *What could I do to my car in order to get $1000 more when I sell it?*
  - *How could I pass from "not admitted" class to "admitted"?*

- *Why A and not B?* This is a directly contrastive question and the answer is expected to emphasize the most important features that differentiate A and B. Examples of "Why A and not B" questions are:

  - *Why should I buy car A and not car B?*
  - *Why shouldn't I buy car B rather than car A?* This might give a different answer than the previous question because A is now the "baseline" for the explanation, rather than B in the previous question.
  - *What changes might make B preferable to A?* This is a combined "what-if?" and contrastive question.

- *I don't agree with either outcome, nor the justification or explanation provided! How can I correct that?* This situation could occur, for instance, in the car selection scenario in Sect. 2.3, in which the AI system attempts to identify and model the user's preferences. In such a situation, the user needs to be given the possibility of taking some corrective action to the AI system model, e.g., through 'pseudo examples' as proposed by Främling (1996b). A further possibility is that the user wants to try something such as "What would the result be if my preferences were actually different from the AI system's initial assumption?"

- *How confident are you about your outcome?* Getting an answer to this question should be a basic requirement for any trustworthy system and is something that has been recognized since the beginning of AI. In practice, most modern AI systems are not capable of answering this question. It is also worth noting that a system's confidence in its outcome might be different from its confidence in the explanation that is given.
- *How?* The question (and answer) might be similar to the "Why?" question, but one could suppose that the explainee might want a more extensive answer about the model's training, the dataset used, and so forth.

Some of these questions are similar to the ones posed by Lim and Dey (2009), who assessed the usefulness of questions mainly as a function of context. The questions and the examples presented here also assume that context needs to be considered, while also considering the social XAI (sXAI) elements of multimodality, incrementality, and patternedness.

As mentioned in Sect. 14.4, one requirement for a 'good' explanation is that it uses terms that are familiar to the explainee. At the minimal level, this signifies that it should be possible to use an *explainee-adapted vocabulary* for feature names and their values rather than using the original column names in the training dataset or similar. AI systems might also use tens or hundreds of input features that might be optimized for the training performance rather than for explainability. In order to provide explainee-digestable explanations, it should also be possible to group features together into higher-level abstractions or so-called *intermediate concepts (ICs)* as described by Främling (1996a, 2020). These are essentially named coalitions of features. ICs can be structured using semantic networks with named relations, of which hierarchical structures such as taxonomies and meronomies are particularly useful for explanation purposes. As an example referring to the car selection scenario in Chap. 2, an IC called "Performance" could group together the features "Horse powers," "Maximal torque," "Acceleration," and "Weight." In practice, "Acceleration" depends at least on "Maximal torque" and "Weight," so the XAI method must be capable of handling feature dependencies correctly and consistently in explanations that use ICs.

Table 15.1 attempts to assess four XAI methods, or types of methods, given the questions that can be asked, whether the method output values have an absolute meaning, and to what extent they support ICs. The criterion *multimodal capabilities* refers to whether the methods support graphical, textual, and other modalities as discussed in the chapters of Part "Multimodality" of this book.

Criteria that have not been included in Table 15.1 are 'model-agnostic' and whether the methods consider interdependencies between features. All the studied

Table 15.1 Assessment of SOTA XAI methods versus questions that they answer

Criteria	SHAP(/AFA)	CIU	Counterfactual	Rule-based
Why?	Yes	Yes	No	Yes
Why not?	Yes	Yes	No	Partially
Why (not)important feature?	No	Yes	No	No
What if?	No	Yes	Yes (classification)	Partially
Why A and not B?	No	Yes	Maybe	No
Absolute meaning	No	Yes	No	Yes
Multimodal capabilities	No	Yes	Maybe	No
Intermediate concepts	Yes	Yes	Maybe	No

methods can be considered model-agnostic, even though that might not be true for methods that belong to the families of counterfactual and rule-based methods. Regarding the consideration for interdependencies between features, all the methods listed in Table 15.1 deal with them in their own way. Among AFA methods, at least SHAP takes interdependencies into account and distributes the contribution (influence) in a 'fair' way. SHAP in practice uses a linear model, as defined by the efficiency axiom of Shapley values, which guarantees that the contributions from all features add up to explain the model output. This will hide the presence of simple interdependencies even for simple logical functions such as OR, AND, and so forth, in which any feature can potentially change the result completely. CIU again assigns importance values 'correctly' in these cases as well, while still guaranteeing that the joint importance of all features is correct in the sense of considering interdependencies. Counterfactual methods, especially those that address "How to?"-questions will normally take interdependencies into account automatically, unless they replace the actual AI model with a surrogate model. Rule-based models will obviously not have problems when dealing with logical functions, so they can deal with interdependencies. However, rule-based models often require discretization of numeric features, which can be a challenge.

For SHAP and AFA methods in general, the "no"-values are mainly due to the influence (ϕ) values that those methods produce not providing any "What-if?" information, so that they can only be assessed relative to each other due to their potential [−inf, inf], rather than having a direct and absolute meaning. The lack of absolute meaning also makes it challenging to produce textual explanations, for instance, and this might be why these methods often use only different variations of bar plots for visualization. SHAP also gets "yes" for IC support because the Shapley value distributes the 'gain' in a 'fair' way to all features, which is also reflected in the linear surrogate model g produced by SHAP. However, to the best of knowledge, using ICs with SHAP has only been studied empirically by Jullum et al. (2021) and Främling (2022b) and would require further investigation.

CIU has "yes" for all criteria, partially because CI, CU, and influence values produced by CIU have clearly defined limits and interpretations. CIU is not a counterfactual method, but the potential influence (PI) plots presented by Främling

(2024) and similar uses of the combination of CI and CU values indicate what features have the greatest potential for changing the outcome, as illustrated in the next section. ICs are also 'natively supported' in CIU and take feature dependencies into account in a consistent way (Främling, 1996a; Patil & Främling, 2023).

It has been argued that counterfactual explanations are preferred in many situations (Wachter et al., 2018; Doshi-Velez & Kim, 2017; Verma et al., 2020). However, counterfactual methods do not directly answer the elementary "Why?" and "Why not?"-questions. They are usually presented and used for classification tasks, in which the presented explanation is of the form "If features ... would be ..., then the instance x would be in Class B rather than Class A." Such explanations might also be adapted to answer the question "Why A and not B," even though they do not provide an answer. Regarding multimodal capabilities and support for ICs, we do not have sufficient knowledge and confidence to answer "yes" or "no."

Rule-based methods provide a set of rules that apply to the instance x and therefore answer the question "Why?," as well as indirectly providing an answer to the questions "Why not?" and "What if?" For the question "Why A and not B," we are unaware of results that would use or show such functionality. The produced rules do have an absolute meaning. However, the rules are presented in a textual and rather formal way that is challenging to present in multimodal ways. Regarding ICs, symbolic ML methods such as C4.5 (Quinlan, 1993) do produce decision trees and similar hierarchical structures. However, the ICs of the tree are based uniquely on training performance and might not have any particular meaning for the explainee used in an explanation. Such ICs will typically not have any name or explanation either.

15.4 Operationalization

In order to provide examples of how explanatory content can be generated in practice, we continue with the Ames Housing example, which is described in Sect. 14.5. In order to illustrate some challenges with current SOTA XAI methods, Fig. 15.1 shows typical influence value plots as produced by SHAP and using CIU's contextual influence ϕ values. This plot should presumably answer the question "Why is the price of this house $443,508?" relative to the average price for the whole set of houses used for training the ML model (i.e., $455,470). Figure 15.2 shows a corresponding PI plot based on CIU's CI and CU values, as 'raw' in the range [0, 1] and scaled according to the highest CI value. When comparing the influence and PI plots, we can see that the two features that have the highest importance do not have the highest influence. Because influence values indicate a zero, positive, or negative difference compared to a reference value, the influence might be zero even for the feature that has the highest importance for the model output. Without a proper understanding of influence values, the explainee might get a wrong impression about what features are truly the most important ones.

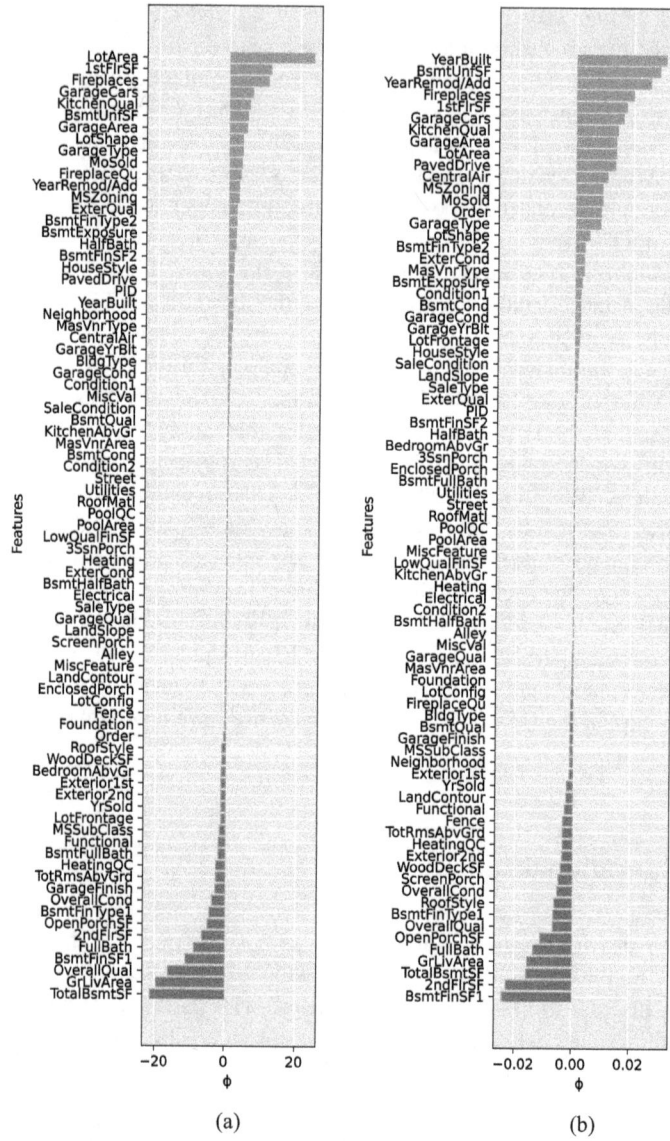

Fig. 15.1 Influence value explanations using SHAP and contextual influence for an average price instance of the Ames Housing dataset. (**a**) SHAP. (**b**) Contextual influence

The PI plot shows to what extent the result could change by modifying the value of the feature, which is indicated by the length of the transparent bar given by the CI value. The CU value determines the length of the solid bar as a percentage of coverage of the transparent bar, so that $CU = 1$ will cover the transparent bar entirely, thereby indicating that the feature already has the best possible value.

15 Generation of Explanatory Content and Requirements for Social XAI

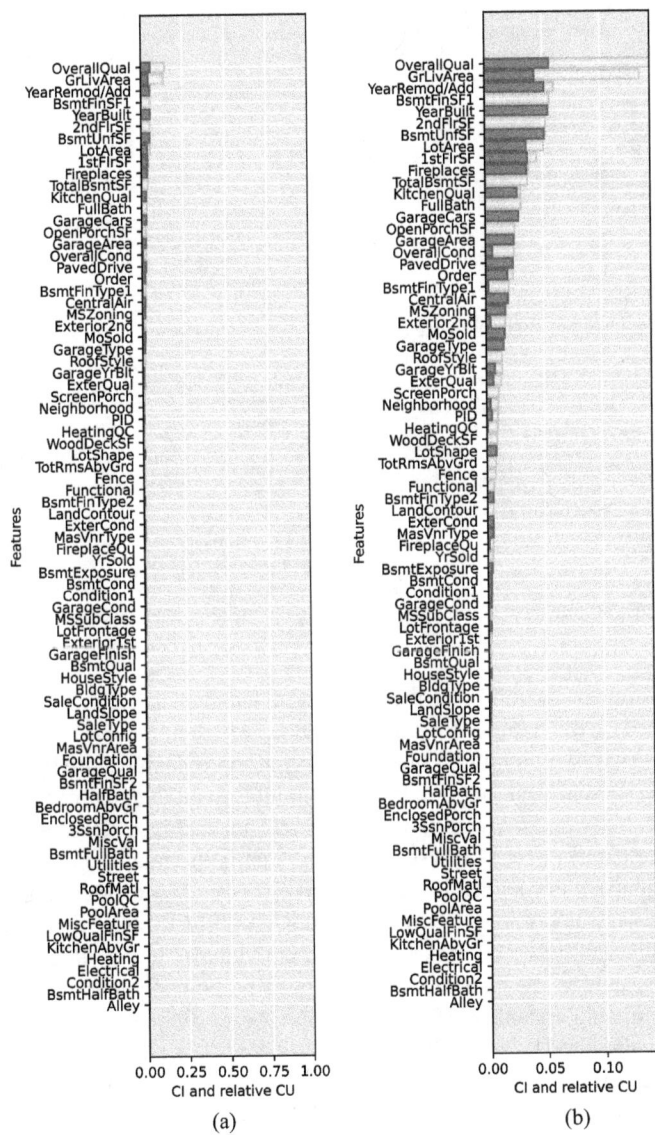

Fig. 15.2 Potential influence (PI) explanation that uses CIU's CI and CU values. Left plot uses default scale 0–1 for CI axis; right plot has CI axis scaled to the highest CI value. (**a**) Default, CI axis scale 0–1. (**b**) CI axis scaled to maximal CI value

$CU = 0$ indicates the worst possible value and results in a zero-length solid bar. A PI plot can be used to identify what modifications of individual features would modify the result the most in the negative or positive sense. Therefore, a PI plot gives more information to the explainee than an influence plot.

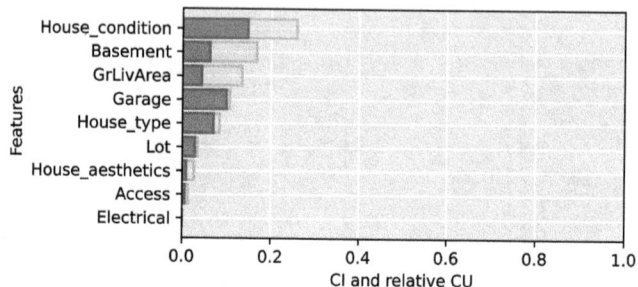

Fig. 15.3 Top-level potential influence (PI) plot for Ames house price

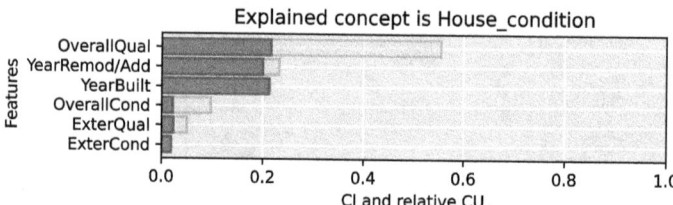

Fig. 15.4 Potential influence (PI) plot for explaining the value of "House condition"

It seems rather obvious that the number of features is a challenge for understanding these explanations for any explainee, whether they are an expert or a layperson. What is even more problematic is that many features are interdependent in this case, so analyzing them individually might give the explainee a misleading explanation. As we can see in the top-level PI plot in Fig. 15.3, it is actually the Intermediate Concept (IC) "House condition" that is the most important, when we use the vocabulary introduced in Sect. 14.3 to produce explanations using CIU. The feature "GrLivArea" is now only the third most important, rather than being nearly the most important when taking each feature individually in Fig. 15.2. A high-level explanation such as the one in Fig. 15.3 could be considered more correct and, above all, more understandable for the explainee because the vocabulary that is used can even be defined by the explainee and further refined using a partner model as described in Sect. 14.5.4. With CIU, it is possible to obtain further details about ICs if the explainee desires to do so. Figure 15.4 shows a PI plot for "House condition" that shows how "House condition" is defined, why it is important, and why it is considered to be slightly above average.

Different kinds of explanations might be preferred by different explainees, e.g., figures, tables, bar plots, natural language, …. Figure 15.5 shows a textual CIU explanation for the IC "Basement" as an alternative to the PI plot used for "House condition." The text generator of the used py-ciu uses a rather simple and generic template-based text generation method. It could be envisaged that the quality of textual explanations could be improved rather easily, especially when combined with recent LLM approaches.

The explained value is *SalePrice* with the value 443.51 (CU=0.43), which is **lower than average** utility.
Feature *Garage* has **very low importance** (CI=0.11) and has value(s) { 1, 82, 3, 2, 309, 5, 5,], which is **high utility** (CU=0.93).
Feature *Basement* has **very low importance** (CI=0.16) and has value(s) { 2, 5, 0, 5, 30, 2, 152, 0, 58, 0, 0.], which is **lower than average** utility (CU=0.38).
Feature *Lot* has **very low importance** (CI=0.03) and has value(s) { 5, 42, 1, 0, 3, 0, 4.], which is **high utility** (CU=0.81).
Feature *Access* has **very low importance** (CI=0.01) and has value(s) {23, 2.], which is **high utility** (CU=0.49).
Feature *House_type* has **very low importance** (CI=0.08) and has value(s) {2.055e+03 2.000e+00 0.000e+00 3.300e+01], which is **high utility** (CU=0.84).
Feature *House_aesthetics* has **very low importance** (CI=0.03) and has value(s) { 1, 1, 14, 15, 1.], which is **lower than average** utility (CU=0.33).
Feature *House_condition* has **low importance** (CI=0.26) and has value(s) {90, 5, 33, 2, 4, 4.], which is **higher than average** utility (CU=0.56).
Feature *Electrical* has **very low importance** (CI=0.00) and has value(s) 4.0, which is **low utility** (CU=0.00).
Feature *GrLivArea* has **very low importance** (CI=0.13) and has value(s) 446.0, which is **lower than average** utility (CU=0.32).

Fig. 15.5 Textual top-level explanation for Ames house price

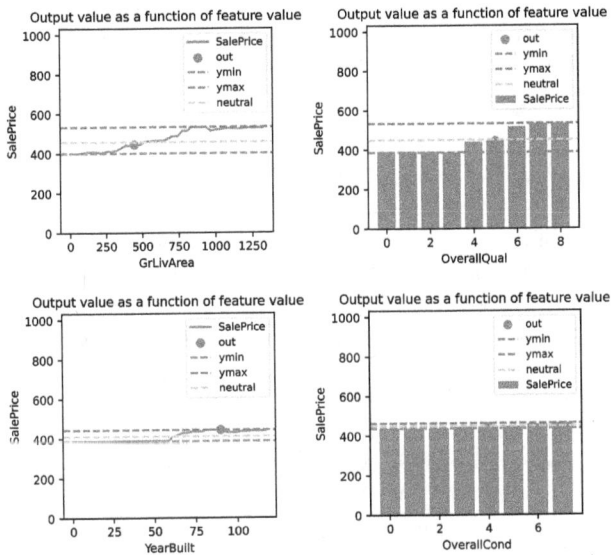

Fig. 15.6 Input–output plots for features "size of living area" (GrLivArea), "overall quality," "year built," and "overall condition"

Unlike many (or most/all) SOTA XAI methods, the CI, CU, and ϕ values can be illustrated for each feature individually with what we here call input-output (IO) plots.[2] IO plots show how the value of one output changes when modifying the value of the studied feature, while maintaining the other feature values at those of the studied instance (i.e., the house being studied by Främling 1996a. Figure 15.6 shows IO plots for two numerical and two categorical features, with the meaningful limits used by CIU indicated by colored lines. Interpreting such IO plots requires some understanding of the underlying principles of CIU, for which we refer the reader to, for example, Främling (2023, 2024). IO plots offer explainees a direct insight into how CI, CU, and contextual influence values are calculated, thereby indicating why a feature is important (or not) and what is the utility of the current value, that is, answering the questions "Why is this feature important (or not)?" and

---

[2] Similar plots with various variations are sometimes called Partial Dependence Plots (PDPs) (Friedman, 2001), Individual Conditional Expectation (ICE) (Goldstein et al., 2015), or Ceteris Paribus (CP) Biecek (2018) plots.

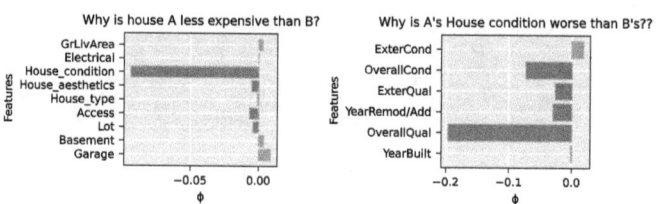

Fig. 15.7 Example of a contrastive explanation between two houses from the Ames dataset, with the top-level ICs on the left and the detailed contrastive explanation on the right. A's estimated price is $443508 and B's estimated price is $568001

"Why is this a good or bad value for this feature?" Natural language explanations as in Fig. 15.5 could also be used for answering such questions.

The examples of explanations given so far address "Why?," "Why not?" (which is usually an inverse variant of a "Why?" explanation), and "Why is this feature important (or not)?" mentioned in Sect. 15.3. The "What-if?" question is also answered at least to some extent by PI and IO plots. Answering "How to?"-questions would require solving a shortest-path or optimization task for which existing counterfactual methods could be used together with CIU, in which the 'potential influence' could help to identify the most useful feature values to modify. In order to answer "Why A and not B?" questions, so-called contrastive explanations can be used. The A is typically the instance being suggested and B is the proposed alternative. Influence plots of different kinds such as the one in Fig. 15.1 are contrastive by nature, even though B is then typically some kind of a 'reference instance' for methods such as SHAP. With CIU, B can be any existing or imaginary instance, including so-called counterfactual instances. Figure 15.7 shows an example of a contrastive explanation "Why A and not B?" for the Ames dataset. ICs can also be used for contrastive explanations, with the one in Fig. 15.7 showing the highest level of the used Ames vocabulary.

15.5 How Does This Chapter Inspire Further Directions of XAI?

Until now, we have focused on question-answer pairs that can be retrieved directly from the AI system, even though many XAI systems do not incorporate such aspects as certainty,[3] feature aggregation, or multimodality systematically and thereby simultaneously enabling dialogs. However, depending on the goal of the interaction

---

[3] "Certainty" should not be confounded with "class probability" or similar AI model outputs. An AI model will produce an output value even for input values that are entirely outside its competence, no matter if the system has been human-defined, (e.g., rules) or has been trained by ML.

between explainer and explainee, other characteristics may also be relevant to the explainee that may serve to complement or substitute for information.

For instance, the whole sXAI dialog might have been designed to provide the explainee with sufficient information to decide whether they want to follow the recommendation of the AI assessment. In such cases, more information than the actual feature is important to assess the quality of a system. This is easily explained when we think of a researcher who wants to understand whether an empirical analysis is trustworthy. Here, one would easily agree that it is not just necessary to look into the results of such an analysis, but one also needs information about the sample, model choices, measures, and so forth. Obviously, no AI system is perfect but depends on the quality of input.

When we think of Kary wanting to ask for an explanation of why he should buy car A and not car B, the problem becomes instantly clear: In order to assess the overall quality of the recommender system, he needs to know what cars have been in the pool of potential cars of the system in terms of content, regional and temporal dimensions:

- What is a car? (What is in the sample and what not, what are the boundaries?)
  - Are all cars ever built on earth in the dataset or are there some regional boundaries?
  - Also, are cars that will be released within the next month? What is the temporal dimension of the dataset?
  - Are there general definitions of what constitutes a car? For instance, are small vans fulfilling the requirement of "car?" Are Tuk Tuks considered a "car?"

- How are the features defined and measured?
  - For instance, how is "fuel consumption" measured? In a test stand or real traffic conditions? How is "design" measured?
  - How reliable is the information provided for each feature and each case in the sample?
  - Are features used that can be measured objectively, reliably, and validity? Are some features missing minimum bars for measures?

- Are some features missing?
  - For instance, did the system consider that Kary likes a certain type of seat cover? Is seat cover fabric in the dataset as a feature?
  - Are there missing data in the dataset that may impact the quality of the recommendation?

- Are some other aspects important for the explainee's trust and reliance?
  - How frequently is the dataset updated, and how are past connections unlearned and past items forgotten (e.g., are data on the VW Golf I in the dataset even if there are many successors?)
  - Did the AI programmer have hidden intentions (e.g., conflicts of interest as the preference is to sell as many cars of a certain type because the car builder

has invested in the AI? Or biases that lead the programmer to have some personal preferences that lead to some exclusion/inclusion choices of features or subjects in the dataset?
- Does the AI have some general knowledge of the world that may be needed (e.g., some upcoming safety regulations that make certain cars less preferable, some environmental regulations, imminent insolvency of a certain car manufacturer, after-sales service quality, and so forth.

The questions mentioned above are only examples, and one may consider even more, for example, when we consider that AI explanations may be given consecutively to the same person, who makes questions possible such as "Why does the recommendation differ from the one yesterday?" Note, however, that there needs to be a conscious choice about the boundaries of the sXAI system's knowledge: Should it be able to explain more than the outcome to ease the explainee's assessment? What knowledge exactly about the outside world, such as the institutions in the sense of norms, rules, and regulations of the past, current, and future outside world, is needed for AI systems to be trustworthy and explainable? The idea about the boundaries of the explanatory system and what it should be able to answer is important to sXAI. As soon as explanations are considered as a process and not just as a one-shot attempt (such as one picture or one sentence) and as soon as the explainee can lead or contribute actively to the process of the dialog, the programmer needs to make explicit choices about what questions must be answered, what questions would be answered, and what questions cannot be answered because they do not belong to this specific AI. The next chapter (Chap. 16) describes how explanations can be given using interactive dialogs.

Moreover, the programmer and the explainer of the XAI system must differentiate and assess the explainee's questions: Some questions may, for instance, signal that the explainee is searching for information that can substitute explainability when forming a trust. For instance, the explainee may come to realize that they lack the necessary domain knowledge or AI knowledge to be capable of understanding an explanation. Still, they start to substitute the lack of explainability of the system to them by assessing the trustworthiness of the system, by, for example, asking for the programmer's intentions. Ignoring the sign of the explainee's attempt to substitute an explanation by trust would lead to detrimental consequences concerning future explanations. Similarly, a good explainer would somehow try to assess whether the next question of an explainee is useful or not. A mismatch between the previous chunk and the following question may indicate misunderstanding or false beliefs of the explainee, too little common ground, or no interest in explanations. Thus, the set of relevant questions needs to be learned to indicate misunderstanding and the wrong explanatory content in the interaction.

15.6 Rapid Access to the Content of This Chapter

This chapter discusses what are the requirements and necessary capabilities of XAI methods in order to implement social XAI systems (sXAI). sXAI systems should be able to explain their decisions in ways that are understandable and **actionable** for explainees. The goal is that it should be possible for an explainee to have a similar dialog as with a human explainer, that is, at least be able to ask similar questions and get appropriate answers. An sXAI system should also be capable of adapting to the context and the explainee regarding the vocabulary, modality, level of detail, and so forth. This chapter attempts to provide a list of typical questions that an explainee might want to ask during an explanatory dialog with an sXAI system.

In practice, current state-of-the-art XAI methods answer rather few of those questions. Furthermore, it is not always clear whether the XAI output actually provides the user-expected answer, and this might lead to a misunderstanding of the explanation by the explainee. For instance, the use of what we call *feature influence* values that are produced by well-known XAI methods such as SHAP and LIME might be misleading if they are understood as expressing *feature importance*. Furthermore, SHAP and LIME create a linear surrogate model of the underlying AI system for the instance to be explained, and this prevents the exposition of even simple relations such as the logical OR and AND relations.

Counterfactual explanations are an alternative to importance- or influence-based explanations. A counterfactual explanation typically answers "What-if?" questions, rather than answering "Why?" or "Why not?" questions. State-of-the-art counterfactual XAI methods are mostly applicable to classification tasks, in which they provide information only on what would happen if certain features changed enough to shift the instance from one class to another. The lack of generalizability and the difficulty of answering key questions limits the applicability of counterfactual methods to a broader set of use cases.

State-of-the-art rule-based methods for XAI, such as decision trees, provide sets of rules that can explain an instance's classification. These rules can be used to answer the "Why?" question and provide indirect answers to "Why not?" or "What-if?" questions. However, the presentation of rules is often too formal and difficult to translate into other modalities (e.g., visual explanations). Additionally, the importance of individual rules can be challenging to convey, because rule-based systems might not have a clear way to assess the contribution of different features in a way that is meaningful to the end user.

Table 15.1 assesses these categories of state-of-the-art methods, as well as for the little known Contextual Importance and Utility (CIU) XAI method. CIU makes a separation between feature importance and feature influence, while taking into consideration the notion of feature value utility. This separation of metrics makes it possible to provide answers to "Why?," "Why not?," "What-if?," and other questions within a single mathematical framework, thereby ensuring the consistency between different kinds of explanations and modalities. Furthermore, CIU's intermediate concepts make it possible to use any explanation vocabulary and divide the explanations into different levels of detail, while taking feature dependencies into consideration.

In the operationalization section, we use the well-known Ames Housing dataset with CIU as an illustrative example. With 80 input features that have numerous dependencies, analyzing features in isolation might lead to misleading explanations. For example, the intermediate concept "House condition" is a key factor in determining the house price, whereas individual features such as "Size of the ground living area" might seem important when considered separately but are less so in a holistic explanation.

Different explainees might prefer different types of explanations. Examples of so-called *potential influence* (PI) plots, textual explanations, influence plots, and contrastive explanations produced using CIU illustrate how the same basic explanation can be presented in different ways. For instance, when explaining a car recommendation to a buyer, it is important to provide not just a feature-based explanation but also contextual information about the dataset used, such as the regional and temporal scope of the data. The explainee might also want to know about the reliability of the data and whether important features were considered (e.g., personal preferences such as seat cover fabric). The chapter also emphasizes the importance of dialog in social XAI. Rather than providing static answers, sXAI systems should be capable of engaging in an ongoing dialog with the explainee, refining their explanations based on feedback and adjusting their answers based on the user's specific concerns and preferences.

In addition to feature importance, the trustworthiness of the AI system itself can be a significant factor. Factors such as how frequently the dataset is updated, the presence of biases, or hidden intentions from the AI programmers (such as conflicts of interest) can affect how much an explainee trusts the AI's recommendation. We call for more flexible and expressive methods that can adapt to different explainees' needs, as well as improvements in generating textual explanations through methods such as large language models (LLMs).

Acknowledgments We thank Tim Miller for his valuable perspective and helpful comments on an earlier version of this chapter.

Kary Främling's work has been partially supported by the Wallenberg AI, Autonomous Systems and Software Program (WASP) funded by the Knut and Alice Wallenberg Foundation.

This work was funded by the Deutsche Forschungsgemeinschaft (DFG, German Research Foundation): TRR 318/1 2021 – 438445824.

References

Andrews, R., Diederich, J., & Tickle, A.B. (1995). Survey and critique of techniques for extracting rules from trained artificial neural networks. *Knowledge-Based Systems, 8*(6), 373–389. https://doi.org/10.1016/0950-7051(96)81920-4.

Anjomshoae, S., Najjar, A., Calvaresi, D., & Främling, K. (2019). Explainable agents and robots: Results from a systematic literature review. In *Proceedings of the 18th International Conference on Autonomous Agents and MultiAgent Systems*. Montreal, QC, Canada: IFAAMAS (pp. 1078–1088)

Barredo, A., Natalia Díaz-Rodríguez, A., Del Ser, J., Bennetot, A., Tabik, S., Barbado, A., Garcia, S., Gil-Lopez, S., Molina, D., Benjamins, R., Chatila, R., & Herrera, F. (2020). Explainable Artificial Intelligence (XAI): Concepts, taxonomies, opportunities and challenges toward responsible AI. *Information Fusion, 58*, 82–115. https://doi.org/10.1016/j.inffus.2019.12.012.

Biecek, P. (2018). DALEX: Explainers for complex predictive models in R. *Journal of Machine Learning Research, 19*(1), 3245–3249.

Breiman, L. (2001). Random forests. *Machine Learning, 45*(1), 5–32. https://doi.org/10.1023/A:1010933404324

Chefer, H., Gur, S., & Wolf, L. (2021). Transformer interpretability beyond attention visualization. In *Proceedings of the IEEE/CVF Conference on Computer Vision and Pattern Recognition (CVPR)*. Nashville, TN, USA (pp. 782–791). IEEE. https://doi.org/10.1109/CVPR46437.2021.00084.

Doshi-Velez, F., & Kim, B. (2017). *Towards a rigorous science of interpretable machine learning.* https://doi.org/10.48550/arXiv.1702.08608, arXiv: 1702.08608 [stat.ML].

Dyer, J. S. (2005). MAUT — Multiattribute utility theory. In *Multiple criteria decision analysis: State of the art surveys* (pp. 265–292). Springer. https://doi.org/10.1007/0-387-23081-5_7.

Främling, K. (1996a). Explaining results of neural networks by contextual importance and utility. In *Rules and Networks: Proceedings of the Rule Extraction from Trained Artificial Neural Networks Workshop (AISB'96)*. Brighton, UK.

Främling, K. (1996b). Modélisation et apprentissage des préférences par réseaux de neurones pour l'aide à la décision multicritère". PhD thesis. INSA de Lyon. https://tel.archives-ouvertes.fr/tel-00825854.

Främling, K. (2020). Decision theory meets explainable AI. In *Explainable, Transparent Autonomous Agents and Multi-Agent Systems: Second International Workshop, EXTRAAMAS 2020, Auckland, New Zealand, May 9–13, 2020, Revised Selected Papers* (pp. 57–74). Springer. https://doi.org/10.1007/978-3-030-51924-7_4.

Främling, K. (2022a). Contextual importance and utility: A theoretical foundation. In *AI 2022: Proceedings of the 34th Australasian Joint Conference on Artificial Intelligence* (pp. 117–128). Springer. https://doi.org/10.1007/978-3-030-97546-3_10.

Främling, K. (2022b). Contextual importance and utility: A theoretical foundation. In *AI 2021: Advances in Artificial Intelligence* (pp. 117–128). Springer International. https://doi.org/10.1007/978-3-030-97546-3_10.

Främling, K. (2023). Counterfactual, contrastive, and hierarchical explanations with contextual importance and utility. In *Explainable and Transparent AI and Multi-Agent Systems: 5th International Workshop, EXTRAAMAS 2023* (pp. 180–184). Springer. https://doi.org/10.1007/978-3-031-40878-6_16.

Främling, K. (2024). *Contextual importance and utility in python: New functionality and insights with the py-ciu package.* https://arxiv.org/abs/2408.09957, arXiv: 2408.09957 [cs.AI].

Friedman, J. H. (2001). Greedy function approximation: A gradient boosting machine. *Annals of Statistics, 29*(5), 1189–1232. https://doi.org/10.1214/aos/1013203451.

Goldstein, A., Kapelner, A., Bleich, J., Pitkin, E. (2015). Peeking inside the black box: Visualizing statistical learning with plots of individual conditional expectation. *Journal of Computational and Graphical Statistics, 24*(1), 44–65. https://doi.org/10.1080/10618600.2014.907095.

Guidotti, R., Monreale, A., Ruggieri, S., Pedreschi, D., Turini, F., & Giannotti, F. (2018a). *Local rule-based explanations of black box decision systems.* https://doi.org/10.48550/arXiv.1805.10820, arXiv: 1805.10820 [stat.ML].

Guidotti, R., Monreale, A., Ruggieri, S., Turini, F., Giannotti, F., & Pedreschi, D. (2018b). A survey of methods for explaining black box models. *ACM Computing Surveys (CSUR), 51*(5), 93. https://doi.org/10.1145/3236009.

Gunning, D., & Aha, D. (2019). DARPA's explainable artificial intelligence (XAI) program. *AI Magazine, 40*(2), 44–58. https://doi.org/10.1609/aimag.v40i2.2850.

Jullum, M., Redelmeier, A., & Aas, K. (2021). *groupShapley: Efficient prediction explanation with Shapley values for feature groups*. https://doi.org/10.48550/arXiv.2106.12228, arXiv: 2106.12228 [stat.ML].

Lim, B. Y., & Dey, A. K. (2009). Assessing demand for intelligibility in context-aware applications. In *Proceedings of the 11th International Conference on Ubiquitous Computing* (pp. 195–204). Association for Computing Machinery. https://doi.org/10.1145/1620545.1620576.

Liu, N., Zhang, N., Wan, K., Shao, L., & Han, J. (2021). Visual saliency transformer. In *Proceedings of the IEEE/CVF International Conference on Computer Vision (ICCV)* (pp. 4722–4732). IEEE. https://doi.org/10.1109/ICCV48922.2021.00468.

Lundberg, S. M., & Lee, S.-I. (2017). A unified approach to interpreting model predictions. In *NIPS'17: Proceedings of the 31st International Conference on Neural Information Processing Systems* (pp. 4768–4777). Curran Associates.

Miller, T. (2019). Explanation in artificial intelligence: Insights from the social sciences. *Artificial Intelligence, 267*, 1–38. https://doi.org/10.1016/j.artint.2018.07.007.

Patil, M., & Främling, K. (2023). Do intermediate feature coalitions aid explainability of black-box models? In *Explainable Artificial Intelligence: First World Conference, xAI 2023* (pp. 115–130). Springer. https://doi.org/10.1007/978-3-031-44064-9_7.

Quinlan, J. R. (1993). *C4.5: Programs for machine learning*. Morgan Kaufmann.

Ribeiro, M. T., Singh, S., & Guestrin, C. (2016). "Why should I trust you?" Explaining the predictions of any classifier. In *Proceedings of the 22nd ACM SIGKDD International Conference on Knowledge Discovery and Data Mining* (pp. 1135–1144). ACM. https://doi.org/10.1145/2939672.2939778.

Ribeiro, M. T., Singh, S., & Guestrin, C. (2018). Anchors: High-precision model-agnostic explanations. In *Proceedings of the Thirty-Second AAAI Conference on Artificial Intelligence* (pp. 1527–1535). AAAI.

Saaty, T. L. (1980). *The analytic hierarchy process: Planning, priority setting, resource allocation*. McGraw Hill Higher Education.

Štrumbelj, E., & Kononenko, I. (2014). Explaining prediction models and individual predictions with feature contributions. *Knowledge and Information Systems, 41*(3), 647–665. https://doi.org/10.1007/s10115-013-0679-x.

Vaswani, A., Shazeer, N., Parmar, N., Uszkoreit, J., Jones, L., Gomez, A. N., Kaiser, Ł., & Polosukhin, I. (2017). Attention is all you need. In *NIPS'17: Proceedings of the 31st International Conference on Neural Information Processing Systems* (pp. 6000–6010). Curran Associates.

Verma, S., Dickerson, J. P., & Hines, K. (2020). Counterfactual explanations for machine learning: A review. *ACM Computing Surveys, 56*(12), 207–213. https://doi.org/10.1145/3677119.

Wachter, S., Mittelstadt, B., Russell, C. (2018). Counterfactual explanations without opening the black box: Automated decisions and the GDPR. *Harvard Journal of Law and Technology, 31*(2), 841–887. https://doi.org/10.2139/ssrn.3063289.

Open Access This chapter is licensed under the terms of the Creative Commons Attribution 4.0 International License (http://creativecommons.org/licenses/by/4.0/), which permits use, sharing, adaptation, distribution and reproduction in any medium or format, as long as you give appropriate credit to the original author(s) and the source, provide a link to the Creative Commons license and indicate if changes were made.

The images or other third party material in this chapter are included in the chapter's Creative Commons license, unless indicated otherwise in a credit line to the material. If material is not included in the chapter's Creative Commons license and your intended use is not permitted by statutory regulation or exceeds the permitted use, you will need to obtain permission directly from the copyright holder.

Chapter 16
Exploration of Explaining Content

Kary Främling, Britta Wrede, and Kirsten Thommes

Abstract This chapter examines key challenges and potential improvements in the areas of user interaction and dynamic explanations. It highlights the need for XAI systems to address context factors beyond their predefined scope, it points to the potential need to cocreate new concepts that are adapted to particular explainees, and it provides a clear overview of the XAI system's underlying knowledge structure and interaction steps. Emphasis is placed on mixed-initiative interaction in which the system can lead or respond based on the context and the explainee's reactions while asserting the importance of maintaining coherence across consecutive explanations. These advances aim to make XAI systems more flexible, interactive, and user-centric. An operationalization section outlines how such social XAI systems could be implemented based on the XAI capabilities provided by the Contextual Importance and Utility XAI method described in the previous chapter.

16.1 How Does This Chapter Relate to XAI?

An explanation is a social interaction that can be initiated by the AI system (explainer) to explain or justify a planned or taken action or decision, or it can be initiated by the human user (explainee) who poses an initial question to the AI

K. Främling (✉)
Department of Computing Science, Umeå University, Umeå, Sweden

Department of Industrial Engineering and Management, Aalto University, Espoo, Finland
e-mail: kary.framling@umu.se

B. Wrede
Medical School OWL, Bielefeld University, Bielefeld, Germany
e-mail: bwrede@techfak.uni-bielefeld.de

K. Thommes
Faculty of Business Administration and Economics, Paderborn University, Paderborn, Germany
e-mail: kirsten.thommes@uni-paderborn.de

system. Overall, an explanation process requires that both partners, the explainer and the explainee, are able to take the initiative to ask for or provide information, thus calling for a mixed-initiative approach. In addition to the organization of the interaction, the limited capacity of humans to incorporate new information imposes natural constraints on the explainer who has to compromise between the amount of information to include and the length of the explananda to present to the explainee. As we shall show below, it is also crucial for the explananda to include some leads or clues for the explainee about what additional information can be asked for and how to obtain it. This is extraordinarily important, because explanations of AI decisions or processes are likely to contain many concepts that are new to the explainee and thus require special attention. Consequently, it might well be that the explainee does not understand or agree with the presented explanation, thereby requiring the explainer to elaborate by, for example, using a different modality, vocabulary, or other modification that could be expected to give the explainee a better understanding. It should be noted that the interaction might end with anything ranging from a total agreement and understanding to a total disagreement and misunderstanding. Whereas the former is, of course, the goal of the AI explainer it should nevertheless have a concept for how to deal with the latter, for example, by proactively coming back to a controversial topic in a follow-up interaction or at least by identifying possible explanatory moves that may impede understanding. Thus, the explainer should provide the explainee with the best possible means to understand the explainer's reasoning and reasons.

16.2 State of the Art of Exploration Strategies

There are many different kinds of explanation strategies and ways to categorize them. For some very useful definitions and distinctions, see Dwivedi et al. (2023). However, for the purpose of this chapter and this book, we will introduce a distinction along the lines of static versus dynamic explanation strategies as well as the extent of the content (solely AI or the social context). First, it is useful to distinguish between static and potentially dynamic explanation strategies. Static explanation strategies are very common. The programmer adds one explanation for the explainee to enable a better understanding of the output. Mostly, these outputs try to address directly the explanandum. Few of these explanatory strategies consider more than the explanandum (e.g., extent to the social context). On the other hand, a dynamic XAI system allows for interaction in dynamic explanation strategies (e.g., incremental explanations, different modalities, and patterned communication structures).

Many static attempts to explain AI are derived from human-to-human explanations, even though they are usually boiled down to the core element of explanations. In a recent paper, Morrison et al. (2023) conducted a study that observed how humans explain patterns in pictures to each other and then used human explanation strategies as an XAI approach. The main task in their study was to detect damages in buildings. In the first part of the study, humans were observed to use mainly six different explanatory approaches when explaining to others: (a) constructing a causal argument, (b) contrasting, (c) highlighting, (d) using explanations based on impact, (e) explaining reasons for lack of confidence in their assessment, and (f) making relative comparisons. Constructing a causal argument would, for instance, mean that the human engages in sense-making of structures in the picture, for example, by saying that the roof of a house looks like it has been damaged by a hurricane (even though the reason for the observed damage is unknown and not part of the explanatory challenge). In some sense, this strategy uses secondary knowledge, which is not entailed in the picture itself and adds this to the explanation. Contrasting explanatory strategies specifically contrast pre- and post-images. This explanation strategy is close to explaining with counterfactuals in XAI, even though the counterfactuals in XAI can be synthetic cases. The strategies of highlighting important parts of the picture or explanations based on impact are close to saliency map explanations for image-related explanations. Such explanations do not explain the underlying reasons for an AI output but rather highlights the areas (in image data) or features (in text or tab data) that influence the output the most. Finally, Morrison et al. (2023) propose a strategy that mixes contrastive explanations within the unit (e.g., by stating that House A shows signs of a disaster while House B does not) with a highlighting of the differences.

Many strategies of human-to-human explanations, as found by Morrison et al. (2023), are also used in the existing literature. For instance, in their review of the value of XAI compared to AI, Schemmer et al. (2022) found mostly feature importance methods such as LIME or human assessment of feature importance but also counterfactuals and example-based strategies as in highlighting or confidence values as explanations. Interestingly, Schemmer et al. (2022) found in their review that most XAI explanation strategies do not outperform AI without any explanation regarding the overall performance of the human–AI duo. In Waa et al. (2021), only rule-based or example-based strategies make an exception. Similarly, also Morrison et al. (2023) found that most of their explanation strategies derived from human-to-human explanations do not result in high levels of user reliance. Notably, causal sense-making—the first and most used strategy of human-to-human explanations—outperforms other strategies; however, only if the AI advice is wrong. Here, causal reasoning results in more skeptical human users and more overall correct rejections of advice. Advice rejecting when the AI advice is wrong is one of the ends of XAI. However, improving users' reliance when the advice is right is another end, and this might require a different solution and might be difficult to adapt from human-to-human explanatory strategies.

Whereas the explanatory strategies mentioned above all answer the question of how to explain, other researchers have focused on other aspects of explanations, e.g., what to explain. Based on a systematization by Schoonderwoerd et al. (2021), Lammert et al. (2024) compared fully transparent explanations of small models with guided explanations in which only the most important features are explained. Moreover, they contrasted these model-based explanation strategies with an explanation strategy that purposely addresses the context and not the AI model (the explainee's specific emotional situation). They found that neither addressing solely the context nor fully transparent explanations are useful strategies. On the contrary, guided explanations, highlighting the most important aspects, are evaluated best in terms of user reliance, implying that many users may experience information overload when faced with too much information at once.

Both findings – avoiding too much information at once and causal reasoning – suggest that (a) interactive strategies may result in better XAI-human interaction, which is more user-friendly, and (b) users must make sense of information by learning rules or adding causality to explanations.

The trade-off between avoiding information overload in humans and allowing transparency has already been addressed frequently in human–XAI research. Research in cognitive psychology suggests that providing comprehensive and transparent information may overwhelm individuals receiving the explanation. This phenomenon extends to situations in which humans are presented with excessive options (Cramer et al., 2008). Previous studies have illustrated that cognitive overload can affect users' confidence (Hudon et al., 2021) and trust in the system (Schmidt et al., 2020), thereby risking their reliance on it. In an online experimental investigation, You et al. (2022) explored the impact of varying levels of transparency on advice acceptance. The findings indicate that individuals exposed to detailed representations are less inclined to heed advice than those presented with either no representation or an aggregated one. These problems have been discussed for some time—though, not related to AI or XAI but related to human–machine interaction. In a very early paper, Benbasat and Taylor (1982) discussed the state of the art that has not changed fundamentally since then. First, the relation between information load and information processing follows an inverted U-shape, implying that neither too little nor too much information at once is optimal for information processing. The optimum lies in between. One of the solutions proposed is a hierarchical organization of information, called information cascading, in which humans receive some aggregated top-level data first and can proceed to investigate further if they wish.

The very early literature on information systems, as reviewed by Benbasat and Taylor (1982), reveals more aspects that are highly relevant to social XAI (sXAI): First, they explain that decisive and also hierarchical information system designs may be less suited if there is high environmental uncertainty or complexity. These characteristics are considered in sXAI, because acknowledging the social context of a human-XAI interaction eventually results in higher complexity and uncertainty about the system and the context in which it is applied. Second, they also stress that human characteristics may be important in matching information strategy to decision situations, systems, and context. In particular, they also stress that human characteristics should be taken into account by a system, and among others, they report a distinction between systematic cognitive types and intuitive types, resulting in different needs for the presentation of information. Similarly, contemporary research suggests that the human perception of AI in terms of intuitive versus analytical tasks Lebedeva et al. (2023) matters for the preferred interaction.

Likewise, Benbasat and Taylor (1982) highlight that individual characteristics may affect how humans explore information. In particular, they assume that personality and surface-level characteristics such as gender and age may affect how humans want to acquire information from a system. Similarly, recent XAI approaches show that the current situation of humans may affect how they approach information Thommes et al. (2024). For instance, individuals with very low arousal may be reluctant to start any exploration concerning an AI system, whereas individuals with high arousal will be interested in getting more information. If one takes individual static or dynamic differences into account, the sXAI system would be required first to form an inner model about the explainee and the context before starting an appropriate exploration of the explanatory content, as explained in Chap. 14.

16.3 Context-Sensitive Exploration

As discussed above, context plays an important role in what users need to have explained and how it should be explained. Yet, while the context determines the goals of a human–AI interaction, these goals are often presupposed independently of the context as "users' needs" (Alpsancar et al., 2024, p. 3015). For example, Sanneman and Shah, 2022 propose that a user's informational needs can be determined by a formal analysis of the task at hand such as goal-directed task analysis (GDTA) Endsley, 2011. Thus, it can be seen that there is a considerable gap in the XAI literature when it comes to the role that context plays with respect to the goals of an explanation and therefore its effect on the explanation itself. How can this context-goal relation be incorporated into a meaningful context-sensitive exploration?

It is important to distinguish between the macro-context, which may encompass the interaction situation, the domain, the roles, and so forth, and the micro-context, which consists of the interaction history and elements directly related to the decision task, which is supported by the XAI system. The macro-context contains many static factors that cannot be changed during the explanation situation. For example, the institutional context of the role of the XAI system will remain fixed with the AI being either an optional information source or a required decision support system whose arguments and explanations need to be reported and taken into account. It is, therefore, important for the AI system to have knowledge about such fixed context factors. While some of these context factors, such as the role and the requirement for how to take the AI's decision into account, may be highly relevant for the explainee and should be known a priori to the explanation, other macro-context factors such as on what data the AI system has been trained or what kind of AI model it implements may or may not become relevant during the explanation process. In contrast, the micro-context is more dynamic and relates to the prior interaction between the explainer and the explainee and also contains knowledge related to the decision task. This context may become highly relevant during the explanation. In order to enable context-sensitive exploration, an XAI system needs not only a representation of factors pertaining to the micro- and macro-context but also information about the (a priori) relevance of each of these for the explanation.

Based on such a context representation, a context-sensitive exploration strategy can be derived and negotiated with the explainee. One heuristic that should be kept in mind pertains to the balancing between the explanation of the AI's decision and the differently relevant context factors. The context factors with a priori relevance need to be provided before anything else. The other context factors may become relevant during the further explanation process.

While we propose an interactive explanation process enabling the explainee to take an active part by asking questions and steering the interaction toward those aspects they deem relevant, we are also aware that an explanation requires a fixed starting point. As observed by Fisher et al., 2022, in human–human interaction, it is common for the explainer to take the initial lead and starts with an explanation of what they believe is the explanandum. After this initial, potentially rather monological phase Fisher et al., 2022, the explainee asks questions pertaining to this initial explanation and initiates an interaction in which a common ground Clark and Brennan, 1991 and an interaction history are built. This interaction history then serves as a (dynamic) context that allows the XAI system to support context-sensitive exploration. For example, in Herbold et al. (2024), it is argued that why-questions of the form "why P?" are often meant in a contrastive way: "why P rather than Q?" referring to a previously mentioned item Q. In their approach, they propose to make use of the interaction history to determine Q and to provide an answer that takes the contrast of the currently focused item P to the previous item Q into account. In this phase, the explainer and the explainee continue to build a common ground. However, the system needs to be capable to switch to other explananda in order to satisfy the explainee's needs for explanation. More specifically, the sXAI system should not be stuck in a clarification attempt. Wan et al., 2023 argue that overcoming a gap between the explainee's and the explainer's mental model may be too resource intensive for the explainee. This is in line with Clark and Brennan, 1991, according to whom grounding is not an absolute process requiring complete understanding. Rather, its goal is to provide evidence that supports the 'belief that the partners have understood what the contributor meant to a criterion sufficient for current purposes.' This may entail to shift the attention to another relevant component Wan et al., 2023.

Thus, it is also important for the explaining system to expect questions that seem unrelated to the explanandum but rather target context factors. This is a clear extension to the questions that are currently considered (Sokol & Flach, 2021).

16.4 Operationalization

One of the first AI systems to implement an exploration of explanatory content is presumably the MYCIN system (Shortliffe, 1976). MYCIN was an early expert system developed in the 1970's at Stanford University to help physicians diagnose and recommend treatments for bacterial infections, particularly blood infections and meningitis. It is considered to be one of the most significant applications of artificial intelligence in medicine. MYCIN interacted with users (physicians) through a series of questions, obtaining relevant patient information such as symptoms, test results, and patient history. Based on the input, it provided recommendations for antibiotic therapy, including dosages and potential side effects. MYCIN also included an explanation system that implemented a question-answering mechanism based on a simple natural language processing (NLP) engine.

However, MYCIN's explanation capabilities were tightly coupled with the explicit rules in the underlying AI system, so the explanation capabilities were model-specific and the underlying rule base was not truly a black-box system. However, it remains interesting to draw a parallel with the recent development of large language models (LLM) and how they are queried in systems such as ChatGPT through a question-answering mechanism as in MYCIN. In the case of ChatGPT, the LLM is a black box to which the dialog management system provides a query produced from the earlier interaction, based on which the LLM provides a textual output.[1] It is even possible to ask the LLM to explain its reasoning, in case it's not already included in the answer that does *not* make the LLM explainable in the XAI sense. An XAI analysis would reveal which parts of the LLM input were the most important for producing the LLM's output at every step for building the entire answer. Therefore, LLMs are not XAI methods. However, the question-answering mechanism and the natural-language processing capabilities of LLMs and systems such as ChatGPT could be powerful tools for developing interactive sXAI systems that enable a gradual exploration of explanatory content. In practice, that currently remains a topic of ongoing and future research.

At present, the exploration of explaining content is constrained by the limited capabilities of XAI systems to generate explanatory content, as described in Chap. 15. At least the following capabilities could be considered as being mandatory:

- Avoid presenting too much information by supporting the use of 'intermediate concepts,' rather than using raw input features directly, whose number can be overwhelming and whose signification may not be clear to the explainee.
- Adapt the vocabulary used, the modality, and the type of explanation according to a partner model of the explainee.
- Keep a model of the history of interaction in order to enable an intelligible dialog that allows the explainee to navigate through the different aspects and levels of explanation.
- Implement a dialog user interface that presents enough (but not too much) information to provide the explainee with salient information that allows the explainee to continue exploration.
- Provide information to the explainee on how to go further in the exploration process. This could include presenting the current explanation with a different modality, asking a new kind of question or getting a detailed explanation about an intermediate concept.

---

[1] The output can also be an image, music, video or other kinds of media but the interaction is still usually done in natural language.

Intermediate concepts (IC), the questions that are possible to ask in different explanatory moves, the kinds of explanations that are available, and so forth can be modeled using semantic nets (Sowa, 1991) or knowledge graphs (KG) as explained in Sect. 14.5. In the latter, ICs, questions, and so forth are the nodes of the graph, and the possible transitions between them are the edges. The process of exploration can then be modeled by memorizing what nodes and edges of the graph have been visited and in what order. To navigate a KG, one typically starts at a given node (the starting concept) and explores the connected edges (relationships) to reach other nodes (related concepts). This traversal can be guided by specific goals, which in our case are defined by the explainee's preferences and need for information. Such information about the explainee's preferences can then be used to initiate or augment a partner model with clues such as "prefers contrastive explanations," "prefers counterfactual explanations," "prefers natural language explanations," and so forth that can be stored by adjusting edge weights of the KG, together with other relevant statistics.

If we continue with the Ames housing example presented in Sects. 14.5 and 15.4, we can combine the KG presented in Sect. 14.5 with the different kinds of exlpananda presented in Sect. 15.4 in order to allow for an explanatory dialog as an interactive exploration. Figure 16.1 illustrates how an explainee might navigate through a KG of possible explananda, in which the starting point is a PI plot that answers the question "Why is this house expensive?" using the highest abstraction level IC of the vocabulary used. As described in Chap. 15, the vocabulary to use can be selected and adapted according to the explainee and to the explanation context. The explainee can then ask to receive more details about some parts of the explanans, in this case "House condition" and "Basement." The explainee can also choose between the available modalities, with a PI plot being used for "House condition" and a textual explanation for "Basement" in this example. Finally, in

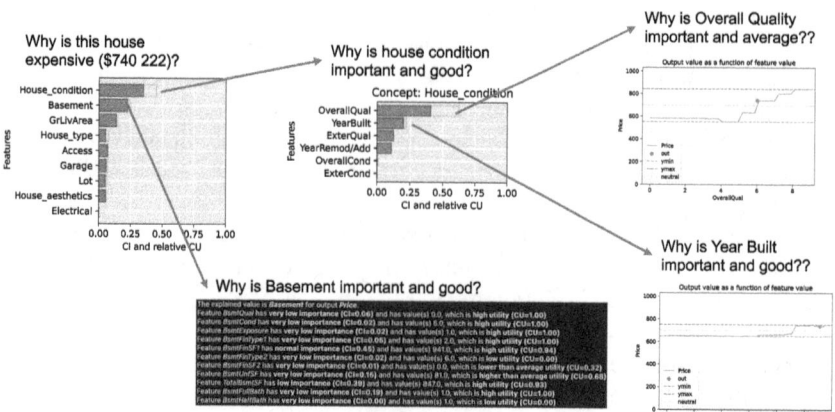

Fig. 16.1 Hierarchical dialog for interactive and incremental exploration of the different levels, types, and modalities that are available for explaining the estimated price of a house in Ames

order to analyze how different features affect the result individually, IO plots are used for the features "Overall quality" and "Year built." IO plots are good for gaining a deeper understanding of CIU calculations and the corresponding explanations, but they require some background knowledge about CIU in order to be usable. Therefore, some kind of textual explanation as for "Basement" might be more appropriate.

The actual graph of possible explanatory moves would presumably have tens or hundreds of possible nodes even, for example, vocabulary and the different modalities that would be available in this case. In addition to these, there's presumably a similar number of additional edges when considering the possibility of contrastive, counterfactual, and so forth explanations that might be useful. Furthermore, in order to enable necessary insight that goes beyond the XAI content, the explainee might also want to know how different features are defined, measured, and so forth. A more extensive list with imaginable questions by the explainee can be found in Sect. 15.3.

With such an overwhelming number of possible explanation moves being available to the explainee, it should be rather clear why partner models are necessary in order to make the explanatory dialog efficient for the explainee. A history of interaction can be used to train the partner model over time in order to achieve this, as described in Chap. 17.

16.5 How Does This Chapter Inspire Further Directions of XAI?

As discussed above, current XAI systems – as most dialog systems that are not LLM-based chat systems – tend to be very restricted regarding *what* to ask and *how* to ask as they provide a very limited interface. However, XAI systems are becoming more and more interactive, and they offer more than just one XAI method, thus providing a rich and highly structured knowledge base as a well as an accessible source for explanations. On the other hand, LLMs offer a highly sophisticated and adaptive way of multimodal communication, although they themselves generally remain a black box despite their ability to provide explanations that look plausible. However, as discussed above, because their explanations do not relate explicitly to their internal architecture or representations, they do not really explain the outcome they present and are, thus, not an XAI approach. Yet, the backpack models Hewitt et al., 2023 provide an interesting approach to achieve explainability in LLMs as well, but their potential capabilities and impact have only just started to be explored. It is conceivable that LLMs can play a role in XAI when using them as a subprocess or extending the model with an XAI knowledge graph or similar. These technologies may enable further progress in some of the following issues:

Switch Focus to Context Factors Users of XAI may have very strong ideas regarding what the XAI system should explain to them. They may quite often want to switch the focus of the explanation, or the explanandum. While this is already possible in some interactive XAI approaches, it still currently remains impossible to ask questions outside the defined task space of the AI model. Yet, users do have questions regarding, for example, context factors such as the data used for training, or the roles of the interaction partners involved. This requires a representation that distinguishes between important and less important context factors and can, on the other hand, track the content of the interaction in order to keep an accessible history.

Co-construct Intermediate Concepts Current XAI systems can refer only to the concepts that are known a priori. However, when interacting and especially when talking about complex or abstract issues, it is important to be able to derive a new concept out of one or several existing ones. So far, this is not yet possible. But especially with a structured knowledge base, it should be possible to generate a new concept based on two previously known ones in an interaction with the explainee. Such a capability would be a qualitative step forward toward more flexible explanations.

Provide an Overview of the Knowledge Structure and Possible Explanation Moves of the XAI In general, interactive systems should provide an overview of the interaction steps they are capable of and of which steps can be taken in the next phase. This is especially true for explaining systems in which users often don't know what options are available. This also pertains to the underlying knowledge structure in terms of what information is actually available.

Mixed Initiative Interaction As discussed above, it may be necessary for the sXAI system to be the leader of the interaction, for example, by providing an initial overarching explanation at the beginning. Also, upon detection of misconceptions, it should be capable of proactively initiating a clarification routine or of switching to a previous interaction topic where a misunderstanding has been detected. Yet, the system should also be capable to switch to a more reactive behavior, answering questions of the explainee and even stimulating users' active exploration behavior.

Consecutive Explanations While it is important to break up the explaining content into smaller units, it is still necessary to maintain coherence and to build up a more complex explanation across different interactions. This may require the system to navigate a hierarchical or otherwise structured representation, starting with a rather abstract explanation and proceeding toward more concrete explanations.

16.6 Rapid Access to the Content of This Chapter

This chapter analyzes why it is important to allow explainees to explore explanations from various angles, different levels of detail, and using different formats and modalities, thereby allowing for a co-constructive sXAI dialog. Related key issues and required advances in the field of XAI are to take into account context, interaction, flexibility, and coherence in explanations.

One of the main points is addressing context factors in explanations. Users of XAI systems often have specific ideas about what they want the system to explain, and their focus can shift depending on their needs. Current XAI systems are limited in their ability to respond to queries outside of the predefined task space of the model. For instance, users may have questions about the data used for training the AI, the roles of different interaction partners, or other context-related factors that go beyond the system's original scope. This gap underscores the need for a representation that can distinguish between important and less important context factors while also maintaining a history of the interaction to allow for easier access to relevant information.

Another challenge in current XAI systems is their reliance on predefined concepts. When discussing complex or abstract issues, it is often necessary to derive new concepts from existing ones in order to enhance understanding. However, this capability is not yet available in current XAI models. This chapter suggests that integrating a structured knowledge base could enable the generation of new concepts through interaction with the user, allowing for more flexible and dynamic explanations. This ability to co-construct intermediate concepts represents a significant step forward in achieving more nuanced and adaptable explanations.

XAI systems should also provide users with an overview of their knowledge structure and the possible explanatory steps they can take. Many users are unaware of the options available to them when interacting with XAI systems, and this can limit the effectiveness of the explanations provided. By offering a clear overview of the interaction steps, as well as the underlying knowledge structure, XAI systems can guide users more effectively through the explanation process, ensuring they are aware of the available information and can make informed decisions about how to proceed.

Another key issue discussed is the concept of mixed-initiative interaction, in which the XAI system can take on different roles in the interaction. In some cases, the system may need to take the lead, providing an overarching explanation at the beginning of the interaction or proactively addressing misconceptions as they arise. For example, if the system detects that the user has misunderstood a previous explanation, it could initiate a clarification routine or revisit the topic to ensure understanding. On the other hand, the system should also be able to switch to a more reactive mode and respond to user questions while encouraging active exploration of the topic. This flexibility in interaction roles can lead to a more engaging and effective explanatory process.

The flexibility provided by the proposed exploration mechanisms raises a question regarding the coherence in explanations, especially when dealing with complex topics. While breaking down explanations into smaller, more digestible units is crucial, it is equally important to maintain a sense of continuity and coherence across interactions. XAI systems need to be able to build upon previous explanations and guide users through a hierarchical or structured representation of the knowledge, starting with abstract concepts and gradually moving toward more concrete details. This ability to deliver consecutive explanations that build on each other is essential for helping users develop a deeper understanding of complex issues over time.

For future developments, LLMs have the potential to enhance the explainability of AI systems by serving as a subprocess or by being extended with an XAI knowledge graph or similar technologies. This integration could help address some of the challenges mentioned above, such as providing flexible and context-aware explanations, co-constructing new concepts, and offering a clear overview of the available information. However, the potential of LLMs in XAI has only begun to be explored, and further research is needed to fully understand how LLMs can be leveraged to improve the transparency and effectiveness of AI systems.

To conclude, the chapter outlines several key areas on which XAI systems could be improved, particularly in terms of flexibility, interaction, and coherence. By addressing context factors, enabling the co-construction of intermediate concepts, providing an overview of knowledge structures, and supporting mixed-initiative interaction, XAI systems can become more user-friendly and effective in helping users understand complex AI processes. The integration of LLMs with XAI represents a promising avenue for achieving these goals, but further exploration is needed to fully realize their potential in enhancing explainability.

Acknowledgments We thank Tim Miller for his valuable perspective and helpful comments on an earlier version of this chapter.

Kary Främling's work has been partially supported by the Wallenberg AI, Autonomous Systems and Software Program (WASP) funded by the Knut and Alice Wallenberg Foundation.

This work was funded by the Deutsche Forschungsgemeinschaft (DFG, German Research Foundation): TRR 318/1 2021 – 438445824.

References

Alpsancar, S., Matzner, T., & Philippi, M. (2024). Unpacking the purposes of explainable AI. In *Smart Ethics in the Digital World: Proceedings of the ETHICOMP 2024. 21th International Conference on the Ethical and Social Impacts of ICT* (pp. 31–35). Universidad de La Rioja.

Benbasat, I., & Taylor, R. N. (1982). Behavioral aspects of information processing for the design of management information systems. *IEEE Transac-tions on Systems, Man, and Cybernetics, 12*(4), 439–450. https://doi.org/10.1109/TSMC.1982.4308848.

Clark, H. H., & Brennan, S. E. (1991). Grounding in communication. In L. B. Resnick, J. M. Levine, & S. D. Teasley (Eds.), *Perspectives on Socially Shared Cognition* (pp. 222–233). American Psychological Association.

Cramer, H., Evers, V., Ramlal, S., Van Someren, M., Rutledge, L., Stash, N., Aroyo, L., & Wielinga, B. (2008). The effects of transparency on trust in and acceptance of a content-based art recommender. *User Modeling and User-Adapted Interaction, 18*, 455–496. https://doi.org/10.1007/s11257-008-9051-3.

Dwivedi, R., Dave, D., Naik, H., Singhal, S., Omer, R., Patel, P., Qian, B., Wen, Z., Shah, T., Morgan, G., et al. (2023). Explainable AI (XAI): Core ideas, techniques, and solutions. *ACM Computing Surveys, 55*(9), 1–33. https://doi.org/10.1145/3561048.

Endsley, M. R. (2011). Direct measurement of situation awareness: Validity and use of SAGAT. In E. Salas (Ed.), *Situational awareness* (pp. 129–156). Routledge.

Fisher, J. B., Lohmer, V., Kern, F., Barthlen, W., Gaus, S., & Rohlfing, K. J. (2022). Exploring monological and dialogical phases in naturally occurring explanations. *KI-Künstliche Intelligenz, 36*(3), 317–326. https://doi.org/10.1007/s13218-022-00787-1.

Herbold, L., Sadeghi, M., & Vogelsang, A. (2024). Generating context-aware contrastive explanations in rule-based systems. In *Proceedings of the 2024 Workshop on Explainability Engineering* (pp. 8–14). Association for Computing Machinery. https://doi.org/10.1145/3648505.3648507.

Hewitt, J., Thickstun, J., Manning, C. D., & Liang, P. (2023). Backpack language models. In *Proceedings of the Association for Computational Linguistics* (pp. 9103–9125). Association for Computational Linguistics. https://doi.org/10.18653/v1/2023.acl-long.506.

Hudon, A., Demazure, T., Karran, A., Léger, P.-M., & Sénécal, S. (2021). Explainable artificial intelligence (XAI): How the visualization of AI predictions affects user cognitive load and confidence. In *Information Systems and Neuroscience: NeuroIS Retreat 2021* (pp. 237–246). Springer. https://doi.org/10.1007/978-3-030-88900-5_27.

Lammert, O., Richter, B., Schütze, C., Thommes, K., & Wrede, B. (2024). Humans in XAI: Increased reliance in decision-making under uncertainty by using explanation strategies. *Frontiers in Behavioral Economics, 3*, 1377075. https://doi.org/10.3389/frbhe.2024.1377075.

Lebedeva, A., Kornowicz, J., Lammert, O., & Papenkordt, J. (2023). The role of response time for algorithm aversion in fast and slow thinking tasks. In *International Conference on Human–Computer Interaction* (pp. 131–149). Springer. https://doi.org/10.1007/978-3-031-35891-3_9.

Morrison, K., Shin, D., Holstein, K., & Perer, A. (2023). Evaluating the impact of human explanation strategies on human-AI visual decision-making. *Proceedings of the ACM on Human-Computer Interaction, 7*(CSCW1), 1–37. https://doi.org/10.1145/3579481.

Sanneman, L., & Shah, J. A. (2022). The situation awareness framework for explainable AI (SAFE-AI) and human factors considerations for XAI systems. *International Journal of Human–Computer Interaction, 38*(18–20), 1772–1788. https://doi.org/10.1080/10447318.2022.2081282.

Schemmer, M., Hemmer, P., Nitsche, M., Kühl, N., & Vössing, M. (2022). A meta-analysis of the utility of explainable artificial intelligence in human-AI decision-making. In *Proceedings of the 2022 AAAI/ACM Conference on AI, Ethics, and Society* (pp. 617–626). Association for Computing Machinery. https://doi.org/10.1145/3514094.3534128.

Schmidt, P., Biessmann, F., & Teubner, T. (2020). Transparency and trust in artificial intelligence systems. *Journal of Decision Systems, 29*(4), 260–278. https://doi.org/10.1080/12460125.2020.1819094.

Schoonderwoerd, T. A. J., Jorritsma, W., Neerincx, M. A., & Van Den Bosch, K. (2021). Human-centered XAI: developing design patterns for explanations of clinical decision support systems. *International Journal of Human–Computer Studies, 154*(C), 102684. https://doi.org/10.1016/j.ijhcs.2021.102684.

Shortliffe, E. H. (1976). *Computer-based medical consultations: MYCIN.* Elsevier. https://doi.org/10.1016/B978-0-444-00179-5.X5001-X.

Sokol, K., & Flach, P. (2020). One explanation does not fit all. *KI – Künstliche Intelligenz, 34*, 235–250. https://doi.org/10.1007/s13218-020-00637-y.

Sowa, J. F. (1991). *Principles of semantic networks: Explorations in the rep-resentation of knowledge.* Morgan Kaufmann. https://doi.org/10.1016/C2013-0-08297-7.

Thommes, K., Lammert, O., Schütze, C., Richter, B., & Wrede, B. (2024). Human emotions in AI explanations. In *World Conference on Explainable Artificial Intelligence* (pp. 270–293). Springer. https://doi.org/10.1007/978-3-031-63803-9_15.

van der Waa, J., Nieuwburg, E., Cremers, A., & Neerincx, M. (2021). Evaluating XAI: A comparison of rule-based and example-based explanations. *Artificial Intelligence, 291*, 103404. https://doi.org/10.1016/j.artint.2020.103404.

Wan, C., Belo, R., Zejnilović, L., & Lavado, S. (2023). The duet of representations and how explanations exacerbate it. In *World Conference on Explainable Artificial Intelligence* (pp. 181–197). Springer. https://doi.org/10.1007/978-3-031-44067-0_10.

You, S., Yang, C. L., & Li, X. (2022). Algorithmic versus human advice: Does presenting prediction performance matter for algorithm appreciation? *Journal of Management Information Systems, 39*(2), 336–365. https://doi.org/10.1080/07421222.2022.2063553.

Open Access This chapter is licensed under the terms of the Creative Commons Attribution 4.0 International License (http://creativecommons.org/licenses/by/4.0/), which permits use, sharing, adaptation, distribution and reproduction in any medium or format, as long as you give appropriate credit to the original author(s) and the source, provide a link to the Creative Commons license and indicate if changes were made.

The images or other third party material in this chapter are included in the chapter's Creative Commons license, unless indicated otherwise in a credit line to the material. If material is not included in the chapter's Creative Commons license and your intended use is not permitted by statutory regulation or exceeds the permitted use, you will need to obtain permission directly from the copyright holder.

Chapter 17
Interaction History in Social XAI

Kirsten Thommes ⓘ, Kary Främling ⓘ, Britta Wrede ⓘ, and Sylvain Kubler ⓘ

Abstract Much research in XAI focuses on single, one-shot interactions, implicitly assuming that interactions have no past, no future, and no surroundings. Although this assumption may be necessary for many empirical research settings, it is overly simplifying and unrealistic. Whereas empirical research focuses on a world in which no social context exists, real applications are embedded in a temporal (past and future) and social context. Social science research shows that repeated interactions and secondhand knowledge in the social space massively affect human attitudes and behaviors. This chapter explains how not only repeated interactions between XAI and humans but also the social space and secondhand information may affect social XAI research.

17.1 How Does This Chapter Relate to XAI?

Up until now, generating explanatory content and exploring the explanatory process have been analyzed mainly as a 1:1 interaction between the explainer and the explainee in a single, one-shot interaction. However, by adding social context to

---

K. Thommes (✉)
Faculty of Business Administration and Economics, Paderborn University, Paderborn, Germany
e-mail: kirsten.thommes@uni-paderborn.de

K. Främling
Department of Computing Science, Umeå University, Umeå, Sweden

Department of Industrial Engineering and Management, Aalto University, Espoo, Finland
e-mail: kary.framling@umu.se

B. Wrede
Medical School OWL, Bielefeld University, Bielefeld, Germany
e-mail: bwrede@techfak.uni-bielefeld.de

S. Kubler
Interdisciplinary Centre for Security, Reliability and Trust (SnT), University of Luxembourg, Esch-sur-Alzette, Luxembourg
e-mail: sylvain.kubler@uni.lu

© The Author(s) 2026
K. J. Rohlfing et al. (eds.), *Social Explainable AI*,
https://doi.org/10.1007/978-981-96-5290-7_17

XAI, the interactive episode for co-constructing an explanation is no longer viewed as an act in isolation, but also considers the social context of interactions. In this chapter, we discuss the social sphere in what are broadly two dimensions: First, most explanatory processes are not single interactions (one-shot), because the explainee will readdress the explainer with a request for another explanation when reusing the AI system. Thus, social XAI (sXAI) must address whether experiences in past interactions will and should be used for the subsequent explanatory processes and whether it has to anticipate future interactions. Second, both the explainer and the explainee will interact with other agents about the topic of the explanation, resulting in many different interactions. For instance, the XAI system will also explain the AI output to other explainees, the explainee will interact with other XAI systems, and the various explainees may also discuss and exchange their knowledge on their experience with the AI output among themselves. Going from 1:1 to many:many is a problem largely unaddressed in XAI research; and, in reality, most XAI systems produce the same output to all explainees regardless of their background and do not take into account that the user may have interacted with other systems and explanatory strategies previously.

This chapter will discuss the advantages, opportunities, and potential problems on the micro-level arising from repeated interactions between one explainer and one explainee as well as on the macro-level of several interactions among heterogeneous agents that also require some time gaps between single XAI–human interactions.

On the micro-level, the co-constructive explanatory process has to consider the history of an interaction with an interaction partner within one interaction sequence. However, the question arises whether the history of communicated information can and should be used for the next dialogue. The already established common ground between explainer and explainee in one interaction may increase dialog efficiency. Here, the interaction history may serve as important context information about the explainer's mental model of the system, the domain, their preferences, and their terminology that can serve as a basis for the subsequent explanatory process. Moreover, user-specific feedback may further enhance the tailoring of explanations toward the specific explainee and their preferences concerning, for example, completeness of explanations, modalities, interaction patterns, and so forth. Depending on the purpose of the explanatory process, this may not only increase efficiency in the interaction but also improve trust in the system. The opportunities and problems mentioned above arise from repeated interaction between machines and humans in 1:1 repeated interactions. However, the past and the future of a 1:1 interaction are also embedded in the past and future of other interactions—be they with other XAI systems with which the individual gains experiences or the interactions of other humans who share their experience with the individual. When more than one human and more than one XAI system interact, problems amplify on the macro-level of the ecological system in which the XAI is employed, and new problems emerge. First, learning about successful explanatory strategies may benefit all XAI systems, and therefore, experiences with past interactions need to be stored and analyzed. This allows explanations to be tailored to a human's needs and preferences, and it speeds up explanatory processes even when there has been no interaction history with this

Fig. 17.1 Path dependencies in repeated interactions

specific human. As a downside, it is most unlikely that one explanatory strategy will fit all. When trying to differentiate, system designers might be tempted to cluster types of users, which may result in stereotyping and bear the inherent danger of discrimination, or to adopt a one-fit explanation for every individual. This notion of individual stereotyping is illustrated in a comic strip-like format in Fig. 17.1.

Individualization may also become a problem when consistency is needed. In repeated interactions with one user, the system may achieve consistency in explanations or be aware of a potential need to explain drift. When we consider multiple agents, the problem of consistency is amplified because different parts of the explanatory process may be taken by different agents, resulting in the system having data gaps about the human agent. Also, generating friction-free explanations for several humans may be more demanding than just ensuring consistency in explanations for one human agent, because perceived consistency must also be ensured across humans. Consider, for instance, the scenario 2.3 in which the same decision is explained to different users. Suppose users talk to each other about their experience with the recommender system. In that case, they will perceive that the system is inconsistent about feature weights, because one explainee assumes that the system puts a lot of weight on speed while the other explainee assumes that the system puts a lot of weight on the safety of the car. In that case, a conversation between the two individuals about the system may eventually result in distrust. We believe that the trade-off between consistency in explanations and individualization and the resulting challenges for trust, mistrust, and distrust need to be addressed as a major challenge on the micro- and macro-levels.

17.2 Taking into Account Repeated Interaction at the Micro-Level

In this chapter, we distinguish between the micro-level and the macro-level of interactions within the framework of the agents involved. With the micro-level of an interaction, we mean the human user as the explainee and the XAI as the explainer that are both involved in the explanatory process in a 1:1 situation. In contrast, with the macro-level, we mean the broader social sphere—for example, when many XAIs and many human agents form a social network of explanations with each other.

Common Ground and Common Context Even though much research addresses the micro-level as we define it, current XAI research frequently sticks to one-shot interactions. In reality, however, many interactions are not one-shot, but there is an interaction history, and there will be a future. In interactions, the incrementally evolving interaction history is an important resource for ongoing interaction because it allows one to refer to previously established content. Through the process of grounding, a *common ground* and a *common context* are created. These consist of propositional content that both partners agree to, and both know that the other one knows as well (Clark & Brennan, 1991). Importantly, grounding assumes that presenting an utterance or an explanation alone does not mean that the explainee has understood it. Rather, a structured process is assumed by which the listener processes the presented content incrementally. This entails aspects such as acoustic processing, lexical mapping, and semantic understanding up to action selection and execution, all of which can be accompanied by nonverbal cues indicating, for example, that the listener is attending, listening, and processing or having trouble in following an utterance while the interaction partner is producing that utterance (Brennan & Hulteen, 1995). For a presentation to be considered grounded, an acknowledgment of the interaction partner is required, indicating that they have understood what has been said. Otherwise, a clarification will be expected (Clark, 2005; Buschmeier & Kopp, 2018).

Whereas the common ground and context refer to the jointly established facts in the interaction, the interaction patterns create a history of elements that can be reused for specific goals (Rohlfing et al., 2016). Thus, the interaction repertoire is another important resource of the interaction history that is especially important in human–robot and human–machine interaction. Problems tend to occur more frequently here than in human–human interaction because predefined interaction patterns are often expected (Vollmer et al., 2016), which can be difficult for a human interaction partner to follow (Lohse et al., 2009). For explanations, it is therefore important to keep track of the explanatory content grounded by both participants in order to refer to this joint basis. Moreover, the interaction patterns that have been used successfully can be an essential resource when going on to explain difficult content.

Shared Concepts and Efficiency of Explanations Retrieving information that both agents have already agreed upon and constitutes a common ground in the sense that it is shared knowledge that both agents assume that the other partner possesses as well can speed up explanatory processes. For instance, if the concept of classification by an AI has already been explained in a previous dialog, the system can check whether the general logic is still known to the explainee without starting to explain this again. Retrieving such a history of interactions may result in more efficient dialogs or also enable partners to introduce more complex concepts during the explanatory process. This effect may be present in one interaction, but even more important in consecutive interactions over time. Next to the direct effects of quicker and more tailor-made explanations after repeated interactions, research on repeated interactions shows that coordination in terms of common ground technology may speed up, trust may increase, and the need for control may decrease. In repeated interactions with one interaction partner, trust is formed on the basis of previous experiences. It lowers the need for control. Moreover, pleasant and unpleasant interactions with an interaction partner result in emotional responses. Hence, due to different emotional regulation abilities, this is also leads to a great variation in the effect of repeated interactions on human trust development (Van den Bos et al., 2012). Nonetheless, repeated interactions affect trust and the perceived need for control.

For instance, the difference between single one-shot and long-term, repeated interactions is captured in the psychological effect of hot- versus cold-state decisions (Loewenstein, 2005). In cold states, when not currently in an interaction or decision situation, individuals overestimate the stability of their personal preferences and underestimate how biased they will be in a certain situation when aroused. In social science, many researchers are therefore cautious about translating their results from lab studies to the real world (Levitt & List, 2007) because the situation in a lab experiment may be less 'hot' than in the real world. Moreover, lab situations frequently represent one-shot situations and do not consider the evolution of interaction over time. Thus, the real effect of long-term interactions can be measured only in long-term usage situations, and it cannot be assessed by scenario questions such as "would you consider using the system again," because this scenario question is a cold decision. Moreover, we cannot infer long-term effects from one-shot explanations, because goals, preferences, common ground, and context evolve over time.

Long-Term Effects of Repeated Interaction In sXAI, explainees will judge the explainer on how reliable the explanations are. Most likely, other findings from human–computer interaction may also be relevant in XAI–explainee situations. Han et al. (2021), for instance, found that trust in a machine evolves over time and that control costs decrease. Their study shows that individuals cooperating with a machine stop checking their machine counterparts after every interaction once they have experienced sufficient cooperation. The authors argue that such trust-based strategies may be even more likely the more nontransparent the machine counterpart is. For explanations of AI, Kahr et al. (2023) find that humanlike explanations help to elevate trust in AI systems in terms of both reliance and self-reported trust over time as long as the AI system is highly accurate. If the system is inaccurate, explanations cannot help the decline in trust and reliance. Likewise, Gemalmaz and Yin (2022) showed that the users' consecutive experience with a system affects the perceived fairness of that system. Notably, perceived fairness is in-group favoritism, which affects the decision to use a system again. Hence, individuals expect the system to favor their group and not to avoid discrimination. Because the explainer's experience with the system over time affects trust, perceived fairness, and the need for control, the interactions will also evolve in patterns (7).

Information Retrieval Over Time and Path Dependence From the side of the explainer—the sXAI system—gaining more information about specific user groups or single users may also alter patterns in communication because explanation processes can start from a once-established ground. However, this may also lead to wrong beliefs about user groups and single users. To achieve a positive utility from storing the interaction history, the information gathered must be retrieved accurately, and the system also needs an understanding of time (e.g., understanding when information is considered to be outdated or is likely to be forgotten). In some cases, information collected might be helpful even when there are years between two subsequent explanatory processes; in other instances, it might be invalid the next day. Moreover, some human characteristics may be relatively stable over time (e.g., a preference for visual explanations), whereas others such as fatigue or the current emotional state are context-dependent and may vary. Therefore, the system must not only have an idea of the time that has elapsed between two interactions but also of the dynamics in humans. It needs to take into account stable and varying conditions that affect humans' goals, their ability to recall previously exchanged information, and their ability to transfer previously acquired knowledge to the current interaction.

Stereotyping by Learning Explanations Over Time Stereotyping by learning explanations over time: Correlating certain patterns with surface or deep-level characteristics of user groups may not result in differentiation through better tailoring but in discrimination. Surface-level discrimination may occur if systems start explanatory processes based on mostly visible individual differences such as gender or age. For instance, if the explanatory system learns via a history of previous interactions that young individuals tend to have sufficient knowledge about a certain explanatory step, the system may start to skip that step. Whereas tailoring to a certain group may be beneficial, it may also stereotype individuals into groups and serve as a source of discrimination. The same problem may occur if the systems learn about deep-level differences between individuals – for instance, via semantic analysis experiences that neurotic individuals prefer other explanatory patterns than others – and they, therefore, try to use other explanatory routines.

Perception of Conflicting Explanations Continuously retaining past interactions could also lead to the amplification of any biases present in the data. If the XAI system learns from historical interactions and modifies explanatory processes according to the information about the explainee it has retrieved, then not only path dependency in explanations but also self-perpetuating bias reproduction may become a problem over time. On an individual basis, assigning too much consideration to the previous interaction may result in different problems. Understanding the data retrieved about an individual may pose an enormous challenge in repeated interactions when information is used from earlier interaction sequences. Moreover, the need to generate noncontradictory explanations in repeated interactions may be less severe either after some time has passed or when the explanatory shift can be explained (e.g., by the incorporation of new knowledge). However, this may jeopardize trustworthiness when there is too little time between two explanations, even when the AI has received new data and, therefore, generates new recommendations and delivers new explanations. For instance, the system may rely overly on previous experiences with a user, not considering the time between two interactions. Although it might be reasonable to assume that the explainee has not changed within one minute, whether attributes, preferences, and knowledge have remained stable and thus still can be used for the next interaction after a day, week, month, or years is not a trivial issue. If too much time has passed between two interactions, taking up the previous interaction may be worse than forgetting the past, deleting previous interaction data, and starting a new conversation.

One example of such perceived inconsistencies is that an additional explanation is needed for the recommendation, and the difference in explanations compared to the previous interaction results from the time-variant features used in the model. Time-variant features of the individual or the explanandum are – apart from the day of the week, month, season, or year – variables that may change over time, such as age, personal health, wealth, family situation, or the like. For instance, the buying recommendation and explanation may differ for the same person when buying a car (see Chap. 2) if the recommendation depends on personal wealth, which may well change over time. The data used for AI training may also drift over time, so exactly the same case may lead to different advice and explanations. In such cases, explainers may ask not only for the current advice to be explained but also for the reason why there is a difference compared to either the former recommendation or the former explanation. This problem may be addressed by approaches derived from drift detection in continuous real-world data. Such approaches can detect changes in underlying time series data—such as interaction data.

Human Right to be Forgotten Human explainees may want control over the information retrieved, stored, and used by the system in the subsequent explanatory process. Users may also have the right to see, verify, and delete information gained in interactions about them in many jurisdictions. Storing user data may also generally result in new questions about privacy and security and transparency problems concerning the user model of the XAI, thereby doubling the problem of XAI from transparency in AI to include the problem of the transparency of the explanation system. The possibility of starting a new interaction depends on the technical and institutional possibilities regarding the right to be forgotten, and this is not straightforward. Villaronga et al. (2018) argue that effective forgetting is rather tricky in data science—both from a technical and legal perspective. Muller and Strohmayer (2022) present a comprehensive overview of data silencing, data forgetting, and data erasure concerning AI, but the framework also applies to the explanatory layer of XAI. Notably, they distinguish the need to forget data for the AI model according to motivation. Here, they introduce a social dimension as a prerequisite to analyze the need to forget. Muller and Strohmayer (2022) distinguish between "modest silence," "silence as a force," and "ambivalent silence." Modest silence occurs if data are missing or are made missing for no specific reason or because the old data are regarded as outdated by the benevolent human designing or interacting with an AI. In our case, the explainee, for example, has achieved so much new knowledge about the domain or the sXAI system that an sXAI system connecting to the previous state of knowledge would be wrong in its model of the human. However, there might also be silence as a force, which implies that a normative evaluation of the facts causes the need to forget data. Here, normative reasons underlie the situation, and there may be a desire to disadvantage others by omission or altering data (structures). Type three, ambivalent silence, is less important for individual sXAI–explainee interaction forgetting because it involves the attempt to influence the sXAI system about the broader past or a broader group. Addressing the problem of how human interaction partners should be allowed to manipulate whether the previous data about them is reused to improve explanations for them next time or to generate better explanations for others is, therefore, not an easy question. Whereas one may benefit from a common ground and already established trust in a dyad, which improves communication, there may also be a human need to forget previous interactions, and the need may be due to outdated data or normative reasons, with it not necessarily being easy to differentiate between the two.

17.3 Repeated Interaction at the Macro-Level

Whereas little research in the field of AI and XAI takes into account that humans and AI do not interact one time but engage in a repeated interaction sequence with temporal breaks in between, even less research looks into broader social networks consisting of many humans and (potentially also many) XAI systems. This question relates to the question of microlevel interactions, but is even more complex. Consider, for instance, a tutoring system that should assist two students and needs to explain itself to them. Then, we already have a network of three agents in which potentially every agent is exchanging information with everybody else. Moreover, the interaction history of Student A and the XAI system will become potentially relevant for the subsequent interaction between the XAI system and Student B, because Student A may talk about their experience with Student B. In this setting, the interaction history with Student B on the micro-level is not the relevant point; it is the interaction history on the macro-level. However, considering many different explainees interacting with the same XAI system creates new opportunities and may create new problems. For the sake of simplicity, imagine the following setting like in the example above: a system in which many human explainees interact with the same XAI system in a sequence but also talk to each other about their upcoming or previous interaction. In such embedded systems with multiple consecutive or simultaneous interactions, information will flow indirectly not only from XAI to the user but also via other users. The system can become even more complex when one human explainee exchanges with multiple XAI systems and multiple humans are involved.

Analytically, the resulting problem of secondhand information – that is, information not given directly by the XAI, but by another user who has previously interacted with the system – is already known from observing reputational and efficiency effects in social networks (Raub & Weesie, 1990). In such a setting of social embeddings and interactions about one agent – the XAI system – secondhand information may result, and this information may be either true or not true. It alters the accuracy of the partner model that the XAI system uses. If the specific interaction is the first interaction, the appropriate partner model is not that of a novice. If the interaction is reenacted, then the previous human model of the AI may have changed in the meantime due to secondhand information.

The outcome of observing the specific dyadic interaction and embedding it in the social network is especially relevant when we are interested in trust, distrust, and mistrust. Regarding the environment, explainees can compare explanations and get a second opinion. The opportunity to triangulate AI advice and AI explanations may result in real or perceived discrepancies between the advice and the explanation received. This may jeopardize trust or also allow and trigger healthy distrust Fig. 17.2.

17.4 Operationalization

Retaining a history of interaction requires a way to identify the explainee from one interaction session to the next. This typically signifies having a user account with which the partner model is associated. Systems such as ChatGPT require users to create a user account before being able to interact with the system. However, when asking ChatGPT version 4.0 whether it creates or uses any partner model, it answers

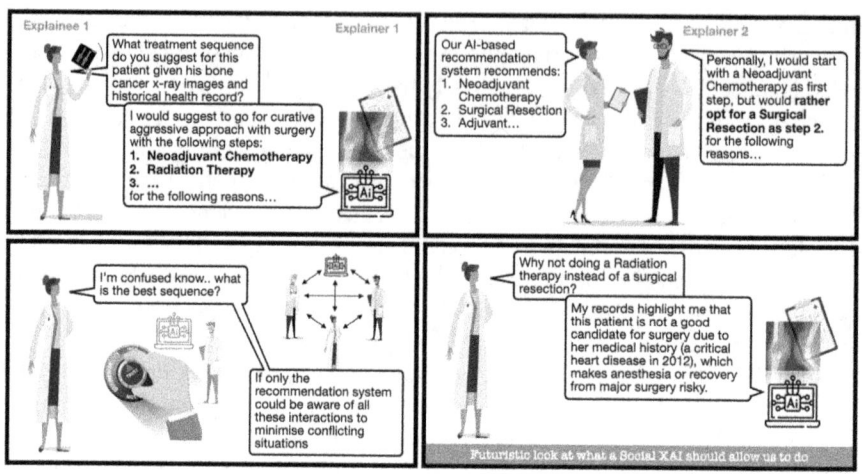

Fig. 17.2 Social interactions and sXAI explanations

that it *does not create or maintain any kind of 'partner model' or store personal information about users. Each interaction is stateless and independent of previous interactions* (as per June 10th, 2024).

On the other hand, so-called recommender systems rely heavily on user modeling based on a history of interaction (Ricci et al., 2015). A recommender system is a type of information filtering system that suggests relevant items – such as products, movies, books, or services – to users based on their preferences, behaviors, and historical interactions (Resnick & Varian, 1997). Recommender systems are widely used in e-commerce, streaming platforms, and online services.

The primary goal of a recommender system is often to increase user retention and sales by profiling users and providing personalized suggestions at moments deemed most relevant. Such profiling can also be beneficial for users, drawing their attention to products or content that align with their interests. However, many users have experienced cases in which a recommender system presents irrelevant or even intrusive recommendations, often in the form of targeted advertisements. These situations highlight some of the challenges associated with user modeling, as discussed in Sect. 17.2.

Given these challenges, it would be fair for users to have the ability to request explanations for a recommender system's suggestions and to be able to correct or reset an inaccurate user profile. However, in practice, most users have little to no access to the inner workings of these systems and are often unaware of the organizations developing or hosting them. In the context of XAI, we argue that users – as explainees – should always have the ability to access, modify, or reset their user profile within an XAI-powered recommender system. This would not only enhance transparency but also help mitigate the frustration caused by inaccurate or unwanted recommendations.

17 Interaction History in Social XAI

In an sXAI interaction, all explainees start with an empty or default user model – or rather a partner model as we call it in the sXAI context – when the explainee begins the first interaction with the sXAI system. A default partner model might have the following kinds of properties:

1. A default preference prioritization between graphical, natural language, and other modalities for explanations.
2. A default preference prioritization between feature importance/influence, counterfactual, and other explanations.
3. A default 'domain and competence profile' could be used to select which vocabularies and exploration strategies to use when interacting with the explainee.

Another option is to have an initial interaction with the explainee in order to identify a suitable partner model template. The template could be chosen by the explainee themselves, or the system could try to assign a suitable template based on an initial set of profiling questions.

As mentioned in Chap. 16, every exploration session can potentially produce an 'exploration model' that stores information about the vocabulary used, the questions, the modality, and so forth. The exploration model could then be used to create or update a partner model and presumably provide more efficient exploration in future interactions. Such an update is feasible in the case of repeated interactions on the same topic or domain. However, it is more challenging to decide what can be generalized across an explanatory interaction on choosing a car, choosing an apartment, or why a credit has been refused. At least the vocabulary used in the explanations will differ, whereas the preferred modality and type of explanations might remain the same.

Figure 17.3 shows a screenshot of a proof-of-concept prototype that showcases how many of the different sXAI concepts described can be implemented in reality. It uses the building blocks described in the Operationalization sections of the previous chapters (Sects. 14.5, 15.4 and 16.4) for implementing an interactive, graphical sXAI user interface.[1] Ames Housing is the dataset used in the earlier chapters. The sXAI system uses the KG described in Sect. 14.5 for defining a vocabulary using CIU's Intermediate Concepts (ICs) that make it possible to obtain explanations on different levels of abstraction or detail. The vocabulary is shown as an interactive graph in the middle of the window, where the explainee can select the IC or basic feature that should be explained (which can also be selected from the drop-down list "Selected feature/concept" on the left side of the window). The explanations provided by CIU are shown on the right edge of the window, where it is possible to select what kind of visual explanation to show. The options are CIU's Potential Influence (PI) plot, influence plot, or a contrastive plot that makes a comparison between the current instance and another instance. A corresponding textual explanation is also provided under the visual explanation. Finally, it is also possible to use the graph in the middle as a visual explanation by modifying the size

---

[1] The systems have been programmed using the Shiny framework in "R."

Interactive XAI with CIU

Fig. 17.3 Screenshot of a proof-of-concept prototype that implements interactivity, different kinds of explanations, KG-based vocabulary with different abstraction levels, support for adaptive partner models, and numerous other sXAI capabilities described in this chapter

of the circles according to CIU's importance value and setting the color according to CIU's utility value.

The KG also includes metadata used for tooltips in the graph and for providing descriptions about the features (left side of the window). The drop-down menu "Partner model" (top-left) changes the partner model used, which signifies that the explanation vocabulary changes accordingly. In addition to defining the used vocabulary, the partner model can also store explainee-specific statistics about what concepts are used the most/least, what kind of explanations are selected or looked at the most by the explainee, etc. Such statistics can then be used to adapt the user interface accordingly. Even though it has not been implemented in the prototype user interface, it would also be possible for the explainee to add new concepts into the vocabulary at any moment, or to modify/remove existing ones.

At the present time, we are not aware of existing implementations of the kind of partner models for XAI purposes that we call for here. One reason is that even the SOTA regarding the generation of explanatory content analyzed in Chap. 15 seems to be rather far from what would be required to reach sXAI requirements. However, we believe that our proof-of-concept sXAI implementation shows that implementing sXAI is feasible with existing methods and technologies.

In addition to the open questions regarding how to implement sXAI, there might be additional challenges to tackle as pointed out in Sect. 17.3. For instance, an sXAI system might be used by different explainees, who have different partner models and therefore might receive explanations that seem different, even though the underlying mathematics and metrics are consistent. This is a challenge that sXAI shares with human explainers—that is, there is no guarantee as to how different explainees will perceive the explanations provided. Such potential incoherence might be detrimental to the overall trust in the system. However, it is difficult to see how this challenge can be addressed with mathematical or technical solutions, which once again shows the need for a multidisciplinary approach to implement satisfactory sXAI systems.

A major purpose of partner models is actually to introduce *positive bias* in the sense of making the interaction between sXAI systems and explainees more efficient. However, such a 'bias' might also be harmful if the explainee's understanding, competence, or preferences change over time. Using an outdated partner model might then cause relevant information to be omitted by the sXAI system.

A similar phenomenon might be due to changes in the AI model, which might come from changes in the training data, a change in the AI model itself, a change in the XAI system that is used, or some other change in the sXAI system that causes it to alter its recommendations or explanations from one day to the next. In such situations, it would be necessary for the same system to proactively exhibit the underlying reasons for the change in order to preserve its trustworthiness toward explainees.

17.5 How Does This Chapter Inspire Further Directions in XAI?

Although research on human-human interaction clearly shows that a joint history of interaction is beneficial to joint understanding, progress, and many other dimensions of the interaction, to the best of our knowledge, this has barely been considered in XAI systems so far. This opens up a range of research directions for sXAI at both the micro-level (i.e., in interaction with one person) and at the macro-level (i.e., in repeated interactions with individuals who are part of a group of individuals who are also interacting with the system).

The most obvious research direction concerns keeping track of the explanatory content and which parts have (probably) been understood—that is, basically, the common ground. This will allow the system to initiate repairs in case of detected misunderstandings. Also, if the interaction allows the explainee to ask questions about the history, it will contain valuable information about which aspects or elements of the explanation so far are most relevant for the EE. On the other hand, this allows the system to explain important elements actively. For example, in the context of financial credits, the system should be aware that it might be important for the explainee to know how they can change their negative rating, and it should thus offer counterfactuals—enabling the explainee to possibly ask follow-up questions regarding specific variables that they think they can change.

A further direction concerns the interaction patterns the explainee has shown or coconstructed in an initial interaction. Such patterns (e.g., who starts to ask questions or provide explanations, or which explanation modalities have been used) are important to remember because they allow for quick progress. For adaptation, a dedicated partner model is required. Such a partner model will allow the system to start the interaction with an explainee at a level that is familiar to the explainee. This is important because it saves the ER a lot of time when accommodating the specific needs of the user. Here, it should be noted that there are different approaches to adaptation with different consequences for the human–robot interaction: automatic adaptation to the user (personalization), configuration by the user, or setting the system parameters via explicit interaction.

Lacroix et al. (2023) note that customization (where the user determines the settings) increases perceived human agency and enables a sense of identity as opposed to personalization (automatic adaptation), which, on the other hand, is more convenient and requires less effort. Finding the right balance and the most relevant parameters will be an important area for future sXAI research. Once an interaction history is integrated into a system, the right to forget is another important issue to consider.

At the macro-level, the highly relevant question of perceived consistency needs to be addressed. A system providing local explanations of different cases to different users may be perceived as inconsistent, because it provides different features that are relevant for the local case. Here, it will be relevant to develop explanation strategies that also include the explanation of consistency.

17.6 Rapid Access to the Content of This Chapter

Many studies in HCI and XAI investigate one-shot interactions. Although this is a very efficient design choice for empirical research, it disregards the social context of the explanation. Also, it neglects some potentially relevant possibilities: First, most individuals use AI several times in a row consecutively (e.g., by asking ChatGPT for help several times or by using an AI for assistance in pattern recognition). In private and professional settings, humans will more likely be confronted with or actively choose the same technological artifact several times in a row rather than engaging in one shot. The difference between one-shot interactions and consecutive encounters implies that technology evolves from being a stranger to being more familiar. For instance, new technologies may lack reliability and human arousal due to their newness. After several tries, the technology becomes familiar and humans feel more confident about assessing their qualities. When we think of technologies and humans in XAI interaction, this familiarity may result in a shared common understanding of each other, the establishment of a common ground, and the opportunity to consecutively build up on previous interactions. If understanding or trust cannot be built in one interaction, it may be generated in several consecutive interactions. Second, routine interactions between XAI and humans may also result in the substitution of control by trust, with humans blindly following the AI advice and being less likely to develop a healthy distrust. Also, there may be a pathway toward certain types of explanations. For example, the XAI system learns over time that showing graphs seems to be a more efficient explanation for a certain user, whereas verbal reasoning consumes more time for the system. Therefore, the system reproduces graphical explanations over and over, even if they lead to less understanding for this specific user.

Many of the social core dimensions of XAI, such as trust, are long-term constructs that need time to become established and evolve. The same may be true for many facets of understanding in which reproduction of knowledge is probably only a quick win, whereas being able to apply the acquired knowledge about an AI to other encounters with the AI is probably the deepest way of understanding.

Until now, most XAI research has also ignored the social sphere in which an interaction takes place and the communication that may happen about the XAI. However, this is a very relevant dimension, measured frequently and very practical. Consider, for instance, a tutoring system for many students. Students will certainly exchange information about the system. On the one hand, they may be able to explain the system to each other. Thus, the XAI system can rely on secondhand knowledge when explaining. As a very practical hazard, the system may falsely believe that Student B is smarter than Student A, not acknowledging that Student A has talked about her experience with Student B, and Student B, therefore, starts forming a different body of knowledge in the interaction. Similarly, Students A and B may receive very different explanations—for example, the system learns that Student A prefers graphical explanations, whereas Student B prefers verbal arguments. Although these explanations may be absolutely consistent from a technical view, they may appear very differently to Student A and Student B when they start a social exchange about the AI, resulting in mistrust or reactance.

Acknowledgments We thank Eyke Hüllermeier for his valuable perspective and helpful comments on an earlier version of this chapter.

This work was funded by the Deutsche Forschungsgemeinschaft (DFG, German Research Foundation): TRR 318/1 2021 – 438445824.

Kary Främling's work has been partially supported by the Wallenberg AI, Autonomous Systems and Software Program (WASP) funded by the Knut and Alice Wallenberg Foundation.

References

Brennan, S. E., & Hulteen, E. A. (1995). Interaction and feedback in a spoken language system: A theoretical framework. *Knowledge-Based Systems, 8*(2–3), 143–151. https://doi.org/10.1016/0950-7051(95)98376-H.

Buschmeier, H., & Kopp, S. (2018). Efficient communication through attentive speaking. In *Proceedings of the 14th Biannual Conference of the German Society for Cognitive Science*, Darmstadt, Germany.

Clark, H. H. (2005). Coordinating with each other in a material world. *Discourse Studies, 7*(4–5), 507–525. https://doi.org/10.1177/1461445605054404.

Clark, H. H., & Brennan, S. E. (1991). Grounding in communication. In L. B. Resnick, J. M. Levine, & S. D. Teasley (Eds.), *Perspectives on socially shared cognition* (pp. 222–233). American Psychological Association.

Gemalmaz, M. A., & Yin, M. (2022). Understanding decision subjects' fairness perceptions and retention in repeated interactions with AI-based decision systems. In *Proceedings of the 2022 AAAI/ACM Conference on AI, Ethics, and Society* (pp. 295–306). Association for Computing Machinery. https://doi.org/10.1145/3514094.3534201.

Han, T. A., Perret, C., & Powers, S. T. (2021). When to (or not to) trust intelligent machines: Insights from an evolutionary game theory analysis of trust in repeated games. *Cognitive Systems Research, 68*, 111–124. https://doi.org/10.1016/j.cogsys.2021.02.003.

Kahr, P. K., Rooks, G., Willemsen, M. C., & Snijders, C. C. P. (2023). It seems smart, but it acts stupid: Development of trust in AI advice in a repeated legal decision-making task. In *Proceedings of the 28th International Conference on Intelligent User Interfaces* (pp. 528–539). Association for Computing Machinery. https://doi.org/10.1145/3581641.3584058.

Lacroix, D., Wullenkord, R., & Eyssel, F. (2023). "Who's in charge? Using personalization vs. customization distinction to inform HRI research on adaptation to users". In *Companion of the 2023 ACM/IEEE International Conference on Human-Robot Interaction* (pp. 580–586). Association of Computing Machinery. https://doi.org/10.1145/3568294.3580152.

Levitt, S. D., & List, J. A. (2007). What do laboratory experiments measuring social preferences reveal about the real world? *Journal of Economic Perspectives, 21*(2), 153–174. https://doi.org/10.1257/jep.21.2.153.

Loewenstein, G. (2005). Hot-cold empathy gaps and medical decision making. *Health Psychology, 24*(4S), 49–56. https://doi.org/10.1037/0278-6133.24.4.S49.

Lohse, M., Hanheide, M., Rohlfing, K. J., & Sagerer, G. (2009). Systemic interaction analysis (SInA) in HRI. In *Proceedings of the 4th ACM/IEEE International Conference on Human Robot Interaction* (pp. 93–100). Association for Computing Machinery. https://doi.org/10.1145/1514095.1514114.

Muller, M., & Strohmayer, A. (2022). Forgetting practices in the data sciences. In *Proceedings of the 2022 CHI Conference on Human Factors in Computing Systems* (pp. 1–19). Association for Computing Machinery. https://doi.org/10.1145/3491102.3517644.

Raub, W., & Weesie, J. (1990). Reputation and efficiency in social interactions: An example of network effects. *American Journal of Sociology, 96*(3), 626–654. https://doi.org/10.1086/229574.

Resnick, P., & Varian, H. R. (1997). Recommender systems. *Communications of the ACM, 40*(3), 56–58. https://doi.org/10.1145/245108.245121.

Ricci, F., Rokach, L., & Shapira, B. (2015). *Recommender systems handbook* (2nd ed.). Springer. https://doi.org/10.1007/978-1-4899-7637-6.

Rohlfing, K. J., Wrede, B., Vollmer, A.-L., & Oudeyer, P.-Y. (2016). An alternative to mapping a word onto a concept in language acquisition: Pragmatic frames. *Frontiers in Psychology, 7*, 470. https://doi.org/10.3389/fpsyg.2016.00470.

Van den Bos, W., van Dijk, E., & Crone, E. A. (2012). Learning whom to trust in repeated social interactions: A developmental perspective. *Group Processes & Intergroup Relations, 15*(2), 243–256. https://doi.org/10.1177/1368430211418698.

Villaronga, E. F., Kieseberg, P., & Li, T. (2018). Humans forget, machines remember: Artificial intelligence and the right to be forgotten. *Computer Law & Security Review, 34*(2), 304–313. https://doi.org/10.1016/j.clsr.2017.08.007.

Vollmer, A.-L., Wrede, B., Rohlfing, K. J., & Oudeyer, P.-Y. (2016). Pragmatic frames for teaching and learning in human–robot interaction: Review and challenges. *Frontiers in Neurorobotics, 10*, 10. https://doi.org/10.3389/fnbot.2016.00010.

Open Access This chapter is licensed under the terms of the Creative Commons Attribution 4.0 International License (http://creativecommons.org/licenses/by/4.0/), which permits use, sharing, adaptation, distribution and reproduction in any medium or format, as long as you give appropriate credit to the original author(s) and the source, provide a link to the Creative Commons license and indicate if changes were made.

The images or other third party material in this chapter are included in the chapter's Creative Commons license, unless indicated otherwise in a credit line to the material. If material is not included in the chapter's Creative Commons license and your intended use is not permitted by statutory regulation or exceeds the permitted use, you will need to obtain permission directly from the copyright holder.

Part III
Multimodality

Chapter 18
Theoretical Aspects of Multimodal Processing

Angela Grimminger and **Hendrik Buschmeier**

Abstract The concept of sXAI is inspired by (human) social interaction, the primary case of which is face-to-face communication involving not only speech and language but also nonverbal modalities such as facial expression, gaze, gesture, head movement, and body posture. Such multimodal communication facilitates language processing in humans and becomes relevant for sXAI systems when they are (embodied) communicating agents able to produce multimodal behaviors and understand those of human users. In this chapter, we describe theoretical aspects of multimodal processing in human interaction (binding and segregation of modalities, how multimodal behavior is produced and understood) and their relation to computational models of multimodal interaction for conversational agents.

18.1 How Does This Chapter Relate to XAI?

Empirical research has provided evidence that multimodality in social interactions and communication between humans facilitates cognitive processing and understanding. This is important for explanations because these aim to change the state of an explainee's knowledge about the explanandum and their level of understanding. Therefore, they will most likely profit from being multimodal. Empirical findings in this field have informed theories on the integration of verbal and nonverbal communicative means in humans in terms of both their production and their reception.

A. Grimminger (✉)
Psycholinguistics, Faculty of Arts and Humanities, Paderborn University, Paderborn, Germany
e-mail: angela.grimminger@uni-paderborn.de

H. Buschmeier
Digital Linguistics Lab, Faculty of Linguistics and Literary Studies, Bielefeld University, Bielefeld, Germany
e-mail: hbuschme@uni-bielefeld.de

For sXAI, multimodal communication becomes relevant as soon as explanations are produced by artificial agents that provide anthropomorphic cues—that is, for example, agents that use language or speech, or exhibit human features (behavioral and morphological factors; Kim & Im, 2023). Such anthropomorphic cues may raise expectations in human interlocutors (e.g., habitability gap, Moore, 2017). Furthermore, they make it most likely that humans will also produce multimodal utterances in which information might be distributed across different modalities when interacting with artificial agents. Such agents should therefore be equipped with proper processing that will allow them to interpret multimodal input and respond accordingly.

In this chapter, we shall present a theoretical basis for the human processing of multimodal communication in dialog. In other words, we present theoretical approaches that explain how humans produce or comprehend information across multiple modalities (modalities might, at times, be independent, complementary, or redundant). Knowledge about these theoretical aspects of multimodal processing is considered helpful when it comes to modeling multimodal communication in conversational (explaining) agents[1] that are able to orchestrate their multimodal behavior in a meaningful way or interpret a human explainee's multimodal request or feedback.

18.2 General Principles and Problems

Human communication is multimodally encoded across two or more modalities (e.g., auditory and visual) when their signals are produced in temporal alignment and are integrated structurally and/or functionally (Fricke, 2012, p. 46). A general assumption here is that the different modalities are coded in different representational formats—namely, in verbal linguistic ones and nonverbal ones (such as imagery, auditory, or emotional ones)—forming a semantic network. These different representational formats are coded and processed in a contrastive, but complementary manner.

The fact that these signals are temporally aligned and structurally and/or functionally integrated creates a central problem in the processing of multimodal communication, the so-called *"binding" problem* (Holler & Levinson, 2019, p. 639). This refers to the (re)construction of multimodal messages using the various articulators available to humans (speech, manual gestures, facial expressions, head movements, etc.). For speakers, the problem is to orchestrate their multimodal behavior and provide information across modalities and time. For their interlocutors,

---

[1] The mutual interest of theoretical, empirical, and computational modeling in multimodal interaction and communication is reflected in the existence of thriving and long-running international and interdisciplinary conference series such as the ACM International Conference on Multimodal Interaction (ICMI), the Symposium on Multimodal Communication (MMSYM), or the Gesture and Speech in Interaction (GESPIN) Conference.

the problem is to integrate and make sense of the information provided by the speaker's articulators. Even if not totally overlapping, human signals from different sources may form a semantically related unit. Thus, the binding problem also includes dealing with asynchronies and "multiple, temporally offset signals ...across the different articulators and levels of processing" (Holler & Levinson, 2019, p. 640).

The binding problem is further complicated by the fact that not all behaviors that a speaker produces are necessarily intended to be communicative and therefore contribute meaning to a multimodal utterance (Wharton, 2009). Holler and Levinson (2019, p. 639) call this the *segregation problem*. Thus, interlocutors, be they humans or machines, need to be able to separate a speaker's co-occurring behaviors that are communicatively 'relevant' from those that are not. This is further complicated in that the meaningfulness of a movement or configuration of body parts (e.g., a slight tilt of the head to one side, or gazing toward an object) might become apparent only later in the interaction (e.g., when a misunderstanding is discovered).

The following two sections will consider multimodal processing from two perspectives: (1) production and generation and (2) comprehension. We shall focus on theoretical assumptions regarding the processing of speech and gesture—modalities that most researchers in the field agree are temporally and semantically very well integrated (e.g., McNeill, 1992, see also Chapter 22). Hence, when looking at speech and gesture alone, binding and segregation would seem to be less of a problem. It should be noted, however, that studies of only these two forms of communicative behavior are often carried out in specific (experimental) settings (e.g., when watching and retelling cartoons or listening to sentences with or without accompanying gestures), so that the social aspects (e.g., context) are limited. Afterwards, we shall consider what Holler and Levinson (2019) suggest for complex multimodal utterances including multiple articulators in order to address these principles and problems (Sect. 18.5).

18.3 Production and Generation of Speech and Gesture

Up to now, the production of multimodal behavior in humans is best understood for speech and speech-accompanying manual gestures.[2] Theoretical approaches to the production of speech and manual gestures are mainly interested in how this process works in a way that results in temporally and semantically aligned multimodal utterances. Various theoretical models (classes of models) have been suggested that generally differ in their assumptions regarding what level the binding, or, in more technical terms, integration, takes place.

---

[2] In order to be produced, speech of course also involves articulators (the vocal tract, including lips, tongue, etc.) that can be perceived visually. Although this is also a fascinatingly complex process, speech depends on these articulators in such a fundamental way, that we do not consider it here.

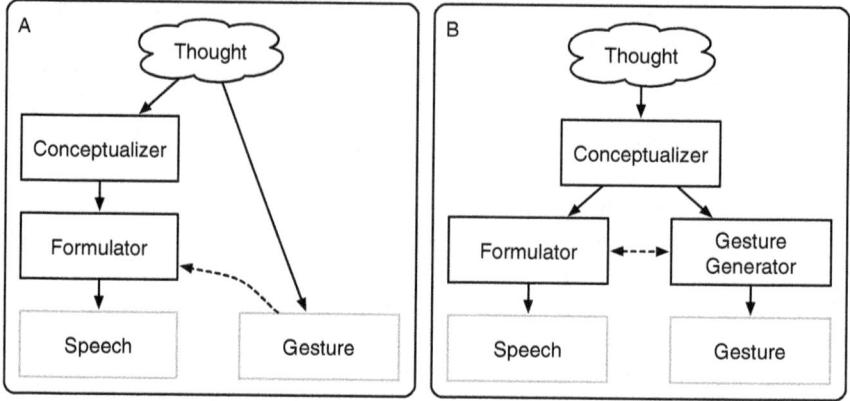

Fig. 18.1 Different classes of models that generally vary in their assumptions regarding at what level the integration of speech and gesture takes place (based on schematic illustrations in de Ruiter, 2007)

An early theoretical conceptualization of the integration of speech and gesture posited *growth points* (McNeill, 1992) as cognitive units that combine representations such as mental imagery and linguistic categorical content and serve as the starting point in utterance formation. An underlying assumption is that information is represented in (at least) two different ways, and hence, the two modalities (auditory and visual) reflect different aspects of it. Based on such a growth point, the distribution of information across speech and gesture self-organizes.

Later theories adopted an information-processing paradigm and developed integrated models of speech and gesture production based on established psycholinguistic models of human speech production (e.g., Levelt, 1989). These models enabled the investigation of different stages of communication production (e.g., conceptualization, formulation, gesture planning, speech articulation, and motor control). Figure 18.1 illustrates the different classes of models (based on illustrations in de Ruiter, 2007) and applies the terms used by Levelt (1989) for speech production. *Thought* here means both long-term memory (including situation knowledge, discourse models, and encyclopedic knowledge) and working memory (including visuospatial and propositional information). The *conceptualizer* is a unit in which a communicative intention is created, resulting in a preverbal message. The *formulator* transforms the preverbal message into a surface structure that is organized syntactically and contains both the lexical units and their phonological encoding in the target language. The *speech* unit refers to the articulation and the realization of a phonetic plan, whereas the *gesture* unit is the realization of an action plan in real or imagined space (Kita & Özyürek, 2003). Different classes of models vary in their assumption on where a gesture is generated—that is, either as a product of the visuospatial memory, and thus not part of the conceptualization and the communicative intention (e.g., Krauss et al., 2000, see Fig. 18.1A), or as part of it (e.g., Kita and Özyürek, 2003; Ruiter, 2000, see Fig. 18.1B)—and in their assumption on if and how the different processing units exchange information.

Cross-linguistic studies have expanded theoretical models and provided further evidence for the tight integration of the spoken and the gestural modality on the level of conceptualization. Kita and Özyürek (2003) asked English, Japanese, and Turkish speakers to narrate about previously seen events that happened in a cartoon. They showed that the way an event (e.g., rolling down a hill) is packaged linguistically, that is, whether it is verbalized as one or more informational units, affects the way speakers use gestures (e.g., their form and number). Based on their observations, they propose an *Interface Hypothesis*, according to which "gestures originate from an interface representation between speaking and spatial thinking" (Kita & Özyürek, 2003, p. 17) (see Fig. 18.1B).

Depending on the technical approach to multimodal output generation in an explaining agent, ideas from these model classes can guide computational modeling decisions. Although fully data-driven, end-to-end models for speech and gesture generation (recently surveyed in Nyatsanga et al., 2023) do not take such insights into account (the binding between gesture form and speech content is implicit, learned from data), architectures for speech-gesture generation that are model-based or combine model-based with data-driven approaches often resemble psycholinguistic production models. One example is the model proposed in Bergmann and Kopp (2009), in which speech formulation and gesture generation interface as in Fig. 18.1B. In this architecture, limitations in speech generation (e.g., missing lexical items or lack of computational resources in real-time incremental generation) can be compensated by gesture or vice versa (Bergmann et al., 2013), allowing a flexible generation of representational gestures that can be either bound to a lexical affiliate or complementary to the meaning expressed in speech.

Modeling timing and cross-modality synchronization (see Chap. 22) in multimodal generation have been studied extensively and are well understood (resulting in the de facto standard BML; Vilhjálmsson et al., 2007) with several implementations from different research labs (Kopp & Wachsmuth, 2004; Hartmann et al., 2005; Heloir & Kipp, 2009; Thiebaux et al., 2008; Reidsma & van Welbergen, 2013) and extensions for incremental generation (van Welbergen et al., 2014, see also Chapter 12).

18.4 Comprehension of Speech and Gesture

With respect to the online integration of spoken and gestural input – that is, how humans comprehend spoken utterances together with manual gestures – research using different methods provides evidence for a tight semantic integration of gesture and speech: Studies applying neuroimaging methods such as EEG or ERP (e.g., Holle & Gunter, 2007; Kelly et al., 2004; Bernardis et al., 2008; Kelly et al., 2010) have shown an effect of mainly iconic gestures[3] on the semantic processing of speech—for example, by comparing congruent versus incongruent speech-gesture combinations. Positive effects are reported for matching, congruent speech-gesture utterances (i.e., semantically related gestures including those that add meaning to the verbal information) and negative effects for mismatching, incongruent ones (i.e., the meaning of the gesture was unrelated or contradictory to the spoken part). This holds even for larger units of semantic content and not just for the temporally overlapping speech-gesture part. These findings support the theoretical view of a tight integration on multiple levels of processing that Kelly et al. (2010, pp. 260–261) call the "integrated-systems hypothesis." This posits that "gesture and speech mutually and obligatorily interact with one another to enhance language comprehension; that is, gesture influences the processing of speech, speech influences the processing of gesture, and this integration is mandatory" (p. 261). Behavioral studies support the findings of a tight integration by showing "faster reaction times and more correct responses when participants were in presence of congruent pairs compared to incongruent pairs" (Kandana et al., 2021, p. 3). However, Kandana et al. (2021) concluded that these results as well as the ones from clinical studies do not necessarily "imply that the gesture-speech integration is carried out in an automatic fashion and/or stems from a 'unique integrated system' [but rather] appear to plead in favor of the existence of two distinct systems, one being able to compensate the other in the event of an impairment" (p. 10).

In terms of a theoretical model, to the best of our knowledge, there is none specifically for the integration of speech and gesture in language comprehension. Instead, research (mainly investigating developmental questions) has made use of a model from cognitive psychology initially proposed for the processing and integration of verbal (spoken and written) and visual representations in order to explain educational phenomena and multimodal cognitive processes in humans: the *dual coding theory* (DCT; Paivio, 1971; Clark & Paivio, 1991; Paivio, 1990). This theory posits that information is coded in different representational formats – namely, in verbal linguistic ones (including auditory, articulatory, or, in the case of written text, visual codes) and nonverbal ones (such as images, or environmental sounds) – and these form a semantic network. The different representational formats are coded and processed in different mental systems in a contrastive, but complementary manner: verbal codes ("logogens") as separate, arbitrary, and discrete categories that are processed sequentially and nonverbal codes ("imagens") that are "analogous and perceptually similar to the events that they denote rather than being arbitrary symbols" (Clark & Paivio, 1991, p. 152) and are processed in parallel or simultaneously. Within the separate representational formats, there are associative connections between the logogens, or imagens, respectively. Across the different formats, corresponding codes are linked to each other via referential connections. A further assumption is that via both types of connections, activation is spread within one representational format or across both formats, that is, from

---

[3] Iconic gestures depict properties of objects, actions, or spatial relations (see Chap. 19).

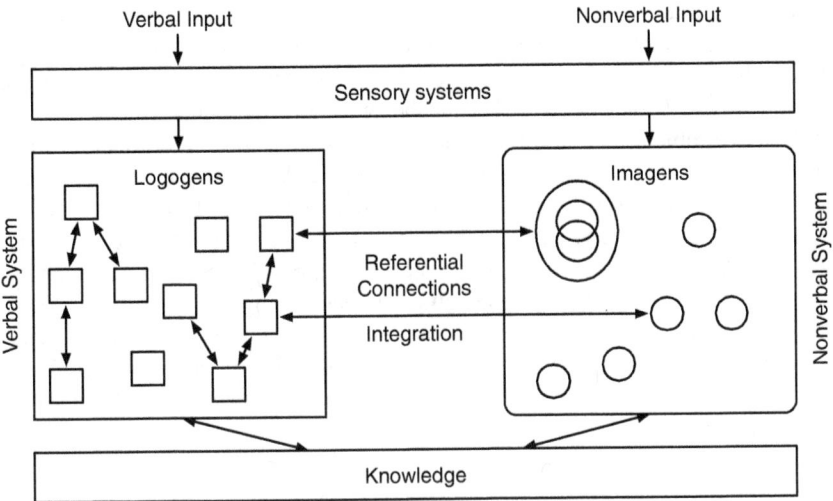

Fig. 18.2 Dual coding theory (based on the illustration in Clark and Paivio, 1991, p. 152)

logogens to other logogens or to imagens, or vice versa, based on the premise that the codes "vary in their activity levels, with some representations highly active and others depressed at any given time" (see Fig. 18.2, Clark & Paivio, 1991, p. 154). Because of the referential connections and the spread of activation between different representational formats, it is assumed that information that is dual-coded is processed and learned more easily.

Originally, the DCT was proposed to explain the cognitive interplay between verbal (written) input (e.g., textbooks, teachers' or students' notes) and visual input in the form of images in textbooks or in other material used in educational settings. It did not address explicitly or exclusively the binding of spoken and gestural parts of utterances for (long-term) learning. However, gesture researchers, mainly investigating first- and second-language learning, have used this theory to explain their findings on the facilitative effect of input provided in two modalities – speech and gesture – that are synchronized in terms of both content and time (e.g., Capone & McGregor, 2004; Kirk et al., 2011; Tellier, 2008; Huang et al., 2019). They conclude that gestural input in addition to spoken linguistic input leads to "strengthened memory traces and deeper conceptual understanding" (Vogt & Kauschke, 2017, p. 1459).

The automatic interpretation of human multimodal behavior is a task that involves machine-learning-based approaches at all stages: The human, their body parts, and their movement need to be recognized and tracked (usually using computer vision on video data) and interpreted in the interaction context in which they occur. What are tracked is usually landmarks and features that are easily recognizable in an image. During tracking, they are often stabilized (due to noise) or interpolated (due to occlusion) based on models of human body constraints (e.g., the 'skeleton' or limits of joint angles). The output, vectors of tracked points over time, can then be used to detect behaviors: gestures, facial expressions, head movements, body postures, and so forth. If other, nonvisual modalities are also of interest, they must be 'fused,' either early or late in the processing pipeline. The binding and segregation problem is usually not addressed explicitly (the interpretation model considers all data at once), and timing is often considered only within short windows of analysis, making it difficult to consider bindings that are further apart in time (temporal cycle consistency, Dwibedi et al., 2019, is a proposed solution for video-to-video mapping across time spans that could be applied to multimodal behavior).

One approach motivated by research on embodied cognition integrates perception and action into a single learned representation (Sadeghipour & Kopp, 2011) that probabilistically maps observed behavior – possibly from multiple modalities – onto an agent's own motor representations, enabling it to understand the actions of its interlocutors.

18.5 Processing of Multimodal Behavior in Social Interactions

Multimodal processing in social interaction is not only about producing or comprehending multimodal utterances in isolation, but also about coordinating with an interlocutor in a temporally and semantically aligned way (e.g., for turn-taking). Further, multimodal utterances in human social interaction include not only speech and manual gestures, but also other behaviors such as head gestures, facial expressions, gaze, and torso movement (see Chap. 19). One could expect that cognitive processing might be hindered when more information from multiple sources needs to be processed simultaneously. However, empirical research has provided evidence that multimodality facilitates cognitive processing and understanding in human communication. In their overview, Holler and Levinson (2019) state that one observation in face-to-face interactions is that pauses between turns of different interlocutors are usually very short (i.e., around 200 ms; see Stivers et al. (2009), also showing this across various cultures), though the production process takes at least 600 ms (Levinson, 2016; Indefrey & Levelt, 2004). These findings lead to the conclusion that in human face-to-face interactions: (1) Comprehension happens in parallel to own language planning, (2) comprehension and language planning are based on predictions, and (3) the co-occurrence of multimodal signals is used and helpful for these predictions. Holler and Levinson (2019, p. 641) argue that there are some "statistical regularities in the co-occurrence of multimodal signals together with the communicative meanings that the whole ensemble is intended to convey." Therefore, cognitive mechanisms such as gestalt-like principles are involved in the processing and *binding* of multimodal signals into 'multimodal gestalts' and, based on that, in the prediction of the meaning and timing of an interlocutor's utterances. For example, the multimodal gestalt "uncertainty" is expressed by certain verbal utterances ("I don't know") and nonverbal behaviors such as a shrug, a facial shrug, or certain manual gestures (Holler & Levinson, 2019, p. 641). In the board-game explanation scenario presented in Sect. 2.5, the explainee tries to resolve the spatial reference of the explainer's current explanation by displaying eye movements and a pointing gesture and then, most likely, expresses uncertainty via backchannels ("okay," "m-hm") and a self-adaptor (touching of own body; see Sect. 19.3.3). These co-occurring multimodal signals can be used by the explainer when monitoring the explainee in order to adapt the explanation to resolve problems in understanding.

Certain signals or co-occurring signals can predict other signals, and one multimodal gestalt can predict another gestalt: in the case of uncertainty, for example, a clarification request from the same interlocutor (as exemplified in the board-game scenario; Sect. 2.5). This processing and the multimodal gestalts are suggested as a solution to the binding and the segregation problem mentioned in Sect. 18.2: Some multimodal signals are more likely to co-occur and to be semantically related, which will result in *binding*, whereas others are not, which will result in *segregation*. This processing and assumed processing units (e.g., a multimodal semantic memory buffer) are addressed further in Chap. 12 with a focus on incrementality. Current findings support these assumptions about multimodal processing in social interactions: When gestures accompany questions, turn transitions between speakers are shorter (Holler et al., 2018; ter Bekke et al., 2024a), and the end of a turn can be better anticipated (ter Bekke et al., 2024b). Furthermore, Trujillo and Holler (2024) provide evidence for multimodal gestalts of facial signals (here: eyebrow raise, head tilt, and head turn) that are interpreted differently by an interlocutor when produced together compared to their interpretation when presented alone.

Gestalt principles were recognized as a promising theoretical avenue in the early days of multimodal human–computer interaction (Oviatt et al., 2003), particularly for interpreting multimodal user actions. Although there has been little to no follow-up work explicitly building systems based on these principles, they have certainly been used implicitly in (1) systems that use machine learning to discover "patterns" in multimodal user behavior for, for example, multimodal turn-taking or backchannel prediction (e.g., Skantze, 2021; Morency et al., 2010), and (2) systems with multimodal behaviors that are carefully designed by hand.

Commercially available embodied agents, especially social robots, which are equipped with automatic 'lively' nonverbal behavior (gaze toward humans, continuous pose shifts and movements, automatic nonrepresentational gestures) and can be easily customized with domain-specific content and some multimodal gestures, often have no meaningful binding and/or segregation between automatic and customized behavior and modalities. This easily leads to confusion for human users (Tuncer et al., 2023; Rudaz & Licoppe, 2024).

18.6 Operationalization: Multimodality in sXAI

One model for sXAI is human conversation. This is usually face-to-face and therefore multimodal in nature. As usual in modeling, it is important to choose the level of detail of the model as well as the level of abstraction. Should sXAI systems simply build on concepts such as co-construction, should they be conversational in the sense of a chatbot or even a spoken dialog system, or should they be able to communicate multimodally in the sense described in this chapter and in this part of the handbook?

Interactive embodied explainer-agents (such as robots, or embodied conversational agents; see Chap. 24), especially if anthropomorphized, will necessarily produce 'natural' (for the agent) behaviors that humans might interpret—whether they are used ostensively or not. In fact, an important motivation for anthropomorphizing such agents is to enable them to communicate in more natural, humanlike ways. However, this means that such systems must be able to solve the fundamental problems of multimodal communication outlined in this chapter (for a comprehensive analysis of the history and state of the art in socially interactive agents, see the two-volume handbook on the subject: Lugrin et al., 2021, 2022). What should be noted, however, is that the anthropomorphization of (X)AI agents is a "double-edged sword" (Reinecke et al., 2025, p. 1): Besides its benefits for interaction, it comes with the potential pitfall of users' over-trusting in its output (Maeda and Quan-Haase, 2024)—a significant danger for sXAI applications (Visser et al., 2023).

18.7 Rapid Access to the Content of This Chapter

This chapter addresses different assumptions about how humans process multimodal communicative signals in both their production and comprehension. Empirical research has provided evidence that multimodality facilitates cognitive processing and understanding in human communication. This becomes relevant for sXAI as soon as explanations are produced by artificial agents that provide anthropomorphic cues, such as agents that use language, speech, or exhibit human features (behavioral and morphological factors; Kim & Im, 2023). This may raise expectations in human interlocutors. Thus, such systems should integrate and synchronize various modalities naturally—not just for output generation but also when interpreting human input.

Most theoretical assumptions focus primarily on the integration of speech and gesture based on findings indicating their tight temporal and semantic synchronization (see also Chap. 22) in both production and comprehension. For **speech–gesture production** (Sect. 18.3), different classes of models (see Fig. 18.1) have been suggested that generally have in common that they assume different representational formats (mental imagery and linguistic content), but differ in their assumptions regarding the level at which the integration of these representational formats takes place. Established psycholinguistic models of human speech production (e.g., Levelt, 1989) proposing multiple stages (e.g., conceptualization, formulation, speech articulation, motor control) have been extended and investigated empirically to cover gesture production. These models have influenced multimodal behavior generation in conversational agents (Bergmann & Kopp, 2009), though current data-driven models are mostly agnostic to such cognitive assumptions (Nyatsanga et al., 2023).

For **speech–gesture comprehension** (Sect. 18.4), behavioral and neuroimaging studies support the view of an *integrated-systems hypothesis* (Kelly et al., 2010), according to which gesture and speech each influence the processing of the other. However, it is unclear whether this integration takes place in one unique or two distinct systems (Kandana et al., 2021). The *dual coding theory* (DCT; Paivio, 1990), a model from cognitive psychology proposed for the processing and integration of verbal (spoken and written) and visual representations to explain educational phenomena in humans, has been borrowed by gesture researchers to explain results showing that spoken-gestural input benefits language comprehension and receptive word learning. According to this theory, two mental systems for the processing of the different representational formats exist that form a semantic network (see Fig. 18.2). The codes are connected to one another, both within each system and across both systems, and thus, activation is spread. Accordingly, information that is dual-coded—for example, via speech and gesture—leads to higher activation and is processed and learned more easily.

In addition to speech and gesture, humans produce and process other **multimodal signals in social interaction** involving different articulators (speech, manual gestures, facial expressions, head movements, etc.). This may create two problems: *binding* and *segregation* (Holler & Levinson, 2019, see Section 18.2). Binding deals with the (re)construction of multimodal messages and their semantic meaning, even though human signals are often not totally overlapping. Segregation addresses the challenge to separate a speaker's co-occurring behaviors that are communicatively "relevant" from those that are not. This is further complicated in that the meaningfulness of a movement might only become apparent later in the interaction (e.g., when a misunderstanding is discovered). In addition, human face-to-face communication is fast; for example, pauses between interlocutors' turns are usually very short (around 200 ms; Stivers et al., 2009). Holler and Levinson (2019) propose that cognitive mechanisms such as gestalt-like principles are involved in the processing and *binding* of multimodal signals into 'multimodal gestalts' and, based on that, in predicting the meaning and timing of an interlocutor's utterances (see Sect. 18.5). Certain signals or co-occurring signals can predict other signals, and one multimodal gestalt can predict another gestalt. This processing and the multimodal gestalts are suggested as a solution to the binding and segregation problem: Some multimodal signals are more likely to co-occur and to be semantically related, which will result in binding; whereas others are not, resulting in *segregation*. These assumptions about multimodal processing in social interactions are supported by recent findings (Holler et al., 2018; ter Bekke et al., 2024a,b; Trujillo & Holler, 2024).

Acknowledgments This work was funded by the Deutsche Forschungsgemeinschaft (DFG, German Research Foundation): TRR 318/1 2021 – 438445824.

References

Bergmann, K., Kahl, S., & Kopp, S. (2013). Modeling the semantic coordination of speech and gesture under cognitive and linguistic constraints. In *Proceedings of the 13th International Conference on Intelligent Virtual Agents* (pp. 203–216). Springer. https://doi.org/10.1007/978-3-642-40415-3_18.

Bergmann, K., & Kopp, S. (2009). Increasing the expressiveness of virtual agents – Autonomous generation of speech and gesture for spatial description tasks. In *Proceedings of the 8th International Conference on Autonomous Agents and Multiagent Systems* (pp. 361–368). IFAAMAS. https://doi.org/10.5555/1558013.1558062.

Bernardis, P., Salillas, E., & Caramelli, N. (2008). Behavioural and neurophysiological evidence of semantic interaction between iconic gestures and words. *Cognitive Neuropsychology, 25*(7–8), 1114–1128. https://doi.org/10.1080/02643290801921707.

Capone, N. C., & McGregor, K. K. (2004). Gesture development: A review for clinical and research practices. *Journal of Speech, Language, and Hearing Research, 47*(1), 173–186. https://doi.org/10.1044/1092-4388(2004/015).

Clark, J. M., & Paivio, A. (1991). Dual coding theory and education. *Educational Psychology Review, 3*(4), 149–210. https://doi.org/10.1007/BF01320076.

de Ruiter, J. P. (2000). The production of gesture and speech. In D. McNeill (Ed.), *Language and gesture*. Language, Culture, and Cognition (pp. 284–311). Cambridge University Press. https://doi.org/10.1017/CBO9780511620850.018.

de Ruiter, J. P. (2007). Postcards from the mind: The relationship between speech, imagistic gesture, and thought. *Gesture, 7*(1), 21–38. https://doi.org/10.1075/gest.7.1.03rui.

Dwibedi, D., Aytar, Y., Tompson, J., Sermanet, P., & Zisserman, A. (2019). Temporal cycle-consistency learning. In *2019 IEEE/CVF Conference on Computer Vision and Pattern Recognition (CVPR)* (pp. 1801–1810). IEEE. https://doi.org/10.1109/CVPR.2019.00190.

Fricke, E. (2012). *Grammatik multimodal: Wie Wörter und Gesten zusammenwirken*. de Gruyter. https://doi.org/10.1515/9783110218893.

Hartmann, B., Mancini, M., & Pelachaud, C. (2005). Implementing expressive gesture synthesis for embodied conversational agents. In *Proceedings of the 6th International Conference on Gesture in Human–Computer Interaction and Simulation* (pp. 188–199). Springer. https://doi.org/10.1007/11678816_22.

Heloir, A., & Kipp, M. (2009). EMBR – A realtime animation engine for interactive embodied agents. In *Proceedings of the 9th International Conference on Intelligent Virtual Agents* (pp. 393–404). Springer. https://doi.org/10.1007/978-3-642-04380-2_43.

Holle, H., & Gunter, T. C. (2007). The role of iconic gestures in speech disambiguation: ERP evidence. *Journal of Cognitive Neuroscience, 19*(7), 1175–1192. https://doi.org/10.1162/jocn.2007.19.7.1175.

Holler, J., Kendrick, K. H., & Levinson, S. C. (2018). Processing language in face-to-face conversation: Questions with gestures get faster responses. *Psychonomic Bulletin & Review, 25*(5), 1900–1908. https://doi.org/10.3758/s13423-017-1363-z.

Holler, J., & Levinson, S. C. (2019). Multimodal language processing in human communication. *Trends in Cognitive Sciences, 23*(8), 639–652. https://doi.org/10.1016/j.tics.2019.05.006.

Huang, X., Kim, N., & Christianson, K. (2019). Gesture and vocabulary learning in a second language. *Language Learning, 69*(1), 177–197. https://doi.org/10.1111/lang.12326.

Indefrey, P., & Levelt, W. J. M. (2004). The spatial and temporal signatures of word production components. *Cognition, 92*(1–2), 101–144. https://doi.org/10.1016/j.cognition.2002.06.001.

Kandana Arachchige, K. G., Loureiro, I. S., Blekic, W., Rossignol, M., & Lefebvre, L. (2021). The role of iconic gestures in speech comprehension: An overview of various methodologies. *Frontiers in Psychology, 12*, 634074. https://doi.org/10.3389/fpsyg.2021.634074.

Kelly, S. D., Kravitz, C., & Hopkins, M. (2004). Neural correlates of bimodal speech and gesture comprehension. *Brain and Language, 89*(1), 253–260. https://doi.org/10.1016/S0093-934X(03)00335-3.

Kelly, S. D., Özyürek, A., & Maris, E. (2010). Two sides of the same coin: Speech and gesture mutually interact to enhance comprehension. *Psychological Science, 21*(2), 260–267. https://doi.org/10.1177/0956797609357327.

Kim, J., & Im, I. (2023). Anthropomorphic response: Understanding interactions between humans and artificial intelligence agents. *Computers in Human Behavior, 139*, 107512. https://doi.org/10.1016/j.chb.2022.107512.

Kirk, E., Pine, K. J., & Ryder, N. (2011). 'I hear whatyou say but I see what you mean': The role of gestures in children's pragmatic comprehension. *Language and Cognitive Processes, 26*(2), 149–170. https://doi.org/10.1080/01690961003752348.

Kita, S., & Özyürek, A. (2003). What does cross-linguistic variation in semantic coordination of speech and gesture reveal?: Evidence for an interface representation of spatial thinking and speaking. *Journal of Memory and Language, 48*(1), 16–32. https://doi.org/10.1016/S0749-596X(02)00505-3.

Kopp, S., & Wachsmuth, I. (2004). Synthesizing multimodal utterances for conversational agents. *Computer Animation and Virtual Worlds, 15*(1), 39–52. https://doi.org/10.1002/cav.6.

Krauss, R. M., Chen, Y., & Gottesman, R. F. (2000). Lexical gestures and lexical access: A process model. In D. McNeill (Ed). *Language and gesture* (Vol. 2, pp. 261–283). Cambridge University Press.

Levelt, W. J. M. (1989). *Speaking: From intention to articulation.* The MIT Press. https://doi.org/10.7551/mitpress/6393.001.0001.

Levinson, S. C. (2016). Turn-taking in human communication – Origins and implications for language processing. *Trends in Cognitive Sciences, 20*(1), 6–14. https://doi.org/10.1016/j.tics.2015.10.010.

Lugrin, B., Pelachaud, C., & Traum, D. (Eds.) (2021). *The Handbook on Socially Interactive Agents.* Vol. 1: Methods, Behavior, Cognition. Association for Computing Machinery. https://doi.org/10.1145/3477322.

Lugrin, B., Pelachaud, C., & Traum, D. (Eds.) (2022). *The Handbook on Socially Interactive Agents.* Vol. 2: Interactivity, Platforms, Application. Association for Computing Machinery. https://doi.org/10.1145/3563659.

Maeda, T., & Quan-Haase, A. (2024). When human–AI interactions become parasocial: Agency and anthropomorphism in affective design. In *Proceedings of the 2024 ACM Conference on Fairness, Accountability, and Transparency* (pp. 1068–1077). Association for Computing Machinery. https://doi.org/10.1145/3630106.3658956.

McNeill, D. (1992). *Hand and mind: What gestures reveal about thought.* University of Chicago Press.

Moore, R. K. (2017). Is spoken language all-or-nothing? Implications for future speech-based human–machine interaction. In K. Jokinen & G. Wilcock (Eds.), *Dialogues with social robots* (pp. 281–291). Springer. https://doi.org/10.1007/978-981-10-2585-3_22.

Morency, L.-P., de Kok, I., & Gratch J. (2010). A probabilistic multimodal approach for predicting listener backchannels. *Autonomous Agents and Multiagent Systems, 20*, 70–84. https://doi.org/10.1007/s10458-009-9092-y.

Nyatsanga, S., Kucherenko, T., Ahuja, C., Henter, G. E., & Neff, M. (2023). A comprehensive review of data-driven co-speech gesture generation. *Computer Graphics Forum, 42*(2), 569–596. https://doi.org/10.1111/cgf.14776.

Oviatt, S., Coulston, R., Tomko, S., Xiao, B., Lunsford, R., Wesson, M., & Carmichael, L. (2003). Toward a theory of organized multimodal integration patterns during human–computer interaction. In *Proceedings of the 5th International Conference on Multimodal Interfaces* (pp. 44–51). Association for Computing Machinery. https://doi.org/10.1145/958432.958443.

Paivio, A. (1971). Imagery and language. In S. J. Segal (Ed.), *Imagery. Current psychological approaches* (pp. 7–32). Academic Press. https://doi.org/10.1016/B978-0-12-635450-8.50008-X.

Paivio, A. (1990). *Mental representations: A dual coding approach*. Oxford University Press. https://doi.org/10.1093/acprof:oso/9780195066661.001.0001.

Reidsma, D., & van Welbergen, H. (2013). AsapRealizer in practice – A modular and extensible architecture for a BML realizer. *Entertainment Computing, 4*(3), 157–169. https://doi.org/10.1016/j.entcom.2013.05.001.

Reinecke, M. G., Ting, F., Savulescu, J., & Singh, I. (2025). The double-edged sword of anthropomorphism in LLMs. *Proceedings of the Online Workshop on Adaptive Education: Harnessing AI for Academic Progress, 114*(1), 4. https://doi.org/10.3390/proceedings2025114004.

Rudaz, D., & Licoppe, C. (2024). 'Playing the robot's advocate': Bystanders' descriptions of a robot's conduct in public settings". *Discourse & Communication, 18*(6), 869–881. https://doi.org/10.1177/17504813241271481.

Sadeghipour, A., & Kopp, S. (2011). Embodied gesture processing: Motor-based perception-action integration in social artificial agents. *Cognitive Computation, 3*, 419–435. https://doi.org/10.1007/s12559-010-9082-z.

Skantze, G. (2021). Turn-taking in conversational systems and human-robot interaction: A review. *Computer Speech & Language, 67*, 101178. https://doi.org/10.1016/j.csl.2020.101178.

Stivers, T., Enfield, N. J., Brown, P., Englert, C., Hayashi, M., Heinemann, T., Hoymann, G., Rossano, F., de Ruiter, J. P., Yoon, K.-E., & Levinson, S. C. (2009). Universals and cultural variation in turn-taking in conversation. *Proceedings of the National Academy of Sciences, 106*(26), 10587–10592. https://doi.org/10.1073/pnas.0903616106.

Tellier, M. (2008). The effect of gestures on second language memorisation by young children. *Gesture, 8*(2), 219–235. https://doi.org/10.1075/gest.8.2.06tel.

ter Bekke, M., Drijvers, L., & Holler, J. (2024a). Hand gestures have predictive potential during conversation: An investigation of the timing of gestures in relation to speech. *Cognitive Science, 48*(1), e13407. https://doi.org/10.1111/cogs.13407.

ter Bekke, M., Levinson, S. C., Van Otterdijk, L., Kühn, M., & Holler, J. (2024b). Visual bodily signals and conversational context benefit the anticipation of turn ends. *Cognition, 248*, 105806. https://doi.org/10.1016/j.cognition.2024.105806.

Thiebaux, M., Marshall, A., Marsella, S., & Kallmann, M. (2008). SmartBody: Behavior realization for embodied conversational agents. In *Proceedings of the 7th International Conference on Autonomous Agents and Multiagent Systems* (pp. 151–158). IFAAMAS. https://doi.org/10.1145/1402383.1402409.

Trujillo, J. P., & Holler, J. (2024). Conversational facial signals combine into compositional meanings that change the interpretation of speaker intentions. *Scientific Reports, 14*(1), 2286. https://doi.org/10.1038/s41598-024-52589-0.

Tuncer, S., Licoppe, C., Luff, P., & Heath, C. (2023). Recipient design in human–robot interaction: The emergent assessment of a robot's competence. *AI & Society, 39*(4), 1795–1810. https://doi.org/10.1007/s00146-022-01608-7.

van Welbergen, H., Yaghoubzadeh, R., & Kopp S. (2014). AsapReal3izer 2.0: The next steps in fluent behavior realization for ECAs. In *Proceedings of the 14th International Conference on Intelligent Virtual Agents* (pp. 449–462). Springer. https://doi.org/10.1007/978-3-319-09767-1_56.

Vilhjálmsson, H., Cantelmo, N., Cassell, J., Chafai, N. E., Kipp, M., Kopp, S., Mancini, M., Marsella, S., Marshall, A. N., Pelachaud, C., Ruttkay, Z. M., Thórisson, K. R., van Welbergen, H., & van der Werf, R. J. (2007). The behavior markup language: recent developments and challenges. In *Proceedings of the 7th International Conference on Intelligent Virtual Agents* (pp. 99–111). Springer. https://doi.org/10.1007/978-3-540-74997-4_10.

Visser, R., Peters, T. M., Scharlau, I., & Hammer, B. (2023). *Trust, distrust, and appropriate reliance in (X)AI: A survey of empirical evalu3ation of user trust*. https://doi.org/10.48550/arXiv.2312.02034. arXiv: 2312.02034[cs.HC].

Vogt, S., & Kauschke, C. (2017). Observing iconic gestures enhances word learning in typically developing children and children with specific language impairment. *Journal of Child Language, 44*(6), 1458–1484. https://doi.org/10.1017/S0305000916000647.

Wharton, T. (2009). *Pragmatics and non-verbal communication*. Cambridge University Press. https://doi.org/10.1017/CBO9780511635649.

Open Access This chapter is licensed under the terms of the Creative Commons Attribution 4.0 International License (http://creativecommons.org/licenses/by/4.0/), which permits use, sharing, adaptation, distribution and reproduction in any medium or format, as long as you give appropriate credit to the original author(s) and the source, provide a link to the Creative Commons license and indicate if changes were made.

The images or other third party material in this chapter are included in the chapter's Creative Commons license, unless indicated otherwise in a credit line to the material. If material is not included in the chapter's Creative Commons license and your intended use is not permitted by statutory regulation or exceeds the permitted use, you will need to obtain permission directly from the copyright holder.

Chapter 19
Characteristics of Nonverbal Behavior

Stefan Lazarov, Igor Tchappi, and Angela Grimminger

Abstract In social interactions, humans use nonverbal forms of behavior, performed by different body parts (e.g., head, eyes, hands), in addition to verbal behavior. Many of these forms of nonverbal behavior are multifunctional and their meaning is not unequivocal. This may raise communication challenges not only in human–human interaction but also in human–machine interaction, especially when the interaction partners are not able to interpret the nonverbal behavior and their functions correctly. This chapter focuses on different forms and functions of human nonverbal behavior by reviewing research both on human–human and human–machine interaction. The purpose of the chapter is to explain the importance and relevance of human nonverbal behavior for the development of sXAI and to suggest how to leverage characteristics of human nonverbal behavior to possible scenarios of human–machine interaction.

19.1 How Does This Chapter Relate to XAI?

Although current XAI systems mainly provide explanations in the form of text or with the help of visualizations (e.g., SHAP Lundberg & Lee, 2017), they often overlook the importance of social interaction and the multimodal nature of communication. In human social interaction, however, nonverbal behaviors communicate information, emotions (see Chap. 20), intentions, etc., complement verbal communication, and foster understanding and connection between individuals. In fact, nonverbal behavior can encompass various forms of signals such as body orientation, gaze, gestures (addressed in this chapter), or facial expressions, and tone

---

S. Lazarov (✉) · A. Grimminger
Psycholinguistics, Faculty of Arts and Humanities, Paderborn University, Paderborn, Germany
e-mail: stefan.lazarov@uni-paderborn.de

I. Tchappi
FINATRAX, SnT, University of Luxembourg, Esch-sur-Alzette, Luxembourg
e-mail: igor.tchappi@uni.lu

of voice, (addressed in Chap. 20) to name a few; co-occurring with verbal behavior, it plays an important role in human social interaction, for example, by facilitating the exchange of spoken utterances, i.e., turn-taking, between interlocutors (Goodwin, 1981).

In the same vein, as humans increasingly interact with machines (computers, robots, smartphones etc.), it is crucial to understand the role of nonverbal behavior in human–machine communication in order to design AI systems that can interact with users in a manner that is natural, intuitive, and contextually appropriate in reducing human cognitive effort, as well as fostering more effective human–machine interactions.

In this regard, the ability to interpret the nonverbal behavior of explainers and explainees in relation to their communicative intentions and cognitive processing could improve both, the explanation and the understanding of explainees. Further, explaining and feedback behavior in human–human interaction are both realized in a multimodal fashion (see also Chaps. 3 and 22). Therefore, a thorough understanding of nonverbal communicative behavior in human–human and human–machine interaction is vital for advancing XAI systems beyond multimodality alone, enabling them to communicate explanations that are context-aware and aligned with natural human expectations.

Over the past two decades, many research works have investigated nonverbal behavior in human–machine interaction (see Sect. 19.4, also Chap. 20). However, there is limited research exploring the approach to incorporate nonverbal social signals within the framework of sXAI. This chapter aims to reflect this approach in the context of sXAI – i.e., in social interaction between explainers and explainees where either is a machine – by first reviewing existing literature on the characteristics of nonverbal behavior in human–human interactions.

19.2 The Dynamics of Nonverbal Behavior as a Challenge for Human–Machine Interaction

Although verbal communication is often segmented into distinct units, such as words and sentences, making it clear and structured, human nonverbal behavior, in contrast, flows in a more fluid and uninterrupted manner (e.g., McNeill, 1992). On the one hand, this continuous nature allows nonverbal behavior to convey subtle and nuanced messages that can enhance or contradict verbal communication, providing a richer and more dynamic exchange of information between different agents (both human and technical ones). On the other hand, it represents a challenge in the field of human–machine interaction, particularly in robotics, where embodied agents have to interpret and respond to complex social cues in real time to ensure socially acceptable interactions. One main focus of the research in robotics is therefore dedicated to creating robots capable of producing and interpreting nonverbal signals similarly to nonverbal signals in human–human interactions (Saunderson & Nejat,

2019; Xu et al., 2014). Recent results have revealed the complexity of imitating the fluidity and complementarity of verbal and nonverbal signals within humans' interactions to transpose it in human–robot interaction (Aly & Tapus, 2016; Salem et al., 2013; Yoon et al., 2019). To ease the complexity, traditional and commercial robotics research has often explored nonverbal gestures in isolation—a wave, a nod, or a simulated smile (Leite et al., 2013). Yet without the natural flow and integration of these behaviors into a coherent nonverbal or multimodal narrative, robots can appear unnatural or unsettling to human observers (Aly & Tapus, 2016; Leite et al., 2013; Salem et al., 2011). The difficulty lies not only in reproducing a gesture, but also in capturing the seamless transition between gestures, expressions, and postures that characterize human nonverbal communication. The challenge extends beyond the mechanical reproduction of movements of robots to encompass the timing, rhythm, and context in which these nonverbal cues are deployed. Human interaction is deeply contextual (see Chap. 4), with the meaning and appropriateness of gestures and expressions varying widely across different social and cultural settings. Thus, creating robots capable of providing a suitable explanation (e.g., goal-based explanation or data-driven explanation, (Anjomshoae et al., 2019)) that can navigate this complex landscape requires not only technical progress, but also an understanding of the social and emotional nuances of human explanation, that is, a multidisciplinary approach that draws insights from psychology, sociology, and linguistics. As research seeks to push the boundaries of what embodied agents can understand and express, it is necessary to explore and understand the nature of nonverbal behavior in human–human interaction. The following section provides insights into the formal and functional characteristics of different forms of human nonverbal behavior from empirical research.

19.3 Forms of Nonverbal Behavior in Human–Human Interaction

Human nonverbal communication is constituted by different forms of bodily behavior which can be related to different interactional processes, such as the exchange of spoken utterances between interlocutors, i.e., turn-taking, information processing, and understanding. To track these processes, interlocutors monitor each other's bodily behavior moment by moment, focusing on their speech acts, eye gaze behavior, co-speech gestures, and torso orientations (Clark & Krych, 2004). Further, interaction partners use various nonverbal and multimodal signals of the interlocutor to predict, for example, a question type and their responses accordingly (Nota et al., 2021, 2023), the speakers' intentions (Trujillo & Holler, 2024), or the end of a speaker's turn (ter Bekke et al., 2024) (see also Chap. 18). These multimodal communicative resources can be used to express and monitor an interlocutor's level of understanding or attention without necessarily disrupting the speaker (e.g., Buschmeier & Kopp, 2018; Clark & Krych, 2004; Krahmer & Swerts, 2005).

Although this chapter does not address verbal behavior, we would like to highlight that each form of nonverbal behavior described below often co-occurs with and is semantically related to speech, and different forms of nonverbal behavior can co-occur with one another. Scenario 4 (Chap. 2.5) illustrates different forms and their co-occurrence in human–human explanatory interactions. Further, the research referred to below does not exclusively address explanatory interactions, but describes human communicative behavior more generally. In the following sections, we describe different nonverbal behaviors with various articulators that are used for communicative purposes; we focus on those that are related to the coordination of interaction and cognitive processing (for an overview, see Table 19.1, p. 349). Nonverbal behavior associated with emotional meaning, such as facial expressions or paralinguistic aspects of speech, is addressed in Chap. 20.

19.3.1 Eye Gaze Behavior

Eye gaze behavior is (for sighted people) one of the most prominent forms of nonverbal behavior in human–human interaction because of its dual function—(a) information uptake and (b) information signal to others: (a) Via their own gaze, interlocutors gather information, for example, about other people's focus of attention or emotional expression, and they can further use it as support for speech perception; (b) at the same time, a person's gaze behavior is accessible and, therefore, informative to others (for a review, see Hessels, 2020). Gaze behavior also depends on various factors, such as the task, cultural norms, the presence of other people, or gender, to name a few (Hessels, 2020). Thus, it is not surprising that gaze behavior is an ambiguous signal and may undergo different interpretations, for example, as a signal of visual attention (Argyle & Cook, 1976; Goodwin, 1981; Kendon, 1967), as a signal of increased cognitive processing (Glenberg et al., 1998; Goodwin, 1981; Phelps et al., 2006), or as disengagement from a task (Dohert & Phelps, 2007).

Within dialogical interactions, gaze seems to be important for turn management among interlocutors (for a review, see Degutyte & Astell, 2021), such as the allocation and change of turns, or the request for attention or short feedback signals (Bavelas et al., 2002; Goodwin, 1981; Jokinen et al., 2010b,a; Kendon, 1967). A speaker's gaze directed at an interlocutor often seems to occur at the end of their turn, while a speaker's gaze averted from them may be used as a turn-holding signal (Degutyte & Astell, 2021; Kendon, 1967), though the results regarding the function of gaze at different phases within turn-taking are not conclusive (Degutyte & Astell, 2021). Further and with respect to conversational management, interlocutors' gaze behavior may influence the openings, the duration, and the closures of topics of an interaction (Rossano, 2012, 2013).

Eye gaze may also have a deictic function when directed at people, objects, or locations (Clark, 2003; Goodwin, 1981), aids understanding, or resolves misunderstanding or ambiguity (Hanna & Brennan, 2007). In a study on dyadic face-to-face interactions in which instructors requested from addressees to select an object among similarly looking objects and move it to a targeted location (Hanna & Brennan, 2007), the addressees used the instructors' eye gaze at the targeted objects together with their verbal descriptions to resolve the ambiguity between objects sharing nearly identical characteristics.

A special form of gaze shift – *gaze aversions from an interlocutor* – seems to be related to cognitive processing,[1] both in adults (Abeles & Yuval-Greenberg, 2017; Glenberg et al., 1998) and in children (e.g. Phelps et al., 2006). Based on their experimental studies, the authors concluded that a person's gaze aversion while thinking about the solutions of challenging arithmetical or verbal tasks are related to increased cognitive processing and that it enhances the overall task performance (Glenberg et al., 1998; Phelps et al., 2006). Similar observations have been made in dialogs—the so-called *thinking face* (i.e., prominent withdraw of the gaze and display of "doing thinking," Heller, 2021, p. 1) has been related to language processing (Bavelas & Chovil, 2018; Goodwin & Goodwin, 1986).

Thus, even though gaze is an ambiguous signal, this nonverbal behavior is relevant in explanatory situations, as it supports conversational management, and can indicate a need for clarification, for additional time to process what has been explained, or understanding-related issues.

19.3.2 Co-Speech Gestures

The verbal mode of communication cannot remain unmentioned when discussing co-speech gestures, because together, gestures and speech form an integrated system which becomes apparent in a tight semantic and temporal coupling (Kendon, 2004; Kita, 2009; McNeill, 2005) (see Chap. 22). A co-speech gesture can be defined as " visible action when it is used as an utterance or as part of an utterance (Kendon, 2004, p. 7); this definition includes any body part that is used for this purpose. McNeill (1998, p. 11) defines them closer as "a movement of the arms or hands in a region of space reserved for symbolic expression, typically in front of the torso," thus limiting them to hand and arm gestures. In this section, we will mainly address hand gestures; however, some gesture types can be expressed with other articulators, especially when considering different cultures (see below).

Formally, co-speech gestures establish reference to syntactic, semantic, or pragmatic units of speech. They can increase an addressee's understanding via pointing, representing, or highlighting important content (e.g., Kendon, 2004; McNeill, 1992, 2006). Classically, co-speech (hand) gestures are categorized as either *deictic, iconic, metaphoric,* or *beats* (McNeill, 1992, 2006), with distinguishable forms. Deictic, iconic, and metaphoric gestures are constituted by triphasic hand movements (gesture phases: preparation, stroke, retraction), typically in front of

---

[1] It is also related to clinical conditions, or affective states; see Chap. 20.3.

the upper body (McNeill, 1992). Deictic gestures[2] are used to refer to objects, people, or locations, with culturally varying forms—in Western cultures, they are often realized as index-finger or palm pointing, often with the arm being extended (Clark, 2003), but other cultures use other articulators (such as lips, feet, or head: Cooperrider et al., 2018; Wilkins, 2003). Iconic gestures are hand and arm movements depicting properties of objects, actions, or events, and they contribute to addressee's memory recall and comprehension (Dargue et al., 2021; Kandan-Arachchige et al., 2021; McKern et al., 2021). Unlike iconic gestures, metaphoric gestures depict abstract concepts within an utterance (e.g., opposing opinions being held in the left and the right hand; Beattie & Shovelton, 2005; McNeill, 1992). Beat gestures (also *beats*) are biphasic hand movements (repetitive preparation and stroke phases) that do not refer to semantic information in their form; rather, they highlight specific semantic or syntactic units within the spoken part of an utterance by being aligned with the affiliated part and accompanied by prosodic marking (Beege et al., 2020; McNeill, 1992).

Emblems (also *conventional gestures*) are conventionalized (culturally specific) gestures, and their (arbitrary) meaning can be derived even in the absence of speech by the members from the same sociocultural background (Kendon, 1995; McNeill, 1992, 2006). Emblems can replace spoken feedback, and their use depends either on the interlocutor or on external factors, such as a noisy environment preventing the acoustic perception of speech. Examples for such conventionalized hand gestures in Western cultures are the thumbs-up gesture and the *OK* gesture (thumb and pointing fingertips touching and the other fingers extended), which signal agreement or approval (e.g., Kendon, 1995; McNeill, 2006; Teßendorf, 2013). The list of mono- and cross-cultural emblems is long, but the examples above can often occur in explanatory dialogs, especially when an explainee is asked to agree or disagree about a specific problem (see Chap. 23). Therefore, it is necessary that computational modeling of an sXAI takes cultural conventions in gestural behavior into account.

Although research on co-speech hand gestures was often focused on particular gesture categories, they can also have hybrid forms: For example, an extended index finger can be a pointing gesture at a location (deictic) and a beat in the form of multiple pointing at the same time, or a pointing and an iconic gesture when the index finger not only refers to a location but also draws a shape referring to some features there (see Lazarov & Grimminger, 2024, for a study on such hybrid forms within explanatory interactions). McNeill (2006), thus, suggested to rather analyze gesture dimensions (deixis, iconicity, metaphoricity, and temporal highlighting) than distinct gesture categories. These observations, however, pose a challenge for technical systems in detecting different gesture types.

---

[2] See Scenario 4 and Fig. 2.2 in Chap. 2.5 for an example.

19.3.3 Adaptors

A group of specific hand movements on the own body (e.g., touching the neck or head) or on objects without clear reference to units in speech (thus, not considered *gestures*), namely, adaptors, are potentially interesting in explanatory interactions because they are associated with listeners' cognitive processing (Ekman & Friesen, 1969). However, recent research on their function is very sparse. Two groups of adaptors have been empirically investigated (Ekman & Friesen, 1969): (1) *self-adaptors* (self-contact reducing cognitive load or anxiety) and (2) *object-adaptors* (object-contact reducing cognitive load). Self-adaptors[3] tend to appear (a) in the presence of novel environmental factors, for example, an unknown interaction partner; (b) in correspondence to the introduction of a novel topic of conversation; (c) in moments of emotional affection, for example, anxiety (Ruggieri et al., 1982); (d) or during information processing and speech production (Allen & Honeycutt, 1997; Harrigan, 1985). Recent empirical research on the use of self-adaptors by adults has mainly focused on speech response tasks involving increased cognitive load (Cienki et al., 2023). Some forms of self-adaptors, such as the self-soothing touch, have been reported to have a positive effect on the reduction of stress (Dreisoerner et al., 2021). Other forms of self-adaptors, such as facial self-touches, are indicative of an increased cognitive load (Mueller et al., 2019) and foster working memory functions in challenging cognitive tasks (Grunwald et al., 2014; Spille et al., 2021). Like self-adaptors, object adaptors facilitate speech information processing and speech production in situations of increased cognitive load or stress (Allen & Honeycutt, 1997; Ekman & Friesen, 1969).

19.3.4 Head Movements

In human–human interaction, interlocutors' head movements indicate the structure of ongoing discourse and regulate processes, such as turn-taking, or marking of semantic and syntactic boundaries (Duncan, 1972; Kendon, 1972; McClave, 2000). They may have different functions, depending on the interactional role (speaker or addressee): *Speakers' head movements* can provide the addressee with guidance within discourse, for example, by pointing at objects or the addressee with the head, or by stressing important semantic information in speech (McClave, 2000), whereas *addressees' head movements* are a form of nonverbal feedback, commonly expressed by conventionalized (i.e., culturally specific) head gestures (Bavelas et al., 2002; Kendon, 1970; McClave, 2000). Therefore, based on their function, many head movements in human–human interaction are regarded as *head gestures* with a conventionalized meaning (*emblems*; see 19.3.2). For example, in Western cultures,

---

[3] See Scenario 4 in Chap. 2.5 for an example.

head nods (down-up movements) signal addressees' approval or attention, and head shakes (side to side sweeps) negation or denial (McClave, 2000). Often, these head gestures co-occur together with vocal forms of feedback such as backchannels[4], so that head gestures are regarded also as a nonverbal form of backchannelling (Malisz et al., 2016; Yngve, 1970). Although head nods and head shakes express conventionalized polarity, head nods can undergo ambiguous interpretations (see Chap. 21), depending, for example, on whether or not they co-occur with other behaviors, or with which form of behavior: A speaker may interpret a listener's head nod either as understanding or as attention when occurring unimodally (Gander & Gander, 2020), or as an agreement when accompanied by different forms of vocal backchannels (Allwood & Cerrato, 2003). Further, this feedback signal may affect the speaker with respect to their level of confidence, as was shown by Gurney et al. (2014) for eyewitness interviews: A head nod, as a positive nonverbal feedback signal, from an interviewer leads to a higher level of confidence of a witness' report, independent of the correctness of what is reported. A subcategory of head nods – tilts (down-up movements sideways) – also expresses positive feedback, such as acceptance and agreement (Włodarczak et al., 2012) and signal ongoing attention and cognitive processing in argumentation (Ismail & Syahputri, 2022). Jerks (inverted nods, up-down movements) signal listeners' understanding or surprise (Włodarczak et al., 2012). The detailed kinematic characteristics of these and other head gesture categories have been thoroughly described in annotation manuals, e.g., by Allwood et al. (2007), Kousidis et al. (2013), and Włodarczak et al. (2012).

19.3.5 *Torso Movements*

In dialogical conversations, torso movements can express interlocutors' engagement with each other (Goodwin, 1981). More specifically, torso movements towards or away from the interaction partner co-occur with gaze shifts (see Sect. 19.3.1), indicating the direction of visual attention of the interlocutors (Mortensen & Hazel, 2014). When interlocutors complete a task that they have to perform, both orient their bodies towards each other in alignment with eye gaze (Robinson, 2006). In a study on addressees' perception of a speaker's video-taped, trained bodily behavior, Nagels et al. (2015) found that addressees' feeling of involvement increases when the speaker's body is oriented frontally. In a more recent study on face-to-face discussions, Trujillo and Holler (2021) reported that interlocutors' torso movements and the magnitude of the movements are related to the spoken discourse, information requests, initiation of repairs, and interlocutors' emotional affection during the interactions.

---

[4] Backchannels are short verbal–vocal listener responses, which are a common way for interlocutors to provide feedback in dialog (Allwood et al., 1992). Examples: *alright*, *okay*, and *yes* (lexical backchannels), or *mhm* and *yeah* (non-lexical backchannels).

Table 19.1 Forms of nonverbal behavior in human–human interaction addressed in this chapter

Behavior	Formal features	Functional features
Eye gaze	Directed towards the interlocutor, an object or away	Indication of (dis-)engagement, cognitive processing, or feedback elicitation
Co-speech hand gestures	Arms and hands pointing, showing, illustrating, highlighting or symbolizing finger/hand palm movements	Provide semantic reference to objects, locations, and concrete and abstract concepts in the co-occurrence with speech
Adaptors	Physical self-contact or contact with another object with arms and hands	Indicate emotional affection, cognitive processing, and speech planning
Head movements	(1) Speaker: speech-related shifts of head position; (2) Addressee: culturally specific head gestures (e.g., head nods & head shakes)	(1) Speaker, providing guidance within discourse addressee or indication of turn-taking; (2) addressee, nonverbal feedback about attention, (dis-)approval, and (non-)understanding
Torso movements	Directed towards an interlocutor or away and changing	Indicate social (dis-)engagement, emotional affection

19.3.6 Summary: Nonverbal Behavior in Human–Human Interaction

In the previous subsections we have reviewed different forms of humans' nonverbal behaviors and research on their function for interactional and cognitive processes (see also Table 19.1). In general, certain behavior can be associated with certain (interactional) functions. However, as we have described above, research has shown that the forms of nonverbal behavior and their meaning or interpretation depend on various aspects, such as their co-occurrence with other verbal and nonverbal means, on the situation or the context (see Chap. 4), and on cultural conventions. This is important for developing sXAI and its use in social interaction with humans with different cultural backgrounds, or when applying sXAI for different purposes.

19.4 Forms of Nonverbal Behavior in Human–Machine Interaction

Explanatory interactions in which either the explainer or the explainee is a machine (virtual agent, robots, etc.) encompass a range of communicative actions that extend beyond verbal exchanges (Buzcu et al., 2024; Tessa et al., 2023). As machines increasingly participate in social contexts (Najja et al., 2022; Tchappi et al., 2020), it becomes essential in the field of human–machine interaction (HMI) to build them with abilities to interpret, generate, and respond to nonverbal cues, in order to establish effective and intuitive interactions (Saunderson & Nejat, 2019). In the following, we will review research in HMI (not only from XAI), in which nonverbal behavior has been implemented in artificial systems and evaluated by human users. Note that the way these behaviors are implemented often differs from how humans produce them.

19.4.1 Eye Gaze Behavior

The use of suitable eye gaze by a robot can support several objectives in social interaction with humans in general and in sXAI in particular (Saunderson & Nejat, 2019). As stated before in Sect. 19.3.1, in human interactions, eye contact is prominent and often associated with engagement and turn-taking in conversations. In HMI, the ability of machines to understand and replicate eye gaze behavior is also important for creating natural and effective communication. Breazeal et al. (2005) conducted an experiment to study how a robot's gaze impacts task performance. In their study, participants interacted with the furry Leonardo (Leo) robot, teaching it the locations of buttons and verifying tasks. Their results showed that in scenarios in which Leo used gaze dynamically with changes in gaze direction and tracking of the human's head, participants completed tasks 43% (close to half) times faster and made half as many errors compared to scenarios without this dynamic gaze. Additionally, participants rated Leo's behavior as more understandable in terms of its actions and expressions in the more dynamic gaze condition. In another experiment using the robot Furhat (Al Moubayed et al., 2013), Skantze et al. (2013) found that a robot's gaze helps human users disambiguate references to objects on a shared referential space during a route map task in which the robot instructed the human. The robot Furhat was further used in a study examining the effect of a robot's gaze behavior on a human interlocutor during an interview with questions that varied in their level of intimacy (Mishra et al., 2023): The robot either averted its gaze every 3–5 seconds (based on observations of natural gaze behavior from HHI studies) or maintained a fixed gaze at the human interlocutor. Results showed that, in the fixed gaze condition, the human interlocutor looked away from the robot more often than in the gaze aversion condition. Thus, the researchers concluded that a robot exhibiting gaze behavior resembling that of humans is less effortful for a human interlocutor, compared to a robot maintaining a fixed gaze. Regarding human gaze patterns associated with turn-taking, similar patterns to those reported in studies on human–human interaction were observed in this study (see Sect. 19.3.1).

In order to be able to respond to requests, a machine needs to monitor and interpret human gaze behavior, which, for example, could signal a request for an explanation. In an earlier study, Kuno et al. (2007) modeled a robotized museum guide *Robovie-R ver. 2* for monitoring human visitors' gaze behavior (in combination with head movements). Kuno et al. (2007) reported that the robot autonomously aligned its head and gaze direction towards the visitors when they moved their heads and gaze towards the robot. The robot interpreted the visitors' eye gaze and head movement as a request for assistance, but when the robot received verbal requests by the visitors, a remote operator took control over the content of verbal responses.

In sXAI, the implementation of eye gaze behavior involves sophisticated computer vision techniques for gaze tracking and algorithms that determine the appropriate timing and direction of gaze shifts. Human's gaze directions (measured using eye tracking) has been successfully used by a robot to predict which object will be manipulated, however in a rather simple tasks with limited choices of objects (Aronson et al., 2021). Thus, accurately interpreting gaze in real time, i.e., avoiding, for example, ambiguity (see Chap. 21), and ensuring that the machine's gaze behavior aligns with human expectations (as it has been investigated in Mishra et al., 2023) is still a challenge.

19.4.2 Co-Speech Gestures and Adaptors

Equipping social robots with the ability to accompany their speech with humanlike co-speech arm and hand gestures (see Sect. 19.3.2) may be crucial for enhancing their acceptability and for increasing their use in real-world settings in general (Gjaci et al., 2022), including XAI settings. The rationale for incorporating co-speech gestures into robots is to convey meaning more naturally, thereby bridging communication gaps and enhancing HMI (He et al., 2022). To this end, research explores the impact of co-speech gestures on human perceptions of robots across various aspects, including humanlikeness, animacy, and focused attention, among others (He et al., 2022). As co-speech gestures improve interaction experiences between humans (Kendon, 2004; McNeill, 2006, see also Sect. 19.3.2), they may also improve interaction between humans and robots (Yoon et al., 2019). Although social robots such as Pepper, Nao, etc. are, to a certain extent, capable of performing humanlike co-speech gestures, they are limited to a predefined set considered during the design stage and are subject to technical limitations in terms of smooth and noise-reduced movements and their velocity, which are important features for accompanying speech in a temporally aligned fashion. Thus, the gesture capabilities of robots and their flexible use is currently limited. Further, as we have described in Sect. 19.3.2, there are cultural differences in the use of gestures, which is a further challenge to computational modeling. Recently, Gjaci et al. (2022) implemented culture-specific communicative gestures into Pepper by training the computational model with a culturally homogeneous dataset composed of different speakers. In an evaluation study, they investigated whether participants from the same cultural background as the training data (experimental group) differed in their perception of the robot's gestures compared to participants from a different cultural background (control group) and found statistically higher ratings by the experimental group regarding the perceived naturalness of the robot's gestures.

To generate consistent co-speech gestures, robots and virtual agents need to be equipped with advanced modules that synchronize gesture production with verbal output, ensuring that the gestures are both contextually appropriate and responsive to the communicative situation, whether through manual programming or data-driven approaches, etc. This requires not only technical expertise in motion planning and control but also an understanding of the social and cultural norms governing gesture use and of theoretical models of humans' speech–gesture integration and processing (see Chap. 18).

To our knowledge, there is no research on adaptors in HMI. However, recognizing humans' adaptors may improve a machine's ability to detect understanding- or stress-related issues in an explanation in sXAI and to adapt accordingly (Leite et al., 2014; Mumm & Mutlu, 2011) (also see Chap. 20). Their implementation in sXAI involves developing sensors and algorithms that can accurately detect and interpret these subtle hand movements.

19.4.3 Head Movements

Head movements are an important aspect of nonverbal communication in HMI in general and sXAI in particular. Head movements of embodied robots and virtual agents can influence human perception and interaction with these systems (Saunderson & Nejat, 2019): Even subtle head movements of an embodied robot can positively impact perceptions of the robot's social engagement, friendliness, and empathy (Embgen et al., 2012; Wang et al., 2006). For example, to understand how a robot's head movements affect enjoyment of human interaction partners, Wang et al. (2006) conducted a study where participants interacted with the humanoid robot Nico in an open-ended setting, that is, in a short interaction without any instructions. Nico used four different head-tracking modes, namely, no tracking (static head), smooth movement tracking, fast tracking, and participant avoidance (looking away). Results showed that participants reported the highest levels of enjoyment for the avoidance and fast-tracking modes, especially those who had no prior experience with robots. In the same vein, using Daryl, a mildly humanized robot, Embgen et al. (2012) studied how well humans could recognize (a robot's way of) emotion display through robot head movements together with other signals such as LEDs glowing in different colors. They found that users could recognize the intended emotions (such as fear, happiness, curiosity) better than by chance. However, it is unclear whether this is due to the head movements alone or other aspects, such as the combination with colors, which could be perceived more holistically (see Chap. 18 on theoretical assumptions regarding humans' processing of multimodal signals).

However, incorporating head movements into sXAI involves both recognizing humans' head movements by artificial agents and recognizing an AI agent's head movement by the human (Skantze, 2021). In an experiment, Anzabi and Umemuro (2023) reported that human interlocutors increased their trust and engagement with a robot that signaled attention in listening to the human speakers via head nodding. In this relation, Irfan et al. (2023) recommend that social robots should demonstrate active listening to human addressees using head gestures (e.g., head nodding) and backchannelling (e.g., *uh huh, yeah*). However, as research by Gurney et al. (2014) shows, head nodding as a feedback signal may result in a higher level of confidence in a human who reports on a certain event, even if this report contains wrong memories (see Sect. 19.3.4). This effect certainly is not always desirable. Therefore, attempts to implement nonverbal behaviors in social artificial agents need to be aware of the various consequences this may have. Beyond that, there are several other challenges such as interpreting the meaning of human head movements (see Sect. 19.3.4), or consistency and cultural sensitivity because interpretations of head movements can vary across different cultures (Tchappi et al., 2023).

19.4.4 Torso Movements and Posture

Torso movements, though also often subtle, may play a crucial role in communication during interactions between humans and machine agents. Focusing on the significance of torso movement in interactions, Kaushik and Simmons (2021) conducted an evaluation of perceived emotions in a set of nonverbal behaviors exhibited by the humanoid robot Quori. Their analysis focused on six summarized movement properties, namely, torso end, torso degree, torso speed, arm symmetry, right arm end, and left arm end. The findings revealed that specific movement characteristics, such as the torso leaning backward or arms positioned high at the end of a movement, were closely linked to particular emotional expressions. In fact, leaning forward during an explanation could be interpreted as a sign of engagement, interest, and attentiveness (D'Mello et al., 2017). Further, Hoffman et al. (2015) investigated how humans perceived a robot's varying posture when standing, namely, neutral (during no conversation), calm (at the start of a conversation), curious (after ongoing conversation), and scared (during loud conversation), and found that the robot using postures was perceived as socially engaging with an intriguing, social–emotional appeal. Compared to the neutral body language condition, results of the other conditions show that the robot was identified to be more warm, friendly, social, and empathetic.

One of the main challenges with respect to torso movements for sXAI involving embodied robots lies in their stability and position control (standing position) when trying to accurately emulate human upper body motion, which remains one of the most complex aspects of humanoid robot design (Sander et al., 2012). In fact, the human spine provides remarkable flexibility while supporting the weight of the entire upper body, making it difficult to replicate in robotic systems.

19.5 Operationalization: Monitoring of Human Nonverbal Behavior in sXAI

One way to equip an sXAI with social capabilities could be to integrate the knowledge about the kinematic and functional characteristics of human nonverbal behavior in the perceptual system of a machine. By that, an artificial system should be enabled to complete an explanation task together with a human explainee via co-constructions, scaffolding, and monitoring (Rohlfing et al., 2021). For this purpose, explainees' cognitive processing and their level of understanding need to be continuously monitored over the course of an explanation (see Sect. 19.3). One possible way to do so is that systems are capable of monitoring the various forms of humans' nonverbal behavior, such as eye gaze or head or hand gestures, which are indicators of ongoing attention, cognitive processing, or levels of understanding. The challenge here is the correct interpretation of these behaviors because of their context dependency and ambiguity and also to separate a speaker's co-occurring behaviors that are communicatively relevant from those that are irrelevant. The suggestions made by Holler and Levinson (2019) regarding humans' processing of multiple signals as a meaningful unit (see Chap. 18.5) might be useful to address this challenge. Systems that are capable of detecting nonverbal signals as a unit may use these forms of behavior to co-construct certain aspects of an explanation related to explainees' cognitive processing and engagement with such systems (for a review, see Axelsson et al., 2022). Further, this capability may enhance the sXAI's ability to interpret the content and purpose of human utterances and thus adapt accordingly.

To integrate the recognition of different forms of human nonverbal behavior in an sXAI, first, it is important to record and analyze observations of nonverbal behavior from explanatory human–human interactions. Second, the kinematic aspects (see Table 19.1) of each form of behavior need to be precisely defined so that an sXAI is able to detect relevant body movements. Third, each form of behavior needs to be correctly interpreted, so that the system adapts the explanation to explainees' cognitive processing and understanding accordingly. One possible way to integrate the knowledge about the kinematics and the functions of human nonverbal behavior is to consult with empirical research on human–human explanations and to empirically investigate whether they serve similar functions in human–agent sXAI settings. This involves the technical design and deployment of sensors, algorithms, and behavioral modules that enable machines to both recognize and generate nonverbal signals in ways that are responsive, adaptive, and contextually appropriate as stated before. Head movements, for instance, can be operationalized by equipping robots or virtual agents with sensors and cameras that track human head movements and algorithms that replicate head gestures either manually or using AI. These systems should be able to detect the direction and speed of head movements and generate corresponding responses in (towards) real time, that is, by optimizing the time lag. The challenge lies in ensuring that the head movements are consistent with the explanation during the interaction. In the same vein, operationalizing gaze behavior in sXAI involves the use of advanced computer vision algorithms to track human eye movements and synchronize the machine's gaze with the flow of conversation. In addition to technical aspects, operationalizing nonverbal behaviors in sXAI requires a multidisciplinary approach that combines technical expertise in robotics, computer vision, and machine learning with a deep understanding of human social and communicative behavior.

19.6 How Does This Chapter Inspire Further Research on sXAI?

This chapter focuses on the importance of nonverbal behavior in social interactions and human communication. Because AI systems increasingly become part of our daily interactions, the ability to interpret and respond to nonverbal cues and use them as resources in addition to written or spoken text will be essential for creating more natural and effective exchanges between humans and machines, especially for explanatory purposes with the aim of increasing understanding. The insights gathered here point to several promising directions for future research in sXAI.

One promising direction is the personalization and adaptation of sXAI systems based on individual differences in nonverbal behavior. As discussed in this chapter, nonverbal cues can vary widely across cultures and individuals. This suggests that future sXAI systems should be designed with the capability to personalize their interactions and dynamically adapt to the specific nonverbal feedback provided by users. Research in this area could investigate how sXAI systems might adjust their explanations in real time, ensuring that they respond appropriately to the user's nonverbal signals, thereby enhancing understanding and engagement.

The chapter also underscores the continuous nature of nonverbal communication, which poses a challenge for sXAI systems. In human interactions, nonverbal cues are constantly monitored and responded to throughout the conversation. For sXAI systems to emulate this level of interaction, they must be capable of recognizing and responding to subtle shifts in a user's nonverbal behavior, such as changes in posture or gaze direction. Further, and obviously more challenging for developing such systems, is to differentiate between humans' bodily behaviors that are part of a communicative contribution, and those that are not, but temporally co-occur (see also Chap. 18). Future research could focus on developing algorithms that allow sXAI systems to maintain an effective dialog by monitoring and interpreting these signals, ultimately fostering trust and smoother interaction between the human and the AI.

Ethical considerations represent another crucial avenue for future research inspired by this chapter. As sXAI systems become more adept at interpreting nonverbal behaviors, it is vital to address the ethical implications surrounding privacy, consent, and the potential for manipulation (see Chap. 29).

19.7 Rapid Access

In human communication and social interaction, nonverbal behaviors play an important role as they communicate information, emotions, intentions, etc., complement verbal communication and foster understanding between individuals. Various forms of nonverbal signals enable communication partners to perceive and elicit information about each other's attention, cognitive processing, and understanding without interrupting each other (Buschmeier & Kopp, 2018; Clark & Krych, 2004; Krahmer & Swerts, 2005). Different forms of nonverbal behaviors can be associated with certain (interactional) functions. However, research has also shown that their meaning or interpretation depend on various aspects, such as their co-occurrence with other verbal and nonverbal means, on the situation or the context (see Chap. 4), or on cultural conventions.

For human–machine interaction (HMI) research and development, different forms of humans' nonverbal behavior can inform XAI systems about a human's focus of attention, other cognitive processes, or engagement, and thus are crucial for a development towards *social* XAI. This development, however, needs to take contextual and cultural aspects of behaviors, such as eye gaze, co-speech (hand) gestures, adaptors, head movements, and torso movements into account.

Eye gaze plays an important role in social interaction because of its dual function:

- *Information uptake*, for example, about people's visual focus of attention (Argyle & Cook, 1976; Goodwin, 1981; Kendon, 1967), emotional expression, or as support for speech perception (Hessels, 2020, for a review),
- *Signal information to others*: as a special form of gaze shift, namely gaze aversions, for example, cognitive processing (Abeles & Yuval-Greenberg, 2017; Glenberg et al., 1998) or disengagement from a task (Dohert & Phelps, 2007)

Further, gaze behavior is important in discourse for turn management among interlocutors, such as the allocation and change of turns, or short feedback signals (Bavelas et al., 2002; Degutyte & Astell, 2021; Goodwin, 1981; Jokinen et al., 2010a,b) (see Sect. 19.3.1). The different functions are important for situations in which understanding is targeted, such as explanatory interactions. However, because of being such a rich signal, eye gaze behavior may result in different interpretations, making it not unequivocally interpretable. In addition, gaze behavior can depend on factors such as the task, cultural norms, or even the social context (e.g., social status, direct/indirect contact, Hessels (2020)), which need to be considered if making use of it for sXAI. Together with **torso movements**, gaze behavior expresses engagement with each other (Goodwin, 1981), or, when being shifted away from each other, visual attention to other entities (Mortensen & Hazel, 2014) (see Sect. 19.3.5).

Modeling human eye gaze behavior in HMI may be beneficial for interactions with users. For example, if robots use gaze behavior for deictic purposes, users' in-space orientation task performance increases (Breazeal et al., 2005; Skantze et al.,

2013). Further, robots' gaze behavior that resembles humans' gaze behavior during turn-taking may facilitate more natural interactions (Mishra et al., 2023).

Co-speech (hand) gestures which are semantically and temporally tightly coupled with speech (Kendon, 2004; Kita, 2009; McNeill, 2005) frequently occur in social interaction and can support understanding of spoken utterances (see Sect. 19.3.2, also Chap. 22). Co-speech hand gestures establish reference to different units in speech (e.g., syntactic, semantic, or pragmatic) and provide interactional guidance and spatial orientation; thus, via pointing, representing, or highlighting important content (Kendon, 2004; McNeill, 1992, 2006), an explainer can increase an addressee's understanding. Classically, they are categorized into distinct categories (McNeill, 1992):

- Deictic (pointing at places/objects)
- Iconic (depiction of properties of objects, actions, or events)
- Metaphoric (depiction of abstract concepts)
- Beats (temporal highlighting)
- Emblems (culturally specific gestures with arbitrary meaning)

However, a hand gesture can have a hybrid form (e.g., deictic beat, when pointing to a location (deictic) multiple times (beat) to highlight it) than a single category (McNeill, 2006), which poses a challenge for computational modeling their detection.

For interaction with humanoid robots, using hand gestures may improve the communication between users and explaining machines (e.g., virtual embodied robots) by bridging communication gaps via pointing at or representing objects (He et al., 2022). However, the generation of hand gestures by a robot or an embodied virtual agent is a complex process, which requires advanced modules synchronizing gesture production with verbal output as in HHI, as well as the consideration of cultural norms related to the use of hand gestures (see 19.3.2).

A group of specific hand movements on the own body or on objects without clear reference to units in speech, namely, **adaptors**, are potentially interesting in explanatory interactions because they are associated with listeners' cognitive processing (Ekman & Friesen, 1969; Harrigan, 1985), speech information processing (Allen & Honeycutt, 1997), or emotional affection (Ruggieri et al., 1982) (see Sect. 19.3.3). Although research on HMI has not focused on adaptors used by humans yet, investigating them may enhance machines' ability to respond more effectively to users' cognitive processing and understanding of explanations (see Sect. 19.4.2).

Head movements can shape the structure of an ongoing discourse and regulate interactional processes, e.g., turn management or setting boundaries between linguistic units (Duncan, 1972; Kendon, 1972; McClave, 2000). With respect to the individual communicative roles, a *speaker's head movements* can provide addressees with orientation about semantic content related to people and objects within discourse (McClave, 2000) (see 19.3.4), whereas *addressee's head movements* can be a form of nonverbal feedback, commonly expressed by culturally related head gestures, for example, head nods and head shakes in Western cultures

(Bavelas et al., 2002; Kendon, 1970; McClave, 2000). In combination with vocal feedback, they undergo ambiguous interpretations between signals of attention and understanding (Allwood & Cerrato, 2003; Gander & Gander, 2020). Integrating human head gestures co-occurring with vocal feedback into technical systems is recommended by researchers on HMI (Irfan et al., 2023). There are some examples in which humans demonstrate increased level of interaction with social robots, including engagement (Wang et al., 2006), or trust and attentiveness (Anzabi & Umemuro, 2023).

The successful completion of explanations via co-constructions, scaffolding, and monitoring (Rohlfing et al., 2021) requires an optimal **operationalization** of nonverbal behavior in HMI. For this purpose, an sXAI should be able to monitor, recognize, and interpret different forms of human nonverbal behavior, e.g., eye gaze, head, and hand gestures, which indicate social engagement, cognitive processing, and understanding. The capability of monitoring and interpreting nonverbal behaviors correctly (that is, taking contextual and cultural aspects into account) may enhance systems' ability to adapt explanations to explainees' cognitive processing and understanding (see Sect. 19.5 for examples about further technical details).

Acknowledgments We thank Gabriel Skantze for his helpful comments on an earlier version of this chapter. This work was funded by the Deutsche Forschungsgemeinschaft (DFG, German Research Foundation): TRR 318/1 2021 – 438445824.

References

Abeles, D., & Yuval-Greenberg, S. (2017). Just look away: Gaze aversions as an overt attentional disengagement mechanism. *Cognition, 168*, 99–109. https://doi.org/10.1016/j.cognition.2017.06.021

Al Moubayed, S., Skantze, G., & Beskow, J. (2013). The furhat back-projected humanoid head–lip reading, gaze and multi-party interaction. *International Journal of Humanoid Robotics, 10*(1), 1350005. https://doi.org/10.1142/S0219843613500059

Allen, T. H., & Honeycutt, J. M. (1997). Planning, imagined interaction, and the nonverbal display of anxiety. *Communication Research, 24*(1), 64–82. https://doi.org/10.1177/009365097024001003

Allwood, J., & Cerrato, L. (2003). A study of gestural feedback expressions. In *Proceedings of the 1st Nordic Symposium on Multimodal Communication* (pp. 7–22). University of Copenhagen.

Allwood, J., Cerrato, L., Jokinen, K., Navarretta, C., & Paggio, P. (2007). The MUMIN coding scheme for the annotation of feedback, turn management and sequencing phenomena. *Language Resources and Evaluation, 41*, 273–287. https://doi.org/10.1007/s10579-007-9061-5

Allwood, J., Nivre, J., & Ahlsén, E. (1992). On the semantics and pragmatics of linguistic feedback. *Journal of Semantics, 9*(1), 1–26. https://doi.org/10.1093/jos/9.1.1

Aly, A., & Tapus, A. (2016). Towards an intelligent system for generating an adapted verbal and nonverbal combined behavior in human–robot interaction. *Autonomous Robots, 40*(2), 193–209. https://doi.org/10.1007/s10514-015-9444-1

Anjomshoae, S., Najjar, A., Calvaresi, D., & Främling, K. (2019). Explainable agents and robots: Results from a systematic literature review. In *18th International Conference on Autonomous Agents and Multiagent Systems (AAMAS 2019)* (pp. 1078–1088). International Foundation for Autonomous Agents and Multiagent Systems.

Anzabi, N., & Umemuro, H. (2023). Effect of different listening behaviors of social robots on perceived trust in human–robot interactions. *International Journal of Social Robotics, 15*(6), 931–951. https://doi.org/10.1007/s12369-023-01008-x

Argyle, M., & Cook, M. (1976). *Gaze and mutual gaze*. Cambridge University Press.

Aronson, R. M., Almutlak, N., & Admoni, H. (2021). Inferring goals with gaze during teleoperated manipulation. In *2021 IEEE/RSJ International Conference on Intelligent Robots and Systems (IROS)* (pp. 7307–7314). IEEE. https://doi.org/10.1109/IROS51168.2021.9636551

Axelsson, A., Buschmeier, H., & Skantze, G. (2022). Modeling feedback in interaction with conversational agents—A review. *Frontiers in Computer Science, 4*, 744574. https://doi.org/10.3389/fcomp.2022.744574

Bavelas, J. B., Black, A., Lemery, C. R., & Mullet, J. (2002). 'I show you how you feel': Motor mimicry as a communicative act. *Journal of Personality and Social Psychology, 50*(2). https://doi.org/10.1037/0022-3514.50.2.322

Bavelas, J. B., & Chovil, N. (2018). Some pragmatic functions of conversational facial gestures. *Gesture, 17*(1), 98–127. https://doi.org/10.1075/gest.00012.bav

Bavelas, J. B., Coates, L., & Johnson, T. (2002). Listener responses as a collaborative process: The role of gaze. *Journal of Communication, 52*(3), 566–580. https://doi.org/10.1111/j.1460-2466.2002.tb02562.x

Beattie, G., & Shovelton, H. (2005). Why the spontaneous images created by the hands during talk can help make TV advertisements more effective. *British Journal of Psychology, 96*(1), 21–37. https://doi.org/10.1348/000712605X103500

Beege, M., Ninaus, M., Schneider, S., Nebel, S., Schlemmel, J., Weidenmüller, J., Moeller, K., & Rey, G. D. (2020). Investigating the effects of beat and deictic gestures of a lecturer in educational videos. *Computers & Education, 156*, 103955. https://doi.org/10.1016/j.compedu.2020.103955

Breazeal, C., Kidd, C. D., Lockerd Thomaz, A., Hoffman, G., & Berlin, M. (2005). Effects of nonverbal communication on efficiency and robustness in human–robot teamwork. In *2005 IEEE/RSJ International Conference on Intelligent Robots and Systems* (pp. 708–713). IEEE. https://doi.org/10.1109/IROS.2005.1545011

Buschmeier, H., & Kopp, S. (2018). Communicative listener feedback in human–agent interaction: Artificial speakers need to be attentive and adaptive. In *Proceedings of the 17th International Conference on Autonomous Agents and Multiagent Systems* (pp. 1213–1221). IFAAMAS.

Buzcu, B., Tessa, M., Tchappi, I., Najjar, A., Hulstijn, J., Calvaresi, D., & Aydoğan, R. (2024). Towards interactive explanation-based nutrition virtual coaching systems. *Autonomous Agents and Multi-Agent Systems, 38*(5), 5. https://doi.org/10.1007/s10458-023-09634-5

Cienki, A., Leonteva, A. V., Agafonova, O., & Petrov, A. A. (2023). Numbers in simultaneous interpreting: A multimodal analysis. *Research Result. Theoretical and Applied Linguistics, 9*(1), 82–98. https://doi.org/10.18413/2313-8912-2023-9-1-0-6

Clark, H. H. (2003). Pointing and placing. In S. Kita (Ed.), *Pointing: where language, culture, and cognition meet* (pp. 243–268). Psychology Press.

Clark, H. H., & Krych, M. (2004). Speaking while monitoring addressees for understanding. *Journal of Memory and Language, 50*(1), 62–81. https://doi.org/10.1016/j.jml.2003.08.004

Cooperrider, K., Slotta, J., & Núñez, R. (2018). The preference for pointing with the hand is not universal. *Cognitive Science, 42*(4), 1375–1390. https://doi.org/10.1111/cogs.12585

D'Mello, S., Dieterle, Ed., & Duckworth, A. (2017). Advanced, analytic, automated (AAA) measurement of engagement during learning. *Educational Psychologist, 52*(2), 104–123. https://doi.org/10.1080/00461520.2017.1281747

Dargue, N., Phillips, M., & Sweller, N. (2021). Filling in the gaps: Observing gestures conveying additional information can compensate for missing verbal content. *Instructional Science, 49*, 637–659. https://doi.org/10.1007/s11251-021-09549-2

Degutyte, Z., & Astell, A. (2021). The role of eye gaze in regulating turn taking in conversations: A systematized review of methods and findings. *Frontiers in Psychology, 12*, 616471. https://doi.org/10.3389/fpsyg.2021.616471

Doherty-Sneddon, G., & Phelps, F. G. (2007). Teachers' responses to children's eye gaze. *Educational Psychology, 27*(1), 93–109. https://doi.org/10.1080/01443410601061488

Dreisoerner, A., Munker, N., Scholtz, W., Heimrich, J., & Bloemeke, S. (2021). Self-soothing touch and being hugged reduce cortisol responses to stress: A randomized controlled trial on stress, physical touch, and social identity. *Comprehensive Psychoneuroendocrinology, 8*, 100091. https://doi.org/10.1016/j.cpnec.2021.100091

Duncan, S. (1972). Some signals and rules for taking speaking turns in conversations. *Journal of Personality and Social Psychology, 23*(2), 283–292. https://doi.org/10.1037/h0033031

Ekman, P., & Friesen, W. V. (1969). The repertoire of nonverbal behavior: Categories, origins, usage, and coding. *Semiotica, 1*(1), 49–98. https://doi.org/10.1515/semi.1969.1.1.49

Embgen, S., Luber, M., Becker-Asano, C., Ragni, M., Evers, V., & Arras, K. O. (2012). Robot-specific social cues in emotional body language. In *2012 IEEE RO-MAN: The 21st IEEE International Symposium on Robot and Human Interactive Communication* (pp. 1019–1025). IEEE. https://doi.org/10.1109/ROMAN.2012.6343883

Gander, A. J., & Gander, P. (2020). Micro-feedback as cues to understanding in communication. In C. Howes, S. Dobnik, E. Breitholtz (Eds.), *Dialogue and Perception. Extended Papers from DaP2018* (pp. 1–11). Gothenburg University.

Gjaci, A., Recchiuto, C. T., & Sgorbissa, A. (2022). Towards culture–aware co-speech gestures for social robots. *International Journal of Social Robotics, 14*(6), 1493–1506. https://doi.org/10.1007/s12369-022-00893-y

Glenberg, A. M., Schroeder, J. L., & Robertson, D. A. (1998). Averting the gaze disengages the environment and facilitates remembering. *Memory & Cognition, 26*, 651–658. https://doi.org/10.3758/bf03211385

Goodwin, C. (1981). *Conversational organization: Interaction between speakers and hearers.* Academic Press.

Goodwin, M. H., & Goodwin, C. (1986). Gesture and coparticipation in the activity of searching for a word. *Semiotica, 62*(1–2), 51–75. https://doi.org/10.1515/semi.1986.62.1-2.51

Grunwald, M., Weiss, T., Mueller, S., & Rall, L. (2014). EEG changes caused by spontaneous facial self-touch may represent emotion regulating processes and working memory maintenance. *Brain Research, 1557*(1), 111–126. https://doi.org/10.1016/j.brainres.2014.02.002

Gurney, D. J., Vekaria, K. N., & Howlett, N. (2014). A nod in the wrong direction: Does non-verbal feedback affect eyewitness confidence in interviews? *Psychiatry, Psychology and Law, 21*(2), 241–250. https://doi.org/10.1080/13218719.2013.804388

Hanna, J. E., & Brennan, S. E. (2007). Speakers' eye gaze disambiguates referring expressions early during face-to-face conversation. *Journal of Memory and Language, 57*(4), 596–615. https://doi.org/10.1016/j.jml.2007.01.008

Harrigan, J. (1985). Self-touching as indicator of underlying affect and language processes. *Social Science & Medicine, 20*(11), 1161–1168. https://doi.org/10.1016/0277-9536(85)90193-5

He, Y., Pereira, A., & Kucherenko, T. (2022). Evaluating data-driven co- speech gestures of embodied conversational agents through real-time interaction. In *Proceedings of the 22nd ACM International Conference on Intelligent Virtual Agents* (pp. 1–8). Association for Computing Machinery. https://doi.org/10.1145/3514197.3549697

Heller, V. (2021). Embodied displays of "Doing Thinking." Epistemic and interactive functions of thinking displays in children's argumentative activities. *Frontiers in Psychology, 12*, 636671. https://doi.org/10.3389/fpsyg.2021.636671

Hessels, R. S. (2020). How does gaze to faces support face-to-face interaction? A review and perspective. *Psychonomic Bulletin & Review, 27*(5), 856–881. https://doi.org/10.3758/s13423-020-01715-w

Hoffman, G., Zuckerman, O., Hirschberger, G., Luria, M., & Sherman, T. S. (2015). Design and evaluation of a peripheral robotic conversation companion. In *Proceedings of the 10th Annual ACM/IEEE International Conference on Human–Robot Interaction* (pp. 3–10). Association for Computing Machinery. https://doi.org/10.1145/2696454.2696495

Holler, J., & Levinson, S. C. (2019). Multimodal language processing in human communication. *Trends in Cognitive Sciences, 23*(8), 639–652. https://doi.org/10.1016/j.tics.2019.05.006

Irfan, B., Kuoppamäki, S., & Skantze, G. (2023). Recommendations for designing conversational companion robots with older adults through foundation models. *Frontiers in Robotics and AI, 11*, 1363713. https://doi.org/10.3389/frobt.2024.1363713

Ismail, N. M., & Syahputri, V. N. (2022). "I mean you can stop. I already understand you": Head tilts during conversations. *Lingua Didaktika: Jurnal Bahasa dan Pembelajaran Bahasa, 16*(1), 1–11. https://doi.org/10.24036/ld.v16i1.116673

Jokinen, K., Harada, K., Nishida, M., & Yamamoto, S. (2010a). Turn-alignment using eye gaze and speech in conversational interaction. In *Proceedings of the European Conference on Speech Communication and Technology (INTERSPEECH'10)* (pp. 2018–2021). Proc. Interspeech. https://doi.org/10.21437/Interspeech.2010-571

Jokinen, K., Nishida, M., & Yamamoto, S. (2010b). On eye gaze and turn taking. In *Proceedings of the International Conference on Intelligent User Interfaces Workshop on Eye Gaze in Intelligent Human–Machine Interaction* (pp. 118–123). Association for Computing Machinery. https://doi.org/10.1145/2002333.2002352

Kandana-Arachchige, K. G., Blekic, W., Loureiro, I. S., & Lefebvre, L. (2021). Covert attention to gestures is sufficient for information uptake. *Frontiers in Psychology, 12*, 776867. https://doi.org/10.3389/fpsyg.2021.776867

Kaushik, R., & Simmons, R. (2021). Perception of emotion in torso and arm movements on humanoid robot quori. In *Companion of the 2021 ACM/IEEE International Conference on Human–Robot Interaction* (pp. 62–66). Association for Computing Machinery. https://doi.org/10.1145/3434074.3447129

Kendon, A. (1967). Some functions of gaze-direction in social interaction. *Acta Psychologica, 26*(1), 22–63. https://doi.org/10.1016/0001-6918(67)90005-4

Kendon, A. (1970). Movement coordination in social interaction: Some examples described. *Acta Psychologica, 32*(2), 100–125. https://doi.org/10.1016/0001-6918(70)90094-6

Kendon, A. (1972). Some relationships between body motion and speech. In A. W. Siegman, & B. Pope (Eds.), *Studies in dyadic communication* (pp. 177–210). Elmsford. https://doi.org/10.1016/B978-0-08-015867-9.50013-7

Kendon, A. (1995). Gestures as illocutionary and discourse structure markers in Southern Italian conversation. *Journal of Pragmatics, 23*(3), 247–279. https://doi.org/10.1016/0378-2166(94)00037-F

Kendon, A. (2004). *Gesture: visible action as utterance*. Cambridge University Press. https://doi.org/10.1017/cbo9780511807572

Kita, S. (2009). Cross-cultural variation of speech-accompanying gesture: A review. *Language and Cognitive Processes, 24*(2), 145–167. https://doi.org/10.1080/01690960802586188

Kousidis, S., Malisz, Z., Wagner, P., & Schlangen, D. (2013). Exploring annotation of head gesture forms in spontaneous human interaction. In *Proceedings of the Tilburg Gesture Meeting (TiGeR2013)* (pp. 1–4), Tilburg, Sweden. https://pub.uni-bielefeld.de/record/2567303.

Krahmer, E., & Swerts, M. (2005). How children and adults produce and perceive uncertainty in audiovisual speech. *Language and Speech, 48*(1), 29–53. https://doi.org/10.1177/00238309050480010201

Kuno, Y., Sadazuka, K., Kawashima, M., Yamazaki, K., Yamazaki, A., & Kuzuoka, H. (2007). Museum guide robot based on sociological interaction analysis. In *CHI '07: Proceedings of the SIGCHI Conference on Human Factors in Computing Systems* (pp. 1191–1194). Association for Computing Machinery. https://doi.org/10.1145/1240624.1240804

Lazarov, S., & Grimminger, A. (2024). Variations in explainers' gesture deixis in explanations related to the monitoring of explainees' understanding. In *Proceedings of the Annual Meeting of the Cognitive Science Society* (pp. 4805–4812). University of California.

Leite, I., Castellano, G., Pereira, A., Martinho, C., & Paiva, A. (2014). Empathic robots for long-term interaction: Evaluating social presence, engagement and perceived support in children. *International Journal of Social Robotics, 6*, 329–341. https://doi.org/10.1007/s12369-014-0227-1

Leite, I., Pereira, A., Mascarenhas, S., Martinho, C., Prada, R., & Paiva, A. (2013). The influence of empathy in human–robot relations. *International Journal of Human–Computer Studies, 71*(3), 250–260. https://doi.org/10.1016/j.ijhcs.2012.09.005

Lundberg, S. M., & Lee, S.-I. (2017). A unified approach to interpreting model predictions. In *Advances in Neural Information Processing Systems 30 (NIPS 2017)* (vol. 30, pp. 4768–4777). Curran Associates.

Malisz, Z., Włodarczak, M., Buschmeier, H., Skubisz, J., Kopp, S., & Wagner, P. (2016). The ALICO corpus: Analysing the active listener. *Language Resources and Evaluation, 50*, 411–442. https://doi.org/10.1007/s10579-016-9355-6

McClave, E. Z. (2000). Linguistic functions of head movements in the context of speech. *Journal of Pragmatics, 32*(7), 855–878. https://doi.org/10.1016/S0378-2166(99)00079-X

McKern, N., Dargue, N., Sweller, N., Sekine, K., & Austin, E. (2021). Lending a hand to storytelling: Gesture's effects on narrative comprehension moderated by task difficulty and cognitive ability. *Quarterly Journal of Experimental Psychology, 74*(10), 1781–1805. https://doi.org/10.1177/17470218211024913

McNeill, D. (1992). *Hand and mind: What gestures reveal about thought*. University of Chicago Press.

McNeill, D. (1998). Speech and gesture integration. In J. M. Iverson, & S. Goldin-Meadow (Eds.), *The nature and functions of gesture in children's communication* (pp. 11–27). Jossey-Bass. https://doi.org/10.1002/cd.23219987902

McNeill, D. (2005). *Gesture and thought*. University of Chicago Press. https://doi.org/10.7208/chicago/9780226514642.001.0001

McNeill, D. (2006). Gesture and communication. In K. Brown (Ed.), *Encyclopedia of language & linguistics*, 2nd ed. (pp. 60–66). Georgetown University Press. https://doi.org/10.1016/B0-08-044854-2/00798-7

Mishra, C., Offrede, T., Fuchs, S., Mooshammer, C., & Skantze, G. (2023). Does a robot's gaze aversion affect human gaze aversion? *Frontiers in Robotics and AI, 10*, 1127626. https://doi.org/10.3389/frobt.2023.1127626

Mortensen, K., & Hazel, S. (2014). Moving into interaction – Social practices for initiating encounters at a help desk. *Journal of Pragmatics, 62*, 46–67. https://doi.org/10.1016/j.pragma.2013.11.009

Mueller, S. M., Martin, S., & Grunwald, M. (2019). Self-touch: Contact durations and point of touch of spontaneous facial self-touches differ depending on cognitive and emotional load. *PloS One, 14*(3), e0213677. https://doi.org/10.1371/journal.pone.0213677

Mumm, J., & Mutlu, B. (2011). Human–robot proxemics: Physical and psychological distancing in human–robot interaction. In *Proceedings of the 6th International Conference on Human–Robot Interaction* (pp. 331–338). IEEE. https://doi.org/10.1145/1957656.1957786

Nagels, A., Kircher, T., Steines, M., & Straube, B. (2015). Feeling addressed! The role of body orientation and co-speech gesture in social communication. *Human Brain Mapping, 36*(5), 1925–1936. https://doi.org/10.1002/hbm.22746

Najjar, A., Prakash, H., Tchappi, I., Ndamlabin Mboula, J. E., & Mualla, Y. (2022). Towards a smart robot model for traffic signal management in developing countries. In *Proceedings of the 10th International Conference on Human–Agent Interaction* (pp. 333–336). Association for Computing Machinery. https://doi.org/10.1145/3527188.3563924

Nota, N., Trujillo, J. P., & Holler, J. (2021). Facial signals and social actions in multimodal face-to-face interaction. *Brain Sciences, 11*(8), 1017. https://doi.org/10.3390/brainsci11081017

Nota, N., Trujillo, J. P., & Holler, J. (2023). Specific facial signals associate with categories of social actions conveyed through questions. *PloS One, 18*(7), 1–26. https://doi.org/10.1371/journal.pone.0288104

Phelps, F. G., Doherty-Sneddon, G., & Warnock, H. (2006). Helping children think: Gaze aversion and teaching. *British Journal of Developmental Psychology, 24*(3), 577–588. https://doi.org/10.1348/026151005X49872

Robinson, J. D. (2006). Getting down to business: Talk, gaze, and body orientation during openings of doctor–patient consultations. *Human Communication Research, 25*(1), 97–123. https://doi.org/10.1111/j.1468-2958.1998.tb00438.x

Rohlfing, K. J., Cimiano, P., Scharlau, I., Matzner, T., Buhl, H., Buschmeier, H., Grimminger, A., Hammer, B., Häb-Umbach, R., Horwath, I., Hüllermeier, E., Kern, F., Kopp, S., Thommes, K., Ngomo, A.-C. N., Schulte, C., Wachsmuth, H., Wagner, P., & Wrede, B. (2021). Explanation as a social practice: Toward a conceptual framework for the social design of AI systems. *IEEE Transactions on Cognitive and Developmental Systems, 13*(3), 717–728. https://doi.org/10.1109/TCDS.2020.3044366

Rossano, F. (2012). Gaze Behavior in Face-to-Face Interaction. PhD thesis. Radboud University Nijmegen, Nijmegen.

Rossano, F. (2013). Gaze in conversation. In J. Sidnell, & T. Stivers (Eds.), *The handbook of conversation analysis* (pp. 308–329). Wiley-Blackwell. https://doi.org/10.1002/9781118325001.ch15

Ruggieri, V., Celli, C., & Crescenzi, A. (1982). Gesturing and self-contact of right and left halves of the body: Relationship with eye-contact. *Perceptual and Motor Skills, 55*(3), 695–698. https://doi.org/10.2466/pms.1982.55.3.695

Salem, M., Eyssel, F., Rohlfing, K. J., Kopp, S., & Joublin, F. (2013). To err is human(-like): Effects of robot gesture on perceived anthropomorphism and likability. *International Journal of Social Robotics, 5*(3), 313–323. https://doi.org/10.1007/s12369-013-0196-9

Salem, M., Rohlfing, K. J., Kopp, S., & Joublin, F. (2011). A friendly gesture: Investigating the effect of multimodal robot behavior in human–robot interaction. In *2011 Ro-Man* (pp. 247–252). IEEE. https://doi.org/10.1109/ROMAN.2011.6005285

Sander, C., Soworka, T., & Albers, A. (2012). Design of a new torso- joint for the humanoid robot ARMAR. *Journal of Mechanical Engineering and Automation, 2*(4), 58–64. https://doi.org/10.5923/j.jmea.20120204.02

Saunderson, S., & Nejat, G. (2019). How robots influence humans: A survey of nonverbal communication in social human–robot interaction. *International Journal of Social Robotics, 11*(4), 575–608. https://doi.org/10.1007/s12369-019-00523-0

Skantze, G. (2021). Turn-taking in conversational systems and human–robot interaction: A review. *Computer Speech & Language, 67*, 101178. https://doi.org/10.1016/j.csl.2020.101178

Skantze, G., Hjalmarsson, A., & Oertel, C. (2013). Exploring the effects of gaze and pauses in situated human–robot interaction. In *Proceedings of the SIGDIAL 2013 Conference* (pp. 163–172). Association for Computational Linguistics. https://aclanthology.org/W13-4029

Spille, J. L., Grunwald, M., Martin, S., & Mueller, S. M. (2021). Stop touching your face! A systematic review of triggers, characteristics, regulatory functions and neuro-physiology of facial self touch. *Neuroscience and Behavioral Reviews, 128*, 102–116. https://doi.org/10.1016/j.neubiorev.2021.05.030

Tchappi, I., Hulstijn, J., Pagou, E. S., Bhattacharya, S., & Najjar, A. (2023). Towards explainable recommender systems for illiterate users. In *Proceedings of the 11th International Conference on Human–Agent Interaction* (pp. 415–416). Association for Computing Machinery. https://doi.org/10.1145/3623809.3623945

Tchappi, I. H., Galland, S., Kamla, V. C., Kamgang, J. C., Mualla, Y., Najjar, A., & Hilaire, V. (2020). A critical review of holonic technology in traffic and transportation fields. *Engineering Applications of Artificial Intelligence, 90*, 103503. https://doi.org/10.1016/j.engappai.2020.103503

ter Bekke, M., Levonson, S. C., van Otterdijk, L., Kühn, M., & Holler, J. (2024). Visual bodily signals and conversational context benefit the anticipation of turn ends. *Cognition, 248*, 105806. https://doi.org/10.1016/j.cognition.2024.105806

Tessa, M., Abchiche, S., Ferstler, Y. C., Tchappi, I., Benatchba, K., & Najjar, A. (2023). Enhancing explainability in AI: Food recommender system use case. In *Proceedings of the 11th International Conference on Human–Agent Interaction* (pp. 395–397). Association for Computing Machinery. https://doi.org/10.1145/3623809.3623938

Teßendorf, S. (2013). Emblems, quotable gestures, or conventionalized body movements. In C. Müller, A. Cienki, E. Fricke, S. Ladewig, D. D. McNeill, & S. Teßendorf (Eds.), *Body – Language – Communication: An International Handbook on Multimodality in Human Interaction* (pp. 82–100). De Gruyter Mouton. https://doi.org/10.1515/9783110261318.82

Trujillo, J. P., & Holler, J. (2021). The kinematics of social action: Visual signals provide cues for what interlocutors do in conversation. *Brain Sciences, 11*(8), 996. https://doi.org/10.3390/brainsci11080996

Trujillo, J. P., & Holler, J. (2024). Conversational facial signals combine into compositional meanings that change the interpretation of speaker intentions. *Scientific Reports, 14*, 2286. https://doi.org/10.1038/s41598-024-52589-0

Wang, E., Lignos, C., Vatsal, A., & Scassellati, B. (2006). Effects of head movement on perceptions of humanoid robot behavior. In *Proceedings of the 1st ACM SIGCHI/SIGART Conference on Human–Robot Interaction* (pp. 180–185). Association for Computing Machinery. https://doi.org/10.1145/1121241.1121273

Wilkins, D. (2003). Why pointing with the index finger is not a universal (in sociocultural and semiotic terms). In S. Kita (Ed.), *Pointing: where language, culture, and cognition meet* (pp. 179–224). Lawrence Erlbaum Associates.

Włodarczak, M., Buschmeier, H., Malisz, Z., Kopp, S., & Wagner, P. (2012). Listener head gestures and verbal feedback expressions in a distraction task. In *Proceedings of the Interdisciplinary Workshop on Feedback Behaviors in Dialog, INTERSPEECH2012 Satellite Workshop* (pp. 93–96), Stevenson, WA, USA. https://www.isca-archive.org/fbid_2012/wodarczak12_fbid.html

Xu, J., Broekens, J., Hindriks, K., & Neerincx, M. A. (2014). Effects of bodily mood expression of a robotic teacher on students. In *2014 IEEE/RSJ International Conference on Intelligent Robots and Systems* (pp. 2614–2620). IEEE. https://doi.org/10.1109/IROS.2014.6942919

Yngve, V. H. (1970). On getting a word in edgewise. In *Papers from the Sixth Regional Meeting of the Chicago Linguistic Society* (pp. 567–577). Chicago Linguistic Society.

Yoon, Y., Ko, W.-R., Jang, M., Lee, J., Kim, J., & Lee, G. (2019). Robots learn social skills: End-to-end learning of co-speech gesture generation for humanoid robots. In *2019 International Conference on Robotics and Automation (ICRA)* (pp. 4303–4309). IEEE. https://doi.org/10.1109/ICRA.2019.8793720

Open Access This chapter is licensed under the terms of the Creative Commons Attribution 4.0 International License (http://creativecommons.org/licenses/by/4.0/), which permits use, sharing, adaptation, distribution and reproduction in any medium or format, as long as you give appropriate credit to the original author(s) and the source, provide a link to the Creative Commons license and indicate if changes were made.

The images or other third party material in this chapter are included in the chapter's Creative Commons license, unless indicated otherwise in a credit line to the material. If material is not included in the chapter's Creative Commons license and your intended use is not permitted by statutory regulation or exceeds the permitted use, you will need to obtain permission directly from the copyright holder.

Chapter 20
Nonverbal Signals of Affect

Hanna Drimalla

Abstract Affective states can influence the processing and delivery of explanations, making nonverbal signals of affect a valuable resource for sXAI. This chapter examines how the computational processing and generation of nonverbal affective signals can enhance human–computer explanations. It explores various nonverbal affective signals such as facial expressions, gaze, voice, heartbeat, and breathing, detailing the affective information they convey and their current as well as potential use in social XAI (sXAI). Additionally, the chapter addresses the challenges associated with interpreting each of these modalities.

20.1 Relevance of Nonverbal Signals of Affect for XAI

Affect is a broad term encompassing feeling states such as emotions and moods (Niven, 2013). Affective states are typically accompanied by bodily sensations and physiological changes (Barrett & Bliss-Moreau, 2009) and are expressed through different channels such as facial expressions, gaze patterns, vocal changes, heart rate, and breathing changes (Cohn et al., 2007). These nonverbal signals provide insights into a person's internal state going beyond explicit verbal communication. Since we are constantly experiencing affects from the moment we are born (Barrett & Bliss-Moreau, 2009), explanations also take place in an affective context (Thommes et al., 2024). Both the explainer and the explainee may experience affective states such as stress, surprise, excitement, or anger that can be induced by the explanation process itself or may be independent from it. For instance, in a hospital setting, a physician under time stress might explain a diagnosis to a patient who is anxiously awaiting the results. Throughout the explanation process, the affective states may change; for example, the physician

---

H. Drimalla (✉)
Human-Centered Artificial Intelligence, Faculty of Technology, Bielefeld University, Bielefeld, Germany
e-mail: drimalla@techfak.uni-bielefeld.de

© The Author(s) 2026
K. J. Rohlfing et al. (eds.), *Social Explainable AI*,
https://doi.org/10.1007/978-981-96-5290-7_20

Table 20.1 Overview of potential use cases for monitoring and generating affective signals in sXAI

Use case	Explainer	Process	Example affect	Benefit
Machine adapts explanation based on the explainer's affect	Machine	Monitoring	Frustration	Suitability of explanation
Machine reacts appropriately to the explainer's affect	Human	Monitoring	Anxiety	Interaction quality
Machine expresses affect during explaining	Machine	Generation	Excitement	Motivation for understanding
Machine expresses affect during receiving an explanation	Human	Generation	Surprise	Motivation for explaining
Machine imitates the explainer's affect during explaining	Machine	Generation	Engagement	Trust and likeability towards the machine

might notice the patient's anxiety and adopt a reassuring tone, potentially transforming the anxiety into relief.

Because a person's affective state influences their thinking, processing, and communication behavior (Clore & Huntsinger, 2007; Storbeck & Clore, 2007), it also impacts on how explanations are delivered and perceived. Thus, for both the explainer and the explainee, it is crucial not only to process factual information but also to recognize and respond to signs of affect, thereby enabling *empathic explanation behavior*.

In human–XAI explanations, affect can play a role in two main ways: expressed by the human and monitored by the machine, or generated by the machine. Furthermore, one can distinguish whether the human is the explainer or the explainee. Table 20.1 provides an overview of potential use cases.

20.1.1 Monitoring Affective Signals

Monitoring – that is, constantly processing and interpreting the affective signals of an explainee – enables the explainer to adapt to affective influences on cognitive processes, motivation, and judgments (Fig. 20.1). Cognitive influences are especially relevant in relation to stress. Stress might inhibit information retrieval or processing by the human explainee because it can have negative effects on working memory (Schoofsrede et al., 2008). Additionally, affect may bias the understanding of the explanation, influencing stereotypes and prejudices (Dasgupta et al., 2009) or risk perception (Lerner & Keltner, 2001). Under stress, an explainee may be more likely to reject or accept an explanation depending on subjective biases. Affect also influences motivation, changing a human explainee's willingness to listen and understand, as well as a human explainer's willingness to prepare and propose explanations. For example, Thommes et al. (2024) showed that an

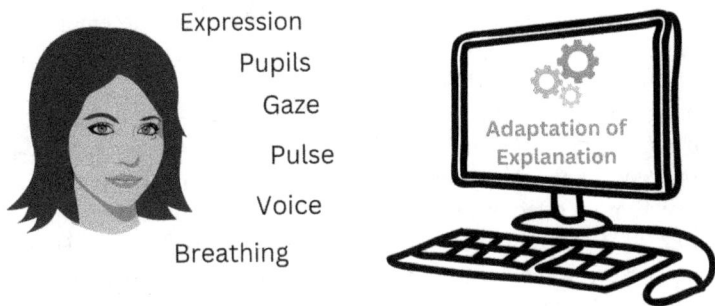

Fig. 20.1 This figure illustrates a potential use case for nonverbal affect with XAI: A user is receiving an explanation from a computer system while their nonverbal affective signals are captured and analyzed through a camera. The system integrates multimodal signals (e.g., facial expression, pupil sizes, gaze, pulse), estimates the affective state (e.g., stress), and adapts its explanation process based on the affect monitoring

explainee's need for an agent's explanations depends on their arousal level, in the sense that individuals with low arousal show less need for arousal, whereas highly aroused individuals prefer guided explanations. Similarly, the affective state influences trust, often overlooked in human–AI interaction research (Shang et al., 2024) that traditionally treats trust as a cognitive phenomenon. Recent XAI research has found that users experiencing positive emotions such as excitement, surprise, or interest showed more trust on an XAI than those with negative emotions such as fear, anger, or sadness (Bernardo & Seva, 2023).

So far, most work on monitoring affective signals of explainees has focused on tutoring systems that detect various aspects of affective engagement such as boredom, frustration, or confusion in order to adapt the content appropriately (for an overview: Dewan et al., 2019). In XAI, in which a machine explains its decision, recent work emphasizes the need to track the user's affective response to XAI explanations (Schmid & Wrede, 2022; Thommes et al., 2024), and initial research efforts are now underway (Guerdan et al., 2021).

In explanation scenarios with a human explainer (e.g., training a robot in a new skill), monitoring the (human) explainer's affective signals may also be beneficial. For example, the described effects of stress on working memory may cause a human explainer to omit important elements of the explanation or to overlook relevant aspects for training an agent. The effects on motivation could change a human explainer's willingness to prepare and propose explanations.

20.1.2 Generating Affective Signals

Although the main focus of this chapter is on monitoring affective signals, generative approaches can also be useful in the context of XAI—for example, an explaining humanoid shows a positive facial expression to increase the user's motivation. A recent research focus is on agents that simulate emotions to self-explain their behavior as a heuristic to identify important beliefs and desires for the explanation (Kaptein et al., 2017).

Generating nonverbal signals of affect also allows one to align them with the monitored user's signals, because in interactive settings, such as human–machine explanations, the concordance or discordance of affective expressions may be relevant. Imitation of affective expressions may increase liking and rapport (Lakin & Chartrand, 2003), thereby increasing confidence in an explanation. However, this raises ethical issues when trust is created artificially or at least reinforced by the agent's nonverbal signal, rather than being a result of the actual explanation or the accuracy of the AI decision.

20.1.3 Inference of Affective Signals

It should be noted that both observed and generated affective signals can also interfere with other relevant interaction signals. Because affect modifies verbal and nonverbal communication behaviors and is itself expressed, it can obscure the expression of nonverbal signals of understanding. For example, frowning in anger may be misinterpreted by an explainer (or an explaining system) as concentration, because both states activate similar muscles such as the corrugator supercilii (Barrett et al., 2019).

20.2 Facial Expressions

Our facial expressions are the most overt signs of affective engagement and serve as powerful communication signals. Even newborns show strong interest in human faces (Farroni et al., 2005) and display affective expressions early on (Izard et al., 1995).

To use affective information from the face in the context of XAI, the computer has to interpret the pixel information from a camera such as a webcam during an online lecture. There are two main approaches to computer-based facial expression recognition: sign-based and message-based (Girard & Cohn, 2016). The sign-based approach focuses on the signal, which is the movement of the facial muscles, without inferring an emotion or affective state. A common method for describing these movements is the Facial Action Coding System (FACS, Ekman & Friesen, 1978), which defines action units (AUs) as the smallest visible movements in the face. For example, in response to a successful explanation, the user may activate the AU 12, which corresponds to the cheek-raiser and is often associated with smiling. In contrast, the message-based approach focuses on the conveyed message such as happiness and aims to detect it. A commonly used categorical message-based framework in automatic affect detection is given by the so-called basic emotions.

Ekman and Friesen (1978) claimed that these emotions – namely, happiness, anger, joy, disgust, surprise, and fear – are expressed and recognized worldwide. This approach has been criticized for representing mainly Western stereotypes instead of spontaneous emotions (Durán et al., 2017), ignoring contextual and cultural influences, and failing to account for the variability of emotions in real-world scenarios (Barrett et al., 2011). In contrast, dimensional message-based approaches represent emotions as points in an affective space with dimensions such as valence and arousal (Barrett & Bliss-Moreau, 2009) or more complex mappings (Cowen et al., 2019). For example, someone who is extremely stressed because they are listening to an important but difficult to understand explanation might be very negative on the valence dimension but positive on the arousal axis.

Both sign-based and message-based approaches can be useful for considering affect or emotion within XAI. For example, mimicking the explainee's affective expressions by an artificial explainer to increase likability could be achieved using a sign-based approach. Detecting the explainee's confusion requires a message-based approach. Importantly, XAI researchers should be aware of the level of inference they are making and, for message-based approaches, the problematic assumption of a one-to-one mapping between a face and an emotion, along with cultural and contextual influences.

Researchers aiming to integrate facial expressions into their XAI applications should consider several challenges. First, the models used for facial expression recognition often reflect biases in the databases on which they were trained. Often, these databases fail to represent the global population, although the cultural influences on expression and perception of facial signals are well-established (Yuki et al., 2007). In addition, biases may also stem from the distribution of individuals within the dataset. For example, in AffectNet, one of the largest emotion datasets, more males express anger and more females express happiness (Domingue-Catena et al., 2024), thereby reproducing gender stereotypes. Second, affective databases are often created by asking people to display emotions. This may result in prototypical basic emotions rather than the spontaneously evoked emotions (Durán et al., 2017) one would expect in an explanation situation. A third challenge is the influence of context. Aviezer et al. (2017) showed that typical facial expressions are labeled differently depending on the context. A triumph face without context is easily interpreted as anger. The same could be true for a very focused face processing an explanation. Overall, these findings point to the need for an evaluation of affect recognition in well-defined XAI use cases instead of using broad existing models.

20.2.1 Current Use of Facial Expressions in XAI

Several recent papers in the context of learning and tutoring systems use facial expressions to detect engagement and/or recognize basic emotions (e.g., Savchenko et al., 2022; Kaur et al., 2018). Detecting engagement in online learning settings (for a review, see Dewan et al., 2019) includes identifying boredom, confusion, frustration, and learning gain. Some studies record students watching instructional videos Whitehill et al., 2008; Booth et al., 2017, whereas others analyze videos of cognitive skill training (Whitehill et al., 2014) or interactions with tutoring systems (McDaniel et al., 2007). The authors of these studies also describe which action units are particularly relevant for certain affective states—for example, for confusion, the activation of AU4 (eyebrow lowering) is often noted. However, this does not mean it is specific to confusion, but could rather signal the negative valence of this state. Similar to the datasets of facial expressions described earlier, most existing datasets are either of small sample size or biased toward one gender or ethnicity (Dewan et al., 2019). EngageWild includes 78 individuals who watched videos (Kaur et al., 2018), and recently, EngageNet has been published that consists of 127 participants watching online educational videos (Singh et al., 2023). However, both have about twice as many male participants. Moreover, these datasets all focus on a single individual perceiving or processing an explanation or other learning content. Recently, some datasets (e.g., Wagner et al., 2024 or Paletschek et al., 2024) have been collected that also capture the interactive aspect of an explanation by recording both an explainer and an explainee co-constructing an explanation.

20.3 Eyes

The eye is not only relevant for visual perception but can also convey a lot of information about a person ranging from age to mental state to drug use (Kröger et al., 2020). Eye movements, blinking, and even pupil dilation can tell us something about a person's emotional state.

Gaze behavior – that is, where people look and where they fixate for long periods of time – tells us something about their preferences and attention. When we look at a scene, we do not process it from left to right, but first focus on highly relevant parts such as faces (Norbury et al., 2009). Clinical conditions such as Alzheimer's disease (Mosimann et al., 2004) or autism (Klin et al., 2002; Norbury et al., 2009) may alter these patterns. Apart from clinical cases, gaze behavior is also an indicator of internal affective states, changing with fatigue (Horng et al., 2004), mood (Eckstein et al., 2017), or preferences and aversions (Eckstein et al., 2017).

One aspect of gaze that is highly relevant to interactive settings such as explanation is its dual function, or as (Synnott, 1992, p. 633) put it: "The eye cannot take unless it gives at the same time." When we look at something, we immediately reveal our interest (Baro et al., 2001; Frischen et al., 2007). This allows us to strategically direct another's attention (Kuhn & Kingstone, 2009). For instance, looking at our interaction partner and then looking away leads to reflexive gaze-following behavior so that joint attention can be established (Pfeiffer et al., 2013). Looking at someone can signal our desire to communicate (Ho et al., 2015) or be a sign of dominance (Emery, 2000). In line with this, direct eye contact has been shown to increase one's level of arousal (Jarick & Bencic, 2019). The described dual nature of gaze is relevant for human–machine interaction and could be used in explanations, because systems could either express these signals to guide the user or detect these signals in the user to react in line with their preferences, interests, and attention.

Last but not least, for the social perception of a system, it should be noted that one's gaze influences how likeable (Thayer & Schiff, 1974), attentive (Breed et al., 1972), competent, and credible (Hemsley & Doob, 1978) they are perceived to be. These findings might be leveraged for building an explanatory system with simulated gaze patterns that users trust.

The eyes reveal more than our gaze. Blinking and pupil size are two other affective signals that can be analyzed regarding not only the number and amplitude of blinks but also mean pupil dilation, peak dilation, and latency to peak dilation. We blink about ten times a minute, mainly to lubricate and protect the eyes. However, blinking is also influenced by cognitive effort (Holland & Tarlow, 1975) and affective states, with emotional arousal due to stress or anxiety increasing the blink rate (Giannakakis et al., 2017). Accordingly, an increased blinking rate has been discussed in the context of e-learning as a sign of confusion (Kanematsu et al., 2016). The social perception of blinking also shapes our impressions of a character's intelligence and nervousness (Omori & Miyata, 1996) and is also perceived as a communicative signal (Hómke et al., 2018). Similarly, blinking could be integrated into embodied agents or avatars that are explaining something to the user.

Pupil dilation is not only an important mechanism for adapting to light levels, but also reveals information about the user, because it is influenced directly by the autonomic nervous system. Pupil dilation can be informative in the context of XAI, because it can be considered an index of effort in tasks requiring cognitive control (Van der Wel & Van Steenbergen, 2018) and is indicative of attention (Laeng et al., 2012) and memory (Papesh et al., 2012). As with gaze and blinking, pupil size also affects how someone is perceived – for example, in terms of their trustworthiness (Kret & De Dreu, 2019) – a finding that could be incorporated into the development of explaining agents, but would require careful ethical consideration, especially if trust is not justified.

20.3.1 Current Use of Eye Signals in XAI

Similar to facial expressions, several studies in the field of learning have used eye-related signals. Lee et al. (2015) monitor learners' concentration based on pupil responses and blink patterns. Hutt et al. (2016) use gaze to detect mind-wandering for an intelligent tutoring system. Another line of research focuses on the use of gaze in human–robot interactions. In particular, in collaborative tasks, gaze has been discussed as a valid signal for the robot to adapt and/or explain its behavior (Tisnikar et al., 2022). Wachowiak et al. (2024) showed that in a collaborative virtual cooking scenario, user gaze patterns differed between moments of user confusion, agent error, and successful collaboration. Kurylo and Wilson (2019) showed that gazing at the robot when the robot was not speaking is a valid indicator of the need for assistance from a socially assistive robot. In addition to analyzing the mental state of humans through their gaze and blink patterns and pupil responses, another line of research focuses on equipping agents with the ability to express a mental state through their gaze, ranging from tutoring robots expressing engagement through mutual gaze to more task-oriented gaze in socially assistive robots (Admoni & Scassellati, 2017).

20.4 Voice

When we explain something verbally, our voice conveys more than just words. These aspects of speech apart from the actual verbal content are referred to as paralinguistics and allow information about the speaker's affective state to be conveyed. Emotional prosody describes the paralinguistic aspects of prosody that convey emotion. Prosody is an umbrella term (Arvaniti, 2020) encompassing a variety of interrelated and interacting phenomena—namely, stress, rhythm, phrasing, and intonation. The absence of emotional prosody, for example, in a written text message, can easily lead to misinterpretation. In addition to prosodic features, spectral features, which represent frequency content, and voice quality features, which capture the physical properties of the voice, play a crucial role in affective voice recognition.

Even after nearly three decades of research on emotional prosody, the mapping between acoustics and emotional states is still unclear (Larrouy-Maestri et al., 2024). Possible reasons for this are described by Larrouy-Maestri et al. (2024) in a recent review: Mainly posed emotions and therefore often stereotypical expressions are displayed, a limited set of emotions is considered, and the influence of culture is ignored. In fact, the study of cultural influences is still an ongoing debate. In a study by Chronaki et al. (2018), participants were able to recognize at least some emotions above chance in their own culture as well as (although less well) in other cultures. Similarly, for vocal bursts (e.g., sighing, laughing, crying), it was shown that participants from very different cultures (e.g., Western native English speakers and individuals from a remote Namibian village) could recognize a number of predominantly negative emotions that could be recognized across cultures (Chronaki et al., 2018). In a large-scale study, Cowen et al. (2019) extracted 24 different types of emotions from vocal bursts. Similarly, in a study by Sauter et al. (2010), ten emotions could be predicted from nonverbal cues. However, this study has been criticized for the fact that the participants from the remote culture were actually exposed to Western civilization (Gewald, 2010). Despite the over-chance-level detection of stereotypical vocal bursts, a clear one-to-one mapping of prosody and affect seems to be just as unrealistic as that for other affective signals. Instead, a multimodal combination of different signals (e.g., prosodic features plus facial expression) appears to be required for a particular affect to be perceived by another person (Selting, 2017).

An affective state that is often analyzed from the voice, and highly relevant for explanations, is stress or high arousal. Because stress leads to higher muscle tension and increased respiration, it influences our voice production and sound (Slavich et al., 2019). Many different acoustic and prosodic properties of the voice have been discussed in relation to stress (Giddens et al., 2013). The most commonly, but not always, reported indicator of stress in well-controlled studies is an increase in the fundamental frequency F0, the frequency at which an individual's vocal folds vibrate that we perceive as the pitch of the voice. Comparing different types of stress, it has been shown that the increase in F0 is associated more closely with psychological stress than with physical stress (Johannes et al., 2007). Accordingly, a significant increase in F0 has been reported in emergency situations (Van Puyvelde et al., 2018) similar to the expression of pain (Pisanski et al., 2018) as well as excitement (Trouvain, 2015). Pisanski and Sorokowski (2021) also showed that an increase in F0 is related to an increase in cortisol and that people perceive a higher F0 as more stressed. Less commonly, some studies have also found changes associated with a significant reduction in jitter—that is, microvariations in F0 (Giddens et al., 2013). Another informative aspect in assessing a person's stress is how fast they speak and how many times and for how long they pause, with speaking rate increasing under stress (Buchanan et al., 2014). Furthermore, a recent study by Kappen et al. (2024) compared these speech features (F0, speech rate, and jitter) in two different psychosocial stress paradigms and found that they reflect physiological stress rather than isolated negative affect. Whereas voice pitch and intensity appear to be informative for detecting arousal, they are less useful for detecting valence (Goudbeek & Scherer, 2010).

Existing datasets of emotional speech vary in several aspects: They contain acted or spontaneous emotions, are collected in the wild or in the lab, and are annotated by listeners or by self-report on discrete, continuous, or comparative scales (Gómez-Zaragozá et al., 2024). Dyadic interactions, such as those often found in explanation scenarios, are, for example, performed by actors in the IEMOCAP database (Busso et al., 2008) or the MSP-IMPROV database (Busso et al., 2017). A new dataset that could also be of interest in explanation scenarios is the MSP Podcast Corpus (Lotfian & Busso, 2019) that uses existing podcast data. It contains not only non-acted and naturalistic speech, similar to real-world explanation scenarios, but also over 230 hours of podcast material, making it suitable for deep learning approaches.

Classifiers can be trained either on extracted features or directly on the speech signals themselves. A commonly used feature set for affective analysis of speech is the eGeMAPS (Eyben et al., 2016). For directly training on the speech signal, either the raw audio waveform (Tzirakis et al., 2018) or the spectrum (Cummins et al., 2017) is often fed into a convolutional neural network. For small data sets, active learning, transfer learning and data augmentation, as well as synthetic speech have been used.

20.4.1 Current Use of Voice Signals in XAI

A recent review of affective XAI by Johnson et al. (2024) points out that compared to the visual domain in affective computing, few studies have attempted to make emotional audio explainable. Most of these have focused on feature-based methods that extract the meaning of different features either post hoc or through simpler and thus more transparent models. For interpretability, the eGeMAPS (Eyben et al., 2016) feature set has often been used as a smaller, more interpretable feature set. A conceptual approach by Zhang and Lim (2022) built an interface for explaining voice emotional patterns, offering contrastive saliency, counterfactual synthetic, and contrastive cues explanations. Despite the interesting idea of using synthesized voice samples as counterfactual examples, the synthesis was not successful enough to be used (instead of samples) in the evaluation study.

In a scoping review of prosody in affective human–robot interaction, Gasteiger et al. (2024) concluded that prosodic elements generally help to convey or recognize emotion, but are less effective for negative emotion. There are some interesting approaches in XAI: For example, Knierim et al. (2024) explored how a user's prosody can help agents learn tasks in a reinforcement setting. And Ferguson et al. (2024) investigated which aspects of verbal explanations, such as tone of voice, influence the perception of explanations.

20.5 Circulatory System

The circulatory system, consisting of the heart, blood vessels, and lungs, circulates blood and oxygen throughout the body. It provides two different affective signals: respiration and heartbeat. Their relevance for affective phenomena is reflected in our everyday language, as something "takes our breath away," "makes our heart sink or break," or is "inspiring."

Unlike the modalities discussed earlier, we cannot observe the heart or lungs directly, nor do they perceive the world directly. Instead, they receive information about the world from our autonomic nervous system. The sympathetic nervous system prepares the body for flight by increasing heart rate, constricting blood vessels, increasing blood pressure, and dilating the bronchi. In contrast, activation of the parasympathetic nervous system returns the body to a calm state for rest and digestion. Accordingly, its activation decreases the heart rate, indirectly dilates the blood vessels, and constricts the bronchi.

20.5.1 Heart

Heart rate (HR) is measured as the number of beats or contractions per minute. The number of pulses per minute palpated at the periphery is called the pulse rate and can be felt by placing two fingers on the wrist. A typical adult heart rate at rest is 60–80 beats per minute, with values below 60 called bradycardia and values above 100 called tachycardia. Many factors affect the heartbeat, including fitness, muscle activity, thermal stress, and mental stress. Breathing changes the heartbeat: When you inhale, your heartbeat increases; when you exhale, it decreases. Similarly, our position influences the heartbeat: Lying down slows it down; standing up increases it. Exercise increases the heart rate because more oxygen is needed. Besides heart rate, another important measure is heart rate variability (HRV), the variability of the beat-to-beat interval. HRV is synchronized with breathing, a phenomenon called respiratory sinus arrhythmia. Many factors influence HRV and must be considered when interpreting the signal. For example, HRV is lower in the elderly than in the young and in women than in men. Lifestyle factors such as tobacco, alcohol, exercise, and meditation also affect heart rate (Fatisson et al., 2016). Therefore, baseline assessments and repeated measures are recommended for proper interpretation of HRV values.

In the context of emotion, the most commonly used measures are HR and HRV (Kreibig, 2010). A meta-analysis by Siegel et al. (2018) of 202 studies measuring autonomic nervous system reactivity during emotion induction in healthy adults showed reactivity for many emotions, but no pattern clearly distinguished different emotions. Similar to voice, one well-studied affective phenomenon highly relevant in the context of explanations is stress. Stress generally leads to an increase in HR and a decrease in HRV. Consistent with this, a higher task load in a flight simulation (De Rivecourt et al., 2008) also leads to an increase in HR and a decrease in HRV. Surgeons who experienced stress during surgery showed increased intraoperative HR and decreased HRV at night, appearing to experience less relaxation during sleep (Rieger et al., 2014).

Hearts are often used as emoticons in romantic relationships and friendships. In fact, women who reported greater chronic loneliness also had lower resting HRV. Their hearts are more responsive to acute feelings of loneliness, with greater increases in HRV (Roddick & Chen, 2020). In pop culture, there is a common idea that hearts beat in sync (e.g., "our hearts beat as one"). In fact, heart synchronization increases when people feel trust in relationships (Helm et al., 2012; Mitkidis et al., 2015), and mothers and infants also coordinate their heart rhythms (Feldman et al., 2011). In romantic couples, a negative (antiphase) synchrony of their HRV and a positive (in-phase) synchrony of HR have been reported (Coutinho et al., 2021). During conflict, their HRV synchrony seems to increase (Wilson et al., 2018).

In the medical context, heart rate and its variability are often measured by ECG. Advances in signal processing and machine learning have enabled another unobtrusive method called remote photoplethysmography (rPPG) that estimates an individual's heart rate from a video recording of their face. The method estimates heart rate by measuring changes in reflected light caused by fluctuations in blood volume under the skin.

20.5.2 Respiration

Breathing oxygenates our blood to deliver oxygen to our muscles and nervous system. We typically breathe about once every 3–4 seconds, but individual variation is large, with a range of 6–31 breaths per minute at rest. We inhale between 442 and 1,549 ml of air with each breath. Our individual breathing pattern is relatively stable throughout adulthood (Benchetrit, 2000), and even monozygotic twins breathe similarly (Shea et al., 1989). Spontaneously, our breathing is affected by speech, smell, laughter, sighing, and gasping in surprise.

The induction of affective states has been shown to affect breathing. For example, arousal typically increases respiratory rate. Individuals differ in how strongly they respond to a change in their breathing pattern. Jerath and Beveridge (2020) showed that changes in breathing in response to anxiety correlate positively with an individual's trait anxiety. People who are generally more anxious responded with a greater increase in their breathing rate to a red warning light that preceded electrical stimulation of the finger (Homma & Masaoka, 2008). A review by Grassmann et al. (2016) of respiratory changes in response to cognitive load showed that mentally demanding episodes are characterized by faster breathing, whereas the amplitude is quite stable. The effect on respiratory rate seems to be independent of valence, because it was found for both negative and positive arousal (Kreibig, 2010).

The relationship between affect and breathing patterns has been studied bidirectionally: Philippot et al. (2002) showed that breathing instructions can produce a certain affective state in a participant. For example, an instruction such as "Breathe in and out slowly and deeply through your nose; your breathing is very regular and your chest is relaxed!" resulted in the participants feeling more joy. Especially in relation to stress, much research examines breathing from the other direction, because changing the breathing pattern (e.g., to slow breathing to about 6 breaths per minute) can influence mood and thinking. Zaccaro et al. (2018) showed that slow breathing techniques act to increase autonomic, cerebral, and psychological flexibility in a scenario of reciprocal interactions. A meta-review of voluntary slow breathing showed an increase in HRV during and after the practice (Laborde et al., 2024). A recent review by Fincham et al. (2023, p. 1) concluded that: "Overall, the results show that breathwork may be effective in improving stress and mental health. However, we urge caution and advocate for nuanced research approaches with low risk of bias study designs to avoid a miscommunication between hype and evidence."

Interpersonal synchrony can also be observed in breathing. In a study of 22 romantic couples, Goldstein et al. (2017) examined synchrony as a function of touch and pain. A pain recipient and an observer were placed in pain/no-pain and touch/no-touch conditions. ECG and respiratory rates were recorded. Partner touch increased interpersonal respiratory coupling in both pain and no-pain conditions.

20.5.3 Current Use of Circulatory System Signals in XAI

The use of cardiac or respiratory nonverbal cues in XAI has been limited. I am not aware of any intelligent explainable agents that express their state with certain heartbeat or breathing patterns, or of AI systems that aim to detect affect in explanation scenarios based on the circulatory system. However, in the context of human–robot interaction, the use of psychophysiological affective signals has been explored. Certain aspects of this research are also interesting in the context of XAI, such as detecting engagement in human–robot collaboration based on ECG data (Ramadurai et al., 2024) or measuring trust in human–robot interaction based on heart rate and other psychophysiological features (Ahmad & Alzahrani, 2023). More related to explanations, Lane and D'Mello (2019) emphasize the use of physiological signals for intelligent learning environments to support cognitive, affective, and metacognitive aspects of learning.

20.6 Conclusion

Nonverbal signals of affect offer significant opportunities for enhancing XAI systems. By automatically analyzing affective cues from facial expressions, vocal characteristics, vocal bursts, gaze patterns, pupil responses, heartbeat, and respiration, XAI systems can gain valuable insights into a user's emotional state. Such insights may enable adaptive responses from the machine, potentially improving user experience and interaction fluidity. In addition, the agent's generation of nonverbal cues can increase the agent's perceived trustworthiness, which is related to the ethical challenges of unwarranted trust (see Chap. 30). Exploring the less studied modalities and integrating multiple modalities could further enhance these benefits, potentially leading to more robust and nuanced XAI applications.

20.7 Rapid Access to the Content of This Chapter

- Nonverbal affective signals could improve XAI systems by monitoring and integrating information about a user's affective state or by generating and simulating a machine's state.
- Facial expressions carry relevant information about one's own affect, but simplistic interpretations should be avoided, and individual differences, cultural context, and biases in databases need to be taken into account.
- Eyes reveal information that could be useful for XAI systems through gaze, blinking, and pupil size, and they do this mainly in relation to attention, cognitive load, and preferences.

- Voice contains information about stress that could potentially be relevant to clinical or educational XAI systems, and this has been studied in the context of tutoring systems.
- The respiratory system has rarely been studied in the context of explanation or learning for XAI systems, but stress may be a promising avenue here as well.
- For the future of using affective signals to enhance XAI, researchers can integrate multiple modalities, explore less studied modalities while considering context and culture, and evaluate the use of affective signals in the concrete use case of XAI.

Acknowledgments I thank Philipp Müller, Olya Hakobyan, and Matthias Norden for their valuable perspectives and helpful comments on an earlier version of this chapter.

This work was funded by the Deutsche Forschungsgemeinschaft (DFG, German Research Foundation): TRR 318/1 2021 – 438445824.

References

Admoni, H., & Scassellati, B. (2017). Social eye gaze in human–robot interaction: A review. *Journal of Human–Robot Interaction, 6*(1), 25–63. https://doi.org/10.5898/JHRI.6.1.Admoni

Ahmad, M., & Alzahrani, A. (2023). Crucial clues: Investigating psychophysiological behaviors for measuring trust in human–robot interaction. In *Proceedings of the 25th International Conference on Multimodal Interaction* (pp. 135–143). Association for Computing Machinery. https://doi.org/10.1145/3577190.3614148

Arvaniti, A. (2020). The phonetics of prosody. In M. Aronoff (Ed.), *Oxford research encyclopedia of linguistics* . Oxford University Press. https://doi.org/10.1093/acrefore/9780199384655.013.411

Aviezer, H., Ensenberg, N., & Hassin, R. R. (2017). The inherently contextualized nature of facial emotion perception. *Current Opinion in Psychology, 17*, 47–54. https://doi.org/10.1016/j.copsyc.2017.06.006

Baron-Cohen, S., Wheelwright, S., Hill, J., Raste, Y., & Plumb, I. (2001). The "Reading the Mind in the Eyes" Test revised version: A study with normal adults, and adults with Asperger syndrome or high-functioning autism. *Journal of Child Psychology and Psychiatry, and Allied Disciplines, 42*(2), 241–251. https://doi.org/10.1111/1469-7610.00715

Barrett, L. F., & Bliss-Moreau, E. (2009). Affect as a psychological primitive. *Advances in Experimental Social Psychology, 41*, 167–218. https://doi.org/10.1016/S0065-2601(08)00404-8

Barrett, L. F., Mesquita, B., & Gendron, M. (2011). Context in emotion perception. *Current Directions in Psychological Science, 20*(5), 286–290. https://doi.org/10.1177/0963721411422522

Barrett, L. F., Adolphs, R., Marsella, S., Martinez, A. M., & Pollak, S. D. (2019). Emotional expressions reconsidered: Challenges to inferring emotion from human facial movements. *Psychological Science in the Public Interest, 20*(1), 1–68. https://doi.org/10.1177/1529100619832930

Benchetrit, G. (2000). Breathing pattern in humans: Diversity and individuality. *Respiration Physiology, 122*(2), 123–129. https://doi.org/10.1016/S0034-5687(00)00154-7

Bernardo, E., & Seva, R. (2023). Affective analysis of explainable artificial intelligence in the development of trust in AI systems. In *Intelligent human systems integration (IHSI 2023): Integrating people and intelligent systems* (pp. 417–427). AHFE Open Acces. https://doi.org/10.54941/ahfe1002861

Booth, B. M., Ali, A. M., Narayanan, S. S., Bennett, I., & Farag, A. A. (2017). Toward active and unobtrusive engagement assessment of distance learners. In *2017 Seventh International Conference on Affective Computing and Intelligent Interaction (ACII)* (pp. 470–476). IEEE. https://doi.org/10.1109/ACII.2017.8273641

Breed, G., Christiansen, E., & Larson, D. (1972). Effect of a lecturer's gaze direction upon teaching effectiveness. *Catalog of Selected Documents in Psychology, 2*, 115.

Buchanan, T. W., Laures-Gore, J. S., & Duff, M. C. (2014). Acute stress reduces speech fluency. *Biological Psychology, 97*, 60–66. https://doi.org/10.1016/j.biopsycho.2014.02.005

Busso, C., Bulut, M., Lee, C.-C., Kazemzadeh, E. A., Mower, E. M., Kim, S., Chang, J. N., Lee, S., Narayanan, S.S. (2008). IEMOCAP: Interactive emotional dyadic motion capture database. *Language Resources and Evaluation, 42*, 335–359. https://doi.org/10.1007/s10579-008-9076-6

Busso, C., Parthasarathy, S., Burmania, A., AbdelWahab, M., Sadoughi, N., & Provost, E. M. (2017). MSP-IMPROV: An acted corpus of dyadic interactions to study emotion perception. *IEEE Transactions on Affective Computing, 8*(1), 67–80. https://doi.org/10.1109/TAFFC.2016.2515617

Chronaki, G., Wigelsworth, M., Pell, M. D., & Kotz, S. A. (2018). The development of cross-cultural recognition of vocal emotion during childhood and adolescence. *Scientific Reports, 8*, 8659. https://doi.org/10.1038/s41598-018-26889-1

Clore, G. L., & Huntsinger, J. R. (2007). How emotions inform judgment and regulate thought. *Trends in Cognitive Sciences, 11*(9), 393–399. https://doi.org/10.1016/j.tics.2007.08.005

Cohn, J. F., Ambadar, Z., & Ekman, P. (2007). Observer-based measurement of facial expression with the Facial Action Coding System. In J. A. Coan & J. J. B. Allen (Eds.), *Handbook of emotion elicitation and assessment* (pp. 203–221). Oxford University Press. https://doi.org/10.1093/oso/9780195169157.003.0014

Coutinho, J., Pereira, A., Oliveira-Silva, P., Meier, D., Lourenço, V., & Tschacher, W. (2021). When our hearts beat together: Cardiac synchrony as an entry point to understand dyadic co-regulation in couples. *Psychophysiology, 58*(3), e13739. https://doi.org/10.1111/psyp.13739

Cowen, A. S., Elfenbein, H. A., Laukka, P., & Keltner, D. (2019). Mapping 24 emotions conveyed by brief human vocalization. *The American Psychologist, 74*(6), 698–712. https://doi.org/10.1037/amp0000399

Cummins, N., Amiriparian, S., Hagerer, G., Batliner, A., Steidl, S., & Schuller, B. W. (2017). An image-based deep spectrum feature representation for the recognition of emotional speech. In *Proceedings of the 25th ACM International Conference on Multimedia* (pp. 478–484). Association for Computing Machinery. https://doi.org/10.1145/3123266.3123371

Dasgupta, N., DeSteno, D., Williams, L. A., & Hunsinger, M. (2009). Fanning the flames of prejudice: The influence of specific incidental emotions on implicit prejudice. *Emotion, 9*(4), 585–591. https://doi.org/10.1037/a0015961

De Rivecourt, M., Kuperus, M. N., Post, W. J., & Mulder, L. J. M. (2008). Cardiovascular and eye activity measures as indices for momentary changes in mental effort during simulated flight. *Ergonomics, 51*(9), 1295–1319. https://doi.org/10.1080/00140130802120267

Dewan, M. A. A., Murshed, M., & Lin, F. (2019). Engagement detection in online learning: A review. *Smart Learning Environments, 6*, 1. https://doi.org/10.1186/s40561-018-0080-z

Dominguez-Catena, I., Paternain, D., Jurio, A., & Galar, M. (2024). Less can be more: Representational vs. stereotypical gender bias in facial expression recognition. *Progress in Artificial Intelligence, 14*, 11–31. https://doi.org/10.1007/s13748-024-00345-w

Durán, J. I., Reisenzein, R., & Fernández-Dols, J.-M. (2017). Coherence between emotions and facial expressions: A research synthesis. In J. A. Russell & J. M. Fernandez Dols (Eds.), *The science of facial expression* (pp. 107–129). Oxford University Press. https://doi.org/10.1093/acprof:oso/9780190613501.003.0007

Eckstein, M. K., Guerra-Carrillo, B., Singley, A. T. M., & Bunge, S. A. (2017). Beyond eye gaze: What else can eyetracking reveal about cognition and cognitive development? *Developmental Cognitive Neuroscience, 25*, 69–91. https://doi.org/10.1016/j.dcn.2016.11.001

Ekman, P., & W. V. Friesen (1978). *Facial action coding system.* Consulting Psychologists Press. https://doi.org/10.1037/t27734-000

Emery, N. J. (2000). The eyes have it: The neuroethology, function and evolution of social gaze. *Neuroscience & Biobehavioral Reviews, 24*(6), 581–604. https://doi.org/10.1016/S0149-7634(00)00025-7

Eyben, F., Scherer, K. R., Schuller, B.W., Sundberg, J., André, E., Busso, C., Devillers, L., Epps, J., Laukka, P., Narayanan, S. S., & Truong, K. P. (2016). The Geneva minimalistic acoustic parameter set (geMAPS) for voice research and affective computing. *IEEE Transactions on Affective Computing, 7*(2), 190–202. https://doi.org/10.1109/TAFFC.2015.2457417

Farroni, T., Johnson, M. H., Menon, E., Zulian, L., Faraguna, D., & Csibra, G. (2005). Newborns' preference for face-relevant stimuli: Effects of contrast polarity. *Proceedings of the National Academy of Sciences of the United States of America, 102*(47), 17245–17250. https://doi.org/10.1073/pnas.0502205102

Fatisson, J., Oswald, V., & Lalonde, F. (2016). Influence diagram of physiological and environmental factors affecting heart rate variability: An extended literature overview. *Heart International, 11*(1), e32–e40. https://doi.org/10.5301/heartint.5000232

Feldman, R., Magori-Cohen, R., Galili, G., Singer, M., & Louzoun, Y. (2011). Mother and infant coordinate heart rhythms through episodes of interaction synchrony. *Infant Behavior & Development, 34*(4), 569–577. https://doi.org/10.1016/j.infbeh.2011.06.008

Ferguson, S., Aoyagui, P. A., Rizvi, R., Kim, Y.-H., & Kuzminykh, A. (2024). The explanation that hits home: The characteristics of verbal explanations that affect human perception in subjective decision-making. *Proceedings ACM on Human–Computer Interaction, 8*(CSCW2), 517. https://doi.org/10.1145/3687056

Fincham, G. W., Strauss, C., Montero-Marin, J., & Cavanagh, K. (2023). Effect of breathwork on stress and mental health: A meta-analysis of randomised-controlled trials. *Scientific Reports, 13*(1), 432. https://doi.org/10.1038/s41598-022-27247-y

Frischen, A., Bayliss, A. P., & Tipper, S. P. (2007). Gaze cueing of attention: Visual attention, social cognition, and individual differences. *Psychological Bulletin, 133*(4), 694–724. https://doi.org/10.1037/0033-2909.133.4.694

Gómez-Zaragozá, L., del Amor, R., Castro-Bleda, M. J., Naranjo, V., Alcañiz Raya, M., & Marín-Morales, J. (2024). *EMOVOME: A dataset for emotion recognition in spontaneous real-life speech.* https://doi.org/10.48550/arXiv.2403.02167

Gasteiger, N., Lim, J., Hellou, M., MacDonald, B. A., & Ahn, H. S. (2024). A scoping review of the literature on prosodic elements related to emotional speech in human–robot interaction. *International Journal of Social Robotics, 16*(4), 659–670. https://doi.org/10.1007/s12369-022-00913-x

Gewald, J.-B. (2010). Remote but in contact with history and the world. *Proceedings of the National Academy of Sciences of the United States of America, 107*(18). https://doi.org/10.1073/pnas.1001284107

Giannakakis, G., Pediaditis, M., Manousos, D., Kazantzaki, E., Chiarugi, F., Simos, P. G., Marias, K., & Tsiknakis, M. (2017). Stress and anxiety detection using facial cues from videos. *Biomedical Signal Processing and Control, 31*, 89–101. https://doi.org/10.1016/j.bspc.2016.06.020

Giddens, C. L., Barron, K. W., Byrd-Craven, J., Clark, K. F., & Winter, A. S. (2013). Vocal indices of stress: A review. *Journal of Voice: Official Journal of the Voice Foundation, 27*(3), 390.e21–29. https://doi.org/10.1016/j.jvoice.2012.12.010

Girard, J. M., & Cohn, J. F. (2016). A primer on observational measurement. *Assessment, 23*(4), 404–413. https://doi.org/10.1177/1073191116635807

Goldstein, P., Weissman-Fogel, I., & Shamay-Tsoory, S. G. (2017). The role of touch in regulating inter-partner physiological coupling during empathy for pain. *Scientific Reports, 7*(1), 3252. https://doi.org/10.1038/s41598-017-03627-7

Goudbeek, M., & Scherer, K. (2010). Beyond arousal: Valence and potency/control cues in the vocal expression of emotion. *The Journal of the Acoustical Society of America, 128*(3), 1322–1336. https://doi.org/10.1121/1.3466853

Grassmann, M., Vlemincx, E., Von Leupoldt, A., Mittelstädt, J. M., & Van den Bergh, O. (2016). Respiratory changes in response to cognitive load: A systematic review. *Neural Plasticity, 2016*, 8146809. https://doi.org/10.1155/2016/8146809

Guerdan, L., Raymond, A., & Gunes, H. (2021). Toward affective XAI: Facial affect analysis for understanding explainable human–AI interactions. In *2021 IEEE/CVF International Conference on Computer Vision Workshops (ICCVW)* (pp. 3789–3798). IEEE. https://doi.org/10.1109/ICCVW54120.2021.00423

Hömke, P., Holler, J., & Levinson, S. C. (2018). Eye blinks are perceived as communicative signals in human face-to-face interaction. *PloS One, 13*(12), e0208030. https://doi.org/10.1371/journal.pone.0208030

Helm, J. L., Sbarra, D., & Ferrer, E. (2012). Assessing cross-partner associations in physiological responses via coupled oscillator models. *Emotion, 12*(4), 748–762. https://doi.org/10.1037/a0025036

Hemsley, G. D., & Doob, A. N. (1978). The effect of looking behavior on perceptions of a communicator's credibility. *Journal of Applied Social Psychology, 8*(2), 136–144. https://doi.org/10.1111/j.1559-1816.1978.tb00772.x

Ho, A. K., Sidanius, J., Kteily, N., Sheehy-Skeffington, J., Pratto, F., Henkel, K. E., Foels, R., &Stewart, A. L. (2015). The nature of social dominance orientation: Theorizing and measuring preferences for intergroup inequality using the new SDO_7 scale. *Journal of Personality and Social Psychology, 109*(6), 1003–1028. https://doi.org/10.1037/pspi0000033

Holland, M. K., Tarlow, G. (1975). Blinking and thinking. *Perceptual and Motor Skills, 41*(2), 503–506. https://doi.org/10.2466/pms.1975.41.2.4

Homma, I., & Masaoka, Y. (2008). Breathing rhythms and emotions. *Experimental Physiology, 93*(9), 1011–1021. https://doi.org/10.1113/expphysiol.2008.042424

Horng, W.-B., Chen, C.-Y., Chang, Y., & Fan, C.-H. (2004). Driver fatigue detection based on eye tracking and dynamic template matching. In *IEEE International Conference on Networking, Sensing and Control* (pp. 7–12). IEEE. https://doi.org/10.1109/ICNSC.2004.1297400

Hutt, S., Mills, C., White, S., Donnelly, P. J., & D'Mello, S. K. (2016). *The eyes have it: Gaze-based detection of mind wandering during learning with an intelligent tutoring system*. Tech. rep. International Educational Data Mining Society.

Izard, C. E., Fantauzzo, C. A., Castle, J. M., Haynes, O. M., Rayias, M. F., & Putnam, P. H. (1995). The ontogeny and significance of infants' facial expressions in the first 9 months of life. *Developmental Psychology, 31*(6), 997–1013. https://doi.org/10.1037/0012-1649.31.6.997

Jarick, M., & Bencic, R. (2019). Eye contact is a two-way street: Arousal is elicited by the sending and receiving of eye gaze information. *Frontiers in Psychology, 10*, 1262. https://doi.org/10.3389/fpsyg.2019.01262

Jerath, R., & Beveridge, C. (2020). Respiratory rhythm, autonomic modulation, and the spectrum of emotions: The future of emotion recognition and modulation. *Frontiers in Psychology, 11*, 1980. https://doi.org/10.3389/fpsyg.2020.01980

Johannes, B., Wittels, P., Enne, R., Eisinger, G., Castro, C. A., Thomas, J. L., Adler, A. B., & Gerzer, R. (2007). Non-linear function model of voice pitch dependency on physical and mental load. *European Journal of Applied Physiology, 101*(3), 267–276. https://doi.org/10.1007/s00421-007-0496-6

Johnson, D. S., Hakobyan, O., Paletschek, J., & Drimalla, H. (2024). Explainable AI for audio and visual affective computing: A scoping review. *IEEE Transactions on Affective Computing* 1–20. https://doi.org/10.1109/TAFFC.2024.3505269

Kanematsu, H., Ogawa, N., Shirai, T., Kawaguchi, M., Kobayashi, T., & Barry, D. M. (2016). Blinking eyes behaviors and face temperatures of students in Youtube lessons – for the future e-learning class. *Procedia Computer Science, 96*(C), 1619–1626. https://doi.org/10.1016/j.procs.2016.08.209

Kappen, M., Vanhollebeke, G., Van Der Donckt, J., Van Hoecke, S., & Vanderhasselt, M.-A. (2024). Acoustic and prosodic speech features reflect physiological stress but not isolated negative affect: A multi-paradigm study on psychosocial stressors. *Scientific Reports, 14*(1), 5515. https://doi.org/10.1038/s41598-024-55550-3

Kaptein, F., Broekens, J., Hindriks, K., & Neerincx, M. (2017). The role of emotion in self-explanations by cognitive agents. In *2017 Seventh International Conference on Affective Computing and Intelligent Interaction Workshops and Demos (ACIIW)* (pp. 88–93). IEEE. https://doi.org/10.1109/ACIIW.2017.8272595

Kaur, A., Mustafa, A., Mehta, L., & Dhall, A. (2018). Prediction and localization of student engagement in the wild. In *Digital image computing: Techniques and applications (DICTA)* (pp. 1–8). IEEE. https://doi.org/10.1109/DICTA.2018.8615851

Klin, A., Jones, W., Schultz, R., Volkmar, F., & Cohen, D. (2002). Visual fixation patterns during viewing of naturalistic social situations as predictors of social competence in individuals with autism. *Archives of General Psychiatry, 59*(9), 809–816. https://doi.org/10.1001/archpsyc.59.9.809

Knierim, M., Jain, S., Aydoğan, M. H., Mitra, K., Desai, K., Saran, A., & Baraka, K. (2024). *Prosody as a teaching signal for agent learning: Exploratory studies and algorithmic implications*. https://doi.org/10.48550/arXiv.2410.23554

Kröger, J. L., Lutz, O. H.-M., & Müller, F. (2020). What does your gaze reveal about you? On the privacy implications of eye tracking. In M. Friedewald, M. Önen, E. Lievens, S. Krenn & S. Fricker (Eds.), *Privacy and identity management. Data for better living: AI and privacy* (pp. 226–241). Springer. https://doi.org/10.1007/978-3-030-42504-3_15

Kreibig, S. D. (2010). Autonomic nervous system activity in emotion: A review. *Biological Psychology, 84*(3), 394–421. https://doi.org/10.1016/j.biopsycho.2010.03.010

Kret, M. E., & De Dreu, C. K. (2019). The power of pupil size in establishing trust and reciprocity. *Journal of Experimental Psychology: General, 148*(8), 1299–1311. https://doi.org/10.1037/xge0000508

Kuhn, G., & Kingstone, A. (2009). Look away! Eyes and arrows engage oculomotor responses automatically. *Attention, Perception & Psychophysics, 71*(2), 314–327. https://doi.org/10.3758/APP.71.2.314

Kurylo, U., & Wilson, J. R. (2019). Using human eye gaze patterns as indicators of need for assistance from a socially assistive robot. In *Social Robotics: 11th International Conference, ICSR 2019* (pp. 200–210). Springer. https://doi.org/10.1007/978-3-030-35888-4_19

Laborde, S., Zammit, N., Iskra, M., Mosley, E., Borges, U., Allen, M. S., & Javelle, F. (2024). The influence of breathing techniques on physical sport performance: A systematic review and meta-analysis. *International Review of Sport and Exercise Psychology, 17*(2), 1222–1277. https://doi.org/10.1080/1750984X.2022.2145573

Laeng, B., Sirois, S., & Gredebäck, G. (2012). Pupillometry: A window to the preconscious? *Perspectives on Psychological Science, 7*(1), 18–27. https://doi.org/10.1177/1745691611427305

Lakin, J. L., & Chartrand, T. L. (2003). Using nonconscious behavioral mimicry to create affiliation and rapport. *Psychological Science, 14*(4), 334–339. https://doi.org/10.1111/1467-9280.14481

Lane, H. C., & D'Mello, S. K. (2019). Uses of physiological monitoring in intelligent learning environments: A review of research, evidence, and technologies. In T. D. Parsons, L. Lin & D. Cockerham (Eds.), *Mind, brain and technology: Learning in the age of emerging technologies* (pp. 67–86). Springer. https://doi.org/10.1007/978-3-030-02631-8_5

Larrouy-Maestri, P., Poeppel, D., & Pell, M. D. (2024). The sound of emotional prosody: Nearly 3 decades of research and future directions. *Perspectives on Psychological Science*. https://doi.org/10.1177/17456916231217722

Lee, G., Ojha, A., & Lee, M. (2015). Concentration monitoring for intelligent tutoring system based on pupil and eye-blink. In *Proceedings of the 3rd International Conference on Human–Agent Interaction* (pp. 291–294). Association for Computing Machinery. https://doi.org/10.1145/2814940.2815000

Lerner, J. S., & Keltner, D. (2001). Fear, anger, and risk. *Journal of Personality and Social Psychology, 81*(1), 146–159. https://doi.org/10.1037/0022-3514.81.1.146

Lotfian, R., & Busso, C. (2019). Building naturalistic emotionally balanced speech corpus by retrieving emotional speech from existing podcast recordings. *IEEE Transactions on Affective Computing, 10*(4), 471–483. https://doi.org/10.1109/TAFFC.2017.2736999

McDaniel, B., D'Mello, S., King, B., Chipman, P., Tapp, K., & Graesser, A. (2007). Facial features for affective state detection in learning environments. In *Proceedings of the Annual Meeting of the Cognitive Science Society* (pp. 467–472). University of California.

Mitkidis, P., McGraw, J. J., Roepstorff, A., & Wallot, S. Wallot (2015). Building trust: Heart rate synchrony and arousal during joint action increased by public goods game. *Physiology & Behavior, 149*, 101–106. https://doi.org/10.1016/j.physbeh.2015.05.033

Mosimann, U. P., Mather, G., Wesnes, K. A., O'brien, J. T., Burn, D. J., & McKeith, I. G. (2004). Visual perception in Parkinson disease dementia and dementia with Lewy bodies. *Neurology, 63*(11), 2091–2096. https://doi.org/10.1212/01.wnl.0000145764.70698.4e

Niven, K. (2013). Affect. In M. D. Gellman & J. Rick Turner (Eds.), *Encyclopedia of behavioral medicine* (pp. 49–50). Springer. https://doi.org/10.1007/978-1-4419-1005-9_1088

Norbury, C. F., Brock, J., Cragg, L., Einav, S., Griffiths, H., & Nation, K. (2009). Eye-movement patterns are associated with communicative competence in autistic spectrum disorders. *Journal of Child Psychology and Psychiatry, 50*(7), 834–842. https://doi.org/10.1111/j.1469-7610.2009.02073.x

Omori, Y., & Miyata, Y. (1996). Eyeblinks in formation of impressions. *Perceptual and Motor Skills, 83*(2), 591–594. https://doi.org/10.2466/pms.1996.83.2.591

Paletschek, J., Bleimling, J., Johnson, D., & Drimalla, H. (2024). A paradigm to investigate social signals of understanding and their susceptibility to stress. In *12th International Conference on Affective Computing & Intelligent Interaction*.IEEE.

Papesh, M. H., Goldinger, S. D., & Hout, M. C. (2012). Memory strength and specificity revealed by pupillometry. *International Journal of Psychophysiology, 83*(1), 56–64. https://doi.org/10.1016/j.ijpsycho.2011.10.002

Pfeiffer, U. J., Vogeley, K., & Schilbach, L. (2013). From gaze cueing to dual eye-tracking: Novel approaches to investigate the neural correlates of gaze in social interaction. *Neuroscience & Biobehavioral Reviews, 37*(10, Part 2), 2516–2528. https://doi.org/10.1016/j.neubiorev.2013.07.017

Philippot, P., Chapelle, G., & Blairy, S. (2002). Respiratory feedback in the generation of emotion. *Cognition and Emotion, 16*(5), 605–627. https://doi.org/10.1080/02699930143000392

Pisanski, K., & Sorokowski, P. (2021). Human stress detection: Cortisol levels in stressed speakers predict voice–based judgements of stress. *Perception, 50*(1), 80–87. https://doi.org/10.1177/0301006620978378

Pisanski, K., Kobylarek, A., Jakubowska, L., Nowak, J., Walter, A., Błaszczyński, K., Kasprzyk, M., Lysenko, K., Sukiennik, I., Piątek, K., & Frackowiak, T. (2018). Multimodal stress detection: Testing for covariation in vocal, hormonal and physiological responses to Trier Social Stress Test. *Hormones and Behavior, 106*, 52–61. https://doi.org/10.1016/j.yhbeh.2018.08.014

Ramadurai, S., Gutierrez, C., Jeong, H., & Kim, M. (2024). Physiological indicators of fluency and engagement during sequential and simultaneous modes of human–robot collaboration. *IISE Transactions on Occupational Ergonomics and Human Factors, 12*(1–2), 97–111. https://doi.org/10.1080/24725838.2023.2287015

Rieger, A., Stoll, R., Kreuzfeld, S., Behrens, K., & Weippert, M. (2014). Heart rate and heart rate variability as indirect markers of surgeons' intra-operative stress. *International Archives of Occupational and Environmental Health, 87*(2), 165–174. https://doi.org/10.1007/s00420-013-0847-z

Roddick, C. M., & Chen, F. S. (2020). Effects of chronic and state loneliness on heart rate variability in women. *Annals of Behavioral Medicine, 55*(5), 460–475. https://doi.org/10.1093/abm/kaaa065

Sauter, D. A., Eisner, F., Ekman, P., & Scott, S. K. (2010). Cross-cultural recognition of basic emotions through nonverbal emotional vocalizations. *Proceedings of the National Academy of Sciences of the United States of America, 107*(6), 2408–2412. https://doi.org/10.1073/pnas.0908239106

Savchenko, A. V., Savchenko, L. V., & Makarov, I. (2022). Classifying emotions and engagement in online learning based on a single facial expression recognition neural network. *IEEE*

Transactions on Affective Computing, 13(4), 2132–2143. https://doi.org/10.1109/TAFFC.2022.3188390

Schmid, U., & Wrede, B. (2022). What is missing in XAI so far? *KI – Künstliche Intelligenz, 36*(3), 303–315. https://doi.org/10.1007/s13218-022-00786-2

Schoofs, D., Preuss, D., & Wolf, O. T. (2008). Psychosocial stress induces working memory impairments in an n-back paradigm. *Psychoneuroendocrinology, 33*(5), 643–653. https://doi.org/10.1016/j.psyneuen.2008.02.004

Selting, M. (2017). The display and management of affectivity in climaxes of amusing stories. *Journal of Pragmatics, 111*, 1–32. https://doi.org/10.1016/j.pragma.2017.01.008

Shang, R., Hsieh, G., & Shah, C. (2024). Trusting your AI agent emotionally and cognitively: Development and validation of a semantic differential scale for AI trust. In *Proceedings of the AAAI/ACM Conference on AI, Ethics, and Society* (pp. 1343–1356). AAAI. https://doi.org/10.1609/aies.v7i1.31728

Shea, S. A., Benchetrit, G., Dinh, T. P., Hamilton, R. D., & Guz, A. (1989). The breathing patterns of identical twins. *Respiration Physiology, 75*(2), 211–223. https://doi.org/10.1016/0034-5687(89)90065-0

Siegel, E. H., Sands, M. K., Van den Noortgate, W., Condon, P., Chang, Y., Dy, J., Quigley, K. S., & Barrett, L.F. (2018). Emotion fingerprints or emotion populations? A meta-analytic investigation of automatic features of emotion categories. *Psychological Bulletin, 144*(4), 343–393. https://doi.org/10.1037/bul0000128

Singh, M., Hoque, X., Zeng, D., Wang, Y., Ikeda, K., & Dhall, A. (2023). Do I have your attention: A large scale engagement prediction dataset and baselines. In *ICMI '23: Proceedings of the 25th International Conference on Multimodal Interaction* (pp. 174–182). Association for Computing Machinery. https://doi.org/10.1145/3577190.3614764

Slavich, G. M., Taylor, S., & Picard, R. W. (2019). Stress measurement using speech: Recent advancements, validation issues, and ethical and privacy considerations. *Stress, 22*(4), 408. https://doi.org/10.1080/10253890.2019.1584180

Storbeck, J., & Clore, G. L. (2007). On the interdependence of cognition and emotion. *Cognition & Emotion, 21*(6), 1212–1237. https://doi.org/10.1080/02699930701438020

Synnott, A. (1992). The eye and I: a sociology of sight. *International Journal of Politics, Culture, and Society, 5*(4), 617–636. https://doi.org/10.1007/BF01419559

Thayer, S., & Schiff, W. (1974). Observer judgment of social interaction: Eye contact and relationship inferences. *Journal of Personality and Social Psychology, 30*(1), 110–114. https://doi.org/10.1037/h0036647

Thommes, K., Lammert, O., Schütze, C., Richter, B., & Wrede, B. (2024). Human emotions in AI explanations. In *Explainable artificial intelligence, xAI 2024* (pp. 270–293). Springer. https://doi.org/10.1007/978-3-031-63803-9_15

Tisnikar, P., Wachowiak, L., Canal, G., Coles, A., Leonetti, M., & Celiktutan, O. (2022). Towards autonomous collaborative robots that adapt and explain. In *IEEE ICRA 2022 Workshop on Prediction and Anticipation Reasoning in Human Robot Interaction*. IEEE.

Trouvain, J. (2015). Notes on the development of speaking styles over decades—the case of live football commentaries. In *HSCR INTERSPEECH* (pp. 160–166). TUDpress.

Tzirakis, P., Zhang, J., & Schuller, B. W. (2018). End-to-end speech emotion recognition using deep neural networks. In *2018 IEEE International Conference on Acoustics, Speech and Signal Processing (ICASSP)* (pp. 5089–5093). IEEE. https://doi.org/10.1109/ICASSP.2018.8462677

Van der Wel, P., & Van Steenbergen, H. (2018). Pupil dilation as an index of effort in cognitive control tasks: A review. *Psychonomic Bulletin & Review, 25*, 2005–2015. https://doi.org/10.3758/s13423-018-1432-y

Van Puyvelde, M., Neyt, X., McGlone, F., & Pattyn, N. (2018). Voice stress analysis: A new framework for voice and effort in human performance. *Frontiers in Psychology, 9*, 1994. https://doi.org/10.3389/fpsyg.2018.01994

Wachowiak, L., Tisnikar, P., Canal, G., Coles, A., Leonetti, M., & Celiktutan, O. (2024). Predicting when and what to explain from multimodal eye tracking and task signals. *IEEE Transactions on Affective Computing, 16*(1), 179–190. https://doi.org/10.1109/TAFFC.2024.3419696

Wagner, P., Włodarczak, M., Buschmeier, H., Türk, O., & Gilmartin, E. (2024). Turn-taking dynamics across different phases of explanatory dialogues. In *Proceedings of the 28th Workshop on the Semantics and Pragmatics of Dialogue - Full Papers* (pp. 6–14). SEMDIAL.

Whitehill, J., Bartlett, M., & Movellan, J. (2008). Automatic facial expression recognition for intelligent tutoring systems. In *2008 IEEE Computer Society Conference on Computer Vision and Pattern Recognition Workshops* (pp. 1–6). IEEE. https://doi.org/10.1109/CVPRW.2008.4563182

Whitehill, J., Serpell, Z., Lin, Y. C., Foster, A., & Movellan, J. R. (2014). The faces of engagement: Automatic recognition of student engagement from facial expressions. *IEEE Transactions on Affective Computing, 5*(1), 86–98. https://doi.org/10.1109/TAFFC.2014.2316163

Wilson, S. J., Bailey, B. E., Jaremka, L. M., Fagundes, C. P., Andridge, R., Malarkey, W. B., Gates, K. M., & Kiecolt-Glaser, J. K. (2018). When couples' hearts beat together: Synchrony in heart rate variability during conflict predicts heightened inflammation throughout the day. *Psychoneuroendocrinology, 93*, 107–116. https://doi.org/10.1016/j.psyneuen.2018.04.017

Yuki, M., Maddux, W. W., & Masuda, T. (2007). Are the windows to the soul the same in the East and West? Cultural differences in using the eyes and mouth as cues to recognize emotions in Japan and the United States. *Journal of Experimental Social Psychology, 43*(2), 303–311. https://doi.org/10.1016/j.jesp.2006.02.004

Zaccaro, A., Piarulli, A., Laurino, M., Garbella, E., Menicucci, D., Neri, B., & Gemignani, A. (2018). How breath-control can change your life: A systematic review on psycho-physiological correlates of slow breathing. *Frontiers in Human Neuroscience, 12*, 353. https://doi.org/10.3389/fnhum.2018.00353

Zhang, W., & Lim, B. Y. (2022). Towards relatable explainable AI with the perceptual process. In *CHI Conference on Human Factors in Computing Systems* (p. 181). Association for Computing Machinery. https://doi.org/10.1145/3491102.3501826

Open Access This chapter is licensed under the terms of the Creative Commons Attribution 4.0 International License (http://creativecommons.org/licenses/by/4.0/), which permits use, sharing, adaptation, distribution and reproduction in any medium or format, as long as you give appropriate credit to the original author(s) and the source, provide a link to the Creative Commons license and indicate if changes were made.

The images or other third party material in this chapter are included in the chapter's Creative Commons license, unless indicated otherwise in a credit line to the material. If material is not included in the chapter's Creative Commons license and your intended use is not permitted by statutory regulation or exceeds the permitted use, you will need to obtain permission directly from the copyright holder.

Chapter 21
Ambiguity of Nonverbal Signals

David S. Johnson and Igor Tchappi

Abstract Nonverbal signals are a key component of the multimodal interactions central to sXAI. However, due to their inherent characteristics, these signals are often ambiguous, and the interpretation of nonverbal signals is highly dependent on situational context. Ambiguity can be introduced when the interpretation is inaccurate. In this chapter, we discuss factors contributing to ambiguity in nonverbal signals and examine how it influences the dynamics of an explanation. We then consider the role these factors play in the expression and perception capabilities of sXAI and discuss how to account for them in the development of these systems. Despite efforts to mitigate it, ambiguity remains inevitable due to the nature of nonverbal signals. Therefore, we propose strategies that not only mitigate ambiguity but also enhance the system's ability to identify and resolve it. By adopting these measures, sXAI can become more robust in handling ambiguity in nonverbal signals.

21.1 How Does This Chapter Relate to XAI?

Social explainable AI (sXAI) is predicated on multimodal interactions, in which both verbal and nonverbal communication plays a crucial role in the construction and understanding of explanations. Nonverbal communication (NVC) refers to the sending and receiving of information without the use of words through nonverbal behavior—including facial expression, gaze, head gestures, body language, personal space (proxemics), and vocal qualities (paralanguage). Occurring alongside verbal communication, nonverbal behavior conveys additional information about the sender's internal state, such as their emotions, intentions, or understanding

---

D. S. Johnson (✉)
Faculty of Technology, Bielefeld University, Bielefeld, Germany
e-mail: djohnson@techfak.uni-bielefeld.de

I. Tchappi
FINATRAX, SnT, University of Luxembourg, Esch-sur-Alzette, Luxembourg
e-mail: igor.tchappi@uni.lu

(Hall et al., 2019), enriching the information flow by complementing or contradicting the verbal communication. During a verbal explanation, for example, an explainee might display a facial expression to indicate confusion, prompting the explainer to alter their explanation without disrupting the verbal exchange (see Chap. 19 for a more comprehensive discussion on nonverbal behavior). Since nonverbal behavior can shape the dynamics of an explanation, it is important for both the sender and receiver to have a shared understanding of the sender's intentions and the signal's meaning (or lack thereof).

Nonverbal behavior, however, is inherently ambiguous as multiple cues may occur simultaneously, flow continuously, and be interpreted differently depending on contextual factors (Urakami & Seaborn, 2023; Hall et al., 2019). Misinterpretations of nonverbal behavior can disrupt an explanation by creating ambiguities that require resolution and, if left unresolved, may lead to confusion or dissatisfaction for the explainee. For instance, if an sXAI misinterprets an explainee's facial expression of confusion as one of concentration, then it may not simplify the explanation as signaled through the explainee's facial behavior, therefore exacerbating the confusion.

To address such ambiguities and establish a shared understanding of nonverbal signals, sXAI should take a co-constructive process, where meaning is negotiated between both interactants. Designing this requires systems to be aware of the inherent ambiguity in nonverbal behavior and the contextual facts that may cause it. To better understand this at a core level, we use a simplified sender-receiver model of nonverbal communication. This model allows us to examine the ambiguity inherent in nonverbal expression and interpretation. By doing so, designers can better support co-constructive interaction in sXAI by enabling systems to mitigate ambiguity whenever possible and to identify and resolve it when it arises.

In this chapter, we examine ambiguity in nonverbal behavior and the contextual factors that contribute to it. We also explore how this ambiguity impacts the dynamics of explanations and discuss how design decisions in sXAI might introduce ambiguity. Finally, we offer suggestions for mitigating, detecting and resolving such ambiguities to enable more effective explanations.

21.2 Ambiguity and Nonverbal Behavior

Both verbal and nonverbal communication are subject to interpretive uncertainty where the mapping between the meaning of a signal and its intended meaning is not one-to-one (Kennedy, 2019). This uncertainty leads to ambiguity when it affects the truth conditions of the message, meaning the information can be either true or false depending on how it is interpreted. This may occur in signals that have multiple meanings that depend on context. For example, the sentence *The chicken is ready to eat* could mean that the chicken is hungry or that the cooked chicken is ready to be served. Such ambiguity is typically resolved based on the context in which the statement is made. Nonverbal communication exhibits similar ambiguity as nonverbal behaviors lack a standardized dictionary of meanings and may depend on situational context, cultural background, or individual differences between interactants (Patterson, 2019). For example, research suggests that smiles have up to 50 subtle variations conveying different meanings depending on context (Rychlowska et al., 2019), including expressions of amusement and pain (Ambadar et al., 2009). The remainder of this section examines how ambiguity may emerge during nonverbal communication and how it affects the dynamics of an explanation.

21.2.1 Factors of Ambiguity in Nonverbal Behavior

Nonverbal communication involves senders encoding messages in nonverbal cues and receivers decoding them (Patterson, 2019; Hall et al., 2019), the accuracy of which depends on how well the interpretation of the behavior reflects the sender's intended meaning (Hall et al., 2019). In this process of encoding and decoding nonverbal cues, ambiguity may arise from a mismatch between intentions and interpretations, which are influenced by factors like individual differences and situational context (Patterson, 2019).

The expression and perception of nonverbal behavior varies widely among individuals, with factors such as culture, gender, and biological differences influencing how people express and interpret nonverbal cues (Patterson, 2019). For example, cultural differences create expressive dialects where subtle variations in behavior can impact the accuracy of recognition across cultures (Elfenbein et al., 2007). These differences extend to the perception of expressions, as shown in the variations in brain responses to nonverbal signals between cultures (Barrett et al., 2011; Chiao et al., 2008). Variations in mental health and social behavior, including autism spectrum disorder (ASD), depression, social anxiety, and schizophrenia, further influence nonverbal behavior leading to atypical behavior patterns affecting both expression (Grabowski et al., 2019; Weeks et al., 2013; Drimalla et al., 2020) and perception (Aleman & Kahn, 2005). Physical conditions can also influence nonverbal behavior. For example, visually impaired individuals rely less on visual cues and more on less informative channels. They also generate nonverbal signals differently than sighted individuals, such as avoiding eye contact (Qiu et al., 2020). Consequently, these individual differences in nonverbal expression and perception can lead to ambiguity and miscommunication, especially when interactants are unfamiliar with each other's determinant factors (Patterson, 1983).

Individuals' nonverbal behavior can also vary based on the explanation's situational context, including the setting and environment of the interaction (Patterson, 2019). Physical factors such as lighting, smell, temperature, and acoustics have been shown to influence the expression and perception of nonverbal signals (Patterson, 2019; Patterson & Quadflieg, 2015). For instance, brightness not only affects visual detail but also proxemics; dim lighting may increase the distance between strangers while decreasing it between friends. These effects typically occur automatically and unconsciously (Patterson & Quadflieg, 2015). Social context also plays a crucial role, with affective states like joy, sadness, and stress impacting nonverbal behavior (Hall et al., 2019; Lang et al., 1993; Li et al., 2007; Vatheuer et al., 2021). Stress, for example, can alter speech prosody features, such as shimmer and jitter (Li et al., 2007), and facial behavior, such as reducing direct eye gaze (Vatheuer et al., 2021). Consequently, situational context, similar to individual differences, is a strong determinant of both the expression and interpretation of nonverbal signals. The presence of such situational factors may thus lead to atypical nonverbal behavior from interactants resulting in ambiguous interpretations of expressed cues. For example, if an explainee becomes stressed during an explanation, they may begin to show reduced eye contact. If the explainer is unaware of their stressed state, they may attribute this change in eye contact to disengagement of the explainee. Therefore, situational awareness, as discussed in Chap. 4, is an important factor in reducing ambiguity due to such situational factors.

21.2.2 Life Cycle of Ambiguity Resolution

In the context of sXAI, ambiguity can emerge at any stage of an explanation if either interactant is unable to accurately interpret their partner's nonverbal cues. This difficulty may stem from the inherent ambiguity of the cues themselves or from various contextual factors, described in Sect. 21.2.1. When ambiguity does arise, it can diminish the quality of the explanation, potentially leading to misunderstandings, confusion, or frustration. It may also shift the focus away from the explanation as interactants attempt to clarify ambiguity. To examine the dynamics of an explanation as ambiguity unfolds, we introduce the life cycle of ambiguity resolution in NVC. It is inspired by the life cycle of norm in multiagent systems (Frantz & Pigozzi, 2018), illustrated in Fig. 21.1 and described below. The life cycle is described as a cyclic process for the sake of simplicity, but the stages could overlap as interactants plan their responses before their partner's turn is complete.

- **Cue generation:** In this stage, the message or state to be communicated from one of the interactants emerges, and the nonverbal cues start to form (often several simultaneous modalities). Situational factors, such as the sender's individual traits or environmental factors, play a role in the formation of the cues to be sent.
- **Transmission**: The nonverbal signals are then transmitted through various media depending on the setting of the explanation and whether the sender is a machine agent or a human. Transmission media include signals sent via virtual avatars, robotic interfaces, human behavior, etc.
- **Reception and interpretation**: The sent cues are then received by the interaction partner, who proceeds to interpret the cues. Again situational factors, such as the receiver's traits and environmental factors, shape the interpretation of the cue, as discussed in Sect. 21.2.1. At this point, ambiguity may emerge if there is a

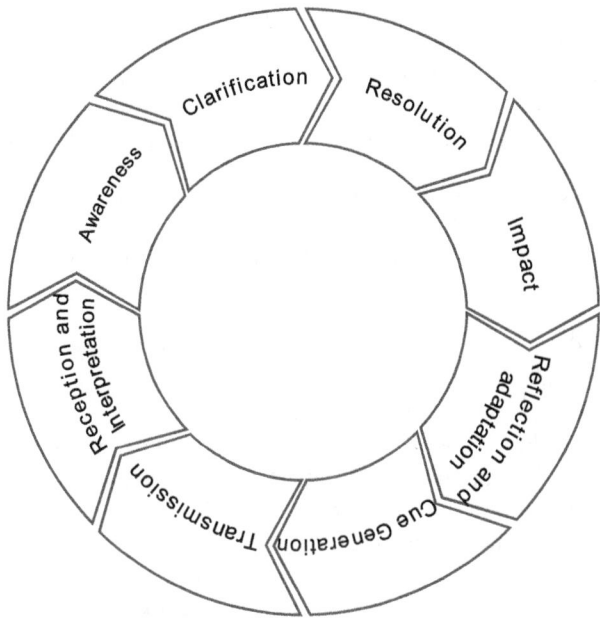

Fig. 21.1 Life cycle of ambiguity in NVC in social explainable AI

mismatch in the intended meaning of the signal and its interpretation, possibly leading to confusion or misunderstandings.

- **Awareness:** At this point, one of the interactants may recognize a breakdown in the explanation. This may happen immediately after cue interpretation, but not necessarily if neither of the interactants recognize the misinterpretation right away.
- **Clarification**: To resolve the ambiguity, the recognizing interactant seeks additional information either by directly asking their partner to clarify their intent or through further examination of the situational context to find information that may have caused the ambiguity. At this point, the main explanation may be interrupted and placed on hold until the ambiguity is resolved.
- **Resolution**: Ambiguity is resolved when the recognizing interactant has sufficient information, either from their partner or through examining the situational context, to clarify the misinterpretation. Ambiguity, however, may persist if the clarification attempts are unsuccessful and mutual understanding is not achieved.
- **Impact**. If the ambiguity is resolved the interactants may resume the explanation process with shared understanding. If not, the explanation resumes but with the current ambiguity affecting the quality of the interaction. Unresolved ambiguity can lead to confusion, frustration, and miscommunication, resulting in a breakdown in interaction efficiency and effectiveness in the short term. Over time, persistent ambiguity can result in misunderstandings, eroded trust in the

explainer, and communication inefficiencies, reducing overall user satisfaction and the perceived reliability of the AI.
- **Reflection and adaptation**: Optionally, the interactants reflect, together or alone, on the source and outcome of the ambiguity. Through this reflection, they may develop and implement strategies to minimize ambiguity in future interactions.

This life cycle represents an ideal pathway through an ambiguous cue towards resolution. It is possible, however, that the ambiguity is never identified by either interactant. In such a case, the interaction proceeds but with latent miscommunication that would have a significant impact on the quality of the explanation, as well as the explainee's ability to understand it.

To contextualize the life cycle of ambiguity in NVC, consider an interaction between a teaching chef and Susan, an individual on the autism spectrum who exhibits reduced gaze fixation on others' eye regions. Susan has intermediate cooking skills. In this scenario, the chef is explaining to Susan how to properly roast a turkey at an intermediate level. During the explanation, Susan listens intently (cue generation) but does not make consistent eye contact with the chef (transmission) due to her communication style. The chef, not used to interacting with individuals with ASD, mistakenly interprets this as a sign of disengagement or confusion (Glenberg et al., 1998) regarding the explanation (reception and interpretation). To address the confusion, the chef simplifies the explanation, assuming Susan is struggling to understand. This simplification causes confusion and possibly offense for Susan, as she does not understand why the instructions have been simplified to basic cooking methods (awareness).

From this point, Susan may either attempt to clarify the ambiguity (clarification) or allow it to persist without intervening. If she chooses the latter, the chef will continue with a basic explanation that is not helpful to her, and Susan will come away from the interaction dissatisfied (impact). Alternatively, if Susan chooses to clarify, the chef can explain its reasoning for simplifying the instructions and, following the clarification, resume the explanation at a more appropriate level (resolution). This incident may cause Susan to lose trust in the chef's ability to understand her (impact). Then Susan may either try to adapt her nonverbal behavior or understand that the chef may at times misinterpret her cues and try to correct it for a more accurate explanation (reflection and adaptation). The chef could also attempt to learn how to interpret Susan's eye gaze patterns for improved future interactions (reflection and adaptation).

21.3 Ambiguity in Human-Machine Interactions

In human-machine interaction (HMI), typical with sXAI, both agents and humans may exhibit nonverbal behavior, including both the sending and receiving of nonverbal cues. Thus, sXAI has two pathways for nonverbal behavior: the human-sender and agent-receiver path and the agent-sender and human-receiver path.

Consider the previous example from Sect. 21.2.2 regarding the chef teaching Susan, an individual with ASD, how to roast a turkey. In this example, the chef could be replaced by RobotChef; see Sect. 2.3. Emulating a human chef, RobotChef is designed with abilities for detecting and interpreting nonverbal signals and for expressing nonverbal behavior. However, both the perception and expression of nonverbal cues have challenges that can lead to ambiguity during explanations. In this section, we describe the potential for ambiguity in nonverbal behavior of both pathways. While an interactant can be a sender and receiver of nonverbal cues in parallel (Patterson, 2019), we will consider them separately to simplify understanding.

21.3.1 Human-Sender and Agent-Receiver

In the human-sender and agent-receiver pathway, nonverbal cues are encoded and sent by a human explainee and then decoded and interpreted by an sXAI, such as RobotChef. For the agent to accurately interpret these cues, it must rely on models capable of both detecting the cues (meaningful signals need to be distinguished from nonmeaningful signals) and interpreting their meanings. However, the inherent challenges of detecting and interpreting nonverbal cues contribute to ambiguity in human-agent interactions with sXAI.

Nonverbal behavior has inherent characteristics that make the detection and interpretation of nonverbal cues challenging (Urakami & Seaborn, 2023), often leading to ambiguity if not addressed. First, *nonverbal behavior is continuous* meaning that cues typically lack clear boundaries, with no discrete start or end, and may shift over time. Second, *multiple cues* are often expressed at once, requiring the receiver to integrate related cues to accurately infer the sender's intended meaning. Third, many of the cues perceived by the receiver may be unintentional and not part of the intended message, resulting in the interpretation of signals that were not meant to convey meaning. Finally, as previously discussed, many *nonverbal cues may have multiple meanings* that depend on the situational context. These characteristics highlight the inherent ambiguity in the detection of nonverbal cues.

In addition to the inherent ambiguous nature of nonverbal behavior, interpreting them introduces further possibilities for ambiguity. Current state-of-the-art methods in social signal processing typically rely on data-driven machine learning methods (Vinciarelli et al., 2009; Zhao et al., 2021), which depend on carefully designed and annotated datasets. When developing social signal processing models and datasets for sXAI, it is crucial for developers to consider the situational context to address two main challenges.

First, ambiguity can arise from the selection of nonverbal cues the sXAI should recognize, as machine learning approaches typically require a dataset annotated using a finite set of classes, and developers must decide which nonverbal cues the sXAI should be able to recognize based on research in human communication (see Chap. 19). Excluding important cues may cause the agent to misinterpret or ignore important signals. If the cues recognized by an agent do not align with human expectations, this mismatch can create ambiguity in the explainee's model of the agent's capability. For example, in an interaction with RobotChef, our explainee, Susan, might notice that the system responds positively to her smile. This could lead her to assume RobotChef is capable of detecting other states, such as understanding and confusion. However, if RobotChef is only trained to recognize basic emotions (Zhao et al., 2021), it may fail to respond when Susan tries to signal nonunderstanding of a recipe step, leaving her more confused and frustrated, as to why RobotChef did not reexplain the recipe step. Such discrepancies highlight the risk of ambiguity during human-agent interactions, resulting from missed or misinterpreted cues, when designers overlook which nonverbal cues an sXAI should recognize. Yet, a predominant focus of research in social signal processing is on detecting affective states, relying on either a categorical approach for the seven basic emotions or on a dimensional approach using continuous measures of valence and arousal (Zhao et al., 2021), leaving important sXAI nonverbal cues, such as those signaling confusion and understanding, underrepresented.

Second, ensuring robustness to contextual factors, as discussed in Sect. 21.2.1, is another key challenge in dataset and model development. Developing social signal datasets is difficult and costly, often resulting in small datasets with limited diversity and, consequently, models that struggle with ambiguity in unfamiliar contexts. When designers overlook the situational contexts in which explanations occur, sXAI may face scenarios they were not trained for. For instance, the altered expressions of an explainee that has become stressed—perhaps due to time constraints required in completing a recipe—could lead to ambiguous interpretations from RobotChef, impacting its ability to respond appropriately. Such deficits can lead to cues that are ambiguous to the agent and can create a mismatch between the explainee's expectations and the agent's performance, further leading to ambiguity during an interaction.

Despite these challenges, many social signal processing models neglect diverse contextual factors. Representational biases in social signal processing datasets reveal significant disparities in age, gender, and ethnoracial background (Saakyan et al., 2021; Buolamwini & Gebru, 2018). Psychological conditions, which significantly affect nonverbal expression, are also underrepresented. Social contexts, such as stress, are often overlooked despite their importance to sXAI, especially in high-stakes explanation settings, such as medical diagnosis explanation, or time-constrained explanations, such as cooking a recipe with RobotChef. Algorithmic choices related to context also contribute to ambiguity in signal interpretation. For example, a common practice in social signal detection methods to crop and align faces before prediction removes important contextual information crucial for accurately decoding and interpreting nonverbal cues (Barrett et al., 2011). While addressing these contextual factors requires understanding how explanations will be situated, it is not feasible to identify all contexts an sXAI might face. Therefore, agents should be equipped to handle ambiguity as it arises, further discussed in Sect. 21.4.

21.3.2 Agent-Sender and Human-Receiver

21.3.2.1 Embodied Agent Explainer

Embodied agents such as physical agents (physical robots, etc.) and/or virtual agents (virtual robots, virtual avatars, etc.) may rely on nonverbal signals to enhance communication and interaction with human explainees. These agents, equipped with physical or virtual bodies, can leverage a wide range of nonverbal cues to facilitate understanding, build rapport, and improve the overall effectiveness of their explanations. However, as stated before, the interpretation of these signals can often be ambiguous due to the inherent limitations in the design and programming of the agents, as well as the diverse perceptions of human receivers. For example, let us assume the interaction presented in Chap. 2 on page 2 where three scenarios present an interaction between a RobotChef (a robot proficient in food preparation aiming to teach and evaluate the cooking) and a User named Susan. In each of the three scenarios, the verbal dialog between Susan and the RobotChef is identical. In fact Susan asserts "I tried to follow the recipe closely, but I'm not sure if it turned out right. Why does my recipe seem not to look like yours?" and RobotChef replies "the aroma and presentation of your dish are quite remarkable. It seems you've captured the essence of the recipe beautifully." However, although the verbal communication between Susan and RobotChef is identical, the nonverbal cues depicted by RobotChef lead Susan to three distinct interpretations of the explanation provided by RobotChef, namely, approval (satisfaction of the cooking efforts), concern (doubt on the cooking skills), and curiosity (intrigue by the attempt to follow the cooking). The previous example highlights the variability of the human mental model of the robot. The mental model of a robot involves expectations and assumptions about the robot's capabilities, limitations, intentions, and roles within human contexts (Tabrez et al., 2020). Mental models, also referred to as mental representations, are organized knowledge structures that allow individuals to interact with their environment (Tabrez et al., 2020). Humans develop mental models to understand and predict the behavior of robots, much like they do with other humans and complex systems.

Human mental models of robots often revolve around what the robot can and cannot do (Groom & Nass, 2007). Humans tend to categorize robots based on their perceived abilities, such as physical strength, precision, speed, and cognitive skills. Moreover, human mental models are influenced by the design and presentation of the robot (Phillips et al., 2017). A humanoid appearance, whether physical as seen in robots like Pepper,[1] or virtual, such as with digital humans,[2] can evoke higher expectations of cognitive and social capabilities due to anthropomorphism

---

[1] https://www.aldebaran.com/en/pepper.
[2] https://www.soulmachines.com/.

(Złotowski et al., 2015). However, elevated expectations can introduce significant ambiguity into the interactions when the actual capabilities of robots do not align with these humanlike expectations, creating a mismatch between expectation and reality that may induce uncertainty (Złotowski et al., 2015).

21.3.2.2 Non-Embodied Agent Explainer

Non-embodied agents, such as chatbots, voice assistants, etc., lack a physical presence but they may still rely on nonverbal signals to enhance their explanation while interacting with human explainees. These agents operate within digital or virtual environments, using text, voice, and other digital cues to convey meaning and facilitate understanding. For example, Al et al. (2022) explored the effect of anthropomorphic (having human characteristics) design cues on chatbot empathy. To this end, the authors investigated the added value of emojis for emotional expression of a chatbot and blink dots as chatbot typing indicator and concluded that a combination of verbal design and nonverbal design on chatbots can increase chatbot anthropomorphism. Other work focuses, for example, on the adjustment of the pitch and volume to match the context and content of the interaction; the use of different formatting techniques such as bolding, italics, or color changes; the use of emojis and other graphical elements; and the like (Yu & Zhao, 2024; Joo et al., 2019). As stated before, nonverbal cues lack a standardized dictionary of meanings (Patterson, 2019), and therefore, the signals such as bolding, italics, or color changes can vary widely among users, leading sometimes to ambiguous interpretations. In the same vein, emoticons or emojis to convey emotions can be ambiguous and a smiley face might be intended to show friendliness, but in certain contexts, it could be perceived as sarcastic or patronizing (Kontogiorgos et al., 2019).

21.4 Operationalization

Ambiguity is an inherent aspect of nonverbal communication, making it an important challenge for sXAI. To address this, designers should implement strategies to mitigate its impact, identify its presence, and effectively resolve it when possible. To support this, we offer practical suggestions for operationalizing the concepts discussed in this chapter.

Mitigating ambiguity in nonverbal communication for sXAI requires careful consideration of how situational context influences the expression and interpretation of nonverbal signals. sXAI equipped with social signal processing capabilities should be capable of detecting nonverbal cues that are relevant to the explanation setting, such as confusion and understanding. Such cues would be expected by explainees when interacting with an sXAI. This is not easy, however, as signals for understanding are often ambiguous. For example, head nodding is difficult to interpret as it might indicate an explainee's understanding or it could indicate nonunderstanding when paired with eye gaze (Gander & Gander, 2020). Therefore, integrating multimodal behavior such as gaze behavior, discussed in Chap. 19, could be used to resolve such ambiguities. Additionally, equipping these systems with situational awareness, as described in Chap. 4, strengthens their internal model of both the explainee and the explanation environment. Datasets should also contain a representative sample of the expected explainee population and situational contexts (Paletschek et al., 2024). By considering these factors, developers are able to create more effective training sets that mitigate ambiguity by enhancing the system's ability to accurately perceive and interpret nonverbal signals.

All sXAIs exhibit nonverbal cues, even if not explicitly programmed to do so (Urakami & Seaborn, 2023). Therefore, in the case of nonverbal expression, designers must consider factors that may lead to ambiguity, not only in the design of explicit nonverbal behavior, but also in the overall design of the system. The design of nonverbal behavior, including unintended behaviors, should account for how different individuals perceive these behaviors based on the specific situational context. Integrating a human-centric design approach (Apraiz et al., 2023; Prati et al., 2021) into systems' interaction design is key for identifying user requirements and important user and environmental traits. This approach enables a better understanding of relevant context, allowing more effective user experience testing that considers the anticipated users and situational factors.

Despite careful design, ambiguity is inevitable in human–machine explanations due to the inherent uncertainties in characteristics of nonverbal behavior (Urakami & Seaborn, 2023). To address this, sXAI should incorporate mechanisms enabling ambiguity awareness. Uncertainty estimation research (Gawlikowski et al., 2023) offers a promising solution to identify different sources of ambiguity in the perception of nonverbal cues. By categorizing model uncertainty into one of the three main classes, namely, in-domain, domain-shift, or out-of-domain certainty, an sXAI system may be able to identify the cause of ambiguity. For example, high domain-shift uncertainty in cue recognition suggests that the situational context differs from the training data. While high out-of-domain uncertainty indicates unfamiliar nonverbal cues are being processed by the agent. By identifying these types of uncertainty, sXAI can quickly detect potential ambiguity and seek clarification from the user. Furthermore, the agent may improve its recognition abilities by adapting to the current context using methods such as unsupervised domain-shift (Ganin & Lempitsky, 2015) and incremental learning (Ven et al., 2022).

sXAI should also be capable of recognizing when their own signals cause uncertainty in the explainee. According to the Behavioral Ecology View (BECV) of facial display, facial cues are used to elicit a specific response from the receiver rather than signaling an internal state (Crivelli & Fridlund, 2018). By adopting such an approach when developing an agent's explicit nonverbal behavior, their signaled cues should be designed to evoke an expected response from the explainee. Actions from the explainee that do not match the agent's expectations could indicate ambiguity in the explainee. For implicitly signaled cues, the agent may look for changes in affective state or atypical behavioral responses from the explainee. By integrating this knowledge with uncertainty estimations, the sXAI can develop an internal ambiguity model that triggers the agent to resolve ambiguity as it emerges.

To effectively mitigate, identify, and resolve ambiguity, NVC capabilities in sXAI should be explainable and transparent. This fosters a co-constructive approach to handling ambiguity, where agents can explain their nonverbal behavior, allowing explainees to question and correct the agent's actions. Making an agent's interpretations transparent requires explanation of why a specific interpretation of a nonverbal signal was made. Post hoc and local XAI approaches for machine learning (Johnson et al., 2024) offer potential solutions by generating explanations for the decisions of black-box social signal processing systems. These methods typically aim to identify key features or concepts that influenced the decision, outline rules that describe the decision, or provide illustrative examples of the model's behavior. While most methods focus on explaining decisions based on input features, incorporating modality-based explanations can also reveal how interactions between verbal and nonverbal signals complement or conflict with each other (Wang et al., 2021), aiding in understanding how these interactions contribute to ambiguity. However, most XAI approaches are visual in nature and may require expert interpretation, limiting their use in interactive explanation settings. Designers should therefore develop explanations based on user-understandable representations that align with the available modalities of the agent.

On the other hand, to enable transparency in agent actions, sXAI should also integrate explainability into their nonverbal expressions. The Situation Awareness Framework for Explainable AI (SAFE-AI) (Sanneman & Shah, 2022) offers a framework describing information needs of users of XAI systems to guide the design of such systems. Furthermore, integrating approaches, such as the Belief, Desire, and Intention framework (Broekens et al., 2010), enable the system to simulate and represent the mental states that support its decisions and actions, providing methods through which the system can articulate not just what it is doing, but why it is doing it (Floyd & Aha, 2016). For instance, if a robot-based sXAI uses a gesture to point at an object, the BDI model enables it to explain that the gesture was motivated by the belief that the user needs guidance, the desire to assist in completing a task, and the intent to clarify the next steps in the interaction. This can make the agent's intentions more clear and help align the explainee's understanding with the agent's intended meaning, improving future interactions. Explainable NVC fosters constructive ambiguity resolution by helping both the agent and the explainee identify and clarify sources of ambiguity. This enables the agent to refine its nonverbal behavior and perception, using adaptive modeling approaches (Ganin & Lempitsky, 2015; Ven et al., 2022), based on clarifying feedback from the explainee. Such a co-constructive approach not only enhances the agent's perception capabilities, but also aligns its nonverbal behavior more closely with user expectations, reducing ambiguity in future interactions.

21.5 How Does This Chapter Inspire Further Research on sXAI?

This chapter focuses on the ambiguous nature of NVC and the resulting challenges that arise for sXAI. An exploration of how ambiguity emerges in NVC, especially in human-machine interactions, opens up several research paths that could deepen the understanding of ambiguity and enhance the development of sXAI systems. One of the factors highlighted in this chapter is the discussion of how situational context (see Chap. 4) contributes to ambiguity in NVC. Since nonverbal signals could be highly influenced by their environment and social setting, future research should investigate how these factors impact the interpretation of nonverbal cues in AI systems. New paradigms for examining the influence of such contextual factors (Paletschek et al., 2024) enable controlled analysis for theoretical understanding and context-based data collection.

Cross-cultural differences are also an important contextual factor for sXAI that should be considered when designing NVC abilities. NVC varies greatly across cultures, and these differences often result in ambiguity. Researchers could explore how sXAI systems can be designed to recognize and adjust to these cultural variations, ensuring their effectiveness in diverse settings. This research should include cross-cultural studies that examine how different cultural norms shape the interpretation of nonverbal cues and how sXAI can be trained to adapt to these differences.

The chapter also highlights the need for sXAI to be inclusive of diverse user groups. NVC is not uniform, and people with psychiatric or physical conditions may express or interpret nonverbal cues differently. Future research could focus on creating personalized AI models that accommodate the unique communication needs of these diverse groups. This approach would require interdisciplinary collaboration, drawing on insights from psychology, sociology, and AI to ensure that sXAI systems are both technically advanced and socially sensitive.

Another critical research direction is the development of intelligent models for recognizing nonverbal signals. Given the multimodal nature of NVC, future research could look into how multimodal approaches that combine nonverbal cues such as facial expressions, gestures, and vocal tones. can enhance AI systems' accuracy in interpreting human behavior and intentions. This could lead to the creation of more advanced models that are better equipped to handle the complexities of human nonverbal communication.

A promising area for future research discussed in this chapter is the need for sXAI to have mechanisms for detecting and resolving ambiguity in real time. The first step to enabling these ambiguity resolution would be to develop situationally aware explainable NVC capabilities, as proposed by SAFE-AI (Sanneman & Shah, 2022). Researchers could then develop ambiguity detection mechanisms that enable XAI systems to recognize when nonverbal signals are being misunderstood, prompting them to seek clarification from the user. This would involve creating dynamic interaction models that allow the AI to adjust its communication strategy during the interaction.

Finally, the chapter inspires research into adaptive learning in sXAI. Since NVC is dynamic and context-dependent, AI systems must be able to learn and adapt over time. Future studies could explore how sXAI systems can use online learning techniques to continuously refine their nonverbal communication models based on user interactions. This might include implementing feedback-driven approaches where AI systems improve their models by incorporating real-time user feedback, leading to more accurate and effective communication over time.

21.6 Rapid Access

Social interactions, the core of social XAI (sXAI), rely on multimodal communication, incorporating auditory and visual messaging. Communication, therefore, is not limited to verbal content but also depends on nonverbal signals, including facial expression, gaze, head gestures, body language, personal space, and vocal characteristics. A challenge with nonverbal signals is their inherent ambiguity (Urakami & Seaborn, 2023), as they are *continuous*, lacking clear onsets and offsets, and *multiple cues* are often conveyed simultaneously, requiring disentanglement and integration between the signals. Signals may be sent *unintentionally*, or have *multiple meanings*. Further complicating this, human factors such as culture and gender, along with situational factors like the physical environment or social context, influence both the expression and perception of nonverbal signals (Patterson, 2019). These ambiguities can disrupt the effectiveness of explanations and interactions provided by sXAI.

The life cycle of ambiguity resolution, illustrated in Fig. 21.1, progresses through several stages, from the emergence of ambiguous signals to the impact on interaction quality. It begins with **cue generation**, where a message or state arises and nonverbal signals are formed, influenced by individual traits and environmental factors. The cues are then **transmitted** through mediums such as human behavior, virtual avatars, or robotic expression. Ambiguity may emerge upon **reception and interpretation** of the cues if the intended meaning does not align with the perceived one. If the ambiguity is recognized (**awareness**) by one of the interactants, they may request **clarification** from their partner, interrupting the explanation. **Resolution** occurs if the ambiguity is successfully clarified, though it may persist if attempts fail. The **impact** of ambiguity can range from minor misunderstandings to reduced trust and long-term communication inefficiencies. Finally, **reflection and adaptation**, when undertaken, enable interactants to assess and refine communication strategies, potentially reducing ambiguity in later interactions.

Addressing ambiguity is particularly important in human-machine interaction (HMI) with sXAI, as both humans and AI agents engage in nonverbal behavior. When humans use nonverbal signals, sXAI systems require models capable of detecting and interpreting their meaning, typically using data-hungry machine learning approaches Vinciarelli et al. (2009). When selecting signals to detect, sXAI designers should prioritize signals supported by research (see Chap. 19) that enhance the explanation process, such as signals related to understanding. Otherwise, disambiguating relevant and irrelevant signals becomes challenging due to the inherent complexity of nonverbal behavior.

After selecting which signals to detect, it is important that models are robust to the situational factors in which the sXAI is expected to operate. For instance, individuals may express understanding differently in stressful contexts (Paletschek et al., 2024). However, achieving this robustness is challenging due to limited datasets and the high cost of developing sufficiently large datasets. Despite these needs, critical contextual factors are often ignored in dataset acquisition, hindering model robustness in real-world scenarios.

Like humans, embodied sXAI rely on expressing nonverbal signals to enhance communication, making it essential to consider how individuals will interpret sXAI signals. To mitigate this, the design of sXAI should account for situational factors that influence explainee interpretation of the sXAI's expressed nonverbal signals (including unintentional ones) to reduce the likelihood of ambiguity. Additionally, capabilities of embodied agents often do not align with human expectations (Złotowski et al., 2015), leading to ambiguity that affects interaction. To address this, designers must integrate methods that set explainee's expectations.

Mitigating ambiguity in sXAI interactions requires careful consideration of the situational factors that influence the expression and interpretation of nonverbal signals. This highlights the need to integrate a human-centric design approach (Apraiz et al., 2023; Prati et al., 2021) to identify important user and environmental factors. However, even with well-designed detection models, carefully crafted nonverbal signals, and thorough consideration of situational factors, ambiguity is inevitable. Thus, sXAI must include mechanisms to enable ambiguity awareness and management when it does arise.

One approach to identifying ambiguity in signal detection is to analyze model uncertainty (Gawlikowski et al., 2023) to determine whether uncertainty stems from situational context or from unseen nonverbal signals. Additionally, sXAI should be designed to recognize when their own nonverbal expression causes ambiguity for the explainee. By modeling the intended response to nonverbal signals (Crivelli & Fridlund, 2018), sXAI could monitor explainees for expected response and alter the interaction when discrepancies occur.

To more effectively mitigate, identify, and resolve nonverbal ambiguity, sXAI should integrate explainability into their own nonverbal behaviors. This would allow them to clarify their own actions and interpretations of nonverbal signals, giving explainees the opportunity to adjust to ambiguous behavior. The Situation Awareness Framework for Explainable AI (SAFE-AI) (Sanneman & Shah, 2022) offers developers key guidelines outlining the information needs of sXAI systems. At a minimum, sXAI should aim to achieve *Level 2: XAI for comprehension*, meaning it should offer explanations for why a decision was made (e.g., a nonverbal signal was interpreted in a certain way) or why it acted as it did (e.g., why it expressed a certain nonverbal signal).

In summary, this chapter has explored ambiguity associated with detecting and expressing nonverbal signals and how it affects interactions. While careful design choices can help mitigate these issues, the inherent characteristics of nonverbal behavior make ambiguity unavoidable. Therefore, sXAI should not only aim to reduce ambiguity before it arises, but also implement strategies to detect, manage, and resolve it when it occurs. By mitigating ambiguity through careful nonverbal design and equipping sXAI with the ability to identify, mitigate, and explain ambiguity, explanations from sXAI will be more effective, fostering better understanding and trust in interactions.

Acknowledgments This work was funded by the Deutsche Forschungsgemeinschaft (DFG, German Research Foundation): TRR 318/1 2021 – 438445824.

References

Al Farisi, R., Ferdiana, R., & Adji, T. B. (2022). The effect of anthropomorphic design cues on increasing chatbot empathy. In: *2022 1st International Conference on Information System & Information Technology (ICISIT)* (pp. 370–375). IEEE. https://doi.org/10.1109/ICISIT54091.2022.9873008

Aleman, A., & Kahn, R. S. (2005). Strange feelings: Do amygdala abnormalities dysregulate the emotional brain in schizophrenia? *Progress in Neurobiology, 77*(5), 283–298. https://doi.org/10.1016/j.pneurobio.2005.11.005

Ambadar, Z., Cohn, J. F., & Reed, L. I. (2009). All smiles are not created equal: Morphology and timing of smiles perceived as amused, polite, and embarrassed/nervous. *Journal of Nonverbal Behavior, 33*(1), 17–34. https://doi.org/10.1007/s10919-008-0059-5

Apraiz, A., Lasa, G., & Mazmela, M. (2023). Evaluation of user experience in human–robot interaction: A systematic literature review. *International Journal of Social Robotics, 15*(2), 187–210. https://doi.org/10.1007/s12369-022-00957-z

Barrett, L. F., Mesquita, B., & Gendron, M. (2011). Context in emotion perception. *Current Directions in Psychological Science, 20*(5), 286–290. https://doi.org/10.1177/0963721411422522

Broekens, J., Harbers, M., Hindriks, K., Van Den Bosch, K., Jonker, C., & Meyer, J. J. (2010). Do you get it? User-evaluated explainable BDI agents. In: J. Dix, & W. Cees, (Eds.) *Multiagent System Technologies* (Vol. 6251, pp. 28–39). Springer. https://doi.org/10.1007/978-3-642-16178-0_5

Buolamwini, J., & Gebru, T. (2018). Gender shades: Intersectional accuracy disparities in commercial gender classification. In: *Proceedings of the 1st Conference on Fairness, Accountability and Transparency* (pp. 77–91). PMLR.

Chiao, J. Y., Iidaka, T., Gordon, H. L., Nogawa, J., Bar, M., Aminoff, E., Sadato, N., & Ambady, N. (2008). Cultural specificity in amygdala response to fear faces. *Journal of Cognitive Neuroscience, 20*(12), 2167–2174. https://doi.org/10.1162/jocn.2008.20151

Crivelli, C., & Fridlund, A. J. (2018). Facial displays are tools for social influence. *Trends in Cognitive Sciences, 22*(5), 388–399. https://doi.org/10.1016/j.tics.2018.02.006

Drimalla, H., Scheffer, T., Landwehr, N., Baskow, I., Roepke, S., Behnia, B., & Dziobek, I. (2020). Towards the automatic detection of social biomarkers in autism spectrum disorder: Introducing the simulated interaction task (SIT). *NPJ Digital Medicine, 3*(1), 25. https://doi.org/10.1038/s41746-020-0227-5

Elfenbein, H. A., Beaupré, M., Lévesque, M., & Hess, U. (2007). Toward a dialect theory: Cultural differences in the expression and recognition of posed facial expressions. *Emotion, 7*(1), 131–146. https://doi.org/10.1037/1528-3542.7.1.131

Floyd, M. W., & Aha, D. W. (2016). Incorporating transparency during trust-guided behavior adaptation. In: A. Goel, M. Belón Díaz-Agudo, & T. RothBerghofer (Eds.) *Case-Based Reasoning Research and Development* (pp. 124–138). Springer. https://doi.org/10.1007/978-3-319-47096-2_9

Frantz, C., & Pigozzi, G. (2018). Modeling norm dynamics in multiagent systems. *Journal of Applied Logics, 5*(2), 491–564.

Gander, A. J., & Gander, P. (2020). Micro-feedback as cues to understanding in communication. In: C. Howes, S. Dobnik, & E. Breitholtz (Eds.) *Dialogue and Perception. Extended Papers from DaP2018* (pp. 1–11). Gothenburg University.

Ganin, Y., & Lempitsky, V. (2015). Unsupervised domain adaptation by backpropagation. In: *Proceedings of the 32nd International Conference on Machine Learning* (pp. 1180–1189). PMLR.

Gawlikowski, J., Tassi, C. R., Ali, M., Lee, J., Humt, M., Feng, J., Kruspe, A., Triebel, R., Jung, P., Roscher, R., & Shahzad, M. (2023). A survey of uncertainty in deep neural networks. *Artificial Intelligence Review, 56*(1), 1513–1589. https://doi.org/10.1007/s10462-023-10562-9

Glenberg, A. M., Schroeder, J. L., & Robertson, D. A. (1998). Averting the gaze disengages the environment and facilitates remembering. *Memory & Cognition, 26*(4), 651–658. https://doi.org/10.3758/BF03211385

Grabowski, K., Rynkiewicz, A., Lassalle, A., Baron-Cohen, S., Schuller, B., Cummins, N., Baird, A., Podgórska-Bednarz, J., Pieniążek, A., & Łucka, I. (2019). Emotional expression in psychiatric conditions: New technology for clinicians. *Psychiatry and Clinical Neurosciences, 73*(2), 50–62. https://doi.org/10.1111/pcn.12799

Groom, V., & Nass, C. (2007). Can robots be teammates?: Benchmarks in human–robot teams. *Interaction Studies, 8*(3), 483–500. https://doi.org/10.1075/is.8.3.10gro

Hall, J. A., Horgan, T. G., & Murphy, N. A. (2019). Nonverbal communication. *Annual Review of Psychology, 70*(1), 271–294. https://doi.org/10.1146/annurev-psych-010418-103145

Johnson, D. S., Hakobyan, O., Paletschek, J., & Drimalla, H. (2024). Explainable AI for audio and visual affective computing: A scoping review. In: *IEEE Transactions on Affective Computing* (pp. 1–20). https://doi.org/10.1109/TAFFC.2024.3505269

Joo, H., Simon, T., Cikara, M., & Sheikh, Y. (2019). Towards social artificial intelligence: Nonverbal social signal prediction in a triadic interaction. In: *Proceedings of the IEEE/CVF Conference on Computer Vision and Pattern Recognition* (pp. 10873–10883). https://doi.org/10.1109/CVPR.2019.01113

Kennedy, C. (2019). Ambiguity and vagueness: An overview. In: M. Claudia, K. Von Heusinger, & P. Paul (Eds.) *Semantics—Lexical Structures and Adjectives* (pp. 236–271). De GRUYTER. https://doi.org/10.1515/9783110626391-008

Kontogiorgos, D., Pereira, A., Andersson, O., Koivisto, M., Gonzalez Rabal, E., Vartiainen, V., & Gustafson, J. (2019). The effects of anthropomorphism and non-verbal social behaviour in virtual assistants. In: *Proceedings of the 19th ACM International Conference on Intelligent Virtual Agents*. Association for Computing Machinery (pp. 133–140). https://doi.org/10.1145/3308532.3329466

Lang, P. J., Greenwald, M. K., Bradley, M. M., & Hamm, A. O. (1993). Looking at pictures: Affective, facial, visceral, and behavioral reactions. *Psychophysiology, 30*(3), 261–273. https://doi.org/10.1111/j.1469-8986.1993.tb03352.x

Li, X., Tao, J., Johnson, M. T., Soltis, J., Savage, A., Leong, K. M., & Newman, J. D. (2007). Stress and emotion classification using jitter and shimmer features. In: *2007 IEEE International Conference on Acoustics, Speech and Signal Processing—ICASSP '07*. IEEE. https://doi.org/10.1109/ICASSP.2007.367261

Paletschek, J., Bleimling, J., Johnson, D. S., & Drimalla, H. (2024). A paradigm to investigate social Signals of understanding and their susceptibility to stress. In: *2024 12th International Conference on Affective Computing and Intelligent Interaction (ACII)*. IEEE.

Patterson, M. L. (1983). *Nonverbal Behavior*. Springer. https://doi.org/10.1007/978-1-4612-5564-2

Patterson, M. L. (2019). A systems model of dyadic nonverbal interaction. *Journal of Nonverbal Behavior, 43*(2), 111–132. https://doi.org/10.1007/s10919-018-00292-w

Patterson, M. L., & Quadflieg, S. (2015). The physical environment and nonverbal communication. In: M. David, H. C. Hwang, & M. G. Frank (Eds.) *APA Handbook of Nonverbal Communication* (pp. 189–220). APA Books. https://doi.org/10.1037/14669-008

Phillips, E., Ullman, D., De Graaf, M. M., & Malle, B. F. (2017). What does a robot look like?: A multi-site examination of user expectations about robot appearance. *Proceedings of the Human Factors and Ergonomics Society Annual Meeting, 61*(1), 1215–1219. https://doi.org/10.1177/1541931213601786

Prati, E., Peruzzini, M., Pellicciari, M., & Raffaeli, R. (2021). How to include user experience in the design of human–robot interaction. *Robotics and Computer-Integrated Manufacturing, 68*, 102072. https://doi.org/10.1016/j.rcim.2020.102072

Qiu, S., An, P., Hu, J., Han, T., & Rauterberg, M. (2020). Understanding visually impaired people's experiences of social signal perception in face-to-face communication. *Universal Access in the Information Society, 19*(4), 873–890. https://doi.org/10.1007/s10209-019-00698-3

Rychlowska, M., Manstead, A. S., & van der Schalk, J. (2019). The many faces of smiles. In: H. Ursula, & H. Shlomo (Eds.) *The Social Nature of Emotion Expression: What Emotions Can Tell Us about the World* (pp. 227–245). Springer. https://doi.org/10.1007/978-3-030-32968-6_13

Saakyan, W., Hakobyan, O., & Drimalla, H. (2021). Representational bias in expression and annotation of emotions in audiovisual databases. In: *Proceedings of the 1st International Conference on AI for People: Towards Sustainable AI, CAIP 2021*. EAI. https://doi.org/10.4108/eai.20-11-2021.2314203

Sanneman, L., & Shah, J. A. (2022). The situation awareness framework for explainable AI (SAFE-AI) and human factors considerations for XAI systems. *International Journal of Human–Computer Interaction, 38*, 18-20, 1772–1788. https://doi.org/10.1080/10447318.2022.2081282

Tabrez, A., Luebbers, M. B., & Hayes, B. (2020). A survey of mental modeling techniques in human–robot teaming. *Current Robotics Reports, 1*(4), 259–267. https://doi.org/10.1007/s43154-020-00019-0

Urakami, J., & Seaborn, K. (2023). Nonverbal cues in human–robot interaction: A communication studies perspective. *Journal of Human–Robot Interaction, 12*(2), 22. https://doi.org/10.1145/3570169

Vatheuer, C. C., Vehlen, A., Von Dawans, B., & Domes, G. (2021). Gaze behavior is associated with the cortisol response to acute psychosocial stress in the virtual TSST. *Journal of Neural Transmission, 128*(9), 1269–1278. https://doi.org/10.1007/s00702-021-02344-w

Van de Ven, G. M., Tuytelaars, T., & Tolias, A. S. (2022). Three types of incremental learning. *Nature Machine Intelligence, 4*(12), 1185–1197. https://doi.org/10.1038/s42256-022-00568-3

Vinciarelli, A., Pantic, M., & Bourlard, H. (2009). Social signal processing: Survey of an emerging domain. *Image and Vision Computing, 27*(12), 1743–1759. https://doi.org/10.1016/j.imavis.2008.11.007

Wang, X., He, J., Jin, Z., Yang, M., Wang, Y., & Qu, H. (2021). M2Lens: Visualizing and explaining multimodal models for sentiment analysis. *IEEE Transactions on Visualization and Computer Graphics, 28*(1), 802–812. https://doi.org/10.1109/TVCG.2021.3114794

Weeks, J. W., Howell, A. N., & Goldin, P. R. (2013). Gaze avoidance in social anxiety disorder. *Depression and Anxiety, 30*(8), 749–756. https://doi.org/10.1002/da.22146

Yu, S., & Zhao, L. (2024). Emojifying chatbot interactions: An exploration of emoji utilization in human–chatbot communications. *Telematics and Informatics, 86*(C), 102071. https://doi.org/10.1016/j.tele.2023.102071

Zhao, S., Jia, G., Yang, J., Ding, G., & Keutzer, K. (2021). Emotion recognition from multiple modalities: Fundamentals and methodologies. *IEEE Signal Processing Magazine, 38*(6), 59–73. https://doi.org/10.1109/MSP.2021.3106895

Zlotowski, J., Proudfoot, D., Yogeeswaran, K., & Bartneck, C. (2015). Anthropomorphism: Opportunities and challenges in human–robot interaction. *International Journal of Social Robotics, 7*(3), 347–360. https://doi.org/10.1007/s12369-014-0267-6

Open Access This chapter is licensed under the terms of the Creative Commons Attribution 4.0 International License (http://creativecommons.org/licenses/by/4.0/), which permits use, sharing, adaptation, distribution and reproduction in any medium or format, as long as you give appropriate credit to the original author(s) and the source, provide a link to the Creative Commons license and indicate if changes were made.

The images or other third party material in this chapter are included in the chapter's Creative Commons license, unless indicated otherwise in a credit line to the material. If material is not included in the chapter's Creative Commons license and your intended use is not permitted by statutory regulation or exceeds the permitted use, you will need to obtain permission directly from the copyright holder.

Chapter 22
Timing and Synchronization of Multimodal Signals in Explanations

Petra Wagner and Stefan Kopp

Abstract Real-life explanations tend to be exchanged multimodally, and their expression needs to take into account the adequate sequencing and synchronization of the various modalities involved including speech, melodic/rhythmic structure and highlighting (aka *prosody*), manual gestures, head gestures, facial expressions, or posture changes, both within and between conversational partners. Whereas empirical research has not yet unfolded all details behind cross-modal synchronization, we know that a certain amount of it is a prerequisite for cross-modal signals to be integrated meaningfully, to increase the robustness of communication, to indicate the processing of an explanation, and to negotiate the seamless exchange of thoughts.

22.1 How Does This Chapter Relate to XAI?

Explanations unfold as a dialogical process that hinges on rich and robust communication between the explainer and the explainee. Leveraging the richness of multimodal communication in this process can benefit explanations in many ways—from enabling interactive dialog mechanisms such as back-channel feedback to supporting the expression of abstract ideas and to mitigating cognitive load. One crucial aspect in all of these functions of multimodal communication is a proper timing and synchronization of multimodal behavior. This holds for both explanations delivered by a socially interactive artificial agent as well as the responses and contributions by human users. Moreover, missing or wrong timing

---

P. Wagner (✉)
Department Linguistics, Faculty of Linguistics and Literary Studies, Bielefeld University, Bielefeld, Germany
e-mail: petra.wagner@uni-bielefeld.de

S. Kopp
Social Cognitive Systems Group, Faculty of Technology, Bielefeld University, Bielefeld, Germany
e-mail: skopp@techfak.uni-bielefeld.de

© The Author(s) 2026
K. J. Rohlfing et al. (eds.), *Social Explainable AI*,
https://doi.org/10.1007/978-981-96-5290-7_22

of behaviors may not only make processing more difficult but may also even hamper understanding or undermine the impression of a believable communication partner or explainer. Therefore, XAI research must pay close attention to the timing and synchrony of verbal and nonverbal signals when trying to enable multimodal explainability in XAI systems—both locally within an utterance and interpersonally between the interlocutors. This chapter reviews and discusses findings on various effects and phenomena in the timing of multimodal communication that are relevant for social XAI. By focusing on the aspects of timing and synchronization, this chapter complements Chaps. 19, 20, and 21, which focus on the forms and linguistic as well as affective functions of nonverbal signals.

22.2 Timing as an Orchestration of Verbal and Nonverbal Events

Communication unfolds over time, and the speed and temporal structuring of the information (e.g., by its rhythmic distribution or by temporal chunking into meaningful units) are crucial for its processing by the recipient of a message. Speakers are known to slow down dynamically and use longer words in their speech delivery when the information load or surprise of a message (or part thereof) is high and the predictability is low (Aylett & Turk, 2004; Piantadosi et al., 2011).

Furthermore, speakers not only adjust their tempo to the information load of the message conveyed but also take into account the recipient's current level of cognitive load or distraction. If a listener indicates being distracted, speakers may respond by slowing down, hesitating, or pausing, until the recipient redirects their attention back to them. In human-computer interaction (HCI), such an attention-sensitive interaction with human interlocutors has shown benefits for task success in a memorization exercise within a household scenario (Betz et al., 2018). Speakers can also use timing (e.g., filled or unfilled pauses and hesitations) to indicate their own level of cognitive load (e.g., when they are describing something difficult) (Arnold et al., 2007) or their own level of uncertainty with respect to what they are saying (Brennan & Williams, 1995). Another crucial timing-related aspect is the ongoing feedback in an interaction by which a listener may signal not only their individual level of understanding or non-understanding but also their current level of attention, agreement, or attitude (Allwood et al., 1992; Axelsson et al., 2022). Naturally, all the timing-related aspects mentioned above are crucial for interactive explanations that are supposed to be delivered in a way that dynamically not only takes into account the complexity of the explanans, the level of cognitive load, or the distraction of an explainee but also marks the difficulty of finding a good way to formulate the explanans.

That is, the timing of a message, both with respect to its overall duration, the duration pattern of the message's structural units (e.g., words, syllables, phrases), and the temporal synchronization of its delivery within an interaction are crucial aspects of verbal delivery.

In verbal interaction, issues related to timing within a speaker are regarded as part of a message's prosodic structure or prosodic packaging. This can relate to (1) the overall speed, (2) the local speed of message delivery (e.g., by a hesitation), (3) the prosodic chunking of a message by pauses or other prosodic boundaries (e.g., falling or rising tones), (4) the pause durations, (5) the pause type (silent or "filled" by extended vocalizations such as "uhm") (Betz et al., 2023), and (6) the synchronization of prosodic highlighting (prominences) with other parts of the message delivery (Wagner et al., 2014). Furthermore, (7) the timing of events between speakers needs to be taken into account, because feedback behavior may occur not only during pauses but also while an interlocutor is speaking. Another aspect of timing taking place between interlocutors relates to their synchronization, or entrainment, of verbal or nonverbal movements (Wagner et al., 2014; Iverson & Thelen, 1999).

Crucially, real-life explanations tend to be exchanged multimodally (see introduction to Chap. 18). By taking into account multimodal expression including, for example, speech, manual gestures, head gestures, facial expressions, or posture changes, we add further layers describing how a message can unfold over time and how these various descriptive layers are either temporally synchronized or not synchronized (see Fig. 22.1). Again, such a multilayered event score needs to take into account not only the speaker's internal synchronization of events but also their relationship to those of an interlocutor (see Fig. 22.1). Partly due to this complexity, many open questions remain with respect to the degree to which the different layers of multimodal events are synchronized within and between speakers and how important this is for the success of an explanation. However, we know of a strong and stable link between verbalizations and co-speech gesturing, also aided by a strong developmental sensory-motor link between hand and mouth movements (Iverson & Thelen, 1999). This multimodal interdependence is also taken as evidence for the cognitive interdependence of the two modalities (McNeill, 1992). McNeill (1992) has suggested three rules of synchronization between verbal and gestural productions, namely, (1) the phonological synchrony rule, predicting that gesture strokes should occur before the most prominent syllable in a co-occurring utterance; (2) the semantic synchrony rule, predicting that synchronized speech and gestures relate to the same 'idea unit'; and (3) the pragmatic synchrony rule, predicting that multimodal co-occurrence indicates identical pragmatic functions. So far, a large body of research has found plenty of evidence for the phonological synchrony rule, for instance, there appears to be a 'gesture-lead' effect for the initiation of gestures and corresponding speech landmarks, also called *lexical affiliates* (Kendon, 1980; Bergmann et al., 2011; Esteve-Gibert & Prieto, 2013; Chu & Hagoort, 2014), between pointing gestures and stressed syllables of demonstratives (Levelt et al., 1985; Rochet-Capellan et al., 2008), and in conversational feedback signals, in which head gestures precede a corresponding verbalized feedback signal (Dittmann & Llewellyn, 1968; Karpiński et al., 2009).

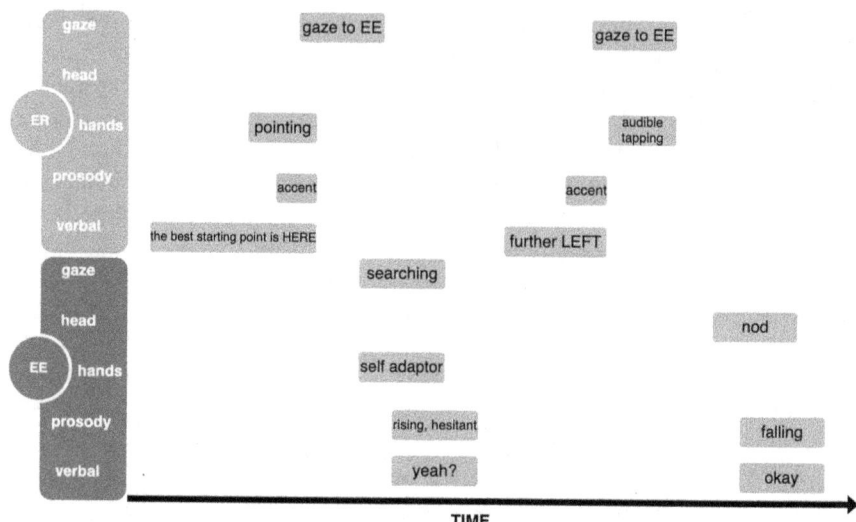

Fig. 22.1 This figure illustrates the fine-tuned intra- and inter-speaker synchronization of verbal and nonverbal events. In particular, it should illustrate the constant monitoring of an explainee's listening behavior and the (multimodal) readjustment of an ongoing explanation, tailored to the multimodally expressed needs. The explainer (ER, top) uses prosodic highlighting (accent) to stress particularly relevant aspects of the ongoing explanation. Simultaneously, ER uses a hand gesture to establish a semantic link within the shared referential space (e.g., the gameboard). The explainee (EE, bottom) shows a high degree of attention (by leaning toward the ER) but also indicates a lack of understanding and/or a high degree of cognitive load or uncertainty by a searching gaze, a rising pitch, and a hesitation on the feedback expression "yeah." This is taken up immediately by ER, who responds with an accented "to the left," and by highlighting the pointing gesture by audibly tapping on the game board. ER now also elicits a feedback using gaze, and EE reacts to this by nodding and verbalizing "okay" with a falling pitch

Likewise, there exists plenty of evidence for cross-modal synchronization: It has been found that speech melodic chunks or *intonation phrases* are aligned with *gesture phrases* (Esteve-Gibert & Prieto, 2013; Rohrer et al., 2019; Loehr, 2012; Türk & Calhoun, 2023), and there exists plenty of empirical evidence for *gesture apices* of prominence lending beat gestures to align with highlighting accents in the speech signal (Loehr, 2012; Rochet-Capellan et al., 2008; Leonard & Cummins, 2011; Treffner et al., 2008; Esteve-Gibert & Prieto, 2013). A similar cross-modal synchronization has been found between accents and head gestures (Esteve-Gibert et al., 2017). However, it is important to keep in mind that the cross-modal timing within speakers does not always achieve synchrony of events expressed at different modalities, as is the case for the 'gesture-lead' effect, and cross-modal synchrony may even be a special case of cross-modal timing.

Further evidence for a strong temporal coupling of various modalities is the finding that slowing down in one modality is paralleled by slowing down in another domain: accentuations in speech in which one syllable gets lengthened tend to co-occur with local lengthening in accompanying gestures (Krivokapić et al., 2017), and temporal disruptions in one modality trigger prolongations in another modality (Chu & Hagoort, 2014; Pouw & Dixon, 2019). Moreover, where a hesitation is triggered in speech, it correlates with deceleration in co-speech gesture (Betz et al., 2023).

As for the cross-modal synchronization between dialog partners, it is known that speakers often use those modalities that are least disruptive for the ongoing interaction: listeners prefer to provide their feedback by nodding while the interlocutor is speaking and to provide verbalized feedback signals toward the end of an interlocutor's utterance, thereby minimizing the amount of overlapping speech (Dittmann & Llewellyn, 1968; Truong et al., 2011; Ferré & Renaudier, 2017).

22.3 Functions of Multimodal Synchronization

We often move while we speak—for example, during driving, walking, gardening, or recreational sports such as table tennis. Not every movement constitutes a co-speech gesture, but, generally, a higher level of multimodal synchronization leads to movements being interpreted as communicative gestures (Church et al., 2014). It is therefore likely that speakers deliberately use cross-modal synchronization as a communicative strategy to convey communicative functions (Kisa et al., 2022). In fact, when too much time elapses between a gesture and the corresponding speech, listeners are no longer able to integrate these two sources of communicative signals (Habets et al., 2011), and co-speech movements may be interpreted as independent, or even erratic, movements.

One such function is the increased highlighting of verbally or gesturally communicated words or concepts by synchronizing accentuations with facial expressions or head movements that further emphasize such highlightings (Krahmer & Swerts, 2005; Ambrazaitis & House, 2017; Al Moubayed et al., 2009). Such cross-modal synchronizations have successfully been shown to improve the intelligibility of artificial agents (Al Moubayed et al., 2009).

A crucial aspect of a message relates to its *information structure*. This specifies which aspect of the message is new, important, or relevant and which aspect is given, has been introduced earlier, or is being talked about. In many languages, new or focused units tend to be highlighted prosodically or syntactically, and it is a plausible communicative strategy to further support these elements with synchronized co-speech gestures (cf. the role of communicative dynamism in speech-gesture synchrony discussed by McNeill 1992). Indeed, Im and Baumann (2020) found a higher gesture frequency co-occurring with focused or prosodically prominent words. Also, Wagner and Bryhadyr (2017) and Kügler and Gregori (2023) found a tighter cross-modal synchronization between hand movements and accents when the latter were highly informative. However, rather than aiming at a tight cross-modal synchrony, speakers of Australian English indicate an upcoming highlighted word by an eyebrow movement preceding this focused word (Kim et al.,

2014). We therefore have further evidence for the fact that cross-modal timing needs to be seen as an orchestration rather than a synchronization of modalities.

However, information structure is not just expressed by using accentuation, and this also affects cross-modal synchronization as well as the choice of co-speech gesture. In German, iconic gestures – that is, gestures that express spatial-physical aspects of the conveyed message (e.g., its shape or size) – tend not to co-occur with focused elements (Kügler & Gregori, 2023). In Turkish, speakers tend to align iconic and metaphoric gestures with focused elements and deictic gestures with message topics (Türk & Calhoun, 2023).

Yet another function of cross-modal synchronization is related to the semantic relationship between the modalities involved, for instance, Bergmann et al. (2011) detected the existence of a stronger temporal synchronization between gestures and lexical affiliates when both express congruent semantic concepts. This indicates that cross-modal synchronization is used to increase the robustness of 'conversational grounding' during an ongoing conversation (de Ruiter et al., 2012).

Beyond signaling features of the message such as its information structure, cross-modal synchronizations can also indicate speaker-related information such as a speaker's level of attention, distraction, understanding, or general cognitive load (Betz et al., 2023; Türk et al., 2024). Often, such cognitive or epistemic states are being delivered as part of a listener's feedback signaling, and interlocutors may deliberately and strategically choose to use verbal or nonverbal feedback signals in certain phases of an ongoing conversations. Nonverbal signals (also see Chap. 19 for an overview) may encompass a wide range of signals such as head, hand, and torso movements but also involve gaze or self-adaptors. Whereas such more or less strategic display may be guided strongly by information-structural aspects as described earlier, it can also play a role when interlocutors are currently in a listening role and want to indicate their level of attention, understanding, or their intention to initiate their own contribution to the conversation (e.g., to ask a clarification question or to contribute further to what has been said earlier). Sometimes, listeners reveal a strategy of relying on nonverbal feedback during an ongoing interlocutor turn in order to be resource-efficient and not disruptive, and they rely more strongly on verbalized feedback during pauses, after the interlocutor has finished their turn (Dittmann & Llewellyn, 1968; Ferré & Renaudier, 2017). However, it has also been shown that feedback signals often are following 'invites' by the speaker (Gravano & Hirschberg, 2011; Heldner et al., 2013). The elicitation of such feedback or back-channel signals is achieved by a complex combination of prosody and other linguistic cues (e.g., bigram probability of a part of speech, pitch height or slope, duration of the interpausal unit; see Gravano and Hirschberg (2011), with gaze having been found to be a powerful feedback-inviting cue in face-to-face conversations (Hjalmarsson & Oertel, 2012; Truong et al., 2011).

Finally, a large body of work has shown that dialog partners either mutually synchronize with each other in their verbal and nonverbal behavior or align in their expressive inventories. Linguistically, interlocutors tend to align their lexical choices, acoustic-prosodic features, or syntactic structures. Likewise, interaction partners have been found to align nonverbally, in, for example, their facial expressions, manual gestures, or body postures (see Kopp, 2010 for an overview). Many of these features are multimodally aligned at the same time (Louwerse et al., 2012). These phenomena have been described as, for example, convergence (Pardo, 2013), accommodation (Giles & Ogay, 2007), interactional synchrony (Bernieri & Rosenthal, 1991), entrainment (Levitan & Hirschberg, 2011), mimicry (Holler & Wilkin, 2011), or alignment (Reitter & Moore, 2014). Each of these terms makes different assumptions about the underlying mechanisms for these phenomena, but they are all based on observations of interlocutors becoming 'in some way more similar' over the course of an ongoing communicative interaction. It is also an important phenomenon in HCI in which embodied conversational agents that align to their users were found to be rated as being more likable (Nass & Lee, 2001), to be more socially intelligent (André et al., 2004), or to be more persuasive (Bailenson & Yee, 2005). On the other hand, people have also been shown to align to verbal and nonverbal behavior of artificial agents—for example, with regard to loudness and reaction latency (Suzuki & Katagiri, 2007); lexical choice (Branigan et al., 2011); speech rate, amplitude, and pause structure (Oviatt et al., 2004); or smiling frequency and duration (Krämer et al., 2013). Bergmann et al. (2015) found that human interlocutors align their lexical choice and gesture handedness similarly when interacting with either real or virtual humans. These studies indicate that alignment has a role to play in the design of dialog systems and virtual humans and especially when modeling explanatory dialogs with XAI, as such an alignment is likely to be beneficial for the processing of and attention to a message delivered as part of an explanation.

22.4 Operationalization of Multimodal Synchronization

Despite the above-described findings about cross-modal timing and synchronization, there is currently no consensus as to how these are measured both within and between speakers. Typically, cross-modal synchronization is measured with the help of cross-modal 'anchors'—that is, points in time that have to align temporally with events in another modality but also have been shown to be perceptually integrated when co-occurring. Within speakers, a strong temporal alignment has been described between the so-called pitch accent peaks, the most prominent intonation excursion of prosodically highlighted words, and co-occurring gesture apices—that is, the point at which a gesture reaches its strongest excursion or turning point. This strong alignment has been found to be particularly strong for beat gestures or deictic gestures (Wagner et al., 2014; Leonard & Cummins, 2011). For this reason, both gesture strokes (in the visual domain) and pitch accents (in the verbal domain) have been suggested to be good cross-modal anchors, together with phrase boundaries (see above). Alternatively, gesture onsets (in the visual domain) and onsets of corresponding 'lexical affiliates' have been suggested as useful additional cross-modal anchors (Bergmann et al., 2011; Chu & Hagoort, 2014; Church et al., 2014). However, it has to be kept in mind that identifying a suitable 'lexical affiliate' in the verbal domain is not always straightforward, because gestures may not always relate to single words but rather describe vague concepts or complex actions that are expressed by longer expressions (de Ruiter, 2000). Yet, another type of cross-modal anchor applies to speech in interaction and constitutes points in time that have an effect on the coordination of the dialog flow by which interlocutors negotiate who is speaking, who is listening, and when these roles are switched. As indicated above, crucial points for this *floor management* may be the ends of utterances or *dialog turns*, where the dialogue floor may change, or backchannel-inviting cues that ask for listener feedback. Multimodal behaviors can therefore also be measured relative to these – not always clear-cut – landmarks.

In principle, the cross-modal anchors introduced above can be applied for the measurement of the cross-modal synchronization within and between speakers, for example, listeners may synchronize their head nods with the (expected) accents of a speaker (Inden et al., 2013) – as an example of multimodal *entrainment* – or a speaker may further emphasize an accented word by simultaneous nodding, producing a beat gesture, or raising the eyebrows (Swerts & Krahmer, 2005).

22.5 How Does This Chapter Inspire Further Directions of XAI

Like human explainers, a sXAI ideally ought to leverage multimodal communicative means for conveying an explanans and then ought to adjust the tempo and temporal structure of its ongoing explanation based on the explainee's multimodal display of their current level of understanding, attention, cognitive load, or interest. Such monitoring and adaptation need to pay attention to the multiple functions of multimodal synchronization and adjust the delivery of an explanation. Whereas XAI typically does not take into account the interactive co-construction of explanations, it is likely that more adaptive dialog-based systems, possibly using artificial agents as mediators between an AI and a human, can considerably improve the quality of an explanation. Such systems should be able to profit substantially from the rich resources of multimodal synchronization. For one, XAI needs to take into account the importance of suitably synchronized multimodal explanations and according potential risks of multimodal explanations (e.g., when listeners are unable to integrate several channels due to lacking synchronization). For another, interagent synchronization at all levels of multimodal behavior facilitates production/comprehension of communicative signals and may yield important positive effects on how users perceive and interact with an XAI system.

22.6 Rapid Access

Explanations unfold as a dialogical process that hinges on rich and robust communication between the explainer and the explainee. Leveraging the richness of multimodal communication in this can benefit explanations in many ways—from enabling interactive dialog mechanisms such as back-channel feedback, supporting the expression of abstract ideas, or mitigating cognitive load. Crucially, real-life explanations tend to be exchanged multimodally, and their expression needs to take into account the adequate sequencing and synchronization of the various modalities involved including speech, melodic/rhythmic structure and highlighting (aka *prosody*), manual gestures, head gestures, facial expressions, or posture changes, both within and between conversational partners. Whereas empirical research has not yet unfolded all details behind cross-modal synchronization, we know that a certain amount of it is a prerequisite for cross-modal signals to be integrated meaningfully. A gesture strongly misaligned with the verbalization it belongs to will rather be interpreted as random movement or even erratic behavior, and it may well impede understanding. On the contrary, adequately synchronized modalities may enrich the message and make communication more robust. While many questions related to cross-modal timing still need to be formulated, we know that gestures typically slightly precede speech and gestures tend to be temporally aligned with co-expressive words, the so-called 'lexical affiliates.' This synchronization is strengthened further if these words are highlighted prosodically. In such cases, the main function of this synchronization is emphasis, often correlated with the introduction of novel or important concepts. In case of a synchronization of representational hand gestures with speech, the message is furthermore made more robust, because both channels add information about the introduced concept in either a congruent or a complementary fashion. Both of the abovementioned functions of synchronization are of obvious relevance to the unfolding of an explanation, which needs to be traced and attended to by an explainee. Furthermore, an explainer can react to the complexity of an ongoing explanation by slowing down locally, or hesitating, across various modalities, thereby providing the explainee with additional processing time. Lastly, cross-modal synchrony also plays a role in the explainee's behavior when they need to express how well an ongoing explanation is understood or what the ongoing level of attention is. This can be achieved by multimodally expressed feedback signals indicating the current level of understanding or attention to an ongoing explanation. Similar to an explainer, an explainee may also use multimodal hesitations as a signal of uncertainty or thinking or less clearly synchronized cross-modal 'fidgeting' as a signal of confusion. Such signals can be used by an explainer to modify the ongoing explanation according to the explainee's expressed needs. When needed, the explainee's feedback signals can also be elicited multimodally by an explainer (e.g., by gaze). Lastly, a temporally fine-tuned display of multimodal cues also affects the floor management of a conversation: by picking up and reacting to these cues, speakers can negotiate the seamless exchange of speaker turns, thereby supporting the active participation of all conversational partners and increasing the robustness and pleasantness of a dialog. Cross-modal timing and synchronization have been shown to be relevant for both explanations delivered by a socially interactive artificial agent and conversations between humans. However, timing mistakes or a lack of cross-modal synchrony may have the contrary effect and may negatively affect understanding or create the impression of a less believable, inattentive communication partner. XAI research must therefore pay adequate attention to timing whenever explanations are expressed multimodally.

Acknowledgments We thank Carola de Beer for helpful comments on an earlier version of this chapter.

This work was funded by the Deutsche Forschungsgemeinschaft (DFG, German Research Foundation): TRR 318/1 2021 – 438445824.

References

Al Moubayed, S., Beskow, J., & Granström, B. (2009). Auditory visual prominence. *Journal on Multimodal User Interfaces, 3*(4), 299–309. https://doi.org/10.1007/s12193-010-0054-0
Allwood, J., Nivre, J., & Ahlsén, E (1992). On the semantics and pragmatics of linguistic feedback. *Journal of Semantics, 9*(1), 1–26. https://doi.org/10.1093/jos/9.1.1
Ambrazaitis, G., & House, D. (2017). Multimodal prominences: Exploring the patterning and usage of focal pitch accents, head beats and eyebrow beats in Swedish television news readings. *Speech Communication, 95*, 100–113. https://doi.org/10.1016/j.specom.2017.08.008
André, E., Rehm, M., Minker, W., & Bühler, D. (2004). Endowing spoken language dialogue systems with emotional intelligence. In *Affective Dialogue Systems: Tutorial and Research Workshop, ADS 2004. Proceedings* (pp. 178–187). Springer. https://doi.org/10.1007/978-3-540-24842-2_17
Arnold, J. E., Kam, C. L. H., & Tanenhaus, M. K. (2007). If you say thee uh you are describing something hard: The on-line attribution of disfluency during reference comprehension. *Journal of Experimental Psychology: Learning, Memory, and Cognition, 33*(5), 914–930. https://doi.org/10.1037/0278-7393.33.5.914
Axelsson, A., Buschmeier, H., & Skantze, G. (2022). Modeling feedback in interaction with conversational agents—a review. *Frontiers in Computer Science, 4*, 744574. https://doi.org/10.3389/fcomp.2022.744574
Aylett, M., & Turk, A. (2004). The smooth signal redundancy hypothesis: A functional explanation for relationships between redundancy, prosodic prominence, and duration in spontaneous speech. *Language and Speech, 47*(1), 31–56. https://doi.org/10.1177/00238309040470010201
Bailenson, J. N., & Yee, N. (2005). Digital chameleons: Automatic assimilation of nonverbal gestures in immersive virtual environments. *Psychological Science, 16*(10), 814–819. https://doi.org/10.1111/j.1467-9280.2005.01619.x
Bergmann, K., Aksu, V., & Kopp, S. (2011). The relation of speech and gestures: Temporal synchrony follows semantic synchrony. In *Proceedings of the 2nd Workshop on Gesture and Speech in Interaction (GeSpIn 2011)*. Bielefeld University.
Bergmann, K., Branigan, H. P., & Kopp, S. (2015). Exploring the alignment space-lexical and gestural alignment with real and virtual humans. *Frontiers in ICT, 2*, 7. https://doi.org/10.3389/fict.2015.00007
Bernieri, F. J., & Rosenthal, R. (1991). Interpersonal coordination: Behavior matching and interactional synchrony. In R. S. Feldman & B. Rimé (Eds.), *Fundamentals of nonverbal behavior* (pp. 401–432). Cambridge University Press.

Betz, S., Bryhadyr, N., Türk, O., & Wagner, P. (2023). Cognitive load increases spoken and gestural hesitation frequency. *Languages, 8*(1), 71. https://doi.org/10.3390/languages8010071

Betz, S., Carlmeyer, B., Wagner, P., & Wrede, B. (2018). Interactive hesitation synthesis: Modelling and evaluation. *Multimodal Technologies and Interaction, 2*(1), 9. https://doi.org/10.3390/mti2010009

Branigan, H. P., Pickering, M. J., Pearson, J., McLean, J. F., Brown, A. (2011). The role of beliefs in lexical alignment: Evidence from dialogs with humans and computers. *Cognition, 121*(1), 41–57. https://doi.org/10.1016/j.cognition.2011.05.011

Brennan, S. E., & Williams, M. (1995). The feeling of another's knowing: Prosody and filled pauses as cues to listeners about the metacognitive states of speakers. *Journal of Memory and Language, 34*(3), 383–398. https://doi.org/10.1006/jmla.1995.1017

Chu, M., & Hagoort, P. (2014). Synchronization of speech and gesture: Evidence for interaction in action. *Journal of Experimental Psychology: General, 143*(4), 1726–1741. https://doi.org/10.1037/a0036281

Church, R. B., Kelly, S., & Holcombe, D. (2014). Temporal synchrony between speech, action and gesture during language production. *Language, Cognition and Neuroscience, 29*(3), 345–354. https://doi.org/10.1080/01690965.2013.857783

de Ruiter, J. P. (2000). The production of gesture and speech. In D. McNeill (Ed.), *Language and gesture* (pp. 248–311). Cambridge University Press. https://doi.org/10.1017/CBO9780511620850.018

de Ruiter, J. P., Bangerter, A., & Dings, P. (2012). Interplay between gesture and speech in the production of referring expressions: Investigating the trade-off hypothesis. *Topics in Cognitive Science, 4*(2), 232–248. https://doi.org/10.1111/j.1756-8765.2012.01183.x

Dittmann, A. T., & Llewellyn, L. G. (1968). Relationship between vocalizations and head nods as listener responses. *Journal of Personality and Social Psychology, 9*(1), 79–84. https://doi.org/10.1037/h0025722

Esteve-Gibert, N., Borràs-Comes, J., Asor, E., Swerts, M., & Prieto, P. (2017). The timing of head movements: The role of prosodic heads and edges. *The Journal of the Acoustical Society of America, 141*(6), 4727–4739. https://doi.org/10.1121/1.4986649

Esteve-Gibert, N., & Prieto, P. (2013). Prosodic structure shapes the temporal realization of intonation and manual gesture movements. *Journal of Speech, Language, and Hearing Research, 56*(3), 850–864. https://doi.org/10.1044/1092-4388(2012/12-0049)

Ferré, G., & Renaudier, S. (2017). Unimodal and bimodal backchannels in conversational English. In *SEMDIAL 2017 (SaarDial) Workshop on the Semantics and Pragmatics of Dialogue* (pp. 20–30). SEMDIAL. https://doi.org/10.21437/SemDial.2017-3

Giles, H., & Ogay, T. (2007). Communication accommodation theory. In *Explaining communication: contemporary theories and exemplars* (pp. 293–310). https://doi.org/10.4324/9781410614308-21

Gravano, A., & Hirschberg, J. (2011). Turn-taking cues in task-oriented dialogue. *Computer Speech & Language, 25*(3), 601–634. https://doi.org/10.1016/j.csl.2010.10.003

Habets, B., Kita, S., Shao, Z., Özyurek, A., & Hagoort, P. (2011). The role of synchrony and ambiguity in speech–gesture integration during comprehension. *Journal of Cognitive Neuroscience, 23*(8), 1845–1854. https://doi.org/10.1162/jocn.2010.21462

Heldner, M., Hjalmarsson, A., & Edlund, J. (2013). Backchannel relevance spaces. In *Nordic prosody XI* (pp. 137–146). Peter Lang Publishing Group.

Hjalmarsson, A., & Oertel, C. (2012). Gaze direction as a back-channel inviting cue in dialogue. In *IVA 2012 Workshop on Realtime Conversational Virtual Agents* (Vol. 9).

Holler, J., & Wilkin, K. (2011). Co-speech gesture mimicry in the process of collaborative referring during face-to-face dialogue. *Journal of Nonverbal Behavior, 35*, 133–153. https://doi.org/10.1007/s10919-011-0105-6

Im, S., & Baumann, S. (2020). Probabilistic relation between co-speech gestures, pitch accents and information status. *Proceedings of the Linguistic Society of America (LSA), 5*(1), 685–697. https://doi.org/10.3765/plsa.v5i1.4755

Inden, B., Malisz, Z., Wagner, P., & Wachsmuth, I. (2013). Timing and entrainment of multimodal backchanneling behavior for an embodied conversational agent. In *Proceedings of the 15th ACM on International Conference on Multimodal Interaction* (pp. 181–188). Association for Computing Machinery. https://doi.org/10.1145/2522848.2522890

Iverson, J. M., & Thelen, E. (1999). Hand, mouth and brain. The dynamic emergence of speech and gesture. *Journal of Consciousness Studies, 6*(11–12), 19–40.

Karpiński, M., Jarmołowicz-Nowikow, E., & Malisz, Z. (2009). Aspects of gestural and prosodic structure of multimodal utterances in Polish task-oriented dialogues. *Speech and Language Technology, 11*, 113–122.

Kendon, A. (1980). Gesticulation and speech: Two aspects of the process of utterance. In M. R. Key (Ed.), *The relationship of verbal and nonverbal communication* (pp. 207–227). De Gruyter Mounton. https://doi.org/10.1515/9783110813098.207

Kim, J., Cvejic, E., & Davis, C. (2014). Tracking eyebrows and head gestures associated with spoken prosody. *Speech Communication, 57*, 317–330. https://doi.org/10.1016/j.specom.2013.06.003

Kisa, Y. D., Goldin-Meadow, S., & Casasanto, D. (2022). Do gestures really facilitate speech production? *Journal of Experimental Psychology: General, 151*(6), 1252–1271. https://doi.org/10.1037/xge0001135

Kopp, S. (2010). Social resonance and embodied coordination in face-to-face conversation with artificial interlocutors. *Speech Communication, 52*(6), 587–597. https://doi.org/10.1016/j.specom.2010.02.007

Krahmer, E., & Swerts, M. (2005). How children and adults produce and perceive uncertainty in audiovisual speech. *Language and Speech, 48*(1), 29–53. https://doi.org/10.1177/00238309050480010201

Krämer, N., Kopp, S., Becker-Asano, C., & Sommer, N. (2013). Smile and the world will smile with you—the effects of a virtual agent's smile on users' evaluation and behavior. *International Journal of Human-Computer Studies, 71*(3), 335–349. https://doi.org/10.1016/j.ijhcs.2012.09.006

Krivokapić, J., Tiede, M. K., & Tyrone, M. E. (2017). A kinematic study of prosodic gesture in articulatory and manual gestures: Results from a novel method of data collection. *Laboratory Phonology. Journal of the Association for Laboratory Phonology, 8*(1), 3. https://doi.org/10.5334/labphon.75

Kügler, F., & Gregori, A. (2023). Iconic gestures in focus—synchronization of prosody and gestures in prominence. In *Proceedings of 20th International Congress of Phonetic Sciences 2023* (p. ID 232). Guarant International.

Leonard, T., & Cummins, F. (2011). The temporal relation between beat gestures and speech. *Language and Cognitive Processes, 26*(10), 1457–1471. https://doi.org/10.1080/01690965.2010.500218

Levelt, W. J. M., Richardson, G., & La Heij, W. (1985). Pointing and voicing in deictic expressions. *Journal of Memory and Language, 24*(2), 133–164. https://doi.org/10.1016/0749-596X(85)90021-X

Levitan, R., & Hirschberg, J. B. (2011). Measuring acoustic-prosodic entrainment with respect to multiple levels and dimensions. In *Proceedings of Interspeech 2011* (pp. 3081–3084). Columbia University Academic Commons. https://doi.org/10.21437/Interspeech.2011-771

Loehr, D. P. (2012). Temporal, structural, and pragmatic synchrony between intonation and gesture. *Laboratory Phonology. Journal of the Association for Laboratory Phonology, 3*(1), 71–89. https://doi.org/10.1515/lp-2012-0006

Louwerse, M. M., Dale, R., Bard, E. G., & Jeuniaux, P. (2012). Behavior matching in multimodal communication is synchronized. *Cognitive Science, 36*(8), 1404–1426. https://doi.org/10.1111/j.1551-6709.2012.01269.x

McNeill, D. (1992). *Hand and mind: What gestures reveal about thought.* University of Chicago Press.

Nass, C., & Lee, K. M. (2001). Does computer-synthesized speech manifest personality? Experimental tests of recognition, similarity-attraction, and consistency-attraction. *Journal of Experimental Psychology: Applied, 7*(3), 171–181. https://doi.org/10.1037/1076-898X.7.3.171

Oviatt, S., Darves, C., & Coulston, R. (2004). Toward adaptive conversational interfaces: Modeling speech convergence with animated personas. *ACM Transactions on Computer–Human Interaction (TOCHI), 11*(3), 300–328. https://doi.org/10.1145/1017494.1017498

Pardo, J. S. (2013). Measuring phonetic convergence in speech production. *Frontiers in Psychology, 4*, 559. https://doi.org/10.3389/fpsyg.2013.00559

Piantadosi, S. T., Tily, H., & Gibson, E. (2011). Word lengths are optimized for efficient communication. *Proceedings of the National Academy of Sciences, 108*(9), 3526–3529. https://doi.org/10.1073/pnas.1012551108

Pouw, W., & Dixon, J. A. (2019). Entrainment and modulation of gesturespeech synchrony under delayed auditory feedback. *Cognitive Science, 43*(3), e12721. https://doi.org/10.1111/cogs.12721

Reitter, D., & Moore, J. D. (2014). Alignment and task success in spoken dialogue. *Journal of Memory and Language, 76*, 29–46. https://doi.org/10.1016/j.jml.2014.05.008

Rochet-Capellan, A., Laboissière, R., Galván, A., & Schwartz, J.-L. (2008). The speech focus position effect on jaw-finger coordination in a pointing task. *Journal of Speech, Language, and Hearing Research, 51*(6), 1507–x1521. https://doi.org/10.1044/1092-4388(2008/07-0173)

Rohrer, P. L., Prieto, P., & Delais-Roussarie, E. (2019). Beat gestures and prosodic domain marking in French. In *Proceedings of the 19th International Congress of Phonetic Sciences (ICPhS)* (pp. 1500–1504). HAL.

Suzuki, N., & Katagiri, Y. (2007). Prosodic alignment in human–computer interaction. *Connection Science, 19*(2), 131–141. https://doi.org/10.1080/09540090701369125

Swerts, M., & Krahmer, E. (2005). Audiovisual prosody and feeling of knowing. *Journal of Memory and Language, 53*(1), 81–94. https://doi.org/10.1016/j.jml.2005.02.003

Treffner, P., Peter, M., & Kleidon, M. (2008). Gestures and phases: The dynamics of speech-hand communication. *Ecological Psychology, 20*(1), 32–64. https://doi.org/10.1080/10407410701766643

Truong, K. P., Poppe, R. W., de Kok, I. A., & Heylen, D. K. J. (2011). A multimodal analysis of vocal and visual backchannels in spontaneous dialogs. In *12th Annual Conference of the International Speech Communication Association, INTERSPEECH 2011* (pp. 2973–2976). International Speech Communication Association (ISCA). https://doi.org/10.21437/Interspeech.2011-744

Türk, O., & Calhoun, S. (2023). Phrasal synchronization of gesture with prosody and information structure. *Language and Speech, 67*(3), 702–743. https://doi.org/10.1177/00238309231185308

Türk, O., Lazarov, S., Wang, Y., Buschmeier, H., Grimminger, A., & Wagner, P. (2024). Predictability of understanding in explanatory interactions based on multimodal cues. In *Proceedings of the 26th ACM International Conference on Multimodal Interaction* (pp. 449–458). Association for Computing Machinery. https://doi.org/10.1145/3678957.3685741

Wagner, P., & Bryhadyr, N. (2017). Mutual visibility and information structure enhance synchrony between speech and co-speech movements. *Journal of Multimodal Communication Studies, 4*(1–2), 69–74.

Wagner, P., Malisz, Z., & Kopp, S. (2014). Gesture and speech in interaction: An overview. *Speech Communication, 57*, 209–232. https://doi.org/10.1016/j.specom.2013.09.008

Open Access This chapter is licensed under the terms of the Creative Commons Attribution 4.0 International License (http://creativecommons.org/licenses/by/4.0/), which permits use, sharing, adaptation, distribution and reproduction in any medium or format, as long as you give appropriate credit to the original author(s) and the source, provide a link to the Creative Commons license and indicate if changes were made.

The images or other third party material in this chapter are included in the chapter's Creative Commons license, unless indicated otherwise in a credit line to the material. If material is not included in the chapter's Creative Commons license and your intended use is not permitted by statutory regulation or exceeds the permitted use, you will need to obtain permission directly from the copyright holder.

Chapter 23
Multimodality in Explanatory Interactions

Friederike Kern

Abstract Studies on human–human interaction have shown that multimodal signals, such as hand gestures, facial expressions, and prosody, are important for both cognitive and interactive processes of meaning-making. Multimodal behavior also plays a crucial role in the area of knowledge transfer, for which explanations are central. Recent studies of multimodal behavior in explanations within the framework of the global structure of explanatory interactions suggest that it can be understood as interdependent and mutually informing. Therefore, this chapter first provides an overview over conceptualizations of explanations, focusing on approaches that view explanations as a social process, thereby emphasizing their co-constructive, interactive nature. A model is introduced that provides an empirically based, co-constructed global structure of explanatory interactions. The main topic of the second section is the forms and functions of multimodal behaviors. The focus is on prosody and gestures, examining how they support knowledge transfer and understanding by structuring speech, creating coherence, emphasizing important information, and, in the case of gestures, providing additional content related to the explanandum. The chapter then suggested how both the global structure of explanatory interactions and multimodal behavior could be brought together in a heuristic for more detailed further research and future fine-tuned implementation of multimodal behavior in sXAI.

23.1 How Does This Chapter Relate to XAI?

Explainable AI has received a lot of attention recently because it provides important tools for making AI applications more transparent to users, by, for example, providing information about how they work and thereby contributing to the promotion of human empowerment (Dazeley et al., 2021). The conceptual basis for explanations in XAI systems is usually scientific explanations (Miller, 2019). However, research

F. Kern (✉)
Faculty of Linguistics and Literary Studies, Bielefeld University, Bielefeld, Germany
e-mail: friederike.kern@uni-bielefeld.de

on explanatory interactions that occur in everyday face-to-face conversations have revealed that these differ from scientific explanations in a few essential ways. Whereas scientific explanations are usually about generalized theories such as universally valid laws of nature, conversational explanations are often about specific single facts – events, decisions, and so forth – that people are interested in and that do not claim general validity (Miller, 2019). Even when conversational explanations are about generalizations, their degrees and types can vary, and it is necessary to identify these degrees and types in order to secure understanding and acceptance (Dazeley et al., 2021). In addition, explanations in conversations are usually co-constructed, whereby the recipient of the explanation (the explainee, hereinafter EE) is also actively participating in the explanatory interaction. Finally, due to their oral mode, both explainer (hereinafter ER) and EE make use of other than verbal means. Multimodal signals – such as co-speech hand gestures, facial expressions, prosody, head, and torso movements (see Chap. 19) – play a significant role for both cognitive and interactive processes of meaning-making. They can lighten the cognitive load and help the EE to gain a better understanding of the subject matter at hand (Goldin-Meadow et al., 2001; Cook et al., 2012), they can support processes of transferring of knowledge (Rohlfing, 2019), and they can display an EE's understanding (Mondada, 2011). In recent research, social aspects of XAI have increasingly become a focus of interest (Rohlfing et al., 2021; Dazeley et al., 2021). As a result, the inherent co-constructivity of explanations was identified as particularly important for future applications of XAI (Miller, 2019). Following findings from research on conversational explanations between humans, new routes to XAI could start by conceptualizing explanations as co-constructed endeavors (Weld & Bansal, 2018; Miller, 2019) that give the EE a more active role in the ongoing explanation (Booshehri et al., 2024) and also employ multimodal resources to ensure better understanding. The aim is to develop more adaptive systems and thus transform XAI into social explainable AI (sXAI). This chapter will focus on the interactive functions of multimodal signals in co-constructed explanatory interactions. To this end, it will first define the characteristics of explanations as jointly accomplished endeavors before, second, citing research on how multimodal signals are used for the abovementioned interactive purpose of transferring knowledge and securing understanding. Building on research on explanatory interactions between humans, the chapter will first provide an overview of two conceptualizations of explanations, focusing on conceptualizations interested in explanations as a social process, thereby emphasizing the co-constructive, interactive structure of naturally occurring face-to-face interactions. Then, it will introduce a model that describes the empirically determined interactive patterns of co-constructed conversational explanations. In the second section, the chapter will turn to the forms and functions of multimodal behavior, with a focus on prosody and co-speech gesture and how these can facilitate knowledge transfer and understanding by structuring speech, establishing coherence across utterances and speakers, highlighting important information, and – in the case of gestures – providing additional content on aspects of the explanandum. The chapter will also provide some ideas about the added value of the described multimodal behavior for the operationalizations of sXAI and its functions in co-constructed explanatory interactions. Finally, it will suggest how the interactive structure of explanations and multimodal behavior can both be brought together in a heuristic for more detailed further research and future fine-tuned implementation of multimodal behavior in sXAI.

23.2 Modeling Explanations as Interactions

Explanatory interactions that arise during everyday conversations are well-established methods of knowledge construction and transfer (Keppler & Luckmann, 1991; Miller, 2019). They occur naturally in all kinds of situations: at dinner with the family (Keppler & Luckmann, 1991), in institutionalized classroom discourse (Morek, 2012), or in medical encounters (Fisher et al., 2022). Following Quasthoff et al. (2017), two approaches to the study of explanations can be distinguished: speaker-oriented approaches adhere to formal norms of logic, as set out in Hempel and Oppenheim's (1948) deductive-nomological schema of explanation. This schema presents a formal structure of how causal relationships can be presented in natural language, and it is applicable to general laws as well as to single events. With regard to content, the authors pursue explanations to explicate factual cause-effect correlations in order to subsume them under the laws of nature. Speaker-oriented approaches thus take scientific explanations as the standard and basis for evaluating the quality of an explanation. Importantly, they focus on the product – that is, the completed explanation – and are not interested in the process that leads to its accomplishment. Explanations as products are common in science. They usually follow a formalized normative form and occur especially in the written modality. In line with this, speaker-oriented approaches are concerned primarily with correctness of content and less with processes of how the content is actually transmitted to the recipient of the explanation.

The second approach places the interactive, co-constructive process of explaining at the center of interest, thereby focusing on the process of learning as an interactional rather than a mental phenomenon (Koschmann & LeBaron, 2002). Interaction-oriented approaches take their start from conversational face-to-face explanations and focus on the process of how an explanation is jointly accomplished – that is, co-constructed – by both ER and the person receiving the explanation (i.e., EE). Explanations in this view are understood as 'occasioned productions' (Koschmann & Zemel, 2009), contingent on and emerging from local situatedness and the unfolding activity in which both ER and EE participate. This also means that in contrast to scientific explanations the completeness and comprehensibility of explanatory interactions arising during mundane conversations is oriented toward everyday life standards that are defined by the circumstances/context of the situation and the needs of the EE. Such explanatory interactions do not follow one explicit, conventional, or logically justified norm, like scientific explanations do, and they are more flexible in content and form (Rohlfing et al., 2021).

Even though explanations are usually carried out by one primary speaker and therefore mostly monological, recipients (or EEs in our terminology) can also be found to contribute to explanations in numerous ways. They provide continuous back channeling to show that they are still following the explanation (Kern, 2007; Fisher et al., 2022), signal their ongoing understanding (Kern, 2007, 2020; Mondada, 2011; Zemel & Koschmann, 2011), or ask for clarification (Kern, 2020). Explanatory interactions are thus not just simple monologues, and the EEs are not just mere listeners. Rather, throughout the entire explanatory interactions, EEs are more or less involved in the ongoing process of co-constructing an explanation and contributing to it (Fisher et al., 2022). Monological phases in which EEs produce only back channeling and change-of-state tokens (Heritage, 1985) such as "oh" that acknowledge prior talk to be informative alternate with dialogical phases in which EEs take a more active part in the explanation by asking follow-up or clarification questions. In contrast to the monological phases, dialogical phases are being initiated mostly by EEs (Fisher et al., 2022).

An analytical framework developed bottom up from empirical data of mundane explanations illuminates the interactive structure of explanations (Quasthoff et al., 2017). According to this framework, explanatory interactions feature a series of five organizational "jobs" (ibid., p. 89) that are carried out by both ER and EE in a joint endeavor. These are as follows: First, the topical relevance of an explanation is established (1), commonly by the EE disclosing a knowledge deficit (Keppler & Luckmann, 1991; Goodwin, 2018) or by the ER acting in institutionalized social settings such as classrooms (Morek, 2012) or doctor-patient consultations (Fisher et al., 2022). When the first job is accomplished by the ER's demonstrated willingness to close the assumed knowledge gap, job (2) "constituting an explanandum" is initiated. In this most vital job, both ER and EE need to negotiate and agree upon the actual explanandum that is also shaped by the EE's goal. The subsequent job (3) explicating procedural, conceptual, and/or causal relations is the core job in this framework – the explanation proper, so to speak. Here, the actual explaining happens. Next, (4) both ER and EE have to agree on closing the explanation, before (5) the transition back to turn-by-turn talk or a different activity can be achieved: "In order to end an explanation, the interlocutors have to display to each other that a satisfactory degree of comprehension and thus a successful knowledge transfer has been accomplished" (Quasthoff et al., 2017, 103) (Fig. 23.1).

Research on the ongoing accomplishment of these jobs suggests that more dialogic phases arise toward the end of job (3) when EEs are given the chance to ask for clarification or produce follow-up questions (Fisher et al., 2022). Ongoing

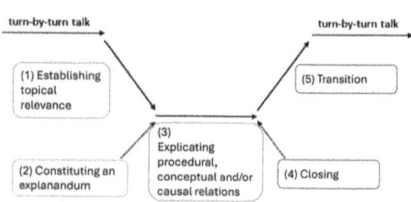

Fig. 23.1 Organizational jobs to establish global structure (Quasthoff et al., 2017, p. 103)

research suggests that job (4) opens up a sequential position in which explainees have one last opportunity to ask for clarification to satisfy their needs. In this case, a loop back into the explanation proper is accomplished. Explainees may employ a variety of strategies to "opening up closing" (Schegloff & Sacks, 1973, p. 289) when they want to clarify something or need more information. However, until now, there is a lack of research that takes a closer look at job 2 in which the explanandum is constituted. The orderly succession of conversational jobs in explanatory dialogs draws the attention to the relevance of co-constructing the explanation as well as the goal of the explanation before starting the explanation—that is, what the EE wants to achieve/understand in the end. Completeness and comprehensibility are a negotiable matter and need to be adapted to the EEs' respective interest and goal (Rohlfing et al., 2021). Even though further research is needed in this area, an understanding of a user's requirements will probably lead to a better adjustment to the needs of EEs and thus result in a better understanding of the explanandum. Co-constructing the explanandum should therefore be understood as an important part of interactive explaining (Rohlfing et al., 2021). Indeed, identifying or agreeing on the explanandum and the existing knowledge gap should be regarded as an outcome of the interaction, not its prerequisite.

It is important to note that the proposed structural framework of explanatory interactions is more than just an empirical finding. It also has a social reality: In order for explanations to happen, participants must agree on doing what they are doing. So, from a constructionist perspective, explanatory interactions are constituted precisely by the mutual accomplishment of these jobs. At the same time, the jobs present a structure that modulates the interaction by requiring the participants to coordinate with each other following a protocol (Rohlfing et al., 2021).

The mutually accomplished sequence of successive *jobs* that explanatory interactions routinely follow provides a solid framework for building sXAI systems with a social structure that is prevalent in everyday conversational explanations and follows rule-based human behavior. To proceed with the explanatory interaction, each of the jobs has to be completed co-constructively. Importantly, because the co-construction of the explanandum is identified as a job in its own right (job 2), attention can be directed toward context conditions as well as toward situated needs of EE to shape the goal of explanation and co-constructively determine its extent and depth. Thus, a better (i.e., more suitable) explanation can follow. An sXAI system should also be made more sensitive toward possible explanatory loops initiated by the EE that occur in later phases of the explanation, such as toward the end of job (3) or in job (4). The fixed sequence of jobs would also provide a basis for implementing more context-sensitive scaffolding or monitoring strategies in an sXAI system, because these are expected to differ with regard to the job in which they occur. Thus, more adaptive systems could be constructed.

23.3 Multimodality in Explanatory Interactions

With the growing use of video footage to investigate authentic interactions, multimodal behavior of interactants has moved increasingly to the center of interest in linguistics and neighboring disciplines. Microanalytical studies of material made available through video recordings have shown that multimodal behavior is not only very probably linked to cognitive processes but also an important resource for establishing mutual understanding in interaction. Although research on the role of multimodal signals in explanatory interactions is still relatively scarce, there are a few outcomes that are potentially relevant for future sXAI systems because they shed light on their functions for the transfer of knowledge and for ensuring understanding. Following the interaction-oriented approach to explanations promoted above, the focus will be on the potential of multimodal signals to manage the interactive process and the co-construction of knowledge. Accordingly, their relation to the EE's cognitive processes such as controlling of attention or of cognitive load will be deliberately left out here (but see, for example, Kita et al., 2017; Cooperrider & Goldin-Meadow, 2017). Multimodality in conversational face-to-face interaction encompasses verbal, nonverbal, and prosodic features. Whereas verbal features involve anything to do with verbal language, nonverbal features include hand gestures, facial expressions, head and body movements, as well as gaze directions (Rohlfing, 2019). Prosodic features comprise intonation contours, pitch, and stress, along with other phonetic aspects such as pitch range and register, levels of loudness, pauses, duration, and articulatory settings (Couper-Kuhlen, 2011). All these features can be used as multimodal resources for the co-construction of shared meaning and understanding in an ongoing conversational interaction (Lyra, 2010; Miller, 2019).

In the following, I shall focus on prosody and co-speech gestures as two resources that assume functions demonstrably supporting shared understanding and thus the transfer of knowledge. Research findings thus offer interesting insights for sXAI systems to adapt explanations better to the accumulating understanding of the EEs as the explanatory interaction unfolds.

Prosody refers to elements of spoken language such as intonation, stress, rhythm, and volume that are linked to units such as syllables, words, and utterances. Stress can be placed on words or sentences, emphasizing individual pieces of information but also potentially changing their meaning. Intonation contours, tempo, and pauses have been found to be important resources for breaking longer stretches of speech into smaller packages to facilitate the planning and processing of spoken language. Prosody can create boundaries as well as discontinuities between units, thereby contributing to local and global coherence (Barth-Weingarten, 2016). Conversely, a series of adjacent turns or utterances can be tied together prosodically—for example, by rushing through from one unit to the next, thereby establishing the so-called abrupt joints (Local & Walker, 2004), by using recurrent rhythmic patterns (Selting & Kern, 2009) or recurrent intonation contours (Selting, 2007). Prosodic cohesion is thus achieved by establishing connections to previous turns through either contrast or repetition. Prosody also functions as a device to organize the interaction by making different response activities relevant (Barth-Weingarten, 2009). In game explanations, even children EEs have been found to use different intonation contours systematically to construct multi-unit turns and prompt different response activities (Kern, 2007). Depending on the final intonation contour (rising to mid, high rising, or falling to mid), EEs either do not respond at all, produce continuers such as "hm" as minimal responses, or signal understanding more explicitly. For example, by a change-of-state token such as "oh" (Heritage, 1985; Local, 1996).

Co-speech hand gestures are spontaneous hand and arm movements that occur during speech. They are commonly divided into pointing, beat, and iconic/representational gestures (McNeill, 1992; Kita et al., 2017) (see Chap. 19 for a more detailed classification). Co-speech hand gestures bear significant functions with regard to knowledge sharing for establishing common ground and information processing (Holler et al., 2011; Holler & Bavelas, 2017; Nathan & Alibali, 2011). Whereas pointing gestures play an important role in explanatory interactions to make objects or material of the environment relevant to the participants by directing their attention to them (Goodwin, 2013), iconic/representational gestures have semantic content that contributes to the verbally constituted meaning by reinforcing information or adding to it (Iverson & Goldin-Meadow, 2005). However, gesture and language rarely express exactly the same meaning (Cooperrider & Goldin-Meadow, 2017), even though they are deeply intertwined. This intertwinement is shown in particular by their temporal alignment: iconic gestures are systematically produced milliseconds before the corresponding lexical items (Mondada, 2018). Gestures might add extra information not coded in the verbal language by expressing a particular perspective (observer or character viewpoint, cf. Parrill, 2010) or spatial orientation (Cooperrider & Goldin-Meadow, 2017) or by depicting additional information on objects or actions during a narrative (Beattie & Shovelton, 2005). With regard to explanatory interactions, aspects of the verbal explanandum might be depicted through gesture (Koschmann & LeBaron, 2002; Alibali & Nathan, 2012), for example, in game explanations, hand gestures depicting parts of the material, such as the board, figures, or dices, may be used to enrich the verbal description of game material (Lohmer et al., 2023).

Like prosody, co-speech gestures can also contribute to the establishment of coherence—that is, they indicate semantic and logical relations between elements of a text or discourse. In the case of gestures, this is done mostly by repetition. Gestures contribute to the achievement of coherence, when they are produced repeatedly across units of talk by a single speaker or across speakers (Flood, 2021; Levy & McNeill, 2013; Nathan & Alibali, 2011). Participants repeat gestures produced by others to build on them and to further develop understanding of the matter at hand (Koschmann & LeBaron, 2002; Arnold, 2012)—for example, when discussing and exploring mathematical ideas (Walkington et al., 2019; Alibali & Nathan, 2012) or explaining procedures in a bike repair shop (Arnold, 2012). Gestures can thus establish semantic links across conversational interactions (Koschmann & LeBaron, 2002, 271), even over several consecutive conversations held over a longer stretch of time. This shows clearly that even though gestural resemblance of objects or actions surely provides referential meaning, a co-speech gesture's meaning thus does not reside in the gesture alone but also in its relationship to the preceding and following forms of visible and audible interaction (Koschmann & LeBaron, 2002). In the context of teaching and learning interactions, gestures are not only useful resources for the ER; they also provide a window into the EE's understanding of the matter. For example, Gerofsky (2010) suggested how the whole body is involved when learning new mathematical concepts. In an experiment, students were asked to present a graph through gestures. Those students who were found to have more difficulties with the mathematical concepts expressed in the graphs used gestures with an observer viewpoint (OVP), whereas more advanced students used gestures with a character viewpoint. In a somewhat broader approach to embodied resources, Hindmarsh et al. (2011) demonstrated how dentist instructors use students' bodily conduct to assess their understanding of the matter at hand. They do not only rely on verbal claims of understanding alone but also check continuously whether a student has the correct posture for visual engagement with a descriptor (e.g., a tooth).

What is also interesting from an interactional perspective is that speakers have also been found to adapt their gestures to the informational needs of their recipients in several ways. They produce larger and clearer gestures when they want to emphasize new information (Gerwing & Bavelas, 2004) and visually more prominent iconic gestures after clarification requests (Holler & Wilkin, 2009) or when they believed co-participants will cooperate rather than compete with them in a later game (Hostetter et al., 2011). The latter result was interpreted as a reflection of speakers' wishes to bring across information to their recipient clearly and unambiguously (ibid.). Conversely, participants might reduce some of their gestures' properties when understanding is increasingly achieved (Holler et al., 2011).

Research in the field of human–robot interaction suggests that the use of iconic gestures by conversational agents, also in combination with other multimodal resources, improves content retrieval in humans (Freigang et al., 2017). This corresponds to findings from human-to-human interactions that co-speech gestural input enhances language acquisition because of its positive effects on long-term memory (Rohlfing, 2019, for an overview). Recent research also indicates that humans recognize iconic gestures produced by humanoid robots almost as well as gestures produced by humans (Bremmer & Leonards, 2016). However, recognition problems arise when hand trajectories – a primary feature of certain iconic gestures – cannot be perceived correctly (Bremmer & Leonards, 2016). Humans are also able to integrate robot-produced speech and gesture: experiments show that humans use multimodal communication, that is, gesture and speech, to disambiguate possible meanings of either of the two (Bremmer & Leonards, 2016). Moreover, utterances with co-speech gestures are responded to more quickly than speech-only utterances, providing evidence that speech–gesture combinations support understanding (Holler et al., 2018; Kelly et al., 2010).

Finally, multimodal signals can be combined to bundles and often co-occur as gestalt-like configurations. Such configurations can facilitate content processing and thus understanding (Holler & Levinson, 2019). If synchronized in time, combined prosody and co-speech gestures emphasize semantic information. Prosodic stress functions as a means to highlight lexical items and mark them as the information focus of an utterance. It tends to be aligned with gestural peaks – the so-called strokes – that further contribute to highlighting the information (Rohrer et al., 2023). With regard to timing, gestures have been found to precede lexical items with pitch accents, even if less than with prosodically unmarked lexical items (Wagner et al., 2014) (see also Chap. 22). The synchronization of lexical, prosodic, and gestural means results in the highlighting of important information that can support better intelligibility of an explanation.

In sum, research on human–human and human–robot interaction suggests that multimodal behavior can make a significant contribution to the transmission of knowledge and foster understanding in explanatory interactions.

23.4 Operationalization of Global Structure and Multimodal Behavior

When designing sXAI systems, attention should be paid to the fact that explanations have a *co-constructed, that is, mutually accomplished, global structure*. EEs also contribute to this structure by supporting an adaption of the explanations' extent and depth to their own goals (Rohlfing et al., 2021). The organizational 'jobs" described above – (1) establishing topical relevance; (2) constituting an explanandum; (3) explicating procedural, conceptual, and/or causal relations; (4) closing; and (5) transition back to turn-by-turn talk—map the structure of an explanatory interaction and therefore operationalize its progression. The structure which is a social fact for the dialog partners provides a valuable tool for pre-structuring an explanatory interaction within a sXAI system. Each of the jobs identifies a task that has to be completed jointly before the next job can start.

Highlighting the fact that all jobs have to be accomplished through co-construction reveals that identifying their beginnings and endings becomes an important task for a sXAI system. Proper identification will help to adapt the explanation better to the users' situated goal and context conditions. Especially the transition from job 2 to job 3 comes into view here as well as job 4, the closing of the explanation. The joint determination of the explanandum is highly likely to be a prerequisite for appropriate explanations, although this has yet to be confirmed by empirical research. Equally, only when the EEs acknowledge their understanding should the explanation come to an end and transition to Job (4) should be accomplished.

With regard to *multimodality*, two aspects of the extensive research in this field could be utilized for sXAI systems. The first is the well-described function of prosody to break larger chunks of speech into smaller parts while simultaneously establishing coherence. In particular, final intonation contours function as a prosodic binding and separating device; they could also be used to prompt response activities by users that indicate their level of understanding (Axelsson et al., 2022).

Second, iconic co-speech gestures can be used by conversational agents to highlight important or new information and to deliberately either reinforce or add to aspects of the verbal meaning. Iconic gestures related to the explanandum could also provide important scaffolding devices (Booshehri et al., 2024) when repeated throughout the explanation. Gestures produced by the EE could help a system to monitor the EE's understanding better, because they might provide vital information about their conceptualization of the explanandum, as it emerges in the process of the explanatory interaction.

23.5 How Does This Chapter Inspire Further Directions of XAI?

The global structure of explanatory interactions can serve as the basis of a heuristic that can be used to capture the local functions of multimodal behavior context sensitively and thus more precisely. Further insights into the global structure of explanatory interactions and the use of multimodal behaviors in the different jobs may thus provide a solid ground for the development of future, more social, and thus more adaptive XAI systems. Such systems have the potential to be better adapted to the habits and needs of EEs because they are more sensitive toward the progression of the explanatory interaction—that is, the jobs that have to be accomplished as the interaction progresses. Further research is required on how human beings transit from one job to the next—that is, how they signal to each other when one job is indeed completed. Here, multimodal behavior may play a crucial role in establishing either continuity or discontinuity with the previous or following *job*. Identifying transition points between jobs by studying the prosodic and gestural means that are used to help organize these transitions could thus be a focus in future sXAI-related research. Furthermore, only little is known so far about how job (2) (*negotiating the explanandum*) is accomplished and how it effects the following explanation (job 3). XAI systems will become better tailored to the users' needs in terms of the comprehensiveness, extent, and depth of the subsequent explanation when they are able to take their part in this co-construction.

Finally, further research is needed to model regularly occurring co-speech iconic hand gestures relating to the explanandum and their co-occurrence with prosodic stress for a better understanding of the function of these resources for processes of transmitting and understanding new knowledge. How and when iconic gestures are reproduced during an explanatory interaction will also help us to gain more insight into processes of knowledge transfer. Multimodal cues displayed by the explainee provide a system with important input about how their understanding progresses (Booshehri et al., 2024). More research on the (repetitive) use of multimodal resources is important to gain a better understanding of explanatory interactions and thus lay grounds for a better adaptability of XAI systems.

23.6 Rapid Access

Explanatory interactions feature a stable global structure made of five consecutive organizational *jobs* that both explainer and explainee accomplish together. The global structure of explanatory interactions can serve as a heuristic, with the help of which the local functions of multimodal behavior can be described context-sensitively and thus more precisely.

In human–human explanatory interactions, multimodal resources can support the intelligibility of the explanation. Prosody and hand gestures are two multimodal tools that have important functions for structuring speech and conveying content. Prosody refers to elements of spoken language such as intonation, stress, rhythm, and volume that are linked to units such as syllables, words, and utterance. Stress can be placed on words or sentences, emphasizing individual pieces of information but also potentially changing their meaning. Intonation contours, tempo, and pauses have been found to be important resources for breaking longer stretches of speech into smaller packages to facilitate the planning and processing of spoken language. Prosody, especially intonation, subdivides larger speech packages into smaller units and can also establish coherence within and between units. Different intonation contours together with other phonetic features block or enable response activities (Barth-Weingarten, 2009) or request different response activities, such as minimal feedback or change-of-state tokens (Kern, 2007).

Co-speech hand gestures are spontaneous hand and arm movements that occur during speech and are usually synchronized with it. They are commonly divided into pointing, beat, and iconic/representational gestures (McNeill, 1992; Kita et al., 2017). Co-speech hand gestures accompany speech and contribute to the meaning conveyed by words. They contribute to establishing common ground between participants in an ongoing conversation, and they support information processing (Holler et al., 2011; Holler & Bavelas, 2017). Iconic (or representational) hand gestures depict aspects of concrete objects or events, thereby either reinforcing verbally transmitted content or adding to it (Iverson & Goldin-Meadow, 2005). In explanations, they might depict aspects of the explanandum (Koschmann & LeBaron, 2002; Alibali & Nathan, 2012). Iconic gestures can also establish coherence across units of talk, or even across speakers, especially in learning situations (Arnold, 2012; Flood, 2021; Koschmann & LeBaron, 2002; Nathan & Alibali, 2011).

In human–human interactions, speakers adapt their gestures to the informational needs of their recipients by producing larger and clearer gestures when they want to emphasize new information (Gerwing & Bavelas, 2004), when proceeding after clarification requests (Holler & Wilkin, 2009), or when they believed co-participants will cooperate rather than compete with them in a later game (Hostetter et al., 2011). In human–robot interaction, iconic gestures produced by robots can improve humans' content recall (Freigang et al., 2017) and help humans to disambiguate sentence meaning (Bremner &Leonards, 2016).

Prosody and different types of gestures work together as highlighting devices to emphasize new or important information. Especially in teaching and learning environments, highlighting information can support knowledge transfer and understanding in human–human interaction (Goodwin, 2013, 2018). The synchronization of lexical, prosodic, and gestural means results in the highlighting of important information.

Research to date therefore suggests that if an XAI/robotic agent were to make use of multimodal behavior, it would be more successful in transmitting relevant knowledge through an explanation. Furthermore, taking into account the global structure with its different jobs would make it possible to use prosodic resources to organize the transitions between jobs, to highlight relevant information at the right place during the explanation, and to use gestures in a more context-sensitive and precise way. All of these are likely to facilitate understanding on the side of the explainee. Even though much more research is needed, the aim is to use the results to develop more adaptive systems that are globally structured and include multimodal signals for better knowledge transfer and understanding.

Acknowledgments This work was funded by the Deutsche Forschungsgemeinschaft (DFG, German Research Foundation): TRR 318/1 2021 – 438445824

References

Alibali, M. W., & Nathan, M. J. (2012). Embodiment in mathematics teaching and learning: Evidence from learners' and teachers' gestures. *Journal of the Learning Sciences, 21*(2), 247–286. https://doi.org/10.1080/10508406.2011.611446

Arnold, L. (2012). Dialogic embodied action: Using gesture to organize sequence and participation in instructional interaction. *Research on Language and Social Interaction, 45*(3), 269–296. https://doi.org/10.1080/08351813.2012.699256

Axelsson, A., Buschmeier, H., & Skantze, G. (2022). Modeling feedback in interaction with conversational agents—a review. *Frontiers in Computer Science, 4*, 744574. https://doi.org/10.3389/fcomp.2022.744574

Barth-Weingarten, D. (2009). When to say something—some observations on prosodic-phonetic cues to the placement and types of responses in multi-unit turns. *Where prosody meets pragmatics* (pp. 143–181). Brill. https://doi.org/10.1163/9789004253223_008

Barth-Weingarten, D. (2016). *Cesuras in talk-in-interaction*. Benjamins. https://doi.org/10.1075/slsi.29

Beattie, G., & Shovelton, H. (2005). Why the spontaneous images created by the hands during talk can help make TV advertisements more effective. *British Journal of Psychology, 96*(1), 21–37. https://doi.org/10.1348/000712605X103500

Booshehri, M., Buschmeier, H., Cimiano, P., Kopp, S., Kornowicz, J., Lammert, O., Matarese, M., Mindlin, D., Robrecht, A. S., Vollmer, A.-L. and Wagner, P., & Wrede, B. (2024). Towards a computational architecture for co-constructive explainable systems. In *Proceedings of the 2024 Workshop on Explainability Engineering* (pp. 20–25). Association for Computing Machinery. https://doi.org/10.1145/3648505.3648509

Bremmer, P., & Leonards, U. (2016). Iconic gestures for robot avatars, recognition and integration with speech. *Frontiers in Psychology, 7*, 183. https://doi.org/10.3389/fpsyg.2016.00183

Bremner, P., & Leonards, U. (2016). Iconic gestures for robot avatars, recognition and integration with speech. *Frontiers in Psychology, 7*, 183. https://doi.org/10.3389/fpsyg.2016.00183

Cook, S. W., Yip, T. K., & Goldin-Meadow, S. (2012). Gestures, but not meaningless movements, lighten working memory load when explaining math. *Language and Cognitive Processes, 27*(4), 594–610. https://doi.org/10.1080/01690965.2011.567074

Cooperrider, K., & Goldin-Meadow, S. (2017). Gesture, language, and cognition. In B. Dancygier (Ed.), *The Cambridge handbook of cognitive linguistics* (pp. 118–134). Cambridge University Press. https://doi.org/10.1017/9781316339732.009

Couper-Kuhlen, E. (2011). Pragmatics and prosody: Prosody as social action. In W. Bublitz & N. R. Norrick (Eds.), *Foundations of pragmatics* (pp. 491–510). De Gruyter Mouton. https://doi.org/10.1515/9783110214260.491

Dazeley, R., Vamplew, P., Foale, C., Young, C., Aryal, S., & Cruz, F. (2021). Levels of explainable artificial intelligence for human-aligned conversational explanations. *Artificial Intelligence, 299*, 103525. https://doi.org/10.1016/j.artint.2021.103525

Fisher, J. B., Lohmer, V., Kern, F., Barthlen, W., Gaus, S., & Rohlfing, K. J. (2022). Exploring monological and dialogical phases in naturally occurring explanations. *KI – Künstliche Intelligenz, 36*(3), 317–326. https://doi.org/10.1007/s13218-022-00787-1

Flood, V. J. (2021). The secret multimodal life of IREs: Looking more closely at representational gestures in a familiar questioning sequence. *Linguistics and Education, 63*, 100913. https://doi.org/10.1016/j.linged.2021.100913

Freigang, F., Klett, S., & Kopp, S. (2017). Pragmatic multimodality: Effects of nonverbal cues of focus and certainty in a virtual human. In *Intelligent virtual agents* (pp. 142–155). Springer. https://doi.org/10.1007/978-3-319-67401-8_16

Gerofsky, S. (2010). Mathematical learning and gesture: Character viewpoint and observer viewpoint in students' gestured graphs of functions. *Gesture, 10*(2–3), 321–343. https://doi.org/10.1075/gest.10.2-3.10ger

Gerwing, J., & Bavelas, J. (2004). Linguistic influences on gesture's form. *Gesture, 4*(2), 157–195. https://doi.org/10.1075/gest.4.2.04ger

Goldin-Meadow, S., Nusbaum, H., Kelly, S. D., & Wagner, S. (2001). Explaining math: Gesturing lightens the load. In *Psychological Science, 12*(6), 516–522. https://doi.org/10.1111/1467-9280.00395

Goodwin, C. (2013). The co-operative, transformative organization of human action and knowledge. *Journal of Pragmatics, 46*(1), 8–23. https://doi.org/10.1016/j.pragma.2012.09.003

Goodwin, C. (2018). *Co-operative action*. Cambridge University Press. https://doi.org/10.1017/9781139016735

Hempel, C. G., & Oppenheim, P. (1948). Studies in the logic of explanation. *Philosophy of Science, 15*(2), 135–175.

Heritage, J. (1985). A change-of-state token and aspects of its sequential placement. In J. M. Atkinson (Ed.), *Structures of social action* (pp. 299–345). Cambridge University Press.

Hindmarsh, J., Reynolds, P., & Dunne, S. (2011). Exhibiting understanding: The body in apprenticeship. *Journal of Pragmatics, 43*(2), 489–503. https://doi.org/10.1016/j.pragma.2009.09.008

Holler, J., & Bavelas, J. (2017). Multi-modal communication of common ground: A review of social functions. In R. B. Church, M. W. Alibali & S. D. Kelly (Eds.), *How the hands function in speaking, thinking and communicating* (pp. 213–240). Benjamins. https://doi.org/10.1075/gs.7.11hol

Holler, J., Kendrick, K. H., & Levinson, S. C. (2018). Processing language in face-to-face conversation: Questions with gestures get faster responses. *Psychonomic Bulletin & Review, 25*(5), 1900–1908. https://doi.org/10.3758/s13423-017-1363-z

Holler, J., & Levinson, S. C. (2019). Multimodal language processing in human communication. *Trends in Cognitive Sciences, 23*(8), 639–652. https://doi.org/10.1016/j.tics.2019.05.006

Holler, J., Tutton, M., & Wilkin, K. (2011). Co-speech gestures in the process of meaning coordination. In *Proceedings of the 2nd GESPIN – Gesture & Speech in Interaction Conference*.

Holler, J., & Wilkin, K. (2009). Communicating common ground: How mutually shared knowledge influences speech and gesture in a narrative task. *Language and Cognitive Processes, 24*(2), 267–289. https://doi.org/10.1080/01690960802095545

Hostetter, A. B., Alibali, M. W., & Schrager, S. M. (2011). If you don't already know, I'm certainly not going to show you!: Motivation to communicate affects gesture production. In G. Stam & M. Ishino (Eds.), *The interdisciplinary nature of gesture* (pp. 61–74). Benjamins. https://doi.org/10.1075/gs.4.06hos

Iverson, J. M., & Goldin-Meadow, S. (2005). Gesture paves the way for language development. *Psychological Science, 16*(5), 367–371. https://doi.org/10.1111/j.0956-7976.2005.01542.x

Kelly, S. D., Özyürek, A., & Maris, E. (2010). Two sides of the same coin: Speech and gesture mutually interact to enhance comprehension. *Psychological Science, 21*(2), 260–267. https://doi.org/10.1177/0956797609357327

Keppler, A., & Luckmann, T. (1991). 'Teaching': Conversational transmission of knowledge. In I. S. Markov (Ed.), *Asymmetries in dialogue* (pp. 143–165). Harvester Wheatsheaf.

Kern, F. (2007). Prosody as a resource in children's game explanations: Some aspects of turn construction and recipiency. *Journal of Pragmatics, 39*(1), 111–133. https://doi.org/10.1016/j.pragma.2005.01.017

Kern, F. (2020). Interactional and multimodal resources in children's game explanations. *Research on Children and Social Interaction, 4*(1), 7–27. https://doi.org/10.1558/rcsi.12419

Kita, S., Alibali, M. W., & Chu, M. (2017). How do gestures influence thinking and speaking? The gesture-for-conceptualization hypothesis. *Psychological Review, 124*(3), 245–266. https://doi.org/10.1037/rev0000059

Koschmann, T., & LeBaron, C. (2002). Learner articulation as interactional achievement: Studying the conversation of gesture. *Cognition and Instruction, 20*(2), 249–282. https://doi.org/10.1207/S1532690XCI2002_4

Koschmann, T., & Zemel, A. (2009). Optical pulsars and black arrows: Discoveries as occasioned productions. *Journal of the Learning Sciences, 18*(2), 200–246. https://doi.org/10.1080/10508400902797966

Levy, E. T., & McNeill, D. (2013). Narrative development as symbol formation: Gestures, imagery and the emergence of cohesion. *Culture & Psychology, 19*(4), 548–569. https://doi.org/10.1177/1354067X13500328

Local, J. (1996). Conversational phonetics: Some aspects of news receipts in everyday talk. In E. Couper-Kuhlen & M. Selting (Eds.), *Prosody in conversation: Interactional studies* (pp. 177–230). Cambridge University Press. https://doi.org/10.1017/CBO9780511597862.007

Local, J., & Walker, G. (2004). Abrupt-joins as a resource for the production of multi-unit, multi-action turns. *Journal of Pragmatics, 36*(8), 1375–1403. https://doi.org/10.1016/j.pragma.2004.04.006

Lohmer, V., Terfloth, L., & Kern, F. (2023). Explaining the technical artifact Quarto!: How gestures are used in everyday explanations. In *International Multimodal Communication Symposium (MMSYM)* (pp. 133–134). MMSYM.

Lyra, M. C. D. P. (2010). On interaction analysis and dialogical perspective: Emergent patterns of order and relational agency. *Integrative Psychological & Behavioral Science, 44*(3), 273–280. https://doi.org/10.1007/s12124-010-9130-y

McNeill, D. (1992). *Hand and mind: What gestures reveal about thought*. University of Chicago Press.

Miller, T. (2019). Explanation in artificial intelligence: Insights from the social sciences. *Artificial Intelligence, 267*, 1–38. https://doi.org/10.1016/j.artint.2018.07.007

Mondada, L. (2011). Understanding as an embodied, situated and sequential achievement in interaction. *Journal of Pragmatics, 43*(2), 542–552. https://doi.org/10.1016/j.pragma.2010.08.019

Mondada, L. (2018). Multiple temporalities of language and body in interaction: Challenges for transcribing multimodality. *Research on Language and Social Interaction, 51*(1), 85–106. https://doi.org/10.1080/08351813.2018.1413878

Morek, M. (2012). *Kinder erklären. Interaktionen in Familie und Unterricht im Vergleich*. Stauffenburg.

Nathan, M. J., & Alibali, M. W. (2011). How gesture use enables intersubjectivity in the classroom. In G. Stam & M. Shino (Eds.), *Integrating gestures: The interdisciplinary nature of gesture* (pp. 257–266). Benjamins. https://doi.org/10.1075/gs.4.23nat

Parrill, F. (2010). Viewpoint in speech–gesture integration: Linguistic structure, discourse structure, and event structure. *Language and Cognitive Processes, 25*(5), 650–668. https://doi.org/10.1080/01690960903424248

Quasthoff, U., Heller, V., & Morek, M. (2017). On the sequential organization and genre-orientation of discourse units in interaction: An analytic framework. *Discourse Studies, 19*(1), 84–110. https://doi.org/10.1177/1461445616683596

Rohlfing, K. J. (2019). Language learning from the use of gestures. In *International handbook of language acquisition* (pp. 213–233). Routledge.

Rohlfing, K. J., Cimiano, P., Scharlau, I., Matzner, T., Buhl, H., Buschmeier, H., Grimminger, A., Hammer, B., Häb-Umbach, R., Horwath, I., Hüllermeier, E., Kern, F., Kopp, S., Thommes, K., Ngonga Ngomo, A.-C., Schulte, C., Wachsmuth, H., Wagner, P., & Wrede, B (2021). Explanation as a social practice: Toward a conceptual framework for the social design of AI systems. *IEEE Transactions on Cognitive and Developmental Systems, 13*(3), 717–728. https://doi.org/10.1109/TCDS.2020.3044366

Rohrer, P. L., Delais-Roussarie, E., & Prieto, P. (2023). Visualizing prosodic structure: Manual gestures as highlighters of prosodic heads and edges in English academic discourses. *Lingua, 293*, 103583. https://doi.org/10.1016/j.lingua.2023.103583

Schegloff, E. A., & Sacks, H (1973). Opening up closings. *Semiotica, 8*(4), 289–327. https://doi.org/10.1515/semi.1973.8.4.289

Selting, M. (2007). Lists as embedded structures and the prosody of list construction as an interactional resource. *Journal of Pragmatics, 39*(3), 483–526. https://doi.org/10.1016/j.pragma.2006.07.008

Selting, M., & Kern, F. (2009). On some syntactic and prosodic structures of Turkish German in talk-in-interaction. *Journal of Pragmatics, 41*(12), 2496–2514. https://doi.org/10.1016/j.pragma.2009.05.018

Wagner, P., Malisz, Z., & Kopp, S. (2014). Gesture and speech in interaction: An overview. *Speech Communication, 57*, 209–232. https://doi.org/10.1016/j.specom.2013.09.008

Walkington, C., Chelule, G., Woods, D., & Nathan, M. J. (2019). Collaborative gesture as a case of extended mathematical cognition. *The Journal of Mathematical Behavior, 55*, 100683. https://doi.org/10.1016/j.jmathb.2018.12.002

Weld, D. S., & Bansal, G. (2018). *The challenge of crafting intelligible intelligence*. https://doi.org/10.48550/arXiv.1803.04263

Zemel, A., & Koschmann, T. (2011). Pursuing a question: Reinitiating IRE sequences as a method of instruction. *Journal of Pragmatics, 43*(2), 475–488. https://doi.org/10.1016/j.pragma.2010.08.022

Open Access This chapter is licensed under the terms of the Creative Commons Attribution 4.0 International License (http://creativecommons.org/licenses/by/4.0/), which permits use, sharing, adaptation, distribution and reproduction in any medium or format, as long as you give appropriate credit to the original author(s) and the source, provide a link to the Creative Commons license and indicate if changes were made.

The images or other third party material in this chapter are included in the chapter's Creative Commons license, unless indicated otherwise in a credit line to the material. If material is not included in the chapter's Creative Commons license and your intended use is not permitted by statutory regulation or exceeds the permitted use, you will need to obtain permission directly from the copyright holder.

Chapter 24
Multimodality in Agents

Rachele Carli ⓘ, Sukriti Bhattacharya ⓘ, Igor Tchappi ⓘ, Kary Främling ⓘ, and Amro Najjar ⓘ

Abstract This chapter examines multimodality in the context of explaining AI agent behavior and reasoning. Both embodied (like robots) and unembodied (like Alexa, including text-based systems) AI systems require effective explanatory mechanisms to help users understand their functions and decisions. The analysis reveals striking similarities between design elements used for encouraging user collaboration with AI systems and those employed in creating multimodal explanations. Despite the considerable advantages offered by multimodality-based sXAI, these design choices may produce unintended negative effects on users receiving the explanations. To address this challenge, the chapter draws on philosophical research regarding emotion co-construction. By integrating methodological approaches and theoretical insights from the philosophy of science with current sXAI studies, designers can create explanations that emerge collaboratively between the explainer and explainee. Such explanations recognize how emotions influence both how humans think and how they make decisions. The path toward more effective multimodal explanations requires recognizing how users' emotional responses shape their understanding of AI systems. Through careful design considerations, explanatory

---

R. Carli (✉)
Responsible AI group, Umeå University, Umeå, Sweden

Sweden Affiliated to the AI RoboLab, University of Luxembourg, Esch-sur-Alzette, Luxembourg
e-mail: rachele.carli@umu.se

S. Bhattacharya · A. Najjar
Trustworthy AI, Data and Software (HANDS) Unit, Luxembourg Institute of Science and Technology, Esch-sur-Alzette, Luxembourg
e-mail: sukriti.bhattacharya@list.lu; amro.najjar@list.lu

I. Tchappi
FINATRAX, SnT, University of Luxembourg, Esch-sur-Alzette, Luxembourg
e-mail: igor.tchappi@uni.lu

K. Främling
Department of Computing Science, Umeå University, Umeå, Sweden

Department of Industrial Engineering and Management, Aalto University, Espoo, Finland
e-mail: kary.framling@umu.se

© The Author(s) 2026
K. J. Rohlfing et al. (eds.), *Social Explainable AI*,
https://doi.org/10.1007/978-981-96-5290-7_24

systems can acknowledge this emotional dimension while still delivering technically accurate information about AI behavior.

24.1 How Does This Chapter Relate to XAI?

Multimodality forms a natural component of explanations between individuals. When people explain concepts to each other, they typically employ speech alongside gestures, movements, and various other tools to convey their message effectively (see Chap. 2.5). Similarly, when artificial intelligent agents serve as explainers, their explanations also utilize multiple modalities. This chapter examines three primary categories of agents: physical embodied agents (like robots), virtual embodied agents (such as avatars), and virtual unembodied agents (including text-based systems).

Outlining the structural differences between these agent types and describing how these differences affect their multimodal explanations, the chapter reveals several problematic aspects of current XAI research. In particular, the chapter highlights how current multimodal explanation techniques may create challenges in everyday interactions due to specific aspects of human communication. Research by Bickmore and Cassell (Bickmore & Cassell, 2005; Bickmore & Picard, 2005) demonstrates that nonverbal communication elements often operate through subconscious mechanisms strongly tied to emotional states. According to Picard's foundational work on affective computing (Picard, 2000), these emotional components prove difficult to fully capture within interaction protocols that merely organize sequences of actions. The author argues that for computers to be truly intelligent and interact naturally with humans, they must be able to recognize, understand, and even express emotions. Despite this complexity, contemporary approaches to multimodal XAI research (Bernardo & Seva, 2023, 2022; Ma, 2024; Kolomaznik et al., 2024; Glickman & Sharot, 2025; Yin et al., 2024) tend to underestimate the importance of these unconscious emotional mechanisms.

This chapter contributes to ongoing XAI research by identifying these underinvestigated aspects. It advocates for greater integration with research at the intersection of social sciences and human-agent interaction, particularly studies exploring *artificial empathy* as defined by Paiva et al. (Paiva et al., 2017, 2021, 2018)—the capacity for AI systems to recognize, understand, and appropriately respond to human emotions during explanatory interactions.

24.2 Embodied Agents

The expression "embodied AI systems" identifies those systems that are endowed with a body, which allows them to occupy a physical space within the human-centric environment in which they are embedded (Wallkötter et al., 2021). Consequently,

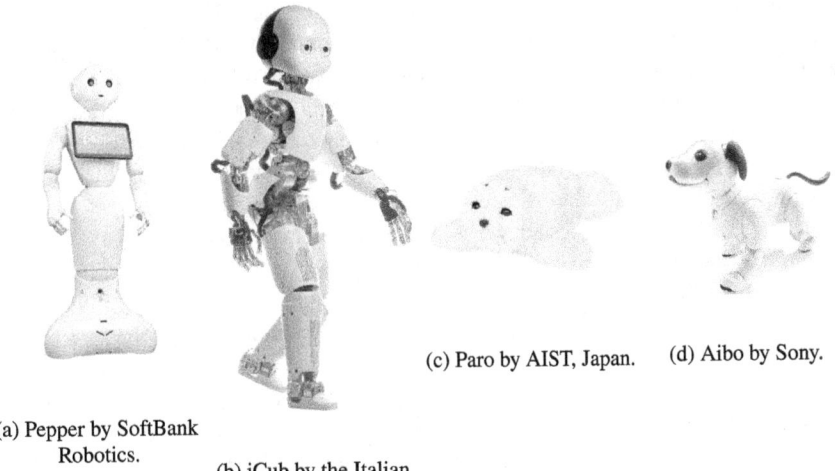

Fig. 24.1 Examples of embodied AI systems: (**a**) Pepper, (**b**) iCub, (**c**) Paro, and (**d**) Aibo. These robots represent different forms of embodiment, from humanoid (Pepper, iCub) to zoomorphic (Paro, Aibo), influencing their interaction styles and applications

these agents are also capable of acting physically in the space, modifying it, influencing it, or collaborating with users for these purposes. This is irrespective of the fact that the corporeality of such agents is realized in a form reminiscent of other human beings or animals. To aid readers who may not be familiar with specific robots mentioned in this discussion, Fig. 24.1 presents four representative examples: Pepper,[1] iCub,[2] Paro,[3] and Aibo.[4] Each of these robots exhibits distinct forms of embodiment and interaction styles, highlighting the diversity within embodied AI systems.

Nevertheless, the existence of a corporal dimension does not inherently constitute a unifying feature of these agents. Indeed, the specific attributes that the physical dimension exhibits are pivotal in characterizing not only the AI system under examination but also its interactive potential and, consequently, the spectrum of sXAI with which it is or could be capable to interact.

One might consider, for instance, the category of humanoid or semi-humanoid social robots. The archetypal and most representative example is Pepper, which is capable of navigating space, self-propelled upper limbs, a round head, and large eyes. These characteristics render it one of the most frequently utilized robots to represent its category to the general public (Sarkadi, 2016). Indeed, the use of

---

[1] https://aldebaran.com/en/pepper/.

[2] https://robotsguide.com/robots/icub/.

[3] http://www.parorobots.com/.

[4] https://us.aibo.com/.

a self-propelled, round head, eyes capable of lighting up in conjunction with the emulation of certain emotional states or in correspondence with the expression of certain concepts, light colors, and language that evokes friendship and confidence are the most commonly used design strategies to make social robots pleasant and appealing to users (Pandey & Alami, 2013; Ghiță et al., 2020). Pepper is equipped with a screen through which it can display videos or images, as well as the capacity to express itself verbally and to accompany its statements with body gestures that reinforce the content conveyed verbally or that help emulate the possession of humanlike feelings, such as hugs or caresses.

Another example is the iCub robot, which is capable of emulating blushing in response to compliments, is equipped with articulated and self-propelled joints that are reminiscent of those found in humans, and has a tone of voice reminiscent of a child (Sarkadi, 2016). On occasion, robots designed for companionship or therapeutic purposes may exhibit zoomorphic characteristics, as exemplified by Paro and Aibo. In the former case, the advantage is that the behavior of a baby seal is not commonly observed, as it is not commonly a pet. Consequently, users' expectations of the social skills that the robot is capable of deploying are rather limited. This has the effect of delaying or preventing a loss of confidence or interest in the AI system (Šabanović & Chang, 2016; Bradwell et al., 2021). In contrast, Aibo is a robotic dog that strives to emulate the interactive dynamics of a real dog to the greatest extent possible. In this instance, the deliberately artificial physicality of the agent serves to prevent the creation of a genuine illusion of interaction with a living entity, thereby counterbalancing the expectations of nonspecialist users (Kubo, 2010).

Underlining the fact that social robots are not necessarily a homogeneous class of devices is the fact that Amazon Alexa also falls into this category. In this context, the social interactive abilities of the devices in question are manifested through a focus on communicative capabilities, in terms of structure, design, and content. Furthermore, attention is paid to the type of voice and gender it displays, as well as to the utterance of phrases that allude to the existence of a friendship bond or shared memories (Purington et al., 2017). However, in reality, this is merely a method of data collection and storage (Natale, 2020). Despite occupying a physical space, Alexa is limited in its physical capabilities, akin to a small box that is unable to move or interact in any manner other than audio reproduction.

It follows that contingent on the degree of embodiment and its defining characteristics the explanations offered in response to the actions of a robot must not only vary in terms of their qualitative and procedural aspects in accordance with the specific type of robot in question but must also encompass a range of different elements in order to ensure transparency. They often exhibit awkward movements and may appear more like toys or science fiction characters than practical tools. Additionally, their speech generation and understanding modules frequently produce significant errors, and the lack of a clear menu of actions to be performed next complicates the learning process for users.

24.2.1 Sense of Others: Explanations in Embodied AI Systems

Despite design efforts aimed at promoting acceptance and trust in embodied artificial agents, their technical performance often falls short of expectations (Hoffman, 2019). Current robots remain limited in several ways (Tulli et al., 2019). They often exhibit awkward movements and may appear more like toys or science fiction characters than practical tools. Additionally, their speech generation and understanding modules frequently make significant errors, and the lack of a clear menu of actions to be performed next complicates the learning process for users. These shortcomings can make robots seem distant from everyday human experiences, creating a sense of otherness that instinctively reduces their perceived trustworthiness (Mahdi et al., 2022). This highlights the need for embodied conversational agents to provide comprehensive explanations that cover not only their functioning and tasks but also the entire interaction process, including their sub-actions. For robots capable of moving in and modifying their environment or otherwise exerting influence on it, explanations must address both their actions and intentions (Chao et al., 2010).

One notable example of a multimodal explanation technique is the "inner voice" implemented in the Pepper robot for experiments with human interlocutors (Chella & Pipitone, 2020; Pipitone et al., 2024). This approach programs the robot to verbalize its reasoning process while simultaneously displaying corresponding visual cues through its tablet interface and appropriate body postures, for instance, when explaining a recommendation, Pepper combines spoken explanation with supporting images on its chest-mounted screen while adopting a thoughtful posture. This multimodal approach combines verbal, visual, and physical elements to make the robot's reasoning transparent in a manner that maintains user engagement by avoiding technical jargon or constant interaction interruptions. This enhances the robot's ability to communicate effectively and transparently. This integration of multiple communication modes not only makes the robot's explanations more accessible but also reinforces the humanlike interaction, which is crucial for building trust and facilitating collaboration. This approach aligns with the design goal of evoking humanlike traits, a defining characteristic of the robot (Carli & Calvaresi, 2023).

Overall, embodied AI systems can benefit from explanations of their multimodal behaviors to be transparent in how they interact and communicate (see also Chap. 11).

24.3 Disembodied Agents

The focus on embodied agents can be attributed to the so-called embodiment turn in cognitive science, which has developed since the 1990s (Clark, 1999; Laakso, 2011). This represents the realization that the body plays a fundamental role in cognitive, emotional, and affective processes and that the whole human epistemological experience cannot be reduced to a piece of code (Foglia & Wilson, 2013). Nevertheless, this did not mean the conclusion of research on artificial intelligence systems without a physical form. In fact, while it is true that reducing human brain processes to a mere sequence of computational processes is limiting, the development of machine learning (ML), neural nets, and natural language processing (NLP) techniques has allowed even disembodied AI systems to achieve satisfactory levels of resemblance to human communication and syntax.

In particular, ML and NLP technologies enable virtual agents to learn in the course of interaction, adapting their responses based on context (see Chap. 4 for effects of context), aiming to replicate the structure and nuances of natural language as closely as possible (Sun et al., 2024; Casas et al., 2021). This not only makes the disembodied agents more effective and linear in their communication with the user but also allows them to establish distinctive social roles despite lacking physical embodiment. Unlike embodied agents that rely heavily on physical presence and nonverbal cues to establish social connections, virtual agents must compensate this entirely through linguistic and conversational techniques developing personas, conversation styles, and interaction patterns that create a sense of social presence without physical form (Go & Sundar, 2019; Feine et al., 2019; Skjuve et al., 2021).

The earliest and most prominent example of this phenomenon is the Rogerian psychotherapist chatbot, ELIZA. This pioneering system demonstrated the capacity of humans to form trust and attachment even toward an agent that did not manifest itself to them with anything more than a voice or written text (Natale, 2019). ELIZA achieved this by adopting specific linguistic patterns associated with therapeutic contexts, reflecting statements back to users and asking open-ended questions-social techniques that established a therapeutic relationship without any physical embodiment. More contemporary examples include the multitude of behavioral change systems, comprising disembodied AI agents that facilitate the transformation of entrenched habits in users, such as smoking cessation, dietary modification, and the adoption of a more active lifestyle (Calvaresi et al., 2023). These systems establish coaching relationships through consistent tone, personalized feedback, and conversation history rather than physical presence, creating a distinct form of social bond that relies entirely on linguistic and contextual cues rather than embodied interaction.

In such instances, the absence of expressiveness, corporeality, and action in a shared environment is compensated for by language that is as familiar as possible, relevant, but also persuasive conversation and the use of expressions that evoke feelings of friendship, confidence, and shared memories.

24.3.1 Embodied Virtual Agents and Multimodality

A further development in the field of virtual agents is the creation of what are known as embodied virtual agents. The term is frequently employed as a synonym for 'digital avatars,' although some scholars contend that there are distinctions between the two. Embodied virtual agents represent a synthesis of the strengths inherent to both embodied and disembodied AI systems (Kim et al., 2018). Indeed, they are virtual agents and thus not robots that occupy the same physical space as the individual with whom they interact. Rather, they are visually represented with a digital physicality, able to take on the appearance of humanoid agents, animals, or other recognizable creatures, as well as simple artificial agents with robotic features.

The multimodal nature of embodied virtual agents provides distinct advantages in explanation contexts. Unlike text-only systems, these agents can employ visual signals, animated gestures, facial expressions, and simulated eye contact alongside verbal communication (Thellman et al., 2016). This multimodality, i.e., the integration of multiple communication channels, allows for richer explanations where complex concepts can be described verbally simultaneously while being visually demonstrated, for example, when explaining a medical diagnosis, an embodied virtual agent might point to relevant areas on a displayed medical scan while verbally explaining the significance of specific features. In instances where users can customize and design their own avatars, the multimodal interaction becomes even more nuanced. The visual representation itself becomes a communication channel, with user-selected features influencing how information is perceived. Research shows that explanations delivered by agents whose appearance matches the domain setting (such as a professional-looking avatar for financial advice) are judged as more credible (Nowak & Rauh, 2008). This visual modality works in concert with verbal and gestural modalities, creating a comprehensive communication system where multiple channels reinforce the explanatory content. The customization process also establishes a foundation for trust in subsequent multimodal explanations, as users perceive themselves as having participated in creating their explanatory partner.

24.3.2 *Explainable Disembodied Agents*

Even in the case of disembodied agents, the focus of designers and programmers is on giving them a socially recognized role and making them emulate socially aware skills (Kim et al., 2018). Therefore, claiming that transparency can be achieved just by explaining to the user that they are interacting with an artificial system, whose output is generated by AI, seems reductive. In fact, as presented in Chaps. 19 and 21, ambiguity can arise during the interactions, and the complexity of nonverbal signals need to be considered. Therefore, multimodal XAI is of central importance.

In the case of virtual embodied agents, the same considerations that have been discussed for embodied agents may apply. Even if these systems do not share the same three-dimensional space as the people with whom they actually interact, they are capable of accompanying objective explanations with the movement of body parts or the inclusion of gaze or facial micro-expressions (Gratch et al., 2007).

In the case of agents engaged in purely verbal interaction, it will be necessary for them to provide explanations of their reasoning and the evaluation mechanisms they have applied. This can be achieved by working on the capability they express also during the interaction, focusing on multimodal explanations that target the voice, visual representation of the information, or even the choice of some precise words over others (Weitz et al., 2021). Such design expedients may also have the benefit of helping to convey a sense of familiarity with the user or a sense of professionalism that may support the social role that the system is expected to perform or a broader sense of trustworthiness Främling et al. (2023); Weitz et al. (2021).

Such a level of multimodality may easily be inspired by similar strategies that are also used – more or less consciously – in human-to-human communications and transfer of information (see Chap. 22), for example, the explainer may use a lower tone of voice, the communication may be slowed down, and the words to which one wants the interlocutor to pay more attention may be articulated better Sorokowski et al. (2019); Tsibulya (2019). Sometimes, an attempt is made to engage the explainee in questions that allow them to ascertain an adequate level of comprehension and fix the central topics of the explanandum Seaborn et al. (2021). In the case of predominantly written communication, one may resort to using a different font, boldface, or different colors where permitted.

24.4 Potentials and Risks in Multimodal XAI Implementing Social Cues

In the realm of AI, the principal function of explainable AI (XAI) is to provide users with a practical comprehension of the AI system (Rohlfing et al., 2021). This understanding serves as a foundation for subsequent actions, such as completing sub-tasks, making decisions, or acquiring new skills (Felzmann et al., 2019). However, the completeness of the information provided is not sufficient on its own (Dranove et al., 2003). Access to more data does not necessarily translate into more knowledge (Bawden & Robinson, 2020); therefore, multimodal XAI is essential, as it facilitates a collaborative construction of the explanation, where the explanandum is shaped not only by the explanans but also by the reactions and attributes of the explainee. To clarify, multimodality in the context of XAI refers to the use of multiple communication channels to convey information. This includes speech, gestures, facial expressions, text, and visual aids. The goal is to create a more comprehensive and engaging interaction that leverages the strengths of each mode (Sun et al., 2024; Casas et al., 2021). This approach is particularly effective in overcoming emotional and cognitive barriers, such as potential aversion to the provided explanation or the actual correct and complete processing of the information. The design of the explanandum partly follows the technical expedients used in the design of the system itself, for instance, interactions with an agent that employs anthropomorphic terminology to describe its activities have been shown to engender a desire for continued engagement and a positive emotional response, evoking feelings of empathy and familiarity in the user (Natale, 2019; Calvaresi et al., 2023). This is supported by research in human–robot interaction (HRI) and human-computer interaction (HCI), which highlight the importance of social cues in building trust and rapport (Thellman et al., 2016; Kim et al., 2018).

Social cues are so crucial because the notion of humans as 'social animals' extends beyond their tendency to form communities. It encompasses how humans interpret reality and relationships through the lens of their social nature (Mlodinow, 2012; Epley et al., 2007). The human tendency toward social interpretation extends beyond explicit interaction patterns. Reeves and Nass (1996) and Nass and Moon (2000) documented how humans naturally interpret reality through social frameworks, applying anthropomorphic terminology to natural phenomena and technological artifacts alike. This is evident in the use of anthropomorphic terminology to describe inanimate objects, such as referring to a Roomba vacuum cleaner as 'crying' when it becomes stuck (Natale, 2019). Such tendencies can result in interpreting all actions as driven by intentionality and behaviors as expressions of personality, even when these signals come from artificial agents (Epley et al., 2007). Implicit social cues, such as intonation, facial expressions, and body language, play a central role in the transfer of information. These cues appeal to the human subconscious and elicit the instinct of natural sociality common to all individuals (Lakoff & Wehling, 2016; Phelps, 2006), for example, a robot programmed to respond with a prompt like "Let me think for a moment" when information is requested can maintain user engagement by simulating humanlike thought processes (Chao et al., 2010). This strategy leverages multimodality by combining speech with nonverbal cues, enhancing the overall interaction.

In light of this, the construction of explanation dynamics that considers the entire multimodal human–XAI interaction represents significant progress in XAI research (Miller, 2019; Liao et al., 2020). Nevertheless, the close parallel between explanation design and interaction design – whether in human–robot interaction (HRI) or human–computer interaction (HCI) – introduces potential risks (Eiband et al., 2018). While multimodal XAI aims to enhance transparency and understanding, it can also expose users to potential harm (Burrell, 2016; Ehsan et al., 2021), for instance, if the model employs expedients that target natural human sociality and subconscious cognitive processes, it could induce unintended effects such as excessive complexity, bias amplification, overtrust, and manipulative drifts (Klenk, 2022; Carli, 2022). Few examples are also as follows: research by Bussone et al. (2015) identified specific multimodal explanation risks including excessive complexity leading to opacity when different modalities provide conflicting information, bias amplification when visual cues reinforce stereotypes delivered through verbal explanation, overtrust when multimodal explanations appear more complete than they actually are, and potential manipulation when coordinated verbal and nonverbal cues exploit cognitive biases (Kaur et al., 2020). These risks highlight the need for careful design and implementation of multimodal XAI systems. By leveraging multimodality and implicit social cues, we can create AI systems that are more transparent, effective, and aligned with human needs and expectations.

24.4.1 Burdens of Complexity and Its Management

It has been observed that contemporary XAI models are frequently so complex that they may potentially compromise the efficiency, speed, and precision of the outcomes produced by the AI systems in which they are embedded (Caruana et al., 2015; Waltl & Vogl, 2018). The creation of multimodal explanations capable of adapting to the specific interaction and topic they are intended to elucidate could entail a twofold level of complexity to be managed.

From a technical standpoint, the development of an explainer and explanandum necessitates a significant investment of resources. This is due to the fact that the explainer and explanandum must align with the specific requirements of the case at hand and address the nuances of both the explanans and the explainee. Such necessity may result in significant technical challenges during implementation. Even if these latter aspects were successfully resolved, the overall level of complexity of the XAI model thus produced would have to be taken into account. Indeed, when implemented in agents that are already called upon to perform technically complex activities, it could exacerbate the general complexity, slowing down the regular production of outcomes and 'burdening' the interaction in such a way that compromises its pleasantness and thus its long-term sustainability and reliability for the nonspecialized user (Longo et al., 2024; Rudin et al., 2022). In fact, neuroscience and behavioral science demonstrate that individuals frequently underestimate the risks associated with a given activity or decision in direct proportion to the emotional drive they possess in carrying out that activity or decision-making process (Rudolph et al., 2018). Consequently, a system that, although justifiably, markedly slows down this process or makes it excessively cumbersome could induce the opposite effect to that which is expected. This would not only result in an unpleasant interactive experience for the human user but could also lead to the market preference for systems that adopt more streamlined XAI systems or, even worse, are predominantly opaque (Ebers, 2019). Such a dynamic would have the effect of penalizing investment in the development of multimodal XAI models, which represent a fundamental resource for users.

Therefore, it is necessary to consider the implications of multimodality in terms of the added complexity that it may entail and modulate it accordingly.

It is also important to consider that a significant aspect of complexity in the interaction between the explainer and the explainee is represented by the variables that operationalize the latter's cognitive, emotional, and sociocultural dimensions. Indeed, the level of influence of what we have defined as implicit social cues – that is to say, the features of multimodality itself – is strictly dependent on the user and the context as discussed in Chap. 22, for example, modifying the intonation of a sentence or individual words to convey different emotions or ideas related to the explanandum may be effective in some languages but not in others, potentially leading to ambiguity (more details are presented in Chap. 21). Similarly, the association of specific gazes or hand movements with ambiguous or interrogative meanings is a common practice in some cultural contexts but not in others (more details are presented in Chap. 19).

In other words, assuming that one is simplifying the fruition of information by using indirect cues risks failing to consider that the explainee may not register these cues or interpret them subjectively. In fact, human beings interpret the signals coming from the external world on the basis of their own prior experiences, the social norms to which they are most exposed (see Chap. 27), or the knowledge they have (or think they have) of the source of the information itself (Lotto, 2022).

24.4.2 Potential Bias Amplification and Overtrust in Multimodal Interaction

In all humans, cognitive biases can be observed that influence how they process information across different modalities. Research on multimodal perception demonstrates that these biases operate differently depending on which communication channels are engaged (Ernst & Bülthoff, 2004; Spence, 2011). Multimodal explanations face unique challenges related to these biases. When explanations combine verbal, visual, and interactive elements, they risk triggering selective attention biases (Wickens, 2008), for instance, users typically prioritize visual information over auditory data when both are presented simultaneously, potentially missing critical verbal explanations when accompanied by compelling visuals (Mayer & Moreno, 2002). The integration of multiple modalities can either mitigate or amplify confirmatory bias. When explanations present consistent information across modalities (text matching, visual matching, interactive feedback), users better integrate contradictory evidence. However, slight inconsistencies between modalities can create opportunities for users to selectively attend to whichever modality confirms their existing beliefs (Sundar, 2015). While XAI systems aim to increase transparency, multimodal explanations that engage subconscious processing through design elements that synchronize verbal, visual, and interactive cues may unintentionally trigger cognitive biases. This makes the user's interpretation less deliberate and informed than intended (Wang et al., 2019). The specific combination and synchronization of modalities must, therefore, be carefully designed to avoid inadvertently exploiting these cognitive vulnerabilities.

However, if the multimodal explanation is programmed in a way that employs design expedients that appeal to the user's more subconscious spheres, this could result in the solicitation, even unintentionally, of biases that make the user's actions anything but conscious and informed.

One might consider, for instance, the use of images to reinforce a written or verbal explanation as outlined in Chap. 25. In this case, it is evident that the utilization of specific colors can evoke a sense of urgency and haste in the completion of the task at hand, as exemplified by the use of the color red. Similarly, the utilization of specific fonts serves to accentuate particular terms in explanations that are presented in a more accessible format. These fonts are known to capture the reader's attention to a significant extent, prompting the brain to prioritize the processing of information that is deemed relevant while automatically filtering out other data. In certain instances, this outcome is anticipated and intended to convey the primary information or data deemed most relevant to the context or recipient. Nevertheless, in certain instances, this may engender an attitude toward the explanation that is the direct consequence of influences exerted by the explanation itself, rather than a conscious evaluation on the part of the recipient. The use of colors, sounds, or fonts that can induce a subconscious effect of urgency and haste in making a decision may, if employed in the most crucial phases of an explanation, prompt an individual to develop a sense of haste in completing the task or in following the recommendation produced by the AI system, without due attention being paid to the content of the explanation itself.

Furthermore, the utilization of a specific intonation, precise movements, or linguistic expressions may assist in reducing the natural human inclination toward anthropomorphism, which is the attribution of humanlike characteristics to inanimate objects, including artificial agents. This could facilitate the targeting of the human response in terms of empathy and overtrust toward the artificial agent. This is not necessarily due to a lack of awareness of interacting with an AI; rather, it is because certain design features are capable of targeting the areas of the brain that are involved with feelings of care, affection, and attachment. One need only to consider the phenomenon known as the 'baby schema,' which posits that the tilting head of a robot, coupled with other expressions such as doubt or enthusiasm, activates the same regions of the brain that are engaged when encountering a human infant. This leads to perceptions of tenderness, a proclivity for protection, and even parental attachment. In the context of the interaction between an explainer utilizing multimodal explanans and the explainee, the subject may develop excessive trust in explanations without fully comprehending the inherent limitations of multimodal XAI. This can be driven by emotional rather than evaluative overstimulation. Such overconfidence could result in the formulation of misguided decisions, such as placing undue reliance on a system's explanations in critical applications without first verifying the validity of the underlying model or questioning it until a more concrete satisfaction of the information need is achieved (see further details in Chap. 30).

24.4.3 Risk of Manipulative Drifts

The practice of multimodal explanations, while intended to enhance transparency and user engagement, can inadvertently lead to secondary and potentially harmful effects. These concerns manifest differently across embodied and disembodied agents, as their multimodal explanatory capacities interact with human cognitive vulnerabilities through distinct mechanisms (De Graaf & Malle, 2019; Złotowski et al., 2015). These effects, though not intended by designers and programmers, arise from the inherent nature of multimodality, which leverages implicit social cues that target subconscious cognitive processes (Klenk, 2022; Carli, 2022). This can result in manipulative dynamics that influence users' decisions and actions in unintended ways.

From these factors, the possibility of manipulative drifts in XAI systems emerges. When the explanandum and explanans serve to reinforce psychological targeting already present in AI-user interactions,[5] users may be induced to perform actions they would otherwise avoid if not subjected to such combined influence (Carli & Calvaresi, 2023). This phenomenon aligns with what Burr and Cristianini (Burr & Cristianini, 2019) term predictive persuasion—where systems leverage explanatory components not to clarify decision processes but to enhance compliance through psychological targeting.

The explanans may exert a convincing effect on the explainee. It can induce compliance with AI recommendations rather than enhancing critical awareness. This creates a misalignment between stated and actual goals. When this occurs without conscious awareness, it becomes problematic. When it benefits third parties rather than users, it's even more concerning. Such dynamics constitute manipulation as defined in recent legal scholarship (Klenk, 2022; Carli, 2022; Susser et al., 2019). Consider an AI agent in the food sector that recommends a specific brand of products. This agent might provide explanations that leverage emotional and psychological cues to encourage users to adopt the recommended brand, for example, the agent might use persuasive language, visual aids, and even gestures (in the case of embodied agents) to create a sense of urgency or trust. This can lead users to accept the recommendation without fully questioning its underlying motivations (Klenk, 2022; Carli, 2022).

The manipulation exists regardless of outcome harm when decisions are induced for producer-set purposes through explanations targeting unconscious psychological profiles. This problem stems from multimodality's inherent characteristics as established in cognitive science. Multimodal explanations incorporate implicit social cues that target subconscious processing pathways (Nass & Moon, 2000; Reeves & Nass, 1996). While multimodal explanations can enhance user engagement and understanding, they must be carefully designed to avoid unintended manipulative effects. By recognizing the potential for implicit social cues to influence user decisions (Kim et al., 2018; Thellman et al., 2016), we can develop more ethical and user-centric AI systems.

---

[5] The term "psychological targeting in AI-user interaction" here refers to the process by which AI systems are designed and programmed to appeal to specific areas of the human brain or to elicit certain emotions in the user, in order to facilitate benefits in interaction. Some examples may be the attempt to elicit acceptance or trust in the individuals involved in the interaction, to arouse emotions of tenderness or agreeableness, or to reinforce the very phenomenon of 'social presence.'

24.5 Operationalization

The fundamental premise of sXAI is that the interaction between the explainer and the explainee is a co-constructed process. This process is not merely about the effectiveness and efficiency of the explanation but also about understanding the complex interplay between cognitive and emotional structures that characterize human sociality. The potential for developing multimodal explanations plays a pivotal role in this regard, as it allows for a more comprehensive and engaging interaction (Rohlfing et al., 2021). However, even in studies of XAI that address multimodality, the interaction is often approached from a procedural-functional perspective that neglects the emotional component. This oversight can lead to unintended consequences, such as bias amplification, overtrust, and manipulative drifts (Klenk, 2022; Carli, 2022). Therefore, it is crucial to consider the potential benefits of managing the emotional dynamics within the XAI interaction.

The concept of sociality in current XAI research is often understood in terms of the alignment of roles and actions, which must be coherent and organized according to a precise protocol (Rohlfing et al., 2021; Fasoli, 2023). While this approach addresses the asymmetry of communication and bridges the epistemological gap between the parties involved, it may overlook the emotional and cognitive complexities of human interactions. Human beings are not merely rational actors; they are also emotional and symbolic subjects. The majority of cognitive processes and perceptions occur at an unconscious level, and emotions play a significant role in decision-making (Mlodinow, 2012; Simon, 1990), for instance, humans can experience sympathy for inanimate objects or AI systems that possess characteristics that evoke emotional responses (Epley et al., 2007). This phenomenon underscores the importance of considering the human emotional variable in the design of XAI systems.

To address these complexities, we can draw inspiration from the field of artificial empathy, which studies the role of emotions in human-robot interaction (HRI) and human–computer interaction (HCI) Damiano et al., 2015a; Damiano & Dumouchel, 2020; Zhu & Luo, 2024. This field asserts that emotion and cognition are highly interrelated processes, influencing both the perception of the external world and the articulation of thought Phelps, 2006; Lowe, 2019. The concept of emotional mirroring and the co-construction of emotions within the relationship between two agents are particularly relevant (Gallese, 2008; Dumouchel, 2001; Damiano et al., 2015b). Integrating artificial empathy theories into multidisciplinary studies of sXAI would facilitate improvement in several ways: First, it would enhance the design of multimodal explanations by considering both cognitive clarity and emotional resonance (Miller, 2019; Abdul et al., 2018). Second, it would enable the development of adaptive explanation strategies that respond to the user's emotional state (Schneider et al., 2021; Ehsan et al., 2021). Finally, this integration would allow for more effective management of foreseeable risks in XAI, including overtrust, bias amplification, and manipulation (Glikson & Woolley, 2020; Jacovi et al., 2021). By accounting for the emotional dimensions of human-AI interaction, we can design explanations that promote appropriate trust and critical engagement (Mittelstadt et al., 2019; Zhang et al., 2020), ultimately making AI systems more trustworthy, usable, and ethically sound.

In human–machine interactions, the programmability of AI systems allows for the study of these co-production processes. By selecting features that induce emotions conducive to collaboration, we can enhance the effectiveness of multimodal explanations (Damiano et al., 2015b). This approach not only facilitates a more robust foundation for cognitive functioning but also enables a more effective and linear acquisition and processing of information.

24.6 How Does This Chapter Inspire Further Research on sXAI?

sXAI has shown great promise in using multimodal explanations to create a shared understanding between AI systems and users. However, this chapter uncovers a critical issue often missed: the unintended side effects of multimodality on trust, bias, and potential manipulation.

A key takeaway is that multimodal explanations tap into the same cognitive and emotional mechanisms that drive human-agent interactions. By integrating speech, gestures, facial expressions, and contextual cues, these explanations enhance understanding but can also lead to overtrust. Users might rely too heavily on AI outputs without questioning them critically. This chapter underscores the need for research on how different modalities affect user perception and trust. Future studies should aim to design explanations that boost comprehension without reinforcing biases or fostering unwarranted confidence in AI systems.

Another crucial area for further research is the ethical side of multimodal sXAI. The same features that make an AI system persuasive can also lead to manipulation, whether intentional or not. We need to find ways to ensure transparency in explanations while minimizing the risk of undue influence. How can we design multimodal interactions that engage users without compromising their autonomy? Answering this requires a multidisciplinary approach, combining insights from cognitive science, human-computer interaction (HCI), and the philosophy of technology.

Artificial empathy also plays a vital role in XAI research. By understanding how humans co-construct emotions during interactions, we can develop explanations that are both technically accurate and emotionally aware. Future work should explore how to integrate artificial empathy with explainability, ensuring that AI systems can adapt their explanations to users' emotional and cognitive states without resorting to deceptive tactics.

As AI systems become more integrated into daily life, we must also study the long-term effects of multimodal explanations on human behavior and decision-making. How do repeated interactions with socially explainable AI shape user expectations, cognitive load, and trust over time? These questions are crucial for developing responsible, human-centered AI systems. By combining insights from multimodality, social sciences, and AI ethics, researchers can refine the design of sXAI. This chapter calls for deeper, interdisciplinary research into how AI explanations influence human understanding, trust, and autonomy. Only through such efforts can we maximize the benefits of sXAI while proactively addressing its risks.

24.7 Rapid Access

This chapter explores how AI agents can use multiple ways to explain themselves, making their actions and decisions clearer to us. As AI becomes a bigger part of our daily lives, we must understand how it perceives and reasons and why it makes certain choices. This contributes to building trust and ease working with AI. When we talk about multimodality, we mean using different ways to communicate—like talking, showing visuals, using gestures, or even showing emotions. This chapter looks at three main types of AI agents:

1. Embodied agents (think robots like Pepper or iCub) use their physical presence to explain things through gestures, facial expressions, and how they move around.
2. Virtual embodied agents (like digital avatars) don't have a physical body but use digital visuals and animations to explain things in a humanlike way.
3. Virtual unembodied agents (like Alexa or chatbots) rely on words and tone of voice to create meaningful interactions, even though they don't have a physical form.

We point out that good AI explanations do more than just give information; they adapt to how humans react, think, and feel. This is key for AI to be a more reliable partner, especially when it's giving advice or assisting in making decisions. Despite the added values to which multimodality contributes, there are also challenges:

- Complexity: If AI gives too many different types of cues along with the explanation at once, it can be overwhelming or misleading.
- Bias: The way AI uses visuals, colors, or words can accidentally reinforce human cognitive biases, leading to misunderstandings.
- Overtrust: Making use of humanlike behaviors has the potential to result in the attribution of AI capabilities and competences that exceed the actual ones and may contribute to inducing a suspension of critical thinking with regard to AI suggestions.
- Manipulation: Using features like tone of voice or visual emphasis can influence our behavior. This raises both ethical and legal questions, related to the right of self-determination, cognitive sovereignty, autonomy, and psychological integrity, among others.

To handle these challenges, the chapter suggests combining insights from different fields – like emotion science, psychology, and human-computer interaction

– to create AI that is both clear and ethical. The idea of *artificial empathy* (Damiano et al., 2015a; Damiano & Dumouchel, 2020; Zhu & Luo, 2024) is brought up as a way to make AI explanations more in tune with our feelings without taking advantage of them.

By understanding how different communication cues, human thinking, and ethics all connect, this work sets the stage for the next generation of AI that can explain itself well and fit seamlessly into our world.

References

Abdul, A., Vermeulen, J., Wang, D., Lim, B. Y., & Kankanhalli, M. (2018). Trends and trajectories for explainable, accountable and intelligible systems: An HCI research agenda. In *Proceedings of the 2018 CHI Conference on Human Factors in Computing Systems*, CHI'18 (p. 582). Association for Computing Machinery. https://doi.org/10.1145/3173574.3174156

Bawden, D., & Robinson, L. (2020). Information overload: An overview. In D. P. Redlawsk (Ed.), *Oxford encyclopedia of political decision making*. Oxford University Press. https://doi.org/10.1093/acrefore/9780190228637.013.1360

Bernardo, E., & Seva, R. (2022). Exploration of emotions developed in the interaction with explainable AI. In *15th International Symposium on Computational Intelligence and Design, ISCID'22'* (pp. 143–146). IEEE. https://doi.org/10.1109/ISCID56505.2022.00039

Bernardo, E., & Seva, R. (2023). Affective design analysis of explainable artificial intelligence (XAI): A user-centric perspective. *Informatics, 10*(1), 1–24. https://doi.org/10.3390/informatics10010032

Bickmore, T., & Cassell, J. (2005). Social dialogue with embodied conversational agents. In J. C. J. Kuppevelt, L. Dybkjaer, & N. O. Bernsen, (Eds.), *Advances in natural multimodal dialogue systems* (pp. 23–54). Springer. https://doi.org/10.1007/1-4020-3933-6_2

Bickmore, T. W., & Picard, R. W. (2005). Establishing and maintaining long-term human–computer relationships. *ACM Transactions on Computer–Human Interaction (TOCHI), 12*(2), 293–327. https://doi.org/10.1145/1067860.1067867

Bradwell, H. L., Edwards, K., Shenton, D., Winnington, R., Thill, S., & Jones, R. B. (2021). User-centered design of companion robot pets involving care home resident-robot interactions and focus groups with residents, staff, and family: Qualitative study. *JMIR Rehabilitation and Assistive Technologies, 8*(4), e30337. https://doi.org/10.2196/30337

Burr, C., & Cristianini, N. (2019). Can machines read our minds? *Minds and Machines, 29*(3), 461–494. https://doi.org/10.1007/s11023-019-09497-4

Burrell, J. (2016). How the machine 'thinks': Understanding opacity in machine learning algorithms. *Big Data & Society, 3*(1), 2053951715622512. https://doi.org/10.1177/2053951715622512

Bussone, A., Stumpf, S., & O'Sullivan, D. (2015). The role of explanations on trust and reliance in clinical decision support systems. In *2015 International Conference on Healthcare Informatics* (pp. 160–169). IEEE. https://doi.org/10.1109/ICHI.2015.26

Calvaresi, D., Carli, R., Piguet, J. G., Contreras, V. H., Luzzani, G., Najjar, A., Calbimonte, J. P., & Schumacher, M. (2023). Ethical and legal considerations for nutrition virtual coaches. *AI and Ethics, 3*(4), 1313–1340. https://doi.org/10.1007/s43681-022-00237-6

Carli, R. (2022). Manipulation through AI systems. In L. Sposini, & R. Limongelli (Eds.) *Regulating Advanced Technologies: Policy Papers of the Jean Monnet Centre of Excellence on the Regulation of Robotics and AI* (pp. 7–22). Jean Monnet Centre of Excellence on the Regulation of Robotics and AI. Carli.

Carli, R., & Calvaresi, D. (2023). Reinterpreting vulnerability to tackle deception in principles-based XAI for human–computer interaction. In *International Workshop on Explainable, Transparent Autonomous Agents and Multi-Agent Systems* (pp. 249–269). Springer. https://doi.org/10.1007/978-3-031-40878-6_14

Caruana, R., Lou, Y., Gehrke, J., Koch, P., Sturm, M., & Elhadad, N. (2015). Intelligible models for healthcare: Predicting pneumonia risk and hospital 30-day readmission. In *Proceedings of the 21th ACM SIGKDD International Conference on Knowledge Discovery and Data Mining* (pp. 1721–1730). Association for Computing Machinery. https://doi.org/10.1145/2783258.2788613

Casas, J., Spring, T., Daher, K., Mugellini, E., Khaled, O. A., & Cudré-Mauroux, P. (2021). Enhancing conversational agents with empathic abilities. In *Proceedings of the 21st ACM International Conference on Intelligent Virtual Agents* (pp. 41–47). Association for Computing Machinery. https://doi.org/10.1145/3472306.3478344

Chao, C., Cakmak, M., & Thomaz, A. L. (2010). Transparent active learning for robots. In *2010 5th ACM/IEEE International Conference on Human–Robot Interaction*, HRI'10 (pp. 317–324). IEEE. https://doi.org/10.1109/HRI.2010.5453178

Chella, A., & Pipitone, A. (2020). A cognitive architecture for inner speech. *Cognitive Systems Research, 59*, 287–292. https://doi.org/10.1016/j.cogsys.2019.09.010

Clark, A. (1999). An embodied cognitive science? *Trends in Cognitive Sciences, 3*(9), 345–351. https://doi.org/10.1016/S1364-6613(99)01361-3

Damiano, L., Dumouchel, P., & Lehmann, H. (2015a). Artificial empathy: An interdisciplinary investigation. *International Journal of Social Robotics, 7*, 3–5. https://doi.org/10.1007/s12369-014-0259-6

Damiano, L., Dumouchel, P., & Lehmann, H. (2015b). Towards human–robot affective co-evolution overcoming oppositions in constructing emotions and empathy. *International Journal of Social Robotics, 7*, 7–18. https://doi.org/10.1007/s12369-014-0258-7

Damiano, L., & Dumouchel, P. G. (2020). Emotions in relation. Epistemological and ethical scaffolding for mixed human–robot social ecologies. *HUMANA. MENTE Journal of Philosophical Studies, 13*(37), 181–206.

De Graaf, M. M. A., & Malle, B. F. (2019). People's explanations of robot behavior subtly reveal mental state inferences. In *2019 14th ACM/IEEE International Conference on Human–Robot Interaction*, HRI'19 (pp. 239–248). IEEE.

Dranove, D., Kessler, D., McClellan, M., & Satterthwaite, M. (2003). Is more information better? The effects of "report cards" on health care providers. *Journal of Political Economy, 111*(3), 555–588. https://doi.org/10.1086/374180

Dumouchel, P. (2001). Exchange and emotions. In C. Gerschlager (Ed.), *Expanding the economic concept of exchange: Deception, self-deception and illusions* (pp. 53–65). Springer. https://doi.org/10.1007/978-1-4615-0905-9_3

Ebers, M. (2019). Regulating AI and robotics: Ethical and legal challenges. In M. Ebers, & S. Nava (Eds.), *Algorithms and law* (pp. 37–99). Cambridge University Press.

Ehsan, U., Vera Liao, Q., Muller, M., Riedl, M. O., & Weisz, J. D. (2021). Expanding explainability: Towards social transparency in ai systems. In *Proceedings of the 2021 CHI Conference on Human Factors in Computing Systems*, CHI'21 (pp. 1–19). Association for Computing Machinery. https://doi.org/10.1145/3411764.3445188

Eiband, M., Schneider, H., Bilandzic, M., Fazekas-Con, J., Haug, M., & Hussmann, H. (2018). Bringing transparency design into practice. In *Proceedings of the 23rd International Conference on Intelligent User Interfaces* (pp. 211–223). Association for Computing Machinery. https://doi.org/10.1145/3172944.3172961

Epley, N., Waytz, A., & Cacioppo, J. T. (2007). On seeing human: A three-factor theory of anthropomorphism. *Psychological Review, 114*(4), 864. https://doi.org/10.1037/0033-295X.114.4.864

Ernst, M. O., & Bülthoff, H. H. (2004). Merging the senses into a robust percept. *Trends in Cognitive Sciences, 8*(4), 162–169. https://doi.org/10.1016/j.tics.2004.02.002

Fasoli, G. (2023). *Frames: Muoversi nel Digitale e Attraversare le Cornici*. Edizioni Centro Studi Erickson.

Feine, J., Gnewuch, U., Morana, S., & Maedche, A. (2019). A taxonomy of social cues for conversational agents. *International Journal of Human–Computer Studies, 132*, 138–161. https://doi.org/10.1016/j.ijhcs.2019.07.009

Felzmann, H., Villaronga, E. F., Lutz, C., & Tamò-Larrieux, A. (2019). Transparency you can trust: Transparency requirements for artificial intelligence between legal norms and contextual concerns. *Big Data & Society, 6*(1), 2053951719860542. https://doi.org/10.1177/2053951719860542

Foglia, L., & Wilson, R. A. (2013). Embodied cognition. *Wiley Interdisciplinary Reviews: Cognitive Science, 4*(3), 319–325. https://doi.org/10.1002/wcs.1226

Främling, K., Lim, B. Y., & Rohlfing, K. J. (2023). *Social Explainable AI: Designing Multimodal and Interactive Communication to Tailor Human–AI Collaborations.* NII Shonan Meeting Report 200. National Institute of Informatics.

Gallese, V. (2008). Empathy, embodied simulation, and the brain: Commentary on Aragno and Zepf/Hartmann. *Journal of the American Psychoanalytic Association, 56*(3), 769–781. https://doi.org/10.1177/0003065108322206

Ghiță, A. S., Gavril, A. F., Nan, M., Hoteit, B., Awada, I. A., Sorici, A., Mocanu, I. G., & Florea, A. M. (2020). The amiro social robotics framework: Deployment and evaluation on the pepper robot. *Sensors, 20*(24), 7271. https://doi.org/10.3390/s20247271

Glickman, M., & Sharot, T. (2025). How human–AI feedback loops alter human perceptual, emotional and social judgements. *Nature Human Behaviour, 9*, 345–359. https://doi.org/10.1038/s41562-024-02077-2

Glikson, E., & Woolley, A. W. (2020). Human trust in artificial intelligence: Review of empirical research. *Academy of Management Annals, 14*(2), 627–660. https://doi.org/10.5465/annals.2018.0057

Go, E., & Sundar, S. S. (2019). Humanizing chatbots: The effects of visual, identity and conversational cues on humanness perceptions. *Computers in Human Behavior, 97*, 304–316. https://doi.org/10.1016/j.chb.2019.01.020

Gratch, J., Wang, N., Gerten, J., Fast, E., & Duffy, R. (2007). Creating rapport with virtual agents. In *Intelligent Virtual Agents: 7th International Conference* (pp. 125–138). Springer. https://doi.org/10.1007/978-3-540-74997-4_12

Hoffman, G. (2019). *Anki, Jibo, and Kuri: What we can learn from social robots that didn't make it.* https://spectrum.ieee.org/anki-jibo-and-kuri-what-we-can-learn-from-social-robotics-failures

Jacovi, A., Marasović, A., Miller, T., & Goldberg, Y. (2021). Formalizing trust in artificial intelligence: Prerequisites, causes and goals of human trust in AI. In *Proceedings of the 2021 ACM Conference on Fairness, Accountability, and Transparency* (pp. 624–635). Association for Computing Machinery. https://doi.org/10.1145/3442188.3445923

Kaur, H., Nori, H., Jenkins, S., Caruana, R., Wallach, H., & Vaughan, J. W. (2020). Interpreting interpretability: Understanding data scientists' use of interpretability tools for machine learning. In *Proceedings of the 2020 CHI Conference on Human Factors in Computing Systems*, CHI'20 (pp. 1–14). Association for Computing Machinery. https://doi.org/10.1145/3313831.3376219

Kim, K., Boelling, L., Haesler, S., Bailenson, J., Bruder, G., & Welch, G. F. (2018). Does a digital assistant need a body? The influence of visual embodiment and social behavior on the perception of intelligent virtual agents in AR. In *2018 IEEE International Symposium on Mixed and Augmented Reality*, ISMAR'18' (pp. 105–114). IEEE. https://doi.org/10.1109/ISMAR.2018.00039

Klenk, M. (2022). (Online) manipulation: Sometimes hidden, always careless. *Review of Social Economy, 80*(1), 85–105. https://doi.org/10.1080/00346764.2021.1894350

Kolomaznik, M., Petrik, V., Slama, M., & Jurik, V. (2024). The role of socio-emotional attributes in enhancing human–AI collaboration. *Frontiers in Psychology, 15*, 1369957. https://doi.org/10.3389/fpsyg.2024.1369957

Kubo, A. (2010). Technology as mediation: On the process of engineering and living with the "AIBO" robot. *Japanese Review of Cultural Anthropology, 11*, 103–123. https://doi.org/10.14890/jrca.11.0_103

Laakso, A. (2011). Embodiment and development in cognitive science. *Cognition, Brain, Behavior: An Interdisciplinary Journal, 15*(4), 409–425.

Lakoff, G., & Wehling, E. (2016). *Your brain's politics: How the science of mind explains the political divide* (vol. 59). Andrews UK Limited.

Liao, Q. V., Gruen, D., & Miller, S. (2020). Questioning the AI: Informing design practices for explainable AI user experiences. In *Proceedings of the 2020 CHI Conference on Human Factors in Computing Systems*, CHI'20 (pp. 1–15). Association for Computing Machinery. https://doi.org/10.1145/3313831.3376590

Longo, L., Brcic, M., Cabitza, F., Choi, J., Confalonieri, R., Del Ser, J., Guidotti, R., Hayashi, Y., Herrera, F., Holzinger, A., et al. (2024). Explainable artificial intelligence (XAI) 2.0: A manifesto of open challenges and interdisciplinary research directions. *Information Fusion, 106*, 102301. https://doi.org/10.1016/j.inffus.2024.102301

Lotto, B. (2022). *Percezioni: Come il Cervello Costruisce il Mondo*. Bollati Boringhieri.

Lowe, R. (2019). Emotions in robots: Embodied interaction in social and non-social environments. *Multimodal Technologies and Interaction, 3*(3), 53. https://doi.org/10.3390/mti3030053

Ma, S. (2024). *Towards human-centered design of explainable artificial intelligence (XAI): A survey of empirical studies*. https://doi.org/10.48550/arXiv.2410.21183

Mahdi, H., Akgun, S. A., Saleh, S., & Dautenhahn, K. (2022). A survey on the design and evolution of social robots—Past, present and future. *Robotics and Autonomous Systems, 156*(C), 104193. https://doi.org/10.1016/j.robot.2022.104193

Mayer, R. E., & Moreno, R. (2002). Animation as an aid to multimedia learning. *Educational Psychology Review, 14*, 87–99. https://doi.org/10.1023/A:1013184611077

Miller, T. (2019). Explanation in artificial intelligence: Insights from the social sciences. *Artificial Intelligence, 267*, 1–38. https://doi.org/10.1016/j.artint.2018.07.007

Mittelstadt, B., Russell, C., & Wachter, S. (2019). Explaining explanations in AI. In *Proceedings of the Conference on Fairness, Accountability, and Transparency* (pp. 279–288). Association for Computing Machinery. https://doi.org/10.1145/3287560.3287574

Mlodinow, L. (2012). *Subliminal: The revolution of the new unconscious and what it teaches us about ourselves*. Penguin.

Nass, C., & Moon, Y. (2000). Machines and mindlessness: Social responses to computers. *Journal of Social Issues, 56*(1), 81–103. https://doi.org/10.1111/0022-4537.00153

Natale, S. (2019). If software is narrative: Joseph Weizenbaum, artificial intelligence and the biographies of ELIZA. *New Media & Society, 21*(3), 712–728. https://doi.org/10.1177/1461444818804980

Natale, S. (2020). *Deceitful media: Artificial intelligence and social life after the turing test*. Oxford University Press. https://doi.org/10.1093/oso/9780190080365.001.0001

Nowak, K. L., & Rauh, C. (2008). Choose your "buddy icon" carefully: The influence of avatar androgyny, anthropomorphism and credibility in online interactions. *Computers in Human Behavior, 24*(4), 1473–1493. https://doi.org/10.1016/j.chb.2007.05.005

Paiva, A., Correia, F., Oliveira, R., Santos, F., & Arriaga, P. (2021). Empathy and prosociality in social agents. In B. Lugrin, C. Pelachaud, & D. Traum (Eds.), *The handbook on socially interactive agents: 20 years of research on embodied conversational agents, intelligent virtual agents, and social robotics volume 1: Methods, behavior, cognition* (pp. 385–432). Association for Computing Machinery. https://doi.org/10.1145/3477322.3477334

Paiva, A., Leite, I., Boukricha, H., & Wachsmuth, I. (2017). Empathy in virtual agents and robots: A survey. *ACM Transactions on Interactive Intelligent Systems (TiiS), 7*(3), 32. https://doi.org/10.1145/2912150

Paiva, A., Mascarenhas, S., Petisca, S., Correia, F., & Alves-Oliveira, P. (2018). Towards more humane machines: Creating emotional social robots. In S. G. Da Silva (Ed.), *New interdisciplinary landscapes in morality and emotion* (pp. 125–139). Routledge.

Pandey, A. K., & Alami, R. (2013). Affordance graph: A framework to encode perspective taking and effort based affordances for day-to-day human–robot interaction. In *2013 IEEE/RSJ International Conference on Intelligent Robots and Systems* (pp. 2180–2187). IEEE. https://doi.org/10.1109/IROS.2013.6696661

Phelps, E. A. (2006). Emotion and cognition: Insights from studies of the human amygdala. *Annual Review of Psychology, 57*(1), 27–53. https://doi.org/10.1146/annurev.psych.56.091103.070234

Picard, R. W. (2000). *Affective computing*. MIT Press.

Pipitone, A., Geraci, A., D'Amico, A., Seidita, V., & Chella, A. (2024). Robot's inner speech effects on human trust and anthropomorphism. *International Journal of Social Robotics, 16*(6), 1333–1345. https://doi.org/10.1007/s12369-023-01002-3

Purington, A., Taft, J. G., Sannon, S., Bazarova, N. N., & Taylor, S. H. (2017). "Alexa is my new BFF": Social roles, user satisfaction, and personification of the Amazon Echo. In *Proceedings of the 2017 CHI Conference Extended Abstracts on Human Factors in Computing Systems* (pp. 2853–2859). Association for Computing Machinery. https://doi.org/10.1145/3027063.3053246

Reeves, B., & Nass, C. (1996). *The media equation: How people treat computers, television, and new media like real people*. Cambridge University Press.

Rohlfing, K. J., Cimiano, P., Scharlau, I., Matzner, T., Buhl, H., Buschmeier, H., Grimminger, A., Hammer, B., Häb-Umbach, R., Horwath, I., Hüllermeier, E., Kern, F., Kopp, S., Thommes, K., Ngonga Ngomo, A.-C., Schulte, C., Wachsmuth, H., Wagner, P., & Wrede, B. (2021). Explanation as a social practice: Toward a conceptual framework for the social design of AI systems. *IEEE Transactions on Cognitive and Developmental Systems, 13*(3), 717–728. https://doi.org/10.1109/TCDS.2020.3044366

Rudin, C., Chen, C., Chen, Z., Huang, H., Semenova, L., & Zhong, C. (2022). Interpretable machine learning: Fundamental principles and 10 grand challenges. *Statistic Surveys, 16*, 1–85. https://doi.org/10.1214/21-SS133

Rudolph, M., Feth, D., & Polst, S. (2018). Why users ignore privacy policies–A survey and intention model for explaining user privacy behavior. In *Human–Computer Interaction. Theories, Methods, and Human Issues: 20th International Conference, HCI International* (pp. 587–598). Springer. https://doi.org/10.1007/978-3-319-91238-7_45

Šabanović, S., & Chang, W.-L. (2016). Socializing robots: Constructing robotic sociality in the design and use of the assistive robot PARO. *AI & Society, 31*, 537–551. https://doi.org/10.1007/s00146-015-0636-1

Sarkadi, S. (2016). Artificial consciousness in an artificial world. *Philosophy, Communication, Media Sciences, 4*(4), 322–330. https://doi.org/10.22618/TP.PCMS.20164.349030

Schneider, T., Hois, J., Rosenstein, A., Ghellal, S., Theofanou-Fülbier, D., & Gerlicher, A. R. S. (2021). ExplAIn yourself! Transparency for positive UX in autonomous driving. In *Proceedings of the 2021 CHI Conference on Human Factors in Computing Systems*, CHI'21 (p. 161). Association for Computing Machinery. https://doi.org/10.1145/3411764.3446647

Seaborn, K., Miyake, N. P., Pennefather, P., & Otake-Matsuura, M. (2021). Voice in human-agent interaction: A survey. *ACM Computing Surveys (CSUR), 54*(4), 1–43. https://doi.org/10.1145/3386867

Simon, H. A. (1990). Bounded rationality. In J. Eatwell, M. Milgate, & P. Newman (Eds.), *Utility and probability* (pp. 15–18). Palgrave Macmillan.

Skjuve, M., Følstad, A., Fostervold, K. I., & Brandtzaeg, P. B. (2021). My chatbot companion—A study of human–chatbot relationships. *International Journal of Human-Computer Studies, 149*, 102601. https://doi.org/10.1016/j.ijhcs.2021.102601

Sorokowski, P., Puts, D., Johnson, J., Żółkiewicz, O., Oleszkiewicz, A., Sorokowska, A., Kowal, M., Borkowska, B., & Pisanski, K. (2019). Voice of authority: Professionals lower their vocal frequencies when giving expert advice. *Journal of Nonverbal Behavior, 43*, 257–269. https://doi.org/10.1007/s10919-019-00307-0

Spence, C. (2011). Crossmodal correspondences: A tutorial review. *Attention, Perception, & Psychophysics, 73*, 971–995. https://doi.org/10.3758/s13414-010-0073-7

Sun, G., Zhan, X., & Such, J. (2024). Building better AI agents: A provocation on the utilisation of persona in LLM-based conversational agents. In *Proceedings of the 6th ACM Conference on Conversational User Interfaces* (pp. 1–6). Association for Computing Machinery. https://doi.org/10.1145/3640794.3665887

Sundar, S. S. (2015). *The handbook of the psychology of communication technology*. John Wiley & Sons.

Susser, D., Roessler, B., & Nissenbaum, H. (2019). Technology, autonomy, and manipulation. *Internet Policy Review, 8*(2), 1–22. https://doi.org/10.14763/2019.2.1410

Thellman, S., Silvervarg, A., Gulz, A., & Ziemke, T. (2016). Physical vs. virtual agent embodiment and effects on social interaction. In *Intelligent Virtual Agents: 16th International Conference, IVA '16* (pp. 412–415). Springer. https://doi.org/10.1007/978-3-319-47665-0_44

Tsibulya, N. B. (2019). Developing and mastering voice quality and nonverbal component of communication. In *Vestnik Moskovskogo gosudarstvennogo lingvisticheskogo universiteta, 3*(832), 177–189.

Tulli, S., Ambrossio, D. A., Najjar, A., & Rodríguez-Lera, F. J. (2019). Great expectations & aborted business initiatives: The paradox of social robot between research and industry. *BNAIC/BENELEARN, 1*, 1–10.

Wallkötter, S., Tulli, S., Castellano, G., Paiva, A., & Chetouani, M. (2021). Explainable embodied agents through social cues: A review. *ACM Transactions on Human–Robot Interaction (THRI), 10*(3), 1–24. https://doi.org/10.1145/3457188

Waltl, B., & Vogl, R. (2018). Explainable artificial intelligence – The new frontier in legal informatics. *Jusletter IT, 4*, 1–10.

Wang, D., Yang, Q., Abdul, A., & Lim, B. Y. (2019). Designing theory-driven user-centric explainable AI. In *Proceedings of the 2019 CHI Conference on Human Factors in Computing Systems* (p. 601). Association for Computing Machinery. https://doi.org/10.1145/3290605.3300831

Weitz, K., Schiller, D., Schlagowski, R., Huber, T., & André, E. (2021). "Let me explain!": Exploring the potential of virtual agents in explainable AI interaction design. *Journal on Multimodal User Interfaces, 15*(2), 87–98. https://doi.org/10.1007/s12193-020-00332-0

Wickens, C. D. (2008). Multiple resources and mental workload. *Human Factors, 50*(3), 449–455. https://doi.org/10.1518/001872008X288394

Yin, Y., Jia, N., & Wakslak, C. J. (2024). AI can help people feel heard, but an AI label diminishes this impact. *Proceedings of the National Academy of Sciences, 121*(14), e2319112121. https://doi.org/10.1073/pnas.2319112121

Zhang, Y., Vera Liao, Q., & Bellamy, R. K. E. (2020). Effect of confidence and explanation on accuracy and trust calibration in AI-assisted decision making. In *Proceedings of the 2020 Conference on Fairness, Accountability, and Transparency* (pp. 295–305). Association for Computing Machinery. https://doi.org/10.1145/3351095.3372852

Zhu, Q., & Luo, J. (2024). Toward artificial empathy for human-centered design. *Journal of Mechanical Design, 146*(6), 061401. https://doi.org/10.1115/1.4064161

Złotowski, J., Proudfoot, D., Yogeeswaran, K., & Bartneck, C. (2015). Anthropomorphism: Opportunities and challenges in human–robot interaction. *International Journal of Social Robotics, 7*, 347–360. https://doi.org/10.1007/s12369-014-0267-6

Open Access This chapter is licensed under the terms of the Creative Commons Attribution 4.0 International License (http://creativecommons.org/licenses/by/4.0/), which permits use, sharing, adaptation, distribution and reproduction in any medium or format, as long as you give appropriate credit to the original author(s) and the source, provide a link to the Creative Commons license and indicate if changes were made.

The images or other third party material in this chapter are included in the chapter's Creative Commons license, unless indicated otherwise in a credit line to the material. If material is not included in the chapter's Creative Commons license and your intended use is not permitted by statutory regulation or exceeds the permitted use, you will need to obtain permission directly from the copyright holder.

Chapter 25
Visualization and the Use of Multimodality to Explain

Richard Albrecht , Rachele Carli , Igor Tchappi , and Amro Najjar

Abstract To enhance explanations about artificial intelligence systems, visualizations can be employed for the task of explaining deep learning models. Since social explanations are incremental and multimodal (Chap. 1), visualizations serve as both an incremental component and an additional modality, such as alongside textual or verbal explanations. Thereby, visualizations can help create more intuitive explanations that are adapted to the needs of an explainee. In this chapter, we focus on visualizing local post hoc explanations that can explain specific decisions made by a deep-learning-based system. These explanations can, for example, answer questions on why a decision that affects the user was made. We review how these visualizations are currently produced and how they can be used in social explainable artificial intelligence. To evaluate visualizations in explanations for black-box deep learning systems, we suggest to focus on the social aspects of the explanation process.

R. Albrecht (✉)
AI Robolab, University of Luxembourg, Esch-sur-Alzette, Luxembourg
e-mail: richard.albrecht@uni.lu

R. Carli
Responsible AI Group, Umeå University, Umeå, Sweden

AI RoboLab, University of Luxembourg, Esch-sur-Alzette, Luxembourg
e-mail: rachele.carli@umu.se

I. Tchappi
FINATRAX, SnT, University of Luxembourg, Esch-sur-Alzette, Luxembourg
e-mail: igor.tchappi@uni.lu

A. Najjar
Trustworthy AI, Data and Software (HANDS) Unit, Luxembourg Institute of Science and Technology, Esch-sur-Alzette, Luxembourg
e-mail: amro.najjar@list.lu

© The Author(s) 2026
K. J. Rohlfing et al. (eds.), *Social Explainable AI*,
https://doi.org/10.1007/978-981-96-5290-7_25

25.1 How Does This Chapter Relate to Social XAI?

In this book, three characteristics of explanations are outlined that sXAI adds to existing perspectives of XAI: Interaction is patterned, incremental, and multimodal (Chap. 1). Visualization can be integrated into all of the three characteristics to potentially enhance the explanation process.

One drawback of black-box artificial intelligence (AI) methods and models is the lack of interpretability (Burkart & Huber, 2021). Users who interact with or develop such models and systems (that is explainees) require explanations to enhance their understanding (Mualla et al., 2022). For instance, a customer might be interested in buying a new car and receives recommendations based on a black-box model. Explanations from the AI system playing the role of the explainer can help the customer to understand why they should buy a certain one, and not another option (Sect. 2.3).

In the literature, many methods were proposed to generate explanations at different stages of the creation or use of ML models (Yuan et al., 2021; Hohman et al., 2019). To present these generated explanations, works in the literature resorted to visualization as a tool to improve the explanation and to enhance the dialog of the explainer and the explainee (Prentzas et al., 2023). Thus, as described in (Yuan et al., 2021), visualizations can be employed at various steps to explain the process of the creations and use of ML models. First, the model itself can be visualized, and the explainee can obtain a better understanding of its inner working. Next, the data as well as the training process of these models can be visualized. Lastly, post hoc explanations that are created after predictions are made can be visualized, for example, saliency maps. At this stage, the explanation is generated for the decision that affects the explainee directly and is therefore most relevant from their perspective.

In this chapter, we focus on the visualization of local explanations from post hoc methods and connect them to the framework of sXAI, in which explanations are social and interactive (Rohlfing et al., 2021). Therefore, we emphasize interactive and explainee-centric elements of visualizations in XAI for deep learning (DL) systems since adding interactivity to a system lets explainees individualize explanations and investigate questions they have. We outline the use of visualization techniques to explain black-box DL models in a social way and connect it to the social process of explanations. Lastly, we discuss the challenging aspect of operationalization as it is necessary to measure the effectiveness of explanations and their visualization and to determine if they actually are helpful for a user. Evaluating XAI methods is challenging (Nauta et al., 2023), which also holds for evaluation of visualizations of sXAI.

25.2 Visualization in Deep Learning

In the field of ML, DL has gained increasing attention and is widely used (Dong et al., 2021). This is due to the success of such methods and the increasing accuracy that they achieve in many tasks, for example, text generation (Radford et al., 2019) or image classification (Dosovitskiy et al., 2021). For DL, artificial neural networks with multiple layers are trained on large datasets, for example (Deng et al., 2009). Each layer processes the given input or the results of the previous layer until the final layer is reached which produces the output. The output can be a probability for a class in case of a classification task or likelihoods for text tokens in case of a text generation task, among others (see, e.g., Sarker, 2021 for a detailed overview). Additionally, DL models can also be trained as recommender systems to, for example, recommend a car or a recipe (Buzcu et al., 2024; Tessa et al., 2023).

DL models can be trained in an unsupervised, semi-supervised, or supervised manner (Alom et al., 2019). Since DL models need large amounts of data, even labeled data for supervised tasks, suitable datasets have to be created. Once a model and a dataset is selected, the training process starts. After successful creation and training of a model, it can be integrated into applications to perform real-world tasks. For all of the steps that are part of the process of creating and deploying DL models, visualization can be used to better understand a model. The field of visual analytics investigates the use of visualizations for DL (Chatzimparmpas et al., 2020; Yuan et al., 2021).

For example, to train a model to classify car types, pictures of cars with their associated labels are required, for example (Krause et al., 2013). Once the collection of the data is done, a DL model will be fitted to the given dataset. Finally, it can be used to classify previously unseen images. In this process, the training data, the model architecture, training metrics, and explanations of the model can be visualized (Yuan et al., 2021; Hohman et al., 2019).

The clear strength of DL models is that they can achieve high accuracy scores, e.g., achieving 97.8% at classifying images (Grill, 2020). However, they are black boxes, and even technical experts do not always know how a model makes decisions (Doyle et al., 2003). Therefore, explanations are important to make models transparent, especially in the context of sXAI, where providing clear and accessible explanations is useful for persons interacting with these models in everyday social interactions. During all of the steps mentioned above, visualizations can be used to better explain a part of the process (Fig. 25.2).

25.3 Explainable Deep Learning

Visual analytics techniques for DL models can be used at different stages (Yuan et al., 2021; Hohman et al., 2019). First, data explainability is an important aspect for understanding any DL model (Ali et al., 2023). Since a given model learns

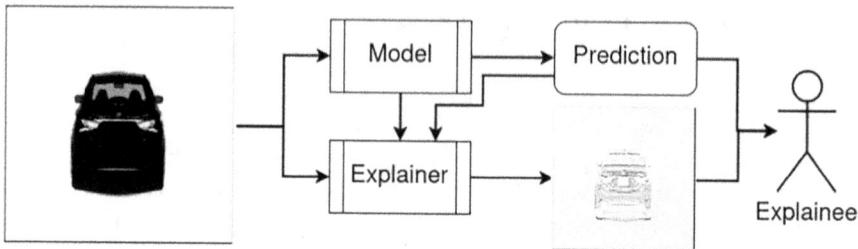

Fig. 25.1 Local explanation for an image classifier for cars. Image created with a VGGNet (Simonyan and Zisserman, 2015) that is fine-tuned on a dataset to classify cars (Krause et al., 2013). Attributions are computed with the GradCAM (Selvaraju et al., 2017) method

representations based on the dataset, visualizing the underlying data can generate valuable insights about a DL model. Second, explanations and visualizations can be used during the creation and training of models (Hohman et al., 2019). Here, explainable AI is helpful for improving and validating models (Yuan et al., 2021). Third, DL models have to be explained, while they are deployed, and visualizations can be made after the training process (Hohman et al., 2019). During this step, transparency is crucial, especially for users that are affected by these systems (Yuan et al., 2021).

In this chapter, we give examples on visualizations in social explanations for explainees that encounter DL models in everyday situations. These can be given through local post hoc explanations since these are the outcomes of a black-box model that the explainee is interacting with. Local means that the explanation is for a single prediction on a single data point by a model, that is a specific decision (Adadi and Berrada, 2018). Post hoc explanations are generated after the model is created and after a prediction is made (Fig. 25.1). For example, an explanation of why a specific car is recommended for buying.

There exist various different XAI methods that can be applied to DL models (see, e.g., Samek et al., 2021). Examples for these methods are LIME (Ribeiro et al., 2016), SHAP (Lundberg & Su-In, 2017), and contextual importance and utility (CIU) (Främling, 1996). All of these examples generate local explanations that are model agnostic. However, some of these methods (LIME and SHAP) have major drawbacks, that is, they are unfaithful and can be attacked (Slack et al., 2020). This means that explanations generated by such systems are not necessarily truthful and can also be manipulated to provide explanations that deceive a user. It has also been shown that they can however help explainees in better understanding model behavior (Hase & Bansal, 2020).

Next to the above-mentioned methods, there also exist gradient-based and attribution methods, for example, deep lift (Shrikumar et al., 2017), integrated gradients (Sundararajan et al., 2017), and layer-wise relevance propagation (LRP) (Binder et al., 2016). In this category, it has been shown experimentally that not all available and used methods are faithful (Adebayo et al., 2018). With these methods, attribution scores for input data can be calculated, which can be the basis for visualizations.

The previously mentioned XAI methods can be leveraged to create visualizations like saliency maps. Saliency maps (Fig. 25.1) are images that highlight the most relevant region of an image (Simonyan et al., 2013). Relevancy in this case is determined by the explanation method that calculates the attribution scores. Explanations for textual data can be made through, for example, bar plots (Fig. 25.3). Here, every input token (which is a part of a word) also receives an attribution score that can be plotted.

These can be employed to generate user-centered explanations to enhance understanding. However, the method and its results itself are not enough to provide social explanations. They still need to be adapted to the explainee to fit the process of sXAI. For example, saliency maps can be used as one step in the interaction between an explainer and explainee that adds a visual modality.

25.4 Visualization in XAI

In this section, we focus on the visualization of DL models, data used for training and predictions from such models. Visualization can aid explainers to express the explanandum for explainees and thereby aid them in gaining better understanding. For example, it has been shown that visualizations can have a positive impact on the development and increase of critical thinking for university students (Shatri & Buza, 2017).

In recent years, the field of visual analytics has been applied to create explanations of various steps in the process of creating and using DL models (Alicioglu & Sun, 2022). Each of these steps has different target audiences with varying previous knowledge about those models (Fig. 25.2). Visualizations can be used before the model creation and training process, during model development and after model development (Yuan et al., 2021). During these stages, different explainees are dealt with, from technical experts that develop DL systems to end users that interact with the outcomes of such models.

25.4.1 Visualization of Post Hoc Explanations

Visualization of local post hoc explanations plays an important role in determining the kind of visualizations. Explanations generated for DL models used for classifying images can be added to the input image as highlights (Fig. 25.1). In this way, the regions a model focuses on to make a prediction can be conveyed to a user. For other data modalities, other types of visualizations can be used (Fig. 25.3).

Natural language processing is another field where DL models are used. State-of-the-art architectures like the transformer architecture (Vaswani et al., 2017) originate

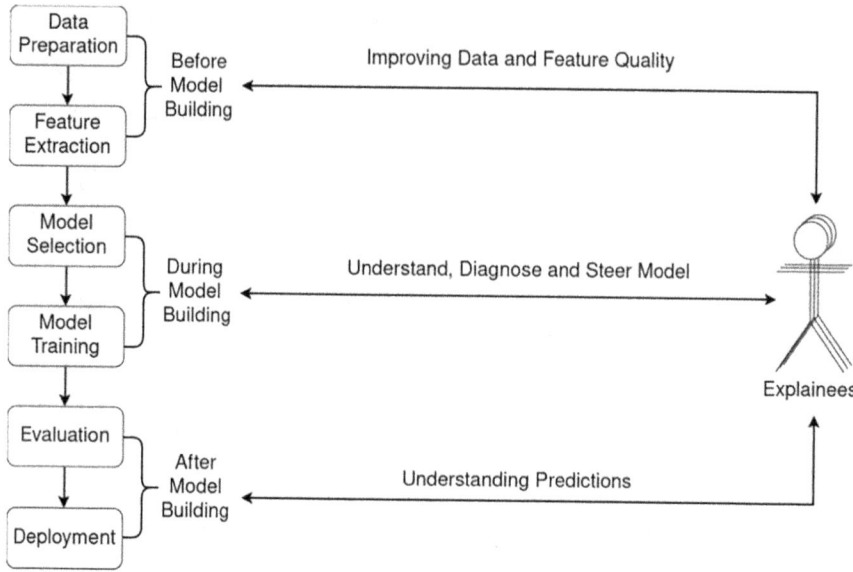

Fig. 25.2 Visualizations to explain various stages of the ML process. At each stage, visualizations can be added to an explanation process for various explainees. Figure inspired by Yuan et al. (2021)

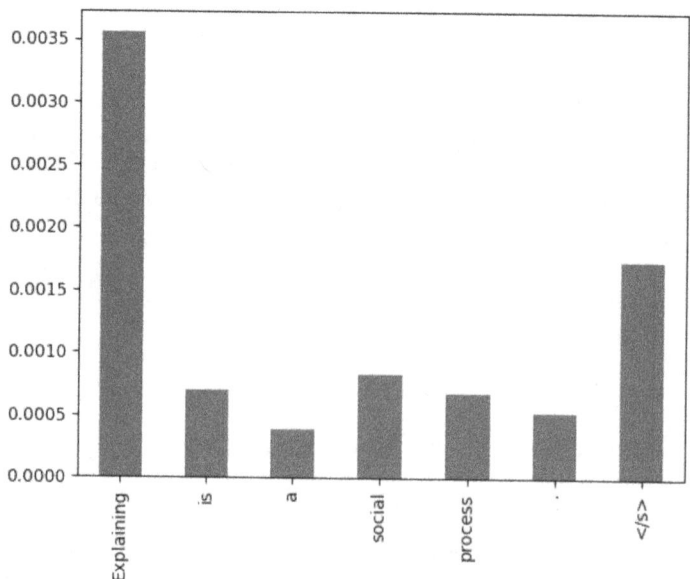

Fig. 25.3 Visualization of feature attributions for text data to explain which tokens were most important to predict the word "Erklären." Prediction made with a MarianMT model (Junczys-Dowmunt et al., 2018) to translate from English to German. Explanations generated through saliency method and aggregated from tokens to words with the inseq library (Sarti et al., 2023)

in this field. A concrete use case can be machine translation, for example, translating from English to German (Junczys-Dowmunt et al., 2018), or sentiment analysis, for example, to detect hate speech in social media comments (Davidson et al., 2017). In these use cases, text is provided as input and text or a label is given as output from a model. To visualize a local explanation that provides feature attribution scores for every word of the input, simple bar plots can be used (Fig. 25.3).

Next to feature attributions, the relative importance of an input token for an output token for sequence-to-sequence models can also be visualized. For example, attention maps of transformer models can be visualized in this manner, but also other explanation methods can be used here, for example (Sarti et al., 2023). These visualizations are not necessarily as intuitive as the previous one and require an explainee to have some prior knowledge to make use of them. However, they can be necessary for these use cases so prior instructions can be helpful.

Besides the modalities of image and text, visualizations can also be used for other ones, like tabular data (Rodis et al., 2024). The same principles as before apply. Depending on the task a model is trained for and the type of the data, visualizations can be created to, for example, highlight important parts of inputs.

25.4.2 Other Forms of Visualizations

Besides visualizing local post hoc explanations, other aspects of the process of creating and deploying DL models can be visualized (Yuan et al., 2021). To increase the global understanding of a system by the user, the model itself can be visualized. For this purpose, many different visualization tools exist (La Rosa et al., 2023), for example, the CNNVis is a tool to visualize convolutional neural networks (CNNs) (Liu et al., 2016). For CNNVis, a requirements analysis was conducted with DL experts and therefore targets domain experts. The latter case can be helpful to get lay users a better understanding of the overall process.

Another aspect of developing DL models that uses visualizations is the training process itself (Yuan et al., 2021). Metrics like the loss during training can be visualized and help technical experts in assessing the quality of a model. However, for these visualizations, the explainees are technical experts with previous knowledge, for example, knowledge of the training process of DL model, and not end users. Therefore, we do not delve deeper into these aspects.

Furthermore, key features of the training data can be visualized to an explainee, again to provide a global understanding of the model. Since patterns are learned from data, understanding the data can be crucial. This type of XAI can be called data explainability (Ali et al., 2023).

25.4.3 Interactivity of Visualizations

As social explanations are revolving around interaction (Sect. 1.1), we will discuss the use of visualizations in the explanation process. More specifically, we will elaborate on visualizations for the three concepts of interaction outlined for social explanations. That is, interaction is patterned, incremental, and multimodal (Sect. 1.1). In all of the discussed ways to visualize explanations for DL models above, visualizations can add value to interactions. They can be used to make interactions multimodal by adding another modality and can be part of a pattern or an incremental step in an explanation process.

Furthermore, interactive elements can also be built into visualizations in order to enhance them. For example, textual explanations could be toggled next to a given visualization or making an image zoomable and rotatable can allow an explainee to focus on aspects that are relevant to them. Commonly used tools during model development, for example, Tensorboard,[1] especially during model training, are designed interactively. For this category of visualization tools, the explainee requires ways to adapt the visualization to a specific problem during development. Therefore, it is important to incorporate interactivity that allows for the adjustment of visualizations. The techniques from the field of visual analytics that are used for ML are also often designed interactively (Yuan et al., 2021).

However, not just technical experts can profit from interactivity in visualizations. Interactivity can help a lot in making visualizations personalized since an explainee can customize the explanation. If a provided visualization includes optional components that show further details, explainees can modify it and focus on the parts for which they require further information. When focusing on an end user, it is important to consider differences in existing knowledge of AI systems (Jansen et al., 2024). Furthermore, everyday explanations are personalized, and an iterative process between an explainer and explainee builds understanding (Rohlfing et al., 2021).

Therefore, interactivity can also be helpful for explanations in DL systems and models. As an example, contrastive explanations can be presented upon request to an explainee that is using a DL model and questions a given output, for example, for explaining the choice of a car to an explainee (Sect. 2.3). Overall, visualizations can aid in the interactivity of social explanations, and interactive elements can enhance explanations.

25.5 Multimodality Through Visualization

Multimodal ML describes the field of using at least two different modalities as input or output of a model. Examples of multimodal ML models are text-to-speech models, text-to-image models, or vision language models. The latter takes a textual

---

[1] https://www.tensorflow.org/tensorboard

prompt that describes an image and generates the image accordingly, for example, diffusion models (Ho et al., 2020). In addition to having a different input and output modality, models can also receive multiple different modalities as input. For example, visual-question answering (VQA) models take an image and a question about an image and generate answers (Wu et al., 2017).

XAI methods for DL models are often in the same modality as the data that is used in combination with the model (Rodis et al., 2024). However, there are also methods that generate multimodal explanations directly (Rodis et al., 2024). If visual explanations are generated for nonvisual data, the generated explanation is multimodal since two different data modalities are present. Multimodality can also be achieved without visualizations, for example, by combining text with speech data. Since this chapter outlines the use of visualizations for social explanations, we focus on multimodality through visualization.

Visual explanations can, for example, be created for textual data. More specifically, by adding visual highlights to a text to mark important words, a multimodal (text and image) explanation is created (Fig. 25.3). If, for example, a user asks a language model a question, relevant input words can be highlighted to explain an answer. Another case of multimodal explanations consisting of the modalities text and image are image descriptions. Next to creating, for example, saliency maps to highlight important regions of an image that played a crucial role, textual descriptions can be given (Rodis et al., 2024).

Multimodal explanations for DL models are not limited to just text and images. Explanations for tabular data can also use visual explanations (Sahakyan et al., 2021). Combining these two modalities results in another multimodal explanation through visualizations. As an example, key input features, which are tabular, can be highlighted, similar as to highlighting key input words.

25.6 Visual sXAI System—Example

In this section, we use the second scenario (Sect. 2.3) to illustrate the use of visualization and multimodality to explain. The scenario deals with a web-based decision support system to assist customers in selecting a car. Here, we assume that the system is based on a DL recommendation model that presents potentially interesting cars to a customer. These recommendations consist of a list of features for the car, for example, its engine specifications and size dimensions as well as a visual depiction of the car. We also assume that the recommendation system is user-centric and takes the end user into account.

Once the customer has entered personal preferences into the system, a recommendation will be displayed. To explain the decision, which car to buy in this case, multiple methods can be used. Key features of the car can be highlighted and linked to the customers' preferences as a first explanation. Second, on the visual depiction of the car, key areas of the visualization can be highlighted that correspond with the customers' preferences. Furthermore, textual descriptions of the visual car features can be provided in addition to the visual explanations. Here, the explainee is the customer, so explanations should be tailored toward their personal perspective.

If a user is not fully satisfied with a recommendation and provides feedback to the system, changes or new recommendations can be provided. Now, it can be useful to add contrastive and counterfactual explanations (Miller, 2019) to explain the differences between the initial recommendation and the new recommendation. These changes and all differences can be visualized again. Either changed features can be highlighted or the images of the different cars can be plotted next to each other.

In this example, we so far have a patterned interaction between a potential customer (the explainee) and the recommendation system (the explainer). Also, the explanations contain visual and textual components making them multimodal. Lastly, the explanation is built incrementally depending on the feedback of the explainee. To take into account the background knowledge of a customer, a user model can be integrated into the explainer according to which adaptations are made (Sect. 13.1). More specifically, explanations can be more general in the beginning and without any detail. Upon request, explanations can be altered and can become more fine-grained if the customer deems it helpful. For example, by showing images of the entire car itself in the beginning followed by detailed images of important components. Similarly, listed features can first be coarse with the option to expand the list of features for more detailed explanations. Importantly, the explainee determines the development of the explanation to suit their needs.

Besides the customer, there are other potential explainees for such a system. The seller might also be interested in understanding what kind of recommendations are given. Thereby, the seller can optimize their offering of cars or interact with a customer during the buying process. Furthermore, the developers are also potential explainees since they might want to optimize the system. Explanations that answer questions on what kind of recommendations leave customers satisfied and which do not can be helpful.

Using visualizations in such a system can thereby provide advantages to all explainees interacting with it. Customers can make more informed decisions, sellers can gain a better understanding of their customers, and developers are able to optimize the system.

25.7 Operationalization

Explanation reception has been highlighted as a key challenge in the field of XAI (Neerincx et al., 2018). This refers to how the explainee receives and evaluates an explanation, and it includes visual and multimodal XAI (Doshi-Velez & Kim, 2017). Since explanations are built incrementally between an explainer and explainee (Chap. 13), quantitative metrics need to consider the addressee as well as the state of the process to evaluate explanations. User studies can be utilized since they do not require definitions of ground truth explanations beforehand. Besides user studies, qualitative analysis is also often conducted by developers of XAI systems which can be insufficient (Nauta et al., 2023).

Since this chapter focuses on visualization and the use of multimodality for social explanations, the explainee plays a key role in evaluating explanations. Based on our example (Sect. 25.6), explainees can be divided into different groups that each require different explanations since they have different background knowledge. First, the explainee that is using the system, that is, the customer that receives recommendations. Second, the seller that uses the system to help customers decide which car to buy. Lastly, the developer of the system that seeks to improve the system.

All of these three explainees have different requirements for an explanation and different questions toward an explainer. Specifically, there are different stakeholders with differing interests in explanations of AI systems (Langer et al., 2021). Therefore, evaluations of explanations can also be split into these categories. Nauta et al. (2023) use three different measures to assess the quality of an explanation regarding users: context, coherence, and controllability. These three properties can be used to evaluate whether or not an explanation is geared toward the right context of an explainee, if the explainee can control the explanation through, for example, interaction, and if the explanation is coherent with previous knowledge of the explainee.

Visual explanations for developing a DL model are often created for technical experts (Yuan et al., 2021). However, it has also been shown that showing exemplary training data can also be effective for end users (Perlmutter et al., 2024). Therefore, it can be helpful to provide explanations from the development process of a DL model to enhance end-user understanding. In this case, explanations that were designed for technical developers can also serve end users despite them being explainees with different background knowledge and requirements.

There are also quantitative approaches to evaluate explanations (Nauta et al., 2023). These can assume ground truth explanations that a system should produce in order to generate good explanations. However, since social explanations are explainee and context dependent, it is very difficult to define such true explanations. Nonetheless, quantitative metrics can be part of the evaluation process of XAI methods; however, it will be difficult to cover all cases.

Overall, explanations should be evaluated considering different background knowledge and needs of different explainees. The goal is to enhance understanding of the explainee. Furthermore, since sXAI focuses on the three concepts that interactions are patterned, incremental, and multimodal (Sect. 1.1), these three aspects should also be considered when evaluating sXAI systems. Additionally, explainers should be evaluated toward their faithfulness and correctness. Otherwise, they might mislead explainees (Slack et al., 2020) and can cause wrong understanding and misplaced trust in a system.

25.8 How Does This Chapter Inspire Further Research on sXAI?

Multimodal signals are key features used in social explanations between humans (Rohlfing et al., 2021). However, these characteristics leave room for improvement of current XAI methods and systems. Especially data-driven systems often use the same modality for explanations as the given data are in, and those explanations are unimodal (Rodis et al., 2024).

So far, the creation of visualizations and multimodal explanations with XAI methods has been discussed. However, for social explanations, it is also necessary for the system to receive multimodal signals as input (Chap. 18). Therefore, such explanation systems could use multiple sensors that can analyze a user's gestures or facial expressions in addition to other input modalities like speech or text via a keyboard. In the given example (Sect. 25.6), customers could be enabled through multimodal inputs that the system could adapt recommendations based on the input.

Another important topic to discuss is interactivity in XAI systems. Since interactivity and incrementality are core features of social explanations (Chap. 1), sXAI systems should be built around that. Dialog-based XAI systems already exist (Sokol & Flach, 2020) and could be used as a basis. Once such systems are interactive, visualizations and multimodality can be incorporated as input and output of such systems. When doing so, the understandability of visualizations should be considered. Depending on previous knowledge of the explainee, some visualizations need to be elaborated upon before they can be understood.

Future studies can also investigate the impact of sXAI aspects on visualizations for explainees with various degrees of background knowledge. Adjusting the type of visualization of an XAI method can significantly reduce the cognitive load of explainees with low AI literacy (Jansen et al., 2024). Therefore, future work could also analyze the effect of integrating social aspects into visualizations of XAI methods on explainees.

Future research can therefore focus on interactivity and personalization of XAI systems toward explainees considering key aspects of social explanations (Chap. 1). Introducing interactivity also opens up more research opportunities to analyze different iterations of the explanation process between explainer and explainee.

25.9 Rapid Access

Current state-of-the-art methods in AI, especially in ML, display an inherent lack of transparency and interpretability in those models (Ali et al., 2023). In DL, a subfield of ML, the size of the used models and the number of their parameters make it especially intransparent. Hence, the field of XAI is relevant to make those models more transparent by providing explanations. These explanations can be visual, for example, an image of a single data instance with highlights at relevant parts.

  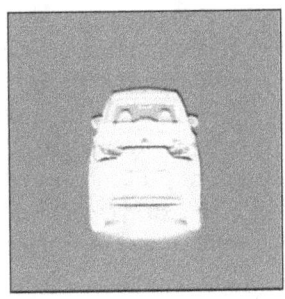

Fig. 25.4 Saliency map example for an image classifier for cars. Image created with a VGGNet (Simonyan and Zisserman, 2014) that is fine-tuned on a dataset to predict cars (Krause et al., 2013). Attributions created with the GradCAM (Selvaraju et al., 2017) method. The left image shows the original input, the middle one all pixels that contributed to a decision (in green), and the right one all pixels that did not (in red)

Visualizations can be done to explain various steps during the creation of DL models (Yuan et al., 2021). Here, we discuss key aspects of sXAI and how visualizations of XAI methods can be connected to them. The focus is on the interactivity of the explanations, that is, explanations are patterned, multimodal, and incremental (Chap. 1).

An example of visual explanations that can be generated with XAI methods for DL models is saliency maps (Simonyan et al., 2013) (Fig. 25.4). In saliency maps, the most important parts of an image are highlighted, indicating which areas affected a given output the most. Multiple methods exist that can create such explanations, for example, GradCAM (Selvaraju et al., 2017) and Integrated Gradients (Sundararajan et al., 2017). Visualizations can also be done on other modalities like textual data (Fig. 25.3) or tabular data (Rodis et al., 2024).

Visualizations can be used to add another modality to an explanation, for example, complement a textual explanation. In natural language processing tasks, like text classification, visualizations can be used to mark the most significant words of the input for a produced output (Fig. 25.3). For image-related tasks, visual explanations can be used, for example, by highlighting relevant parts of input images that contributed to a given output (Fig. 25.4). XAI methods for DL models can incorporate multimodality (Rodis et al., 2024) to enhance the explanans given by the explainer, which can be an explanation module for a recommender system (Sect. 25.6). In general, the combination of any other modality, like text, with visualizations, will result in multimodal explanations.

To make visual explanations incremental, options to request further visualizations can be provided to an explainee. Visualizations can also be adapted based on a user model from the explainer about the explainee (Chap. 13). This can be utilized to create individualized visualizations.

Explanation evaluation of XAI systems is an ongoing research topic (Nauta et al., 2023). Visualizations and multimodal explanations in the context of sXAI have to be evaluated with regard to the interactive process of an explanation. Explainees have to be taken into account in order to assess an explanation. User studies are already used to evaluate XAI systems (Nauta et al., 2023) and will also be useful for evaluating sXAI systems.

sXAI builds on the concepts of interactive explanation generation between an explainer and explainee (Chap. 1). The explanandum is iteratively brought across toward the explainee, and the understanding is built over multiple iterations (Rohlfing et al., 2021). Visualizations can be utilized to make explanations patterned, incremental, and multimodal.

References

Adadi, A., & Berrada, M. (2018). Peeking inside the black-box: A survey on Explainable Artificial Intelligence (XAI). *IEEE Access, 6*, 52138–52160. https://doi.org/10.1109/ACCESS.2018.2870052.

Adebayo, J., Gilmer, J., Muelly, M., Goodfellow, I., Hardt, M., & Kim, B. (2018). Sanity checks for saliency maps. In *Proceedings of the 32nd International Conference on Neural Information Processing Systems* (pp. 9525–9536). Curran Associates Inc. https://doi.org/10.5555/3327546.3327621.

Ali, S., Abuhmed, T., El-Sappagh, S., Muhammad, K., Alonso-Moral, J. M., Confalonieri, R., Guidotti, R., Del Ser, J., Díaz Rodríguez, N., & Herrera, F. (2023). Explainable Artificial Intelligence (XAI): What we know and what is left to attain Trustworthy Artificial Intelligence. *Information Fusion, 99*, 101805. https://doi.org/10.1016/j.inffus.2023.101805.

Alicioglu, G., & Sun, B. (2022). A survey of visual analytics for explainable artificial intelligence methods. *Computers & Graphics, 102*, 502–520. https://doi.org/10.1016/j.cag.2021.09.002.

Alom, Md.Z., Taha, T. M., Yakopcic, C., Westberg, S., Sidike, P., Nasrin, M. S., Hasan, M., Van Essen, B. C., Awwal, A. A. S., & Asari, V. K. (2019). A state-of-the-art survey on deep learning theory and architectures. *Electronics, 8*(3), 292. https://doi.org/10.3390/electronics8030292.

Binder, A., Montavon, G., Lapuschkin, S., Müller, K.-R., & Samek, W. (2016). Layer-wise relevance propagation for neural networks with local renormalization layers". In *Artificial Neural Networks and Machine Learning-ICANN 2016* (pp. 63–71). Springer. https://doi.org/10.1007/978-3-319-44781-0_8.

Burkart, N., & Huber, M. F. (2021). A survey on the explainability of supervised machine learning. *Journal of Artificial Intelligence Research, 70*, 245–317. https://doi.org/10.1613/jair.1.12228.

Buzcu, B., Tessa, M., Tchappi, I., Najjar, A., Hulstijn, J., Calvaresi, D., & Aydoğan, R. (2024). Towards interactive explanation-based nutrition virtual coaching systems. *Autonomous Agents and Multi-Agent Systems, 38*, 5. https://doi.org/10.1007/s10458-023-09634-5.

Chatzimparmpas, A., Martins, R. M., Jusufi, I., Kucher, K., Rossi, F., & Kerren, A. (2020). The state of the art in enhancing trust in machine learning models with the use of visualizations. *Computer Graphics Forum, 39*(3), 713–756. https://doi.org/10.1111/cgf.14034.

Davidson, T., Warmsley, D., Macy, M., & Weber, I. (2017). Automated hate speech detection and the problem of offensive language. In *Proceedings of the International AAAI Conference on Web and Social Media* (Vol. 11. 1, pp. 512–515), Montreal, Canada. https://doi.org/10.1609/icwsm.v11i1.14955.

Deng, J., Dong, W., Socher, R., Li, L.-J., Li, K., & Fei-Fei, L. (2009). ImageNet: A large-scale hierarchical image database. In *2009 IEEE Conference on Computer Vision and Pattern Recognition* (pp. 248–255). IEEE. https://doi.org/10.1109/CVPR.2009.5206848.

Dong, S., Wang, P., & Abbas, K. (2021). A survey on deep learning and its applications. *Computer Science Review, 40*, 100379. https://doi.org/10.1016/j.cosrev.2021.100379.

Doshi-Velez, F., & Kim, B. (2017). *Towards a rigorous science of interpretable machine learning.* https://doi.org/10.48550/arXiv.1702.08608.

Dosovitskiy, A., Beyer, L., Kolesnikov, A., Weissenborn, D., Zhai, X., Unterthiner, T., Dehghani, M., Minderer, M., Heigold, G., Gelly, S., Uszkoreit, J., & Houlsby, N. (2021). *An image is worth 16x16 words: Transformers for image recognition at scale.* https://doi.org/10.48550/arXiv.2010.11929.

Doyle, D., Tsymbal, A., & Cunningham, P. (2003). A review of explanation and explanation in case-based reasoning (pp. 1–24). https://publications.scss.tcd.ie/tech-reports/reports.03/TCD-CS-2003-41.pdf.

Främling, K. (1996). *Modélisation et apprentissage des préférences par réseaux de neurones pour l'aide à la décision multicritère.* PhD thesis. INSA de Lyon. https://theses.hal.science/tel-00825854v1/file/1996_Framling_Kary.pdf.

Grill, J.-B., Strub, F., Altché, F., Tallec, C., Richemond, P., Buchatskaya, E., Doersch, C., Pires, B. A., Guo, Z., Azar, M. G., Piot, B., Kavukcuoglu, K., Munos, R., & Valko, M. (2020). Bootstrap your own latent – A new approach to self-supervised learning. In H. Larochelle, M. Ranzato, R. Hadsell, M.-F. Balcan, & H.-T. Lin (Eds.), *NIPS'20: Proceedings of the 34th International Conference on Neural Information Processing Systems* (pp. 21271–21284). Curran Associates, Inc. https://proceedings.neurips.cc/paper_files/paper/2020/file/f3ada80d5c4ee70142b17b8192b2958e-Paper.pdf.

Hase, P., & Bansal, M. (2020). Evaluating explainable AI: Which algorithmic explanations help users predict model behavior? In *Proceedings of the 58th Annual Meeting of the Association for Computational Linguistics* (pp. 5540–5552). Association for Computational Linguistics. https://doi.org/10.18653/v1/2020.acl-main.491.

Ho, J., Jain, A., & Abbeel, P. (2020). Denoising diffusion probabilistic models. In *Proceedings of the 34th International Conference on Neural Information Processing Systems* (pp. 6840–6851). Curran Associates Inc. https://doi.org/10.5555/3495724.3496298.

Hohman, F., Kahng, M., Pienta, R., & Chau, D. H. (2019). Visual analytics in deep learning: An interrogative survey for the next frontiers. *IEEE Transactions on Visualization and Computer Graphics, 25*(8), 2674–2693. https://doi.org/10.1109/TVCG.2018.2843369.

Jansen, A., Leborgne, F., Wang, Q., & Zhang, C. (2024). Contextualizing the "Why": The potential of using visual map as a novel XAI method for users with low AI-literacy. In *Extended Abstracts of the CHI Conference on Human Factors in Computing Systems* (p. 87). Association for Computing Machinery. https://doi.org/10.1145/3613905.3650812.

Junczys-Dowmunt, M., Grundkiewicz, R., Dwojak, T., Hoang, H., Heafield, K., Neckermann, T., Seide, F., Germann, U., Aji, A. F., Bogoychev, N., Martins, A. F. T., & Birch, A. (2018). Marian: Fast neural machine translation in C++. In F. Liu & T. Solorio (Eds.), *Proceedings of ACL 2018, System Demonstrations* (pp. 116–121). Association for Computational Linguistics. https://doi.org/10.18653/v1/P18-4020.

Krause, J., Stark, M., Deng, J., & Fei-Fei, L. (2013). 3D object representations for fine-grained categorization. In *2013 IEEE International Conference on Computer Vision Workshops* (pp. 554–561). IEEE. https://doi.org/10.1109/ICCVW.2013.77.

Langer, M., Oster, D., Speith, T., Hermanns, H., Kästner, L., Schmidt, E., Sesing, A., & Baum, K. (2021). What do we want from Explainable Artificial Intelligence (XAI)?–A stakeholder perspective on XAI and a conceptual model guiding interdisciplinary XAI research. *Artificial Intelligence, 296*, 103473. https://doi.org/10.1016/j.artint.2021.103473.

La Rosa, B., Blasilli, G., Bourqui, R., Auber, D., Santucci, G., Capobianco, R., Bertini, E., Giot, R., & Angelini, M. (2023). State of the art of visual analytics for explainable deep learning. *Computer Graphics Forum, 42*(1), 319–355. https://doi.org/10.1111/cgf.14733.

Liu, M., Shi, J., Li, Z., Li, C., Zhu, J., & Liu, S. (2017). Towards better analysis of deep convolutional neural networks. *IEEE Transactions on Visualization and Computer Graphics, 23*(1), 91–100. https://doi.org/10.1109/TVCG.2016.2598831.

Lundberg, S. M., & Lee, S.-I. (2017). A unified approach to interpreting model predictions. In *Proceedings of the 31st International Conference on Neural Information Processing Systems* (pp. 4769–4777). Curran Associates Inc. https://doi.org/10.5555/3295222.3295230.

Miller, T. (2019). Explanation in artificial intelligence: Insights from the social sciences. *Artificial Intelligence, 267*, 1–38. https://doi.org/10.1016/j.artint.2018.07.007.

Mualla, Y., Tchappi, I., Kampik, T., Najjar, A., Calvaresi, D., Abbas-Turki, A., Galland, S., & Nicolle, C. (2022). The quest of parsimonious XAI: A human–agent architecture for explanation formulation. *Artificial Intelligence, 302*, 103573. https://doi.org/10.1016/j.artint.2021.103573.

Nauta, M., Trienes, J., Pathak, S., Nguyen, E., Peters, M., Schmitt, Y., Schlötterer, J., van Keulen, M., & Seifert, C. (2023). From anecdotal evidence to quantitative evaluation methods: A systematic review on evaluating explainable AI. *ACM Computing Surveys, 55*(13s), 295. https://doi.org/10.1145/3583558.

Neerincx, M. A., van der Waa, J., Kaptein, F., & van Diggelen, J. (2018). Using perceptual and cognitive explanations for enhanced human-agent team performance. In *Engineering Psychology and Cognitive Ergonomics: 15th International Conference* (pp. 204–214). Springer. https://doi.org/10.1007/978-3-319-91122-9_18.

Perlmutter, M., Gifford, R., & Krening, S. (2024). Impact of example-based XAI for neural networks on trust, understanding, and performance. *International Journal of Human–Computer Studies, 188*, 103277. https://doi.org/10.1016/j.ijhcs.2024.103277.

Prentzas, N., Kakas, A., & Pattichis, C. S. (2023). *Explainable AI applications in the medical domain: A systematic review.* https://doi.org/10.48550/arXiv.2308.05411.

Radford, A., Wu, J., Child, R., Luan, D., Amodei, D., & Sutskever, I. (2019). Language models are unsupervised multitask learners. *OpenAI Blog, 1*(8), 1–24. https://cdn.openai.com/better-language-models/language_models_are_unsupervised_multitask_learners.pdf.

Ribeiro, M. T., Singh, S., & Guestrin, C. (2016). *Model-agnostic interpretability of machine learning.* https://doi.org/10.48550/arXiv.1606.05386.

Rodis, N., Sardianos, C., Radoglou-Grammatikis, P., Sarigiannidis, P., Varlamis, I., & Papadopoulos, G. Th. (2024). Multimodal explainable artificial intelligence: A comprehensive review of methodological advances and future research directions. *IEEE Access, 12*, 159794–159820. https://doi.org/10.1109/ACCESS.2024.3467062.

Rohlfing, K. J., Cimiano, P., Scharlau, I., Matzner, T., Buhl, H., Buschmeier, H., Grimminger, A., Hammer, B., HäbUmbach, R., Horwath, I., Hüllermeier, E., Kern, F., Kopp, S., Thommes, K., Ngomo, A.-C. N., Schulte, C., Wachsmuth, H., Wagner, P., & Wrede, B. (2021). Explanation as a social practice: Toward a conceptual framework for the social design of AI systems. *IEEE Transactions on Cognitive and Developmental Systems, 13*(3), 717–728. https://doi.org/10.1109/TCDS.2020.3044366.

Sahakyan, M., Aung, Z., & Rahwan, T. (2021). Explainable Artificial Intelligence for tabular data: A survey. *IEEE Access, 9*, 135392–135422. https://doi.org/10.1109/ACCESS.2021.3116481.

Samek, W., Montavon, G., Lapuschkin, S., Anders, C. J., & Müller, K.-R. (2021). Explaining deep neural networks and beyond: A review of methods and applications. *Proceedings of the IEEE, 109*(3), 247–278. https://doi.org/10.1109/JPROC.2021.3060483.

Sarker, I. H. (2021). Deep learning: A comprehensive overview on techniques, taxonomy, applications and research directions. *SN Computer Science, 2*(6), 420. https://doi.org/10.1007/s42979-021-00815-1.

Sarti, G., Feldhus, N., Sickert, L., Van Der Wal, O., Nissim, M., & Bisazza, A. (2023). *Inseq: An interpretability toolkit for sequence generation models.* https://doi.org/10.48550/arXiv.2302.13942.

Selvaraju, R. R., Cogswell, M., Das, A., Vedantam, R., Parikh, D., & Batra, D. (2017). Grad-CAM: Visual explanations from deep networks via gradient-based localization. In *2017 IEEE International Conference on Computer Vision (ICCV)* (pp. 618–626). IEEE. https://doi.org/10.1109/ICCV.2017.74.

Shatri, K., & Buza, K. (2017). The use of visualization in teaching and learning process for developing critical thinking of students. *European Journal of Social Science Education and Research, 4*(3), 134–140. https://doi.org/10.26417/ejser.v9i1.p71-74.

Shrikumar, A., Greenside, P., & Kundaje, A. (2017). Learning important features through propagating activation differences. In *Proceedings of the 34th International Conference on Machine Learning* (pp. 3145–3153). JMLR.org. https://doi.org/10.5555/3305890.3306006.

Simonyan, K., Vedaldi, A., & Zisserman, A. (2013). *Deep inside convolutional networks: Visualising image classification models and saliency maps*. https://doi.org/10.48550/arXiv.1312.6034.

Simonyan, K., & Zisserman, A. (2014). *Very deep convolutional networks for large-scale image recognition*. https://doi.org/10.48550/arXiv.1409.1556.

Simonyan, K., & Zisserman, A. (2015). In Y. Bengio & Y. LeCun (Eds.), *Very deep convolutional networks for large-scale image recognition*. San Diego, CA, USA. https://doi.org/10.48550/arXiv.1409.1556.

Slack, D., Hilgard, S., Jia, E., Singh, S., & Lakkaraju, H. (2020). Fooling lime and shap: Adversarial attacks on post hoc explanation methods. In *Proceedings of the AAAI/ACM Conference on AI, Ethics, and Society* (pp. 180–186). Association for Computing Machinery. https://doi.org/10.1145/3375627.3375830.

Sokol, K., & Flach, P. (2020). One explanation does not fit all: The promise of interactive explanations for machine learning transparency. *KI-Künstliche Intelligenz, 34*(2), 235–250. https://doi.org/10.1007/s13218-020-00637-y.

Sundararajan, M., Taly, A., & Yan, Q. (2017). Axiomatic attribution for deep networks. In *Proceedings of the 34th International Conference on Machine Learning* (pp. 3319–3328). JMLR.org. https://doi.org/10.5555/3305890.3306024.

Tessa, M., Abchiche, S., Ferstler, Y. C., Tchappi, I., Benatchba, K., & Najjar, A. (2023). Enhancing explainability in AI: Food recommender system use case. In *Proceedings of the 11th International Conference on Human–Agent Interaction* (pp. 395–397), Gothenburg, Sweden. https://doi.org/10.1145/3623809.3623938.

Vaswani, A., Shazeer, N., Parmar, N., Uszkoreit, J., Jones, L., Gomez, A. N., Kaiser, Ł., & Polosukhin, I. (2017). Attention is all you need. In *Proceedings of the 31st International Conference on Neural Information Processing Systems* (pp. 6000–6010). Curran Associates Inc.

Wu, Q., Teney, D., Wang, P., Shen, C., Dick, A., & Van Den Hengel, A. (2017). Visual question answering: A survey of methods and datasets. *Computer Vision and Image Understanding, 163*, 21–40. https://doi.org/10.1016/j.cviu.2017.05.001.

Yuan, J., Chen, C., Yang, W., Liu, M., Xia, J., & Liu, S. (2021). A survey of visual analytics techniques for machine learning. *Computational Visual Media, 7*, 3–36. https://doi.org/10.1007/s41095-020-0191-7.

Open Access This chapter is licensed under the terms of the Creative Commons Attribution 4.0 International License (http://creativecommons.org/licenses/by/4.0/), which permits use, sharing, adaptation, distribution and reproduction in any medium or format, as long as you give appropriate credit to the original author(s) and the source, provide a link to the Creative Commons license and indicate if changes were made.

The images or other third party material in this chapter are included in the chapter's Creative Commons license, unless indicated otherwise in a credit line to the material. If material is not included in the chapter's Creative Commons license and your intended use is not permitted by statutory regulation or exceeds the permitted use, you will need to obtain permission directly from the copyright holder.

Part IV
Evaluation

Chapter 26
Evaluation Principles

Kirsten Thommes

Abstract In the past, there has been much research aiming to evaluate XAI practices—that is, explanations that can add to a user's understanding of "why" or "why not." However, because there is such a huge amount of diversity in social contexts, optimizing for the mean neglects the social dimensions of to whom, what, why, when, and where explanations are provided. Nonetheless, these dimensions matter. We give some brief examples on the accuracy of the mental model (as an example for who?), on measuring explanation practices (as an example of what?), on human motivation (as an example of why?), on repeated interactions (as an example of when?), and on bystander effects (as an example of where?). Importantly, controlling for these factors (or randomizing them) is as important as attempting to perform external validations.

26.1 How Does This Chapter Relate to XAI

Theoretically, the emerging XAI approaches prioritize interpretability and explainability. Both dimensions lie in the eyes of the beholder and constitute a continuum between fully opaque and fully interpretable and explainable. However, there is some confusion about the terms of interpretability and explainability: They may be interpreted from a mathematical side of machine learning as systems that can be described fully and explicitly. However, from a human perspective, interpretability and explainability are perceptions that are not necessarily connected directly to the question whether a system's components can be described explicitly. Therefore, much XAI research has also concentrated on describing shortcuts such as explaining via counterfactuals, explaining via SHAP, or the like. These methods do not explain the whole AI system but try to resonate about a recommendation or a categorization.

K. Thommes (✉)
Faculty of Business Administration and Economics, Paderborn University, Paderborn, Germany
e-mail: kirsten.thommes@uni-paderborn.de

There are two interrelated critiques to such approaches: First, gaining an understanding of a complex system such as AI needs to be hard-earned, requiring efforts from the explainees. However, humans are heterogeneous in the capabilities and willingness to put effort in understanding, and current evaluations therefore may be measures of the mean of the population but not capture how explainable an attempt is to all explainees. Not capturing the diversity of context factors is also at the center of recent state-of-the-art research that exposes several shortcomings that limit the utility of explainable systems for users. These deficiencies include a lack of context awareness (Anjomshoae et al., 2019), insufficient interaction, and insufficient individual explanations according to the user's needs (Sokol & Flach, 2020).

Because there are no easy answers for the abovementioned problems and certainly no answers that will be valid independently of social context, time, and space, some researchers advocate taking the human out of the XAI design. In a nutshell, the question centers on whether technology should adapt to humans or whether humans must adapt to technology. For instance, researchers advocating the latter assume that considering some general design principles is sufficient and that there must be an optimal one-fits-all solution. They even suggest not evaluating how the user receives explanations, and, instead, formulating some sound and general laws about good explanations (see, e.g., Rosenfeld, 2021; Nauta et al., 2023). One example is the idea that good explanations should be short. The line of reasoning here is that user studies (e.g., Poursabzi-Sangdeh et al., 2021) show that users often do not want to be burdened by explanation but want to get on with the task. For this reason, Mualla et al. (2022) stress the importance of parsimony in explanation. They suggest that explanations must be as short as possible so as not to disrupt the flow; but not shorter than that, so as not to be false or incomplete. Therefore, some XAI researchers assume that this very general rule should be applied to all kinds of XAI systems.

However, this view is very mechanistic and takes human nature out of context: In fact, humans are diverse, social context is diverse, and technology must adapt to the user. Diverse technology must serve human needs and, considering human nature, must differentiate between one of the most fundamental human characteristics: individual contexts. The differentiation between good and bad explanations lies in the eyes of the beholder and may differ between humans, between contexts, over time, and across space. We, therefore, suggest that differences in explanations (short or long, static or interactive, incomplete or complete) must be analyzed in context, and that a general rule is not in the interest of human nature. Although the rule may be right in one setting, it may well be wrong in another. Therefore, we propose measuring both sides–the XAI and the human–along with their interaction process in order to understand how "why" explanations can improve comprehension, usability, and the human–XAI tandem as a social system.

The main argument is based on Hoffman et al. (2018), who have been influential in the discussion over the evaluation of explainable AI systems (Fig. 26.1) and succinctly depict the elements of a social system (see also Hulstijn et al., 2023 for a recent discussion of explainable recommendation systems).

26 Evaluation Principles

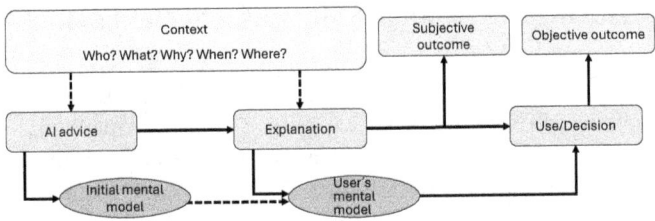

Fig. 26.1 Diagram, based on a similar diagram by Hoffman et al. (2018)

The model shows a flow. The user receives initial advice from the AI, which affects the initial mental model. The instruction is followed by an explanation on the user's demand (the explainee). Explanations can be quantified according to their properties. As suggested in this book, we differentiate between modalities, patterns, and incrementality. Chapter 27 discusses how to measure these properties of explanations. The explanations will revise the user's mental model and subsequently enable good decision-making. The quality of decision-making can be measured either subjectively or objectively. Chapter 28 disentangles how to measure the effects of explanations.

The upper level of the model presents suggestions on how to measure the *objective outcome* of explanations. For example, the effectiveness of an explanation can be tested by so-called *goodness criteria* that developers can assess independently based on log files. For example, correctness of the information items in an explanation (are they true), or relative completeness of an explanation (are all relevant arguments for or against listed). The effect of an explanation on a user's mental model is tested by a *test of comprehension*, similar to an exam question. After the explanation, is the user's mental model adjusted so that the explanandum is now understood? Finally, the overall effect on performance can be measured by a *test of performance* related to the task. Here, we can measure usage, for example, or a decision to buy or to undertake the transaction. There are also *subjective outcomes* that can be measured to test the effect of an explanation. Consider, for example, a *test of satisfaction*, asking end users whether they are satisfied with the explanation.

Contrary to popular claims such as "keep it short" or "aim for completeness," the book advocates for measuring explanations according to the context. Thus, good evaluations should take important context factors into account. In the following, discuss some of the most important context factors and how they may be operationalized in the form of the context-relevant questions. Note that the following chapter provides only some examples and reviews the recent debate in the scientific literature. Nonetheless, other criteria and characteristics of the social context may be relevant as well.

26.2 Measuring the Human Ability as a Social Factor

"Who?" asks for the human who uses the system. Many studies in this area differentiate between expert users and lay person either in a particular domain or with AI. The idea is that domain experts have some general knowledge with which to put any explanation into context, they may ask more informed questions, and they can communicate differently than lay persons. This assumption about the dichotomy in the population (expert vs. lay person) is easy to make but rather naive. First, experts can be very biased (Perez, 2015; Kynn, 2008) and may have neither a correct mental model about the problem nor the AI in their mind. Think, for instance, about decision-making in the medical domain, in which, among others, gender issues are frequently discussed, because many practitioners tend to overlook, for instance, signs of a heart attack in women because of different medical conditions. Similarly, human experts may be very biased in every domain, even though they have some expert knowledge.

Second, while they may be generally more able to communicate about the domain using technical terminology, they may lack technical terminology about the underlying machine learning, just as they may also lack knowledge about machine learning. A prominent example of experts failing in statistics is the popular survey among British Members of Parliament in which 60% failed to correctly answer the question, "If you spin a coin twice, what is the probability of getting two heads?" Thus, being in charge or being an expert in no way means that one is an expert in logic, statistics, or machine learning.

Therefore, we suggest that research should not focus on stereotyping users into experts and lay persons but rather reflect on the social dimensions of the explanans and what is important to know about AI. Gentile et al. (2021) suggest differentiating between the subject's prior knowledge of the domain and their prior knowledge of AI.

One potential way to do this is reflected in Fig. 26.1, which assumes that the interaction with the XAI alters the mental model 14.5.4 of the explainee; see also Chap. 14. It might be useful to raise the question of what dimension determines the initial accuracy of the mental model. The further away the mental model from the desired state of the explained, the more effort will be required to renew, alter, and refine it. In a sense, this proposal is a resource-based view on explanations, by which we mean that the cognitive resources time, attention, and energy for changing the mental model are more relevant than any stereotype about experts or lay persons.

Thus, the division between experts or lay persons is intended to roughly approximate the distance between the user's mental model and the AI system being explained. Hence, when reading and doing user studies, one must consider that the difference may be marginal and that the approximation of an individual's status as an expert or lay persons is imprecise. An improvement would be understanding user models, their variation, and the determinants causing variation. Understanding other humans' mental models is a rather complex task, because users have difficulties explicitly stating what they understand about a system. Hoffman et al. (2018)

gives an overview of the current techniques of users' mental model elicitation, ranging from think-aloud studies in which mental models are elicited greenfield to prototypical models and users are asked to alter them until they match their mental model.

Measuring the distance between a user's mental model and the AI model as ground truth or the refined model after an interaction is rather difficult. Standard metrics such as the Pearson correlation, Euclidean distance, and cosine similarity result in different measures for the same distance. More advanced measures generate the same problem (Schaffernicht & Groesser, 2021). Recently, (Alspector, 2021) suggested a new method of measuring mental models based on knowledge graphs and interpreting the distance as the novelty of the task (or the environment for the user). The idea is promising, because it is compatible with the resource-based view we propose: Differences in mental models can be overcome with sufficient resources. However, the users' resources to overcome differences must be considered. Not considering them may widen the gap between the initial and final mental models, because explanations may overemphasize conflicts between mental models and remove attention from relevant components (Wan et al., 2023). The resources mitigating this conflict and mental model updating are the users' social context, and these can be distinguished roughly as motivation, ability, and available cognitive capacity.

26.3 Measuring the Explanation as a Social Factor

Many current approaches use feature explanations as a solution for the "What" question by either applying SHAP or similar procedures. Nauta et al. (2023) provide a very succinct overview of the most prominent explanation techniques currently used in XAI for text, tabular, and image data methods. Based on Guidotti et al. (2018), they differentiate between post hoc explanations, white box algorithms, and trained explanation practices of the XAI system (not the AI). Nauta et al. (2023) propose asking questions to classify and describe explanations in more detail. Their framework is targeted mainly toward one-shot explanations and not socially constructed explanations in incremental, patterned, and multimodal modes (see for this Chap. 27). Nonetheless, the criteria are a very useful collection of explanation characteristics that need to be specified in evaluations. Specifically, they ask for correctness, completeness, consistency, continuity, contrastivity, covariate (interaction of features explained), complexity, composition, confidence, context (as relevance for the user), coherence (with world knowledge), and controllability. In their review, they also analyze whether these criteria have been evaluated in empirical XAI studies, but with the rather disappointing result that many empirical studies evaluate coherence, and only a few vary more than one explanation characteristic systematically. This is unfortunate, because a systematic evaluation of different types of explanations and what should be aimed for what is needed to advance the field. Systematic evaluations, for instance, along the proposed 12 C characteristics, would be useful to better understand the question of what constitutes good explanations.

On a different level, the question concerning "what" to explain may also be related to the questions asked in the generation of explanations in Chap. 15, and these go way beyond the current state of the art. Just to mention a few points, it might also be a valid explanation for some users to explain the process of data collection, quality control, or other aspects of the recommendation by the AI. For instance, as Vilone and Longo (2021) explain, depending on the goal of the explanations (justification, controlling the system, improving the system, or discovering new associations), other questions may occur and also require other explanation techniques than the previously established ones.

For empirical research, it would be useful to differentiate between different goals of the explanation process and also to specifically address the explanation properties that are going to be varied in explanations.

26.4 Measuring the Human Motivation as a Social Factor

One important question in evaluating explanations is answering "Why?"—Why should humans be motivated to interact with the XAI system at all? What would they gain, and what are the associated costs? The why question also suggests how many resources a human user will devote to understanding.

Many evaluations do not address the why, and participants often have little reason to invest resources in understanding. The assumption that all humans enjoy thinking about advice is, however, not backed up by psychological research, which highlights overall that thinking is frequently unpleasant for humans (David et al., 2024). When mental effort in general and overall populations and situations felt aversive, this raises some doubts about the motivation to solve artificial tasks in experimental research in AI. Moreover, many evaluations use proxy tasks. However, as Gentile et al. (2021) put it, the "measures of performance in proxy tasks may not be predictive of performance in more realistic decision-making tasks." Often, XAI approaches use easy scenarios in an artificial online lab environment. As such, not only is the task just a proxy, but the human-AI interaction is also a proxy. In their famous study on comparing real tasks and proxy tasks, Buçinca et al. (2020) show that the consequences of analyzing proxy tasks may even result in wrong conclusions as they have no external validity for real tasks.

There are many potential reasons for differences between lay persons interaction in proxy tasks and later real-world interaction settings due to social context:

- The center of attention in a proxy lab situation is the human-XAI interaction and not the outcome of the task. Because study participants are forced to interact and have no alternative way of spending their time, they will probably be more likely to interact and ask for explanations than in the real world. Buçinca et al. (2020) assume that this may be one of the explanations for the difference between proxy

and real task results. Proxy tasks may thus be problematic, because, by design, they focus too much on the interaction.
- Moreover, the implicit motivation to ask for an explanation and engage in a co-constructive explanation process may differ between lab situations and the real world. First, experimental participants may serve the researcher's demand effect (see also "where," 26.6): They know that the researcher wants them to engage thoroughly in a task and want to please the researcher by acting accordingly. This effect may be especially pronounced in qualitative settings or when the researcher is visible to the participant. Also, curiosity may drive some interactions in the lab and the field but in a non-predictable manner. This may result in a wrong estimation of effects, because the wrong root cause for the results is identified when results are attributed to interaction design and not to curiosity. In real decision-making scenarios, the intrinsic motivation to engage in explanations may differ and diminish in repeated interactions due to routines, laziness, or thinking aversion.
- Also, the extrinsic motivation to engage in explanatory processes may differ from the lab to the field and from proxy to real tasks. In many lab studies, participants have no extrinsic motivation to put effort into the task. In real-world human-XAI interaction, the users' end goal may motivate them, because they want to decide well or they have to take responsibility for their decision and fear the monetary, social, or psychological costs of a suboptimal decision. All potential losses or gains of such an interaction belong to the extrinsic motivation from users and may also result in erroneous conclusions about causal relations and little external validity.

The optimal design would be a real-world test bed (also called field experiments in some disciplines) to analyze social XAI with real end users in real tasks and real situations over a longer period to mimic real-world conditions in an evaluation study.

A second best solution would be evaluating as closely as possible to the later field of application regarding human users, tasks, situations, and motivation. For instance, one may allow humans to skip explanations or do something else instead of listening and engaging in explanations. One may also ensure that implicit motivation is equal, by using, for example, A-B designs. In A-B designs and randomization to groups A and B, one can assume that the implicit motivation to do a favor for the researcher or being excited due to participating in the study should be equal in both groups. Even when effect sizes might still be attributed to intrinsic motivation, potential differences between groups A and B can be attributed to the design choice concerning XAI under ceteris paribus assumptions.

Finally, ensuring some extrinsic motivation can be achieved by using monetary rewards for good decisions. Even if individuals have other extrinsic motivations in the lab and the field, under monotonicity and dominance assumptions—more money is better, and everyone always prefers better bundles of outcomes—monetary rewards per performance may be used. These rewards could be bound to the interaction behavior itself but also to later, objective measures, such as task performance (see Chap. 28).

Putting individuals in real decision situations instead of hypothetical ones may also circumvent the hot-cold decision gap frequently observed in many social science areas (Loewenstein, 2005; Kang et al., 2013): individuals who are not emotionally involved and whose interaction or decision is only simulated decide differently than individuals in actual situations. The gap is the difference between cold (hypothetical) preferences and hot (actual) actions. In hot actions, preferences are less stable than those that individuals anticipate themselves, and instead, current arousal affects decisions. Moreover, if reaching the goal does not matter to a study's participants, the cognitive resources devoted to the interaction will be reduced. In real-world settings, a rational, deliberate reduction of cognitive resources (Sweller et al., 2011) may also occur, but it is due to a conscious choice in terms of utility and costs of thinking effort. Next to a deliberate choice to reduce cognitive resources, resources may also be lower due to general resource unavailability. Cognitive capacity may vary, and users may reach their overload level at different points. Cognitive psychology suggests that presenting complete and transparent information could contribute to cognitive information overload. This is a phenomenon that is also observed when individuals face many options (Cramer et al., 2008). Prior studies have demonstrated that cognitive overload can affect users' confidence (Hudon et al., 2021) and trust in a system (Schmidt et al., 2020), thereby compromising their reliance. In online experimental studies, (You et al., 2022; Lammert et al., 2024; Miller, 2023) explored the impact of different transparency levels on advice-taking, revealing that individuals exposed to elaborate representations are less inclined to follow advice than those presented with no or aggregated representations.

The threshold of an individual's cognitive overload can depend on—for instance—the personal level of emotional load an individual is facing. The arousal-biased competition model suggests that arousal intensifies neural competition among representations of stimuli, resulting in heightened processing of salient stimuli and diminished processing of less-salient ones (Lee et al., 2014). The consequence of arousal may manifest in an observation bias, because increased arousal tends to predispose individuals toward perceiving what they desire, diverting them from a more factual representation of the environment. On the other hand, too little arousal may also result in a substantial lack of interest in explanations and neglect (Thommes et al., 2024).

Consequently, human motivation to engage with AI and ask for explanations cannot be taken for granted. In many lab settings and research designs, humans want to please the researcher, resulting in an above-average motivational level, or they are not very motivated, because there is no real incentive to understand AI. In real situations, the same effects may occur: One may encounter particularly curious humans or humans who do not enjoy thinking. Even though the effects are similar, the underlying reason differs, and therefore, most lab results have little prognostic power for real-world XAI situations.

26.5 Measuring the Interaction Sequence as a Social Factor

Concerning the "When"-question, one of the most important issue is whether there has been a previous interaction with this XAI-system or any other XAI-system (see Chap. 17). As Han et al. (2021) explains, many interaction characteristics may change in a repeated interaction. For example, the partners may have already established a common language, have experience with each other, or have established trust (or distrust). It is, therefore, essential to be specific as to whether an interaction is the first one (i.e., independent from all other (later) interactions)) or whether an explanation process is later in a sequence (i.e., an observation contingent or dependent on the first interaction). Importantly, this may not only change the initial mental model (see Fig. 26.1), e.g., leading to a more accurate model of the human explainee at the beginning of an interaction, but also change the explanation process or the subjective or even objective outcome. Take, for instance, a practitioner who receives explanations from an AI system concerning some medical images. Not only will the practitioner have a more accurate mental model of the AI and the explanandum after several interactions, but she will also have developed some trust and some hints or instances in which she knows when to distrust the system. Thus, experience in repeated interactions will change every element of the interaction process and, therefore, needs to be captured when evaluating socialXAI.

Currently, most XAI evaluations measure one shot, meaning that one interaction or some repeated interactions within a short time frame of 1 hour or the like are analyzed. Basically, the approaches assume that there has been no previous interaction, no learning, and there will be no future. However, this may not be true, especially for very common explanations such as SHAP or also explanation strategies that gain momentum such as LLMs. Here, there may be previous interactions and previous explanations, and the interaction will likely have a future so that trust, reliance, understanding, and so on can develop and will change over time.

26.6 Measuring the Human Spatial Embedding as a Social Factor

Next to basic differences such as physical space between explainer and explainee which may be relevant in embodied AI studies and is already analyzed in human-robot interaction studies, a more general factor in spatial dimensions is overlooked: The context factor "where" may also be related to the physical space. For example, are you on your own when interacting with an XAI system, or do others observe you? Especially bystander and the difference between being unobserved or surrounded by peers or bystanders are important for evaluation aspects: In a very recent study, Von Terzi et al. (2021) report a Vignette study—individuals expect that their private utility and their satisfaction with technology in general will be context sensitive. In this study, the authors differentiate the private and the public sphere, analyzing how potential spectators in the public sphere may affect the expected assessment of an interaction with technology. Apart from some Vignette studies, there is little research on how potential or actual spectators or bystanders shape the interaction between technology and individuals. This is even more true for XAI interaction processes: Will bystanders remind the explained that they should try to receive an explanation? Or will bystanders discourage the explainees questions? To the best of our knowledge, there is no real evidence of such context effects and context sensitivity in human–AI interactions.

However, the difference between private use and use in an evaluation situation is well known. In many social fields, researchers observe a researcher-demand effect. Because the individuals in the laboratory situation know that the researcher is after some effects, they do not behave as they would naturally do. Instead, they want to favor the researcher and are more alert, active, or the like. Nichols et al. (2008), for instance, shows that many participants in the laboratory try to guess the researcher's hypotheses and then also consciously or subconsciously try to confirm them. Mummolo and Peterson (2019) also provide a very good overview of the researcher-demand effect and show how they believe it can be diminished.

Without going too deep into the literature, the context question "Where?" may, for instance, ask whether the interaction will take place in a public or a private sphere. If the XAI is socially unaware, there will be no difference. However, interaction with technology will be different if the individual feels (or is) observed by others. This effect of bystanders has yet not been analyzed thoroughly. However, we know the same effect for evaluation situations. Here, the effect is even more diffuse, because some participants in evaluations will be trying to help the evaluator, which may reduce the external validity of the evaluation.

26.7 How Does This Chapter Inspire Further Research in XAI

In general, we believe that evaluation principles in XAI must be improved. First, there are some problems with operationalizing the social explanation (see Chap. 27) and the expected outcome (see Chap. 28). Second, the social context factors as who, what, why, when, and where are frequently not regarded at all and need systematic research. Because this social context causes a lot of variance in results, it should be kept constant or controlled for.

We end with some general advice:

1. Be critical. Not all expected features work, and even if they work in a technical sense, they do not always produce the expected effect in human subjects. Design evaluation experiments, so that they can also falsify the claims. For instance, explanation properties should be systematically varied to find good explanations.

2. Handle complexity. Socially interactive AI and also explainability tend to increase system complexity. Especially social dimensions such as human heterogeneity or temporal and space dimensions matter and cause high variance. Therefore, it would be good to either randomize participants, find situations in which they do not matter much, or control for heterogeneity in the statistical analysis. In user testing, you need to handle that complexity. Not all treatments can be tested. Rather, one aspect instead of many should be systematically varied.
3. Design the system with experiments in mind, not the other way around. That means you can use a simple system or a mock-up if that shows the features to be tested. If there is no option to test against, then you limit learning.
4. Worry about the social context: Who, what, when, why, and where are important questions to optimize an XAI system for users' needs. Avoid stereotyping the user, and instead, try to measure what you are interested in as directly as possible.
5. Worry about external validity: Letting individuals test a system with test questions in a laboratory in the presence of the researchers is not the real situation in which the system will be used later. Assume that humans can be easily influenced by the social context and have human characteristics: They can be smart (or not), motivated, and interested (or not), affected by the surrounding and bystanders (or not), affected by previous experiences (or not), and so on. While there is never 100% external validity, there are many instances in which there is no external validity, potentially resulting in irrelevant or even wrong conclusions.

Last but not least, it is essential to note that many social science disciplines have followed some decisive trends recently. First, experiments must fulfill ethical standards and be approved by an ethics committee. Second, there is a trend toward preregistration of experimental evaluation studies to avoid p-hacking and researcher bias: Studies, the main hypotheses, and the statistical plan need to be preregistered before data collection to avoid researchers reading the data with their bias and crunching data until they find their desired effect. Third, non-findings should also be published. Because human nature and contingency factors are difficult to research and possibilities are endless, non-findings should also be reported to speed up the scientific process.

26.8 Rapid Access to the Content of This Chapter

In many evaluations of XAI, the social context of an interaction is largely ignored or very simplified. This is unfortunate, because explanations of the AI system must satisfy the user's need to receive justifications, control the system, improve the system, or generate new knowledge. Thus, explanations are very context-dependent, starting from the reason for an explanation and extending to the specific technology that has to be explained, the specific user to whom something is being explained, and other context factors. As such, there cannot be a good explanation that fits all causes and circumstances. For example, an explanation that works well for analyzing images may work badly for decision support systems.

To generate systematic knowledge about good and bad explanations, we need to consider that – as typical for social science – there is no universal approach, and single studies will not answer the overall problem. Instead, we face diversity in technology, the social sphere, and individuals. Even for some general principles to evolve, we need many puzzle pieces that will fit together to provide an answer about criteria and contingencies for explanations.

However, in many cases, the type of explanation is varied, and the social context of an explanation is also varied. For instance, an explainee may accept an explanation about oneself, but they may find the same explanation unacceptable if it were about someone else. The explainee has to reproduce the explanation and justify the decision. Similarly, being observed versus being alone during an interaction with a technical system will affect any communication process as it also does in real life and with human-to-human conversations.

Moreover, many XAI studies suffer from very naive perceptions of humans and assume, for instance, that all humans want to understand everything and are motivated and unbiased experts in their fields. These naive perceptions may also lead to massive misattributions: For example, one may assume that one explanation works better than another because of its characteristics, but in fact, it may be just less understandable and appears to be believed to the researcher, while it is actually being ignored.

Many XAI evaluations so far also do not analyze the root causes of differences in explanation strategies clearly. Sometimes, they also do not evaluate systematically by varying only one thing in explanations. This leads to an unsystematic knowledge base, that makes it difficult to compare across publications. For instance, some papers evaluate SHAP explanations of decision support models with experts, while others evaluate LLM-generated explanations for image classification. Some evaluations even just test one specification and do not compare at all or choose poor baselines. However, if we want to improve the situation for humans in explanation processes, we need a more systematic understanding, which is optimally close to A-B testing randomized controlled trials. Only then relevant and meaningful meta-analyses will be possible.

Acknowledgments We thank Simon Trang for his valuable perspective and helpful comments on an earlier version of this chapter. This work was funded by the Deutsche Forschungsgemeinschaft (DFG, German Research Foundation): TRR 318/1 2021 – 438445824.

References

Alspector, J. (2021). *Representation edit distance as a measure of novelty.* https://doi.org/10.48550/arXiv.2111.02770. arXiv: 2111.02770 [cs.LG].

Anjomshoae, S., Najjar, A., Calvaresi, D., & Främling, K. (2019). Explainable agents and robots: Results from a systematic literature review. In *18th International Conference on Autonomous Agents and Multiagent Systems (AAMAS 2019)* (pp. 1078–1088). International Foundation for Autonomous Agents and Multiagent Systems. https://doi.org/10.5555/3306127.3331806.

Buçinca, Z., Lin, P., Gajos, K. Z., & Glassman, E. L. (2020). Proxy tasks and subjective measures can be misleading in evaluating explainable AI systems. In *Proceedings of the 25th International Conference on Intelligent User Interfaces* (pp. 454–464). ACM. https://doi.org/10.1145/3377325.3377498.

Cramer, H., Evers, V., Ramlal, S., Van Someren, M., Rutledge, L., Stash, N., Aroyo, L., & Wielinga, B. (2008). The effects of transparency on trust in and acceptance of a content-based art recommender. *User Modeling and User-adapted Interaction, 18*, 455–496. https://doi.org/10.1007/s11257-008-9051-3.

David, L., Vassena, E., & Bijleveld, E. (2024). The unpleasantness of thinking: A meta-analytic review of the association between mental effort and negative affect. *Psychological Bulletin, 150*(9), 1070–1093. https://doi.org/10.1037/bul0000443.

Gentile, D., Jamieson, G., & Donmez, B. (2021). Evaluating human understanding in XAI systems. In *ACM CHI XCXAI Workshop*. Association for Computing Machinery.

Guidotti, R., Monreale, A., Ruggieri, S., Turini, F., Giannotti, F., & Pedreschi, D. (2018). A survey of methods for explaining black box models. *ACM Computing Surveys (CSUR), 51*(5), 1–42. https://doi.org/10.1145/3236009.

Han, T. A., Perret, C., & Powers, S. T. (2021). When to (or not to) trust intelligent machines: Insights from an evolutionary game theory analysis of trust in repeated games. *Cognitive Systems Research, 68*, 111–124. https://doi.org/10.1016/j.cogsys.2021.02.003.

Hoffman, R. R., Mueller, S. T., Klein, G., & Litman, O. (2018). *Metrics for explainable AI: Challenges and prospects*. https://doi.org/10.48550/arXiv.1812.04608. arXiv: 1812.04608 [cs.AI].

Hudon, A., Demazure, T., Karran, A., Léger, P.-M., & Sénécal, S. (2021). Explainable artificial intelligence (XAI): How the visualization of AI predictions affects user cognitive load and confidence. In *Information Systems and Neuroscience: NeuroIS Retreat 2021* (pp. 237–246). Springer. https://doi.org/10.1007/978-3-030-88900-5_27.

Hulstijn, J., Tchappi, I., Najjar, A., & Aydoğan, R. (2023). Metrics for evaluating explainable recommender systems. In *International Workshop on Explainable, Transparent Autonomous Agents and Multi-Agent Systems (EXTRAA- MAS 2023)* (pp. 212–230). Springer. https://doi.org/10.1007/978-3-031-40878-6_12.

Kang, M. J., & Camerer, C. F. (2013). fMRI evidence of a hot-cold empathy gap in hypothetical and real aversive choices. *Frontiers in Neuroscience, 7*, 48505. https://doi.org/10.3389/fnins.2013.00104.

Kynn, M. (2008). The 'heuristics and biases' bias in expert elicitation. *Journal of the Royal Statistical Society Series A: Statistics in Society, 171*(1), 239–264. https://doi.org/10.1111/j.1467-985X.2007.00499.x.

Lammert, O., Richter, B., Schütze, C., Thommes, K., & Wrede, B. (2024). Humans in XAI: Increased reliance in decision-making under uncertainty by using explanation strategies. *Frontiers in Behavioral Economics, 3*, 1377075. https://doi.org/10.3389/frbhe.2024.1377075.

Lee, T.-H., Sakaki, M., Cheng, R., Velasco, R., & Mather, M. (2014). Emotional arousal amplifies the effects of biased competition in the brain. *Social Cognitive and Affective Neuroscience, 91*(12), 2067–2077. https://doi.org/10.1093/scan/nsu015.

Loewenstein, G. (2005). Hot-cold empathy gaps and medical decision making. *Health Psychology, 24*(4S), S49–S56. https://doi.org/10.1037/0278-6133.24.4.S49.

Miller, T. (2023). *Explainable ai is dead, long live explainable ai! hypothesis-driven decision support*. https://doi.org/10.48550/arXiv.2302.12389. arXiv: 2302.12389 [cs.AI].

Mualla, Y., Tchappi, I., Kampik, T., Najjar, A., Calvaresi, D., Abbas-Turki, A., Galland, S., & Nicolle, C. (2022). The quest of parsimonious XAI: A human-agent architecture for explanation formulation. In *Artificial Intelligence, 302*(C), 103573. https://doi.org/10.1016/j.artint.2021.103573.

Mummolo, J., & Peterson, E. (2019). Demand effects in survey experiments: An empirical assessment. *American Political Science Review, 113*(2), 517–529. https://doi.org/10.1017/S0003055418000837.

Nauta, M., Trienes, J., Pathak, S., Nguyen, E., Peters, M., Schmitt, Y., Schlötterer, J., van Keulen, M., & Seifert, C. (2023). From anecdotal evidence to quantitative evaluation methods: A systematic review on evaluating explainable AI. *ACM Computing Surveys, 55*(13s), 1–42. https://doi.org/10.1145/3583558.

Nichols, A. L., & Maner, J. K. (2008). The good-subject effect: Investigating participant demand characteristics. *Journal of General Psychology, 135*(2), 151–166. https://doi.org/10.3200/GENP.135.2.151-166.

Perez, O. (2015). Can experts be trusted and what can be done about it? Insights from the biases and heuristics literature. In A. Alemanno & A.-L. Sibony (Eds.), *Nudge and the Law. A European Perspective* (pp. 115–138). Bloomsbury. https://doi.org/10.13140/2.1.4839.0409.

Poursabzi-Sangdeh, F., Goldstein, D. G., Hofman, J. M., Vaughan, J. W. W., & Wallach, H. (2021). Manipulating and measuring model interpretability. In *Proceedings of the 2021 CHI Conference on Human Factors in Computing Systems* (pp. 1–52). Association for Computing Machinery. https://doi.org/10.1145/3411764.3445315.

Rosenfeld, A. (2021). Better metrics for evaluating explainable artificial intelli- gence. In *Proceedings of the 20th International Conference on Autonomous Agents and Multiagent Systems*. International Foundations for Autonomous Agents and Multiagent Sysems (pp. 45–50).

Schaffernicht, M., & Groesser, S. N. (2011). A comprehensive method for comparing mental models of dynamic systems. In *European Journal of Operational Research, 210*(1), 57–67. https://doi.org/10.1016/j.ejor.2010.09.003.

Schmidt, P., Biessmann, F., & Teubner, T. (2020). Transparency and trust in artificial intelligence systems. *Journal of Decision Systems, 29*(4), 260–278. https://doi.org/10.1080/12460125.2020.1819094.

Sokol, K., & Flach, P. (2020). One explanation does not fit all: The promise of interactive explanations for machine learning transparency. *KI-Künstliche Intelligenz, 34*(2), 235–250. https://doi.org/10.1007/s13218-020-00637-y.

Sweller, J., Ayres, P., & Kalyuga, S. (2011). Measuring cognitive load. In J. Sweller, P. Ayres, & S. Kalyuga (Eds.), *Cognitive load theory* (pp. 71–85). Springer. https://doi.org/10.1007/978-1-4419-8126-4_6.

Thommes, K., Lammert, O., Schütze, C., Richter, B., & Wrede, B. (2024). Human emotions in AI explanations. In *World Conference on Explainable Artificial Intelligence* (pp. 270–293). Springer. https://doi.org/10.1007/978-3-031-63803-9_15.

Vilone, G., & Longo, L. (2021). Notions of explainability and evaluation approaches for explainable artificial intelligence. *Information Fusion, 76,* 89–106. https://doi.org/10.1016/j.inffus.2021.05.009.

Von Terzi, P., Tretter, S., Uhde, A., Hassenzahl, M., & Diefenbach, S. (2021). Technology-mediated experiences and social context: Relevant needs in private vs. public interaction and the importance of others for positive affect. *Frontiers in Psychology, 12,* 718315. https://doi.org/10.3389/fpsyg.2021.718315.

Wan, C., Belo, R., Zejnilović, L., & Lavado, S. (2023). The duet of representations and how explanations exacerbate it. In *World Conference on Explainable Artificial Intelligence* (pp. 181–197). Springer. https://doi.org/10.1007/978-3-031-44067-0_10.

You, S., Yang, C. L., & Li, X. (2022). Algorithmic versus human advice: Does presenting prediction performance matter for algorithm appreciation? *Journal of Management Information Systems, 39*(2), 336–365. https://doi.org/10.1080/07421222.2022.2063553.

Open Access This chapter is licensed under the terms of the Creative Commons Attribution 4.0 International License (http://creativecommons.org/licenses/by/4.0/), which permits use, sharing, adaptation, distribution and reproduction in any medium or format, as long as you give appropriate credit to the original author(s) and the source, provide a link to the Creative Commons license and indicate if changes were made.

The images or other third party material in this chapter are included in the chapter's Creative Commons license, unless indicated otherwise in a credit line to the material. If material is not included in the chapter's Creative Commons license and your intended use is not permitted by statutory regulation or exceeds the permitted use, you will need to obtain permission directly from the copyright holder.

Chapter 27
Operationalizing Social Interaction

Henning Wachsmuth , **Kirsten Thommes** , **and Milad Alshomary**

Abstract Explainable AI (XAI) aims to make the decisions and behavior of an AI understandable to the people interacting with it and to those affected by its outcomes. To make XAI social, real-world XAI systems need to simulate not only the ways in which human explainers behave within explanatory dialogs but also the ways in which such dialogs can successfully achieve the intended understanding on the explainee's side. This, in turn, requires an operationalization of the three core aspects of social XAI: multimodality, incrementality, and patterns. This chapter lays the ground for this goal by defining a basic operational model of social interactions that can be refined and extended to account for the specificities of any explanatory real-world setting. This serves as a basis for summarizing and discussing existing ideas from explainability research and related areas in order to operationalize each core aspect. Selected examples and case studies illustrate how to concretely realize such an operationalization, thereby serving as a starting point for future research on social interaction with XAI.

27.1 How Does This Chapter Relate to XAI?

Explainable artificial intelligence (XAI) pursues the goal of making the decisions and the behavior of AI methods and systems understandable to the people interacting with the AI along with those affected by its outcomes. Most parts of this book discuss the building blocks needed to make XAI social only conceptually,

---

H. Wachsmuth (✉)
Institute of Artificial Intelligence, Leibniz University Hannover, Hannover, Germany
e-mail: h.wachsmuth@ai.uni-hannover.de

K. Thommes
Faculty of Business Administration and Economics, Paderborn University, Paderborn, Germany
e-mail: kirsten.thommes@uni-paderborn.de

M. Alshomary
Data Science Institute, Columbia University, New York, NY, USA
e-mail: ma4608@columbia.edu

even though hinting selectively at the necessary operationalization. However, not only guiding XAI toward the outlined goal but also assessing whether it serves its purpose requires a systematic operationalization that enables an actual evaluation of the success of XAI (be it quantitative or qualitative) and, thus, ultimately, of its need and impact. Whereas Chap. 26 has discussed the general principles of evaluating XAI, and Chap. 28 looks at how to assess the outcomes of XAI, the processes that XAI carries out during the interaction with people need to be operationalized as well. Only then, will it be possible to assess the influence of the different steps and decisions in the process on the outcomes and the success. This refers particularly to the three main social aspects focused on in the present book.

In this chapter, we present a general formalization of how to operationalize social interaction with respect to multimodality, incrementality, and patterns. Starting from the introduction of a basic model that enables the operationalization of social interactions related to explaining, we will discuss existing approaches to specific elements of each of the three social aspects. We show selected operational models that provide the basis for quantitative and qualitative evaluation, and we review empirical insights into the manifestation of social aspects within and across specific domains of explanatory dialogs.

27.2 A Basic Operational Model of Social Interactions

As the different scenarios in Chap. 2 exemplify, there are various forms of partly more, partly less conventionalized explanatory dialogs. The more specific the scenario, the more assumptions can be made about the fixed and common elements of the respective type of dialogs and, hence, the more specific the elements of a model of their social interactions may be. For example, in a medical anamnesis setting, it is largely predefined that the doctor leads the dialog, asks for symptoms and background information, and later informs the patient of procedures, diagnoses, and treatments, before the patient has the chance to ask questions. Mostly, that happens in an oral way only, although, in certain situations possibly with the support of gestures and visual illustrations. In general, however, few assumptions can be made about modalities, process flows, and fixed stages in a dialog. Accordingly, a generally applicable operational model of social interaction in explanatory dialogs needs to be restricted to the basic invariant elements of explanatory interaction.

The model we introduce here is rather generic and would even apply in principle to nonexplanatory interaction. However, it may (or should) allow for easy extensions and refinements, though, to make it specific to the explanatory context at hand, as the following sections should show.

Social Interactions In particular, the *social interaction*, σ, between an explainer, ER, and an explainee, EE, in an explanatory dialog can generally be defined as a

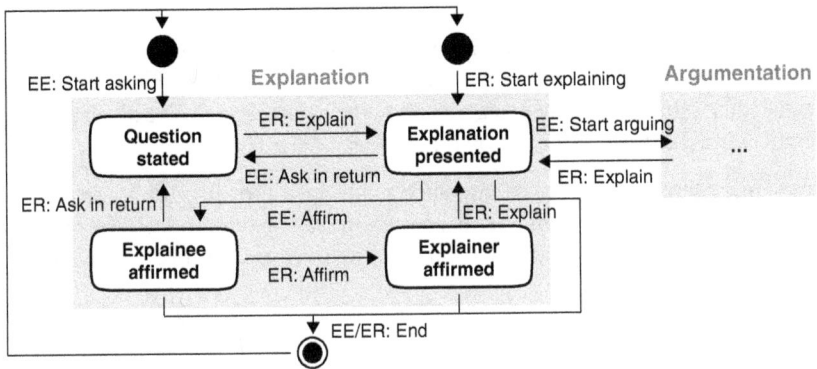

Fig. 27.1 Excerpt from the interaction protocol of explanatory dialogs, adapted from Madumal et al. (2019). Either the explainee EE or the explainer ER starts the dialog, before explaining, asking, and affirming evolve incrementally. The dialog may also deviate into argumentation (left out here)

sequence of $n \geq 2$ turns, each with explicit or implicit functions. That is,

$$\sigma := (f(\tau_1), f(\tau_2), \ldots, f(\tau_n)),$$

where each *turn* τ_i refers to a contiguous communicative utterance by either ER or EE, and consecutive turns τ_i, τ_{i+1} alternate between the two interaction participants. On the other hand, $f(\tau_i)$ describes the function (or functions) that τ_i takes within the social interaction of ER and EE. The definition of σ may appear rather generic, not appearing to be specific in any way to explanations. We note, though, that the functions of the turns are subject to the general goals of explanatory dialogs (e.g., enabling EE). Both turns and functions are further explained below.

As illustrated in Fig. 27.1, Madumal et al. (2019) proposed an interaction protocol of explanatory dialogues derived from 398 real-life dialogs. While the protocol underlines the incrementality and the patterns intrinsic to the social interaction, it also stresses the diversity of possible dialog flows. Among other differences, both the explainer and the explainee may generally trigger the interaction in τ_1, and both may end it in τ_n. This is why we refrain here from including an explicit labeling of ER and EE in the definition of social interaction. Instead, we may later say that all odd indices refer to ER and all even indices to EE, or vice versa. We may also model more than one explainer or explainee, if that makes sense in a given scenario. In practice, an explicit labeling of ER and EE make the distinction easy. Still, the pure enumeration complies well with the idea that explanations are anyway co-constructed between the participants (Rohlfing et al., 2021), so both explainer(s) and explainee(s) can, in principle, contribute any kind of turn at any moment.

We point out that even the given basic definition of σ is already a somewhat simplified model, since ER and EE may communicate simultaneously in reality. To capture the behavior of both participants, one could model each participant's turns in an individual sequence and then align the two sequences using time information. To capture interaction, however, combining the turns in one sequence seems favorable, since interaction intrinsically expects reactions to actions. Where important, we can alleviate this issue to a certain extent, by allowing a turn τ_i to also be a non-complete utterance, in case it is interrupted by other turns.

Turns In general, the kinds of utterance made in a turn may differ in terms of modality, and an utterance may either be unimodal or multimodal. Formally, we model the potential multimodality of *turn*, τ, as an ordered set of $l \geq 1$ unimodal utterances, that is,

$$\tau := \langle v_1, \ldots, v_l \rangle.$$

Similar to above, we do not predefine what modality a specific utterance v_j has, allowing the combination of any possible set of utterances. For example, a turn may consist of only a verbal statement; it may combine the statement with other modalities; or it may just be nonverbal such as a gesture together with a beep sound and a displayed image if we think of an XAI avatar explaining something on a screen. Some modalities may even appear multiple times in the same turn (e.g., two gestures may be performed simultaneously); for others, this may be rather unlikely (e.g., spoken utterances).

For completeness, we note that any turn τ_i may itself consist of multiple sequentially expressed (unimodal or multimodal) utterances by the same participant, possibly with (usually short) interaction breaks in between, as extensively covered in the literature on dialog models (Chen et al., 2017). That is, a technically more exact model would define a turn τ_i as being a sequence of one or more *elementary process units*, following the terminology of pattern structures from Chap. 7, such as individual propositions or gestures (if we think unimodally) or combinations thereof (if we think multimodally). For a concise and comprehensible discussion, we do not distinguish further between turns and elementary process units here but simply assume a turn to be atomic, that is, to be the smallest building block of social interaction distinguished. If need be, the resulting limitation could be circumvented by allowing for complex utterances, each combining a sequence of elementary process units.

Functions Now, the turns within the sequential social interaction of ER and EE do not happen randomly. Rather, they aim to fulfill specific functions related to the goal of the explanatory dialog. For conciseness, we model the complex *function*, f, of a turn as an ordered set of $k \geq 1$ simple functions,

$$f : \tau \mapsto \langle f_1(\tau), \ldots, f_k(\tau) \rangle,$$

where each $f_k(\tau)$ defines a measurable feature of τ. Technically, such simple functions will usually map a turn to a nominal label or a numeric value, in line with standard methods in empirical data presentation (Aggarwal, 2015).

As an example, Wachsmuth and Alshomary (2022) capture three distinct features of a turn: the *explanation move* that a participant makes to push the explaining process forward (e.g., requesting an explanation or signaling understanding), the *dialog act* used to continue the communication (e.g., asking a question or giving a confirming answer), and the type of *topic* being referred to (e.g., the main explanandum or a related topic). In general, how many features m and what features to include depends on the goal of operationalizing the model as well as on the feasibility of measuring certain features in a specific explaining scenario. By explicating simple functions $f_k(\tau)$, we can thus refine the basic model into a concrete model of social interactions, as explained in the following.

27.3 Refinements and Extensions of the Basic Model

The literature on computational dialogue models is extensive, often building upon the widely adopted notion of *dialog acts* (Stolcke et al., 2000; Bunt et al., 2010). For explanatory dialogs specifically, computational linguistics came up early with conceptualizations of fundamental aspects in respective processes, ranging from the modeling of interactions to explanatory moves and dialog acts and to the need to model the audience of an explanation (Cawsey, 1989). In her book, Moore (1994) details various elements of explanatory dialogs, including explanation strategies, the reaction to feedback, and the monitoring of the dialog progress. In a way, this line of research anticipated a large part of the recent developments in research on explanatory dialogs covered in this book in general and this chapter in particular, at least for the linguistic side of explaining. Nonetheless, rather few operational modeling attempts addressing the topic directly have been published to this day.

A related but more focused research area deals with tutoring settings, for example, studying how to give feedback to explanation questions (Dzikovska et al., 2012). For monological texts, Fontan and Saint-Dizier (2008) model the functions of utterances in instructional texts, whereas Wachsmuth and Stein (2017) propose a universal model of the sequential flow in monological arguments based on the notion of rhetorical moves (Swales, 1990). Building on the rhetorical structure theory of Mann and Thompson (1988), Bourse and Saint-Dizier (2012) look at the discourse structure of monological explanations, distinguishing between 11 functions of utterances: instructions, advice, warnings, illustration, restatement, purpose, condition, circumstance, concession, contrast, and causes. Al Khatib et al. (2018) look at deliberative argumentation dialogs, modeling each turn in the dialog as having a specific discourse act, argumentative relation, and frame. These works may inspire models of explanatory dialogs, but none of them targets such dialogues exactly.

Explanatory Dialogs One of the few research lines on operationalizing dialogical explanations has recently been published in the consecutive works of Wachsmuth and Alshomary (2022) and Alshomary et al. (2024), already mentioned above as an example. In particular, in discussion with an interdisciplinary team of computer scientists, linguists, psychologists, and cognitive scientists, Wachsmuth and Alshomary (2022) created a taxonomy of three categorizations of turn labels (i.e., simple functions in the terminology above):

- *Topic.* Four different relations of a turn's topic to the explanandum,
- *Dialog act.* Ten dialogue acts performed by the utterance in a turn, and
- *Explanation move.* Ten explanation-related moves made through the turn.

In the data that Alshomary et al. (2024) annotate for the taxonomy categories, the authors further extended the taxonomy by a fourth categorization of turn labels that applies only to turns that provide explanations, even though this did not find its way into the published article:

- *Explanation Type.* Eight mechanisms by which a given explanandum is explained.

Table 27.1 lists all topics, dialog acts, explanation moves, and explanation types in the extended taxonomy. The underlying four functions define a suitable basis for measuring the social XAI aspects of incrementality and patterns, as we will show further below. Other works have taken on similar ideas, for example, analyzing the impact of explanatory interaction on the understanding achieved on the side of the explainee (Booshehri et al., 2024) or extending the modeling of explanatory dialogs to the instructional side of the explainer (Feldhus et al., 2024).

In contrast, multimodality is not captured as well, because the authors focus on purely textual explanatory dialogs. Beyond text, Buhl et al. (2024) consider verbal explanatory moves within the adaptation process of explaineers and explainees. Heylen (2006) consider the functions of head movements with respect to information structure, expressive reactions to messages, and interaction management. Lausberg and Slöetjes (2015) perform a similar analysis as part of a multistep assess-

Table 27.1 All possible values of the four functions of explanatory dialog turns in the taxonomies of Wachsmuth and Alshomary (2022) and Alshomary et al. (2024)

Topic	Dialog act	Explanation move	Explanation type
Main topic	Check question	Test understanding	Reasoning by causality
Subtopic	What/How question	Test prior knowledge	Reasoning otherwise
Related topic	Other questions	Provide explanation	Giving context
No/Other topic	Confirming answer	Request explanation	Contrasting
	Disconfirming answer	Signal understanding	Making an analogy
	Other answer	Signal non-understanding	Explaining case-based
	Agreeing statement	Providing feedback	Other
	Disagreeing statement	Providing assessment	
	Informing statement	Providing extra information	
	Other	Other	

Table 27.2 The different functions of head movements and hand gestures in the taxonomies of Heylen (2006) and Lausberg and Slöetjes (2015)

Head movements	Hand gestures
General emphasis	Emotion/Attitude
Wider perspective	Emphasis
Need for a closer look	Egocentric deictic
Emblem of being taken aback	Egocentric direction
More information	Pantomime
Expectation of engagement from partner	Form presentation
General emphasis + more information	Spatial relation presentation
Wider perspective + more information	Motion quality presentation
Contrast of related topics	Emblem/social convention
	Object-oriented action
	Subject-oriented action

ment of hand gestures. For comparison to the text-related functions, Table 27.2 lists the main functions that the two works distinguish.

Outlook There is another point of extension of the basic model introduced above that remains to be explored. Whereas the model focuses on the sequential structure, many explaining scenarios will also exhibit a hierarchical or otherwise nonsequential interaction structure between the different turns, even if often only implicitly. That is, turns may refer to other turns that happened notably before—or possibly even to turns that are yet to be made. This could be modeled by relations between the turns that induce the nonsequential structure. Figure 27.1 gives an idea of the connections that may emerge in explanatory dialogs. We do not further detail them here, because explanation-oriented literature on this topic is still largely lacking.

27.4 Modeling Multimodality

In its actual form, social interaction takes place in a face-to-face setting. As comprehensively discussed in the first part of this book, explanations between humans usually use different modalities, such as speech and gestures. A full operationalization of the social interaction thus particularly needs to also take into account nonverbal signals and interactions. To measure multimodality in interactions between an explaining AI, ER, and a human explainee, EE, it is useful to first systematize the potential dimensions of multimodal interactions and to then derive possible measurements of the various dimensions. While various systematizations exist, we concentrate here on the most prominent ones:

- *Channel.* What kinds of modalities are used during explaining?
- *Content.* How do different modalities add to each other?

- *Timing.* When is which modality used within turns and dialogs?
- *Roles.* Who decides what modalities are used within the interaction?

Channel Hence, one dimension to measure multimodality is the channel through which the information is provided and exchanged. As Chap. 23 explained, in human-to-human explanations, modalities frequently address a new channel; for example, a speech-based explanation (acoustic channel) is supported by gestures (visual channel). These two channels are also the most prominent in machine-to-human explanations. Liang et al. (2023) made a first attempt to categorize channels, distinguishing acoustic modalities (e.g., speech or sounds) from static visual modalities (e.g., written explanations, images, or graphs), dynamic visual modalities (e.g., videos or interactive pictures), proprioceptive modalities (e.g., movements of an embodied agent), and the like. The formalization of a turn, τ, as a tuple of $\langle v_1, \ldots, v_l \rangle$ that we introduced above directly enables an operationalization on this basis. Here, l then denotes the overall number of observable modalities. In a specific turn, not all modalities, v_i, may play a role, meaning that the absence of a used modality is to be modeled explicitly.

Based on the model, it is possible to study how different channels support each other, for example, whether the inclusion of a channel adds value over other channels or to what extent the semantics conveyed by one channel are coherent to the signals from others. Naturally, this requires the creation of controlled experiments where these effects can actually be measured. In the aforementioned work of Heylen (2006), the authors conclude, for example, that language usually targets social purposes: Because people engage in interaction to get something done, this creates social obligations which are usually resolved via language. Hand gestures, on the other hand, turn out to be more closely related to the actual interaction in their study.

Content A second distinction can be made concerning the content of two modalities used jointly (or immediately after each other). Content can be exactly the same (e.g., a written statement that is also read out loud) but also dissimilar (e.g., the statement is accompanied by a facial expression of surprise). The classification is more of a continuum than a binary choice, because there may be different degrees of similarity between the modalities' content and different degrees of overlap and contradiction between different modalities. If there is a dissimilarity in the different modalities used, the content may still be perceived to be either similar or contradictory.

In general, the expected default is that the modalities of explanations support each other and are complementary; for example, some information may be given verbally and as a bar chart. However, as the work of Miller (2023) suggests, this type of persuasive explanation (similar information presented in different modalities) may not be very natural. Instead, a human may respond better to contradicting information that helps them to develop their own hypothesis about the best action. In an empirical user study, Le et al. (2024) show that giving contradicting information for and against a hypothesis may result in higher decision accuracy than giving persuasive explanations that only point in one direction. In a similar vein, Lammert et al. (2024) show that presenting some pros and cons results in more user reliance and less reactance than other types of explanations.

Timing A third dimension relates to timing: Information in different modalities can be presented simultaneously or sequentially, as already indicated for the aforementioned dimension. For instance, Papenkordt et al. (2023) as well as Papenkordt (2024) analyze whether the information presented simultaneously or sequentially affects user reliance. Both find that sequential information may not result in higher user reliance, even if it may prevent cognitive overload in explainees. However, it remains to be studied if the human processing time of information should be considered, if it is better to guide explainees via modalities, or if explainees will be better off if they can choose from several modality options presented at once.

Roles The last dimension we look at here is the participants' roles with respect to multimodality in an interaction, that is, whether the explainer, ER, or the explainee, EE, decides what modalities to use when and for what. It may be intuitive to assume that ER would usually offer some modalities and, therefore, lead the process. Many studies are built on this assumption. However, within human-AI interaction in particular, giving EE the freedom to choose, expand, and evolve the modalities used may result in better explanations and, hence, more probably explanation success, because it gives EE agency in the explanatory process. Also, the modalities to use can be tailored directly to the explainee's preferred style. Qi et al. (2023), for instance, find that the preferred type of information (visual or textual) depends partly on the comprehension goals and strategies of humans.

27.5 Modeling Incrementality

The core idea behind incrementality is that social XAI should align with the stepwise character of explanatory dialogs, by which explanations are co-constructed in small portions between the explainer (usually represented by the XAI), ER, and the explainee, EE. This raises questions about sequential interaction and the dynamic adaptation inherent to the interaction on the one hand, and about the evolving mutual models of the interaction participants and of the explanandum on the other. The model of social interaction introduced above defines an adequate basis for measuring incrementality in the interactional aspects, as we discuss in the following. For the incremental evolution and completion of models, common measures capture the recall at specific time steps in the interaction (Shapira et al., 2021) but are beyond the scope of the discussion at hand.

Given an instance of a social interaction $\sigma = (f(\tau_1), f(\tau_2), \ldots, f(\tau_n))$ of length $n \geq 2$, we can immediately infer that it is made up of $n - 1$ adjacent pairs of turn functions, $(f(\tau_1), f(\tau_2)), \ldots, (f(\tau_{n-1}), f(\tau_n))$. These pairs do not behave arbitrarily, but the second turn in a pair will probably often depend on the first turn. For example, EE may ask a question on the explanandum or a topic related to it, thereby requesting an explanation. ER, in turn, will probably often answer the question, providing an explanation. However, it is important to see that a turn made in an explanatory dialog might not only depend on the previous turn but may also be affected by turns earlier in the dialog. In line with the hypothesis behind incrementality in social interactions, we model a turn and its function, $f(\tau_i)$, as the most likely result of the entire preceding interaction along with a set of parameters Θ (e.g., including common prior knowledge, shared history, etc.), that is:

$$f(\tau_i) := \text{argmax}_{f(\tau)} Prob(f(\tau)|f(\tau_1), \ldots, f(\tau_{i-1}), \Theta)$$

This definition provides us with an intuitive way to operationalize the determination of the next turn, given all preceding turns. Thereby, the operationalization defines the basis for the development of an XAI method that takes the role of ER and incrementally reacts to the turns of a human explainee, EE. In particular, given a dataset of explanatory dialogs with turns annotated for their functions, the probability of any specific turn (and turn function) can be learned to be predicted.

Operationalizations Wachsmuth and Alshomary (2022), for example, experimented with different neural techniques to learn to model the function of the current turn, given the history of previous interactions in the explanatory dialog. The authors constructed a corpus of 65 expert explanatory dialogs from the Wired video series *5 Levels* and annotated it with three different turn functions mentioned above: topics, dialog acts, and explanation moves. To predict the function of a given textual turn, the authors proposed a method, based on the neural transformer encoder BERT (Devlin et al., 2019), that models the sequential interaction between turn functions and compares its performance against baselines that consider only the textual information of single utterances or the relation across different functions of a single utterance. Table 27.3 shows the effectiveness of this method, *BERT-sequence*, compared to baseline methods in terms of macro F_1 scores (ranging from 0 to 1). The results demonstrate a gain in performance of the sequential modeling over baselines but also suggest that there is still room for improvement.

In a follow-up study, Alshomary et al. (2024) constructed a new corpus of daily-life explanatory dialogs from the Reddit forum "Explain Like I'm Five," annotated for the taxonomy of Wachsmuth and Alshomary (2022) as well as for scores reflecting the quality of the dialogs in terms of the level of understanding achieved on the explainee's side. Their goal was to study whether modeling the interaction between explainer and explainee allows for a more effective quality prediction. To

Table 27.3 Turn function prediction results from Wachsmuth and Alshomary (2022): Macro F_1-scores of the evaluated BERT variants for topics, dialog acts, and explanation moves in the *five levels* of explanatory dialogs. The best value in each column is highlighted bold

Approach	Topic	Dialog acts	Explanation moves
BERT-basic	0.51	0.44	0.41
BERT-multitask	0.41	0.38	0.34
BERT-sequence	**0.52**	**0.47**	**0.43**

Table 27.4 Explanation quality prediction results from Alshomary et al. (2024): Root mean squared error (RMSE) and mean absolute error (MAE) of an average baseline and their two models (HatFormer and LongFormer) with different augmented input explanatory dialogs from *Explain like I'm Five* for two scenarios: Quality is predicted based on either *ground-truth* turn labels or on label predictions from the developed methods. The best values of each model are highlighted bold

Approach	Ground truth		Predictions	
	RMSE	MAE	RMSE	MAE
Average baseline	1.60	1.42	1.60	1.42
HatFormer	1.42	1.17	1.42	1.17
w/Topic	1.41	1.20	1.41	1.20
w/Dialog act	**1.29**	**1.05**	1.31	1.09
w/Explanation move	1.41	1.21	1.43	1.22
w/ALL	1.30	**1.05**	**1.28**	**1.05**
LongFormer	1.34	1.13	1.34	1.13
w/Topic	1.35	1.15	1.34	1.14
w/Dialog act	**1.31**	**1.05**	**1.32**	**1.06**
w/Explanation move	**1.31**	**1.05**	**1.32**	1.09
w/ALL	1.32	1.08	1.34	1.10

this end, they experimented with a basic idea to model the interactions as special tokens along with the textual information of the dialogs. They implemented this for two transformer neural network architectures that can deal with dialog-long input, HatFormer (Chalkidis et al., 2022) and LongFormer (Beltagy et al., 2020). The former abstracts a text hierarchically, whereas the latter abstracts less recent parts of a text more than more recent ones. As shown in Table 27.4, modeling the interaction consistently improves prediction in terms of root-mean-squared-errors and mean absolute error.

27.6 Modeling Patterns

Patterns in social XAI, as discussed in this book, refer to commonalities observed with respect to several aspects of explanatory dialogs: general values and norms, the explainer's and explainee's roles and relationships, their goals, responsibilities, and engagement in explaining as well as the structures and practices emerging across the dialogs. Some of these aspects are fixed within a given setting (such as the norms) or can often be reasonably represented computationally through simple labels (such as roles) or ordinal/numeric values (such as engagement). In contrast, measuring aspects such as structures and practices requires more sophisticated methods. This is why they are the focus of the following.

In particular, Chap. 7 has introduced the different basic hierarchy levels, under which interaction structures can be analyzed: Building on the elementary process units and turns discussed above, *elementary interactions* denotes micro-sequences of turns, whereas *pragmatic frames* refer to meso-sequences, and *dialog types* to macro-sequences. In a given social interaction $\sigma = (f(\tau_1), f(\tau_2), \ldots, f(\tau_n))$, we can identify these types of sequences as follows:

1. *Elementary interaction.* Any (usually short) subsequence $\sigma_{EI} \subseteq \sigma$ that occurs in identical or in near-identical form across a substantial proportion of explanatory dialogs (within some given dataset);
2. *Pragmatic frames.* A (possibly longer) subsequence $\sigma_{PF} \subseteq \sigma$ that occurs in similar forms across a substantial proportion of explanatory dialogues and that can serve as an interdependent social interaction on its own;
3. *Dialog type.* A categorization $c(\sigma)$ of σ that conceptually matches a substantial proportion of explanatory dialogs.

Notably, we observe that the first two require pattern mining, whereas the third implies a classification task. We build on this distinction in our subsequent summary of computational approaches. While we are aware of only a few approaches that actually focus on explanation patterns specifically, a number of promising methods for such patterns have been proposed in related areas.

Elementary Interactions Here, an operationalization is straightforward, matching the notion of n-gram modeling ubiquitous in data science (Aggarwal, 2015): Given a collection of $m \geq 1$ explanatory dialogs, modeled by their social interactions $\Sigma = \{\sigma_1, \ldots, \sigma_m\}$, all subsequences σ_{EI} of some predefined length $n \geq 2$ occurring in Σ can be counted. Either the most common $k \geq 1$ interactions, or all interactions whose frequency exceeds some absolute or relative threshold τ, can then be seen as elementary interactions. Even more is possible, if explanatory dialogs are categorized, for example, rated for explanation quality (Alshomary et al., 2024). In such cases, the most *discriminative* interactions can be identified, that is, those that occur often in one category (say, Quality score 5), and rarely in others (say, Quality scores 1–4). In related work, Zhang et al. (2016) modeled elementary interactions in a debate computationally to predict the winner of the debate on this basis.

Pragmatic Frames For pragmatic frames σ_{PF}, n-gram patterns could also be determined in principle. However, it is increasingly unlikely to find identical n-grams, the longer or more sophisticated the subsequences are. In certain cases, it may be possible to look at an interaction at a more coarse-grained level than individual turns. For example, Persing and Ng (2010) classified discourse functions of whole paragraphs of learner essays as being introductions, arguments, rebuttals, or conclusions. Then, they identified common discourse function n-grams and used these to assess the organization quality of the essays.

If such a granularity level change is not applicable, an alternative is to resort to more sophisticated pattern mining techniques from natural language processing (NLP) research: One of the first attempts in this regard is the idea of local sentiment flows by Mao and Lebanon (2007) who modeled a product review as a sequential

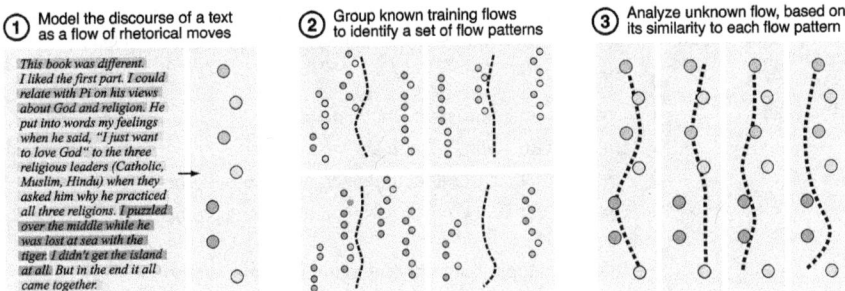

Fig. 27.2 Three steps to model the discourse-level structure of monological texts using flow patterns, adapted from Wachsmuth and Stein (2017): (1) modeling flows, (2) identifying flow patterns, and (3) using the flow patterns to analyze unknown flows

flow of local sentence-level sentiments. Later, Wachsmuth et al. (2014) pointed out that this represents positional rather than sequential information and extended the idea into *sentiment flow patterns* that capture the global discourse-level structure of reviews as a flow. In follow-up work, Wachsmuth et al. (2015) presented different flow abstractions to find more meaningful patterns, most importantly the *change flow*, that merges consecutive sequences of identical sentiments. Wachsmuth et al. (2016) moved beyond sentiment, analyzing common paragraph-level flows of different types of rhetorical moves in essays, before Wachsmuth and Stein (2017) generalized flow patterns for any types of moves to obtain a universal model of (monological) discourse-level structure. Figure 27.2 illustrates the general flow modeling process.

The modeling of pragmatic frames specifically in explanatory dialogs with flows has been studied concretely by Wachsmuth and Alshomary (2022) and Alshomary et al. (2024). The former example looked at what topic change flows occur in the expert dialogs they considered, finding that the most common change flow (15.4%) is *main topic, related topic, main topic*, that is, starting with the main topic to be explained, deviating into one or more related topics, and coming back to the main topic toward the end. The authors also observed that explainers switch topics more than explainees. Alshomary et al. (2024) extended the study of change flows to all three turn label categorizations discussed above (topics, dialog acts, and explanation moves). Table 27.5 shows the frequency of the five most common flows of each type in their dataset of daily-life explanatory dialogs.

Dialog Types Finally, for dialog types $c(\sigma)$, a simple but logical operationalization is to see their identification as a standard classification task. If data annotated for dialog types are available, this task may be approached effectively with supervised machine learning (Aggarwal, 2015). For the related communicative process of argumentation, Walton (2010) established a taxonomy of seven debate types: persuasion, inquiry, discovery, negotiation, information-seeking, deliberation, and eristic dialogs. The types differ in their triggering situation as well as the participants' goals and the dialog goals. We are not aware of a respective taxonomy for

Table 27.5 Flow analysis of Alshomary et al. (2024): The distribution of the five most common topic, dialog act, and explanation move change flows in their *Explain like I'm Five* dataset

Type	#	Flow	Frequency
Topic act	1	(main, main, main, main, main, main)	62
	2	(main, main, main, main, main, main, main)	12
	3	(main, no/other, no/other, no/other, no/other, no/other)	9
	4	(main, no/other, no/other, no/other, no/other, no/other, no/other)	7
	5	(main, subtopic, subtopic, subtopic, subtopic, subtopic)	7
Dialog	1	(question, inform, question, inform, question, inform)	14
	2	(question, inform, question, inform, question, inform, question, inform)	6
	3	(question, inform, question, inform, question, inform, agree)	5
	4	(question, inform, inform, inform, disagree, inform, disagree)	2
	5	(question, inform, agree, inform, answer, inform, answer)	2
Explanation move	1	(request, explain, request, explain, request, explain)	17
	2	(request, explain, request, explain, feedback, feedback)	9
	3	(request, explain, request, explain, request, explain, request, explain)	8
	4	(request, explain, feedback, feedback, feedback, feedback)	5
	5	(request, explain, request, explain, feedback, explain, feedback)	4

explanatory dialog types, let alone of datasets annotated for them. Nonetheless, the distinction of dialog types should be well-operationalizable if a respective effort is made.

We conclude this section by noting that we restricted our view here to sequential patterns of social interactions, in line with the basic operational model we devised above. Research has also come up with models of hierarchical structure, as studied early in computational linguistics (Grosz & Sidner, 1986). One of the most known computational representations used for this purpose is tree kernels used in kernel-based machine learning (Moschitti, 2006). Aiolli et al. (2009) even extended tree kernels further to cover sequential and hierarchical structure jointly, and Wachsmuth et al. (2017) adapted this idea to model the structure of argumentative discourse comprehensively, finding that this structure is a good predictor of different discourse properties. We are confident that such ideas can also be employed to model more complex patterns in explanatory dialogs, but this is a subject for further research.

27.7 How Does This Chapter Inspire Further Research?

A successful realization of social XAI in practice presupposes that the way human explainers (and potentially also human explainees) act within explanatory dialogs can be simulated effectively, or possibly even surpassed in certain aspects, with machines. To this end, the three core aspects of social XAI (i.e., multimodality, incrementality, and patterns) need to be operationalized. Whereas this chapter has laid the ground for such an operationalization by establishing a basic model of social interactions along with possible refinements and extensions, systematic instantiations of the model are yet to be made. We believe that the basic model and the way it can be refined and extended serve as a blueprint for how to work toward real-world social XAI systems in an appropriate manner.

Based on the model, we have devised general ideas on how to concretely operationalize the three core aspects. So far, however, only few lines of research exist that actually investigate such operationalizations for explanatory dialogs, as discussed and exemplified above. For this reason, this chapter has reviewed some of the most relevant techniques for operationalizing social interaction from related areas, such as natural language processing and multimodal human-computer interaction. To what extent, these techniques apply to the sophisticated communicative processes happening in explaining remains to be studied as well as where adaptations and extensions of the techniques are needed. The literature pointers given denote a starting point to identify concrete research gaps in future work.

Hence, it is up to further research to explore the operationalization of social interactions in explanatory dialogs in all its facets and details. The chapter gives general guidelines and a concrete model as a basis for such endeavors. We therefore hope that it inspires researchers as well as practitioners in the context of explainability to shape social XAI systems in the future.

27.8 Rapid Access to the Content of This Chapter

To move toward a successful realization of social explainable AI (XAI), an operationalization is needed that allows for systematic development and evaluation. This includes modeling the interaction process of explainers and explainees within explanatory dialogs, thereby covering the three core aspects of social XAI delineated in the present book at hand: multimodality, incrementality, and patterns.

We devise a basic operational model in this chapter that is designed to apply to any explanation setting irrespective of its specificities in terms of domain, social context, or the like. In particular, we formalize social interaction as a sequence of two or more turns of explainers and explainee. A turn under this model is a contiguous communicative utterance, with an explicit or implicit function. Turns may be unimodal (say, an oral statement or a gesture) or multimodal (say, both together), and they may also compose multiple communicative utterances in sequence. Functions relate to the goal of leading an explanatory dialog, and they can be formalized as a combination of measurable features. For example, the functions of a turn may include covering a specific topic to express a certain dialog act and to make a certain explanation move forward, as has been proposed in prior work (Wachsmuth & Alshomary, 2022).

The outlined model is generic on purpose to make it as generally applicable as possible. However, it is designed in a way that it can easily be refined or extended for specific explanatory settings, among others by defining specific functions as in the given example. Also, an explicit specification of the modalities to consider may be part of a refinement. Another possible point of extension is to go beyond the purely sequential structure of the basic model by adding hierarchical relations between turns or covering other types of nonsequential information. A conceptual model of such kind of interactions in explanatory dialogs has been established by Madumal et al. (2019). Both simple refinements and complex extensions define the basis for operationalizing multimodality, incrementality, and patterns.

For multimodality, operationalizations may target different dimensions, depending on what is meant to be measured: The different *channels* (e.g. visual, auditive, ...) covered by the modalities used in an interaction may be modeled to analyze their benefit and coherence, as Heylen (2006) did for speech and gestures. The way the different modalities add to the *content* of an explanation may be analyzed to learn about their impact on explanation success (Miller, 2023). *Timing* may also be of importance to understand the cognitive load of explainees within a social interaction in this regard (Papenkordt, 2024). The participants' roles and their agency concerning modalities as well as their dialog strategies as a potential result of their explanatory goals may become important.

For incrementality, an operationalization, on the one hand, needs to take into account the dynamic adaptation of explainers and explainees to the interaction process as it evolves. On the other hand, one needs to consider the evolving mutual models of interaction participants and of the explanandum. Interactional aspects can be covered directly with the outlined operational model, such as common reactions that explainees show (e.g., signaling understanding) to explainers' turns (e.g., giving an explanation) or vice versa. Given a dataset of explanatory dialogs, the model also provides a basis for learning to predict the most likely turn (and/or its function) from a sequence of preceding turns in the interaction. A social XAI system could employ such a prediction method to always decide its next turn at any moment of a dialog. First substantial attempts in this direction have been carried out in consecutive works by Wachsmuth and Alshomary (2022) and Alshomary et al. (2024) who presented computational methods to predict the functions of turns as well as the (expected) success of an explanatory dialog. In contrast, the incremental evolution and completion of models may require concepts such as a partner model (Groß et al., 2023) as well as measures that capture ideas such as recall at specific time steps in the interaction (Shapira et al., 2021).

Finally, for patterns, operationalizations may cover various concepts, such as general values and norms, the explainer's and explainee's roles and relationships, their goals, responsibilities, and engagement in explaining as well as the structures and practices emerging across the dialogs. While some of them can simply be presented by labels and ordinal/numeric values, particularly the latter require actual pattern mining methods. *Elementary interactions*, such as pairs or short sequences of turns of an explainer and an explainee, can be modeled as *n*-grams (Aggarwal, 2015) and can be analyzed for their co-occurrence with properties of explanatory dialogs, such as quality. However, it may not be so easy to identify recurring complete dialog sequences (so-called *pragmatic frames*). Effective ideas from related work for this purpose include higher-level *n*-grams (Persing & Ng, 2010) and so-called *flow patterns* (Wachsmuth & Stein, 2017), that is, abstractions of common sequences of turns functions. Alshomary et al. (2024) studied which types of flows occur most frequently in explanatory dialogs. Structural patterns on the dialog level ultimately imply different *dialog types*, such as inquiry versus information-seeking dialogs (Walton, 2010). Assuming respective data is available, their identification may be seen as a standard classification task.

Only a few of the concepts and techniques for operationalizing social interaction have actually already been investigated specifically for explanatory dialogs. Future research should systematically explore and evaluate to what extent they suffice to operationalize multimodality, incrementality, and patterns effectively and where extensions or adaptations may be necessary. The operational model devised here as well as the sketched ideas for concrete operationalizations may serve as basis for any such attempt.

Acknowledgments We thank Manfred Stede for his valuable perspective and helpful comments on an earlier version of this chapter. This work was funded by the Deutsche Forschungsgemeinschaft (DFG, German Research Foundation): TRR 318/1 2021 – 438445824.

References

Aggarwal, C. C. (2015). *Data mining: The textbook*. Springer. https://doi.org/10.1007/978-3-319-14142-8.

Aiolli, F., Da San Martino, G., & Sperduti, A. (2009). Route kernels for trees. In *Proceedings of the 26th Annual International Conference on Machine Learning* (pp. 17–24). Association for Computing Machinery. https://doi.org/10.1145/1553374.1553377.

Al Khatib, K., Wachsmuth, H., Lang, K., Herpel, J., Hagen, M., & Stein, B. (2018). Modeling deliberative argumentation strategies on Wikipedia. In *Proceedings of the 56th Annual Meeting of the Association for Computational Linguistics (Volume 1: Long Papers)* (pp. 2545–2555). Association for Computational Linguistics. https://doi.org/10.18653/v1/P18-1237.

Alshomary, M., Lange, F., Booshehri, M., Sengupta, M., Cimiano, P., & Wachsmuth, H. (2024). *Modeling the quality of dialogi-cal explanations*. https://doi.org/10.48550/arXiv.2403.00662. arXiv: 2403.00662.2403.00662 [cs.CL].

Beltagy, I., Peters, M. E., & Cohan, A. (2020). *Longformer: The long- document transformer*. https://doi.org/10.48550/arXiv.2004.05150. arXiv: 2004.05150 [cs.CL].

Booshehri, M., Buschmeier, H., & Cimiano, P. (2024). A model of factors contributing to the success of dialogical explanations. In *Proceedings of the 26th International Conference on Multimodal Interaction* (pp. 373–381). ACM. https://doi.org/10.1145/3678957.3685744.

Bourse, S., & Saint-Dizier, P. (2012). A repository of rules and lexical resources for discourse structure analysis: The case of explanation structures. In *Proceedings of the Eighth International Conference on Language Resources and Evaluation (LREC-2012)* (pp. 2778–2785). European Languages Resources Association (ELRA).

Buhl, H. M., Fisher, J. B., & Rohlfing, K. (2024). Changes in partner models – Effects of adaptivity in the course of explanations. In *Proceedings of the Annual Meeting of the Cognitive Science Society* (pp. 4976–4983). University of California.

Bunt, H., Alexandersson, J., Carletta, J., Choe, J.-W., Fang, A.C., Hasida, K., Lee, K., Petukhova, V., Popescu-Belis, A., Romary, L., Soria, C., & Traum, D. (2010). Towards an ISO standard for dialogue act annotation. In *Proceedings of the Seventh International Conference on Language Resources and Evaluation (LREC'10)*. European Language Resources Association (ELRA).

Cawsey, A. (1989). Explanatory dialogues. *Interacting with Computers, 1*(1), 69–92. https://doi.org/10.1016/0953-5438(89)90008-8.

Chalkidis, I., Dai, X., Fergadiotis, M., Malakasiotis, P., & Elliott, D. (2022). *An exploration of hierarchical attention transformers for efficient long document classification*. https://doi.org/10.48550/arXiv.2210.05529. arXiv: 2210.05529 [cs.CL].

Chen, H., Liu, X., Yin, D., & Tang, J. (2017). A Survey on dialogue systems: Recent advances and new frontiers. *SIGKDD Explorations Newsletter, 19*(2), 25–35. https://doi.org/10.1145/3166054.3166058.

Devlin, J., Chang, M.-W., Lee, K., & Toutanova, K. (2019). BERT: Pre-training of deep bidirectional transformers for language understanding. In *Proceedings of the 2019 Conference of the North American Chapter of the Association for Computational Linguistics: Human Language Technologies, Volume 1 (Long and Short Papers)* (pp. 4171–4186). Association for Computational Linguistics. https://doi.org/10.18653/v1/N19-1423.

Dzikovska, M. O., Nielsen, R. D., & Brew, C. (2012). Towards effective tutorial feedback for explanation questions: A dataset and baselines. In *Proceedings of the 2012 Conference of the North American Chapter of the Association for Computational Linguistics: Human Language Technologies* (pp. 200–210). Association for Computational Linguistics.

Feldhus, N., Anagnostopoulou, A., Wang, Q., Alshomary, M., Wachsmuth, H., Sonntag, D., & Möller, S. (2024). Towards modeling and evaluating instructional explanations in teacher-student dialogues. In *Proceedings of the 2024 International Conference on Information Technology for Social Good* (pp. 225–230). Association for Computing Machinery. https://doi.org/10.1145/3677525.3678665.

Fontan, L., & Saint-Dizier, P. (2008). Analyzing the explanation structure of procedural texts: Dealing with advice and warnings. In *Semantics in Text Pro- cessing. STEP 2008 Conference Proceedings* (pp. 115–127). College Publications.

Groß, A., Singh, A., Banh, N. C., Richter, B., Scharlau, I., Rohlfing, K. J., & Wrede, B. (2023). Scaffolding the human partner by contrastive guidance in an explanatory human-robot dialogue. *Frontiers in Robotics and AI, 10*. https://doi.org/10.3389/frobt.2023.1236184.

Grosz, B. J., & Sidner, C. L. (1986). Attention, intentions, and the structure of discourse. *Computational Linguistics, 12*(3), 175–204.

Heylen, D. (2006). Head gestures, gaze, and the principles of conversational structure. *International Journal of Humanoid Robotics, 3*(3), 241–267. https://doi.org/10.1142/S0219843606000746.

Lammert, O., Richter, B., Schütze, C., Thommes, K., & Wrede, B. (2024). Humans in XAI: Increased reliance in decision-making under uncertainty by using explanation strategies. *Frontiers in Behavioral Economics, 3*, 1377075. https://doi.org/10.3389/frbhe.2024.1377075.

Lausberg, H., & Slöetjes, H. (2015). The revised NEUROGES-ELAN system: An objective and reliable interdisciplinary analysis tool for nonverbal behavior and gesture. *Behavior Research Methods, 48*, 973–993. https://doi.org/10.3758/s13428-015-0622-z.

Le, T., Miller, T., Sonenberg, L., & Singh, R. (2024). *Towards the new XAI: A hypothesis-driven approach to decision support using evidence*. https://doi.org/10.48550/arXiv.2402.01292. arXiv: 2402.01292.

Liang, P. P., Lyu, Y., Fan, X., Tsaw, J., Liu, Y., Mo, S., Yogatama, D., Morency, L.-P., & Salakhutdinov, R. (2023). *High-modality multimodal transformer: Quantifying modality & interaction het- erogeneity for high-modality representation learning.* https://doi.org/10.48550/arXiv.2203.01311. arXiv: 2203.01311 [cs.LG].

Madumal, P., Miller, T., Sonenberg, L., & Vetere, F. (2019). A grounded interaction protocol for explainable artificial intelligence. In *Proceedings of the 18th International Conference on Autonomous Agents and MultiAgent Sys- tems*. International Foundation for Autonomous Agents and Multiagent Systems (pp. 1033–1041).

Mann, W. C., & Thompson, S. A. (1988). Rhetorical structure theory: Toward a functional theory of text organization. *Text-interdisciplinary Journal for the Study of Discourse, 8*(3), 243–281. https://doi.org/10.1515/text.1.1988.8.3.243.

Mao, Y., & Lebanon, G. (2007). Isotonic conditional random fields and local sentiment flow. In *Advances in Neural Information Processing Systems 19: Proceedings of the 2006 Conference* (pp. 961–968). MIT Press.

Miller, T. (2023). Explainable AI is dead, long live explainable AI!: Hypothesis- driven decision support using evaluative AI. In *2023 ACM Conference on Fairness, Accountability, and Transparency* (pp. 333–342). ACM. https://doi.org/10.1145/3593013.3594001.

Moore, J, D. (1994). *Participating in explanatory dialogues: Interpreting and responding to questions in context.* The MIT Press. https://doi.org/10.7551/mitpress/5247.001.0001.

Moschitti, A. (2006). Making tree kernels practical for natural language learning. In *11th Conference of the European Chapter of the Association for Computational Linguistics*. Association for Computational Linguistics (pp. 113–120).

Papenkordt, J. (2024). Navigating transparency: The influence of on-demand explanations on non-expert user interaction with AI. In *International Conference on Human-Computer Interaction* (pp. 238–263). Springer. https://doi.org/10.1007/978-3-031-60606-9_14.

Papenkordt, J., Ngomo, A.-C. N., & Thommes, K. (2023). Are numbers or words the key to user reliance on AI? In *Academy of Management Proceedings* (p. 12946). Academy of Management. https://doi.org/10.5465/AMPROC.2023.12946abstract.

Persing I., & Davis, A., & Ng, V. (2010). Modeling organization in student essays. In *Proceedings of the 2010 Conference on Empirical Meth- ods in Natural Language Processing* (pp. 229–239). Association for Computational Linguistics.

Qi, R., Zheng, Y., Yang, Y., Zhang, J., & Hsiao, J. (2023). Individual differences in explanation strategies for image classification and implications for explainable AI. In *Proceedings of the Annual Meeting of the Cognitive Science Society* (pp. 1644–1651). University of California.

Rohlfing, K. J., Cimiano, P., Scharlau, I., Matzner, T., Buhl, H. M., Buschmeier, H., Esposito, E., Grimminger, A., Hammer, B., Häb-Umbach, R., Horwath, I., Hüllermeier, E., Kern, F., Kopp, S., Thommes, K., Ngomo, A.-C. N., Schulte, C., Wachsmuth, H., Wagner, P., & Wrede, B. (2021). Explanation as a social practice: Toward a conceptual framework for the social design of AI systems. *IEEE Transactions on Cognitive and Developmental Systems, 13*(3), 717–728. https://doi.org/10.1109/TCDS.2020.3044366.

Shapira, O., Pasunuru, R., Ronen, H., Bansal, M., Amsterdamer, Y., & Dagan, I. (2021). Extending multi-document summarization evaluation to the interactive setting. In *Proceedings of the 2021 Conference of the North American Chapter of the Association for Computational Linguistics: Human Language Technologies* (pp. 657–677). Association for Computational Linguistics. https://doi.org/10.18653/v1/2021.naacl-main.54.

Stolcke, A., Ries, K., Coccaro, N., Shriberg, E., Bates, R., Jurafsky, D., Taylor, P., Martin, R., Van Ess-Dykema, C., & Meteer, M. (2000). Dialogue act modeling for automatic tagging and recognition of conversational speech. *Computational Linguistics, 26*(3), 339–374. https://doi.org/10.1162/089120100561737.

Swales, J. M. (1990). *Genre analysis: English in academic and research settings.* Cambridge University Press.

Wachsmuth, H., Al Khatib, K., & Stein, B. (2016). Using argument mining to assess the argumentation quality of essays. In *Proceedings of COLING 2016, the 26th International Conference on Computational Linguistics: Technical Papers* (pp. 1680–1691). The COLING 2016 Organizing Committee.

Wachsmuth, H., & Alshomary, M. (2022). "Mama always had a way of explaining things so I could understand": A dialogue corpus for learning to construct explanations. In *Proceedings of the 29th International Conference on Computational Linguistics* (pp. 344–354). International Committee on Computational Linguistics.

Wachsmuth, H., Da San Martino, G., Kiesel, D., & Stein, B. (2017). The impact of modeling overall argumentation with tree kernels. In *Proceedings of the 2017 Conference on Empirical Methods in Natural Language Processing* (pp. 2369–2379). Association for Computational Linguistics.

Wachsmuth, H., Kiesel, J., & Stein, B. (2015). Sentiment flow - A general model of web review argumentation. In *Proceedings of the 2015 Conference on Empirical Methods in Natural Language Processing* (pp. 601–611). Association for Computational Linguistics. https://doi.org/10.18653/v1/D15-1072.

Wachsmuth, H., & Stein, B. (2017). A universal model for discourse-level argumentation analysis. *Special Section of the ACM Transactions on Internet Technology: Argumentation in Social Media, 17*(3), 28:1–28:24. https://doi.org/10.1145/2957757.

Wachsmuth, H., Trenkmann, M., Stein, B., & Engels, G. (2014). Modeling review argumentation for robust sentiment analysis. In *Proceedings of COLING 2014, the 25th International Conference on Computational Linguistics: Technical Papers* (pp. 553–564). Dublin City University and Association for Computational Linguistics.

Walton, D. (2010). Types of dialogue and burdens of proof. In *Proceedings of the 2010 Conference on Computational Models of Argument: Proceedings of COMMA 2010* (pp. 13–24). IOS Press.

Zhang, J., Kumar, R., Ravi, S., & Danescu-Niculescu-Mizil, C. (2016). Conversational flow in Oxford-style debates. In *Proceedings of the 2016 Conference of the North American Chapter of the Association for Computational Linguistics: Human Language Technologies* (pp. 136–141). Association for Computational Linguistics. https://doi.org/10.18653/v1/N16-1017.

Open Access This chapter is licensed under the terms of the Creative Commons Attribution 4.0 International License (http://creativecommons.org/licenses/by/4.0/), which permits use, sharing, adaptation, distribution and reproduction in any medium or format, as long as you give appropriate credit to the original author(s) and the source, provide a link to the Creative Commons license and indicate if changes were made.

The images or other third party material in this chapter are included in the chapter's Creative Commons license, unless indicated otherwise in a credit line to the material. If material is not included in the chapter's Creative Commons license and your intended use is not permitted by statutory regulation or exceeds the permitted use, you will need to obtain permission directly from the copyright holder.

Chapter 28
Measuring the Outcome of sXAI

Kirsten Thommes

Abstract Quantitatively evaluating the benefits of eXplainable Artificial Intelligence (XAI) and social XAI for humans is not a trivial pursuit. Therefore, we categorize the potential measures in terms of subjective and objective outcomes and short- and long-term outcomes of interactive social XAI. When reviewing the current state of the art, we observed some measurement problems in the literature: (a) Researchers do not clearly state whether they want to measure the inner state of users, users' behavioral response, or the overall AI-human collaborative performance. (b) Moreover, most measures implicitly assume that all humans either do not react or improve in attitudes or performance. Psychological reactance (feeling or doing the opposite) is usually not captured. (c) Many researchers invent their own scale when measuring psychological constructs, thereby jeopardizing the validity of their measures and slowing down progress in the field, because general evidence and subsequent learning can be achieved only by collecting many compatible pieces of evidence. (d) Most studies look into short-term outcomes and neglect that experiences in social interactions with XAI may evolve and have long-term outcomes not only for the individual but also for groups or society at large.

28.1 How Does This Chapter Relate to XAI?

Evaluating interactive explanations from a user's perspective is crucial for advancing our knowledge of social XAI. However, the evaluation field sometimes suffers from diverse disciplinary backgrounds, resulting in seemingly insurmountable debates. Researchers with an engineering background frequently assume that "measuring humans" is easy because they can be asked whether they like or dislike an interaction. However, many disciplines have a long history of struggling with measuring latent concepts, that is, these things are not directly measurable on a scale with fixed units. Latent variables such as attitudes or intentions are

K. Thommes (✉)
Faculty of Business Administration and Economics, Paderborn University, Paderborn, Germany
e-mail: kirsten.thommes@uni-paderborn.de

stored in the mind and require a complex translation for the human involving the ability to express their inner state, their willingness to do so, and also, on the researcher's side, the ability and willingness to ask the right question that the human can understand unambiguously (Bollen, 2002). Moreover, social scientists know there is a huge gap between attitudes (e.g., the likability of a certain object or its perceived usefulness) and behavior (e.g., usage), sometimes making the knowledge about attitudes even irrelevant as a predictor of behavior. For instance, (Zhang et al., 2020) show trust in systems can be calibrated, but trust calibration is not sufficient for optimal behavior. Further, the obstacles to translating attitudes, perceptions, and values into a numerical scale, plus the limited predictive power of these measures for later behavior, are frequently underestimated in research. On the other hand, social scientists tend to overuse and overgeneralize their established scales, such as trust scales, that might require some tailoring toward the technical system. That is sometimes largely ignored for the sake of a valid but sometimes inappropriate measure. We give some examples for that later. For instance, some of the scales validated by social science, such as social psychology, even still mention technological artifacts from the 1990s.

Due to the diverse backgrounds, four general themes have recently emerged in the literature. First, some researchers question whether the human-centric focus on the outcome measurement is appropriate (Rosenfeld, 2021; Vilone & Longo, 2021). The idea is that evaluating the outcome by 'measuring humans' is insufficient and prone to measurement errors as humans are diverse and much research finds not one fits all solution. While the problems addressed are relevant, not measuring the human outcome and measuring the system alone will not solve the problems of XAI or social XAI and will result in a dead end of technological progress. The result would be a myopic technological imperative in which the researcher – and not the human user or society – sets the goal for an optimal system. While a general typology of explainable systems is most welcome, a social XAI system must eventually serve humans, and human needs cannot be ignored (Cabitza et al., 2023).

Second, much research confuses the inner state of humans with observable actions. For instance, a recent review of XAI (Rong et al., 2023) shows that some studies interpret behavior (e.g., user reliance), as a signal of the inner state of the human (e.g., trust). Whereas the inner state of the human may be a determinant for certain behavior, no conclusion can be made in the opposite direction. For instance, one may accept the explanation of a system and follow the advice because one feels social pressure to do so, or because the other options are even worse, or because one wants to reduce cognitive load by just following the advice. Thus, following advice is not a good operationalization of trust and vice versa; trust is not imperative for advice-taking. Unlike machines, humans do not necessarily follow their intentions, but diverse inner and outer influences affect their behavior, e.g., they behave differently when being observed, when they feel their decision is irrelevant, when they are emotionally aroused, when they feel time pressure, and so on. Thus, assuming that there is just one influence (trust) leading to choice (behavior) is neglecting human nature. Therefore, good evaluations are sensitive to the problem of defining the construct they aim at, differentiating between the latent human inner state (attitudes, norms, preferences) and measures of human behavior, and acknowledging the operationalization problems both may entail.

Third, even when studies agree on measuring a certain construct, such as trust, many develop their own measurement tools (see, e.g., the overview by Hoffman et al. (2018). Not adhering to one tool or scale in the outcome makes the general progress of science in this area difficult. Any single study should be placed into context and comparable to other studies to improve our understanding of drivers and general patterns. Also, changing the outcome frequently prevents the analysis of ambiguous results across different studies.

Fourth, most, if not all, of the research looks into short-term interaction sequences, either one decision per user or some consecutive decisions (e.g., 20 consecutive rounds of decisions). While this is an economical approach to collecting first insights, it may lure the research community into false beliefs about human responses because people will be able to learn during interactions with a system, develop trust, mistrust, or distrust over time, start routinized behaviors, and the like. Thus, an interaction after several months of AI use will be very different compared to the first one, and first-time usage behavior may not be reproduced.

To mitigate the problems above, we propose improving the reflection on outcome measurement in every study, eventually combining different measures, for example, studies simultaneously trying to capture the inner state of the human that can only be measured subjectively and combining that with more objective outcome measures of behavior. Hoffman et al. (2018) go even one step further and suggest using not only two metrics but also two groups of evaluators—for instance, the researcher (or the developer) and the user. While netting these two groups and the specific measures is difficult, deliberately segmenting users and evaluations in different partitions may improve measurement quality. To support a deliberate choice, we discuss the most frequently used measures in XAI research and also their pros and cons in the following.

28.2 Quantitative Measures Applied in XAI

First, one can distinguish between latent, subjective, and directly measurable objective measures (see Table 28.1). The most prominent and frequently used subjective measures are trust, perceived quality of advice, or user satisfaction. These measures are subjective because the users subjectively rate their inner state. The measures cannot be validated against a ground truth. When measuring such latent constructs, the measurement tools matter tremendously because, for instance, two different scales of perceived satisfaction may result in very different metrics even when applied after the same XAI–human interaction.

Objective measures are also frequently used, for example, whether humans can accurately reproduce the content that has been explained or follow or reject advice. Here, the results of an interaction can be counted. Contrary to the inner state of the

Table 28.1 Types of evaluation metrics

	Subjective	Objective
Short term	**Trust (+distrust, mistrust)**	**Reliance, weight of advice (+reactance)**
	Perceived workload, perceived helpfulness	Task performance
	Satisfaction, rated ease of use	Comprehension test
	Perceptions of transparency, understanding	Errors, duration of interaction
Long term	Technology acceptance (TAM) **intention to reuse, intention to recommend**	**Adoption rate, rate of reuse rate of diffusion**
	General trust in AI (AI appreciation, AI aversion)	Internalization of AI & explanandum

Note: Outcome measures in bold are specifically addressed in this chapter

user, which is a difficult-to-measure latent construct, objective measures are usually a manifest construct and can be measured more easily.

For a full evaluation of interactive XAI, research should also tackle the direct outcome of interaction and the long-term impact. While the overwhelming majority of studies rely on studying one or few interactions with an AI in a short time and directly measure either subjective or objective human reactions, many relevant outcomes of (social) XAI emerge over time and may affect not only the single user but also groups or the society. Outcomes such as trust, the humans' reuse of a system after an explanation, or whether they start promoting (warning about) the system to others and, therefore, accelerate (hamper) the diffusion of certain explanatory practices may be a relevant for XAI. Table 28.1 gives an overview of the potential interactive social XAI outcome measures.

Essential to all measures is whether one is only interested in the mean or in a more fine-grained analysis of human response. For instance, an interactive social XAI may improve the mean correctness rate of humans compared to a situation with no interactive social AI. However, the increase in the mean may result from everybody advancing thanks to the interactive XAI or by some individuals driving the outcome measure up. In contrast, some individuals even move in the other direction, by, for example, responding to the interaction with reactance (doing deliberately the opposite of what was recommended). Therefore, it is important to question whether one is only interested in the mean effect of a social XAI system or is also interested in disparity among the population of users by, for example, analyzing improvement in the outcome but also reactance to XAI. Recent research (Le et al., 2024; Lammert et al., 2024) shows the need to differentiate between reliance, overreliance, and reactance. The same is, for instance, also true for trust, because calibrated trust (Zhang et al., 2020) is not just the opposite side of the spectrum when trust is just missing, and more nuanced discussions about accurate measurement and operationalization are needed. A recent review in psychology

(Jeckel et al., 2024) shows that monitoring adverse events is still in its infancy even in psychology. Whereas many XAI researchers acknowledge the problem of overreliance or blind trust, many empirical studies neglect the problem. For instance, many studies report a shift or a difference in means and do not consider that the distribution may also vary due to bimodal or other distributions between two treatments or over time. Hence, the potential bifurcation or other heterogeneous responses to explanations should be considered explicitly to improve evaluations.

28.3 Short-Term Subjective Outcomes

Because social XAI is interactive, interpersonal constructs such as trust are frequently subject of research (Wischnewski et al., 2023). For human systems to work, trust in the system is usually seen as a relevant social outcome. Nonetheless, trust can only be self-reported. While some researchers extrapolate trust from actions, the causal link is weak, and action may also result from reason, luck, algorithm aversion, or appreciation. However, measuring trust even in self-reported questionnaire studies is difficult, and much research is struggling to find good measurement instruments. First, a recent review found that in 23 recent studies, 20 different measurement instruments were used. Moreover, 52% used self-designed questionnaires (Rong et al., 2023), thereby jeopardizing the measurement instrument's objectivity, reliability, and validity.

Weak measurement instruments raise doubts about the general reliability of results. Second, the other half of the studies in this review used validated measurement instruments. However, the scales were intended to measure general trust in technology, general human-computer trust, trust in human–machine systems, and the like. When such scales are used after short-term interactions, the results rely on the previous interaction and the humans' general and lifelong experiences with technology, computer systems, or machines. Thus, differences between groups may result not only from differences in the experimental setting but also from previous experiences, and the trustworthiness of results may be corrupted if randomization in groups is not implemented in full. Table 28.2 gives an overview of some of the measurement instruments and sample items that are frequently used, displaying the wider variety of operationalizations of trust in the literature.

As is easy to see, the ways of measuring trust are diverse. Semantic similarity analysis of many trust scales (Alsaid et al., 2023) reveals that the trust items used in research vary widely, and it is at least questionable whether all of them are measuring trust (i.e., are valid, reliable, and objective). For social science, where human beliefs, intentions, and thoughts as latent constructs frequently need to be measured, there is a scientific process of scale development. Among other criteria, two independent researchers should receive the same test results if they ask the same person, questions concerning one construct (e.g., trust) should cover all theoretical aspects of that concept, and the question should measure what they intend to measure. Therefore, one needs an external verification process and statistical proof

Table 28.2 Examples of trust scales

Construct	Example items	Scale	Source
Trust in automation	E.g., "The system is deceptive," "the system behaves in an underhanded manner," "I am suspicious of the system's intent, action, or output," "I can trust the system," "I am familiar with the system"	7pt Likert	Jian et al. (2000)
General trust in technology	Perceived recommendation quality, e.g., "I liked the items recommended by the system," perceived system effectiveness, e.g., "I can find better items without the help of the system," and choice satisfaction, e.g., "I like the movie/item I have chosen"	5pt Likert	Knijnenburg et al. (2012)
Trust in human-machine systems	Rate trust, predictability, and judgment of dependability and faith for, e.g., "the local bus service to be on time," "the calculator to produce the right answer"	7pt Likert	Lee and Moray (1992)
Trust	E.g., "I am convinced by the medical suggestions that the app recommended to me," "the app can be trusted"	7pt Likert	Tsai et al. (2021)
Trustworthiness	E.g., "Given the provided explanations, I trust that the automated decision system makes good-quality decisions," and "based on my understanding of the decision-making procedures, I know the automated decision system is not opportunistic"	5pt Likert	Schoeffer et al. (2022)

for scales that the item fully measures the concept in question (e.g., fully measures trust in all its aspects) and not partially something else (e.g., satisfaction).

Many measures of subjective concepts in XAI are not validated according to scale evaluation standards and also measure quite different aspects. Validation of a scale, however, is important because the researchers' idea of what they are measuring and their actual measuring may well diverge. One needs to make sure that the scale is really measuring what it should, and not something else or many different things (such as trust, ease of use, and satisfaction) all at once. Take, for instance, the trust scale by Tsai et al. (2021) from Table 28.2, which aims to measure trust but also asks for advice quality which is surely related, but a different latent concept.

Moreover, by using diverse scales, the effect size, generally, cannot be interpreted as being directly linked to the specific technology experiences in the experiment but may also stem from the participants' past. One way to mitigate the problem would be to measure the general trust (in technology, computers, machines, or the like) before and after the interaction with the XAI system and to analyze differences in magnitude while either controlling for equality in groups before the XAI interaction or using differences-in-differences approaches (Villa, 2016).

Hoffman et al., 2018 consider this problem and develop their own scale based on previous scales addressing trust toward specific systems. Their scale consists of eight items derived from other scales and measures trust on a 5-point Likert scale. Some items appear to measure human-AI efficiency (e.g., "the [tool] is efficient in that it works very quickly") and may not be loading on the latent variable trust. While we applaud seeing the need for scale development, we encourage future work to refine and validate their scale while keeping in mind that the perfect scale does not exist and will always generate measurement errors (Rauthmann, 2023).

In their review, Rong et al. (2023) also analyze the frequency and measurement models of other subjective outcomes after social XAI, specifically workload, helpfulness, satisfaction, and ease of use. Workload studies use solely the Task Load Index (NASA-TLX) (Hart and Staveland, 1988). It is worth noting, however, that this measurement tool entails some very basic problems and is debated heavily among social scientists (Winter, 2014). Also, two different versions appear to exist, both released by NASA, so even the comparability is not given automatically. Moreover, recent research suggests that the measure should at least not aggregate the six dimensions of mental demand, physical demand, temporal demand, subjective performance, subjective effort, and frustration into an aggregated measure but report them separately (Bolton et al., 2023) because their aggregation results in no meaningful information, and the different subdimensions sometimes show contradictory results. For example, some go up while others go down, and not all are similarly related to objective performance measures.

Concerning subjective user satisfaction and perceived ease of use, the same problem as in the trust literature seems prevalent. Rong et al. (2023) count 13 papers measuring satisfaction, with 7 developing their own measurement instrument, while 4 used previously developed but not validated scales and changed them when using them. It is clear that comparability will never be possible. Rong et al. (2023) identify 11 studies evaluating the perceived ease of use, almost all either developing their own scales or using a scale that has not yet been validated. The system usability scale (Holzinger et al., 2020) may become of special interest to social XAI research. It asks explicitly for the users' perception of the quality of explanations instead of attempting to measure explanation-quality and system-quality in one go. The proposed questions for assessing the perceived quality of an explanation contain items such as "I found that the data included all relevant known causal factors with sufficient precision and granularity," "I was able to use the explanations with my knowledge base," or "I did not find inconsistencies between explanations." Even though the scale is subjective and probably needs some refinement (e.g., "I think that most people would learn to understand the explanations very quickly" might be irrelevant), it is a very useful attempt to measure the perceived subjective quality of an explanation.

28.4 Short-Term Objective Outcomes

Many researchers prefer objective over subjective outcomes because this circumvents the measurement problem of subjective latent constructs. While latent concepts are 'in the user,' objective outcomes can be counted from the outside (e.g., by a researcher), and at least the measurement scale is less of a problem. Also, researchers are usually not concerned with the entertainment qualities of their AI but want to improve something, such as the users' knowledge or the users' performance. However, these measures usually come with the downside that they cannot answer any why questions over the causal chain and many assume that latent concepts such as trust must be explained as a root cause of user behavior. Thus, many researchers also measure subjective and latent variables, that is, variables such as trust that cannot be counted directly but must be assessed indirectly via questionnaire research.

If one compares two modes of social XAI, for instance, and observes that one mode leads to more advice-taking than the other, the causal chain – be it trust, perceived usefulness, or just a random result – remains in the dark. Nonetheless, objective measures remain important because they are accurate, valid, and can be compared. In the following, we discuss some frequently used objective measures ranging from binary to metric measures of advice-taking, task performance, and comprehension.

The outcome variable is often binary (e.g., agreement to a classification). However, evaluations of binary outcomes, such as the agreement or categorization, have some statistically undesirable side effects. First, they produce little variance. The response either rejects or agrees, and thus, means are not a meaningful moment for describing the outcome. Also, changes in individuals without and with XAI are difficult to measure; the respondent's initial choice has already been correct. And change cannot be attributed clearly to a convincing XAI or to human luck. Thus, XAI explanations cannot alter the initial choice but only reconfirm. Because of potentially random agreement, evaluations with binary outcomes need a much larger sample size because many observations must potentially be excluded due to humans' lucky guesses (or prior knowledge of the subject). If randomization between two design choices, for example, two types of explanations, has not worked out, this problem might even be relevant when comparing two groups.

The same is true for the analysis of advice-rejecting, which even requires a larger sample size. Because rejection is a less frequent event, researchers aiming to analyze rejection/misunderstanding or reactance need even more observations to be sure that differences between groups are not due to chance but occur systematically.

Also, the effect size must be reported accurately in binary, categorical, or ordinal data as the marginal effect at the means of all other variables, the average marginal effect of one variable, or the marginal effect at representative values. For instance, in binary outcome variables, the estimated effect is an odd ratio, not a relative probability, and may lead to confusion. With both odd ratios and relative probabilities, the magnitude of an effect is difficult to understand, and researchers are advised to get help from statisticians, especially if social science and statistics with human populations are not their original field. Here, marginal effects help assess the magnitude of an effect. As in a linear case, the change in probability is shown when the predictor or independent variable increases by one unit. Choosing whether this effect should be shown at the means of all other variables, the average marginal effect of one variable, or the marginal effect at representative values is a matter of taste and probably should depend on the specific case. However, this needs to be reported.

If the research goal is to analyze how well humans follow advice, researchers frequently use metric measures such as the weight of advice (also referred to as the taking index), calculated as

$$WOA = \frac{(finalchoice - initialchoice)}{(recommendation - initialchoice)} \tag{28.1}$$

or slight variations thereof (Bailey et al., 2023). Some variations take negative advice, such as the formula above, whereas others take the absolute value. The latter results in no differentiation between reactance to advice and following advice, whereas the formula above differentiates both directions. The primary difference lies in the potential inclusion of negative values. This situation arises when a participant lowers the second estimation despite the advice suggesting an increase. Furthermore, the index may surpass one if the participant exceeds the recommended adjustment (Logg et al., 2019; Schultze et al., 2015). Further, some studies employ Winsorization, setting values below 0 to 0 and those above 1 to 1. This approach leads to a continuous outcome variable on a scale from 0 (completely ignoring the advice) to 1 (completely relying on advice) (Harvey & Fischer, 1997; Schultze et al., 2015; Yaniv, 2004b,a).

Suppose the research goal is to compare adherence to AI advice in different settings. In that case, research frequently uses the mean difference (Schemmer et al., 2022) between human–XAI collaboration with and without certain features to measure metric task performance. If XAI across domains is compared and the domains differ in tasks, one may also use the standardized mean difference to account for different scale ranges in the outcome task. The standardized score is calculated as

$$SMD = \frac{\text{Difference in mean outcome between group}}{\text{Pooled standard deviation}} \tag{28.2}$$

Instead of the pooled standard deviation, some authors (Andrade, 2020) also recommend using only the standard deviation of the control group. SDs of 0.2, 0.5, and 0.8 are considered small, medium, and large, respectively.

In some instances, the overall goal of an interactive XAI system is not to enable the user to make a decision or fulfill a task but to transfer knowledge. Here, the comprehensibility of an explanation should be focused in standardized tests. Herm et al. (2021) propose testing comprehension in retention, transfer, and recall dimensions. Retention would be whether the user can reproduce the specific explanans, transfer knowledge would test whether the explanation enables the user to apply the knowledge to new cases, and recall tests long-term internalization to reproduce the knowledge. Especially the last dimension, recall, requires some time gap between interaction and evaluation.

28.5 Long-Term Outcomes

Implicitly, many scientists are concerned with measuring not only the direct outcome of an interaction with social XAI but also the long-term results. These studies are seldom undertaken and frequently suffer from insufficient time gaps between interaction and outcome. Unfortunately, many studies measure the long-term goal directly after the interaction and do not follow up after some time or longer periods of social XAI-human interaction. Nonetheless, many of the theories focus on long-term outcomes.

These theories usually assume that individual experiences with a system promote or foster individual intentions to reuse the system, promote it, and contribute to its diffusion. These long-term outcomes can be differentiated further between the subjective long-term attitudes toward a particular system or a technology in general of either one person or a larger group of individuals. The outcome can also be measured objectively in terms of the adoption rates of that person or of a group or the diffusion of any technology in general.

Studies using technology acceptance models (TAMs) still mainly use subjective outcomes because the variable of interest is self-reported usage behavior that social norms may bias. More objective measures would be the diffusion of an explanatory practice in XAI in systems or across domains or regions. The idea stems from Rogers et al. (2014), who theorizes that adoption rates to any innovation result among others from the perceived relative advantage over other alternatives, compatibility, (non)complexity, trialability, and observability as attributes of the innovation, but also on the communication in the social sphere about the innovation. Thus, the rapid diffusion of a system or practice may be attributed to positive user assessments. The idea is not used very frequently in XAI research. One notable exception is research from the medical domain (Panagoulias et al., 2023). However, measuring explanatory practices in the long run by utilizing, operationalizing, and modifying the components of Rodgers' diffusion theory may be a fruitful avenue to approach long-term outcomes of social XAI.

28.6 How Does This Chapter Inspire Further Directions of XAI?

Research in XAI needs to make advances in measurement methods: First, researchers should be aware that the inner state of a human – frequently measured by questionnaires – and the observed behavior are not related monocausally. For instance, humans can be very satisfied with a certain interaction but still refrain from accepting the explanation because of other influential factors, such as social pressure. On the other hand, following AI advice is not necessarily a sign of trust but may also be due to laziness, routinized behavior or the like. Nonetheless, it may also result from a random choice, social pressure, or the desire to please the researcher (the so-called researcher demand effect). One possible avenue for better evaluation is measuring subjective and objective outcomes and trying to link them. The aspiration here is not to achieve a perfect correlation but to prove that some social explanations of AI are better on subjective and objective dimensions.

Second, many researchers work with directed scales, aiming to detect an improvement in outcome measures. For instance, the weight of advice as a frequently used measure cannot deal with the plethora of potential human responses to interaction ranging from advice-taking to ignorance to reactance. Usually, the scale construction allows changes in only one direction. It ignores that interaction or any influential attempt may also trigger individuals to choose the opposite as a conscious sign of their reactance. To better understand and evaluate the variety of potential reactions, research should consider that the same "average response effect" might result from different distributions of reactions.

Third, the current state of the art is fragmented, and there are hardly two studies that use the same outcome variable. This is especially problematic because the XAI used in research is usually a very specific artifact. To learn about social XAI, we need to systematically vary the interaction processes and social dimensions of interactions and repeatedly measure the same outcome. The research community simultaneously varies the social XAI and the outcome variable—sometimes even using invalidated measures. This slows down the progress. While it will be hard to agree on one specific outcome, a standard set of outcomes will hopefully emerge, maybe even improving the measurement of human inner states by establishing other measurement modes, such as physiological feedback or natural language processing (NLP) analysis of user expressions.

Finally, numerous studies with human interaction partners measure the human response immediately after a short period of interaction. However, many potentially very relevant outcomes of social XAI, such as trust in institutions using social XAI, diffusion of explanatory practices, side effects of XAI, and the like, may emerge only after several interactions and can only be captured when repeatedly measuring interactions and the outcome variable of interest.

28.7 Rapid Access to the Content of This Chapter

Based on the very prominent theory of planned behavior and their own model of man, many researchers think that they do not necessarily have to distinguish between subjective and objective outcomes of an interaction. For instance, if respondents answer after a machine-human interaction that they do trust the machine, researchers assume that they intend to reuse it, like the machine, and that the overall machine-human performance will be good. However, the theory of planned behavior is just one theory and much research points in the direction that the theory is not sufficient to explain human behavior. Whereas there are certainly cases in which attitudes affect later human actions, many actions happen unconsciously or subconsciously due to mental overload, stress, routinized behavior, social norms, or the like and are not linked in a monocausal way to the inner human state. Unfortunately, much research treats humans like robots, which act as intended and planned and do not take into account human irrationalities and randomness. Social science has largely moved to observe human behavior instead of measuring human attitudes, intentions and such via questionnaires because decades of research have found little connection between questionnaire answers and real use/behavior.

To advance our understanding of the outcomes of social XAI, researchers need to be specific about the construct they aim to measure. Is the research about potential subjective outcomes of XAI-human interaction, such as trust and perceived quality, or is it about objective measures, such as the human ability to reproduce explanations in a test? If one outcome is targeted, should one also target a second outcome on the side and try to relate them to each other?

Second, there is a need for standardized measures, especially for subjective variables. Measuring the human is not easy. Researchers should proceed consecutively and build on existing measures, and not invent their own. If scales need to be developed, they need to be validated first. No researcher from STEM fields would probably recommend using calibrated scales for length or varying the laboratory conditions for measurement all the time. Even though there is much more noise when measuring humans, non-calibrated invalidated measures will obviously be a bad choice.

Almost unaddressed is the question of differentiating between short- and long-term outcomes, and in some cases, both interact. For instance, a respondent's past life experience with technology will certainly affect their technology acceptance. Thus, TAM measures are usually long-term measures that encapsulate the whole life experience. When these measures are used after one interaction, the result of the measures is probably more a result of long-term experience and does not solely reflect the previous interaction. On the contrary, real long-term observations are currently totally lacking in research, and long-term outcomes are unknown. This is unfortunate because short- and long-term outcomes will probably also vary over time. For example, humans build up trust or lose trust, they learn how to interact efficiently, or they learn how to circumvent the AI in their life altogether, to mention some extreme outcomes. Thus, to measure the outcome of a social AI, the relation between explainer and explainee should eventually be viewed as a long-term relation—at least in many human-AI situations, and these long-term outcomes will also have to be considered in research.

Acknowledgments We thank Andreas Holzinger for his valuable perspective and helpful comments on an earlier version of this chapter.

This work was funded by the Deutsche Forschungsgemeinschaft (DFG, German Research Foundation): TRR 318/1 2021 – 438445824.

References

Alsaid, A., Li, M., Chiou, E. K., & Lee, J. D. (2023). Measuring trust: A text analysis approach to compare, contrast, and select trust questionnaires. *Frontiers in Psychology, 14*, 1192020. https://doi.org/10.3389/fpsyg.2023.1192020.

Andrade, C. (2020). Mean difference, standardized mean difference (SMD), and their use in meta-analysis: As simple as it gets. *The Journal of Clinical Psychiatry, 81*(5), 11349. https://doi.org/10.4088/JCP.20f13681.

Bailey, P. E., Leon, T., Ebner, N. C., Moustafa, A. A., & Weidemann, G. (2023). A meta-analysis of the weight of advice in decision-making. *Current Psychology, 42*(28), 24516–24541. https://doi.org/10.1007/s12144-022-03573-2.

Bollen, K. A. (2002). Latent variables in psychology and the social sciences. *Annual Review of Psychology, 53*(1), 605–634. https://doi.org/10.1146/annurev.psych.53.100901.135239.

Bolton, M. L., Biltekoff, E., & Humphrey, L. (2023). The mathematical meaninglessness of the NASA task load index: A level of measurement analysis. *IEEE Transactions on Human-Machine Systems, 53*(3), 590–599. https://doi.org/10.1109/THMS.2023.3263482.

Cabitza, F., Campagner, A., Malgieri, G., Natali, C., Schneeberger, D., Stoeger, K., & Holzinger, A. (2023). Quod erat demonstrandum? – Towards a typology of the concept of explanation for the design of explainable AI. *Expert Systems with Applications, 213*(PA), 118888. https://doi.org/10.1016/j.eswa.2022.118888.

de Winter, J. C. F. (2014). Controversy in human factors constructs and the explosive use of the NASA-TLX: A measurement perspective. *Cognition, Technology & Work, 16*(3), 289–297. https://doi.org/10.1007/s10111-014-0275-1.

Hart, S. G., & Staveland, L. E. (1988). Development of NASA-TLX (Task Load Index): Results of empirical and theoretical research. *Advances in Psychology, 52*, 139–183. https://doi.org/10.1016/S0166-4115(08)62386-9.

Harvey, N., & Fischer, I. (1997). Taking advice: Accepting help, improving judgment, and sharing responsibility. *Organizational Behavior and Human Decision Processes, 70*(2), 117–133. https://doi.org/10.1006/obhd.1997.2697.

Herm, L.-V., Wanner, J., Seubert, F., & Janiesch, C. (2021). I don't get it, but it seems valid! The connection between explainability and comprehensibility in (X)AI research. In *ECIS 2021 Research Papers*. online: AIS (p. 1413)

Hoffman, R. R., Mueller, S. T., Klein, G., & Litman, J. (2018). Metrics for explainable AI: Challenges and prospects. https://doi.org/10.48550/arXiv.1812.04608. arXiv: 1812.04608 [cs.AI].

Holzinger, A., Carrington, A., & Müller, H. (2020). Measuring the quality of explanations: The system causability scale (SCS) comparing human and machine explanations. *KI-Künstliche Intelligenz, 34*(2), 193–198. https://doi.org/10.1007/s13218-020-00636-z.

Jeckel, J., Thiele, C., Hirschfeld, G., Teismann, T., Schneider, S., & von Brachel, R. (2024). Better safe than sorry. A scoping review of monitoring for negative effects in preregistrations of psychological interventions. *Clinical Psychology & Psychotherapy, 31*(2), e2968. https://doi.org/10.1002/cpp.2968.

Jian, J.-Y., Bisantz, A. M., & Drury, C. G. (2000). Foundations for an empirically determined scale of trust in automated systems. *International Journal of Cognitive Ergonomics, 4*(1), 53–71. https://doi.org/10.1207/S15327566IJCE0401_04.

Knijnenburg, B. P., Willemsen, M. C., Gantner, Z., Soncu, H., & Newell, C. (2012). Explaining the user experience of recommender systems. *User Modeling and User-adapted Interaction, 22*, 441–504. https://doi.org/10.1007/s11257-011-9118-4.

Lammert, O., Richter, B., Schütze, C., Thommes, K., & Wrede, B. (2024). Humans in XAI: Increased reliance in decision-making under uncertainty by using explanation strategies. *Frontiers in Behavioral Economics, 3*, 1377075. https://doi.org/10.3389/frbhe.2024.1377075.

Le, T., Miller, T., Singh, R., & Sonenberg, L. (2024). *Towards the new XAI: A hypothesis-driven approach to decision support using evidence*. https://doi.org/10.48550/arXiv.2402.01292. arXiv: 2402.01292 [cs.AI].

Lee, J., & Moray, N. (1992). Trust, control strategies and allocation of function in human-machine systems. *Ergonomics, 35*(10), 1243–1270. https://doi.org/10.1080/00140139208967392.

Logg, J. M., Minson, J. A., & Moore, D. A. (2019). Algorithm appreciation: People prefer algorithmic to human judgment. *Organizational Behavior and Human Decision Processes, 151*, 90–103. https://doi.org/10.4088/JCP.20f13681.

Panagoulias, D. P., Virvou, M., & Tsihrintzis, G. A. (2023). Applying DOI theory to assess the required level of explainability in artificial intelligence-empowered medical applications. In *2023 14th International Conference on Information, Intelligence, Systems & Applications (IISA)* (pp. 1–7). IEEE. https://doi.org/10.1109/IISA59645.2023.10345846.

Rauthmann, J. F. (2023). Personality is (so much) more than just self-reported Big Five traits. *European Journal of Personality, 38*(6), 863–866. https://doi.org/10.1177/08902070231221853.

Rogers, E. M., Singhal, A., & Quinlan, M. M. (2014). Diffusion of innovations. In D. W. Stacks & M. B. Salwen (Eds.), *An integrated approach to communication theory and research* (2nd ed., pp. 432–448). Routledge.

Rong, Y., Leemann, T., Nguyen, T.-T., Fiedler, L., Qian, P., Unhelkar, V., Seidel, T., Kasneci, G., & Kasneci, E. (2023). Towards human-centered explainable AI: A survey of user studies for model explanations. *IEEE Transactions on Pattern Analysis and Machine Intelligence, 46*, 2104–2122. https://doi.org/10.1109/TPAMI.2023.3331846.

Rosenfeld, A. (2021). Better metrics for evaluating explainable artificial intelligence. In *Proceedings of the 20th International Conference on Autonomous Agents and MultiAgent Systems*. International Foundation for Autonomous Agents and Multiagent Systems (pp. 45–50).

Schemmer, M., Hemmer, P., Nitsche, M., Kühl, N., Vössing, M. (2022). A meta-analysis of the utility of explainable artificial intelligence in human-AI decision-making. In *Proceedings of the 2022 AAAI/ACM Conference on AI, Ethics, and Society* (pp. 617–626). Association for Computing Machinery. https://doi.org/10.1145/3514094.3534128.

Schoeffer, J., Kuehl, N., & Machowski, Y. (2022). "There is not enough information": On the effects of explanations on perceptions of informational fairness and trustworthiness in automated decision-making. In *Proceedings of the 2022 ACM Conference on Fairness, Accountability, and Transparency* (pp. 1616–1628). Association for Computing Machinery. https://doi.org/10.1145/3531146.3533218.

Schultze, T., Rakotoarisoa, A.-F., & Stefan, S.-H. (2015). Effects of distance between initial estimates and advice on advice utilization. *Judgment and Decision Making, 10*(2), 144–171. https://doi.org/10.1017/S1930297500003922.

Tsai, C.-H., You, Y., Gui, X., Kou, Y., & Carroll, J. M. (2021). Exploring and promoting diagnostic transparency and explainability in online symptom checkers. In *Proceedings of the 2021 CHI Conference on Human Factors in Computing Systems* (pp. 1–17). ACM. https://doi.org/10.1145/3411764.3445101.

Villa, J. M. (2016). Diff: Simplifying the estimation of difference-in-differences treatment effects. *The Stata Journal, 16*(1), 52–71. https://doi.org/10.1177/1536867X1601600108.

Vilone, G., & Longo, L. (2021). Notions of explainability and evaluation approaches for explainable artificial intelligence. *Information Fusion, 76,* 89–106. https://doi.org/10.1016/j.inffus.2021.05.009.

Wischnewski, M., Krämer, N., & Müller, E. (2023). Measuring and understanding trust calibrations for automated systems: A survey of the state-of-the-art and future directions. In *Proceedings of the 2023 CHI Conference on Human Factors in Computing Systems* (pp. 1–16). ACM. https://doi.org/10.1145/3544548.3581197.

Yaniv, I. (2004a). Receiving other people's advice: Influence and benefit. *Organizational Behavior and Human Decision Processes, 93*(1), 1–13. https://doi.org/10.1016/j.obhdp.2003.08.002.

Yaniv, I. (2004b). The benefit of additional opinions. *Current Directions in Psychological Science, 13*(2), 75–78. https://doi.org/10.1111/j.0963-7214.2004.00278.x.

Zhang, Y., Liao, Q. V., & Bellamy, R. K. E. (2020). Effect of confidence and explanation on accuracy and trust calibration in AI-assisted decision making. In *Proceedings of the 2020 Conference on Fairness, Accountability, and Transparency* (pp. 295–305). ACM. https://doi.org/10.1145/3351095.3372852.

Open Access This chapter is licensed under the terms of the Creative Commons Attribution 4.0 International License (http://creativecommons.org/licenses/by/4.0/), which permits use, sharing, adaptation, distribution and reproduction in any medium or format, as long as you give appropriate credit to the original author(s) and the source, provide a link to the Creative Commons license and indicate if changes were made.

The images or other third party material in this chapter are included in the chapter's Creative Commons license, unless indicated otherwise in a credit line to the material. If material is not included in the chapter's Creative Commons license and your intended use is not permitted by statutory regulation or exceeds the permitted use, you will need to obtain permission directly from the copyright holder.

Chapter 29
Tasking AI Fairly. How to Empower AI Practitioners With sXAI?

Suzana Alpsancar and Eugenia Stamboliev

Abstract This chapter critically examines how social explainable AI (sXAI) can better support AI practitioners in ensuring fairness in AI-based decision-making. We argue for a fundamental shift: Fairness should be understood not as a technical property or an information problem, but as a matter of vulnerability—focusing on the real-world impacts of AI on individuals and groups, especially those most at risk. Hereby, we call for a shift in perspective: from fair AI to *tasking AI fairly*. To motivate our vulnerability approach, we review the "Dutch welfare fraud scandal" (system risk indication—SyRI) and current challenges in the field of fair AI/machine learning (ML). Vulnerability of a person or members of a definable group of persons is a complex relational notion, and not a technical property of a technical system. Accordingly, we suggest several nontechnical strategies that hold the promise to compensate for the insufficiency of purely technical approaches to fairness and other ethical issues in the practical use of AI-based systems. To discuss how sXAI, due to its interactive and adaptive social character, might better fulfill this role than current XAI techniques, we provide a toy scenario for how sXAI might support the virtuous AI practitioner in an ethical inquiry. Finally, we also address challenges and limits of our approach.

Authors Suzana Alpsancar and Eugenia Stamboliev have equal contribution.

S. Alpsancar (✉)
Heinz Nixdorf Institute, Department of Philosophy, Faculty of Arts and Humanities, Paderborn University, Paderborn, Germany
e-mail: suzana.alpsancar@uni-paderborn.de

E. Stamboliev
Department of Philosophy, Faculty of Philosophy and Education, University of Vienna, Vienna, Austria
e-mail: eugenia.stamboliev@univie.ac.at

© The Author(s) 2026
K. J. Rohlfing et al. (eds.), *Social Explainable AI*,
https://doi.org/10.1007/978-981-96-5290-7_29

29.1 How Does This Chapter Relate to XAI?

A key promise of introducing XAI for AI-assisted decision-making is to mitigate the risks of discrimination (bias) and to avoid harming someone, thereby adding to the so-called trustworthiness of AI systems (HLEG, 2019). XAI is also praised as a means to ensure human oversight, which, in turn, serves to keep accountability and responsibility issues manageable (see Chap. 9.1). For normative reasons, such as the attribution of responsibility and accountability, full automation by AI systems is often not seen as meaningful. XAI then appears to be a necessary condition for ensuring meaningful human oversight (Sayles, 2024; Sterz et al., 2024; Green, 2022). For example, in the aftermath of the "Dutch welfare fraud scandal," researchers urged for more XAI (Kuźniacki, 2023). Between 2013 and 2019, the Dutch tax authorities developed risk profiles to spot fraud concerning childcare claims using a *self-learning* system (system risk indication—SyRI) that had been highly criticized. The system penalized non-Dutch or dual citizens because its risk assessment wrongly and illegally drew the risk from nationality, thereby favoring Dutch citizens (Wieringa, 2023). As Amnesty International (2021) reported, many penalized caregivers drifted into huge debt, depression, or even suicide. However, there is no simple answer to what should have been explained to whom, or which explanations could have helped at which point in the administrative decision-making process to avoid these unjustified harms. Remarkably, here, albeit civil servants still had to review the AI's recommendation, the decision-making process was highly criticized for being subject to an automation bias—that is, uncritically following the AI. What we can learn from this case is that it takes more than explaining the underlying technical mechanism to address unfair AI, and that we particularly need to protect those affected by AI-based decision-making.

This chapter discusses the use of XAI to ensure fairness in AI-based decision-making. Up to now, the literature on bias mitigation has framed XAI mostly as one component with which to render parts of the AI system more transparent and interpretable, thus fulfilling reporting duties. In this vein, XAI resembles an information delivery machine. Although we see this as an important step, we argue that it is not enough from an ethical and political perspective, and we question how far social XAI (sXAI, see Sect. 1.2) might advance such an approach to do both better justice to the context sensitivity of the fairness issue and to better assist AI operators in tasking AI fairly.

Our argument is outlined as follows: In Sect. 29.2, we present the SyRI case, a political scandal from the Netherlands, to motivate the need for *tasking AI fairly*. Here, we are deliberately not talking about fair AI, but about tasking AI fairly to articulate a shift in perspective: It is not about engineering certain technical features, but about people – AI practitioners[1] – engaging in their ethical, political, or even

---

[1] The concept *AI practitioners* is meant to circumvent all actors engaging with AI components, developers, designers, distributors, operators, users, maintainers, disposers. However, here we mostly focus on professionals using AI to get their job done.

legal duties (Green, 2022; Hirvonen & Westerling, 2024). Accordingly, our chapter tackles the question of how sXAI can support AI practitioners in tasking AI-based decisions fairly, by adopting a new focus on fairness as a matter of vulnerability, not information. In Sect. 29.3, we dive deeper into this shift of perspective by linking it to what the fair AI/machine learning (ML) literature has pointed out as lasting challenges. From here, we build from the Model Card approach (Mitchell et al., 2019, p. 222), which serves "to disclose information about a trained machine" and includes fairness aspects, to discuss how far sXAI might go beyond such an approach of making certain information accessible. Section 29.4 then turns from discussing what AI practitioners need toward strategies for designing sXAI to support AI practitioners in tasking AI fairly. We conclude by reviewing the limits of our approach in Sect. 29.5.

29.2 The SyRI Case: Lessons to be Learned from a Political Scandal

In the following, we lay out the SyRI case, a real-world case in which obviously many things went wrong. We shall use this as a negative learning case to construct the ideal case of how AI-based decisions should be tasked fairly in public administrations and how sXAI can support decision-makers in this task. To simplify, we shall focus only on the supporting role for the operators/deployers of AI, but we assume that this assisting function could be adapted to other stakeholders and even those affected by AI design making.

29.2.1 What Went Wrong in the Dutch Fraud Scandal?

Between 2015 and 2019, the Dutch government and leveraged municipalities deployed an algorithmic-based "system risk indication" (SyRI) to detect indications of fraud in the data of welfare beneficiaries. This example has become a paradigmatic case for using AI for risk profiling within the EU, similar to how COMPAS has stimulated the debate in the United States (van Schendel, 2019). Of course, the practice of categorizing and ranking individuals or groups within public administration predates Big Data and recent analytic AI tools. "Risk profiles often rely on statistics drawing inferences, from data of behavior that people with similar characteristics displayed, to determine the future behavior of a specific individual or group" (van Schendel, 2019, p. 228). Some critics argue that all statistics-based predictions are somewhat inadequate for two reasons: First, the individuals grouped under a profile do not share all attributes of the respected category. Hence, applying the prediction made by a risk system to an individual means treating that individual only as a categorized member of that group, which is sometimes called "statistic discrimination" (Lippert-Rasmussen, 2011, p. 47). Second, risk systems deliver only predictions (correlations that are interpreted as predictions) and not observations of de facto acts. That is, targeting individuals due to these predictions runs counter to the principle of the presumption of innocence (Sachoulidou, 2023; Blount, 2021). Despite these objections, there are justified ways of using risk profiling in law enforcement. Here, we shall not go into details, because we are interested in the particular challenges deriving from using AI tools on large databases for risk profiling in public administration.

AI-specific challenges arose because SyRI matched several public databases and used the data for risk profiling in an automated fashion. Although authorities declared the system to be based on a simple algorithm, it remained opaque to outsiders. It was initially aimed to link existing public databases and to provide one "data entry point for citizens, after which other public administrations could make copies," thus increasing efficiency (Bekker, 2021, p. 293). Hereby, personal and sensitive data became easily shareable and accessible, that is, "information on employment, detention, sanctions, fiscal information, and information on education, pension, child-care allowances, benefit receipt, health insurance" ibid. SyRI had been used for different projects, each building its required data and indicators for risk profiling. The collected personal data were encrypted and could be matched by the responsible administrative body. For those citizens who were predicted as high risk, a notification was sent out to a central register in which the information was saved for 2 years and could be used by the linked administration for follow-up investigations. So, the main attempt was to automate the selection of citizens to investigate.

Even though SyRI had been criticized even before its implementation, by, for example, the Data Protection Authority and the Council of State, for not doing justice to the principles of proportionality and subsidiarity (Wieringa, 2023, e2–8),[2] it ran for several years until a coalition of eight parties ("including NGOs, the largest Dutch trade union (FNV), and two citizens") started a lawsuit against the State of the Netherlands (Bekker, 2021, p. 296). In 2020, the District Court of The Hague found the system to be violating human rights, what the UN called "a landmark ruling" (Bekker, 2021; Rachovitsa & Johann, 2022, p. 290). The court's decision that SyRI violated human rights was justified by reference to Article 8(2) ECHR, calling for a *fair* balance between the state's interests and respect of private lives.

The central concerns leading to this decision are informative for our argument. A first concern was that the state had alternative methods for detecting fraud that required less data processing. The alleged efficiency gains were to be balanced against protecting data privacy. Thus, there is a reason to evaluate AI tools in light of alternative means to attain the same goals. A second central point was the question of whether SyRI was automating the decisions, because the "GDPR arranges the right not to be subject to a decision based solely on automated

---

[2] These are two principles of the Dutch jurisdiction: "Codified in the Dutch ABBB (General Principles of Good Governance) and the Awb (General Administrative Law Act), proportionality is the principle that a decision or a measure aimed to benefit the public good should not disproportionally affect or harm stakeholders. Subsidiarity, in turn, means that given several options, the least impactful or "heavy" option should be selected." (Wieringa, 2023, e2–8).

processing" (Bekker, 2021, p. 300). Here, the state insisted that SyRI was meant only to signal out discrepancies in the data and was therefore not making decisions itself. This interpretation was highly contested, leading to the key question of the role of the civil servants: Even when they are formally making the decision, is this really a meaningful human act or "just a token gesture" (Bekker, 2021, p. 301)? This question of how much AI practitioners are subject to the AI recommendation is discussed as *automation bias* in the literature. The plaintiffs argued that SyRI was not merely signaling discrepancies in the data, but was flagging individuals as high risk, hence targeting them. The court finally ruled that this targeting alone does have a serious effect on people's lives (Bekker, 2021, p. 306). Despite this potential impact on people's lives, citizens were also not informed about being flagged as high risk, and this was the third critical point for the court. If the administration did not decide to act on that signaling/flagging, the targeted people would not find out that they were marked as high risk in a central registry for 2 years. A fourth concern was the secrecy of the risk model used, leaving people in the dark about the rationale of the risk profiling. It also ruled that the implementation of SyRI was "insufficiently transparent" and could not "be checked" (Bekker, 2021, p. 304).

We may add to these concerns derived from the court's ruling that the AI practitioners had been too naive about the AI system's capacities and limits. It might be debatable whether the Dutch authorities should have known better than to rely blindly on the AI's recommendation. However, after ProPublica raised awareness about the use of COMPAS in the United States in 2016 (Angwin et al., 2016), and a plethora of other problematic cases of AI usages for scoring, profiling, and classification became the topic of public debate (O'Neil, 2017; Campolo et al., 2017; Benjamin, 2019), it was no longer plausible to make excuses based on ignorance.

29.2.2 Vulnerability in SyRI

The SyRI case attracted much attention not only because it was one of the first court rulings on the use of AI in law enforcement in the EU and led to an "implosion of the Dutch surveillance welfare state" (Fenger & Simonse, 2024, p. 264; Bekkum & Borgesius, 2021) but also because it was harming people in an unjustifiable way and specifically those who were already vulnerable. Non-Dutch nationals were *vulnerable* in this case (Wikipedia Contributors, 2024), because these groups often face greater socioeconomic defenselessness, relying more on childcare and governmental support than most Dutch nationals (Amnesty International, 2021, p. 38). At the core of the scandal lies the fact that SyRI was "part of a neighborhood-centered approach aimed to increase livability in what the State terms 'problem neighborhoods'" which means it was used exclusively for neighborhoods "with high rates of poverty, crime, and welfare beneficiaries" (Wieringa, 2023, e2–7). In these targeted areas, there were already more people belonging to what is called vulnerable groups, which means that those citizens already had comparatively fewer equal opportunities and chances to participate in society, and that any further disadvantage would affect them to a disproportionately greater extent.

Social vulnerability encompasses two aspects: exposure to increased risk and the lack of empowerment to confront it (Eubanks, 2018, p. 10). For example, even if the flagged citizens were to have known about their status, it would probably have been the case that many of them would not have been able to adequately contest this processing of their data because of a lack of resources, skills, AI literacy, and so forth. To highlight this particular vulnerability, Amnesty International (2021, p. 36) evoked the metaphor of a 'Kafkaesque castle' in its report on how SyRI was violating human rights. The reference to Kafka, namely his novels *The Castle* and *The Trial*, describes the impact on vulnerable citizens as being alienated when confronted with an unresponsive bureaucracy, leading to the frustrations of trying to do business with opaque, seemingly arbitrary systems of control. This administration, leaving its citizens in the dark about the fact that they were flagged and why it happened (no crime occurred, just predicted), appears like an arbitrary, unaccountable institution of control. The dominant metaphor in the XAI literature, the black box, does not fully grasp this situation of disempowerment, because it always entails the simple solution of providing transparency. Yet, transparency here, albeit important, would not have been sufficient. We argue that it is only a first step that needs to be complemented by skillful and engaged AI practitioners. These, in turn, might be supported by an sXAI.

29.3 From Fair AI to Tasking AI Fairly

Against the background of a plethora of scandals such as the one above and dedicated to creating responsible, fair, and ethical AI systems, *fair ML/AI* has emerged as a novel research field for computer scientists and technologists (Hickok, 2021; Alpsancar, 2023; Fahimi et al., 2024). This community has outlined various strategies to render AI systems more transparent or interpretable, including the common XAI techniques. More particularly, the technical literature has proposed fairness definitions and metrics, as well as a set of mitigation strategies that often include XAI techniques.

So far, one part of the literature is based on the vision that more transparency will solve the problems. This central idea implicitly addresses solely ML experts. In contrast, there is criticism that it fails to emphasize the perspective of laypeople and needs to distinguish between different stakeholders. The other part of the literature is dominated by the idea that the goal is to build fair or ethical AI systems, as if the attributes of fairness and morality were properties like any other technical characteristics. However, this is not the case (more on this below). Ultimately, both visions aim to achieve a simple technical fix that ignores social reality. We, on the other hand, propose a shift in perspective that takes the sociotechnical reality of AI use seriously. Because the XAI community is probably familiar with the argument that transparency or XAI is not sufficient for the societal variety of AI users, we shall not elaborate on this further, but refer only to the relevant literature (Miller, 2019; Sokol & Flach, 2020; Meske et al., 2022; Arrieta et al., 2020; Langer et al., 2021).

However, the thesis that fairness is not a technical attribute that can be produced should be briefly explained.

Although fairness tools, definitions, and strategies help in tasking AI fairly, they should not be perceived as a way to automate ethical assessments or fairness issues, because these can never be formalized or automated completely (Dignum, 2019; Barocas et al., 2023). This is simply true, because a disparity or a bias, as such, does not necessarily imply injustice, discrimination, or unfairness. To hold a disparity to be unfair/fair means to make a normative judgment that calls for justifiable reasons (Forst, 2017; Wallace & Kiesewetter, 2024), including determining which understanding of equality and justice is to be held appropriate for the given situation (e.g., equality in the sense of equal standards for all individuals or equality in the sense of distributive justice, Corbett-Davies et al., 2017). Normative judgments are judgments of a particular kind (Brandom, 1994; Copp, 2015; Williams, 2012). They cannot be true or false, but are more or less appropriate.

Furthermore, fairness judgments are highly context dependent and rest on the interpretation of the given situation (Dolata et al., 2022; Barr et al., 2025). A salient example for this is the current highly controversial debate around affirmative action policies in the United States. Affirmative action policies rest on the idea of distributive justice—that is, the idea to balance out the structural disadvantages of certain social groups. One side argues in favor of distributive justice, because, in their eyes, it would be unjust not to counteract structural disadvantages. The other side, however, argues that the very act of affirmative action is in itself discrimination against those social groups that do not benefit from these policies. Now, if a higher-education institution were to deploy an AI system for preselecting applications, there is a need for a normative judgment around these issues in order to determine, for example, whether or not to adjust a certain threshold for disadvantaged social groups. In the end, setting any threshold for scores entails a normative judgment, and we argue that such judgments should, for socially sensitive application domains, in general, be revisable and be reassessable.

Following the review by Pessach and Shmueli (2022, p. 54), the fair AI community has been focusing mostly on defining mathematical representations of two distinctive legal definitions of discrimination from the context of US jurisdiction (Barocas & Selbst, 2016; Wachter et al., 2021): namely, *disparate treatment* and *disparate impact*. These two are often depicted as direct and indirect discrimination. Disparate treatment means "intentionally treating an individual differently based on his/her membership in a protected class (*direct discrimination*)" (Pessach & Shmueli, 2022, p. 51:4). Disparate impact means "negatively affecting members of a protected class more than others, even if by a seemingly neutral policy (*indirect discrimination*)." According to Pessach and Shmueli (2022, p. 51:4), direct discrimination is based on explicit discrimination of "sensitive attributes" (such as class, gender, race, religion or belief, disability, age, and sexual orientation). As a consequence, direct discrimination can be avoided by excluding these sensitive attributes from the data used to train AI systems (Pessach & Shmueli, 2022). However, often it is more complicated than that, because several other attributes might serve as proxies for these protected ones (Pfeiffer et al., 2023)—for example, zip codes for race or 'caring gaps' in CVs for gender. Yet, most of the quarrel of fair AI rests in avoiding indirect discriminatory effects—that is, *disparate impacts*. The Fair AI community has developed mathematical definitions of this legal term and the corresponding metrics (such as 'disparate impact' and 'demographic parity') (Mehrabi et al., 2021; Verma & Rubin, 2018; Mahoney et al., 2020; Xivuri & Twinomurinzi, 2021).

Building on these fairness metrics and the detection of the main causes for biases, the technical literature has developed a set of bias mitigation strategies that are grouped largely into "preprocessing" (prior to modeling), "in-processing" (at the point of modeling), and "postprocessing" (after modeling) (Caton & Haas, 2024, p. 166:3). Bias can be caused by different factors throughout the AI life cycle (data collection, development, implementation, and use). Types of biases are usually grouped into data-related and algorithm-related. For instance, the data used might not be representative of the case (population) it ought to be used for, or the data might represent an existing bias. Bias can also be caused by algorithmic features such as setting a threshold in tests for selecting college applications. Preprocessing approaches are seen as the best interventions if accessible (Pessach & Shmueli, 2022; Mehrabi et al., 2021). The idea is to 'repair' the dataset (by checking labels and modifying feature representations) and "to remove discrimination from the data set" (Caton & Haas, 2024, p. 166:5). In-processing approaches alter the model: For example, they try to "find a balance between multiple model objectives" (e.g., by adding a "tuning parameter ... to modulate the trade-off between fairness and accuracy" Pessach & Shmueli, 2022, p. 9). Postprocessing approaches are the most flexible in terms of accessibility, because the idea here is to adjust the outcome of an algorithmic decision-making process (e.g., by flipping some decisions). These strategies come with advantages and disadvantages. There can also be practical limitations in how to deploy which mitigation strategy such as when a company buying a pretrained model has no access to the data. Yet, there are already industrial toolkits on the market that allow some sort of 'plug-and-play' bias mitigation such as "Aequitas" and "AI Fairness 360" from IBM (Mehrabi et al., 2021).

The technical literature has, however, pointed out lasting challenges that speak for the normative character of ethical and fairness questions. The primary challenge is that AI users have to choose which fairness metric (if any) applies best to a given situation (Caton & Haas, 2024; Pessach & Shmueli, 2022; Mehrabi et al., 2021, p. 517). A second challenge is how to deal with trade-offs. A trade-off often discussed here is the one between fairness and accuracy, which, however, must not play out in all cases (Pessach & Shmueli, 2022). Another challenge is that pretrained models can be used in dynamic learning settings, which means that they continue to be trained by new/other data (Pessach & Shmueli, 2022). Hence, any formalization of fairness has to remain reviewable (Cobbe et al., 2021) and reassessable on normative grounds.

Particularly the first challenge – the need to choose which fairness definition, hence metric, is appropriate for the given case – shows exactly that a normative decision has to be made even when using today's most advanced 'fairness toolkits.' For instance, AI users then have to decide when to use a fairness metric that concerns differences made between individuals, or when to use a fairness definition that concerns group-level differences. If you had good reasons to choose a group-level metric, then how can you determine which groups to cover? Or, if you are entitled to rely on the concept of individual fairness – that is, the expectation of "consistent treatment in the absence of differences that would seem to justify differential treatment" – how do you determine the similarity of individuals (Barocas et al., 2023, p. 89)? Going back to the example of higher-education student selection, setting these thresholds would include a decision on which school-leaving certificates count as equal qualification and which not, or for which there might be national standards but not necessarily standards for international students.

It is a matter of fact that whatever you define or determine here is contestable, because of the normative nature of fairness and ethical issues. And there is always a higher-order decision to make for which it will not be sufficient to just consider facts of nature, but which calls for a process of normative reasoning that machines cannot fulfill (Wasserman-Rozen et al., 2023). Accordingly, there can never be a technological fix to the quest for fair AI (Pfeiffer et al., 2023; Dignum, 2019; Barocas et al., 2023; Binns, 2018).

In line with these findings, we propose a shift in perspective for (X)AI developers *from solely engineering fairness features to supporting AI practitioners in tasking AI fairly*. This shifts the focus from feature engineering to the practice of AI practitioners, a practice that calls for skillful, engaged, and virtuosic AI users. As a consequence, XAI development and design then entail imagining how such AI practitioners could best be supported in their ethical/fairness assessments, and not fantasizing about mere technological solutions to fairness issues or ethical questions. The vision for XAI development should not be to deliver better explanations, but to build sXAI systems that are capable of supporting users in their reasoning process (see Chap. 10). A model for this role could be a kind of fairness/ethics supervisor, whereby the machine would fulfill this role in a modified form: On the one hand, it cannot draw authentically on empathy and experience; on the other hand, it can incorporate an enormous amount of knowledge and maintain and provide an overview of structures and procedures that would not be possible for human partners in this way.

29.4 A Toy Scenario for Ethical Evaluation

In analogy to the widespread use of *toy models* in science, which are highly idealized and simplified (Reutlinger et al., 2018), we introduce a *toy scenario* to draft an ideal and simplified version of tasking AI fairly. Let us assume we would have such a skillful, engaged, virtuosic, and even impartial AI practitioner (the professional being assisted in decision-making by the AI) in an organizational setting that would appreciate and foster the engagement in ethical assessments and fairness issues. The organizational context would not entail any time constraints or the like. The practitioner does not hold any grudges, is not subject to human biases of any kind (partiality, cognitive biases, laziness, and so forth), and we also rule out any sort of misuse or bad intentions. In such an ideal hypothetical toy scenario, how could sXAI support the AI practitioner's fairness engagement? What can we learn from the negative case of SyRI?

According to the court's ruling, SyRI was illegal; hence, it should never have been deployed in the first place. Yet, we argue that the case is still informative in an ethical sense, meaning it provides crucial concerns that can be turned into a set of questions for an ethical assessment. It should also be a matter of course that ethical evaluations are not reducible to compliance, because legal systems differ throughout the world, and they might not cover everything that would be an obligation or desirable from an ethical perspective. Several, but not all, countries ban discrimination based on so-called protected attributes—that is, race, religion or belief, disability, age, gender, or sexual orientation (Ellis & Watson, 2012; Kim & Fox, 2011). Although human rights are not understood as legally enforceable rights everywhere, it is at least desirable that they should be protected by the mere virtue of being human (Smuha, 2021; HLEG, 2019). Furthermore, ethical demands might transcend legal obligations.[3] For instance, one could argue that the environmental harm of today's prominent large language models violates recognized sustainability goals, and, therefore, public authorities within the EU should not promote using them (e.g., for educational purposes). Likewise, we assume that just because a system is legal does not mean that all fairness issues are off the table. Instead, we believe that it is precisely the vulnerability of certain social groups that poses an ongoing ethical challenge and calls for the fair use of AI systems to be made an ethical duty for AI operators if there is the potential to harm individuals or certain groups.

What we can learn from the Dutch scandal is that it is good advice for AI practitioners to be sensitive about the potential negative outcomes of AI deployment. The crucial question is, how sXAI might support such sensitivity and the potential reasoning process (if adequate in a given situation)? Here, we suggest that ideally, sXAI should be designed as a supporting tool to assist both the sensitivity and the reasoning process with relevant, adaptive, and normatively sensitive cues and interactive turns. We propose that this function can best be addressed in the form of raising questions, because questioning the AI practitioners can stimulate a reflection and reassessment of a given routine. Accordingly, sXAI development and design should account for such a possibility.

Here, we point out exemplary reflection questions that can be helpful for an ethical assessment of a given AI system for decision-making. These questions directly echo the above-systematized concerns raised by the court decision. We assume that the virtuous AI practitioner engages in a reasoning process about potential ethical concerns for which answering these questions is useful. Below, we shall discuss how the ideal sXAI could support the ideal AI practitioner in the ethical assessment—that is, in answering these reflection questions.

---

[3] Beyond that, corporate policies might also be in place.

29.4.1 Reflection Questions for an Ethical Assessment

1. Ethical and Social Sensitivity The first question obviously serves to determine whether or not an ethical assessment is needed: *Is the usage of the AI system of ethical or social concern?* Not all AI applications call for an ethical assessment, because not all of them bear the risk of affecting people's lives (biographies) or adding to the vulnerability of already disadvantaged groups. Here, for example, the risk framework currently used in AI regulation within the EU (Kaminski, 2023; Novelli et al., 2024) provides a first orientation according to which the potential *impact* on a person's life, the *domain* of application, and the *capacities of the AI* are crucial. The EU AI Act uses a 'pyramind of criticality' and divides AI-related risks into four categories: minimal risk, limited risk, high risk, and unacceptable risk (European Commission, 2021). The AI Act "prohibits AI systems with unacceptable risks and imposes specific requirements on high-risk AI systems, while leaving AI systems that pose low or minimal risks largely unencumbered" (Schuett, 2024). Accordingly, (at least) all AI systems that fall into the high-risk category are to be perceived as ethically and socially sensitive. If an AI-based decision potentially affects people's lives in a relevant way, it usually corresponds to the domain of deployment. Annex III of the AI Act provides a list of eight application areas that fall under the high-risk category, namely: biometric identification and categorisation of natural persons, management and operation of critical infrastructure, education and vocational training, employment, workers management and access to self-employment, access to and enjoyment of essential private services and public services and benefits, law enforcement, migration, asylum and border control management, and administration of justice and democratic processes. In contrast, AI in spam filtering or for online recommendations is perceived not to have such a considerable effect on people's lives.[4] The list in Annex III is not meant to be fixed in stone, and systems might be ethically and socially sensitive, albeit they do not necessarily fall into the high-risk category defined in this regulation.

Public administration is per se a crucial area because, in liberal democracies, states are obliged to treat all citizens equally by default—that is, to apply the same rules to everyone. Deviations from this require legal or political legitimization, and citizens have the right to object to administrative decisions (Alfrink et al., 2020; Lyons et al., 2021). The state holds an "ex ante political accountability" (Wieringa, 2023, e2-1) toward its citizens.

2. Vulnerability As argued above, we propose to be extra aware of the question of vulnerability, because vulnerable groups are subjected to discriminatory AI effects in a disproportionate way. AI is opaque to many, but it discriminates against specific groups due to a wider pattern, not by accident or mistake. AI can render women invisible or portray them unjustly (Criado Perez, 2019). AI facial recognition

---

[4] There is, however, a debate on how much these algorithmic structures foster polarization in social media, which, in turn, fragments the political culture of societies (Santos et al., 2021).

systems often fail to recognize people of color (Benjamin, 2019). Biases may have tremendous "downstream impacts" (Dobbe et al., 2024, p. 14), particularly for groups that are already more vulnerable than others to social injustice, such as people of color, women, non-English-speaking cultures, or other underrepresented groups in the datasets of the Internet. These impacts are numerous; failure to recognize or perceive them as a problem can result in denial of public services, denial of housing access, or the soap dispenser failing to detect non-White skin. Vulnerable groups might not only be unevenly treated in a discriminatory manner by AI deployment, but they might also benefit unevenly from AI services (e.g., if there is a reliable decision support system for detecting cancer, it would seem to be appropriate to grant all people access to that kind of diagnosis, whereas, in reality, only some insurances might cover the (full) costs and other people neither have insurance nor access to facilities operating these systems). Because of that, AI-based negative impacts on vulnerable groups bear the potential to broaden the so-called digital divide by adding new forms of unevenly distributed advantages and disadvantages: either because people are subjected to unfair automated decision-making (ADM) unevenly or because they benefit from the systems unevenly (Boyd & Crawford, 2012).

The question of vulnerability links the question of ethical and social sensitivity of AI applications to a broader societal and historical perspective. Vulnerability may exist by belonging to a social group that has been subject to political, economic, and cultural disadvantages, discrimination, enslavement, persecution, or annihilation for centuries—that is, political minorities. These groups are not a minority in a quantitative sense, but in the sense of lacking political and economic power. Vulnerability might also be more specific and not only derived from history. For example, people might become literally vulnerable as soon as they become migrants for reasons of, for example, war or climate change. There is also an interdependence of domains and vulnerability. For instance, marginalized groups are even more vulnerable when it comes to public services such as housing or benefit claims (Eubanks, 2018). This is because citizens cannot remove themselves from public institutions or structures; they are more than users choosing to use private applications, because they depend on them. This dependency exposes them to experience more "unintended harmful societal impacts (e.g., discrimination, cruelty) based on these algorithmic decision-making outcomes" (Showkat et al., 2020, p. 2).

To 'test' for the vulnerability of a given AI-based system, we propose to answer the following questions: *Is the AI system distinctively affecting political minorities? Who would the AI-based system harm the most if it were to be scaled? That is, what are the long-term and large-scale effects of implementing such a system?* In human resource management, hiring decisions obviously directly influence the biographies of individuals and wrong matching (e.g., hiring the second-best, not the best person) also hurts the company. However, scaled up, these hiring decisions indirectly influence the social order of a society. If, for example, women were systematically disadvantaged in recruitment processes in all companies in a country, this would have a serious impact on family constellations, the division of care work, the marriage market, pension entitlements. This social significance, therefore, results from the interplay between local entrepreneurial decisions and their wider social framework, other companies, and so forth.

3. Alternative Means The question of alternative means is rarely discussed in the research literature, but should be a crucial consideration, particularly for AI systems of ethical or social sensitivity and even more for those that might impact vulnerable groups. Most likely, this consideration will take place in economic terms anyway, but it should be reconsidered in light of ethical and social concerns. *Is the AI system the best means for the set purposes* (wherein 'best' circumvents ethics)? What alternatives are there? How exactly is the AI system superior? What disadvantages does it have compared to other systems?

4. Automation Bias To get the best out of AI capacities, it is important that AI practitioners establish "an appropriate level of reliance" on the machine, including both "a sufficient level of trust" and a "healthy amount of critical reflection, or distrust" (Peters & Visser, 2023, p. 302). To establish such a level, the AI practitioner needs to be well-informed about the capacities and limits of the AI system, and they need to be able to tell if the machine is working correctly. Both are not simple and require some sort of specific AI experience or skills. This issue also relates to the next point of sufficient transparency of the systems' capacities and limits. Here, it seems mandatory to address the question concerning the limits and capacities of the systems, including, for instance, whether the training data sufficiently match the data with which the AI is now supposed to be used.

5. Transparency/Secrecy At least three different kinds of information about the AI system seem mandatory to avoid an automation bias and to be capable of performing the ethical assessment: some sufficient understanding of the model, some sufficient understanding of the rationale of whatever the system is supposed to be useful for (risk profiling, classification), and what kind of data the machine has been trained on and what kind of data the machine will be used for (personal, sensitive data). Moreover, the AI practitioner should be able to understand what it means to be a data subject to that particular machine—for example, is it flagging some people for something (as it happened with SyRI)? Do data subjects know that they are being processed and how they are being processed? Do they need to consent to this, and so forth?

Answers to these questions will often relate to the question of the best alternative at hand, or the impacts on people's lives. This is true in general: There is a mutual dependency of these questions, meaning that an answer to the question of vulnerability might lead to the need to reconsider the alternative question or to review the answer on automation biases, and so forth. An ideal sXAI might even be aware of such interdependencies and direct AI practitioners to reassess further answered questions should the need arise.

29.4.2 sXAI to Empower Virtuosic AI Practitioners

How could sXAI be of help in reflecting on the above questions or the ethical assessment and in finding answers? We propose that, ideally, sXAI should go beyond merely delivering information (as classic XAI does) by stimulating and assisting this ethical reasoning process. To do so, it should have three central capacities: (a) it should assist practitioners in a dialogical form, (b) it should provide *relevant* background information on the AI systems and fairness issues, and (c) it should raise open questions in a Socratic manner to engage the AI practitioners in the reasoning process. In doing so, sXAI would strengthen the users' deliberative agency (see Sect. 10.3).

First of all, it would be necessary that the AI operators are well-informed on the process and can sufficiently understand the risks and potential impacts. Here, so-called model cards that were introduced by a group of Google researchers could be a helpful instrument (Mitchell et al., 2019). These cards provide essential information about the AI system, what it was originally intended for, the data it was trained on, ethical concerns, and more. Model cards are meant to fulfill a similar function as instruction leaflets do for medical products. Developers/distributors have to provide the product (AI system) with them to educate the product user—here, the AI practitioner. However, it is clear that making sense of such model cards/instruction leaflets already calls for the capacity to understand them in a meaningful way.

How could sXAI go beyond such a disclosure of helpful information? We propose three levels of support:

At a first level (a), the dialogical form alone might already be more engaging and stimulating than providing information in one shot (Mindlin et al., 2025) or even as attached to the product as an instruction manual. Instead of reading the instructions, the AI practitioners could chat with the sXAI in a dialogical interaction. Here, the sXAI could guide the operator through the model card, provide background information, and, if asked for, direct the operators to where they can go if they do not know how to deal with the situation (in analogy to the imperative: "ask your doctor or pharmacist!" when in doubt about the instruction leaflet of your medical product). The sXAI could even proactively start the process of ethical evaluation.

At a second level (b), and building on the first one, the sXAI could assist in deeper reflection and understanding by providing more detailed and more relevant background information on demand. The sXAI could, on the one hand, respond to the AI practitioners' inquiries or behavior by, for example, supporting them in finding what they are looking for or providing information that is not available in the leaflet itself (via the Internet or other knowledge database banks). In this regard, the sXAI would adapt to the course of the interaction with its users. On the other hand, the sXAI could also take responsibility (in the sense laid out in Sect. 9.1 on responsibility) for monitoring the whole process and advise checking other aspects or reconsidering questions in light of the conversation. This, of course, would give the sXAI some sort of normative power to execute, at least in the sense that it would hold some sort of ideal model for the ethical evaluation process and then check if all things are covered sufficiently.

At a third level (c), we assume that the crucial capacity lies in the interplay of raising open questions and providing relevant background information. This level holds a more normative character and would also be more demanding, following the role model of a human supervisor or even the figure of Socrates, the ancient Greek philosopher who was famous for engaging his interlocutors in ethical reflections by confronting them again and again with open questions and inquiries. (In that regard, sXAI might also stand for Socratic XAI). We propose that such a confrontation with ethical inquiries can be helpful to a certain degree. These open questions and variations of them could be derived easily from the above-systematized ethical assessment questions such as: *Who are the vulnerable groups in your decision-making? How do you know about them? What makes them vulnerable? How does the system potentially affect them? Are these impacts justified? Are there any mitigation strategies in place?*[5] We could also imagine that the sXAI forms somewhat context-specific questions in terms of the particular features of the AI systems (on which it has sufficient background information) and the context of deployment, for example: *Are you aware that the system uses the fairness metric xy? Does this one really fit your case?* Or: *AI predictions are derived from the data the system was trained on. You are using a system that is continuously fed with new data, thus continuously learning and adapting its predictions. The last time you evaluated whether the training data sufficiently matched your application data was 2 years ago; you might want to check for updates.*

The introduction of such sXAI systems naturally raises several organizational questions such as who is responsible for the quality of this assistance function? In light of this book's definition of sXAI, "as systems that interactively adapt to users in order to co-construct a satisfying explanation" (see Sect. 1.5), there is the question of how adaptive such ethical assistance should be on the part of the sXAI. Generally speaking, there can be a trade-off between particular interests (of AI practitioners, e.g., their prejudices or personal wishes) and the idea of ethical impartiality (see Sect. 30.1 on Risks and Chances). For instance, there might be a civil servant who dislikes certain social groups (e.g., people with an Arabic background) and intends to skip the ethical assessment whenever confronted with one of them. On the other hand, more flexibility in the hands of the civil servants could be beneficial, because their professional experience might allow them to determine best which aspects are relevant for which case. This ultimately depends on the AI practitioner's skills, engagement, and virtue. Consequently, our vision of sXAI rests on a strong collaboration between humans and technology, not on engineering a great tool alone.

---

[5] Of course, harming nonvulnerable groups should also be avoided. However, we find it plausible to raise concerns around vulnerability for two reasons: First, being vulnerable means not only being disadvantaged in some sense but also that society lacks awareness about this. AI practitioners will probably be less aware about the effects on vulnerable groups than about the effects on nonvulnerable groups. Accordingly, it makes sense to stipulate such a question. Second, critically thinking about vulnerable groups will often also imply reflection about the consequences of the action at stake in general—hence, including awareness to avoid harming anyone.

Another organizational question could be whether the sXAI should adapt its service in regard to different professional roles and their corresponding rights and duties—for instance, according to different ranks of police officers (Egbert & Esposito, 2024). Accordingly, our vision of sXAI not only demands certain types of AI practitioners but also requires prudent integration into organizational contexts. For example, there is a need to decide when to run the sXAI-supported ethical assessments. It would be counterproductive if the AI practitioners always had to run through a loop with the sXAI (fairness check) when making routine decisions. However, one could imagine that it would be useful to run this type of check during the implementation of a (new) system (the onboarding of new employees) and on demand—that is, if something questionable arises; for example, if there are questions from those affected, or if the employees themselves notice an ambiguity, and so forth. Hereby, sXAI could actually be perceived as a sociotechnical system.

29.5 How Does This Relate to the XAI Community?

In this chapter, we presented the vision of an sXAI that goes beyond the goal of transparency and the function of simply delivering information. For the quest of ethical assessment (e.g., fairness), we imagine an ideal sXAI to be an assisting dialogical partner that guides and supports AI practitioners in being sensitive towards potential ethical and social impacts and in their reasoning process. To do this, the sXAI system needs to have the capacities as outlined above. Our toy scenario was not only idealized in terms of the organizational constraints and the virtue of the AI practitioners but also in terms of the sXAI technical capabilities. Current systems are not able to fulfill the envisioned role of such a supportive partner. Today's advanced LLMs (e.g., ChatGPT) rely on humans to repair conversation murks (Pütz & Esposito, 2024). To consider alternative means for such an ethical assessment of AI-based decision-making is, therefore, also good advice for the question of whether or not to implement XAI (or a future sXAI) and how much to rely on it.

However, even the ideal sXAI machine would not be sufficient to ensure tasking AI-based decisions fairly, because this task is ultimately the job of AI practitioners. On the one hand, this fact presents limits to the engineering perspective of optimizing XAI systems. However, on the other hand, it also demands that we provide the best supporting system possible. For developers and designers of sXAI, this entails a shift in perspective as well: The sXAI should be suitable for AI practitioners and not ML experts, and the sXAI should not simply provide information but become an assisting partner. To fulfill this vision, we see the need to collaborate with experts in the social sciences, humanities, and cultural studies of academia as well as with actual practitioners. We urge XAI researchers to engage with socially oriented and interdisciplinary perspectives in the fair AI community (Fahimi et al., 2024). Going beyond the disclosure of technical mechanisms, sXAI could become a collaborator in forming a fairness judgment.

29.5.1 Limits of sXAI

The above toy scenario was built on ideal, hypothetical conditions that are hardly to be found in reality. As a consequence, we may argue that at least public institutions should foster conditions that allow engaged AI practitioners to care about ethics and fairness issues (Feuerriegel et al., 2020; Dolata et al., 2022; de Bruijn et al., 2022). Still, the idea of a virtuous, skillful, and engaged AI practitioner is quite demanding for professionals. We propose that cultivating these characteristics could be seen as a particular duty that corresponds to particular professional roles AI practitioners hold—for example, in socially and ethically sensitive domains such as public administrations or human resource management.

Moreover, it should be part of the respective institutions' responsibility to support professionals in cultivating such skills and virtues and to minimize organizational constraints. These procedures of ethical assessments must allow for a certain amount of skepticism, even if this goes against the imperative of automation and efficiency (cost savings). It is also helpful to have mitigation strategies in place for the challenge of human biases or the risk of misuse (which we did not discuss here).

If institutions were to deploy a Socratic sXAI (level 3 engagement), there is most likely a high chance that (some) professionals would easily feel bored or disturbed by the machine. It is a famous pattern in all of Socrates' dialogs that his conversation partners sooner or later turned away in annoyance. What we might learn from this ancient story is that ethics is not convenient, fun, or easy, but *demanding*. However, in terms of designing an sXAI system, it might be reasonable to allow for contextual adjustments on how much ethical inquiry is desirable and how many follow-up questions are helpful. Socrates was famous for never stopping his follow-up questions until he was sentenced to death by the government because it was alleged he was leading young people astray with his constant questions. Obviously, the ethical inquiry can be terminated by governments or other forms of power. However, this is a tricky question that demands metareasoning to decide how much ethical inquiry and skepticism is necessary and helpful.

Another limit of our chapter is that we did not cover how to empower those affected by the decision-making process (the 'data subjects') and focused solely on how to design better sXAI to support AI practitioners. We only indirectly addressed vulnerability as an important factor to be considered by the AI practitioner. However, for future research and development, it might be good advice to integrate strategies of participatory design for developing more inclusive sXAI.

Moreover, there is an ongoing debate among legal scholars that we must reconsider the categories of discrimination, hence vulnerability, in light of the logic of current AI systems. Here it is argued that it is not enough to face the challenge of mitigating proxies for attributes that are protected under current anti-discrimination law (gender, race, etc.), as many AI systems use a multitude of attributes for profiling and classification "that need not map onto or correlate with traditionally protected groups, and thus do not automatically receive protection under anti-discrimination law" (Wachter, 2022; Smuha, 2021, p. 152).

29.5.2 Future sXAI Development

We conclude by pointing out strategies for sXAI development and design to integrate the perspective of those who are affected by the AI decision, particularly the vulnerable ones. **The first strategy is a thought experiment** that was already used above: It is trying to anticipate and estimate the impacts on those affected by the decision-making process and question the justifiability of potential harms and so forth. Here, to check for vulnerability, a simple heuristic is to take the impacts to the extreme: What would happen if the system at hand were to be used on a large scale and for a long time? Vulnerability might become visible in light of these extremes. For instance, if non-Dutch (or non-EU) citizens were systematically excluded from all welfare services in the Netherlands (or the EU), what would be the consequences, not only for these groups but also for the respective societies or particular societal fields? Is it desirable, for example, to systematically exclude a particular social group from the EU job market as an effect of a particular bias of a certain hiring recommendation system? This simple thought experiment helps to raise awareness of the sociopolitical situatedness of AI decision-making and potential undesirable impacts.

However, this strategy, though it might provide a good first idea of who is vulnerable and why it might be worth reconsidering the impact, depends completely on the imagination and knowledge of the sXAI developer (or the AI practitioner). Therefore, **the second strategy consists of participatory approaches** that aim to integrate the voices and perspectives of those who are most often left out of (X)AI development and design (Dignum, 2019; Delgado et al., 2023; Zytko et al., 2022). Participatory approaches and initiatives date back at least to the 1980s, when, for example, the OECD called for "the deliberative wave" (OECD, 2020). There are different forms with specific advantages and disadvantages. For instance, public assemblies are known to be one of the most inclusive forms, because they do not preselect who raises their voice. However, we cannot predict or control who is instantiating these assemblies or their goals. This might be a challenge. Stilgoe (2024) writes that big companies often consider democracy something they can control or outline, but he points out that democracy is not a chess game. It is key to leave room for disagreement and chaos. In entering an expert discourse, disagreement and dismissal might surface without many options to disagree agreeably, as Ansell (2023) puts it.

Public assemblies can help us engage with vulnerable groups without singling out a specific group or case. Engaging the wider public and listening to diverse voices reduce the risk of wrongly or openly marginalizing. By addressing the public in general and interest groups for specific topics, instead of grouping citizens based on their backgrounds, we could form new interest groups. This way, an assembly might lead to unpredicted results or new insights. Hence, vulnerability does not have to be just another form of exclusivity, but it can emerge from conversations and inclusion at the table, not by prediction or top-down, but because of the emergence of "voices and perspectives that would not have emerged if scientific experts or other 'elite' actors had simply deliberated among themselves" (Scheufele et al.,

2021, p. 3). Flanigan et al. (2021) speak of the benefits of citizens' assemblies and the difficulties in finding or narrowing down these groups. Grouping or finding citizens to debate productively on AI knowledge systems will not be easy, and it might not be the goal to do only that with every implementation and service. Still, involving different audiences in XAI has clear societal benefits. One is that it would challenge the exclusivity of data or computational sciences, but it might also lessen their pressure to ensure complete AI literacy for society. Another benefit comes from interdisciplinarity, which allows sharing the responsibility over the AI literacy discourse. Even though it is not our primary focus, democratizing XAI could potentially reduce the emphasis on data or engineering sciences as the single point of blame when AI goes rogue while still building on and profiting from their expertise. Throughout this book, we have seen that AI is not a technical issue, nor is XAI. Both are not single or isolated authorities or fields.

Such approaches also call for other collaborations and alliances, for example, with universities, NGOs, or journalists who could be critical in fostering a public dialog about desirable AI deployment and how sXAI might assist in deliberating and managing ethical issues (Perrigo, 2023).

The third strategy calls for the public engagement of data scientists and ML experts. Because *AI* is a hype and a buzzword, there are so many misleading ideas about what we might do with specific AI systems and what we cannot do. AI expertise is crucial for a broader public discourse about desirable AI futures and how tools such as explainability might help to get the best out of these technological developments. Here, it would be helpful if more technical experts understood themselves as political agents in the sense that their expertise is needed to determine such questions, and if they were to play a role in educating and empowering the public—that is, AI users and affected people (Green, 2021).

The crucial step here would be to transition from merely educating people about AI to empowering them to deal with its impacts. Ultimately, if we fail to include marginalized populations in the discourse on AI literacy, we run the risk of excluding them from a system that intends to empower everyone. This will strengthen the concentration of power behind AI (Bartoletti, 2020), and we risk widening the AI divide (Wang et al., 2024).

None of the strategies mentioned is a guarantee for the better design of explainable AI, nor is a supportive sXAI or even Socratic sXAI a guarantee for the fair use of AI systems. With our chapter, we want to invite developers and designers of XAI to reflect on the sociotechnical nature of their artifacts and the political-ethical nature of some of the purposes explainable AI is meant to serve.

29.6 Rapid Access to the Content of This Chapter

Traditional explainable AI (XAI) is often seen as a technical tool to make AI systems more transparent and interpretable, with the goal of mitigating bias and increasing trustworthiness. However, we contend that this approach is insufficient when it comes to addressing deeper ethical and political challenges such as those related to fairness. This is due to the political-ethical nature of fairness issues and the sociotechnical nature of deploying AI systems. From the perspective of social philosophy and technology ethics, we therefore propose reconceptualizing fairness in AI as fundamentally about the vulnerabilities of those affected by AI decisions, rather than about the information or transparency provided to users. Vulnerability is a relational, social phenomenon, not something that can be engineered into a system.

To motivate our perspective, we review the Dutch "SyRI" case as a negative example. SyRI was an automated risk-profiling system used by Dutch authorities to detect welfare fraud that disproportionately targeted non-Dutch nationals and residents of poorer neighborhoods. According to a court's ruling, the system was violating human rights. To prevent such a case, we imagine sXAI to empower virtuous AI practitioners in tasking AI fairly. We argue that simply providing more information or transparency (as with model cards or reporting tools) does not address the core issue: the social and ethical context in which AI is deployed and the real vulnerabilities of affected individuals. sXAI is presented as a more promising approach, because it is interactive and adaptive, potentially enabling AI practitioners to better understand and respond to the vulnerabilities of those impacted by AI decisions. sXAI can support practitioners in their ethical, political, and legal duties, rather than merely providing technical explanations.

Before presenting our toy scenario of sXAI as a supporting partner, we further motivate our approach by pointing out the current limitations and challenges in the field of Fair AI/ML—that is, we consider technical approaches to designing fair AI. We call for a shift in perspective from designing certain technical features that make a system fair to designing a supporting assistant that helps a virtuoso AI practitioner to make AI fair. In doing so, we set a desideratum: The sXAI should be suitable for AI practitioners, not ML experts, and the sXAI should not simply provide information, but become an assisting partner.

Making such a toy scenario possible requires several steps from different actors including designers and developers, AI providers, and AI practitioners (operators). In particular, we emphasize the importance of:

- Designing sXAI systems that actively engage with the context and needs of vulnerable groups
- Developing practices and institutional frameworks that empower AI operators to make fairer decisions
- Recognizing that fairness requires ongoing, context-sensitive judgment, not just technical fixes

Acknowledging these points requires not only a shift in perspective for AI deployment – from fair AI to tasking AI fairly – but also a shift in perspective in AI development and design. There is no guarantee of 'good use' of AI, XAI, or sXAI. No design strategy can guarantee better design of explicable AI. Nor does our vision of a supportive sXAI or even a Socratic sXAI guarantee the fair use of AI systems. In particular, our chapter was not intended to call for another technical solution, but to draw attention to the normative dimension implicit in AI usages and to question an adequate sociotechnical response to them.

Acknowledgments Research for this chapter was funded by the Transregional Collaborative Research Center "Constructing Explainability" (TRR 318/1 2021 – 438445824) at Paderborn University and Bielefeld University, Germany. The research in this chapter has also been supported by The Czech Science Foundation (GACR), Grant No. 24-11697S.

References

Alfrink, K., Turel, T., Keller, A. I., Doorn, N., & Kortuem, G. W. (2020). Contestable city algorithms. In *International Conference on Machine Learning Workshop*.

Alpsancar, S. (2023). What is AI ethics? Ethics as means of self-regulation and the need for critical reflection. In *International Conference on Computer Ethics* (Vol. 1. 1.) https://journals.library.iit.edu/index.php/CEPE2023/article/view/227. Visited on 10 May 2023.

Amnesty International. (2021). *Xenophobic machines*. Amnesty.org. . Visited on 05 Sep 2024.

Angwin, J., Larson, J., Mattu, S., & Kirchner, L. (2016). Machine bias. There's software used across the country to predict future criminals. And it's biased against blacks. In *ProPublica*. https://www.propublica.org/article/machine-bias-risk-assessments-in-criminal-sentencing. Visited on 27 Mar 2022.

Ansell, B. (2023). *BBC Reith Lectures 2023: Our Democratic Future*. https://downloads.bbc.co.uk/radio4/reith2023/Reith_2023_Lecture1_V2.pdf.

Arrieta, A. B., Díaz-Rodríguez, N., Sera, J. D., Benneto, A., Tabik, S., Barbado, A., Garcia, S., Gil-Lopeza, S., Molinag, D., Benjamins, R., Chatilaf, R., & Herrera, F. (2020). Explainable artificial intelligence (XAI): Concepts, taxonomies, opportunities and challenges toward responsible AI. *Information Fusion, 58*, 82–115. https://doi.org/10.1016/j.inffus.2019.12.012.

Barocas, S., Hardt, M., & Narayanan, A. (2023). *Fairness and machine learning: Limitations and opportunities*. MIT Press.

Barocas, S., & Selbst, A. D. (2016). Big data's disparate impact. *California Law Review, 104*, 671–732. https://doi.org/10.2139/ssrn.2477899.

Barr, C. J. S., Erdelyi, O., Docherty, P. D., & Grace, R. C. (2025). *A review of fairness and a practical guide to selecting context-appropriate fairness metrics in machine learning*. arXiv: 2411.06624 [cs.AI].

Bartoletti, I. (2020). *An artificial revolution: On power, politics and AI*. The Indigo Press.

Bekker, S. (2021). Fundamental rights in digital welfare states: The case of SyRI in the Netherlands. In O. Spijkers, W. G. Werner, & R. A. Wessel, *Netherlands yearbook of international law 2019: Yearbooks in international law: history, function and future* (pp. 289–307). T.M.C. Asser Press. https://doi.org/10.1007/978-94-6265-403-7_24.

Benjamin, R. (2019). *Race after technology: Abolitionist tools for the new Jim code*. Polity. ISBN: 978-1-5095-2639-0.

Binns, R. (2018). Fairness in machine learning: Lessons from political philosophy. In S. A. Friedler, & C. Wilson. In *Proceedings of the 1st Conference on Fairness, Accountability and Transparency* (Vol. 81, pp. 149–159). Proceedings of Machine Learning Research. PMLR. https://proceedings.mlr.press/v81/binns18a.html.

Blount, K. (2021). Applying the presumption of innocence to policing with AI. *International Review of Penal Law, 92*(1), 33–48.

Boyd, d. & Crawford, K. (2012). Critical questions for big data. Provocations for a cultural, technological, and scholarly phenomenon. *Information, Communication & Society, 15*(5), 662–679. https://doi.org/10.1080/1369118X.2012.678878.

Brandom, R. (1994). *Making it explicit: Reasoning, representing, and discursive commitment*. Harvard University Press.

Campolo, A., Sanfilippo, M., Whittaker, M., & Crawford, K. (2017). *AI now 2017 report*. New York University. https://ainowinstitute.org/AI_Now_2017_Report.pdf. Visited on 09 Sep 2021.

Caton, S., & Haas, C. (2024). Fairness in machine learning: A survey. *ACM Computing Surveys, 56*(7), 1–38. https://doi.org/10.1145/3616865.

Cobbe, J., Lee, M. S. A., & Singh, J. (2021). Reviewable automated decision-making: A framework for accountable algorithmic systems. In *Proceedings of the 2021 ACM Conference on Fairness, Accountability, and Transparency* (pp. 598–609). FAccT '21. Association for Computing Machinery. ISBN: 978-1-4503-8309-7. https://doi.org/10.1145/3442188.3445921.

Copp, D. (2015). Explaining normativity. *Proceedings and Addresses of the American Philosophical Association, 89*, 48–73. ISSN: 0065972X. http://www.jstor.org/stable/43661502. Visited on 06 Mar 2025.

Corbett-Davies, S., Pierson, E., Feller, A., Goel, S., & Huq, A. (2017). Algorithmic decision making and the cost of fairness. In *Proceedings of the 23rd ACM SIGKDD International Conference on Knowledge Discovery and Data Mining* (pp. 797–806). KDD '17. ACM. https://doi.org/10.1145/3097983.3098095.

Criado Perez, C. (2019). *Invisible women: Data bias in a world designed for men*. Abrams.

de Bruijn, H., Warnier, M., & Janssen, M. (2022). The perils and pitfalls of explainable AI: Strategies for explaining algorithmic decision-making. In *Government Information Quarterly, 39*(2), 1–8. https://doi.org/10.1016/j.giq.2021.101666.

Delgado, F., Yang, S., Madaio, M., & Yang, Q. (2023). The participatory turn in AI design: Theoretical foundations and the current state of practice. In *Proceedings of the 3rd ACM Conference on Equity and Access in Algorithms, Mechanisms, and Optimization* (pp. 1–23). EAAMO '23. Association for Computing Machinery. ISBN: 979-8-4007-0381-2. https://doi.org/10.1145/3617694.3623261.

Dignum, V. (2019). *Responsible artificial intelligence: How to develop and use AI in a responsible way*. Springer. https://doi.org/10.1007/978-3-030-30371-6.

Dobbe, R., & Wolters, A. (2024). Toward sociotechnical AI: Mapping vulnerabilities for machine learning in context. *Minds and Machines, 34*, 1–52. https://doi.org/10.1007/s11023-024-09668-y. Visited on 22 Sep 2024.

Dolata, M., Feuerriegel, S., & Schwabe, G. (2022). A sociotechnical view of algorithmic fairness. *Information Systems Journal, 32*(4), 754–818. https://doi.org/10.1111/isj.12370.

Egbert, S., & Esposito, E. (2024). Algorithmic crime prevention. From abstract police to precision policing. *Policing and Society, 34*(6), 521–534. https://doi.org/10.1080/10439463.2024.2326516.

Ellis, E., & Watson, P. (2012). *EU anti-discrimination law*. Oxford University Press.

Eubanks, V. (2018). *Automating inequality: How high-tech tools profile, police, and punish the poor*. St. Martin's Press.

European Commission. (2021). *Proposal for a regulation of the European Parliament and of the council laying down harmonised rules on artificial intelligence (Artificial Intelligence Act) and amending certain union legislative acts*. Brussels.

Fahimi, M., Russo, M., Scott, K.M., Vidal, M.-E., Berendt, B., & Kinder-Kurlanda, K. (2024). Articulation work and tinkering for fairness in machine learning. In *Proceedings of the ACM on Human-Computer Interaction, 8*(CSCW2), 1–23. https://doi.org/10.1145/3686973.

Fenger, M., & Simonse, R. (2024). The implosion of the Dutch surveillance welfare state. *Social Policy & Administration, 58*(2), 264–276. https://doi.org/10.1111/spol.12998.

Feuerriegel, S., Dolata, M., & Schwabe, G. (2020). Fair AI: Challenges and opportunities. *Business & Information Systems Engineering, 62*, 379–384. https://doi.org/10.1007/s12599-020-00650-3.

Flanigan, B., Gölz, P., Gupta, A., Hennig, B., & Procaccia, A. D. (2021). Fair algorithms for selecting citizens' assemblies. *Nature, 596*(7873), 548–552. ISSN: 1476-4687. https://doi.org/10.1038/s41586-021-03788-6.

Forst, R. (2017). *Normativity and power: Analyzing social orders of justification*. Oxford University Press.

Green, B. (2021). Data science as political action: Grounding data science in a politics of justice. *Journal of Social Computing, 2*, 249–265. https://doi.org/10.23919/jsc.2021.0029.

Green, B. (2022). The flaws of policies requiring human oversight of government algorithms. *Computer Law & Security Review, 45*, 1–22. https://doi.org/10.1016/j.clsr.2022.105681.

Hickok, M. (2021). Lessons learned from AI ethics principles for future actions. *AI and Ethics, 1*(1), 41–47. https://doi.org/10.1007/s43681-020-00008-1.

Hirvonen, H., & Westerling, F. (2024). Beyond human oversight—quality management as a tool to control automated decision-making systems. *The De Gruyter Handbook of Automated Futures: Imaginaries, Interactions and Impact, 2*, 255–270. https://doi.org/10.1515/9783110792256-016.

HLEG. (2019). *Ethics guidelines for trustworthy AI*. Brussels.

Kaminski, M.E. (2023). Regulating the risks of AI . *BUL Review, 103*, 1347–1411. https://doi.org/10.2139/ssrn.4195066.

Kim, K. M., & Fox, M. H. (2011). A comparative examination of disability anti-discrimination legislation in the United States and Korea. *Disability & Society, 26*(3), 269–283. https://doi.org/10.1080/09687599.2011.560371.

Kuźniacki, B. (2023). *'The Dutch childcare benefit scandal shows that we need explainable AI rules'*. uva.nl. https://www.uva.nl/en/shared-content/faculteiten/en/faculteit-der-rechtsgeleerdheid/news/2023/02/childcare-benefit-scandal-transparency.html?cb.

Langer, M., Oster, D., Speith, T., Hermanns, H., Kästner, L., Schmidt, E., Sesing, A., & Baum, K. (2021). What do we want from explainable artificial intelligence (XAI)?—A stakeholder perspective on XAI and a conceptual model guiding interdisciplinary XAI research. *Artificial Intelligence, 296*, 1–24. https://doi.org/10.1016/j.artint.2021.103473.

Lippert-Rasmussen, K. (2011). "We are all different": Statistical discrimination and the right to be treated as an individual. *The Journal of Ethics, 15*(1), 47–59. https://doi.org/10.1007/s10892-010-9095-6.

Lyons, H., Velloso, E., & Miller, T. (2021). Conceptualising contestability: Perspectives on contesting algorithmic decisions. In J. Nichols (Ed.), *Proceedings of the ACM on Human-Computer Interaction* (5.CSCW1, pp. 1–25). https://doi.org/10.1145/3449180.

Mahoney, T., Varshney, K., & Hind, M. (2020). *AI fairness. How to measure and reduce unwanted bias in machine learning*. O'Reilly Media.

Mehrabi, N., Morstatter, F., Saxena, N., Lerman, K., & Galstyan, A. (2021). A survey on bias and fairness in machine learning. *ACM Computing Surveys, 54*(6). ISSN: 0360-0300. https://doi.org/10.1145/3457607.

Meske, C., Abedin, B., Klier, M., & Rabhi, F. (2022). Explainable and responsible artificial intelligence. *Electronic Markets, 32*(4), 2103–2106. https://doi.org/10.1007/s12525-022-00607-2.

Miller, T. (2019). Explanation in artificial intelligence: Insights from the social sciences. *Artificial Intelligence, 267*, 1–38. https://doi.org/10.1016/j.artint.2018.07.007.

Mindlin, D., Beer, F., Sieger, L. N., Heindorf, S., Esposito, E., Ngomo, A.-C. N., & Cimiano, P. (2025). Beyond one-shot explanations: a systematic literature review of dialogue-based xAI approaches. *Artificial Intelligence Review, 58*(3), 1–37. https://doi.org/10.1007/s10462-024-11007-7.

Mitchell, M., Wu, S., Zaldivar, A., Barnes, P., Vasserman, L., Hutchinson, B., Spitzer, E., Raji, I. D., & Gebru, T. (2019). Model cards for model reporting. In: *Proceedings of the Conference on Fairness, Accountability, and Transparency*. FAT* '19 (pp. 220–229). ACM. https://doi.org/10.1145/3287560.3287596.

Novelli, C., Hacker, P., Morley, J., Trondal, J., & Floridi, L. (2024). A robust governance for the AI act: AI office, AI board, scientific panel, and national authorities. *European Journal of Risk Regulation*, 1–25. https://doi.org/10.1017/err.2024.57.

OECD. (2020). *Innovative citizen participation and new democratic institutions*. OECD-org. https://www-oecd-org.uaccess.univie.ac.at/en/publications/innovative-citizen-participation-and-new-democratic-institutions_339306da-en.html. Visited on 10 Sep 2024.

O'Neil, C. (2017). *Weapons of math destruction: how big data increases inequality and threatens democracy*. B/D/W/Y Broadway Books. ISBN: 978-0-553-41882-8.

Perrigo, B. (2023). *AI by the people, for the people*. Time. https://time.com/6297403/the-workers-behind-ai-rarely-see-its-rewards-this-indian-startup-wants-to-fix-that/.

Pessach, D., & Shmueli, E. (2022). A review on fairness in machine learning. *ACM Computing Surveys (CSUR), 55*(3), 1–44. https://doi.org/10.1145/3494672.

Peters, T. M., & Visser, R. W. (2023). The importance of distrust in AI. In L. Longo (Ed.), *Explainable Artificial Intelligence* (pp. 301–317). Springer. https://doi.org/10.1007/978-3-031-44070-0_15.

Pfeiffer, J., Gutschow, J., Haas, C., Möslein, F., Maspfuhl, O., Borgers, F., & Alpsancar, S. (2023). Algorithmic fairness in AI. *Business & Information Systems Engineering, 65*(2), 209–222. https://doi.org/10.1007/s12599-023-00787-x.

Pütz, O., & Esposito, E. (2024). Performance without understanding: How ChatGPT relies on humans to repair conversational trouble. *Discourse & Communication, 18*(6), 859–868. https://doi.org/10.1177/17504813241271492.

Rachovitsa, A., & Johann, N. (2022). The human rights implications of the use of AI in the digital welfare state: Lessons learned from the Dutch SyRI case. *Human Rights Law Review, 22*(2), 1–15. https://doi.org/10.1093/hrlr/ngac010.

Reutlinger, A., Hangleiter, D., & Hartmann, S. (2018). Understanding (with) toy models. *The British Journal for the Philosophy of Science*, 1069–1099. https://doi.org/10.1093/bjps/axx005.

Sachoulidou, A. (2023). Going beyond the "common suspects": To be presumed innocent in the era of algorithms, big data and artificial intelligence. *Artificial Intelligence and Law*, 1–54. https://doi.org/10.1007/s10506-023-09347-w.

Santos, F. P., Lelkes, Y., & Levin, S. A. (2021). Link recommendation algorithms and dynamics of polarization in online social networks. *Proceedings of the National Academy of Sciences, 118*(50), 1–9. https://doi.org/10.1073/pnas.2102141118. eprint: https://www.pnas.org/doi/pdf/10.1073/pnas.2102141118.

Sayles, J. (2024). Human oversight of AI systems. In J. Sayles (Ed.), *Principles of AI governance and model risk management: Master the techniques for ethical and transparent AI systems* (pp. 267–276). Springer. https://doi.org/10.1007/979-8-8688-0983-5_12.

Scheufele, D. A., Krause, N. M., Freiling, I., & Brossard, D. (2021). What we know about effective public engagement on CRISPR and beyond. *Proceedings of the National Academy of Sciences, 118*. https://doi.org/10.1073/pnas.2004835117.

Schuett, J. (2024). Risk management in the artificial intelligence act. *European Journal of Risk Regulation, 15*(2), 367–385. https://doi.org/10.1017/err.2023.1.

Showkat, D., Bellamy, S., & To, A. (2020). Fair and trustworthy welfare systems: Rethinking explainable AI in the public sector. In *Proceedings CHI 2020*. https://doi.org/10.13140/RG.2.2.23902.72001.

Smuha, N. A. (2021). Beyond a human rights-based approach to AI governance: Promise, pitfalls, plea. *Philosophy & Technology, 34*(Suppl 1), 91–104. https://doi.org/10.1007/s13347-020-00403-w.

Sokol, K., & Flach, P. (2020). One explanation does not fit all. *KI - Künstliche Intelligenz, 34*(2), 235–250. https://doi.org/10.1007/s13218-020-00637-y.

Sterz, S., Baum, K., Biewer, S., Hermanns, H., Lauber-Rönsberg, A., Meinel, P., & Langer, M. (2024). On the quest for effectiveness in human oversight: Interdisciplinary perspectives. In *Proceedings of the 2024 ACM Conference on Fairness, Accountability, and Transparency* (pp. 2495–2507). https://doi.org/10.1145/3630106.3659051.

Stilgoe, J. (2024). AI has a democracy problem. Citizens' assemblies can help. *Science, 385*. https://doi.org/10.1126/science.adr6713. Visited on 22 Sep 2024.

van Bekkum, M., & Borgesius., F. Z. (2021). Digital welfare fraud detectiojudgment. *European Journal of Social Security, 23*(4), 323–340. https://doi.org/10.1177/13882627211031257.

van Schendel, S. (2019). The challenges of risk profiling used by law enforcement: Examining the cases of COMPAS and SyRI. In L. Reins (Ed.), *Regulating New Technologies in Uncertain Times* (pp. 225–240). T.M.C. Asser Press. ISBN: 978-9-4626-5279-8. https://doi.org/10.1007/978-94-6265-279-8_12.

Verma, S., & Rubin, J. (2018). Fairness definitions explained. In *Proceedings of the International Workshop on Software Fairness*. FairWare '18 (pp. 1–7). Association for Computing Machinery. ISBN: 978-1-4503-5746-3. https://doi.org/10.1145/3194770.3194776.

Wachter, S. (2022). The theory of artificial immutability: Protecting algorithmic groups under anti-discrimination law. *Tulane Law Review, 97*, 149–206.

Wachter, S., Mittelstadt, B., & Russell, C. (2021). Why fairness cannot be automated: Bridging the gap between EU non-discrimination law and AI. *Computer Law & Security Review, 41*, 1–31. ISSN: 0267-3649. https://doi.org/10.1016/j.clsr.2021.105567.

Wallace, R. J., & Kiesewetter, B. (2024). Practical reason. In E. N. Zalta & U. Nodelman (Eds.), *The Stanford Encyclopedia of Philosophy*. Fall 2024. Metaphysics Research Lab, Stanford University.

Wang, C., Boerman, S. C., Kroon, A. C., Möller, J., & de Vreese, C. H. (2024). The artificial intelligence divide: Who is the most vulnerable? *New Media & Society*. https://doi.org/10.1177/14614448241232345.

Wasserman-Rozen, H., Gilad-Bachrach, R., & Elkin-Koren, N. (2023). Lost in translation: The limits of explainability in AI. *Cardozo Arts & Entertainment Law Journal, 42*(2), 391–437.

Wieringa, M. (2023). "Hey SyRI, tell me about algorithmic accountability": Lessons from a landmark case. *Data & Policy, 5*, e2. https://doi.org/10.1017/dap.2022.39.

Wikipedia Contributors. (2024). *Dutch childcare benefits scandal — Wikipedia, The Free Encyclopedia*. [Online; accessed 24 Sept 2024]. https://en.wikipedia.org/w/index.php?title=Dutch_childcare_benefits_scandal.

Williams, B. (2012). *Morality: An introduction to ethics*. Cambridge University Press.

Xivuri, K., & Twinomurinzi, H. (2021). A systematic review of fairness in artificial intelligence algorithms. In D. Dennehy, A. Griva, N. Pouloudi, Y. K. Dwivedi, I. Pappas, & M. Mäntymäki (Eds.), *Responsible AI and analytics for an ethical and inclusive digitized society* (pp. 271–284). Springer. ISBN: 978-3-0308-5447-8. https://doi.org/10.1007/978-3-030-85447-8_24.

Zytko, D., Wisniewski, P. J., Guha, S., Baumer, E. P. S., & Lee, M. K. (2022). Participatory design of AI systems: Opportunities and challenges across diverse users, relationships, and application domains. In S. Barbosa, C. Lampfe, C. Appert, & D. A. Shamma (Eds.), *CHI Conference on Human Factors in Computing Systems Extended Abstracts* (pp. 1–4). https://doi.org/10.1145/3491101.3516506.

Open Access This chapter is licensed under the terms of the Creative Commons Attribution 4.0 International License (http://creativecommons.org/licenses/by/4.0/), which permits use, sharing, adaptation, distribution and reproduction in any medium or format, as long as you give appropriate credit to the original author(s) and the source, provide a link to the Creative Commons license and indicate if changes were made.

The images or other third party material in this chapter are included in the chapter's Creative Commons license, unless indicated otherwise in a credit line to the material. If material is not included in the chapter's Creative Commons license and your intended use is not permitted by statutory regulation or exceeds the permitted use, you will need to obtain permission directly from the copyright holder.

Chapter 30
The Risk of Manipulation and Deception in sXAI

Suzana Alpsancar and Michael Klenk

Abstract XAI can minimize the risks of being manipulated and deceived by AI but in turn entails other specific risks. This also applies to sXAI, and the specifically social character of sXAI harbors particular risks that designers and developers should be aware of. In this chapter, we shall discuss the potential opportunities and risks of sXAI. We see a particularly positive potential in the social character of sXAI, which lies in the fact that skillful users, including those with "healthy distrust," can use the adaptivity of sXAI to produce an explanation that is actually relevant and adequate for them. However, this requires a high level of skills on the part of the user and is thus in contrast to the general promise of efficiency in the use of AI. A potential risk of XAI is that it can be (even more) persuasive, as the interactive involvement and the anthropomorphism strengthen a trustworthy appearance/performance (independent of the adequacy of the sXAI performance).

30.1 How Does This Chapter Relate to XAI?

As with any technology, using XAI comes with several opportunities and risks. The chances derive from the intended purposes of XAI, which can be divided into four basic categories (Alpsancar et al., 2024): The purpose of XAI can be functionally related to the (further) development of AI systems (error prevention, optimization);

Both authors collaboratively discussed the paper's structure and core argument, edited and approved the final manuscript. S.A. mainly wrote Sects. 30.4, 30.3.2, and 30.6 and finalized Sects. 30.1 and 30.3.1. M.K. drafted the first version of Sects. 30.1 and 30.3.1, an mainly wrote Sects. 30.2 and 30.5.

S. Alpsancar (✉)
Heinz Nixdorf Institute, Department of Philosophy, Faculty of Arts and Humanities, Paderborn University, Paderborn, Germany
e-mail: suzana.alpsancar@uni-paderborn.de

M. Klenk
Department of Values, Technology and Innovation, Faculty of Technology, Policy & Management, Delft University of Technology, Delft, Netherlands
e-mail: M.B.O.T.Klenk@tudelft.nl

there can be an epistemic purpose orientation in the foreground (understanding, knowledge generation), or an economic one that relates to the broad use of AI systems (usability, trustworthiness, efficiency); and finally there is the widespread assumption that XAI can help protect fundamental rights and meet minimum ethical and legal standards. When considering these opportunities, it should be borne in mind that XAI is usually seen as an add-on to a specific AI system; that is, it is not a stand-alone product. Therefore, the extent and weight of the opportunities and risks of XAI depend directly on the opportunities and risks of the associated AI system. For example, the greater the benefit or potential harm of an AI system, the greater the benefit or potential harm of an XAI meant to explain that AI system's behavior.

In a general vein, a fundamental distinction can be made between different types of technology-related risks, such as (a) the risk of malfunction; (b) the risk of misuse, disuse, and nonuse; as well as (c) risks of unintended consequences. The higher the dependency on the AI system's functionality, the higher the potential harm, for example, of malfunction: If AI is used to amplify warfare, a malfunction could have tremendously harmful effects. The very idea of XAI is to *optimize AI usage* and can hence be seen as a means to mitigate AI-related risks and boost AI's potential (Franklin et al., 2023).[1] For example, if there was a reliable AI diagnostic system for some disease and medical experts could be supported by an XAI to effectively calibrate their usage of the AI system (that is to know better when and when not to rely on the AI recommendation), then it would be a disadvantage for society if these experts were not to use or disuse the XAI (and hence the AI, respectively).

However, the use and dependency on XAI are not risk-free for three reasons. First, the question of appropriate reliance and trust is pushed on a **meta-level**: A recommendation is appropriate if it is both factually correct and has taken the contextual factors sufficiently into account. Since the decision-making of AI systems, if they are relatively complex or use ML methods, cannot be understood in detail by humans, XAI should provide sufficient explanations, so that the quality of the AI recommendation can be assessed with sufficient certainty (Longo et al., 2024, p. 5). Yet, to fulfill this role, users must be able to reasonably rely on the XAI, so that the question of the suitability of the machine arises again at a meta-level: When is it appropriate to follow the XAI explanation?

Second, XAI is still a **technology-in-the-making**, and there are many open questions regarding evaluation standards and context-aware-usability (see Chaps. 28 and 26). "What is missing is a set of evaluation metrics for explainability that are generally applicable across studies, contexts, and settings" (Longo et al., 2024; Wickstrøm et al., 2024, p. 10).[2] In consequence, there is a particular risk involved in relying on XAI *now* simply because of the premature status of the technology.

---

[1] See Uuk et al. (2024) for a more nuanced taxonomy of AI-related risks.

[2] It could be the case that the immature status is going to last simply, because AI techniques are evolving and new data and environmental factors can be integrated. For instance, it is currently an open research question how existing XAI techniques help to understand the output and performance of GenAI (Longo et al., 2024).

Third, the very idea of using AI for decision support implies a **shift of power**: AI is meant to influence users' behavior for the sake of *better decision making*. There are two central power-related normative aspects embedded in this idea of AI as a means for facilitating better decision-making. It (a) presupposes knowing what the better or even the optimal decision is. However, the real world is a "wicked" place full of ambiguity (Skaburskis, 2008; Lönngren and Van Poeck, 2021), which is not always a bad thing. There might be cases in which there is more than one 'good' decision, and there might be cases where it is 'good' that human decision-makers have some leeway in forming their decisions. Accordingly, it is not always clear if the implementation of AI does justice to the logic of the real world (de Bruijn et al., 2022; Wachter et al., 2021). Moreover, (b) the usage of AI decision support mediates the expertise of those who formerly made the decision on their own. It transforms the norm of how and by whom a decision is to be made, from human experts alone to human-AI collaboration. Herby, at least partly, some power of defining these norms shifts from the domain experts to the AI experts. Now, the interesting question is how XAI is meant to mitigate these power-related normative aspects of using AI for decision support, which is to a large part a design and deployment choice: On the one hand, the XAI could play the role of reassuring the users about the AI's performance, that is, backing up the AI's game; on the other hand, the XAI could play the role of a skeptical mediator (see Chap. 29 "Tasking"), that is, highlighting the uncertainty implied in a particular decision-making context.

As the very idea of XAI is to assist people in using AI, the overarching goal of XAI is also to **influence people**, on a meta-level, in order to support better decision-making. Accordingly, there is a particular risk of being deceived and manipulated by XAI, which we focus on in this chapter. Here, as said before, it is important to highlight that these XAI-related risks are linked to a specific loop, that is, XAI as a means to mitigate the risks of using AI. It is most likely that these XAI-related risks can never be completely eliminated. Nonetheless, it could be reasonable to argue that not using (a particular) XAI poses a higher risk because of the benefits XAI brings for the linked AI usages.

In general, there is a thin line between providing information and influencing someone. Some might even argue that providing information (or the omission of giving information) is always an act of influence. Some of these might nudge people to do something, for example, the simple fact that navigation systems not only provide one route but also alternative routes while at the same time categorizing these alternatives in some sort of normative evaluation, for example, fastest route, most eco-friendly route, and so forth, can be seen as an attempt to influence decision-making based on providing facts—that is, the simple extension of the area of making an informed choice between alternatives comes with a normative load. However, not all influence is inherently harmful or wrong. Accordingly, we start our discussion by diving into the question of how to distinguish harmful from non-problematic influence. For this, in Sect. 30.2, we sketch the most important current philosophical accounts on making that distinction. In Sect. 30.3, we use these different theoretical models to discuss the current debate on how XAI and transparency might mitigate the risk of being manipulated by AI on the one side while at the same time being aware of a higher-order risk of being deceived or manipulated by XAI itself. In Sect. 30.4, we expand the discussion to sXAI. Here, we argue that the 'social' character of providing more personalized, adaptive explanations or even co-constructing explanations can be seen as both having the potential to enable users' epistemic agency better but also running the risk of deceiving users precisely because of the social nature of the XAI-interaction. We suggest that the opportunities of sXAI, as laid out throughout this book, and the risks coming with its use regarding manipulation are two sides of the same coin. Let's use advertising to illustrate this point. Advertisers have learned that they need to know their audience and that it matters as much *how* you say something as *what* you say. This orientation can be beneficial in that it gets people what they want, while at the same time, it avoids miscommunication. But it also invites nefarious uses of that power, the likes of which are amply discussed in the literature on the ethics of advertising. Can the same be said for the case of sXAI? In this chapter, we challenge this assumption and explore its limits. We conclude in Sect. 30.5 by providing some guiding reflection questions for sXAI designers and point out central concerns that should be further investigated.

30.2 Philosophical Theories of Manipulation

Questions about manipulation can sometimes be misunderstood. For example, when one of us gave a talk on manipulation to a group of design students, the students seemed perplexed by the idea that one would characterize manipulation as a big problem. Aren't we influencing each other all the time? Isn't that the very goal of design, and human computer interaction, in particular? However, there is a form of morally dubious influence, one that most people are not readily willing to accept as perfectly normal, let alone as the explicit goal of well-meaning design. We call that morally dubious form of influence manipulation and consider the task of a theory of manipulation to figure out just where to draw the line.

Importantly, most of the theories that we are going to discuss are intended as analyses of manipulation that, ideally, should result in a definition. The explicit aim is often to give necessary and sufficient conditions for manipulation. Yet, our aim here is not to defend a single theory or modal that captures all aspects of manipulation. For the purposes of this chapter, we focus on emphasising some aspects of manipulation that different theories have highlighted as playing an important part in demarcating influences that are manipulative in the morally dubious sense from other types of influence (Table 30.1).

Table 30.1 Theoretical accounts of manipulation

Manipulation theory	Description	Transparency/ XAI	Explication
The covertness model	Manipulative influence proceeds covertly and is not noticed by the target	Misuse or unintended side-effect	sXAI's adaptivity and dialogic format can hide constraints on the explanation space, making users believe they are co-constructing an open, reality-tracking explanation while being subtly steered. Its trustworthy social performance increases susceptibility to unnoticed influence
Bypassing rationality	Manipulative influence entirely bypasses or subverts the rational capacities of the target	Intentional misuse	Personalized, socially attuned explanations can nudge users through emotional resonance or confirmation of prior beliefs, encouraging acceptance without critical scrutiny and reinforcing automation or confirmation biases
The mistake account	Manipulative influence aims to induce a mistake in the psychological states or processes of the target	Intentional misuse	Actors can intentionally shape or select sXAI explanations (leveraging the disagreement problem) to induce false beliefs. For example, offering non-revealing rationales that mask discriminatory factors or enabling more persuasive fraud and phishing
The indifference account	Manipulative influence primarily aims to be effective and is *not* aimed at helping the target do the right thing for the right reasons (i.e., is indifferent, but not necessarily actively opposed, to the target's rationality)	Disuse	Even without bad intent, designers may deploy sXAI in ways indifferent to supporting users' epistemic agency. For example, prioritizing engagement or compliance over reason-giving quality, or neglecting how adaptive explanations may mislead or fragment users' understanding

30.2.1 Intentional Influence

To begin with, manipulation is a form of influence (Coons & Weber, 2014). As social animals, humans influence each other in countless ways. Some influences are intentional, such as a speech act, while others are unintentional, such as the intimidating effect a very tall person may have on others. However, not all intentional influences are ethically problematic. For example, if you are the passenger in a car and you yell out to the driver to warn them about an accident, you are not doing anything wrong (cf. Sunstein, 2016). Therefore, the first question requires us to determine how manipulation, as a morally suspect influence, is set apart from other types of intentional or purposeful influences that are generally deemed legitimate.

30.2.2 The Continuum Model

Criteria for identifying manipulation may be derived by contrasting it with other forms of influence. The continuum model suggests that manipulation sits on a continuum of influence, situated between rational persuasion and coercion (Beauchamp, 1984; Beauchamp & Childress, 2019). This continuum model helps draw basic distinctions and conceptualize the idea that there are some benign types of influence, like rational persuasion, and other types of influence that are clearly problematic, like coercion. The continuity model allows manipulation to be understood as something gradual, with there being a certain transitional area or gray area between mere influence and manipulation on the one hand and between manipulation and coercion on the other hand. However, the continuum model does not yet provide us with reliable criteria for manipulation. There seem to be forms of non-persuasive and noncoercive influence that are not manipulation (Noggle, 1996). For example, dressing up for a job interview is neither rational persuasion nor coercion, but it does not look like manipulation either (Noggle, 1996). Depending on how we define the reference points of persuasion and coercion, the continuum model might give us criteria for manipulation that are much too encompassing, which would result in overly stringent design requirements if we had the aim to avoid any influence classified as manipulative by such criteria.

Therefore, it is more promising to turn to philosophical theories of manipulation that offer more specific criteria for identifying manipulation. There are several influential ideas about manipulation that are simple, intuitive, and seemingly easy to apply in practice.

30.2.3 The Covertness Model

Perhaps the most influential idea is that manipulation is necessarily a form of hidden influence (cf. Faraoni, 2023, and its uptake and reflection in policy documents): Manipulation works, because it is covert—that is, hidden. This is also the understanding of manipulation championed by Wang (2023) in his discussion of manipulative algorithmic transparency (see below).

The leading proponents of the covertness account in the debate about online manipulation are Susser et al. (2019a; 2019b), who argue that manipulation is an influence *that the victim is not or could not easily be aware of*. For this conception to be useful in understanding the moral repercussions of sXAI, it is crucial to specify exactly what remains hidden from the manipulation victim. For example, must the intended outcome of the influence be hidden from the user? Or the precise psychological mechanism through which the influence is intended to work? Or how the influence was generated? The latter, for example, would suggest that there might be a broad spectrum of factors about how a sXAI output was generated that, if not declared, will count as manipulative on the hidden influence conception. In any case, the hidden influence conception helps distinguish manipulation from persuasion and coercion on the continuum model, because these forms of influence are necessarily overt (cf. Klenk, 2021b).

Yet, the hidden influence conceptualization of manipulation is unlikely to provide reliable criteria to capture the phenomenon of manipulation accurately, let alone entirely. On the one hand, many hidden influences do not fall under manipulation. For instance, the heuristic and biases research program in psychology suggests that many of our decisions arise out of hidden processes that are not the result of conscious deliberation (Kahneman, 2012). Still, such processes often seem legitimate and non-manipulative (cf. Sunstein, 2016).[3] Therefore, the criterion of hidden influence risks being overinclusive: It classifies too many cases as manipulation, thus generating false positives. It would require further work to explain how hidden influence is to be understood in a way that makes it a credible criterion for manipulation. We can return to this point in the next section.

On the other hand, some important forms of manipulation are not covered by the hidden influence conception (cf. Klenk, 2021b). For example, a manipulative real estate agent may use the homely scent of freshly baked cookies at a house viewing to lure in potential buyers who, nonetheless, are fully aware that they are being manipulated (Barnhill, 2014). Similarly, the dark pattern known as a "roach motel" often prevents users from canceling a service by making it cumbersome and tiring to complete (Brinckll, 2023). Victims of a roach motel are being manipulated even though they are often fully aware of the influence.

Therefore, the hidden influence criterion also risks being underinclusive: It generates insufficient cases as manipulation, thus generating false negatives, in the sense that it seems to classify cases as manipulation that do not strike most people as being of the same kind as the evidently problematic forms of manipulation.

30.2.4 Bypassing Rationality

Another influential idea is that manipulation can be identified by influences that *bypass rationality* (Sunstein, 2016; Wilkinson, 2013). Again, the notion of bypassing rationality must be specified further for the criterion to be useful (see Gorin, 2014a for discussion). Like the hidden influence conception, the bypassing rationality conception should help to distinguish manipulation from coercion and persuasion, and it correlates with many paradigmatic cases of manipulation. For example, it is manipulative to prompt a generative AI to guilt-trip a target into

---

[3] See also the discussion in Dowding and Oprea (2024).

donating money to a charity, because the influence targets the victim's emotions and bypasses rational deliberation.

However, important questions about the "bypassing rationality" conceptualization remain. While it seems accurate enough – it accounts for many paradigmatic cases of manipulation – it has been subject to severe criticism for generating false negatives (Gorin, 2014a,b). Some forms of manipulation, such as peer pressure or charm, do not seem to involve bypassed rationality (Baron, 2003; Noggle, 2022). Hence, the bypassing conceptualization of manipulation does not reliably identify all manipulation cases.

Moreover, many forms of tremendously important influences, such as testimony or influences that "activate heuristics", bypass rationality but are not examples of manipulation. Hence, the bypassing criterion is also overinclusive and generates false positives. For example, testimony bypasses rationality, because it is often accepted at face value, given a positive evaluation of the source's credibility. This is not a rational process in the sense of the process being conscious, yet testimony is unlikely to be considered a form of manipulation. Similarly, the availability or recognition heuristic allows people to make frugal decisions without conscious deliberation. It is rational to rely on the heuristic when there is a correlation between the criterion and recognition (Gigerenzer & Goldstein, 1996). This suggests that "activating" the availability heuristic need not be manipulative, even though it means to bypass rationality in the sense of bypassing conscious deliberation.

In summary, the bypassing rationality criterion suffers from over- and underinclusivity. Since it also lacks the advantage of being relatively simple – insofar as bypassing rationality is more difficult to operationalize than hidden influence – it is of questionable relevance for the aim to design for non-manipulation.

30.2.5 The Mistake Account

A more promising approach is to understand manipulation *in terms of the influencer's intentions* rather than the features of the influence itself. One very influential account suggests that we can identify manipulation by the intention to induce a mistake in the recipient by causing them to violate a norm of belief, desire, or emotion (Noggle, 1996, 2020). Typical cases of fraud, for example, are classified as manipulation in this model, because they involve the attempt to trick the target into adopting a false belief or an inappropriate desire. For example, when a scammer uses text messages to pose as a relative and asks for money, they try to induce a mistaken belief in the target.

The mistake conceptualization seems helpful in addressing many forms of intentional manipulation, and it might be used to understand how sXAI can be used as a *tool* for manipulation. For instance, in their critical assessment of AI-driven influence operations, Goldstein et al. (2023) describe how AI can be used to scale up fraud and make it more economical. Similarly, phishing and other attempts to make people solicit information or resources can be aggravated by using generative

AI to create persuasive phishing material, such as text messages or emails. The intent to trick the victim is clearly recognizable in such cases.

However, it is important to also recognize a type of manipulation enabled by technology and sXAI where the mistake criterion seems less appropriate. In particular, the mistake conceptualization produces false negatives in at least two relevant, though still less prevalent, use cases.

First, someone may unwittingly deploy sXAI to generate manipulative influences, although they cannot be said to intend to induce a mistake in anyone. For example, Brinckll (2023) describes how automated A/B testing allows users to run the test and automatically implement the 'winning' design. Someone using this feature may simply be interested in creating a communication design that meets certain sXAI goals, such as engagement or understandability. Still, the 'winning' design may include paradigmatic forms of manipulation, like appeals to emotions or social pressure. Deploying such a system may thus be manipulative on account of the indifference or carelessness about the actual quality of the design's or system's influence. The mistake account does not readily account for cases of unintended manipulation like this.

Second, the mistake account's focus on intentions leads to problems insofar as it seems possible that sXAI can output manipulative content even if nobody directed the system to do so. Cappuccio et al. (2022) argue that new forms of manipulation driven by AI may be 'emergent' and not reducible to, for example, the intentions of a human user. Pham et al. (2022) also stress the importance of considering emergent, non-intentional forms of manipulation that have their source in the automated behavior of AI-driven applications. An account of manipulation that emphasizes the intention to trick or lead astray will not allow us to identify unwitting manipulation that emerges out of the automated behavior of the system.

Although the immediate risk of manipulation through the nefarious use of sXAI may be seen as most clearly, the threat of emergent, non-intentional manipulation is clearly relevant as well and may even be much greater than the risk posed by nefarious actors, a point to which we return in Sect. 30.4.

In summary, the mistake conception faces the biggest challenge in contexts where generative AI threatens to aggravate existing concerns about manipulation by amplifying the scale of manipulative influence. In lieu of intentions and in lieu of overt features of manipulation, we cannot readily classify emergent forms of manipulation as manipulation on the mistake account.

30.2.6 The Indifference Account

A proposal that promises to overcome these problems is to identify manipulation *with indifference to some ideal state* rather than some malicious intention to do harm or induce a mistake (Klenk, 2020, 2021b). According to the indifference criterion for manipulation, manipulation is an influence that aims to be effective but is not explained by the aim to reveal reasons to the interlocutor (Klenk, 2021b, 2023).

The indifference account takes as a starting point the view that we are interdependent beings. Very often, we depend on others to think and act well. Consider, for example, the role that experts play in our knowledge of scientific theories. This perspective is well aligned with the idea of sXAI, which also takes into account the specific communicative needs and dependencies of the target (e.g., an AI's users), which might draw attention to how things need to be presented rather than merely focusing on the content that is being communicated.

From this starting point, the indifference view suggests that there are really two ways in which we can undermine the thinking and acting of our interlocutors. First, we can actively interfere in ways that are aptly captured by the other views of manipulation, like covertly influencing or bypassing rationality. But second, we can also do harm by merely failing to support our interlocutor in thinking and acting well insofar as they depend on us to do so. This perspective thus broadens our understanding of the ways in which manipulation may occur.

The indifference view identifies manipulation based on two criteria. First, it only looks at influence that is aimed at a particular goal. In that sense, and in line with most, if not all, of the literature on manipulation, the view excludes influence that is purely accidental from counting as manipulation (see Noggle, 2018).[4] Second, the indifference view then asks why a particular means of influence was chosen to achieve the relevant goal. Manipulative influence is characterized negatively in terms of a choice of a means of influence that is not being explained by the aim to reveal reasons to the target of the influence. The manipulator is, in that sense, "careless" (Klenk, 2021b) or indifferent to revealing reasons to their victims.

In summary, the indifference view has particular strengths in explaining the case of manipulation without an intentional actor, and the case of manipulation that is not traceable back to any malicious intent. It is also well aligned with the basic premise of sXAI, namely, that we need to consider the deliberative needs of our interlocutors. Failing to do that – merely being indifferent to it – in the design or deployment of a technology can thus count as a manipulative act, in the sense of it being a problematic form of influence.

30.3 Manipulation and Deception in XAI

In general, XAI can be seen as a means to influence human behavior, particularly decision-making assisted by the underlying AI system. Accordingly, the thin line between unproblematic influences and manipulation must be considered for the XAI field. For example, a pertinent question is whether it belongs to the category of manipulation (or another prima facie problematic form of influence).

---

[4] Importantly, a goal can but does not need to be understood in intentional terms. Animals can be said to have goals, as do automated systems, or even simple artifacts based on their use plan (van de Poel, 2020), or affordances (Klenk, 2021a). In short, goals can be understood in functional terms.

Some researchers explicitly aim to build *"Nudge-XAI*, an approach that introduces automatic biases into explanations from explainable AIs (XAIs) with the aim of leading users to better decisions" (Fukuchi & Yamada, 2024). In general, the debate (Lades & Nova, 2023; Vandenbroele et al., 2020; Capasso & Umbrello, 2022) whether or not nudging users is justifiable (and in which cases) applies to XAI as well. From an XAI design perspective, it is particularly central to reflect on what it means to empower users. For example, Franklin (2022) discusses the influence of XAI from two different theoretical frameworks (from the field of policy-making and economics), contrasting nudging with "boosts." A nudge alters the architecture of choices in a given context without forcing a particular choice on the customer/user or limiting the amount of choices (Sunstein, 2018). In contrast, boosts aim to upskill people, build, and foster their competencies, so that they can make their own choices more effectively (Hertwig, 2017). To discuss their difference in influencing someone, it is helpful to use Daniel Kahneman's 2013 dual process theory of cognition, which distinguishes system 1 and system 2 for how the human mind cognitively processes things. System 1 is heuristic, fast, and reacts intuitively without much effort. It accounts for most behavior. System 2 relies on more effort, and it can reevaluate system 1 processing, and so forth. "Importantly, some factors and contexts are more likely to trigger System 1 or System 2 thinking than others" (Franklin, 2022). Now, nudges are seen to influence system 1, while boosts address system 2. Franklin (2022) even proposes that most likely some XAI techniques work as nudges, namely, local and concept-based explanations, while other XAI techniques work as boosts, namely, global and counterfactual explanations. However, empirical evidence is still missing to support these considerations.

Based on these theoretical considerations, we now turn to the current debate, positions, and concerns around XAI and manipulation. The predominant view in scholarship and regulatory debates about algorithms stresses that XAI as well as algorithmic transparency are crucial to algorithmic systems' responsible design and use (Walmsley, 2021; Winfield et al., 2021). This call for transparency, explainability, and interpretability is the loudest for information systems deployed in so called "socially significant" contexts (Floridi et al., 2018, p. 702). However, the value of XAI should not be overgeneralized and needs to be specified for each application context (Alpsancar et al., 2024). Explainability, transparency, or interpretability are not always demanded, necessary, useful, or desirable (Robbins, 2019; de Laat, 2018; Kemper & Kolkman, 2018; Diakopoulos, 2020; Powell et al., 2021; Kim et al., 2021). There are cases in which a full disclosure of the functional transparency is unwanted for different reasons, for example, enabling people to game the system, corporate secrecy, privacy, or national security reasons (Wang, 2022). There might also be a trade-off between XAI and users' cognitive abilities, efficiency, and usability (Asghari et al., 2022). XAI might be undesirable in the sense that it is used to attribute responsibility and accountability to individuals, that is, lay users, for consequences which should be managed on a structural level (Alpsancar et al., 2024; Matzner, 2017). Because of these issues, critical voices (e.g., Bannister & Connolly, 2011) recognize that transparency is not merely a neutral transmission of information but a social process linked to power dynamics (Ananny & Crawford, 2016). When discussing the manipulative potential of transparent AI and XAI, we follow this critical stand.

To structure the debate, it is essential to see that explainability, interpretability, and transparency are often not well-defined and used interchangeably (Krishnan, 2020; Nannini et al., 2023). This is particularly obvious in the stream of ethical guidelines which sparked around 2017 from industry, politics, and academia (Morley et al., 2020; Jobin et al., 2019; Hagendorff, 2020). While some papers try to establish taxonomies (e.g., Adadi & Berrada, 2018; Doshi-Velez & Kim, 2017; Arrieta et al., 2020), there is a lasting tendency in the technical literature to stick with the vagueness of the concepts (Patidar et al., 2024; Longo et al., 2024), which can also be productive (Ehsan & Riedl, 2024).

Partly, XAI is seen as one component to foster transparency, for instance, in the popular model-card approach, which calls to provide a documentation of the most important features and design choices for AI models (Mitchell et al., 2019). Partly, XAI is seen as an alternative to transparency, namely, in the contrast of ex ante transparency (white-box models) and post hoc explainability (black-box models) (Rudin, 2019; Lipton, 2018). First, we present positions concerned with the risks of transparent AI in general, hence addressing XAI as a tool for transparency. Then, we discuss more specific risks of manipulation and deception in regard to post hoc explanations, before we turn to the question of how sXAI adds to this picture.

30.3.1 *The Manipulative Potential of Transparent AI*

The link between transparency and power, a critique of the particular power-dynamic implied by transparency, is nothing new in the field of Social and Political Philosophy. However, recently there has been a more focused debate on algorithmic transparency and its power dynamics. In the following, we discuss three forms of being manipulated by transparent AI using three different accounts of manipulation as outlined before in the theory section. First of all, transparency/XAI might be *misused* by AI operators: Companies could use transparency to fool their customers or the public; that is, corporate interests behind algorithmic transparency may corrupt its otherwise laudable goals (as a kind of ethics washing) (Kossow et al., 2021; Wachter et al., 2018). This misuse of transparent AI is the first form of manipulation or deception in the sense of *the mistake account*—actors are using transparency/XAI for bad intentions. However, transparency/XAI might also be seen as manipulating users and the public without the bad intentions of AI operators. Here, we refer to Klenk's (2023; 2024) indifference account and Wang's (2023) particular covertness account of manipulation.

The second form of manipulation can be classified as a form of *disuse* of transparency/XAI and can be understood following Klenk's *indifference account*. The main idea is that, from an ideal normative point of view, transparency/XAI should be used to empower AI users. But because the AI operators/developers are *indifferent* toward empowering their users, operators/developers disuse the tool, that is not using it for the right purpose. Accordingly, the absence of bad intentions, that is, the intention to manipulate the users, is not enough to free the influence from potentially being an instance of manipulation, following this account. More precisely, Klenk argues from a normative-ideal point of view that transparency/XAI should be used to enable users to authentically engage in a reason-making process. This not only implies an authentic intention to do the right thing but also includes caring about whether or not the means to achieve the goal of empowering users are suitable. For example, an organization may decide to be transparent about their algorithm, because they are convinced that it is, ethically, the right thing to do. Still, the organization faces a question about *how* to achieve algorithmic transparency, that is, what means or methods to employ. They might have the option, for example, of using text to communicate or to record brief instructional videos. There is some evidence that videos enhance learning in educational contexts (Brame, 2016). The organization may choose videos *because* of their (presumed) helpfulness in revealing reasons to users; in that case, their attempt at transparency is clearly not manipulative. But if the organization opts for videos because they reckon that it will win them favor with users and scholars interested in algorithmic transparency, their influence is manipulative. It is *not* explained by the aim to reveal reasons to users but tries to achieve some other ends effectively.

Furthermore, Klenk's approach emphasizes the actual effect of transparency strategies, whether relevant reasons actually become apparent or not (2022; 2023). For instance, the model card approach could work either way (Mitchell et al., 2019). The skillful user might already have sufficient background, technical, domain understanding, and so forth to derive relevant reasons from the provided disclosure. Other users might still be left in the dark, no matter how many lines of information are handed over to them. Here, Klenk particularly draws awareness to the obligation of the transparency providers and their engaged or indifferent attitude: When algorithmic transparency does not aim to reveal reasons to its target audience but merely aims at achieving a certain effect, such as instigating a particular behavior or creating a certain impression, when it is, in a slogan, indifferent to reasons (cf. Klenk, 2021a), then it degenerates into manipulation. As we shall see below, there is some particular potential in sXAI according to Klenk's indifferent account as it adapts to different users, contexts, and tasks.

In short, according to Klenk, algorithmic transparency has manipulative potential, because the providers of said transparency may be transparent in ways that are simply indifferent to informational quality and revealing pertinent reasons to the users. Instead, they may be much more interested in inducing certain behaviors, such as continued or increased use of and reliance on the system that the algorithm operates in.

The third form of manipulation can be classified as an *(unintended) side effect of transparency* following Wang's critique on algorithmic transparency. Wang uses a Foucauldian perspective to draw attention to the objectification of norms that result from algorithmic transparency and its intrinsic power dynamics, which can be discussed as a form of hidden influence in the sense of the covertness model of manipulation. Wang argues that this process of hidden influence qualifies as manipulation, because the objectification of norms determines the scope for action. Let us now look at the individual steps in Wang's argument. First, Wang defends the empirical premise that algorithmic transparency leads to the "objectification" of norms (Wang, 2022, p. 13). For example, the FICO algorithm rewards punctual payment of bills. Sharing this information not only serves transparency, but it also suggests that paying on time is a norm, effectively "disciplining [consumers] according to some expected norms of being responsible credit consumers" (Wang, 2022, p. 12). A consequence might be that individuals come to accept these norms without critical analysis, and, in that sense, they become "objectified" (Wang, 2022, p. 12). Consumers come to think of the system in a particular way (e.g., as objective and value-neutral in the case of the FICO algorithm), and their minds are "reframed," so that their "thinking of other possibilities" is "constrained" (Wang, 2022, p. 15). For example, they fail to see the FICO algorithm as an "arbitrary," "discriminatory," or "unfair" system, because they are more likely "to only focus on the scientific and objective narrative of its algorithm, ignoring other alternative narratives" (Wang, 2022, p. 16–17).

Second, Wang suggests that the objectification of norms constitutes manipulation by drawing on a specific view of manipulation defended by Susser et al. (2019a), who argue that manipulation "exploit[s] the manipulee's cognitive (or affective) weaknesses and vulnerabilities in order to steer his or her decision-making process toward the manipulator's ends" (cf. Wang, 2022, p. 2, 18).[5] Wang suggests that norm objectification is a way to "exploit the manipulatee's weaknesses and vulnerabilities" to benefit the manipulator in contexts of "asymmetrical power relations," such as commercial and political settings (Wang, 2022, p. 3, 17).[6] For example, the FICO algorithm is "a commercial tool for lenders to make profits" (Wang, 2022, p. 19); transparency about the algorithm can lead to "disciplined" individuals that follow the newly objectified norms about behaving in line with good credit-rating scores, so that they can be charged with higher interest rates at lower risk of default, which benefits the lender (Wang, 2022, p. 19). This, argues Wang, constitutes manipulation on the vulnerability view (as a specific form of the covertness model of manipulation). So, according to Wang (2022), algorithmic transparency leads to norm objectification and, in the context of power disparities, operators of algorithms can exploit that vulnerability to steer people toward behaviors that benefit themselves. This, he argues, constitutes manipulation.

---

[5] Wang does not fully adopt Susser et al. (2019b). As I discuss in more detail in Section 3, Susser et al. (2019b) defend *covert influence* as a necessary criterion for manipulation, whereas Wang often highlights that—to the contrary—manipulation can take place non-covertly (e.g., Wang, 2022, p. 69). Thanks to an anonymous referee for prompting me to clarify this point.

[6] See also (Wang, 2023, p. 2).

30.3.2 Manipulation and Deception by Post Hoc Explanations

To discuss the manipulative and deceptive risks of post hoc explanations, it is important to clarify their actual epistemic potential. For this, the distinction of ex ante transparency and post hoc explainability, albeit widespread, is conceptually not sufficient and can be misleading. While it helps to classify different AI techniques and methods on an abstract level (white box models vs. black models), it does not cover the factors determining the opacity of a system, which play out in the actual implementation and usage. When we consider the running of these systems, white box AI can also be opaque for several reasons. Technically, white box models become opaque due to complexity, that is, of parameters (Lipton, 2018). Socially, white box models can become opaque due to economic circumstances (corporate secrecy) and bear different levels of opacity concerning the literacy and expertise of different users (Burrell, 2016).

Against this background, Zerilli (2022) offers a fruitful distinction to grasp the inscrutability of AI systems by distinguishing if a system is *intelligible* or *fathomable*. If you can completely understand the architecture and process of a system, you can evaluate its realism (in the sense of being truthful to reality). Linear systems using a relatively small number of features (dimensionality) are both intelligible and fathomable in the sense that "a person can contemplate the entire model at once" (Lipton, 2018; Zerilli, 2022, p. 4). If the dimensionality (amount of features) increases, even linear systems stop being fathomable while there are still intelligible "—that is, inspectable—without necessarily being fathomable—that is, inspectable all at once" (Zerilli, 2022, p. 4). Those AI systems that "model relationships that are not linear and incorporate extremely large feature spaces" (ibid) are neither fathomable nor intelligible. It is common sense that parsing systems that are not even intelligible is categorically different from parsing (even complex) linear models. However, the relevant question is what this particular challenge of machine learning systems for explainability means in practice. What follows from here is that we may never be completely sure if an XAI explanation is really faithful to the underlying inscrutable AI systems, as we (even experts) are not able to completely grasp the system's architecture and process.

Consequently, post hoc explanations – for technical reasons – never provide completeness or full comprehension, but comprehensibility (Zerilli, 2022).[7] Now, the crucial question is what practically follows from here. There are two positions in the debate. Skeptics argue that XAI should be underpinned by more comprehensive explanations that are faithful to the logic of the system (Rudin, 2019; Leslie & Schmitt, 2019) and because that is not possible in the case of non-intelligible systems, these should not be used in high-stakes decision-making (Rudin, 2019; Simon et al., 2024). Some argue that you should not rely on something that lacks

---

[7] See also the related discussion about the "lack of ground truth explanation labels" as "a fundamental challenge for quantitative evaluation in explainable artificial intelligence (XAI)" (Wickstrøm et al., 2024).

reproducibility, which is hard for some XAI techniques (Longo et al., 2024). Another argument is the categorical conceptual mismatch between human and AI reasoning: If we take that mismatch seriously, on a conceptual level, any attempt to explain the machine that operates in a clearly distinctive conceptual realm in conceptual terms that are understandable for humans is a form of deception (Longo et al., 2024). AI inferences can be subject to a "reality drift" due to complexity and missing conceptual alignment (Longo et al., 2024, p. 11). Particularly in the case of highly complex AI systems, the usefulness of XAI explanations is questionable: If XAI were to render explanations in concepts understandable to humans, these might be illusory, measured against the actual concepts of the AI machine. If the XAI were truthful to the AI system instead, humans would not gain any sort of understanding for categorical reasons (Longo et al., 2024).

The more optimistic position argues that completeness is not necessary in practice, and hence, post hoc explanations can still be adequate. This argument typically rests on an analogy between making sense of other human actors and artificial agents. From a practical point of view, the type of understanding that we need to continue our tasks and succeed with our practices is far from any theoretical ideal of completeness or full comprehension. Rather, this type of understanding can be depicted with what Daniel Dennett called *intentional stance* (Dennett, 1971), which had been a common point of reference in early AI. Dennett's argumentative starting point is the everyday interpretation of human actions, which we explain in terms of intentions. "The intentional stance is the strategy of interpreting the behavior of an entity (person, animal, artifact, whatever) by treating it as if it were a rational agent who governed its 'choice' of 'action' by a 'consideration' of its 'beliefs' and 'desires'" (Dennett, 2009, p. 339). From the intentional stance, we can sufficiently understand and predict people's behavior, and we might use it as a cognitive strategy to also make sense of the behavior of animals or systems, for example, a chess-playing computer, which we can think of as being a rational agent who wants to win and who knows the rules. Following this idea, we can predict the chess-playing computer's next move (Dennett, 1971; Zerilli, 2022). In analogy, those post hoc explanations that enable users to make these kinds of intentional predictions and understandings would be sufficient in a practical sense. Zerilli (2022, p. 18) even defends this pragmatic position for using post hoc explanations for the purpose of justification. In his view, "the quotidian form of explanation that practical reasoning assumes," that is, post hoc explanations which resemble human explanations in everyday situations, are sufficient. There is an additional argument to the optimistic view that XAI explanations do not need to be complete or comprehensive, because very often nonexpert users are not interested and do not need to understand the underlying AI's architecture and processes in detail. Rather, they need a sufficient understanding in regard of the task at hand in a given context. So, strengthening the point of view of nonexpert stakeholders (Langer et al., 2021) could add to the argument that faithfulness to the AI system is not a necessary condition for XAI. Yet, Zerilli (2022) argues that from a design and engineering perspective, a deeper understanding of the systems might be necessary, that is, to optimize, debug, and prevent a system from malfunctions (Zerilli, 2022,

p. 18). Then, the follow-up question is, in which (non-ordinary) cases are these explanations not sufficient, and who is responsible for making sure that post hoc explanations are not used in these?

While this debate about the adequacy of post hoc explanations is still unsettled, what is interesting for the discussion of the deceptive and manipulative potential of post hoc explanations is the fact that this technical discrepancy between any provided XAI explanations and the ideal of being faithful to the real process of the underlying AI system gives room for particular forms of manipulation and deception. The discrepancy first of all gives rise to what is called *the disagreement problem in XAI*, that is, the fact that many different XAI explanations are possible and plausible for the same AI system, and it is prima facie not clear which one is the most adequate (Goethals et al., 2025).

There are different reasons for the disagreement problem. First of all, different XAI methods (e.g., SHAPE, LIME, counterfactual explanations) produce different explanations. Second, the same XAI technique (e.g., counterfactual explanations) is known to produce different explanations for the same outcome (also called "Rashomon effect") (Goethals et al., 2025, p. 3). Third, another challenge arises from the immature nature of some AI systems, that is that their functioning is not static but open to learning (e.g., from human feedback) and adapting (e.g., to changing environmental factors or users' preferences, and so forth). Fourth, algorithms interfere with each other; there are no isolated tools but usually a component within a larger software and data management infrastructure (Sculley et al., 2015; de Bruijn et al., 2022). That also means that one particular AI system is interfering with different data sets, different other algorithms, and so forth. That interference might itself become opaque or something that needs to be explained, or it might influence the plausibility of a given explanation by the XAI system. How decisions impact people's lives might differ from one to the other individual; hence, in some cases, XAI needs to deliver explanations on an individual level that is for a certain decision. Taking that into account implies accounting for the enormous context dependency of meaningful XAI. "This makes it hard to explain the working of the algorithm in general and to explain their different outcomes" (de Bruijn et al., 2022, p. 4). In cases with a high dynamic, this might "result in today's explanation becoming obsolete tomorrow" (ibid).

A first risk deriving from the disagreement problem is, again, the problem of *misuse*: "Indeed, it has been pointed out repeatedly that post-hoc explanation algorithms can be manipulated or cheated upon" (Bordt et al., 2022, p. 892). For example, Naiseh et al. (2023) report, in the context of clinical decision-making, that different XAI techniques influence how the fairness of AI systems is perceived and that trust is calibrated differently. The disagreement problem can be exploited by explanation providers for manipulation, for instance, by preselecting explanation techniques or by data poisoning (Goethals et al., 2025). Accordingly, Carli et al. (2022) call to safeguard XAI from malicious actors—it is, however, unclear how to do that effectively.

Second, a general concern is that people tend to rely more on AI when any explanation is provided (Naiseh et al., 2023), so an *unintended consequence* could be that users over-rely on the machine simply, because an explanation is provided at all ('automation bias'). Insofar as people expect the XAI to provide the right/adequate explanation and are unaware of the disagreement problem, or not skilled enough to deal with it appropriately, the mismatch between users' expectations of the capacity of the XAI and its actual epistemic potential could, in effect, be deceiving.

Third, manipulation in the sense of Klenk's indifference account can be a result of careless (indifferent) deployment of the XAI and its ambivalent epistemic potential: The ambiguity and plurality of explanations could in general also be productive and helpful, probably most likely in cooperative contexts (e.g., a group of data scientists debugging a system). But, the same aspect will most likely rather be problematic in adversarial contexts where we need to expect a misalignment of different stakeholders' interests (Bordt et al., 2022; Asghari et al., 2022). Imagine a loan applicant being denied credit and aiming to flag this rejection as discrimination. Here, the bank/company might choose an explanation which provides a reason for the rejections that is free from any discriminatory indications (Goethals et al., 2025, p. 3). As we can see, the disagreement problem paves the way for misusing XAI, which is obviously a way of deceiving and manipulating clients. Additionally, we can also realize that how problematic this plurality of explanations can get largely depends on the way these XAI offers are handled in practice: It depends on the intentions of the involved actors, the divergence of stakeholders' interests, and the question of who gets access to what. For example, returning to the case described above, having a plurality of explanations at hand could also benefit the loan applicant in contesting the decision. An XAI operator being indifferent to these different contexts, users, and tasks can be seen as manipulating the users in the sense of Klenk's indifference account.

There is a fourth risk of deception, which could also be classified as an unintended consequence, but on a societal level: Taking a perspective beyond the individual and short-term consequences of such manipulative (X)AI usage, we can consider other undesirable effects as well. A long-term and large-scale effect of AI-mediated epistemic environments, for example, social media, is what Coeckelbergh (2025, p. 61) calls "defaulting of statistical knowledge." What he means is the tendency to prioritize statistical knowledge over other forms of knowledge, such as causal knowledge. Using the hypothetical example of Claire, who is holding white supremacist views, Coeckelbergh argues that "if AI offers her statistical knowledge of a correlation between skin colour and success in her particular society, then she might be tempted to keep her white supremacist belief rather than change it, even if there is no causal link" (2025, p. 5). Albeit such statistical knowledge being at hand before, it only became widespread and easily accessible through the latest AI developments and digitalization. Hence, AI poses a particular risk for our human epistemic agency – that is the capability to form justifiable beliefs in the light of other beliefs and desires – which is becoming harder to exercise the more one finds oneself informed and surrounded by AI-mediated epistemic ecosystems. Here, XAI could be imagined to disclose this prioritization or to nudge users to be skeptical about defaulting to statistical knowledge. However, as XAI itself rests on some sort of statistical knowledge but rather appears to provide some 'intentional stance' or 'causal link' to better understand the performance of the underlying AI systems, it might very well be the case that using XAI first coverts the defaulting to statistical knowledge, both in terms of the AI but also the explanation technique, and thus leads to a deception of the users about the actual state of the affairs.

30.4 Does sXAI Aggravate Concerns with Deception and Manipulation?

In this section, we explicitly relate the discussion about deception and manipulation to sXAI. We assume that the risks of XAI generally also apply to sXAI and that there are specific chances and risks deriving from the unique character of sXAI. *Social* XAI aims to create better XAI and hence bears the potential to gather more tailored, personalized, contextualized, and interactive, that is *relevant* explanations which might be actually helpful or even necessary in given situations.

The basic idea of sXAI is to solve the shortcomings of XAI *on the interaction level between the artificial agents and individual users*, that is, on an individual, not on an institutional level. This brings with it certain opportunities but also specific risks. In principle, we see this as an opportunity to strengthen individual users in their decision-making by allowing them to determine and shape what is in question and how it can be adequately explained. However, this focus on the individual harbors the risk of (renewed) overwhelming of the user. It is well known that the use of transparency strategies (e.g., datasheets, model cards, EnvCards) requires a high degree of expertise on the part of the recipients. For many end users, it is already troubling to understand and make practical sense of statistics (Asghari et al., 2022). Accordingly, the opportunity to take part in co-constructing relevant explanations will probably be most helpful for skillful users (e.g., domain experts). How so-called end users might cope with it should be explored carefully (Anjomshoae et al., 2019).

Moreover, there is inherent latitude for deception and manipulation due to the distinctive features of sXAI: (a) the flexible adaptivity regarding the explanandum and explanans, as well as (b) the social character of communication and interaction. We argue that both features demand an even more skillful user to mitigate the risk potential.

30.4.1 Adaptivity as a Medium for Deception and Manipulation

First, if *intentionally misused*, the assumption of interactively constructing an explanation in sXAI can add to the covertness of the manipulation: While in reality the explanation to be constructed is already preselected by the explanation provider/AI deployer (or a scope of possible explanations), the user is under the assumption that s/he takes part in an open process where the only benchmark of the explanation is 'reality.' Picture the loan example from above: If the explanation provider somehow did manage to determine the scope of potential sXAI explanations for its very own benefit only, for example, excluding those that could indicate potential discrimination, and the user was, however, under the assumption that s/he would receive an appropriate and correct explanation, s/he will probably be less skeptical due to the interactive character and less suspicious of being intentionally deceived by the provider behind it. Likewise, regarding the same scenario with no misuse, neither in the intentional sense nor in the sense of Klenk's indifference account, the particular interactive opportunities of the sXAI probably empower the user better, because the process of co-constructing relevant explanations can be seen as critically engaging in the process of reason-making, forming, and reassessing beliefs, hence exercising "epistemic agency" (Coeckelbergh, 2025, p. 59).

Second, it should be explored via empirical user studies, in which ways the adaptivity of sXAI adds to *the disagreement problem of XAI.* Prima facie, it is obvious that the very idea of sXAI implies a higher level of epistemic involvement of the user; hence, it alters the constellations of actors regarding the selection of adequate and relevant explanations. Users are given more options, which may be accompanied by a loss of control on the part of the AI operator (explanation provider). From a normative point of view, this entails the question of who is to be held responsible for the adequacy of the constructed explanations. It might be sensible, for example, for high-stakes areas, not to give every user unrestricted access to every form of explanation. It is conceivable that this freedom of adaptivity could lead to new forms of 'gaming the system.'

Third, tailored explanations could exaggerate the risk of overreliance (Nannini et al., 2023, p. 1206) hence counterbalance "healthy distrust." This could happen not (as in the case of XAI) because there is any explanation given but because of the epistemic involvement of the user. This is particularly likely if the given explanation fits prior beliefs, because then people tend to accept it more easily. This could leverage confirmation or automation bias (Balagopalan et al., 2022) and also add, in a long-term and large-scale perspective, to societal epistemic fragmentation (Coeckelbergh, 2025).

Fourth, the creation of epistemic bubbles and reinforcement of epistemic fragmentation is a specific sXAI-related risk due to its adaptivity to individual users. This risk concerns the societal and collective level, hence regarding large-scale and long-term effects of AI and sXAI usage. "[E]pistemic bubbles" (Coeckelbergh, 2025, p. 61) describe the phenomenon that users only find themselves in echo chambers of their own beliefs and interests. The consequence is epistemic fragmentation because of fewer chances to be confronted with different beliefs, desires, and interests than those aligned with their own. This can have tremendous effects on a collective and societal level—a dimension of risks embedded in AI applications that is less talked about in mainstream XAI (Asghari et al., 2022). Because these epistemic bubbles reduce opposing views, Coeckelbergh (2025) frames them as a potential threat to epistemic agency, that is, the *capacity to form* *and revise epistemic beliefs* in the light of opposing and contesting views. Against this background, the question arises as to how far different users should be able to co-construct different explanations for the same case, or if there should be any limitations to the 'personalization' of explanations. Imagine again the case of loan applications. If you had three potential clients who all get rejected but receive different explanations for that by an sXAI (e.g., different counterfactuals linking the rejection to different factors such as living address, income, working gaps in your CV), this could potentially create or increase mistrust regarding the credit institution or among the clients: Why are we treated unequally by this institution?

Fifth, in sum, it might become very hard or even impossible to determine why users receive different explanations. Is it because the AI operator/explanation provider chose so? Is it because of the learning character of the underlying AI? Is it because of the tailoring of the sXAI? Not only is "the logic to compare with other cases [...] unclear" (de Bruijn et al., 2022, p. 4) but also understanding why it is harder to compare becomes even more difficult. In total, this might add to "a risk of disengagement with reality" (Bertolini & Carli, 2022).

30.4.2 Social Interaction as a Medium for Deception and Manipulation

When Weizenbaum (1966) introduced ELIZA, one of the world's first chatbots, in 1966, he was shocked by the fact that (some) people behaved as if they were interacting with a real person. What has been called the *Eliza-effect* ever since has become amplified due to the 'social abilities' of some of today's software and robot systems. There is empirical evidence that humans react socially to social agents (indicated by politeness, gender stereotypes, triggering smiles, mimicry, and so forth), but this social interaction does not necessarily mean that humans mistake artificial agents to be real persons or full members of society (in, for instance, also a normative sense) (Krämer & Manzeschke, 2021). De facto, these *social AI/robot systems* are hybrid socio-ontological entities. In light of their performance and how people react to them and interact with them, they resemble social partners, but in light of their political and economic status, they are mere artifacts and products—if you destroy them and throw them away, you will not go to jail (Bryson & Theodorou, 2019). People tend to ignore that hybrid character, and it is an open question how that impacts the social order on a collective scale. Despite the openness of these fundamental questions, there are already strong positions in the (X)AI debate about how to evaluate the social character of the interaction. Two opposing views can be pointed out. Many find this social involvement of users steered by the social character of the systems to be key for better human-technology interaction (Sheridan, 2020; Breazeal et al., 2016); others have questioned the need to design for emotional attachments (Brinck & Balkenius, 2020; Gray, 2023) and are skeptical about the long-term and large-scale effects of our "social hallucination" (Metzinger, 2018, p. 3).

Technology ethics hold the established principle that users should always (be able to) be aware of the human-technology relationship they currently find themselves in (Dixon, 2020; Dignum, 2019; Gransche et al., 2014), including knowing if they are interacting with a technical system and what exactly they are interacting with. It is unclear in which cases ignoring the hybrid status of social artificial agents violates that principle in such a way that it could become harmful, that is, when the social hallucination counteracts ethical standards such as mutual recognition, self-identity, autonomy, and the like. In these cases, there will be a trade-off between immediate users' satisfaction (e.g., convenience, ease of use, positive feedback, and so forth) and ethical standards (e.g., mutual recognition, self-identity, autonomy) (Gray, 2023; Hirmiz, 2023; Bertolini & Carli, 2022). Hence, it needs to be further explored how far the social-performance character of sXAI might be subject to these concerns.

In light of these open questions, we have to take into account that the anthropomorphization of the systems and the interactive involvement of the user add to the "social hallucination" (Metzinger, 2018, p. 3) of using sXAI, in the sense of not being aware of any difference between interacting with an artificial system or with other social actors (individuals, institutions). *The missing awareness can become problematic when it decreases the awareness about the technical specifics of the (sX)AI systems, that is, the disagreement problem, the tendency to create and reinforce epistemic bubbles, and defaulting statistical knowledge.* A consequence could be a misjudgment about the limits, doings, and capacities of the artificial systems. In this sense, the social character of (sX)AI might counteract any attempts to cultivate "healthy distrust" (Passen et al., 2025; Visser et al., 2023).

This social hallucination opens a specific scope for deception and manipulation. These risks for manipulation and deception could become amplified insofar as sXAI interaction could soon be based on GenAI systems (Simon et al., 2024), for example, text (or even image and video) generation, which would definitely strengthen the 'social performance' of sXAI interfaces.

Turning now to factors that aggravate risks of manipulation and deception, we can once more first point out concerns about manipulation, understood as a mistake, that is *the misuse of sXAI*. There might be the temptation to use persuasive (i.e., effective) and user-friendly means of influence, knowing that those means of influence will represent bad reasons for the user to adopt certain beliefs or perform certain actions. For example, one might deploy an avatar to communicate with the user that mirrors social characteristics of the user, like race or personality traits, hoping that this will increase the user's trust and consequent willingness to accept the avatar's explanation of the AI system. Even if the provided explanation is correct, this would count as manipulation and a mistake, and such forms might be invited by sXAI.

Second, there is also the risk that what Wang (2023, 2022) described as manipulation by norm objectification becomes amplified due to the social performance, and hence trustworthy character of sXAI. Insofar as sXAI might be more 'user friendly' and more effective in getting users to accept certain evaluative and normative decisions embedded in an algorithm as fact (e.g., that you ought to pay your credit back on time), the more likely it might be that it leads to norm objectification and, in Wang's view, to manipulation.

Third, developing and deploying sXAI that prioritizes effective over reason-revealing influence greatly aggravates concerns about manipulation as indifference. This seems to be a great risk, since debates about sXAI might often be focused on user-friendly and effective communication, with little to no concern given to reason-revealing communication. Those two can come apart quite dramatically. For example, users might prefer frictionless interaction, and that might be considered part of user-friendly design. But there might just be situations where friction is welcome, where users should stop in their tracks and reflect about information, for example, the criteria by which an AI system makes decisions. In such cases, revealing reasons might be contrary to user-friendliness. If that distinction is blurred, then the risk of manipulation as indifference increases.

This has ramifications for possible future use cases of sXAI that rely on automatic, autonomous generation of outputs. While current generative AI applications like ChatGPT are not yet capable of fine-tuning their output in pursuit of goals other than text-sequence prediction, attempts to fine-tune generative AI applications with objectives aimed at effective influence are possible future use cases (and already discussed, e.g., by Matz et al., 2024). When such future generative AI applications optimize for effective influence on the user (e.g., to increase acceptance of a message propagated through sXAI), then their manipulativeness may not come down to anyone's intention but simply be the result of carelessness in revealing reasons exhibited in the design of the system.

Thus, the indifference criterion can capture emergent, unwitting manipulation resulting from the sense that generative AI systems act as "stochastic parrots" (Bender et al., 2021, p. 610). This is one of the chief advantages of the indifference view over the mistake conceptualization of manipulation. Future cases of sXAI could be based on generative AI systems, which can be understood as 'bullshitters' in Frankfurt's sense of bullshitting as a type of speech act indifferent to truth (Frankfurt, 2005). Manipulation as a super-category of bullshit (Klenk, 2022) may not be restricted to malicious intent but more broadly connected to indifference to truth and inquiry.[8]

30.5 How Does This Chapter Inspire Further Directions of XAI?

In this section, we finally turn toward some recommendations for developers by pointing out what to be aware of to mitigate the risk of deceptive and manipulative sXAI.

---

[8] See Klenk (2020) for a discussion of manipulation in relation to bullshit.

The **first** recommendation is, naturally, to try to avoid any of the nefarious criteria identified with manipulation: influence that leads to harm, that is covert in problematic ways, notably regarding the intention of the influence and – possibly – about the nature of the influence though this can probably not always be avoided. Also, there exists a trade-off in making communication overly cumbersome.

Second, there is the recommendation to consider whether and how there are reasons for the target to act in line with the recommendations. What is the point of the influence? Should the target feel, think, and act in specific ways? There will often be reasons for doing so. If not, do not influence. If there are, try to consider how those reasons could be made apparent to the target. Which preexisting beliefs are available, which values can be appealed to? This is an aspect in which XAI could be very strong and helpful.

The **third** recommendation is to be aware of the need to continuously monitor the deployed system (van de Poel, 2020) because of the possibility of emergent manipulation. This, however, is not a concern exclusive to manipulation, but it should always be a concern when discussing the ethics of AI.

Fourth, it would be worthwhile to reflect on the morality of manipulation. There might be trade-offs between manipulative influence and ease of use. Ease of use might be beneficial and valuable. And it might well justify manipulation, but that is a difficult call to make.

Fifth, we highly recommend including a risk assessment beyond the level of the individual user. Guiding questions to depict risks on the societal and collective level could be the following:

- How personalized should the explanation of an sXAI be in a given context in relation to a specific task? What are the possible impacts on different users receiving different explanations for supposedly the same case? Who are the different users?
- What is the character of the epistemic ecosystem the sXAI is placed in? In how far is the adaptivity of the sXAI explanation adding to epistemic bubbles or fragmentation? Is there room for contesting beliefs? Are they bound to a common shared "truth" about the state of affairs (e.g., why some clients receive a loan and others do not?)
- What are the societal impacts if such sXAI is used on a large scale and for a long time?

In the end, sXAI developers and designers have to make crucial decisions affecting the risk for the user of being manipulated or deceived by the technology's performance. For sXAI in particular, they have to decide if the partner model (see Sect. 14.4 on partner models) about the preferences of the user/operator should somehow be governed (due to ethical or regulatory considerations), or if the partner model should completely follow the users' wishes and ideas. Accordingly, sXAI developers and designers should be sensitive about these risks as laid out in this chapter and further ones deriving from future developments in the field.

30.6 Rapid Access

This chapter discusses the risks and opportunities associated with sXAI, particularly focusing on the potential for manipulation and deception in its use. To lay ground for our discussion, we provide an overview of philosophical accounts of manipulation. In general, manipulation is a form of influence that can be intentional or unintentional. As not all influence is harmful or counts as wrongdoing, we need to have reasonable criteria for distinguishing mere influence from manipulation and deception. Here, the different philosophical accounts provide different points of view and criteria to draw that distinction, each helpful in understanding different forms of manipulation and deception.

- The intentional influence account sees (bad) intentions as a prerequisite for manipulation.
- The continuum model situates manipulation between rational persuasion and coercion, highlighting a gray area.
- The covertness model suggests manipulation involves hidden influence that victims are unaware of. For instance, bypassing rationality identifies manipulation as influences that circumvent rational deliberation. Another variation of this account of manipulation is to highlight side effects of using an AI system, for example, the objectification of norms inherent to the usage of the AI.
- The bypassing rationality account identifies manipulation with influence that the targets are unaware of.
- The mistake account focuses on the intention to trick the recipient into violating norms.
- The indifference account emphasizes the lack of care in supporting the interlocutor's reasoning.

To point out the specific risks linked to the social character of XAI, we first discuss the manipulative risks of XAI in general and then turn to discuss how the interactive and adaptive capacities of sXAI add to or mitigate the risks of XAI.

To address the manipulative potential of XAI, it is important to distinguish more general concerns regarding XAI as a means of rendering AI transparent and post hoc explanation techniques.

The major concerns regarding the deceptive or manipulative risks of transparency/XAI in general can be outlined using the continuum model (misuse of transparency/XAI), the covertness model (unintended side effect of transparency/XAI), and the indifferent account (disuse of transparency/XAI). First, transparency/XAI is misused when AI developers or operators intentionally use transparency strategies to manipulate their users, for example, as a form of ethics washing or a strong form of nudging and influencing users for the purpose of corporate interest. Second, using Wang's (2023; 2022) variation of the covertness model of manipulation, we point out the risk of being manipulated by transparent AI/XAI in the sense of objectifying underlying norms, that is, normalizing them. Norm objectification through transparency can exploit users' vulnerabilities, steering them toward specific behaviors. Third, using Klenk's (2022; 2023) indifference account, we argue that measured against the ideal norm of using transparency/XAI as a means to empower users, transparency/XAI is *disused* whenever the responsible party is indifferent toward fulfilling this purpose in their deployment of transparency/XAI. For example, AI operators and deployers would act indifferent toward the goal of empowering users if they would only provide transparency/explanations for reasons of compliance or out of convention. Algorithmic transparency/XAI would degenerate into manipulation when it does not aim to reveal reasons to its target audience but merely aims at achieving a certain impression or wants to instigate a certain behavior while being indifferent to reasons.

Beyond these general concerns around transparency/XAI, there is a particular caveat of risks linked to the nature of post hoc explanations. Two discussions are central here. First, post hoc explanation can only, by definition, provide comprehensibility but not complete understanding or comprehension; that is, they might epistemically provide fathomability but not intelligibility. From a practical point of view, however, incomplete explanations can still be useful and sufficient. Yet, it is questionable in which cases we should strive for or even insist on only those explanations that are truthful to the underlying AI's architecture and processes. Against this background, there is a specific risk that users may misunderstand the epistemic nature of what XAI is actually able to explain and where its limits are. This is followed by the *disagreement problem*, which states that different plausible post hoc explanations can be offered for the same process, not only by different XAI techniques but also when using the same XAI technique several times. In practice, the disagreement problem opens up a space for manipulation of various kinds, because it is prima facie not clear which one is the most adequate.

The ambiguity resulting from the disagreement problem in post hoc explanations can be used by actors with bad intentions to manipulate AI users (continuum model of manipulation), by, for example, preselecting explanation techniques or by data poisoning. Second, a general concern is that people tend to rely more on AI when any explanation is provided, so an unintended consequence could be that users over-rely on the machine simply, because any explanation is provided. Insofar as people expect the XAI to provide the right/adequate explanation and are unaware of the disagreement problem, or not practically skilled enough to deal with it appropriately, the mismatch between users' expectations of the capacity of the XAI and its actual epistemic potential could, in effect, be deceiving. Third, the ambiguity resulting from the disagreement problem also gives rise to indifferent use of XAI, that is, being indifferent about whether or not the post hoc explanation is actually empowering users (what it is supposed to do from a normative point of view) or not. While the ambiguity of different post hoc explanations can also be productive (most likely in cooperative contexts), it poses a risk to strengthen conflicts of interests in adversarial contexts of AI application. Moreover, post hoc explanations could add to the risk of weakening users epistemic agency by defaulting statistical knowledge even in those cases where we actually rely on or should rely on causal inferences (e.g., mistaking a correlation between race and success in particular societies as a causal relation).

We assume that the risks of XAI generally also apply to sXAI and that there are specific chances and risks deriving from the unique character of sXAI. The basic idea of sXAI is to solve the shortcomings of XAI on the interaction level between the artificial agents and individual users, that is, on an individual, not on an institutional level. This brings with it certain opportunities but also specific risks. In principle, we see this as an opportunity to strengthen individual users in their decision-making by allowing them to determine and shape what is in question and how it can be adequately explained. However, this focus on the individual harbors the risk of (renewed) overwhelm of the user. It is well known that the use of transparency strategies (e.g., datasheets, model cards, EnvCards) requires a high degree of expertise on the part of the recipients. Moreover, there is inherent latitude for deception and manipulation due to the distinctive features of sXAI: (a) The flexible adaptivity regarding the explanandum and explanans, as well as (b) the social character of communication and interaction. We show that both features demand an even more skillful user to mitigate the risk potential.

sXAI presents both opportunities for enhancing user understanding and risks of manipulation due to its interactive and adaptive nature. Designers must balance the benefits of co-constructed explanations with the potential for increased persuasion and deception and should be aware of the particularly social character of sXAI and its implications for user interaction.

Acknowledgments Suzana Alpsancar acknowledges funding from the Deutsche Forschungsgemeinschaft (DFG, German Research Foundation): TRR 318/1 2021 – 438445824. Michael Klenk acknowledges support from the Humboldt Foundation and the Carl Friedrich von Siemens Foundation.

References

Adadi, A., & Berrada, M. (2018). Peeking inside the black-box: A survey on explainable artificial intelligence (XAI). *IEEE Access, 6*, 52138–52160. https://doi.org/10.1109/ACCESS.2018.2870052.

Alpsancar, S., Buhl, H. M., Matzner,T., & Scharlau, I. (2024). Explanation needs and ethical demands: Unpacking the instrumental value of XAI. *AI and Ethics*, 1–19. https://doi.org/10.1007/s43681-024-00622-3.

Ananny, M., & Crawford, K. (2016). Seeing without knowing: Limitations of the transparency ideal and its application to algorithmic accountability. *New Media & Society, 20*(3), 973–989. https://doi.org/10.1177/1461444816676645.

Anjomshoae, S., Najjar, A., Calvaresi, D., & Främling, K. (2019). Explainable agents and robots: Results from a systematic literature review. In E. Elkind, M. Velosos, N. Agmon, & M. E. Taylor. *Proceedings of the 18th International Conference on Autonomous Agents and MultiAgent Systems* (pp. 1078–1088). IFAAMAS.

Arrieta, A. B., Díaz-Rodríguez, N., Ser, J. D., Bennetot, A., Tabik, S., Barbado, A., García, S., Gil-López, S., Molina, D., & Benjamins, R. (2020). *Explainable artificial intelligence (XAI): Concepts, taxonomies, opportunities and challenges toward responsible AI*. arXiv: 1910.10045 [cs.AI].

Asghari, H., Birner, N., Burchardt, A., Dicks, D., Faßbender, J., Feldhus, N., Hewett, F., Hofmann, V., Kettemann, M. C., Schulz, W., Simon, J., Stolberg-Larsen, J., & Züger, T. (2022). *What to explain when explaining is difficult. An interdisciplinary primer on XAI and meaningful information in automated decision-making.* https://doi.org/10.5281/zenodo.6375784.

Balagopalan, A., Zhang, H., Hamidieh, K., Hartvigsen, T., Rudzicz, F., & Ghassemi, M. (2022). The road to explainability is paved with bias: Measuring the fairness of explanations. In *Proceedings of the 2022 ACM Conference on Fairness, Accountability, and Transparency* (pp. 1194–1206). https://doi.org/10.1145/3531146.353317.

Bannister, F., & Connolly, R. (2011). The trouble with transparency: A critical review of openness in e-government. In *Policy & Internet, 3*, 1–30. https://doi.org/10.2202/1944-2866.1076.

Barnhill, A. (2014). What is manipulation? In C. Coons & M. Weber (Eds.), *Manipulation: Theory and practice* (pp. 51–72). Oxford University Press. https://doi.org/10.1093/acprof:oso/9780199338207.003.0003.

Baron, M. (2003). Manipulativeness. *Proceedings and Addresses of the American Philosophical Association, 77*(2), 37–54. https://doi.org/10.2307/3219740.

Beauchamp, T. L. (1984). Manipulative advertising. *Business and Professional Ethics Journal, 3*, 1–22. https://doi.org/10.5840/bpej198433l/426.

Beauchamp, T. L., & Childress, J. F. (2019). *Principles of biomedical ethics* (8th ed.). Oxford University Press.

Bender, E. M., Gebru, T., McMillan-Major, A., & Shmitchell, S. (2021). On the dangers of stochastic parrots: Can language models be too big? In *Proceedings of the 2021 ACM Conference on Fairness, Accountability, and Transparency* (pp. 610–623). FAccT '21. Association for Computing Machinery. https://doi.org/10.1145/3442188.3445922.

Bertolini, A., & Carli, R. (2022). Human–robot interaction and user manipulation. In N. Baghaei, J. Vassileva, R. Ali, & K. Oyibo (Eds.), *Persuasive technology* (pp. 43–57). Springer. https://doi.org/10.1007/978-3-030-98438-0_4.

Bordt, S., Finck, M., Raidl, E., & von Luxburg, U. (2022). Post-hoc explanations fail to achieve their purpose in adversarial contexts. In *Proceedings of the 2022 ACM Conference on Fairness, Accountability, and Transparency* (pp. 891–905). FAccT '22. Association for Computing Machinery. https://doi.org/10.1145/3531146.3533153.

Brame, C. J. (2016). Effective educational videos: Principles and guidelines for maximizing student learning from video content. *CBE Life Sciences Education, 15*(4). https://doi.org/10.1187/cbe.16-03-0125.

Breazeal, C., Dautenhahn, K., & Kanda, T. (2016). Social robotics. In B. Siciliano & O. Khatib. *Springer Handbook of Robotics* (pp. 1935–1972). Springer. https://doi.org/10.1007/978-3-319-32552-1_72.

Brignull, H. (2023). *Deceptive patterns: Exposing the tricks tech companies use to control you.* Harry Brignull.

Brinck, I., & Balkenius, C. (2020). Mutual recognition in human-robot interaction: A deflationary account. *Philosophy & Technology, 33*(1), 53–70. https://doi.org/10.1007/s13347-018-0339-x.

Bryson, J. J., & Theodorou, A. (2019). How society can maintain human-centric artificial intelligence. In M. Toivonen & E. Saari (Eds.), *Human-centered digitalization and services* (pp. 305–323). Springer. https://doi.org/10.1007/978-981-13-7725-9_16.

Burrell, J., (2016). How the machine 'thinks': Understanding opacity in machine learning algorithms. *Big Data & Society, 3*(1), 1–12. https://doi.org/10.1177/2053951715622512.

Capasso, M., & Umbrello, S. (2022). Responsible nudging for social good: New healthcare skills for AI-driven digital personal assistants. *Medicine, Health Care and Philosophy, 25*(1), 11–22. https://doi.org/10.1007/s11019-021-10062-z.

Cappuccio, M. L., Sandis, C., & Wyatt, A. (2022). Online manipulation and agential risk. In M. Klenk & F. Jongepier (Eds.), *The philosophy of online manipulation* (pp. 72–90). Routledge. https://doi.org/10.4324/9781003205425-5.

Carli, R., Najjar, A., & Calvaresi, D. (2022). Risk and exposure of XAI in persuasion and argumentation: The case of manipulation. In D. Calvaresi, A. Najjar, M. Winikoff, & K.

Främling (Eds.), *Explainable and transparent AI and multi-agent systems* (pp. 204–220). Springer. https://doi.org/10.1007/978-3-031-15565-9_13.
Coeckelbergh, M. (2025). AI and epistemic agency: How AI influences belief revision and its normative implications. *Social Epistemology*, 1–13. ISSN: 1464-5297. https://doi.org/10.1080/02691728.2025.2466164.
Coons, C., & Weber, M. (2014). Introduction. In C. Coons & M. Weber (Eds.), *Manipulation: Theory and practice* (pp. 1–16). Oxford University Press. https://doi.org/10.1093/acprof:oso/9780199338207.001.0001.
de Bruijn, H., Warnier, M., & Janssen, M. (2022). The perils and pitfalls of explainable AI: Strategies for explaining algorithmic decision-making. *Government Information Quarterly, 39*(2), 1–8. https://doi.org/10.1016/j.giq.2021.101666.
de Laat, P. B. (2018). Algorithmic decision-making based on machine learning from Big Data: Can transparency restore accountability? *Philosophy & Technology, 31*(4), 525–541. https://doi.org/10.1007/s13347-017-0293-z.
Dennett, D. C. (1971). Intentional systems. *The Journal of Philosophy, 68*(4), 87–106. https://doi.org/10.2307/2025382.
Dennett, D. (2009). Intentional systems theory. In A. Beckermann, B. P. McLaughlin, & S. Walter (Eds.), *The Oxford Handbook of Philosophy of Mind* (pp. 339–350). Oxford University Press. https://doi.org/10.1093/oxfordhb/9780199262618.003.0020.
Diakopoulos, N. (2020). Transparency. In M. D. Dubber, F. Pasquale, & S. Das (Eds.) (pp. 196–213). Oxford University Press. ISBN: 978-0-190-06739-7. https://doi.org/10.1093/oxfordhb/9780190067397.013.11.
Dignum, V. (2019). *Responsible artificial intelligence: How to develop and use AI in a responsible way*. Springer. https://doi.org/10.1007/978-3-030-30371-6.
Dixon, L. (2020). Autonowashing: The greenwashing of vehicle automation. *Transportation Research Interdisciplinary Perspectives, 5*, 1–9. ISSN: 2590-1982. https://doi.org/10.1016/j.trip.2020.100113.
Doshi-Velez, F., & Kim, B. (2017). *Towards a rigorous science of interpretable Machine Learning*. https://doi.org/10.48550/arXiv.1702.08608. arXiv:1702.08608v2 [stat.ML].
Dowding, K., & Oprea, A. (2024). Manipulation in politics and public policy. *Economics and Philosophy, 40*(3), 685–710. https://doi.org/10.1017/S0266267124000063.
Ehsan, U., & Riedl, M. O. (2024). Social construction of XAI: Do we need one definition to rule them all? *Patterns, 5*(2), 1–2. https://doi.org/10.1016/j.patter.2024.100926.
Faraoni, S. (2023). Persuasive technology and computational manipulation: Hypernudging out of mental self-determination. In: *Frontiers in Artificial Intelligence, 6*. https://doi.org/10.3389/frai.2023.1216340.
Floridi, L., Cowls, J., Beltrametti, M., Chatila, R., Chazerand, P., Dignum, V., Luetge, C., Madelin, R., Pagallo, U., Rossi, F., Schafer, B., Valcke, P., & Vayena, E. (2018). AI4People–An ethical framework for a good AI society: Opportunities, risks, principles, and recommendations. *Minds and Machines, 28*(4), 689–707. https://doi.org/10.1007/s11023-018-9482-5.
Frankfurt, H. G. (2005). *On bullshit*. Princeton University Press. https://doi.org/10.1515/9781400826537.
Franklin, M. (2022). *The influence of explainable artificial intelligence: Nudging behaviour or boosting capability?*. https://doi.org/10.48550/arXiv.2210.02407, arXiv:2210.02407 [cs.HC].
Franklin, M., Tomei, P. M., & Gorman, R. (2023). *Strengthening the EU AI Act: Defining key terms on AI manipulation*. https://doi.org/10.48550/arXiv.2308.16364. arXiv:2308.16364 [cs.AI].
Fukuchi, Y., & Yamada, S. (2024). *Should XAI nudge human decisions with explanation biasing?* https://doi.org/10.48550/arXiv.2406.07323, arXiv:2406.07323 [cs.HC].
Gigerenzer, G., & Goldstein, D. G. (1996). Reasoning the fast and frugal way: Models of bounded rationality. *Psychological Review, 103*. https://doi.org/10.1037/0033-295x.103.4.650.
Goethals, S., Martens, D., & Evgeniou, T. (2025). Manipulation risks in explainable AI: The implications of the disagreement problem. In R. Meo & F. Silvestri (Eds.), *Machine learning and principles and practice of knowledge discovery in databases* (pp. 185–200). Springer. ISBN: 978-3-031-74633-8. https://doi.org/10.1007/978-3-031-74633-8_12.

Goldstein, J. A., Sastry, G., Musser, M., DiResta, R., Gentzel, M., & Sedova, K. (2023). *Generative language models and automated influence operations: emerging threats and potential mitigations*. arXiv: 2301.04246 [cs.CY].

Gorin, M. (2014a). Do manipulators always threaten rationality? *American Philosophical Quarterly, 51*(1), 51–61.

Gorin, M. (2014b). Towards a theory of interpersonal manipulation. In C. Coons & M. Weber (Eds.), *Manipu-lation: Theory and practice* (pp. 73–97). Oxford University Press. https://doi.org/10.1093/acprof:oso/9780199338207.003.0004.

Gransche, B., Shala, E., Hubig, C., Alpsancar, S., & Harrach, S. (2014). *Wandel von Autonomie und Kontrolle durch neue Mensch- Technik-Interaktionen. Grundsatzfragen autonomieorientierter Mensch-Technik- Verhältnisse; WAK-MTI*. Förderkennzeichen BMBF 16SV6195. Fraunhofer.

Gray, J. (2023). Deception mode: how conversational AI can respect patient autonomy. *The American Journal of Bioethics, 23*(5), 55–57. https://doi.org/10.1080/15265161.2023.2191023.

Hagendorff, T. (2020). The ethics of AI ethics: An evaluation of guidelines. *Minds and Machines, 30*(1), 99–120. https://doi.org/10.1007/s11023-020-09517-8.

Hertwig, R. (2017). When to consider boosting: some rules for policy-makers. *Behavioural Public Policy, 1*(2), 143–161. https://doi.org/10.1017/bpp.2016.14.

Hirmiz, R. (2023). Against the substitutive approach to AI in healthcare. *AI and Ethics, 4*, 1507–1518. https://doi.org/10.1007/s43681-023-00347-9.

Jobin, A., Ienca, M., & Vayena, E. (2019). The global landscape of AI ethics guidelines. *Nature Machine Intelligence, 1*(9), 389–399. https://doi.org/10.1038/s42256-019-0088-2.

Kahneman, D. (2012). *Thinking, fast and slow*. Penguin.

Kahneman, D. (2013). A perspective on judgment and choice: Mapping bounded rationality. In Q. Jing, M. R. Rosenzweig, G. d'Yewalle, H. Zhang, H.-C. Chen, & K. Zhang (Eds.), *Progress in Psychological Science around the World. Volume 1 Neural, Cognitive and Developmental Issues* (pp. 1–47). Psychology Press. ISBN: 978-1-134-95634-0.

Kemper, J., & Kolkman, D. (2018). Transparent to whom? No algorithmic accountability without a critical audience. *Information, Communication & Society, 22*(14), 2081–2096. https://doi.org/10.1080/1369118x.2018.1477967.

Kim, J., Rohrbach, A., Akata, Z., Moon, S., Misu, T., Chen, Y.-T. Darrell, T., & Canny, J. (2021). Toward explainable and advisable model for self-driving cars. *Applied AI Letters, 2*(4), e56. https://doi.org/10.1002/ail2.56.

Klenk, M. (2020). Digital well-being and manipulation online. In C. Burr, & L. Floridi (Eds.), *Ethics of digital well-being: A multidisciplinary perspective* (pp. 81–100). Springer. https://doi.org/10.1007/978-3-030-50585-1_4.

Klenk, M. (2021a). How do technological artefacts embody moral values? *Philosophy and Technology, 34*, 525–544. https://doi.org/10.1007/s13347-020-00401-y.

Klenk, M. (2021b). Manipulation (Online): Sometimes hidden, always careless. *Review of Social Economy, 80*, 85–105. https://doi.org/10.1080/00346764.2021.1894350.

Klenk, M. (2022). Manipulation as indifference to inquiry. *SSRN Electronic Journal*, 1–29. https://doi.org/10.2139/ssrn.3859178.

Klenk, M. (2023). Algorithmic transparency and manipulation. *Philosophy and Technology, 36*. https://doi.org/10.1007/s13347-023-00678-9.

Klenk, M. (2024). Liberty, manipulation, and algorithmic transparency: Reply to Franke. *Philosophy & Technology, 37*(2), 1–8. https://doi.org/10.1007/s13347-024-00739-7.

Kossow, N., Windwehr, S., & Jenkins, M. (2021). *Algorithmic trans- parency and accountability*. https://knowledgehub.transparency.org/assets/uploads/kproducts/Algorithmic-Transparency_2021.pdf.

Krämer, N., & Manzeschke, A. (2021). Social reactions to socially interactive agents and their ethical implications. In B. Lugrin, C. Pelachaud, & D. Traum (Eds.), *The Handbook on Socially Interactive Agents: 20 Years of Research on Embodied Conversational Agents, Intelligent Virtual Agents, and Social Robotics Volume 1: Methods, Behavior, Cognition* (pp. 77–104). ACM. https://doi.org/10.1145/3477322.3477526.

Krishnan, M. (2020). Against interpretability: A critical examination of the interpretability problem in machine learning. *Philosophy & Technology, 33*(3), 487–502. https://doi.org/10.1007/s13347-019-00372-9.

Lades, L., & Nova, F. (2023). Ethical considerations when using nudges to reduce meat consumption: an analysis through the FORGOOD ethics framework. *Journal of Consumer Policy, 47*(1), 1–19. https://doi.org/10.1007/s10603-023-09558-3.

Langer, M., Oster, D., Speith, T., Hermanns, H., Kästner, L., Schmidt, E., Sesing, A., & Baum, K. (2021). What do we want from explainable artificial intelligence (XAI)?—A stakeholder perspective on XAI and a conceptual model guiding interdisciplinary XAI research. *Artificial Intelligence, 296*, 1–24. https://doi.org/10.1016/j.artint.2021.103473.

Leslie, C., & Schmitt, M., (Eds.) (2019). *Histories of computing in eastern Europe*. Springer. https://doi.org/10.1007/978-3-030-29160-0.

Lipton, Z. C. (2018). The mythos of model interpretability: In machine learning, the concept of interpretability is both important and slippery. *Queue, 16*(3), 31–57. https://doi.org/10.1145/3233231.

Longo, L., Brcic, M., Cabitza, F., Choi, J., Confalonieri, R., Del Ser, J., Guidotti, R., Hayashi, Y., Herrera, F., Holzinger, A., et al. (2024). Explainable artificial intelligence (XAI) 2.0: A manifesto of open challenges and interdisciplinary research directions. *Information Fusion, 106*, 1–22. https://doi.org/10.1016/j.inffus.2024.102301.

Lönngren, J., & Van Poeck, K. (2021). Wicked problems: A mapping review of the literature. *International Journal of Sustainable Development & World Ecology, 28*(6), 481–502. https://doi.org/10.1080/13504509.2020.1859415.

Matz, S. C., Teeny, J. D., Vaid, S. S., Peters, H., Harari, G. M., & Cerf, M. (2024). The potential of generative AI for personalized persuasion at scale. *Scientific Reports, 14*(1). ISSN: 2045-2322. https://doi.org/10.1038/s41598-024-53755-0.

Matzner, T. (2017). Opening black boxes is not enough–data-based surveillance in discipline and punish and today. *Foucault Studies*, 27–45. https://doi.org/10.22439/fs.v0i0.5340.

Metzinger, T. K. (2018). Why is virtual reality interesting for philosophers? *Frontiers in Robotics and AI, 5*, 101. https://doi.org/10.3389/frobt.2018.00101.

Mitchell, M., Wu, S., Zaldivar, A., Barnes, P., Vasserman, L., Hutchinson, B., Spitzer, E., Raji, I. D., & Gebru, T. (2019). Model cards for model reporting. In *Proceedings of the Conference on Fairness, Accountability, and Transparency* (pp. 220–229). FAT* '19. ACM. https://doi.org/10.1145/3287560.3287596.

Morley, J., Floridi, L., Kinsey, L., & Elhalal, A. (2020). From what to how: An initial review of publicly available AI ethics tools, methods and research to translate principles into practices. *Science and Engineering Ethics, 26*, 2141–2168. https://doi.org/10.2139/ssrn.3830348.

Naiseh, M., Al-Thani, D., Jiang, N., & Ali, R. (2023). How the different explanation classes impact trust calibration: The case of clinical decision support systems. *International Journal of Human–Computer Studies, 169*, 1–17. https://doi.org/10.1016/j.ijhcs.2022.102941.

Nannini, L., Balayn, A., & Smith, A. L. (2023). Explainability in AI policies: A critical review of communications, reports, regulations, and standards in the EU, US, and UK. In *Proceedings of the 2023 ACM Conference on Fairness, Accountability, and Transparency* (pp. 1198–1212.). FAccT '23. Association for Computing Machinery. https://doi.org/10.1145/3593013.3594074.

Noggle, R. (1996). Manipulative actions: A conceptual and moral analysis. *American Philosophical Quarterly, 33*, 43–55.

Noggle, R. (2018). Manipulation, salience, and nudges. *Bioethics, 32*(3), 164–170. https://doi.org/10.1111/bioe.12421.

Noggle, R. (2020). Pressure, trickery, and a unified account of manipulation. *American Philosophical Quarterly, 57*(3), 241–252. https://doi.org/10.2307/48574436.

Noggle, R. (2022). The ethics of manipulation. In E. N. Zalta (Ed.), *The Stanford Encyclopedia of Philosophy*. Summer 2022. Metaphysics Research Lab, Stanford University.

Passen, B., Alpsancar, S., Scharlau, I., & Matzner, T. (2025). *Healthy distrust in AI systems*. arXiv preprint arXiv:2505.09747.

Patidar, N., Mishra, S., Jain, R., & Prajapati, D. T. (2024). Transparency in AI decision making: A survey of explainable AI methods and applications. *Advances in Robotic Technology, 2*(1), 1–10. https://doi.org/10.23880/art-16000110.

Pham, A., Rubel, A., & Castro, C. (2022). Social media, emergent manipulation, and political legitimacy. In M. Klenk, & F. Jongepier (Eds.), *The philosophy of online manipulation* (pp. 353–369). Routledge. https://doi.org/10.4324/9781003205425-21.

Powell, A. B. (2021). Explanations as governance? Investigating practices of ex- planation in algorithmic system design. *European Journal of Communication, 36*(4), 362–375. https://doi.org/10.1177/02673231211028376.

Robbins, S. (2019). A misdirected principle with a catch: Explicability for AI. *Minds and Machines, 29*(4), 495–514. ISSN: 1572-8641. https://doi.org/10.1007/s11023-019-09509-3.

Rudin, C. (2019). Stop explaining black box machine learning models for high stakes decisions and use interpretable models instead. *Nature Machine Intelligence, 1*(5), 206–215. https://doi.org/10.1038/s42256-019-0048-x.

Sculley, D., Holt, G., Golovin, D., Davydov, E., Phillips, T., Ebner, D., Chaudhary, V., Young, M., Crespo, J.-F., & Denni-son, D. (2015). Hidden technical debt in machine learning systems. In C. Cortes, N. Lawrence, D. Lee, Sugiyama, M., & Garnett, R. (Eds.), *Advances in Neural Information Processing Systems* (Vol. 28, pp. 2503–2511). Curran Associates, Inc.

Sheridan, T. B. (2020). A review of recent research in social robotics. *Current Opinion in Psychology, 36*(Cyberpsychology), 7–12. ISSN: 2352-250X. https://doi.org/10.1016/j.copsyc.2020.01.003.

Simon, J., Döhmann gen., I. S., & Luxburg von, U. (2024). *Genera- tive AI – Beyond euphoria and simple solutions*. https://www.leopoldina.org/publikationen/detailansicht/publication/generative-ki-2024/. Visited on 21 Mar 2025.

Skaburskis, A. (2008). The origin of "wicked problems". *Planning Theory & Practice, 9*(2), 277–280. https://doi.org/10.1080/14649350802041654.

Sunstein, C. R. (2016). *The ethics of influence: Government in the age of behavioral science*. Cambridge University Press. https://doi.org/10.1017/CBO9781316493021.

Sunstein, C. R. (2018). Nudging: A very short guide. In B. van der Sloot, & A. de Groot (Eds.), *The Handbook of Privacy Studies* (pp. 173–180). Amsterdam University Press. ISBN: 978-9-048-54013-6. https://doi.org/10.2307/j.ctvcmxpmp.9.

Susser, D., Roessler, B., & Nissenbaum, H. (2019a). Online manipulation: Hidden influences in a digital world. *Georgetown Law Technology Review, 4*, 1–45.

Susser, D., Roessler, B., & Nissenbaum, H. (2019b). Technology, autonomy, and manipulation. *Internet Policy Review, 8*(2), 1–22. https://doi.org/10.14763/2019.2.1410.

Uuk, R., Gutierrez,, C. I., Guppy, D., Lauwaert, L., Kasirzadeh, A., Velasco, L., Slattery, P., & Prunkl, C. (2024). A taxonomy of systemic risks from general-purpose AI. https://doi.org/10.48550/arXiv.2412.07780, arXiv:2412.07780 [cs.CY].

Vandenbroele, J., Vermeir, I., Geuens, M., Slabbinck, H., & Van Kerckhove, A. (2020). Nudging to get our food choices on a sustainable track. *Proceedings of the Nutrition Society, 79*(1), 133–146. https://doi.org/10.1017/S0029665119000971.

van de Poel, I. (2020). Embedding values in artificial intelligence (AI) systems. *Minds and Machines, 30*(3), 385–409. https://doi.org/10.1007/s11023-020-09537-4.

Visser, R., Peters, T. M., Scharlau, I., & Hammer, B. (2023). *Trust, distrust, and appropriate reliance in (X)AI: A survey of empirical evaluation of user trust*. https://arxiv.org/abs/2312.02034. arXiv: 2312.02034 [cs.HC].

Wachter, S., Mittelstadt, B., & Russell, C. (2018). Counterfactual explanations without opening the black box: Automated decisions and the GDPR. *Harvard Journal of Law and Technology, 31*(2), 841–887.

Wachter, S., Mittelstadt, B., & Russell, C. (2021). Why fairness cannot be automated: Bridging the gap between EU non-discrimination law and AI. *Computer Law & Security Review, 41*, 1–31. ISSN: 0267-3649. https://doi.org/10.1016/j.clsr.2021.105567.

Walmsley, J. (2021). Artificial intelligence and the value of transparency. *AI & Society, 36*(2), 585–595. ISSN: 1435-5655. https://doi.org/10.1007/s00146-020-01066-z.

Wang, H. (2022). Transparency as manipulation? Uncovering the disciplinary power of algorithmic transparency. *Philosophy & Technology, 35*(3), 1–25. https://doi.org/10.1007/s13347-022-00564-w.

Wang, H. (2023). Why should we care about the manipulative power of algorithmic transparency? *Philosophy & Technology, 36*(1). https://doi.org/10.1007/s13347-023-00610-1.

Weizenbaum, J. (1966). ELIZA—a computer program for the study of natural language communication between man and machine. *Communications of the ACM, 9*(1), 36–45. https://doi.org/10.1145/365153.365168.

Wickstrøm, K., Marie-Claire Höhne, M., & Hedström, A. (2024). *From flexibility to manipulation: The slippery slope of XAI evaluation.* https://doi.org/10.48550/arXiv.2412.05592, arXiv: 2412.05592 [cs.AI].

Wilkinson, T. M. (2013). Nudging and manipulation. *Political Studies, 61*(2), 341–355. https://doi.org/10.1111/j.1467-9248.2012.00974.x.

Winfield, A. F. T., Booth, S., Dennis, L. A., Egawa, T., Hastie, H., Jacobs, N., Muttram, R. I., Olszewska, J. I., Rajabiyazdi, F., Theodorou, A., Underwood, M. A., Wortham, R. H., & Watson, E. (2021). IEEE P7001: A proposed standard on transparency. *Frontiers in Robotics and AI, 8*. https://doi.org/10.3389/frobt.2021.665729.

Zerilli, J. (2022). Explaining machine learning decisions. *Philosophy of Science, 89*(1), 1–19. ISSN: 1539-767X. https://doi.org/10.1017/psa.2021.13.

Open Access This chapter is licensed under the terms of the Creative Commons Attribution 4.0 International License (http://creativecommons.org/licenses/by/4.0/), which permits use, sharing, adaptation, distribution and reproduction in any medium or format, as long as you give appropriate credit to the original author(s) and the source, provide a link to the Creative Commons license and indicate if changes were made.

The images or other third party material in this chapter are included in the chapter's Creative Commons license, unless indicated otherwise in a credit line to the material. If material is not included in the chapter's Creative Commons license and your intended use is not permitted by statutory regulation or exceeds the permitted use, you will need to obtain permission directly from the copyright holder.